WESTERN SOCIETIES

A DOCUMENTARY HISTORY

VOLUME I

352 - 363

WESTERN SOCIETIES

A DOCUMENTARY HISTORY

VOLUME I

BRIAN TIERNEY

Cornell University

JOAN SCOTT

Brown University

ALFRED A. KNOPF NEW YORK

THIS IS A BORZOI BOOK

PUBLISHED BY ALFRED A. KNOPF, INC.

First Edition
987654
Copyright © 1984 by Alfred A. Knopf, Inc.

All rights reserved under International and Pan-American Copyright
Conventions. No part of this book may be reproduced in any form or
by any means, electronic or mechanical, including photocopying, with-
out permission in writing from the publisher. All inquiries should be
addressed to Alfred A. Knopf, Inc., 201 East 50th Street, New York,
N.Y. 10022. Published in the United States by Alfred A. Knopf, Inc.,
New York, and simultaneously in Canada by Random House of Canada
Limited, Toronto. Distributed by Random House, Inc., New York.

Library of Congress Cataloging in Publication Data
Main entry under title:

Western societies, a documentary history.

    1. Civilization, Occidental—Sources. 2. Europe—
Civilization—Sources. I. Tierney, Brian. II. Scott,
Joan.
CB245.W4847 1984   909'.09821   83-19929
ISBN 0-394-32691-1 (v. 1)
ISBN 0-394-32692-X (v. 2)

Manufactured in the United States of America

PREFACE

HISTORIANS are always asking new questions of the past; that is why we need new collections of sources from time to time. This one includes readings drawn from many different types of material—poems, plays, chronicles, government records, letters, diaries, treatises of various kinds. In studying these sources we can enter into the life of past generations on their own terms, so to speak. Such study enhances our own personalities by making us more aware of the whole range of human thought and feeling. Historical study can also help us to understand our present-day society better by learning how its various characteristics—ideas and institutions, achievements and dilemmas—grew out of the life of the past.

Some of the new questions that historians ask arise out of contemporary concerns. Many students nowadays want to know more about women's roles and patterns of family structure in earlier times. Modern interest in ecological problems has led us to ask how people in other ages viewed their relationship to the natural environment. Concern over a possible future era of "diminishing expectations" may stimulate questions about earlier theories of human progress (or regression or cyclical recurrence). Experience of social change in the modern world encourages new forms of writing on social history and especially on the sources of social conflict. The difficulties that many "less developed countries" encounter in seeking to "modernize" their economies redirect our attention to the processes of industrialization, urbanization, and demographic expansion that first created a modern society in the Western world. In making the present collection we have tried to bear in mind all these interests of recent historians.

The most evident change in the teaching of history at American colleges during the past decade has been the great growth of courses in the history of women and the family. This is proving to be more than a mere passing fashion (if it ever seemed to be that). Scholars in the field have explored new ranges of source material and raised significant new problems for research. It seems important that such work should not remain isolated in courses on Women's History but should be drawn into the mainstream of teaching on the evolution of Western society. One purpose of the present book is to make this task easier. Many readings dealing with women's roles and family relationships are included, and every chapter contains material by or about women.

A major problem for makers of anthologies is that new interests do not supplant old ones, but rather supplement them. Historians deal with the whole life of people in society. And to understand the life of any people adequately we need to ask about their religion, their economy, their forms of government, their whole world picture. These are subjects of traditional historical disciplines—"history of religions," "economic history," "political history," "history of ideas." Most teachers of Western Civilization courses will not want to neglect such topics. We have aimed therefore to provide a framework of readings illustrating the traditional themes of Western history, but also to include within the framework many readings related to the newer interests of historians.

The authors wish to thank Saphira Baker for research assistance and Ellen Furlough for her contribution to the organization of materials in Volume II.

CONTENTS

Preface   v

I THE ANCIENT NEAR EAST—NATURE,   2
       GODS, AND HUMANS

IN THE BEGINNINGS   4
Egypt   4
From *The Book of Knowing the Creations*
Mesopotamia   5
From *The Creation Epic*
The Hebrews   8
From *The Book of Genesis*

RELIGION AND NATURE   10
Egypt: The Nile and the Sun   10
From *Hymn to the Nile*
From *Hymn to the Aton*
Mesopotamia: Myth, Fertility, and Worship   14
From *The Epic of Gilgamesh*
Love-Song to a King
The Ecstacy of Love
From *A Psalm*
Hymn to Ishtar
The Hebrews: The Garden of Eden   20
From *The Book of Genesis*

ETHICS AND LAW   24
Egypt: Death and Judgment   24
From *The Book of the Dead*
Mesopotamia: Law and Justice   25
From *The Code of Hammurabi*

GOD, MAN, AND HISTORY: 29
THE HEBREW TRADITION
The Covenant   29
From *The Book of Exodus*
The Law   30
From *The Book of Exodus*

The Prophets   32
From *The Book of Isaiah*
Hebrew Poetry   36
A Psalm
From *The Song of Solomon*

II GREEK CIVILIZATION—   40
FROM MYTH TO POLIS (c. 800–c. 430 BC)

GODS AND HUMANS   42
Homer's World   42
From *The Iliad*
Golden Age to Iron Age   48
From *Hesiod's Works and Days*
Human Love   50
From *Poems of Sappho*

FROM MYTHOLOGY TO PHILOSOPHY   54
Religion   54
From *Xenophanes*
Philosophy   55
From *Empedocles*
From *Parmenides*
Atomism: Leucippus and Democritus
Mathematics: The Pythagoreans

SOCIETY AND GOVERNMENT—THE POLIS   60
Athens   60
From Thucydides. *History of the Peloponnesian War*
Sparta   65
From Plutarch. *Life of Lycurgus*

DIVINE AND HUMAN LAW   70
Sophocles   70
From *Antigone*

III GREEK CIVILIZATION—PHILOSOPHY,   76
POLITICS, AND SOCIETY (c. 430–330 B.C.)

THE IDEA OF THE GOOD   78
Socrates: Critics and Friends   78
From *The Clouds*
From *Phaedo*
Plato's Cave   89
From *The Republic*

FAMILY AND STATE—IDEALISM   92
Platonic Utopianism   92
From *The Republic*

FAMILY AND STATE—REALISM 98
An Athenian Household 98
From Xenophon. *Household Management*
State Finances 101
From Xenophon. *On the Revenues*

ARISTOTLE—NATURAL SCIENCE 104
AND SOCIAL SCIENCE
Scientific Method 104
From *Parts of Animals*
Ethics and Politics 106
From *The Nichomachean Ethics*
From *The Politics*

IV HELLENISM AND ROME— 112
FROM REPUBLIC TO EMPIRE

RELIGION AND NATURE 114
The Mother-Goddess 114
From Apuleius. *Metamorphoses*
Paganism 116
From Vergil. *The Georgics*
Epicureanism 117
From Lucretius. *On the Nature of*
the Universe
Stoicism 120
From *Works of Epictetus*

ROME—REPUBLIC AND REVOLUTION 123
Republican Institutions 123
From *The Histories of Polybius*
From *The Roman History of Appian*
The Roman Revolution 129
From *The Roman History of Appian*
From *Writings of Cicero*
From *The Annals of Tacitus*

ROMAN FAMILIES 135
Patriarchal Tradition 135
From *Roman Antiquities*
From *The Histories of Polybius*
From Plutarch. *Life of Cato*
Legislation of Augustus 138
From *Dio's Roman History*
From *The Institutes of Gaius*
From *Opinions of Julius Paulus*

Roman Wives   *140*
From *Juvenal's Sixth Satire*
From *Praise of Turia*

THE EMPIRE—AUGUSTUS TO TRAJAN   *144*
Imperial Mission   *144*
From Vergil. *Eclogue IV*
From Vergil. *The Aeneid*
Provincial Administration   *145*
From *Letters of Pliny*

V   CHRISTIANITY AND THE FALL OF ROME   *150*

ORIGINS OF CHRISTIANITY   *152*
Judaism   *152*
From *The Jewish War*
The Coming of Jesus   *154*
From *The Gospel According to Luke*
From *The Gospel According to John*
Life and Teaching   *156*
From *The Gospel According to Matthew*
From *The Gospel According to Matthew*
From *The Gospel According to Mark*

THE EARLY CHURCH   *162*
Christian and Pagan   *162*
From *Paul's First Epistle to the Corinthians*
From Minucius Felix. *Octavius*
From Hippolytus. *Apostolic Tradition*
The Nicene Creed
Church and State   *165*
From *The Annals of Tacitus*
From *Letters of Pliny*
From *The "Edict of Milan"*
From Eusebius. *Life of Constantine*
From *The Theodosian Code*
Christian Women: Marriage and Celibacy   *169*
From *Paul's Epistle to the Ephesians*
From *Paul's First Epistle to the Corinthians*
From *The Acts of the Christian Martyrs*
From Jerome. *Against Helvidius*
From *Letter of Pope Damasus on Celibacy*

DECLINE AND FALL   *175*
Imperial Centralization   *175*
From J. W. Thompson. *The Middle Ages*
From *The Death of the Persecutors*
From *The Theodosian Code*

Christian Reactions   *178*
Salvianus. *The Burden of Taxation*
Jerome. *The Barbarian Invasions*
Augustine. *The Two Cities*
Augustine. *The Six Ages of the World*
Epilogue   *184*
From Edward Gibbon. *The Decline and Fall of the Roman Empire*

VI A NEW EUROPE— BARBARIANS AND CHRISTIANS   *186*

THE EARLY GERMANS—SOCIETY AND CULTURE   *188*
A Roman Account   *188*
From Tacitus. *On Germany*
Laws and Customs   *191*
From *Laws of the Salian Franks*
From *Laws of the Burgundians*
A Germanic Hero-King   *195*
From *Beowulf*

CHRISTIAN INSTITUTIONS   *200*
The Papacy   *200*
From *Sermon of Leo I*
From Gelasius I. *Letter to Emperor Anastasius*
Monasticism   *202*
From *The Rule of St. Benedict*

ROMAN CHRISTIANITY AND NORTHERN EUROPE   *208*
Gregory the Great as Teacher   *208*
From *Homily of Gregory I*
From *Pastoral Care*
Mission to England   *210*
Gregory I. *Letter to Mellitus*
From Bede. *Ecclesiastical History*
From Bede. *Ecclesiastical History*
Germany. Wilderness and Monasteries   *212*
Oath of Boniface
From *Life of Boniface*
From *Life of Sturmi*
Walafrid Strabo. *A Monastic Garden*

CHARLEMAGNE   *217*
Charlemagne and His Family   *217*
From Einhard. *Life of Charlemagne*
Economic Foundations   *219*
From *Capitulary De Villis*

Carolingian Government   221
From *General Capitulary for the Missi*
The Imperial Coronation   222
From Einhard. *Life of Charlemagne*
From *Annals of Lorsch*
From *Frankish Royal Annals*

VII MEDIEVAL FOUNDATIONS—   224
FEUDALISM, CHURCH REFORM,
AND CRUSADE

FEUDAL INSTITUTIONS   226
Lords and Vassals   226
From *Annals of Xanten*
Capitulary of Mersen
Oaths of Allegiance
From *Chronicle of Galbert of Bruges*
Liege Homage
The Fief   230
Capitulary of Lestinnes (747)
Grant of Fief with Immunity (815)
Foundation of the Duchy of Normandy (911)
Feudal Obligations   231
From *Fulbert of Chartres*
Feudal Aids
Knight Service
Court Service
Wardship and Marriage
Violence and Restraint   234
From *Suger's Life of Louis VI*
Truce of God (1063)

REFORM OF THE CHURCH   238
Beginnings of Reform   238
Parishes in Italy
Simony in France
Foundation Charter of Cluny
Papal Reform Decrees (1074–1075)
Dictatus Papae (1075)
Empire and Papacy   243
Henry IV to Gregory VII (January 24, 1076)
Deposition of Henry IV (February 22, 1076)
Gregory VII to the Princes of Germany (1077)
Gregory VII to Hermann of Metz (1081)
Concordat of Worms

THE FIRST CRUSADERS   251
Western Views   251
From *The Song of Roland*
Pope Urban's Speech at Clermont
An Arab View   254
From *Autobiography of Ousama*

VIII THE MEDIEVAL WORLD— ECONOMY AND GOVERNMENT 258

RURAL LIFE   260
The Medieval Manor   260
From *A Manor of the Hundred Rolls (1279)*
From *Select Pleas in Manorial Courts*
Peasant Daily Fare   263
From *Piers Plowman*

TOWNS AND TRADE   265
City Life   265
From *Otto of Freising's Chronicle*
From *A Description of London*
Economic Activities   269
Rules of a Merchant Guild (Southampton)
Silk Spinners at Paris
Advice to Merchants

MEDIEVAL MONARCHIES   275
England   275
From *Magna Carta*
Summons of Representatives to Parliament (1295)
From *Rolls of Parliament*
From *Flowers of History*
France   282
From *Joinville. Life of St. Louis*
The Empire   284
From *Otto of Freising's Chronicle*

CHURCH AND STATE   287
Innocent III—Papal Power at Its Zenith   287
From *Letters of Innocent III*
Innocent IV and Frederick II   289
Frederick II According to Salimbene
Deposition of Frederick II (1245)
Boniface VIII—The Crisis of Papal Power   291
Unam Sanctam
Accusations Against Boniface VIII
Decree of Clement V (1306)
Decree of Clement V (1311)

Reflections on Government 295
From Innocent IV. *Commentary on the Decretals*
From John of Paris. *On Royal and Papal Power (1303)*
From Giles of Rome. *On the Rule of Princes*

IX THE MEDIEVAL WORLD— 300
RELIGION AND CULTURE

REASON, FAITH, AND LOVE 302
Abelard and Bernard: Reason and Faith 302
From Abelard. *Sic et Non*
From Bernard. *Letter to Pope Innocent II*
From Abelard. *Dialectica*
From Bernard. *The Love of God*
Abelard and Heloise: Learning and Love 308
From Abelard. *A Story of Calamities*
From Heloise. *Letter to Abelard*
From Peter the Venerable. *Letter to Heloise*

LORDS AND LADIES: EVE AND MARY 314
Troubadour Songs 314
Jaufré Rudel. *To His Love Afar*
Walther Von Der Vogelweide. *A Spring Song*
Countess de Dia. *A Distressed Lover*
Love and Marriage 316
From *The Art of Courtly Love*
Eve and Mary 319
Adam Lay Y-Bounden
From *Liber Exemplorum*

GOD AND NATURE—THE WAY OF THE HEART 321
Franciscan Ideals 321
Francis's Testament
Creator and Creatures 323
From *Thomas of Celano*
The Canticle of the Sun

GOD AND NATURE—THE WAY OF THE MIND 327
Chance and Necessity—Maimonides 327
From *The Guide for the Perplexed*
Nature and Law—Aquinas 330
From *Summa Theologiae*
Heaven and Earth—Dante 333
From *The Banquet*

GOD AND NATURE—THE WAY OF DISSENT 335
Albigensians and Patarins 335

From Raynaldus. *Annales*
Decree of Emperor Frederick II (c. 1235)
From *Montaillou*
Beguins   *338*
From *The Inquisitor's Manual of Bernard Gui*

X AN AGE OF RENAISSANCE—   *340*
DECLINE AND RENEWAL, 1300–1500

THE "WANING" OF THE MIDDLE AGES   *342*
Pestilence, Persecution, and Flagellants   *342*
From *Jean de Venette's Chronicle*
Peasant Rebellion   *344*
From *Froissart's Chronicle*
The Great Schism   *346*
Manifesto of the Cardinals (1378)
Opinion of the University of Paris (1393)
The Decree Haec Sancta (1415)
The Decree Execrabilis (1459)
Joan and Her Judges   *348*
From *The Trial of Jeanne d'Arc*

NEW LIGHT IN ITALY   *352*
The Dignity of Man   *352*
From Pico della Mirandola. *Oration on the
Dignity of Man*
Nature and Art   *353*
From Giorgio Vasari. *Lives of the Most Eminent
Painters (1550)*
Renaissance Types—Man of Letters, Courtier, Artist   *357*
and Patron
From *Petrarch's Letters*
From Baldassare Castiglione. *The Book of the
Courtier (1518)*
From Benvenuto Cellini. *Autobiography*

RENAISSANCE FAMILIES   *364*
A Modern Description   *364*
From *The Western Experience*
Family and Fortune   *365*
From Alberti. *I Libri Della Famiglia*
A Florentine Family—Fact   *369*
From Landucci. *A Florentine Diary*
A Florentine Family—Fiction   *370*
From Machiavelli. *La Mandragola*

RENAISSANCE STATECRAFT 374
Italy: Prince and State 374
From Machiavelli. *The Prince*
France: Louis XI 377
From *Memoirs of Commynes*
England: Henry VII 378
From *Bacon's Life of Henry VII*

XI REFORMATIONS—PROTESTANT AND 380
CATHOLIC

NORTHERN HUMANISTS 382
Papal Failings 382
From Erasmus. *In Praise of Folly*
Religion in Utopia 383
From Thomas More. *Utopia*
Germany and Rome 385
From *Wimpheling's Response*

MARTIN LUTHER 387
Luther as Monk 387
From *Luther's Table Talk*
The Break With Rome 388
From *Tetzel's Sermon*
From *The Ninety-Five Theses* (1517)
From *Disputation Against Scholastic Theology*
From *Address to the Christian Nobility of the German Nation*
From *Luther's Speech at Worms*
Celibacy and Marriage 395
From *What Luther Says*

DEVELOPMENTS OF PROTESTANT THOUGHT 397
Switzerland and France 397
Zwingli on the Eucharist
From John Calvin. *Institutes of the Christian Religion*
Scotland and England 399
From John Knox. *The Book of Discipline*
From *The Thirty-Nine Articles*

THE CATHOLIC REFORMATION 403
Doctrine Reaffirmed 403
From *Decrees of the Council of Trent*
Religious Reformers 405
From Ignatius Loyola. *The Spiritual Exercises*
From Teresa of Avila. *The Way of Perfection*

REFORMATION AND POLITICS 411
Germany 411
From *Twelve Articles of the Peasants*
From Charles V. *Abdication Speech*
Peace of Augsburg (1555)
France 415
St. Bartholomew's Day Massacre
Edict of Nantes

XII NEW WORLDS FOR OLD—EXPLORATION, 418
SCIENCE, AND SUPERSTITION

VOYAGES OF DISCOVERY 420
The New World 420
From *Letter of Columbus*
The Indies 422
From *Letter of King Manoel (1499)*
From *Journal of Gaspar Correa*
Exploration and Anthropology 424
From Montaigne. *Of Cannibals*

SCIENTIFIC METHOD 428
Bacon on Empiricism 428
From *The Great Instauration*
Descartes on Deduction 430
From *Discourse on Method*

SCIENTIFIC ACHIEVEMENT 435
Astronomy 435
From Copernicus. *Commentariolus*
From Galileo. *The Starry Messenger*
From Galileo. *Letters on Sunspots*
From Galileo. *Letter to the Grand Duchess Christina*
Synthesis 442
From *Newton's Principia*
From *Bodin's Methodus*

WITCHCRAFT—SUPERSTITION 446
AND PERSECUTION
The Prevalence of Witches 446
From *Bodin's Demonology*
The Frailty of Women 447
From *The Hammer of Witches*
Confession of Françoise Secretain (1598)
Trial of Geillis Duncane (1591)

XIII   THE SEARCH FOR ORDER—   450
ABSOLUTISM AND ARISTOCRACY

SOCIAL CONDITIONS   452
Germany   452
From *Simplicissimus*
Spain   453
From *Letter to the Queen of Spain*
France   454
From *Report of the Estates of Normandy (1651)*
From *Letters of the Abbess of Port-Royal*

FOUNDATIONS OF ABSOLUTISM   456
Rationalism   456
From Thomas Hobbes. *Leviathan*
Divine Right   459
From Bossuet. *Politics Drawn from the Very Words of Holy Scripture*
Patriarchy   461
From Robert Filmer. *Patriarcha*
From David Hunt. *Parents and Children in History*
From *Journal of Jean Héroard*

THE COURT OF LOUIS XIV   466
Portrait of a Monarch   466
From *Memoirs of the Duke of Saint-Simon*
Life at Versailles   468
From *Memoirs of the Duke of Saint-Simon*
From *Letter of the Duchess of Orleans*
From W. H. Lewis. *The Splendid Century*

ABSOLUTISM IN PRACTICE   472
Religion   472
From *Revocation of the Edict of Nantes 1685*
From *Memoirs of the Duke of Saint-Simon*
From *Declaration of the Gallican Church*
From Louis XIV. *Letter to His Heir*
Military Organization   475
From Voltaire. *The Age of Louis XIV*
Economy and Local Administration   477
From *Colbert's Memoranda*
From *Colbert's Correspondence*

EASTERN EUROPE   483
The Turkish Menace   483
From *The Present State of the German and Turkish Empires*
Peter the Great   484
From *Gilbert Burnett's History*

From *Von Korb's Diary*
From *De Missy's Life of Peter*

XIV THE SEARCH FOR ORDER— 488
CONSTITUTIONALISM AND OLIGARCHY

CROWN AND PARLIAMENT 490
Earlier Views 490
From Fortescue. *The Governance of England (1471)*
From *Elizabeth's "Golden Speech" (1601)*
From James I. *Speech to Parliament (1610)*
From *Petition of Grievances (1610)*

CIVIL WAR 494
Two Modern Views 494
From C. H. George. *Revolution*
From J. H. Hexter. *Storm Over the Gentry*
Charles I. The Break with Parliament 495
From *Petition of Right (1628)*
Commons Protestation (1629)
Acts of Parliament (1641)
Abolition of Ship Money
Case of the Five Members
Militia Ordinance
A "Royal Martyr"? 502
Declaration of Sovereignty
Act Establishing a Court to Try the King
Charles's Defense
The Sentence
Last Words

OLIVER CROMWELL 505
War and Religion 505
From *Letters and Speeches*
Authority and Consent 506
Dismissal of the Rump Parliament
From *Clarendon's History*
From *Ludlow's Memoirs*
Cromwell's Deathbed Prayer
A Royalist View 509
From *Clarendon's History*

SOCIETY AND RELIGION 511
Social Legislation 511
From *Acts and Ordinances*
Radical Dissent 512
From *The Free-Man's Freedom Vindicated*

From *A Fiery Flying Roll*
From Winstanley. *Letter to Lord Fairfax*
A Digger Song (1649)
Women's Roles   515
From *Domesticall Duties*
From *Hudibras*
Women's Petition (1649)
From Mary Cary. *The New Jerusalem's Glory*
From George Fox. *A Collection of . . . Epistles*
From *The Sufferings of the People Called Quakers*
From *Dorothy Osborne's Letters*

FROM RESTORATION TO REVOLUTION: 521
ENGLAND AND HOLLAND
Restoration   521
From *John Evelyn's Diary*
The "Glorious Revolution"   521
From *John Evelyn's Diary*
Patterns of Government   523
From *Observations Upon the United Provinces
of the Netherlands*
From *The Bill of Rights (1689)*

WESTERN SOCIETIES

A DOCUMENTARY HISTORY

VOLUME I

I

IN THE BEGINNINGS
Egypt
  From *The Book of Knowing the*
    Creations
Mesopotamia
  From *The Creation Epic*
The Hebrews
  From *The Book of Genesis*

RELIGION AND NATURE
Egypt: The Nile and the Sun
  From *Hymn to the Nile*
  From *Hymn to the Aton*
Mesopotamia: Myth, Fertility, and
Worship
  From *The Epic of Gilgamesh*
  Love-Song to a King
  The Ecstacy of Love
  From *A Psalm*
  Hymn to Ishtar
The Hebrews: The Garden of Eden
  From *The Book of Genesis*

ETHICS AND LAW
Egypt: Death and Judgment
  From *The Book of the Dead*
Mesopotamia: Law and Justice
  From *The Code of Hammurabi*

GOD, MAN, AND HISTORY:
THE HEBREW TRADITION
The Covenant
  From *The Book of Exodus*
The Law
  From *The Book of Exodus*
The Prophets
  From *The Book of Isaiah*
Hebrew Poetry
  A Psalm
  From *The Song of Solomon*

2

THE ANCIENT NEAR EAST
—NATURE, GODS, AND HUMANS

THE FIRST GREAT civilizations of the Near East grew up in Egypt and Mesopotamia during the fourth and third millennia before Christ. The Hebrew people formed their first kingdom much later, about 1000 B.C. It was a rather petty state, rather trivial in its impact on the great nations of the ancient world. But, for Western culture, the Hebrew experience is all important. For many centuries the beliefs of Western people about the origin and destiny of the human race, their attitudes toward nature, and their views on the proper relationship between men and women were profoundly affected by the books of the Old Testament. The gods of Egypt and Mesopotamia were forgotten for many centuries; the god of Israel has been worshipped continuously. The records of Egypt and Mesopotamia had to be rediscovered by modern archeologists; the sacred writings of the Hebrews were never lost, and they influenced Western civilization during the whole process of its development. This raises an important question for the student of Western origins: In what ways did the Hebrews merely assimilate and transmit elements of earlier Near Eastern cultures? And in what ways did they make a distinctive contribution of their own?

IN THE BEGINNINGS

From the beginning of history humans have tried to understand the origins of the universe. The ancient Near Eastern civilizations recorded several stories of primeval creation. They provide an appropriate first approach to the thought patterns of Egyptian, Mesopotamian, and Hebrew culture.

Egypt

In the third millennium B.C. *the Egyptians conceived of the sun-god as a creator who "spat out" the other gods and the world from his own body. The sun-god, known under various names, is here called Khepri. (The translator points out that there is a play on the name Khepri and the Egyptian word* kheper, *meaning "come into being.")*

From *The Book of Knowing the Creations*

The All-Lord said, after he had come into being:

I am he who came into being as Khepri. When I had come into being, being itself came into being, and all beings came into being after I came into being. Many were the beings which came forth from my mouth, before heaven came into being, before earth came into being, before the ground and creeping things had been created in this place. I put together some of them in Nun [the primordial waters in which creation occurred] before I could find a place in which I might stand. It seemed advantageous to me in my heart; I planned with my face; and I made in concept every form when I was alone, before I had spat out what was Shu, before I had sputtered out what was Tefnut,[1] and before any other had come into being who could act with me.

I planned in my own heart, and there came into being a multitude of forms of beings, the forms of children and the forms of their children. I was the one who copulated with my fist, I masturbated with my hand. Then I spewed with my own mouth:[2] I spat out what was Shu,

---

[1] The first two children of the creator-god were Shu, the air-god, and Tefnut, the goddess of moisture. The statement of their ejection into being contains plays on the words *ishesh* "spit" and Shu, and *tef* "sputter" and Tefnut.

[2] There is here a fusion of two myths, creation by self-pollution and creation by ejection from the mouth.

From John A. Wilson, trans. in James B. Pritchard, ed., *Ancient Near East Texts: Relating to the Old Testament*, 3rd ed. (Princeton, N.J.: Princeton University Press, 1969), p. 6. Copyright © 1969 by Princeton University Press. Reprinted by permission of Princeton University Press.

and I sputtered out what was Tefnut. It was Nun who brought them up, and my Eye followed after them since the ages when they were distant from me.[3]

After I had come into being as the sole god, there were three gods beside me.[4] I came into being in this land, whereas Shu and Tefnut rejoiced in Nun, in which they were. They brought to me my Eye with them. After I had joined together my members, I wept over them. That is how men came into being from the tears which came forth from my Eye[5]. . . and I created all creeping things and whatever lives among them. Then Shu and Tefnut brought forth Geb and Nut. Then Geb and Nut brought forth Osiris, Horus Khenti-en-irti, Seth, Isis, and Nephthys from the body, one of them after another; and they brought forth their multitudes in this land.

[3]The eye of the sun-god was an independent part of himself with a complicated mythological history.
[4]Nun, Shu, and Tefnut.
[5]The labored point of the context is a play on the words *remit* "tears," and *romet* "mankind," in explanation of human creation.

Mesopotamia

The earliest Babylonian story of creation (from the second millennium) is set in a complex tale about warfare among the gods.

In the beginning two primordial beings existed, Apsu and Tiamat, male and female, identified with fresh water and salt water. These two engendered a whole race of gods. The gods chose Marduk as king and rebelled against the first parents. Finally Marduk killed Tiamat and used her remains to make the universe. (Babylonian concern with astronomy is evident in the detailed account of the arrangement of the heavens.) As a kind of afterthought Marduk made man as a servant for the gods.

From *The Creation Epic*

When on high the heaven had not been named,
Firm ground below had not been called by name,
Naught but primordial Apsu, their begetter,
(And) Mummu[1]-Tiamat, she who bore them all,
Their[2] waters commingling as a single body;

[1]Perhaps an epithet in the sense of "mother."
[2]I.e., the fresh waters of Apsu and the marine waters of Tiamat "the sea."

From E. A. Speiser, trans. in James B. Pritchard, ed., *Ancient Near East Texts: Relating to the Old Testament*, 3rd ed. (Princeton, N.J.: Princeton University Press, 1969), pp. 60–61, 67–68. Copyright © 1969 by Princeton University Press. Reprinted by permission of Princeton University Press.

No reed hut had been matted, no marsh land had
    appeared,
When no gods whatever had been brought into being,
Uncalled by name, their destinies undetermined—
Then it was that the gods were formed within them. . . .

Then joined issue Tiamat and Marduk, wisest of gods.
They strove in single combat, locked in battle.
The lord spread out his net to enfold her,
The Evil Wind, which followed behind, he let loose in
    her face.
When Tiamat opened her mouth to consume him,
He drove in the Evil Wind that she close not her lips.
As the fierce winds charged her belly,
Her body was distended and her mouth
    was wide open.
He released the arrow, it tore her belly,
It cut through her insides, splitting her heart.
Having thus subdued her, he extinguished her life.
He cast down her carcass to stand upon it.
After he had slain Tiamat, the leader,
Her band was shattered, her troupe broken up . . . .

When he had vanquished and subdued his adversaries,
Had wholly established Anshar's triumph over the foe,
Nudimmud's desire had achieved, valiant Marduk
Strengthened his hold on the vanquished gods,
And turned back to Tiamat whom he had bound.
The lord trod on the legs of Tiamat,
With his unsparing mace he crushed her skull,
When the arteries of her blood he had severed,
The North Wind bore it to places undisclosed.
On seeing this, his fathers were joyful and jubilant,
They brought gifts of homage, they to him.
Then the lord paused to view her dead body,
That he might divide the monster and do artful works.
He split her like a shellfish into two parts:
Half of her he set up and ceiled it as sky,
Pulled down the bar and posted guards.
He bade them to allow not her waters
    to escape.
He crossed the heavens and surveyed the regions.
The Great Abode, its likeness, he fixed as Esharra,
The Great Abode, Esharra, which he made as the firma-
    ment.
Anu, Enlil, and Ea he made occupy their places.

He constructed stations for the great gods,
Fixing their astral likenesses as the Images.
He determined the year by designating the zones:
He set up three constellations for each of the twelve
    months.
After defining the days of the year by means of
    heavenly figures,
He founded the station of Nebiru[3] to determine their
    heavenly bands,
That none might transgress or fall short.
Alongside it he set up the stations of Enlil and Ea.[4]
Having opened up the gates on both sides,
He strengthened the locks to the left
    and the right.
In her belly he established the zenith.
The Moon he caused to shine, the night to him en-
    trusting.
He appointed him a creature of the night to signify the
    days:
"Monthly, without cease, form designs with a crown.
At the month's very start, rising over the land,
Thou shalt have luminous horns to signify six days,
On the seventh day reaching a half-crown.
At full moon stand in opposition in mid-month.[5]
When the sun overtakes thee at the base of heaven,
Diminish thy crown and retrogress in light.
At the time of disappearance approach thou the
    course of the sun,
And on the thirtieth thou shalt again stand in
    opposition to the sun."

When Marduk hears the words of the gods,
His heart prompts him to fashion artful works.
Opening his mouth, he addresses Ea
To impart the plan he had conceived in his heart:
"Blood I will mass and cause bones to be.
I will establish a savage, 'man' shall be his name.
Verily, savage-man I will create.
He shall be charged with the service of the gods
    That they might be at ease!"

[3]The planet Jupiter.
[4]Enlil (wind-god) and Ea (earth- and water-god) were identified with north and south.
[5]I.e., the moon stands in opposition to the sun.

The Hebrews

The Hebrew account of creation is based on traditions that go back to the twelfth century B.C. *In its present form it was written down in the fifth century* B.C.

From *The Book of Genesis*

In the beginning God created the heavens and the earth. The earth was without form and void, and darkness was upon the face of the deep; and the Spirit of God was moving over the face of the waters. And God said, "Let there be light"; and there was light. And God saw that the light was good; and God separated the light from the darkness. God called the light Day, and the darkness he called Night. And there was evening and there was morning, one day.

And God said, "Let there be a firmament in the midst of the waters, and let it separate the waters from the waters." And God made the firmament and separated the waters which were under the firmament from the waters which were above the firmament. And it was so. And God called the firmament Heaven. And there was evening and there was morning, a second day.

And God said, "Let the waters under the heavens be gathered together into one place, and let the dry land appear." And it was so. God called the dry land Earth, and the waters that were gathered together he called Seas. And God saw that it was good. And God said, "Let the earth put forth vegetation, plants yielding seed, and fruit trees bearing fruit in which is their seed, each according to its kind, upon the earth." And it was so. The earth brought forth vegetation, plants yielding seed according to their own kinds, and trees bearing fruit in which is their seed, each according to its kind. And God saw that it was good. And there was evening and there was morning, a third day.

And God said, "Let there be lights in the firmament of the heavens to separate the day from the night; and let them be for signs and for seasons and for days and years, and let them be lights in the firmament of the heavens to give light upon the earth." And it was so. And God made the two great lights, the greater light to rule the day, and the lesser light to rule the night; he made the stars also. And God set them in the firmament of the heavens to give light upon the earth, to rule over the day and over the night, and to separate the light from the darkness. And God saw that it was good. And there was evening and there was morning, a fourth day.

And God said, "Let the waters bring forth swarms of living crea-

From the *Revised Standard Version Bible* (New York: Oxford University Press, 1973). Genesis 1:1–31; 2:1–4. Copyright 1946, 1952, © 1971, 1973 by the National Council of the Churches of Christ. Reprinted by permission.

tures, and let birds fly above the earth across the firmament of the heavens."

So God created the great sea monsters and every living creature that moves, with which the waters swarm, according to their kinds, and every winged bird according to its kind. And God saw that it was good. And God blessed them, saying, "Be fruitful and multiply and fill the waters in the seas, and let birds multiply on the earth." And there was evening and there was morning, a fifth day.

And God said, "Let the earth bring forth living creatures according to their kinds: cattle and creeping things and beasts of the earth according to their kinds." And it was so. And God made the beasts of the earth according to their kinds and the cattle according to their kinds, and everything that creeps upon the ground according to its kind. And God saw that it was good.

Then God said, "Let us make man in our image, after our likeness; and let them have dominion over the fish of the sea, and over the birds of the air, and over the cattle, and over all the earth, and over every creeping thing that creeps upon the earth." So God created man in his own image, in the image of God he created him; male and female he created them. And God blessed them, and God said to them, "Be fruitful and multiply, and fill the earth and subdue it; and have dominion over the fish of the sea and over the birds of the air and over every living thing that moves upon the earth." And God said, "Behold, I have given you every plant yielding seed which is upon the face of all the earth, and every tree with seed in its fruit; you shall have them for food. And to every beast of the earth, and to every bird of the air, and to everything that creeps on the earth, everything that has the breath of life, I have given every green plant for food." And it was so. And God saw everything that he had made, and behold, it was very good. And there was evening and there was morning, a sixth day.

Thus the heavens and the earth were finished, and all the host of them. And on the seventh day God finished his work which he had done, and he rested on the seventh day from all his work which he had done. So God blessed the seventh day and hallowed it, because on it God rested from all his work which he had done in creation.

These are the generations of the heavens and earth when they were created.

RELIGION AND NATURE

To people of the ancient world the gods were not merely remote creator figures. They played an important part in day-to-day life. The gods required humans to worship them and obey them. They established divine rulers over kingdoms. Their activity was needed to maintain the fertility of nature.

Egypt: The Nile and the Sun

For Egyptians there was no sharp line of distinction between natural and divine. The Nile could be perceived simultaneously as an actual river that watered the crops and as a hidden deity to be worshipped. This hymn probably dates back to the Middle Kingdom (2100–1700 B.C.)

From *Hymn to the Nile*

Hail to thee, O Nile, that issues from the earth and comes to keep Egypt alive! Hidden in his form of appearance,[1] a darkness by day, to whom minstrels have sung. He that waters the meadows which Re created, in order to keep every kid alive. He that makes to drink the desert and the place distant from water: that is his dew coming down from heaven.[2] The beloved of Geb,[3] the one who controls Nepri,[4] and the one who makes the craftsmanship of Ptah to flourish.

The lord of fishes, he who makes the marsh-birds to go upstream. . . . He who makes barley and brings emmer[5] into being, that he may make the temples festive. If he is sluggish, then nostrils are stopped up, and everybody is poor. If there be thus a cutting down in the food-offerings of the gods, then a million men perish among mortals, covetousness is practised, the entire land is in a fury, and great and small are on the execution-block. But people are different when he approaches. . . . When he rises, then the land is in jubilation, then every

[1]The Nile had no regular cult or temple in which he might appear in an image.
[2]Regions cut off from the waters of the Nile had his rain to sustain them.
[3]The earth-god.
[4]The grain-god.
[5]A kind of wheat grain used as fodder.

From John A. Wilson, trans. in James B. Pritchard, ed., *Ancient Near Eastern Texts: Relating to the Old Testament*, 3rd ed. (Princeton, N.J.: Princeton University Press, 1969), pp. 372–373. Copyright © 1969 by Princeton University Press. Reprinted by permission of Princeton University Press.

belly is in joy, every backbone takes on laughter, and every tooth is exposed.[6]

The bringer of food, rich in provisions, creator of all good, lord of majesty, sweet of fragrance. What is in him is satisfaction. He who brings grass into being for the cattle and thus gives sacrifice to every god, whether he be in the underworld, heaven, or earth, him who is under his authority. He who takes in possession the Two Lands, fills the magazines, makes the granaries wide, and gives things to the poor.

He Who Makes every beloved Tree to Grow, without lack of them . . . He cannot be seen; he has no taxes; he has no levies; no one can read of the mystery; no one knows the place where he is; he cannot be found by the power of writing. He has no shrines: he has no portion. He has no service of his desire. But generations of thy children jubilate for thee, and men give thee greeting as a king, stable of laws, coming forth at his season and filling Upper and Lower Egypt. Whenever water is drunk, every eye is in him, who gives an excess of his good.

He Who Was Sorrowful Is Come Forth Gay. Every heart is gay. Sobek, the child of Neith, laughs, and the Ennead,[7] in which thou art, is exalted. Vomiting forth and making the field to drink. Anointing the whole land. . . .

The generations of thy children jubilate for thee. Men equip messengers for thee, who come back bearing treasures to ornament this land. He who makes a ship to prosper before mankind; he who sustains hearts in pregnant women; he who loves a multitude of all kinds of his cattle.

When Thou Risest in the City of the Ruler, then men are satisfied with the goodly produce of the meadows. Oh for the little lotus-blossoms, everything that pours forth upon earth, all kinds of herbs in the hands of children! They have even forgotten how to eat. Good things are strewn about the houses. The land comes down frolicking.

When the Nile Floods, offering is made to thee, oxen are sacrificed to thee, great oblations are made to thee, birds are fattened for thee, lions are hunted for thee in the desert, fire is provided for thee. And offering is made to every other god, as is done for the Nile, with prime incense, oxen, cattle, birds, and flame. . . .

O All Men who uphold the Ennead, fear ye the majesty which his son the All-Lord has made, by making verdant the two banks. So it is "Verdant art thou!" So it is "Verdant art thou." So it is, "O Nile, verdant art thou who makest man and cattle to live!"

Besides the Nile, the other great source of fertility was the sun. Around 1370
B.C. *the Pharaoh Akhnaton instituted a new cult, the worship of the sun-disc*

[6]When the Nile floods, all Egyptians laugh in delight.
[7]Ennead, i.e., the group of nine principal gods.

under the name of Aton. This hymn praises Aton as "sole god" and as the source of all life and fruitfulness on earth. (The cult of Aton as sole god was abandoned after Akhnaton's death.)

Hymn to the Aton

Thou appearest beautifully on the horizon of heaven,
Thou living Aton, the beginning of life!
When thou art risen on the eastern horizon,
Thou hast filled every land with thy beauty.
Thou art gracious, great, glistening, and high over every land;
Thy rays encompass the lands to the limit of all that thou hast
　　　made. . . .
Thou subduest them for thy beloved son.
Though thou art far away, thy rays are on earth;
Though thou are in their faces, no one knows thy going.
When thou settest in the western horizon,
The land is in darkness, in the manner of death. . . .
Every lion is come forth from his den;
All creeping things, they sting.
Darkness is a shroud, and the earth is in stillness,
For he who made them rests in the horizon.

At daybreak, when thou arisest on the horizon,
When thou shinest as the Aton by day,
Thou drivest away the darkness and givest thy rays.
The Two Lands are in festivity every day,
Awake and standing upon their feet,
For thou hast raised them up.
Washing their bodies, taking their clothing,
Their arms are raised in praise at thy appearance.
All the world, they do their work.

All beasts are content with their pasturage;
Trees and plants are flourishing.
The birds which fly from their nests,
Their wings are stretched out in praise to thy *ka*.
All beasts spring upon their feet.
Whatever flies and alights,
They live when thou hast risen for them.
The ships are sailing north and south as well,
For every way is open at thy appearance.

From John A. Wilson, trans. in James B. Pritchard, ed., *Ancient Near Eastern Texts: Relating to the Old Testament*, 3rd ed. (Princeton, N.J.: Princeton University Press, 1969) pp. 370–371. Copyright © 1969 by Princeton University Press. Reprinted by permission of Princeton University Press.

The fish in the river dart before thy face;
Thy rays are in the midst of the great green sea.

Creator of seed in women,
Thou who makest fluid into man,
Who maintainest the son in the womb of his mother,
Who soothest him with that which stills his weeping,
Thou nurse even in the womb,
Who givest breath to sustain all that he has made!
When he descends from the womb to breathe
On the day when he is born,
Thou openest his mouth completely,
Thou suppliest his necessities.
When the chick in the egg speaks within the shell,
Thou givest him breath within it to maintain him.
When thou hast made him his fulfillment within the egg, to
　　break it,
He comes forth from the egg to speak at his completed time;
He walks upon his legs when he comes forth from it.
How manifold it is, what thou hast made!
They are hidden from the face of man.
O sole god, like whom there is no other!
Thou didst create the world according to thy desire,
Whilst thou wert alone:
All men, cattle, and wild beasts.
Whatever is on earth, going upon its feet
And what is on high, flying with its wings. . . .

Thy rays suckle every meadow.
When thou risest, they live, they grow for thee.
Thou makest the seasons in order to rear all that thou hast
　　made,
The winter to cool them,
And the heat that they may taste thee.
Thou hast made the distant sky in order to rise therein,
In order to see all that thou dost make.
Whilst thou wert alone,
Rising in thy form as the living Aton,
Appearing, shining, withdrawing or approaching,
Thou madest millions of forms of thyself alone.
Cities, towns, fields, road, and river—
Every eye beholds thee over against them,
For thou art the Aton of the day over the earth. . . .

Thou art in my heart,
And there is no other that knows thee
Save thy son Nefer-kheperu-Re Wa-en-Re (Akhnaton),

For thou hast made him well-versed in thy plans and in thy
strength.

The world came into being by thy hand,
According as thou hast made them.
When thou hast risen they live,
When thou settest they die.
Thou art lifetime thy own self,
For one lives only through thee.
Eyes are fixed on beauty until thou settest.
All work is laid aside when thou settest in the west.
But when thou risest again,
Everything is made to flourish for the king, . . .
Since thou didst found the earth
And raise them up for thy son,
Who came forth from thy body:
The King of Upper and Lower Egypt, . . . Akhnaton . . . and the
Chief Wife of the King . . . Nefertiti, living and youthful
forever and ever.

Mesopotamia: Myth, Fertility, and Worship

The Babylonian Epic of Gilgamesh *(from the second millennium) presents
the first account of man "in a state of nature." The hero, Gilgamesh, is part
god, part man. His companion Enkidu grew up as a savage, living in the
wilderness with only animals for company. The story of how Enkidu was
tamed and brought to civilization offers points of comparison and contrast
with the biblical story of Adam and Eve.*

From *The Epic of Gilgamesh*

The hunter went forth to Gilgamesh.
He took the road, in Uruk he set his foot:
". . . Gilgamesh . . . ,
There is a fellow who has come from the hills,
He is the mightiest in the land; strength
he has
Like the essence of Anu, so mighty his strength!
Ever he ranges over the hills,
Ever with the beasts he feeds on grass,

Ever sets he his feet at the watering-place.
I am so frightened that I dare not approach him!
He filled in the pits that I had dug,
He tore up my traps which I had set,
The beasts and creatures of the steppe
    He has made slip through my hands.
He does not allow me to engage in fieldcraft!"
Gilgamesh says to him, to the hunter:
"Go, my hunter, take with thee a harlot-lass.
When he waters the beasts at the watering-place,
She shall pull off her clothing, laying bare her ripeness.
As soon as he sees her, he will draw near to her.
Reject him will his beasts that grew up on his steppe!"
Forth went the hunter, taking with him a harlot-lass.
They took the road, going straight on their way.
On the third day at the appointed spot they arrived.
The hunter and the harlot sat down in their places.
One day, a second day, they sat by the
    watering-place.
The wild beasts came to the watering-place to drink.

The creeping creatures came, their heart delighting in
    water.
But as for him, Enkidu, born in the hills—
With the gazelles he feeds on grass,
With the wild beasts he drinks at the watering-place,
With the creeping creatures his heart delights in water—
The lass beheld him, the savage-man,
The barbarous fellow from the depths of the steppe:
"There he is, O lass! Free thy breasts,
Bare thy bosom that he may possess thy ripeness!
Be not bashful! Welcome his ardor!
As soon as he sees thee, he will draw near to thee.
Lay aside thy cloth that he may rest upon thee.
Treat him, the savage, to a woman's task!
Reject him will his wild beasts that grew up on his
    steppe,
As his love is drawn unto thee."
The lass freed her breasts, bared her bosom,
    And he possessed her ripeness.
She was not bashful as she welcomed his ardor.
She laid aside her cloth and he rested upon her.
She treated him, the savage, to a woman's task,
As his love was drawn unto her.
For six days and seven nights Enkidu comes forth,
    Mating with the lass.
After he had had his fill of her charms,

He set his face toward his wild beasts.
On seeing him, Enkidu, the gazelles ran off,
The wild beasts of the steppe drew away from his body.
Startled was Enkidu, as his body became taut,
His knees were motionless—for his wild beasts had gone.
Enkidu had to slacken his pace—it was not as before;
But he now had wisdom, broader understanding.
Returning, he sits at the feet of the harlot.
He looks up at the face of the harlot,
His ears attentive, as the harlot speaks;
The harlot says to him, to Enkidu:
"Thou art wise, Enkidu, art become like a god!
Why with the wild creatures dost thou roam over the
      steppe?
Come, let me lead thee to ramparted Uruk,
To the holy temple, abode of Anu and Ishtar,
Where lives Gilgamesh, accomplished in strength,
And like a wild ox lords it over the folk."
As she speaks to him, her words find favor,
His heart enlightened, he yearns for a friend.
Enkidu says to her, to the harlot:
"Up, lass, escort thou me,
To the pure sacred temple, abode of Anu and Ishtar,
Where lives Gilgamesh, accomplished in strength,
And like a wild ox lords it over the folk.
I will challenge him and will boldly address him. . . ."

In Sumerian religion the sacred matings of the gods, reenacted on earth by kings and priestesses, ensured the continuing fruitfulness of nature. These Sumerian verses (which have been called "the first love songs") are ritual chants of priestesses at the sacred marriage ceremonies. The first one is full of fertility symbols. (The breaks indicated thus, . . . , are missing or indecipherable words.)

Love-Song to a King

He has sprouted, he has burgeoned, he is lettuce planted
      by the water,
My well-stocked garden of the . . . plain, my favored of
      the womb,
My grain luxuriant in its furrow—he is lettuce planted
      by the water,

From S. N. Kramer, trans. in James B. Pritchard, ed., *Ancient Near Eastern Texts: Relating to the Old Testament*, 3rd. ed. (Princeton, N.J.: Princeton University Press, 1969), p. 645. Copyright © 1969 by Princeton University Press. Reprinted by permission of Princeton University Press.

My apple tree which bears fruit up to its top—he is
  lettuce planted by the water.

The "honey-man," the "honey-man" sweetens me ever,
My lord, the "honey-man" of the gods, my favored of
  the womb,
Whose hand is honey, whose foot is honey, sweetens me
  ever.
Whose limbs are honey sweet, sweetens me ever.

My sweetener of the . . . navel, my favored of the
  womb,
My . . . of the fair thighs, he is lettuce planted by the
  water.

The next song was written on both sides of a clay tablet (indicated as "obverse" and "reverse"). The god Dumuzi wants to spend the night making love to the goddess Inanna. She says, "What shall I tell my mother . . . ?" He says, "Tell her you were out with a girl friend. . . ."

The Ecstacy of Love

(Obverse)

Last night, as I, the queen, was shining bright,
Last night, as I, the queen of heaven, was shining bright,
As I was shining bright, as I was dancing about,
As I was uttering a song at the brightening of the
  oncoming night,
He met me, he met me,
The Lord Kuli-Anna[1] met me,
The lord put his hand into my hand,
Ushumgalanna embraced me.

"Come now, wild bull, set me free, I must go home,
Kuli-Enlil, set me free, I must go home,
What shall I say to deceive my mother!
What shall I say to deceive my mother Ningal!"

"Let me inform you, let me inform you.
Inanna, most deceitful of women, let me inform you:
'My girl friend took me with her to the public square,

[1]The various forms of address used from this line onward are all different names of Dumuzi.

From S. N. Kramer, trans. in James B. Pritchard, ed., *Ancient Near Eastern Texts: Relating to the Old Testament*, 3rd. ed. (Princeton, N.J.: Princeton University Press, 1969), pp. 639–640. Copyright © 1969 by Princeton University Press. Reprinted by permission of Princeton University Press.

She entertained me there with music and dancing,
Her chant, the sweet, she sang for me.
In sweet rejoicing I whiled away the time there'—
Thus deceitfully stand up to your mother,
While we by the moonlight indulge our passion,
I will prepare for you a bed pure, sweet, and
    noble,
Will while away the sweet time with you in joyful
    fulfillment."

(remainder of the obverse and first three lines of reverse destroyed)

(Reverse)

I have come to our mother's gate,
I, in joy I walk,
I have come to Ningal's gate,
I, in joy I walk.
To my mother he will say the word,[2]
He will sprinkle cypress oil on the ground,
To my mother Ningal he will say the word,
He will sprinkle cypress oil on the ground,
He whose dwelling is fragrant,
Whose word brings deep joy.

My lord is seemly for the holy lap,
Amaushumgalanna, the son-in-law of Sin,
The lord Dumuzi is seemly for the holy lap,
Amaushumgalanna, the son-in-law of Sin.
My lord, sweet is your increase,
Tasty your plants, and herbs in the plain,
Amaushumgalanna, sweet is your increase,
Tasty your plants and herbs in the plain.

*The Babylonian gods were arbitrary, inscrutable figures. They had to be pla-
cated, but it was hard for human beings to know how to please them.*

From *A Psalm*

Prayer was my practice, sacrificing my law,
The day of worship of the gods the joy of my heart,

[2]I.e., he will ask for Inanna in marriage.

From M. Jastrow, Jr., trans., "Babylonian Parallels to Job," in *Journal of Biblical Literature* 25 (1906), pp. 163, 166.

The day of devotion to the goddess more to me than
    riches;
What, however, seems good to oneself, to a god is dis-
    pleasing,
What is spurned by oneself finds favor with a god;
Who is there that can grasp the will of the gods in
    heaven?
The plan of a god full of mystery—who can un-
    derstand it?
How can mortals learn the way of a god?

Sometimes the great mother-goddess Ishtar was asked to intercede with the other gods.

Hymn to Ishtar

How long, O my Lady, shall my adversaries be looking
    upon me,
In lying and untruth shall they plan evil against me,
Shall my pursuers and those who exult over me rage
    against me?
How long, O my Lady, shall the crippled and weak
    seek me out?
One has made for me long sackcloth; thus I have
    appeared before thee.
The weak have become strong; but I am weak.
I toss about like flood-water, which an evil wind makes
    violent.
My heart is flying; it keeps fluttering like a bird of
    heaven.
I mourn like a dove night and day.
I am beaten down, and so I weep bitterly.
With "Oh" and "Alas" my spirit is distressed.
I—what have I done, O my god and my goddess?
Like one who does not fear my god and my goddess
    I am treated;
While sickness, headache, loss, and destruction are
    provided for me;
So are fixed upon me terror, disdain, and fullness of
    wrath,

From Ferris J. Stephens, trans. in James B. Pritchard, ed., *Ancient Near Eastern Texts: Relating to the Old Testament*, 3rd. ed. (Princeton, N.J.: Princeton University Press, 1969), pp. 384–385. Copyright © 1969 by Princeton University Press. Reprinted by permission of Princeton University Press.

Anger, choler, and indignation of gods and men.
I have to expect, O my Lady, dark days, gloomy months,
    and years of trouble.
I have to expect, O my Lady, judgment of confusion
    and violence.
Death and trouble are bringing me to an end.
Silent is my chapel; silent is my holy place;
Over my house, my gate, and my fields silence is
    poured out.
As for my god, his face is turned to the sanctuary of
    another.
My family is scattered; my roof is broken up.
But I have paid heed to thee, my Lady; my attention
    has been turned to thee.
To thee have I prayed; forgive my debt.
Forgive my sin, my iniquity, my shameful deeds, and
    my offence.
Overlook my shameful deeds; accept my prayer;
Loosen my fetters; secure my deliverance;
Guide my steps aright; radiantly like a hero let me enter
    the streets with the living.
Speak so that at thy command the angry god may be
    favorable;
And the goddess who has been angry with me may
    turn again.
Now dark and smoky, may my brazier glow;
Now extinguished, may my torch be lighted.
Let my scattered family be assembled;
May my fold be wide; may my stable be enlarged.
Accept the abasement of my countenance; hear my
    prayers.
Faithfully look upon me and accept my supplication.

The Hebrews: The Garden of Eden

The story of Adam and Eve follows immediately after the creation narrative given above (p. 8). In the first creation story, God gave man "dominion" over all creatures. Here he gives Adam a garden to "till and keep." Some scholars have seen in such phrases the source of an "exploitative" approach to the natural world in Western culture. However that may be, this ancient story has certainly exercised a profound and continuing influence on Western attitudes to God, nature, man, and (especially) woman.

From *The Book of Genesis*

In the day that the Lord God made the earth and the heavens, when no plant of the field was yet in the earth and no herb of the field had yet sprung up—for the Lord God had not caused it to rain upon the earth, and there was no man to till the ground; but a mist went up from the earth and watered the whole face of the ground—then the Lord God formed man of dust from the ground, and breathed into his nostrils the breath of life; and man became a living being. And the Lord God planted a garden in Eden, in the east; and there he put the man whom he had formed. And out of the ground the Lord God made to grow every tree that is pleasant to the sight and good for food, the tree of life also in the midst of the garden, and the tree of the knowledge of good and evil. . . .

The Lord God took the man and put him in the garden of Eden to till it and keep it. And the Lord God commanded the man, saying, "You may freely eat of every tree of the garden; but of the tree of the knowledge of good and evil you shall not eat, for in the day that you eat of it you shall die."

Then the Lord God said, "It is not good that the man should be alone; I will make him a helper fit for him." So out of the ground the Lord God formed every beast of the field and every bird of the air, and brought them to the man to see what he would call them; and whatever the man called every living creature, that was its name. The man gave names to all cattle, and to the birds of the air, and to every beast of the field; but for the man there was not found a helper fit for him. So the Lord God caused a deep sleep to fall upon the man, and while he slept took one of his ribs and closed up its place with flesh; and the rib which the Lord God had taken from the man he made into a woman and brought her to the man. Then the man said,

> "This at last is bone of my bones
>   and flesh of my flesh;
> she shall be called Woman,
>   because she was taken out of
>   Man."

Therefore a man leaves his father and his mother and cleaves to his wife, and they become one flesh. And the man and his wife were both naked, and were not ashamed.

Now the serpent was more subtle than any other wild creature that the Lord God had made. He said to the woman, "Did God say, 'You shall not eat of any tree of the garden'?" And the woman said to the serpent, "We may eat of the fruit of the trees of the garden; but God said, 'You shall not eat of the fruit of the tree which is in the midst of the garden, neither shall you touch it, lest you die.' " But the serpent said to the woman, "You will not die. For God knows that when you eat of it your eyes will be opened, and you will be like God, knowing good and evil." So when the woman saw that the tree was good for food, and that it was a delight to the eyes, and that the tree was to be desired to make one wise, she took of its fruit and ate; and she also gave some to her husband, and he ate. Then the eyes of both were opened, and they knew that they were naked; and they sewed fig leaves together and made themselves aprons.

And they heard the sound of the Lord God walking in the garden in the cool of the day, and the man and his wife hid themselves from the presence of the Lord God among the trees of the garden. But the Lord God called to the man, and said to him, "Where are you?" And he said, "I heard the sound of thee in the garden, and I was afraid, because I was naked; and I hid myself." He said, "Who told you that you were naked? Have you eaten of the tree of which I commanded you not to eat?" The man said, "The woman whom thou gavest to be with me, she gave me fruit of the tree, and I ate." Then the Lord God said to the woman, "What is this that you have done?" The woman said, "The serpent beguiled me, and I ate." The Lord God said to the serpent,

"Because you have done this,
    cursed are you above all cattle,
    and above all wild animals;
upon your belly you shall go,
    and dust you shall eat
    all the days of your life.
I will put enmity between you and
        the woman,
    and between your seed and her
        seed;
he shall bruise your head,
    and you shall bruise his heel."
To the woman he said,
"I will greatly multiply your pain in
        childbearing;
    in pain you shall bring forth
        children,
yet your desire shall be for your
        husband,
    and he shall rule over you."
And to Adam he said,
"Because you have listened to the
        voice of your wife,
    and have eaten of the tree
of which I commanded you,

'You shall not eat of it,'
cursed is the ground because of you;
   in toil you shall eat of it all the
      days of your life;
thorns and thistles it shall bring
      forth to you;
   and you shall eat the plants of the
      field.
In the sweat of your face
   you shall eat bread
   till you return to the ground,
      for out of it you were taken;
   you are dust,
      and to dust you shall return."

The man called his wife's name Eve, because she was the mother of all living. And the Lord God made for Adam and for his wife garments of skins, and clothed them.

Then the Lord God said, "Behold, the man has become like one of us, knowing good and evil; and now, lest he put forth his hand and take also of the tree of life, and eat, and live for ever"—therefore the Lord God sent him forth from the garden of Eden, to till the ground from which he was taken. He drove out the man; and at the east of the garden of Eden he placed the cherubim, and a flaming sword which turned every way, to guard the way to the tree of life.

ETHICS AND LAW

The moral ideals and legal regulations in these texts from Egypt and Babylon may be compared with the later law of Moses.

Egypt: Death and Judgment

In their dealings with the gods Egyptians were especially concerned with a life after death when they would face a divine judgment. This protestation of innocence was written for the chancellor Nu about the middle of the second millennium.

From *The Book of the Dead*

The following shall be said when the overseer of the palace, the chancellor-in-chief, Nu, triumphant, cometh forth into the Hall of Double Maati[1] so that he may be separated from every sin which he hath done and may behold the faces of the gods. Nu, triumphant, saith: . . .

"I have not done evil to mankind. I have not oppressed the members of my family, I have not wrought evil in the place of right and truth. I have had no knowledge of worthless men. I have not wrought evil. I have not made to be the first consideration of each day that excessive labor should be performed for me. I have not brought forward my name for exaltation to honors. I have not ill-treated servants. I have not thought scorn of God. I have not defrauded the oppressed one of his property. I have not done that which is an abomination unto the gods. I have not caused harm to be done to the servant by his chief. I have not caused pain. I have made no one to weep. I have done no murder. I have not given the order for murder to be done for me. I have not inflicted pain upon mankind. I have not defrauded the temples of their oblations. I have not purloined the cakes of the gods. I have not committed fornication. . . . I have not turned back water at the time [when it should flow]. I have not cut a cutting in a canal of running water. . . . I have not repulsed God in his manifestations. I am pure. I am pure. I am pure. I am pure. . . .

"I have given bread to the hungry man, and water to the thirsty

[1] Justice or Truth.

From E. A. Wallis Budge, trans., *The Book of the Dead According to the Theban Recension* in Epiphanius Wilson, ed., *Egyptian Literature* (London: The Colonial Press, 1901), pp. 102–103.

man, and clothes to the naked man, and a boat to the marooned mariner. I have made holy offerings to the gods, and funeral offerings to the dead. Be you then my deliverers, be you then my protectors, and make no accusation against me in the presence of the great god. I am pure of mouth and pure of hands; therefore let it be said unto me by those who shall behold me, 'Come in peace; come in peace.' "

Mesopotamia: Law and Justice

The Code of Hammurabi was set down about 1750 B.C. and it incorporates still earlier laws. In substance a stern code of retributive justice, it incidentally provides rich information about many aspects of early Babylonian society—social gradations, economic activity, family life, sexual morality.

From *The Code of Hammurabi*

1. If a man weave a spell and bring a charge of murder against another man and has not justified himself, the accuser shall be put to death.

2. If a man has put a spell upon another man, and has not justified himself, the one who is charged with sorcery shall go to the holy river, he shall plunge into the holy river, and if the holy river overcomes him, his accuser shall take his estate. If the holy river shows that man to be innocent and has saved him, he who charged him with sorcery shall be put to death and the man who plunged into the river shall take the estate of him who brought the charge against him.

8. If a man has stolen ox or sheep or ass or pig or ship, whether from the temple or from the palace, he shall pay thirtyfold; if he stole from a commoner, he shall render tenfold. If the thief cannot pay, he shall be put to death.

14. If a man has stolen the son of a freeman, he shall be put to death.

15. If a man has helped a male or female palace slave, or a commoner's male or female slave to escape out of the city gate, he shall be put to death.

21. If a man has broken into a house, he shall be killed before the breach and walled in it.

23. If the robber has not been caught, the man who has been despoiled shall recount before the god what he has lost, and the city and governor in whose territory the robbery took place shall make good to him his loss.

From C. H. W. Johns, trans. *The Oldest Code of Laws in the World* (Edinburgh: T. and T. Clarke, 1901).

24. If a life was lost, the city and governor shall pay one mina of silver to his people.

27. If a soldier or a constable disappears whilst on military service and they have given his field and his orchard to another and he has carried on his obligations, if he returns and regains his city, they shall restore his field and his orchard and he shall fulfill his obligations himself.

48. If a man has a debt upon him and a thunderstorm ravaged his field or carried away the produce, or the corn has not grown for lack of water, in that year he shall make no return of corn to his creditor; he shall alter his contract-tablet and he shall not pay interest for that year.

53. If a man has neglected to strengthen the dyke of his canal, and a breach has opened in his dyke, and the waters have ravaged the meadow, the man in whose dyke the breach has been opened shall make good the corn that he caused to be lost.

104. If a merchant has lent a trader corn, wool, oil or any sort of goods to traffic with, the trader shall write down the price and pay it back; the trader shall take a sealed receipt of the price which he pays to the merchant.

109. If a wine merchant has collected outlaws in her house and has not seized those outlaws and driven them to the palace, that wine merchant shall be put to death.

110. If a nun, a lady of god, who is not living in a convent, has opened the door of a wine shop or entered the wine shop for a drink, that woman shall be burned.

117. If a debt came due against a man, and he has given his wife, his son, his daughter for the money, or handed himself over to work off the debt, for three years they shall work in the house of their buyer or exploiter, in the fourth year they shall be set free.

128. If a man has married a wife and has not drawn up a contract, that woman is no wife.

129. If the wife of a man has been caught lying with another man, they shall bind them and throw them into the waters.

131. If a wife has been accused by her husband and she has not been caught lying with another male, she shall swear by god and shall return to her house.

132. If a wife has the finger pointed at her on account of another male but has not been caught lying with another male, for the sake of her husband she shall throw herself into the holy river.

133. If a man has been taken captive and in his house there is maintenance, if his wife has gone out from her house and entered into the house of another, because that woman has not guarded her body and has entered the house of another, they shall prove it against that woman and throw her into the waters.

134. If a man has been taken captive and in his house there is no

maintenance, and his wife has entered into the house of another, that woman has no blame.

137. If a man has decided to put away his concubine who has borne him children or his wife who has granted him children, to that woman he shall return her marriage portion and shall give her half of the field, orchard and goods, and she shall bring up her children. From the time that her children are grown up, from whatever is given to her children they shall give her a share like that of one son, and she shall marry the husband of her choice.

138. If a man has put away his bride who has not borne him children, he shall return her dowry and pay her the marriage portion which she brought from her father's house, and shall put her away.

141. If the wife of a man who is living in the house of her husband has made up her mind to leave the house to engage in business and has acted the fool, neglecting the house and humiliating the husband, it shall be proved against her; and if her husband has said "I put her away," he shall put her away and she shall go her way, and he shall not give her anything for her divorce.

142. If a woman hates her husband and has said "You shall not possess me," they shall inquire into her record and if she has been economical and has no vice and her husband has gone out and greatly belittled her, that woman has no blame, she will take her marriage portion and go off to her father's house.

143. If she has not been economical, a gadabout, has neglected her house and humiliated her husband, that woman they shall throw into the waters.

153. If a man's wife has caused her husband to be killed on account of another man, they shall impale that woman on a stake.

154. If a man has known his daughter, that man shall be expelled from the city.

157. If a man, after his father, has lain in the bosom of his mother, they shall burn both of them together.

195. If a man has struck his father, his hand shall be cut off.

196. If a man has caused the loss of a gentleman's eye, they shall cause him to lose one eye.

200. If a man has made the tooth of a man that is his equal fall out, they shall make his tooth fall out.

201. If he has made the tooth of a commoner fall out, he shall pay one third of a mina of silver.

202. If a man has struck the cheek of his superior, he shall be struck in the assembly with 60 strokes of a cowhide whip.

203. If a man of gentle birth has struck a man of gentle birth who is his equal, he shall pay one mina of silver.

209. If a man has struck a gentleman's daughter and caused her to have a miscarriage, he shall pay ten shekels of silver for what was in her womb.

210. If that woman has died, they shall put to death his daughter.

211. If by his blows he has caused the daughter of a commoner to have a miscarriage, he shall pay five shekels of silver.

212. If that woman has died, he shall pay half a mina of silver.

213. If he has struck a gentleman's slave and caused a miscarriage, he shall pay two shekels of silver.

214. If that slave has died, he shall pay one third of a mina of silver.

215. If a doctor has treated a gentleman for a severe wound, with a bronze lancet and has cured him, or has opened an abcess of the eye for a gentleman with the bronze lancet and has cured the eye of the gentleman, he shall take ten shekels of silver.

218. If the doctor has treated a gentleman for a severe wound with a lancet of bronze and has caused the gentleman to die or has opened an abcess of the eye of a gentleman with the bronze lancet and has caused the loss of the gentleman's eye, they shall cut off his hands.

229. If a builder has built a house and not made his work strong and the house he built has fallen and so has caused the death of the owner of the house, that builder shall be put to death.

230. If he has caused the son of the owner of the house to die, they shall put to death the son of the builder.

250. If a wild bull in his charge has gored a man, and caused him to die, that case has no remedy.

251. If a man's ox was inclined to gore and it was made known to him that this was so and he took no steps to tie him up or blunt his horns, and that ox has gored a man and caused him to die, he shall pay half a mina of silver for a gentleman, one third of a mina for a slave.

GOD, MAN, AND HISTORY: THE HEBREW TRADITION

The Hebrew people worshipped the god Yahweh (often transliterated into English as Jehovah). They moved from a belief in Yahweh as their own particular tribal deity to a conviction that he was the one supreme being, the one true God. This God, they believed, had made a convenant with their ancestors as a specially chosen people, the "children of Israel." They could cooperate with God (or fail to cooperate) in working out their historic destiny. Hebrew religious writings thus formed a sacred history, an account of God's dealings with his people down the course of the ages.

The Covenant

The Covenant (originally made with Abraham) was renewed at the time of Moses. (Moses lived c. 1200 B.C. The biblical account is based on traditions going back to that period.)

From *The Book of Exodus*

In the course of those many days the king of Egypt died. And the people of Israel groaned under their bondage, and cried out for help, and their cry under bondage came up to God. And God heard their groaning, and God remembered his covenant with Abraham, with Isaac, and with Jacob. And God saw the people of Israel, and God knew their condition. . . .

Then the Lord said, "I have seen the affliction of my people who are in Egypt, and have heard their cry because of their taskmasters; I know their sufferings, and I have come down to deliver them out of the hand of the Egyptians, and to bring them up out of that land to a good and broad land, a land flowing with milk and honey, to the place of the Canaanites, the Hittites, the Amorites, the Perizzites, the Hivites, and the Jebusites. And now, behold, the cry of the people of Israel has come to me, and I have seen the oppression with which the Egyptians oppress them. Come, I will send you to Pharaoh that you may bring forth my people, the sons of Israel, out of Egypt." But Moses said to God, "Who am I that I should go to Pharaoh, and bring the sons of Israel out of Egypt?" He said, "But I will be with you; and this shall be

From the *Revised Standard Version Bible* (New York: Oxford University Press, 1973). Exodus 2:23–25; 3:7–15. Copyright 1946, 1952 © 1971, 1973 by the Council of the Churches of Christ. Reprinted by permission.

the sign for you, that I have sent you: when you have brought forth the people out of Egypt, you shall serve God upon this mountain."

Then Moses said to God, "If I come to the people of Israel and say to them, 'The God of your fathers has sent me to you,' and they ask me, 'What is his name?' what shall I say to them?" God said to Moses, "I AM WHO I AM." And he said, "Say this to the people of Israel, 'I AM has sent me to you.'" God also said to Moses, "Say this to the people of Israel, 'The Lord, the God of your fathers, the God of Abraham, the God of Isaac, and the God of Jacob, has sent me to you': this is my name for ever, and thus I am to be remembered throughout all generations."[1]

The Law

From *The Book of Exodus*

And God spoke all these words, saying,

"I am the Lord your God, who brought you out of the land of Egypt, out of the house of bondage.

"You shall have no other gods before me.

"You shall not make for yourself a graven image, or any likeness of anything that is in heaven above, or that is in earth beneath, or that is in the water under the earth; you shall not bow down to them or serve them; for I the Lord your God am a jealous God, visiting the iniquity of the fathers upon the children to the third and the fourth generation of those who hate me, but showing steadfast love to thousands of those who love me and keep my commandments.

"You shall not take the name of the Lord your God in vain; for the Lord will not hold him guiltless who takes his name in vain.

"Remember the sabbath day, to keep it holy. Six days you shall labor, and do all your work; but the seventh day is a sabbath to the Lord your God; in it you shall not do any work, you, or your son, or your daughter, your manservant, or your maidservant, or your cattle, or the sojourner who is within your gates; for in six days the Lord made heaven and earth, the sea, and all that is in them, and rested the seventh day; therefore the Lord blessed the sabbath day and hallowed it.

"Honor your father and your mother, that your days may be long in the land which the Lord your God gives you.

[1]The Hebrew YHWH, translated above as "The Lord," is a form of the verb "to be." Thus the sentence carries on the thought of the preceding passage. The name of God means "He who is" or "He who causes being."

From the *Revised Standard Version Bible* (New York: Oxford University Press, 1973). Exodus 20:1–17; 21:12–29; 22:5–6, 16–25; 23:23–27. Copyright 1946, 1952, © 1971, 1973 by the National Council of the Churches of Christ. Reprinted by permission.

"You shall not kill.

"You shall not commit adultery

"You shall not steal.

"You shall not bear false witness against your neighbor.

"You shall not covet your neighbor's house; you shall not covet your neighbor's wife, or his manservant, or his maidservant, or his ox, or his ass, or anything that is your neighbor's. . . .

"Whoever strikes a man so that he dies shall be put to death. But if he did not lie in wait for him, but God let him fall into his hand, then I will appoint for you a place to which he may flee. But if a man wilfully attacks another to kill him treacherously, you shall take him from my altar, that he may die.

"Whoever strikes his father or his mother shall be put to death.

"Whoever steals a man, whether he sells him or is found in possession of him, shall be put to death.

"Whoever curses his father or his mother shall be put to death.

"When men quarrel and one strikes the other with a stone or with his fist and the man does not die but keeps his bed, then if the man rises again and walks abroad with his staff, he that struck him shall be clear; only he shall pay for the loss of his time, and shall have him thoroughly healed.

"When a man strikes his slave, male or female, with a rod and the slave dies under his hand, he shall be punished. But if the slave survives a day or two, he is not to be punished; for the slave is his money.

"When men strive together, and hurt a woman with child, so that there is a miscarriage, and yet no harm follows, the one who hurt her shall be fined, according as the woman's husband shall lay upon him; and he shall pay as the judges determine. If any harm follows, then you shall give life for life, eye for eye, tooth for tooth, hand for hand, foot for foot, burn for burn, wound for wound, stripe for stripe.

"When a man strikes the eye of his slave, male or female, and destroys it, he shall let the slave go free for the eye's sake. If he knocks out the tooth of his slave, male or female, he shall let the slave go free for the tooth's sake.

"When an ox gores a man or a woman to death, the ox shall be stoned, and its flesh shall not be eaten; but the owner of the ox shall be clear. But if the ox has been accustomed to gore in the past, and its owner has been warned but has not kept it in, and it kills a man or a woman, the ox shall be stoned, and its owner also shall be put to death. . . .

"When a man causes a field or vineyard to be grazed over, or lets his beast loose and it feeds in another man's field, he shall make restitution from the best in his own field and in his own vineyard.

"When fire breaks out and catches in thorns so that the stacked grain or the standing grain or the field is consumed, he that kindled the fire shall make full restitution.

"If a man seduces a virgin who is not betrothed, and lies with her, he shall give the marriage present for her, and make her his wife. If her father utterly refuses to give her to him, he shall pay money equivalent to the marriage present for virgins.

"You shall not permit a sorceress to live.

"Whoever lies with a beast shall be put to death.

"Whoever sacrifices to any god, save to the Lord only, shall be utterly destroyed.

"You shall not wrong a stranger or oppress him, for you were strangers in the land of Egypt. You shall not afflict any widow or orphan. If you do afflict them, and they cry out to me, I will surely hear their cry; and my wrath will burn, and I will kill you with the sword, and your wives shall become widows and your children fatherless.

"If you lend money to any of my people with you who is poor, you shall not be to him as a creditor, and you shall not exact interest from him. . . .

"When my angel goes before you, and brings you in to the Amorites, and the Hittites, and the Perizzites, and the Canaanites, the Hivites, and the Jebusites, and I blot them out, you shall not bow down to their gods, nor serve them, nor do according to their works, but you shall utterly overthrow them and break their pillars in pieces. You shall serve the Lord your God, and I will bless your bread and your water; and I will take sickness away from the midst of you. None shall cast her young or be barren in your land; I will fulfil the number of your days. I will send my terror before you, and will throw into confusion all your enemies."

The Prophets

From time to time prophets arose who rebuked the sins of rulers and people. They warned of God's wrath but also foretold the coming of a Messiah who would finally exalt Israel after all its trials. The early Christians interpreted these prophecies as references to the coming of Jesus. The prophecy of Isaiah is from the eighth century B.C.

From *The Book of Isaiah*

The vision of Isaiah the son of Amoz, which he saw concerning Judah and Jerusalem in the days of Uzziah, Jotham, Ahaz, and Hezekiah, kings of Judah.

From the *Revised Standard Version Bible* (New York: Oxford University Press, 1973). Isaiah 1:1–9. Copyright 1946, 1952, © 1971, 1973 by the National Council of the Churches of Christ. Reprinted by permission.

Hear, O heavens, and give ear, O
    earth;
  for the Lord has spoken:
"Sons have I reared and brought up,
  but they have rebelled against me.
The ox knows its owner,
  and the ass its master's crib;
but Israel does not know,
  my people does not understand."

Ah, sinful nation,
  a people laden with iniquity,
offspring of evildoers,
  sons who deal corruptly!
They have forsaken the Lord,
  they have despised the Holy One
    of Israel,
  they are utterly estranged.

Why will you still be smitten,
  that you continue to rebel?
The whole head is sick,
  and the whole heart faint.
From the sole of the foot even to the
    head,
  there is no soundness in it,
but bruises and sores
  and bleeding wounds;
they are not pressed out, or bound
    up,
  or softened with oil.

Your country lies desolate,
  your cities are burned with fire;
in your very presence
  aliens devour your land;
  it is desolate, as overthrown by
    aliens.
And the daughter of Zion is left
  like a booth in a vineyard,
like a lodge in a cucumber field,
  like a besieged city.

If the Lord of hosts
  had not left us a few survivors,
we should have been like Sodom,
  and become like Gomorrah.

After the rebuke comes the promise.

> The people who walked in darkness
>   have seen a great light;
> those who dwelt in a land of deep
>   darkness,
>   on them has light shined.
> Thou hast multiplied the nation,
>   thou hast increased its joy;
> they rejoice before thee
>   as with joy at the harvest,
>   as men rejoice when they divide
>   the spoil.
> For the yoke of his burden,
>   and the staff for his shoulder,
>   the rod of his oppressor,
>   thou hast broken as on the day of
>   Midian.
> For every boot of the tramping
>   warrior in battle tumult
>   and every garment rolled in blood
>   will be burned as fuel for the fire.
> For to us a child is born,
>   to us a son is given;
> and the government will be upon
>   his shoulder,
>   and his name will be called
> "Wonderful Counselor, Mighty God,
> Everlasting Father, Prince of
>   Peace."
> Of the increase of his government
>   and of peace
>   there will be no end,
> upon the throne of David, and over
>   his kingdom,
>   to establish it, and to uphold it
> with justice and with righteousness
>   from this time forth and for
>   evermore.
> The zeal of the Lord of hosts will do
>   this.

Thou didst cover it with the deep
    as with a garment;
  the waters stood above the
    mountains.
At thy rebuke they fled;
  at the sound of thy thunder they
    took to flight.
The mountains rose, the valleys
    sank down
  to the place which thou didst
    appoint for them.
Thou didst set a bound which they
    should not pass,
  so that they might not again cover
    the earth.

Thou makest springs gush forth in
    the valleys;
  they flow between the hills,
they give drink to every beast of the
    field;
  the wild asses quench their thirst.
By them the birds of the air have
    their habitation;
  they sing among the branches.
From thy lofty abode thou waterest
    the mountains;
  the earth is satisfied with the fruit
    of thy work.

Thou dost cause the grass to grow
    for the cattle,
  and plants for man to cultivate,
that he may bring forth food from
    the earth,
  and wine to gladden the heart of
    man,
oil to make his face shine,
  and bread to strengthen man's
    heart.
The trees of the Lord are watered
    abundantly,
  the cedars of Lebanon which he
    planted.
In them the birds build their nests.

Hebrew Poetry

The following song was attributed to the hero-king David (c. 1000 B.C.).

A Psalm

Praise the Lord!
Praise the Lord from the
heavens,
praise him in the heights!
Praise him, all his angels,
praise him, all his host!

Praise him, sun and moon,
praise him, all you shining stars!
Praise him, you highest heavens,
and you waters above the
heavens!

Let them praise the name of the
Lord!
For he commanded and they were
created.
And he established them for ever
and ever;
he fixed their bounds which
cannot be passed.

Praise the Lord from the earth,
you sea monsters and all deeps,
fire and hail, snow and frost,
stormy wind fulfilling his
command!

Mountains and all hills,
fruit trees and all cedars!
Beasts and all cattle,
creeping things and flying birds!

Kings of the earth and all peoples,
princes and all rulers of the earth!
Young men and maidens together,
old men and children!

Let them praise the name of the
 Lord,
 for his name alone is exalted;
 his glory is above earth and
 heaven.
He has raised up a horn for his
 people,
 praise for all his saints,
 for the people of Israel who are
 near to him.
Praise the Lord!

This love dialogue has affinities both with earlier fertility songs (see above p. 16) and with later mystical literature (see below p. 306). It was often interpreted as an allegory of the love of God for his people or, later, of Christ for the church.

From *The Song of Solomon*

I am a rose of Sharon,
 a lily of the valleys.

As a lily among brambles,
 so is my love among maidens.

As an apple tree among the trees
 of the wood,
 so is my beloved among young
 men.
With great delight I sat in his shadow,
 and his fruit was sweet to my taste.
He brought me to the banqueting
 house,
 and his banner over me was love.
Sustain me with raisins,
 refresh me with apples;
 for I am sick with love.
O that his left hand were under my
 head,

From the *Revised Standard Version Bible* (New York: Oxford University Press, 1973). Song of Solomon 2:1–27. Copyright 1946, 1952, © 1971, 1973 by the National Council of the Churches of Christ. Reprinted by permission.

and that this right hand embraced
   me!
I adjure you, O daughters of
   Jerusalem,
  by the gazelles or the hinds of the
    field,
that you stir not up nor awaken
   love
   until it please.

The voice of my beloved!
  Behold, he comes,
leaping upon the mountains,
  bounding over the hills.
My beloved is like a gazelle,
  or a young stag.
Behold, there he stands
  behind our wall,
gazing in at the windows,
  looking through the lattice.
My beloved speaks and says to me:
"Arise, my love, my fair one,
  and come away;
for lo, the winter is past,
  the rain is over and gone.
The flowers appear on the earth,
  the time of singing has come,
and the voice of the turtledove
  is heard in our land.
The fig tree puts forth its figs,
  and the vines are in blossom;
  they give forth fragrance.
Arise, my love, my fair one,
  and come away.

O my dove, in the clefts of the rock,
  in the covert of the cliff,
let me see your face,
  let me hear your voice,
for your voice is sweet,
  and your face is comely.
Catch us the foxes,
  the little foxes,
that spoil the vineyards,
  for our vineyards are in blossom."

My beloved is mine and I am his,
   he pastures his flock among the
      lilies.
Until the day breathes
   and the shadows flee,
turn, my beloved, be like a gazelle,
   or a young stag upon rugged
      mountains.

II

GODS AND HUMANS
Homer's World
From *The Iliad*
Golden Age to Iron Age
From *Hesiod's Works and Days*
Human Love
From *Poems of Sappho*

FROM MYTHOLOGY TO PHILOSOPHY
Religion
From *Xenophanes*
Philosophy
From *Empedocles*
From *Parmenides*
Atomism: Leucippus and Democritus
Mathematics: The Pythagoreans

SOCIETY AND GOVERNMENT—THE POLIS
Athens
From Thucydides. *History of the Peloponnesian War*
Sparta
From Plutarch. *Life of Lycurgus*

DIVINE AND HUMAN LAW
Sophocles
From *Antigone*

GREEK CIVILIZATION—FROM MYTH TO POLIS (c. 800–c. 430 B.C.)

HISTORIANS OFTEN NOTE that Western civilization grew from Greek and Hebrew roots. Like most platitudes this is true. Unlike most, it points to a complex and significant reality. Our culture has always been marked by internal tensions. That is in part because it incorporates elements, often hard to reconcile, from two disparate earlier civilizations.

The Greek world of the first millennium B.C. *was very different from the contemporary Old Testament world of the Jews. The Greeks lived in scattered communities—first primitive kingdoms, then ordered city-states—separated by mountains and long arms of the sea. They shared a common language and culture but were often in conflict with one another. They worshipped many gods and thought of the gods as very much like themselves, superhuman only in their greater powers. But from the sixth century onward, some Greek philosophers began to find the old mythology unacceptable, both morally and intellectually. Critical thinkers then faced a new problem. How could one explain the intrinsic nature of reality—of the universe and humankind, and ordered society—without an adequate religious myth to give coherence to the whole world picture? Some playwrights learned to use the old myths in fresh ways to express their deepest moral intuitions. A few philosophers embarked on a new enterprise, an attempt to construct, for the first time, a wholly rational picture of the universe. Meanwhile the growth of many self-conscious political communities, exemplifying different life-styles within a common culture, stimulated new reflections in the field that we would call comparative politics.*

GODS AND HUMANS

Homer's World

The first great work of Greek literature, Homer's Iliad, *was set down in the eighth century* B.C. *It is based on earlier legends about a Greek siege of Troy (which probably took place about 1200* B.C.*). Homer's gods were very human in their behavior. At one point Zeus forbids the other gods to intervene in the fighting. His wife, Hera, who wants her brother Poseidon to help the Greeks, decides to distract his attention.*

From *The Iliad*

Now Hera, she of the golden throne, standing on Olympos'
horn, looked out with her eyes, and saw at once how Poseidon,
who was her very brother and her lord's brother, was bustling
about the battle where men win glory, and her heart was happy.
Then she saw Zeus, sitting along the loftiest summit
on Ida of the springs, and in her eyes he was hateful.
And now the lady ox-eyed Hera was divided in purpose
as to how she could beguile the brain in Zeus of the aegis.
And to her mind this thing appeared to be the best counsel,
to array herself in loveliness, and go down to Ida,
and perhaps he might be taken with desire to lie in love with her
next her skin, and she might be able to drift an innocent
warm sleep across his eyelids, and seal his crafty perceptions.
She went into her chamber, which her beloved son Hephaistos
had built for her, and closed the leaves in the door-posts snugly
with a secret door-bar, and no other of the gods could open it.
There entering she drew shut the leaves of the shining door,
      then
first from her adorable body washed away all stains
with ambrosia, and next anointed herself with ambrosial
sweet olive oil, which stood there in its fragrance beside her,
and from which, stirred in the house of Zeus by the golden
      pavement,

From Richmond Lattimore, trans., *The Iliad of Homer* (Chicago, Ill.: University of Chicago Press, 1961), pp. 298–299, 302–303, 441–445. Copyright © 1961 by the University of Chicago Press. Reprinted by permission.

a fragrance was shaken forever forth, on earth and in heaven.
When with this she had anointed her delicate body
and combed her hair, next with her hands she arranged the
    shining
and lovely and ambrosial curls along her immortal
head, and dressed in an ambrosial robe that Athene
had made her carefully, smooth, and with many figures upon it,
and pinned it across her breast with a golden brooch, and circled
her waist about with a zone that floated a hundred tassels,
and in the lobes of her carefully pierced ears she put rings
with triple drops in mulberry clusters, radiant with beauty,
and, lovely among goddesses, she veiled her head downward
with a sweet fresh veil that glimmered pale like the sunlight. . . .
    Then Hera light-footed made her way to the peak of Gargaros
on towering Ida. And Zeus who gathers the clouds saw her,
and when he saw her desire was a mist about his close heart
as much as on that time they first went to bed together
and lay in love, and their dear parents knew nothing of it.
He stood before her and called her by name and spoke to her:
    'Hera,
what is your desire that you come down here from Olympos?
And your horses are not here, nor your chariot, which you
    would ride in.'
    Then with false lying purpose the lady Hera answered him:
'I am going to the ends of the generous earth, on a visit
to Okeanos, whence the gods have risen, and Tethys our mother,
who brought me up kindly in their own house, and cared for
    me.
I shall go to visit these, and resolve their division of discord,
since now for a long time they have stayed apart from each other
and from the bed of love, since rancour has entered their
    feelings.
In the foothills by Ida of the waters are standing
my horses, who will carry me over hard land and water.
Only now I have come down here from Olympos for your sake
so you will not be angry with me afterwards, if I
have gone silently to the house of deep-running Okeanos.'
    Then in turn Zeus who gathers the clouds answered her:
'Hera, there will be a time afterwards when you can go there
as well. But now let us go to bed and turn to love-making.
For never before has love for any goddess or woman
so melted about the heart inside me, broken it to submission,
as now: not that time when I loved the wife of Ixion
who bore me Peirithoös, equal of the gods in counsel,
nor when I loved Akrisios' daughter, sweet-stepping Danaë,
who bore Perseus to me, pre-eminent among all men,

nor when I loved the daughter of far-renowned Phoinix, Europa
who bore Minos to me, and Rhadamanthys the godlike;
not when I loved Semele, or Alkmene in Thebe,
when Alkmene bore me a son, Herakles the strong-hearted,
while Semele's son was Dionysos, the pleasure of mortals;
not when I loved the queen Demeter of the lovely tresses,
not when it was glorious Leto, nor yourself, so much
as now I love you, and the sweet passion has taken hold of me.'
    Then with false lying purpose the lady Hera answered him:
'Most honoured son of Kronos, what sort of thing have you
    spoken?
If now your great desire is to lie in love together
here on the peaks of Ida, everything can be seen. Then
what would happen if some one of the gods everlasting
saw us sleeping, and went and told all the other immortals
of it? I would not simply rise out of bed and go back
again, into your house, and such a thing would be shameful.
No, if this is your heart's desire, if this is your wish, then
there is my chamber, which my beloved son Hephaistos
has built for me, and closed the leaves in the door-posts snugly.
We can go back there and lie down, since bed is your pleasure.'
    Then in turn Zeus who gathers the clouds answered her:
'Hera, do not fear that any mortal or any god
will see, so close shall be the golden cloud that I gather
about us. Not even Helios can look at us through it,
although beyond all others his light has the sharpest vision.'
    So speaking, the son of Kronos caught his wife in his arms.
    There
underneath them the divine earth broke into young, fresh
grass, and into dewy clover, crocus and hyacinth
so thick and soft it held the hard ground deep away from them.
There they lay down together and drew about them a golden
wonderful cloud, and from it the glimmering dew descended.
    So the father slept unshaken on the peak of Gargaron
with his wife in his arms, when sleep and passion had stilled
    him;
but gently Sleep went on the run to the ships of the Achaians
with a message to tell him who circles the earth and shakes it,
Poseidon, and stood close to him and addressed him in winged
    words:
'Poseidon, now with all your heart defend the Danaans
and give them glory, though only for a little, while Zeus still
sleeps; since I have mantled a soft slumber about him
and Hera beguiled him into sleeping in love beside her.'

[*Toward the end of the poem there is a climactic duel between the Trojan
prince Hektor and the Greek hero Achilles. The goddess Athene appears to*

Hektor in the guise of his brother Deiphobos and promises to help him in the
fight—then she betrays him to Achilleus.]

So Athene spoke and led him on by beguilement.
Now as the two in their advance were come close together,
first of the two to speak was tall helm-glittering Hektor:
'Son of Peleus, I will no longer run from you, as before this
I fled three times around the great city of Priam, and dared not
stand to your onfall. But now my spirit in turn has driven me
to stand and face you. I must take you now, or I must be taken.
Come then, shall we swear before the gods? For these are the
     highest
who shall be witnesses and watch over our agreements.
Brutal as you are I will not defile you, if Zeus grants
to me that I can wear you out, and take the life from you.
But after I have stripped your glorious armour, Achilleus,
I will give your corpse back to the Achaians. Do you do likewise.'
   Then looking darkly at him swift-footed Achilleus answered:
'Hektor, argue me no agreements. I cannot forgive you.
As there are no trustworthy oaths between men and lions,
nor wolves and lambs have spirit that can be brought to
     agreement
but forever these hold feelings of hate for each other,
so there can be no love between you and me, nor shall there be
oaths between us, but one or the other must fall before then
to glut with his blood Ares the god who fights under the shield's
     guard.
Remember every valour of yours, for now the need comes
hardest upon you to be a spearman and a bold warrior.
There shall be no more escape for you, but Pallas Athene
will kill you soon by my spear. You will pay in a lump for all
     those
sorrows of my companions you killed in your spear's fury.'
  So he spoke, and balanced the spear far shadowed, and threw
     it;
but glorious Hektor kept his eyes on him, and avoided it,
for he dropped, watchful, to his knee, and the bronze spear flew
     over his shoulder
and stuck in the ground, but Pallas Athene snatched it, and gave
     it
back to Achilleus, unseen by Hektor shepherd of the people.
But now Hektor spoke out to the blameless son of Peleus:
'You missed; and it was not, o Achilleus like the immortals,
from Zeus that you knew my destiny; but you thought so; or
     rather
you are someone clever in speech and spoke to swindle me,

to make me afraid of you and forget my valour and war
    strength.
You will not stick your spear in my back as I run away from you
but drive it into my chest as I storm straight in against you;
if the god gives you that; and now look out for my brazen
spear. I wish it might be taken full length in your body.
And indeed the war would be a lighter thing for the Trojans
if you were dead, seeing that you are their greatest affliction.'
    So he spoke, and balanced the spear far shadowed, and threw
    it,
and struck the middle of Peleïdes' shield, nor missed it,
but the spear was driven far back from the shield, and Hektor
    was angered
because his swift weapon had been loosed from his hand in a
    vain cast.
He stood discouraged, and had no other ash spear; but lifting
his voice he called aloud on Deïphobos of the pale shield,
and asked him for a long spear, but Deïphobos was not near
    him.
And Hektor knew the truth inside his heart, and spoke aloud:
'No use. Here at last the gods have summoned me deathward.
I thought Deïphobos the hero was here close beside me,
but he is behind the wall and it was Athene cheating me,
and now evil death is close to me, and no longer far away,
and there is no way out. So it must long since have been pleasing
to Zeus, and Zeus' son who strikes from afar, this way; though
    before this
they defended me gladly. But now my death is upon me.
Let me at least not die without a struggle, inglorious,
but do some big thing first, that men to come shall know of it.'
    So he spoke, and pulling out the sharp sword that was slung
at the hollow of his side, huge and heavy, and gathering
himself together, he made his swoop, like a high-flown eagle
who launches himself out of the murk of the clouds on the flat
    land
to catch away a tender lamb or a shivering hare; so
Hektor made his swoop, swinging his sharp sword, and Achilleus
charged, the heart within him loaded with savage fury.
In front of his chest the beautiful elaborate great shield
covered him, and with the glittering helm with four horns
he nodded; the lovely golden fringes were shaken about it
which Hephaistos had driven close along the horn of the helmet.
And as a star moves among stars in the night's darkening,
Hesper, who is the fairest star who stands in the sky, such
was the shining from the pointed spear Achilleus was shaking
in his right hand with evil intention toward brilliant Hektor.

He was eyeing Hektor's splendid body, to see where it might best
give way, but all the rest of the skin was held in the armour,
brazen and splendid, he stripped when he cut down the strength
    of Patroklos;
yet showed where the collar-bones hold the neck from the
    shoulders,
the throat, where death of the soul comes most swiftly; in this
    place
brilliant Achilleus drove the spear as he came on in fury,
and clean through the soft part of the neck the spearpoint was
    driven.
Yet the ash spear heavy with bronze did not sever the windpipe,
so that Hektor could still make exchange of words spoken.
But he dropped in the dust, and brilliant Achilleus vaunted
    above him:
'Hektor, surely you thought as you killed Patroklos you would be
safe, and since I was far away you thought nothing of me,
o fool, for an avenger was left, far greater than he was,
behind him and away by the hollow ships. And it was I;
and I have broken your strength; on you the dogs and the
    vultures
shall feed and foully rip you; the Achaians will bury Patroklos.'
   In his weakness Hektor of the shining helm spoke to him:
'I entreat you, by your life, by your knees, by your parents,
do not let the dogs feed on me by the ships of the Achaians,
but take yourself the bronze and gold that are there in
    abundance,
those gifts that my father and the lady my mother will give you,
and give my body to be taken home again, so that the Trojans
and the wives of the Trojans may give me in death my rite of
    burning.'
   But looking darkly at him swift-footed Achilleus answered:
'No more entreating of me, you dog, by knees or parents.
I wish only that my spirit and fury would drive me
to hack your meat away and eat it raw for the things that
your have done to me. So there is no one who can hold the dogs
    off
from your head, not if they bring here and set before me ten
    times
and twenty times the ransom, and promise more in addition,
not if Priam son of Dardanos should offer to weigh out
your bulk in gold; not even so shall the lady your mother
who herself bore you lay you on the death-bed and mourn you:
no, but the dogs and the birds will have you all for their
    feasting.'
   Then, dying, Hektor of the shining helmet spoke to him:

'I know you well as I look upon you, I know that I could not
persuade you, since indeed in your breast is a heart of iron.
Be careful now; for I might be made into the gods' curse
upon you, on that day when Paris and Phoibos Apollo
destroy you in the Skaian gates, for all your valour.'
    He spoke, and as he spoke the end of death closed in upon
        him,
and the soul fluttering free of the limbs went down into Death's
        house
mourning her destiny, leaving youth and manhood behind her.
Now though he was a dead man brilliant Achilleus spoke to him:
'Die: and I will take my own death at whatever time
Zeus and the rest of the immortals choose to accomplish it.'

Golden Age to Iron Age

*The farmer-poet Hesiod wrote mostly about everyday country life. But, living
in troubled times, he also tried to explain how evil and strife came into the
world. Hesiod saw human history as a degeneration from an original
"golden" age to his own "iron" age.*

From Hesiod's Works and Days

But if you will, another tale will I briefly tell you well and skilfully,
and do you ponder it in your mind, that from the same origin are
sprung gods and mortal men. First of all the immortals holding the
mansions of Olympus made a golden race of men. They indeed lived
under Kronos what time he ruled in heaven. And as gods they were
wont to live, with a life void of care, apart from, and without labours
and trouble: nor was wretched old age at all impending, but ever the
same in hands and feet, did they delight themselves in festivals out of
the reach of all ills: and they died, as if o'ercome by sleep; all blessings
were theirs; of its own will the fruitful field would bear them fruit,
much and ample; and they gladly used to reap the labours of their
hands in quietness along with many good things, being rich in flocks,
and dear to the blessed gods. But after that Earth had covered this
generation by the will of mighty Zeus, they indeed are Spirits, kindly
haunting-earth, guardians of mortal men, who watch both the decisions of justice and harsh deeds, going to and fro everywhere over the

From J. Banks, *The Works of Hesiod, Callimachus, and Theognis* (London: Henry
G. Bohn, 1856), pp. 77–85.

earth, having wrapt themselves in mist, givers of riches as they are: and this is a kingly function which they have.

Afterwards again the dwellers in Olympian mansions formed a second race of silver, far inferior; like unto the golden neither in shape nor mind: but for a hundred years indeed a boy was reared and grew up beside his wise mother, in her house, being quite childish: but when they finally came to age and reached the stature of manhood, but for a brief space used they to live, suffering griefs through their foolishness: for they could not keep off rash insult one from the other, nor were they willing to worship the gods, nor to sacrifice at the holy altars of the blessed, as it is right men should in their abodes. Afterwards, Zeus, son of Kronos, buried these too in his wrath, because they gave not due honours to the blessed gods, who occupy Olympus. Now when earth had covered this race also, they too beneath the ground, are called blessed spirits, second in rank; but still honour attends these also.

And yet a third race of men formed father Zeus of brass, not at all like unto silver, formidable and mighty by reason of their ashen spears; whose care was the ghastly deeds of Mars. Nor did they eat bread alone but also flesh. They had stout-spirited hearts of adamant, unapproachable. Now vast strength and hands unvanquished grew from their shoulders upon sturdy arms. These had brazen weapons, and likewise brazen houses, and with brass they wrought; for there was not yet dark iron. They indeed, destroyed by the hands of one another, entered the squalid abode of chilling Hades, inglorious: for terrible though they were, black Death seized them and they quitted the bright sunlight.

But when earth had covered this race also, again Zeus, son of Kronos, wrought yet another, a fourth, on the fertile ground, more just and more worthy, a godlike race of hero-men, the race before our own upon the boundless earth. But these too baneful war, as well as the dire battle-din, destroyed, a part fighting before seven-gated Thebes, in the land of Kadmos, for the flocks of Oedipus, and part also in ships beyond the vast depths of the sea, when it had led them to Troy for fair-haired Helen's sake. There indeed the end of death enshrouded them; but to them Zeus, son of Kronos, their sire, having given life and settlements apart from men, made them dwell at the end of earth, afar from the immortals. Among these Kronos rules. And they indeed dwell with careless spirit in the Isles of the Blest, beside deep-eddying Ocean; blest heroes, for whom thrice in a year doth the fertile soil bear blooming fruits as sweet as honey.

Would that I had no part with the fifth race of men, but had either died before, or been born afterward. For now in truth is the iron race. They will never cease by day, nor by night, from toil and wretchedness, corrupt as they are: but the gods will give them severe cares: yet nevertheless even for these shall good be mingled with ill. But Zeus will destroy this race of men too when, soon after being born, they become silvery-templed. Nor will sire agree with sons, nor sons at all with parent, nor guest with host, nor comrade with comrade, nor will brother be dear, as it was aforetime, to brother. But quickly will they dishonour parents growing old, and will blame them, addressing them with harsh words, being impious, and unaware of the vengeance of the gods; nor to aged parents would these pay back the price of their nurture. Using the right of might, one will sack the city of another: nor will there be any favour to the trusty; nor the just, nor the good, but rather they will honour a man that doeth evil and is overbearing; and justice and shame will not be in their hands, and the bad man will injure the better speaking in perverse speeches, and swearing a false oath. But on all wretched mortals envy with its tongues of malice, exulting in ill, will attend with hateful look. Then also indeed shall Shame and Retribution, shrouding their fair skin in white mantles, depart from broadwayed earth to Olympus, forsaking the whole race of man: but the baneful griefs shall remain behind, and against evil there shall be no recourse.

Human Love

During the transition from the "heroic age" of Greek civilization to the "classical age," new forms of thought and expression arose. Lyric poets produced verses more intimate and personal than the ancient tales of gods and heroes. The poems of Sappho (active c. 600 B.C.) provide a rare example of a woman's voice speaking to us directly from the world of ancient Greece.

From *Poems of Sappho*

WEDDING SONG

Lucky bridegroom!
Now the wedding you
asked for is over

and your wife is the
girl you asked for;
she's a bride who is

From Mary Barnard, *Sappho, A New Translation* (Berkeley and Los Angeles, Calif.: University of California Press, 1958), Nos. 30, 31, 17, 83, 50, 43. Reprinted by permission of the publisher.

charming to look at,
with eyes as soft as
honey, and a face

that Love has lighted
with his own beauty.
Aphrodite has surely

outdone herself in
doing honor to you!

BRIDESMAIDS' CAROL

O Bride brimful of
rosy little loves!

O brightest jewel of
the Queen of Paphos!

Come now
            to your
bedroom to your
bed
    and play there
sweetly   gently
with your bridegroom

And may Hesperus
lead you not at all
unwilling
            until
you stand wondering
before the silver

Throne of Hera
Queen of Marriage

CLEIS I

I have a small
daughter called
Cleis, who is

like a golden
flower
        I wouldn't
take all Croesus'
kingdom with love
thrown in, for her

CLEIS II

I have no embroidered
headband from Sardis to
give you, Cleis, such as
I wore
      and my mother
always said that in her
day a purple ribbon
looped in the hair was thought
to be high style indeed

but we were dark:
             a girl
whose hair is yellower than
torchlight should wear no
headdress but fresh flowers

ATTHIS I

Atthis, I loved you
long ago while you
still seemed to me a
small ungracious child

I was proud of you, too

In skill I think
you need never
bow to any girl

not one who may
see the sunlight
in time to come

After all this

Atthis, you hate
even the thought

of me. You dart
off to Andromeda

ATTHIS II

It was you, Atthis, who said

"Sappho, if you will not get
up and let us look at you
I shall never love you again!

"Get up, unleash your suppleness,
lift off your Chian nightdress
and, like a lily leaning into

"a spring, bathe in the water.
Cleis is bringing your best
purple frock and the yellow

"tunic down from the clothes chest;
you will have a cloak thrown over
you and flowers crowning your hair . . .

"Praxinoa, my child, will you please
roast nuts for our breakfast? One
of the gods is being good to us:

"today we are going at last
into Mitylene, our favorite
city, with Sappho, loveliest

"of its women; she will walk
among us like a mother with
all her daughters around her

"when she comes home from exile . . ."

But you forget everything

FROM MYTHOLOGY TO PHILOSOPHY

Religion

Xenophanes (c. 570–c. 475 B.C.) was the first Greek writer to challenge the accepted mythology about the many gods of Olympus.

From *Xenophanes*

There is one God, supreme among gods and men, not at all like mortals in body or in mind.

It is the whole (of God) that sees, the whole that thinks, and the whole that hears.

He always remains in the same place, not moving at all; it is not fitting for him to be in different places at different times.

But without effort he sets all things in motion by the thoughts of his mind.

Homer and Hesiod attributed to the gods everything which is shameful and blameworthy among humans—such lawless deeds as stealing, committing adultery and deceiving one another.

Mortals suppose that the gods are born and that they have voices and bodies and clothes like humans.

But if oxen or horses or lions had hands and could draw with their hands and paint pictures as men do, they would portray their gods as having bodies like their own: horses would portray them like horses, and oxen like oxen.

Ethiopians have gods with snub noses and black hair; Thracians have gods with gray eyes and red hair.

Clearly the gods did not reveal everything to mortals at the outset; but, by searching, in the course of time mortals discover for themselves what is better.

There is no man and there will never be one who has plain knowledge about the gods and about all the matters I discuss. For even if

From G. S. Kirk and J. E. Raven, *The Presocratic Philosophers*, B. Tierney, trans. (Cambridge: Cambridge University Press, 1969), Nos. 169–175, 189–190. Reprinted by permission of the publisher.

one happened by chance to say the complete truth, he still would not know for certain that he did so.

These things have seemed to me resemblances of what is true.

Philosophy

The Greeks, it has been said, invented heresy. They also invented philosophy. If we begin to doubt that everything in the universe is the way it is simply because the gods make it so, then new problems arise. How can the intrinsic order of the universe be explained? Is there anything permanent behind the changing phenomena revealed to us by sense experience? How did the universe come to exist at all?

Empedocles (active c. 450 B.C.) held that the universe was composed of four elements: Fire, Earth, Air, and Water. (He sometimes designated the elements by the names of gods.) They interacted with one another through the forces of Love (attraction) and Hate (repulsion).

From *Empedocles*

Hear first the four roots of all things: bright Zeus [Fire] and life-bearing Hera [Earth] and Adoneus [Air] and Nestis [Water] whose tears fill the springs of mortals.

The elements never cease in their continual interplay, sometimes coming together under the influence of Love, sometimes moving apart through the force of Hate. . . .

At one time there grew a single One out of Many, at another time it divided again so as to be Many out of One—that is *Fire* and *Water* and *Earth* and the vast height of *Air,* and also dread Hate apart from them . . . and also Love in their midst. . . . She is known to be implanted also in the limbs of mortals; through her they think kind thoughts and perform harmonious actions, calling her Joy by name and Aphrodite. . . .

All these are equal and of like age, but each has its own function and character and they prevail in turn in the course of time. And besides these nothing comes into being or ceases to be . . . these things alone exist and, interacting with one another, become now this and now that, yet remain always the same.

From G. S. Kirk and J. E. Raven, *The Presocratic Philosophers,* B. Tierney, trans. (Cambridge: Cambridge University Press, 1969), Nos. 417, 423–424. Reprinted by permission of the publisher.

*Parmenides (active c. 475 B.C.) wrestled with the problem of existence itself.
What exists now, he maintained, must have existed eternally. The argument
starts from a point of logic. We cannot say that nothingness or empty space
exists or ever existed or can give rise to existence because empty space is by
definition an area where nothing exists. This led on to a first attempt to construct a theory of the universe by pure thought.*

From *Parmenides*

There remains only one way of inquiry to be discussed: that being *is*.
And on this way there are many signs that *What Is* is uncreated and
indestructible. It is whole, immovable, without end. It *was* not in the
past nor *will* it be since it *is* now, altogether, one, continuous. How can
you seek for its creation? How and from what source could it grow? I
will not let you say or think that it came from not-being, for it cannot
be said or thought that not-being *is*. Besides, what could have stirred it
into activity at a later rather than an earlier time if it came from nothingness? Therefore it must exist absolutely or not exist at all. The force
of our convictions will not allow anything to emerge from nothingness
except nothingness. . . .

How could *What Is* cease to be? And how could it come into being?
For if it came into being or is going to come into being there would be
a time when it *is* not. So coming-into-being is excluded and destruction
is unimaginable.

Nor is it divisible since it is homogeneous. Nor is it more concen-
trated here than there, which would prevent its cohesion, but it is all
full of Being. So the Whole is continuous, for *What Is* is in contact with
What Is. . . .

To think is the same as thinking that being *is*, for you will not find
thought without being which it expresses. Nor is there, nor will there
be anything besides *What Is*, for fate has bound it to be whole and immoveable. Accordingly all these things that mortals accept as true—
coming-into-being and perishing, being and not-being, change of position, and alteration of bright color—these are mere names.

*There is a commonsensical persuasiveness in Parmenides' view that nothing
can come from nothingness. But his assertion that the eternally existing
Whole is unmoving and unchanging seems contrary to sense experience. The
first atomic theories were devised to cope with this problem. We know the
views of Leucippus (active c. 440 B.C.) and Democritus (active c. 430 B.C.)
from surviving fragments of their works and from descriptions by later Greek
authors.*

From G. S. Kirk and J. E. Raven, *The Presocratic Philosophers*, B. Tierney, trans.
(Cambridge: Cambridge University Press, 1969), Nos. 347, 348, 352. Reprinted by permission of the publisher.

Atomism: Leucippus and Democritus

By convention there are sweet and bitter, by convention there are hot and cold, by convention there is color; in reality there are only atoms and the void. (Democritus)

Nothing happens at random; everything for a reason and by necessity. (Leucippus)

The following accounts of early atomic theory are from Aristotle.

Some of the early philosophers thought that *What Is* must necessarily be one and immoveable, for empty space is not-being and there could be no motion without empty space beside matter. Likewise there could not be a plurality of things without something to separate them.

But Leucippus believed he had a theory which would be consistent with sense-perception, in that it did not exclude coming-to-be and perishing, nor motion, nor the multiplicity of things. So far he accepted the testimony of appearances. On the other hand he conceded to the monists that there could be no motion without a void, that a void is not-being, and that *What Is* cannot ever be *What Is Not*. Accordingly he agrees that *What Is* must be a complete, continuously full Whole; but he adds that there is not just one such whole; there are many of them; in fact they are infinite in number. Because of their extremely small bulk they are invisible. They move in the void—for there is a void— and by coming together they cause coming-to-be, while by their separation they cause perishing.

According to the theory of Democritus the eternal objects are tiny substances infinite in number. Accordingly he assigns also a place for them that is infinitesimal in size, which he designates by these names— "the void," "nothing," and "the infinite"; whereas he calls each individual atom "thing," "the compact," and "being." He thinks them so small as to elude our senses, but they have all sorts of forms, shapes, and different sizes. Taking these as elements he thinks of them as combining to produce objects that are visible and otherwise perceptible to the senses. The particles move about and struggle in the void because of their dissimilarity and the other mentioned differences. In their motion they collide or brush against one another, and so they tend to get entangled and interlocked. The process never makes them into a single substance however, for it would be absurd to think that two or more things could ever become one. When these particles remain joined together for some time, it is explained by the fact that they intertwine and so catch hold of one another; for some bodies are angular, others hooked, some concave, others convex, and there are countless other

From G. S. Kirk and J. E. Raven, *The Presocratic Philosophers*, B. Tierney, trans. (Cambridge: Cambridge University Press, 1969), Nos. 589, 568, 552, 555. Reprinted by permission of the publisher.

differences. His theory is that they cling together and remain in combination until some stronger outside force separates them and shakes them apart.

For Pythagoras (active c. 530 B.C.) and his followers in the fifth century B.C. mathematical relationships were the basic reality. The Pythagoreans began from the observation that numerical ratios in the physical world are related to musical harmonies. (A lyre string half as long as another produces a note an octave higher.) They proceeded to construct a whole theory of an ordered harmonious universe based on number. Aristotle described their views rather skeptically.

Mathematics: The Pythagoreans

The Pythagoreans, as they are called, devoted themselves to mathematics and were the first to develop this study; and having been brought up in it they thought that its first principles were the first principles of everything. Now since numbers are naturally the first principles of mathematics, they thought they could find in numbers many resemblances to the things that exist and come into being. . . . Since, again, they saw that the properties and ratios of musical scales can be expressed as numbers, and since they considered that everything else, in its intrinsic nature, was modelled after numbers and that numbers were the basic principles of all nature, they concluded that the elements of numbers were the elements of everything, and that the whole heaven consisted of harmony and number.

Accordingly they collected and fitted into their scheme all the properties of numbers and harmonies that they could relate to the properties and parts and the whole arrangement of the heavens; and if any gaps occurred they made additions of their own so as to keep their whole system coherent. For example, since the number ten is considered to be perfect and to contain in itself the whole system of numbers, they say that there must be ten bodies moving through the heavens. But in fact only nine are discernible. Hence they invent a tenth body, called a "counter-earth. . . ."

In all this they are not seeking reasons and causes to explain observed facts but stretching the facts to fit theories and principles of their own.

The Pythagoreans, discerning that things evident to sense experience have many of the attributes of number, supposed that real things

From G. S. Kirk and J. E. Raven, *The Presocratic Philosophers*, B. Tierney, trans. (Cambridge: Cambridge University Press, 1969), Nos. 289, 329, 306. Reprinted by permission of the publisher.

are numbers—not just that they are associated with numbers as something separable from themselves but that they really consist of numbers. And why so? Because the properties of numbers inhere in musical harmony, in the movements of the heavens, and in many other things. But for those who hold that number is merely mathematical it is impossible to say such a thing.

SOCIETY AND GOVERNMENT—THE POLIS

Athens

By the fifth century different patterns of civic life had grown up in the various Greek city-states. Athens was the most democratic of them, Sparta more authoritarian. From 431 to 404 B.C. these two rivals fought in a long-drawn-out struggle, the Peloponnesian War, with Sparta finally emerging as the victor. Thucydides, who wrote an extensive history of the war, gave a memorable description of the ideals of Athens in a speech attributed to the Athenian leader Pericles.

From Thucydides. *History of the Peloponnesian War*

During the same winter, in accordance with an old national custom, the funeral of those who first fell in this war was celebrated by the Athenians at the public charge. The ceremony is as follows: Three days before the celebration they erect a tent in which the bones of the dead are laid out, and every one brings to his own dead any offering which he pleases. At the time of the funeral the bones are placed in chests of cypress wood, which are conveyed on hearses; there is one chest for each tribe. They also carry a single empty litter decked with a pall for all whose bodies are missing, and cannot be recovered after the battle. The procession is accompanied by any one who chooses, whether citizen or stranger, and the female relatives of the deceased are present at the place of interment and make lamentation. The public sepulchre is situated in the most beautiful spot outside the walls; there they always bury those who fall in war; only after the battle of Marathon the dead, in recognition of their pre-eminent valor, were interred on the field. When the remains have been laid in the earth, some man of known ability and high reputation, chosen by the city, delivers a suitable oration over them; after which the people depart. Such is the manner of interment; and the ceremony was repeated from time to time throughout the war. Over those who were the first buried Pericles was chosen to speak. At the fitting moment he advanced from the sepulchre to a

From Thucydides, *History of the Peloponnesian War*, Benjamin Jowett, trans. (Boston: Lothrop, 1883), pp. 115–124.

lofty stage, which had been erected in order that he might be heard as far as possible by the multitude, and spoke as follows:—

Funeral Speech

"I will speak first of our ancestors, for it is right and becoming that now, when we are lamenting the dead, a tribute should be paid to their memory. There has never been a time when they did not inhabit this land, which by their valor they have handed down from generation to generation, and we have received from them a free state. But if they were worthy of praise, still more were our fathers, who added to their inheritance, and after many a struggle transmitted to us their sons this great empire. And we ourselves assembled here to-day, who are still most of us in the vigor of life, have chiefly done the work of improvement, and have richly endowed our city with all things, so that she is sufficient for herself both in peace and war. Of the military exploits by which our various possessions were acquired, or of the energy with which we or our fathers drove back the tide of war, Hellenic or Barbarian, I will not speak; for the tale would be long and is familiar to you. But before I praise the dead, I should like to point out by what principles of action we rose to power, and under what institutions and through what manner of life our empire became great. For I conceive that such thoughts are not unsuited to the occasion, and that this numerous assembly of citizens and strangers may profitably listen to them.

"Our form of government does not enter into rivalry with the institutions of others. We do not copy our neighbors, but are an example to them. It is true that we are called a democracy, for the administration is in the hands of the many and not of the few. But while the law secures equal justice to all alike in their private disputes, the claim of excellence is also recognized; and when a citizen is in any way distinguished, he is preferred to the public service, not as a matter of privilege, but as the reward of merit. Neither is poverty a bar, but a man may benefit his country whatever be the obscurity of his condition. There is no exclusiveness in our public life, and in our private intercourse we are not suspicious of one another, nor angry with our neighbor if he does what he likes; we do not put on sour looks at him which, though harmless, are not pleasant. While we are thus unconstrained in our private intercourse, a spirit of reverence pervades our public acts; we are prevented from doing wrong by respect for authority and for the laws, having an especial regard to those which are ordained for the protection of the injured as well as to those unwritten laws which bring upon the transgressor of them the reprobation of the general sentiment.

"And we have not forgotten to provide for our weary spirits many relaxations from toil; we have regular games and sacrifices throughout the year; at home the style of our life is refined; and the delight which we daily feel in all these things helps to banish melancholy. Because of the greatness of our city the fruits of the whole earth flow in upon us; so that we enjoy the goods of other countries as freely as of our own.

"Then, again, our military training is in many respects superior to that of our adversaries. Our city is thrown open to the world, and we never expel a foreigner or prevent him from seeing or learning anything of which the secret if revealed to an enemy might profit him. We rely not upon management or trickery, but upon our own hearts and hands. And in the matter of education, whereas they from early youth are always undergoing laborious exercises which are to make them brave, we live at ease, and yet are equally ready to face the perils which they face. And here is the proof. The Spartans come into Attica not by themselves, but with their whole confederacy following; we go alone into a neighbor's country; and although our opponents are fighting for their homes and we on a foreign soil, we have seldom any difficulty in overcoming them. Our enemies have never yet felt our united strength; the care of a navy divides our attention, and on land we are obliged to send our own citizens everywhere. But they, if they meet and defeat a part of our army, are as proud as if they had routed us all, and when defeated they pretend to have been vanquished by us all.

"If then we prefer to meet danger with a light heart but without laborious training, and with a courage which is gained by habit and not enforced by law, are we not greatly the gainers? Since we do not anticipate the pain, although, when the hour comes, we can be as brave as those who never allow themselves to rest; and thus too our city is equally admirable in peace and in war. For we are lovers of the beautiful, yet simple in our tastes, and we cultivate the mind without loss of manliness. Wealth we employ, not for talk and ostentation, but when there is a real use for it. To avow poverty with us is no disgrace: the true disgrace is in doing nothing to avoid it. An Athenian citizen does not neglect the state because he takes care of his own household; and even those of us who are engaged in business have a very fair idea of politics. We alone regard a man who takes no interest in public affairs, not as a harmless, but as a useless character; and if few of us are originators, we are all sound judges of a policy. The great impediment to action is, in our opinion, not discussion, but the want of that knowledge which is gained by discussion preparatory to action. For we have a peculiar power of thinking before we act and of acting too, whereas other men are courageous from ignorance but hesitate upon reflection. And they are surely to be esteemed the bravest spirits who, having the clearest sense both of the pains and pleasures of life, do not on that account shrink from danger. In doing good, again, we are unlike others; we make our friends by conferring, not by receiving favors. Now he who confers a favor is the firmer friend, because he would fain

by kindness keep alive the memory of an obligation; but the recipient
is colder in his feelings, because he knows that in requiting another's
generosity he will not be winning gratitude, but only paying a debt. We
alone do good to our neighbors not upon a calculation of interest, but
in the confidence of freedom and in a frank and fearless spirit. To sum
up: I say that Athens is the school of Hellas, and that the individual
Athenian in his own person seems to have the power of adapting himself to the most varied forms of action with the utmost versatility and
grace. This is no passing and idle word, but truth and fact; and the
assertion is verified by the position to which these qualities have raised
the state. For in the hour of trial Athens alone among her contemporaries is superior to the report of her. No enemy who comes against
her is indignant at the reverses which he sustains at the hands of such
a city; no subject complains that his masters are unworthy of him. And
we shall assuredly not be without witnesses; there are mighty monuments of our power which will make us the wonder of this and of suc-
ceeding ages; we shall not need the praises of Homer or of any other
panegyrist whose poetry may please for the moment, although his representation of the facts will not bear the light of day. For we have compelled every land and every sea to open a path for our valor, and have
everywhere planted eternal memorials of our friendship and of our
enmity. Such is the city for whose sake these men nobly fought and
died; they could not bear the thought that she might be taken from
them; and every one of us who survive should gladly toil on her behalf.

"I have dwelt upon the greatness of Athens because I want to show
you that we are contending for a higher prize than those who enjoy
none of these privileges, and to establish by manifest proof the merit
of these men whom I am now commemorating. Their loftiest praise
has been already spoken. For in magnifying the city I have magnified
them, and men like them whose virtues made her glorious. And of
how few Hellenes can it be said as of them, that their deeds when
weighed in the balance have been found equal to their fame! Methinks
that a death such as theirs has been gives the true measure of a man's
worth; it may be the first revelation of his virtues, but is at any rate
their final seal. For even those who come short in other ways may justly
plead the valor with which they have fought for their country; they
have blotted out the evil with the good, and have benefited the state
more by their public services than they have injured her by their private actions. None of these men were enervated by wealth or hesitated
to resign the pleasures of life; none of them put off the evil day in the
hope, natural to poverty, that a man, though poor, may one day become rich. But, deeming that the punishment of their enemies was
sweeter than any of these things, and that they could fall in no nobler
cause, they determined at the hazard of their lives to be honorably
avenged, and to leave the rest. They resigned to hope their unknown
chance of happiness; but in the face of death they resolved to rely

upon themselves alone. And when the moment came they were minded to resist and suffer, rather than to fly and save their lives; they ran away from the word of dishonor, but on the battle-field their feet stood fast, and in an instant, at the height of their fortune, they passed away from the scene, not of their fear, but of their glory.

"Such was the end of these men; they were worthy of Athens, and the living need not desire to have a more heroic spirit although they may pray for a less fatal issue. The value of such a spirit is not to be expressed in words. Any one can discourse to you for ever about the advantages of a brave defence which you know already. But instead of listening to him I would have you day by day fix your eyes upon the greatness of Athens, until you become filled with the love of her; and when you are impressed by the spectacle of her glory, reflect that this empire has been acquired by men who knew their duty and had the courage to do it, who in the hour of conflict had the fear of dishonor always present to them, and who, if ever they failed in an enterprise, would not allow their virtues to be lost to their country, but freely gave their lives to her as the fairest offering which they could present at her feast. The sacrifice which they collectively made was individually re-paid to them; for they received again each one for himself a praise which grows not old, and the noblest of all sepulchres—I speak not of that in which their remains are laid, but of that in which their glory survives, and is proclaimed always and on every fitting occasion both in word and deed. For the whole earth is the sepulchre of famous men; not only are they commemorated by columns and inscriptions in their own country, but in foreign lands there dwells also an unwritten memorial of them, graven not on stone but in the hearts of men. Make them your examples, and, esteeming courage to be freedom and free-dom to be happiness, do not weigh too nicely the perils of war. The unfortunate who has no hope of a change for the better has less reason to throw away his life than the prosperous who, if he survive, is always liable to a change for the worse, and to whom any accidental fall makes the most serious difference. To a man of spirit, cowardice and disaster coming together are far more bitter than death, striking him unper-ceived at a time when he is full of courage and animated by the general hope.

"Wherefore I do not now commiserate the parents of the dead who stand here; I would rather comfort them. You know that your life has been passed amid manifold vicissitudes; and that they may be deemed fortunate who have gained most honor, whether an honorable death like theirs, or an honorable sorrow like yours, and whose days have been so ordered that the term of their happiness is likewise the term of their life. I know how hard it is to make you feel this, when the good fortune of others will too often remind you of the gladness which once lightened your hearts. And sorrow is felt at the want of those blessings, not which a man never knew, but which were a part of his life before they were taken from him. Some of you are of an age at which they may hope to have other children, and they ought to bear their sorrow better; not only will the children who may hereafter be born make them forget their own lost ones, but the city will be doubly a gainer. She will not be left desolate, and she will be safer. For a man's counsel cannot have equal weight or worth, when he alone has no children to risk in the general danger. To those of you who have passed their prime, I say; 'Congratulate yourselves that you have been happy during the greater part of your days; remember that your life of sorrow will not last long, and be comforted by the glory of those who are gone. For the love of honor alone is ever young, and not riches, as some say, but honor is the delight of men when they are old and useless.'

"To you who are the sons and brothers of the departed, I see that the struggle to emulate them will be an arduous one. For all men praise the dead, and, however pre-eminent your virtue may be, hardly will you be thought, I do not say to equal, but even to approach them. The living have their rivals and detractors, but when a man is out of the way, the honor and good-will which he receives is unalloyed. And, if I am to speak of womanly virtues to those of you who will henceforth be widows, let me sum them up in one short admonition: To a woman not to show more weakness than is natural to her sex is a great glory, and not to be talked about for good or for evil among men.

"I have paid the required tribute, in obedience to the law, making use of such fitting words as I had. The tribute of deeds has been paid in part; for the dead have been honorably interred, and it remains only that their children should be maintained at the public charge until they are grown up; this is the solid prize with which, as with a garland, Athens crowns her sons living and dead, after a struggle like theirs. For where the rewards of virtue are greatest, there the noblest citizens are enlisted in the service of the state. And now, when you have duly lamented, every one his own dead, you may depart."

Such was the order of the funeral celebrated in this winter, with the end of which ended the first year of the Peloponnesian War.

Sparta

Plutarch wrote in the first century A.D., *but his* Life of Lycurgus, *based on earlier sources, described Spartan institutions as they had existed several centuries before. (Lycurgus was the legendary founder of Sparta's constitution.)*

From Plutarch. *Life of Lycurgus*

Among the many changes and alterations which Lycurgus made, the first and of greatest importance was the establishment of the senate,

From *Plutarch's Lives,* The Translation Called Dryden's, rev. A. H. Clough (Boston: Little, Brown and Co., 1872), pp. 90, 93–96, 100–106, 109, 115, 119–120.

which, having a power equal to the kings' in matters of great consequence, and as Plato expresses it, allaying and qualifying the fiery genius of the royal office, gave steadiness and safety to the commonwealth. For the state, which before had no firm basis to stand upon, but leaned one while toward an absolute monarchy, when the kings had the upper hand, and another while toward a pure democracy, when the people had the better, found in this establishment of the senate a central weight, like ballast in a ship, which always kept things in a just equilibrium; the twenty-eight always adhering to the kings so far as to resist democracy, and, on the other hand, supporting the people against the establishment of absolute monarchy. . . .

After the creation of the thirty senators, his next task, and, indeed, the most hazardous he ever undertook, was the making a new division of their lands. For there was an extreme inequality among them, and their state was overloaded with a multitude of indigent and necessitous persons, while its whole wealth had centered upon a very few. To the end, therefore, that he might expel from the state arrogance and envy, luxury and crime, and those yet more inveterate diseases of want and superfluity, he obtained of them to renounce their properties, and to consent to a new division of the land, and that they should live all together on an equal footing; merit to be their only road to eminence, and the disgrace of evil, and credit of worthy acts, the one measure of difference between man and man. . . .

Not contented with this, he resolved to make a division of their movables too, that there might be no odious distinction or inequality left among them; but finding that it would be very dangerous to go about it openly, he took another course, and defeated their avarice by the following stratagem: he commanded that all gold and silver coin should be called in, and that only a sort of money made of iron should be current, a great weight and quantity of which was but very little worth; so that to lay up twenty or thirty pounds there was required a pretty large closet, and, to remove it, nothing less than a yoke of oxen. With the diffusion of this money, at once a number of vices were banished from Lacedaemon; for who would rob another of such a coin? Who would unjustly detain or take by force, or accept as a bribe, a thing which it was not easy to hide, nor a credit to have, nor indeed of any use to cut in pieces? For when it was just red hot, they quenched it in vinegar, and by that mean spoiled it, and made it almost incapable of being worked.

In the next place, he declared an outlawry of all needless and superfluous arts; but here he might almost have spared his proclamation; for they of themselves would have gone after the gold and silver, the money which remained being not so proper payment for curious work; for, being of iron, it was scarcely portable, neither, if they should take the pains to export it, would it pass among the other Greeks, who ridiculed it. So there was now no more means of purchasing foreign goods and small wares; merchants sent no shiploads into Laconian ports; no rhetoric-master, no itinerant fortune-teller, no harlot-monger, or gold or silversmith, engraver, or jeweller, set foot in a country which had no money; so that luxury, deprived little by little of that which fed and fomented it, wasted to nothing, and died away of itself. . . .

The third and most masterly stroke of this great lawgiver, by which he struck a yet more effectual blow against luxury and the desire of riches, was the ordinance he made, that they should all eat in common, of the same bread, and same meat, and of kinds that were specified, and should not spend their lives at home, laid on costly couches at splendid tables, delivering themselves up into the hands of their tradesmen and cooks, to fatten them in corners, like greedy brutes, and to ruin not their minds only but their very bodies, which, enfeebled by indulgence and excess, would stand in need of long sleep, warm bathing, freedom from work, and, in a word, of as much care and attendance as if they were continually sick. It was certainly an extraordinary thing to have brought about such a result as this, but a greater yet to have taken away from wealth, as Theophrastes observes, not merely the property of being coveted, but its very nature of being wealth. For the rich, being obliged to go to the same table with the poor, could not make use of or enjoy their abundance, nor so much as please their vanity by looking at or displaying it. . . .

In order to promote the good education of their youth (which, as I said before, he thought the most important and noblest work of a lawgiver), he went so far back as to take into consideration their very conception and birth, by regulating their marriages. For Aristotle is wrong in saying, that, after he had tried all ways to reduce the women to more modesty and sobriety, he was at last forced to leave them as they were, because that in the absence of their husbands, who spent the best parts of their lives in the wars, their wives, whom they were obliged to leave absolute mistresses at home, took great liberties and assumed the superiority; and were treated with overmuch respect and called by the title of lady or queen. The truth is, he took in their case, also, all the care that was possible; he ordered the maidens to exercise themselves with wrestling, running, throwing the quoit, and casting the dart, to the end that the fruit they conceived might, in strong and healthy bodies, take firmer root and find better growth, and withal that they, with this greater vigor, might be the more able to undergo the pains of child-bearing. And to the end he might take away their over-great tenderness and fear of exposure to the air, and all acquired womanishness, he ordered that the young women should go naked in the processions, as well as the young men, and dance, too, in that condition, at certain solemn feasts, singing certain songs, while the young men stood around, seeing and hearing them. On these occasions, they now and then made, by jests, a befitting reflection upon those who had misbehaved themselves in the wars; and again sang encomiums upon those who had done any gallant action, and by these means inspired the younger sort with an emulation of their glory. Those that were thus commended went away proud, elated, and gratified with their honor among the maidens; and those who were rallied were as sensibly touched with it as if they had been formally reprimanded; and so much the more, because the kings and the elders, as well as the rest of the city, saw and heard all that passed. Nor was there any thing shameful in this nakedness of the young women; modesty attended them, and all wantonness was excluded. It taught them simplicity and a care for good health, and gave them some taste of higher feelings, admitted as they thus were to the field of noble action and glory. Hence it was natural for them to think and speak as Gorgo, for example, the wife of Leonidas, is said to have done, when some foreign lady, as it would seem, told her that the women of Lacedaemon were the only women of the world who could rule men; "With good reason," she said, "for we are the only women who bring forth men." . . .

Lycurgus allowed a man who was advanced in years and had a young wife to recommend some virtuous and approved young man, that she might have a child by him, who might inherit the good qualities of the father, and be a son to himself. On the other side, an honest man who had love for a married woman upon account of her modesty and the well-favoredness of her children, might, without formality, beg her company of her husband, that he might raise, as it were, from this plot of good ground, worthy and well-allied children for himself. And indeed, Lycurgus was of a persuasion that children were not so much the property of their parents as of the whole commonwealth, and, therefore, would not have his citizens begot by the first comers, but by the best men that could be found: the laws of other nations seemed to him very absurd and inconsistent, where people would be so solicitous for their dogs and horses as to exert interest and pay money to procure fine breeding, and yet kept their wives shut up, to be made mothers only by themselves, who might be foolish, infirm, or diseased; as if it were not apparent that children of a bad breed would prove their bad qualities first upon those who kept and were rearing them, and well-born children, in like manner, their good qualities. . . .

Nor was it lawful, indeed, for the father himself to breed up the children after his own fancy; but as soon as they were seven years old they were to be enrolled in certain companies and classes, where they all lived under the same order and discipline, doing their exercises and taking their play together. Of these, he who showed the most conduct and courage was made captain; they had their eyes always upon him, obeyed his orders, and underwent patiently whatsoever punishment he inflicted; so that the whole course of their education was one continued exercise of a ready and perfect obedience. The old men, too, were spectators of their performances, and often raised quarrels and disputes among them, to have a good opportunity of finding out their different characters, and of seeing which would be valiant, which a coward, when they should come to more dangerous encounters. Reading and writing they gave them, just enough to serve their turn; their chief care was to make them good subjects, and to teach them to endure pain and conquer in battle. To this end, as they grew in years, their discipline was proportionably increased; their heads were close-clipped, they were accustomed to go barefoot, and for the most part to play naked. . . . Their lovers and favorers, too, had a share in the young boy's honor or disgrace; and there goes a story that one of them was fined by the magistrate, because the lad whom he loved cried out effeminately as he was fighting. And though this sort of love was so approved among them, that the most virtuous matrons would make professions of it to young girls, yet rivalry did not exist, and if several men's fancies met in one person, it was rather the beginning of an intimate friendship, while they all jointly conspired to render the object of their affection as accomplished as possible. . . . Their discipline continued still after they were full-grown men. No one was allowed to live after his own fancy; but the city was a sort of camp, in which every man had his share of provisions and business set out, and looked upon himself not so much born to serve his own ends as the interest of his country.

One of the greatest and highest blessings Lycurgus procured his people was the abundance of leisure which proceeded from his forbidding to them the exercise of any mean and mechanical trade. Of the money-making that depends on troublesome going about and seeing people and doing business they had no need at all in a state where wealth obtained no honor or respect. The Helots tilled their ground for them, and paid them yearly in kind the appointed quantity, without any trouble of theirs. . . .

And this was the reason why he forbade them to travel abroad, and go about acquainting themselves with foreign rules of morality, the habits of ill-educated people, and different views of government. Withal he banished from Lacedaemon all strangers who could not give a very good reason for their coming thither; not because he was afraid lest they should inform themselves of and imitate his manner of government (as Thucydides says), or learn any thing to their good; but rather lest they should introduce something contrary to good manners. With strange people, strange words must be admitted; these novelties produce novelties in thought; and on these follow views and feelings whose discordant character destroys the harmony of the state. He was as careful to save his city from the infection of foreign bad habits, as men usually are to prevent the introduction of a pestilence.

DIVINE AND HUMAN LAW

Sophocles

In his play Antigone, *Sophocles (c. 495–c. 406* B.C.*) raised moral problems that have persisted in Western culture down to modern times.*

For Sophocles the will of the gods is no longer mere divine caprice (as in Homer) but "unwritten and unfailing" law. Also Sophocles sees loyalty to the state as a necessary safeguard against anarchy in all normal circumstances. But what if the law of the state conflicts with divine law? And what if loyalty to the state conflicts with family loyalties—the loyalty of sister to brother, son to father, husband to bride? The following excerpts illustrate these themes.

(Antigone and Polineices are children of Oedipus, the king of Thebes who offended the gods by unknowingly marrying his own mother. A new king of Thebes, Creon, commands that the body of Polineices be left unburied as a penalty for treason. Antigone, defying the royal edict, sprinkles dust on her brother's corpse.)

From Antigone

Creon
(to Antigone)   You—tell me not at length but in a word.
You knew the order not to do this thing?

Antigone   I knew, of course I knew. The word was plain.

Creon   And still you dared to overstep these laws?

Antigone   For me it was not Zeus who made that order.
Nor did that Justice who lives with the gods below
mark out such laws to hold among mankind.
Nor did I think your orders were so strong
that you, a mortal man, could over-run
the gods' unwritten and unfailing laws.
Not now, nor yesterday's, they always live,

From Sophocles, *Antigone*, Elizabeth Wyckoff, trans. in *The Complete Greek Tragedies*, David Grene and Richmond Lattimore, eds. (Chicago, Ill.: University of Chicago Press, 1954), pp. 174–175, 180–187, 203. Copyright © 1954 by University of Chicago Press. Reprinted by permission of the publisher.

and no one knows their origin in time.
So not through fear of any man's proud spirit
would I be likely to neglect these laws,
draw on myself the gods' sure punishment.
I knew that I must die; how could I not?
even without your warning. If I die
before my time, I say it is a gain.
Who lives in sorrows many as are mine
how shall he not be glad to gain his death?
And so, for me to meet this fate, no grief.
But if I left that corpse, my mother's son,
dead and unburied I'd have cause to grieve
as now I grieve not.
And if you think my acts are foolishness
the foolishness may be in a fool's eye.

Chorus	The girl is bitter. She's her father's child.
	She cannot yield to trouble; nor could he.

Chorus   The girl is bitter. She's her father's child.
She cannot yield to trouble; nor could he.

Creon   These rigid spirits are the first to fall.
The strongest iron, hardened in the fire,
most often ends in scraps and shatterings.
Small curbs bring raging horses back to terms.
Slave to his neighbor, who can think of pride?
This girl was expert in her insolence
when she broke bounds beyond established law.
Once she had done it, insolence the second,
to boast her doing, and to laugh in it.
I am no man and she the man instead
if she can have this conquest without pain . . .

Chorus   Fortunate they whose lives have no taste of pain.
For those whose house is shaken by the gods
escape no kind of doom. It extends to all the kin
like the wave that comes when the winds of Thrace
run over the dark of the sea.
The black sand of the bottom is brought from the depth;
the beaten capes sound back with a hollow cry.

Ancient the sorrow of Labdacus' house, I know.
Dead men's grief comes back, and falls on grief.
No generation can free the next.
One of the gods will strike. There is no escape.
So now the light goes out
for the house of Oedipus, while the bloody knife
cuts the remaining root. Folly and Fury have done this . . .

(Haemon enters from the side.)

Here is your one surviving son.
Does he come in grief at the fate of his bride,
in pain that he's tricked of his wedding?

Creon   Soon we shall know more than a seer could tell us.
Son, have you heard the vote condemned your bride?
And are you here, maddened against your father,
or are we friends, whatever I may do?

Haemon   My father, I am yours. You keep me straight
with your good judgment, which I shall ever follow.
Nor shall a marriage count for more with me
than your kind leading.

Creon   There's my good boy. So should you hold at heart
and stand behind your father all the way.
It is for this men pray they may beget
households of dutiful obedient sons,
who share alike in punishing enemies,
and give due honor to their father's friends.
Whoever breeds a child that will not help
what has he sown but trouble for himself,
and for his enemies laughter full and free?
Son, do not let your lust mislead your mind,
all for a woman's sake, for well you know
how cold the thing he takes into his arms
who has a wicked woman for his wife.
What deeper wounding than a friend no friend?
Oh spit her forth forever, as your foe.
Let the girl marry somebody in Hades.
Since I have caught her in the open act,
the only one in town who disobeyed,
I shall not now proclaim myself a liar,
but kill her. Let her sing her song of Zeus
who guards the kindred.
If I allow disorder in my house
I'd surely have to license it abroad.
A man who deals in fairness with his own,
he can make manifest justice in the state.
But he who crosses law, or forces it,
or hopes to bring the rulers under him,
shall never have a word of praise from me.
The man the state has put in place must have
obedient hearing to his least command
when it is right, and even when it's not.
He who accepts this teaching I can trust,
ruler, or ruled, to function in his place,
to stand his ground even in the storm of spears,

a mate to trust in battle at one's side.
There is no greater wrong than disobedience.
This ruins cities, this tears down our homes,
this breaks the battle-front in panic-rout.
If men live decently it is because
discipline saves their very lives for them.
So I must guard the men who yield to order,
not let myself be beaten by a woman.
Better, if it must happen, that a man
should overset me.
I won't be called weaker than womankind.

Chorus We think—unless our age is cheating us—
that what you say is sensible and right.

Haemon Father, the gods have given men good sense,
the only sure possession that we have.
I couldn't find the words in which to claim
that there was error in your late remarks.
Yet someone else might bring some further light.
Because I am your son I must keep watch
on all men's doing where it touches you,
their speech, and most of all, their discontents.
Your presence frightens any common man
from saying things you would not care to hear.
But in dark corners I have heard them say
how the whole town is grieving for this girl,
unjustly doomed, if ever woman was,
to die in shame for glorious action done.
She would not leave her fallen, slaughtered brother
there, as he lay, unburied, for the birds
and hungry dogs to make an end of him.
Isn't her real desert a golden prize?
This is the undercover speech in town.
Father, your welfare is my greatest good.
What loveliness in life for any child
outweighs a father's fortune and good fame?
And so a father feels his children's faring.
Then, do not have one mind, and one alone
that only your opinion can be right.
Whoever thinks that he is alone is wise,
his eloquence, his mind, above the rest,
come the unfolding, shows his emptiness.
A man, though wise, should never be ashamed
of learning more, and must unbend his mind.
Have you not seen the trees beside the torrent,
the ones that bend them saving every leaf,

while the resistant perish root and branch?
And so the ship that will not slacken sail,
the sheet drawn tight, unyielding, overturns.
She ends the voyage with her keel on top.
No, yield your wrath, allow a change of stand.
Young as I am, if I may give advice,
I'd say it would be best if men were born
perfect in wisdom, but that failing this
(which often fails) it can be no dishonor
to learn from others when they speak good sense.

Chorus   Lord, if your son has spoken to the point
you should take his lesson. He should do the same.
Both sides have spoken well.

Creon   At my age I'm to school my mind by his?
This boy instructor is my master, then?

Haemon   I urge no wrong. I'm young, but you should watch
my actions, not my years, to judge of me.

Creon   A loyal action, to respect disorder?

Haemon   I wouldn't urge respect for wickedness.

Creon   You don't think she is sick with that disease?

Haemon   Your fellow-citizens maintain she's not.

Creon   Is the town to tell me how I ought to rule?

Haemon   Now there you speak just like a boy yourself.

Creon   Am I to rule by other mind than mine?

Haemon   No city is property of a single man.

Creon   But custom gives possession to the ruler.

Haemon   You'd rule a desert beautifully alone.

Creon (to the Chorus)   It seems he's firmly on the woman's side.

Haemon   If you're a woman. It is you I care for.

Creon   Wicked, to try conclusions with your father.

Haemon   When you conclude unjustly, so I must.

Creon   Am I unjust, when I respect my office?

Haemon   You tread down the gods' due. Respect is gone.

Creon   Your mind is poisoned. Weaker than a woman!

Haemon   At least you'll never see me yield to shame.

Creon   Your whole long argument is but for her.

Haemon   And you, and me, and for the gods below.

Creon   You shall not marry her while she's alive.

Haemon   Then she shall die. Her death will bring another . . .

(Haemon leaves, by one of the side entrances.)

Chorus   And what death have you chosen for the other?

Creon   To take her where the foot of man comes not.
There shall I hide her in a hollowed cave
living, and leave her just so much to eat
as clears the city from the guilt of death.
There, if she prays to Death, the only god
of her respect, she may manage not to die.
Or she may learn at last and even then
how much too much her labor for the dead.

(Creon returns to the palace.)

Chorus   Love unconquered in fight, love who falls on our havings.
You rest in the bloom of a girl's unwithered face.
You cross the sea, you are known in the wildest lairs.
Not the immortal gods can fly,
nor men of a day. Who has you within him is mad.
You twist the minds of the just. Wrong they pursue and are
  ruined.
You made this quarrel of kindred before us now.
Desire looks clear from the eyes of a lovely bride:
power as strong as the founded world.
For there is a goddess at play with whom no man can fight.

(Creon is finally persuaded to relent. But by then Antigone has committed suicide in her prison-tomb. Haemon in turn kills himself. At the end of the play Creon is left in despair.)

Creon   Take me away at once, the frantic man who killed
my son, against my meaning. I cannot rest.
My life is warped past cure. My fate has struck me down.

(Creon and his attendants enter the house.)

Chorus   Our happiness depends
on wisdom all the way.
The gods must have their due.
Great words my men of pride
bring greater blows upon them.
So wisdom comes to the old.

III

THE IDEA OF THE GOOD
Socrates: Critics and Friends
　From *The Clouds*
　From *Phaedo*
Plato's Cave
　From *The Republic*

FAMILY AND STATE—
IDEALISM
Platonic Utopianism
　From *The Republic*

FAMILY AND STATE—
REALISM
An Athenian Household
　From Xenophon. *Household
　　Management*
State Finances
　From Xenophon. *On the Revenues*

ARISTOTLE—NATURAL
SCIENCE AND SOCIAL
SCIENCE
Scientific Method
　From *Parts of Animals*
Ethics and Politics
　From *The Nichomachean Ethics*
　From *The Politics*

GREEK CIVILIZATION—PHILOSOPHY, POLITICS, AND SOCIETY
(c. 430–c. 330 B.C.)

*T*HE THREE GREATEST *thinkers of the ancient world—Socrates, Plato, and Aristotle—lived and worked in Athens during the century after 430* B.C.

Socrates (469–399 B.C.*) reoriented the whole tradition of Greek philosophy by turning away from speculation about the external universe to consider the inner nature of man himself. (He held that "the unexamined life is not worth living.") Socrates questioned all the everyday assumptions of respectable Athenian citizens. But the Athenians, especially after their defeat in the Peloponnesian War, were in no mood to accept such probing criticism. In the end they put Socrates to death for "worshipping false gods and corrupting the youth."*

Socrates' disciple, Plato (428–347 B.C.*), believed that the world revealed to us by sense experience was only a shadowy world of half-truths. The pure intellect of the philosopher could rise above these mere appearances to contemplate a world of absolute forms or archetypes—absolute beauty, absolute justice, and, at the furthest reach of the human mind, absolute good.*

Aristotle (384–322 B.C.*) was a more down-to-earth philosopher. He did not despise sense experience but rather collected great masses of information in fields that we would call "natural sciences" and "social sciences" and organized it all in accordance with his own scientific methodology. (Typically, when he wanted to write on politics, he had his students collect for study the constitutions of 158 Greek city-states.)*

To complement the abstract teachings of the philosophers we have included some comments of a hard-headed country gentleman, Xenophon (c. 434–c. 355 B.C.*), on Athenian family life and political affairs.*

THE IDEA OF THE GOOD

Socrates: Critics and Friends

Aristophanes presented a derisive caricature of Socrates in The Clouds *(performed in 423 B.C.). The play, a good specimen of Athenian comedy, may tell us nothing about the real Socrates, but it does convey the exasperation aroused in many ordinary Athenians by Socrates' questioning of their traditional beliefs.*

Strepsiades is a foolish old farmer who has accumulated huge debts through his son's passion for horse racing. He decides to enter the school of Socrates.

From *The Clouds*

Strepsiades.
Throw open the Thinkery! Unbolt the door
and let me see this wizard Sokrates in person.
Open up! I'm MAD for education! . . .

He catches sight of Sokrates
dangling in a basket overhead.

       Look: who's that dangling up there in the basket?
Student.
Himself.

Strepsiades.
       Who's Himself?

Student.
               Sokrates.

Strepsiades.
               SOKRATES!
Then call him down. Go on. Give a great big shout.

Student.

Hastily and apprehensively taking his leave.

       Er . . . *you* call him. I'm a busy man.

Exit Student.

Strepsiades.
             O Sokrates!

No answer from the basket.

       Yoohoo, Sokrates!

From Aristophanes, *The Clouds*, William Arrowsmith, trans. (Ann Arbor, Mich.: University of Michigan Press, 1962), pp. 25–31, 34–38. Copyright © 1962 by William Arrowsmith. Reprinted by permission of the publisher and by arrangement with The New American Library, Inc., New York, N.Y.

Sokrates.

From a vast philosophical height.

> Well, creature of a day?

Strepsiades.
What in the world are you doing up there?

Sokrates.

>   Ah, sir,
I walk upon the air and look down upon the sun
from a superior standpoint.

Strepsiades.

>   Well, I suppose it's better
that you sneer at the gods from a basket up in the air
than do it down here on the ground.

Sokrates.

>   Precisely. You see,
only by being suspended aloft, by dangling
my mind in the heavens and mingling my rare thought
with the ethereal air, could I ever achieve strict
scientific accuracy in my survey of the vast empyrean.
Had I pursued my inquiries from down there on the ground,
my data would be worthless. The earth, you see, pulls down
the delicate essence of thought to its own gross level.

As an afterthought.

> Much the same thing happens with watercress.

Strepsiades.

Ecstatically bewildered.

>   You don't say?
Thought draws down . . . delicate essence . . . into watercress.
O dear little Sokrates, please come down. Lower away,
and teach me what I need to know!

Sokrates is slowly lowered earthwards.

Sokrates.

>   What subject?

Strepsiades.
Your course on public speaking and debating techniques.
You see, my creditors have become absolutely ferocious.
You should see how they're hounding me. What's more, Sokrates,
they're about to seize my belongings.

Sokrates.

>   How in the world
could you fall so deeply in debt without realizing it?

Strepsiades.

>   How?
A great, greedy horse-pox ate me up, that's how.
But that's why I want instruction in your second Logic,

you know the one—the get-away-without-paying argument.
I'll pay you *any* price you ask. I swear it.
By the gods.

Sokrates.

    By the gods? The gods, my dear simple fellow,
are a mere expression coined by vulgar superstition.
We frown upon such coinage here.

Strepsiades.

        What do *you* swear by?
Bars of iron, like the Byzantines?

Sokrates.

      Tell me, old man,
would you honestly like to learn the truth, the *real* truth,
about the gods?

Strepsiades.

    By Zeus, I sure would. The *real* truth.

Sokrates.
And also be admitted to intercourse with their Serene Highnesses,
our goddesses, the Clouds?

Strepsiades.

      Intercourse with *real* goddesses?
Oh yes, I'd *like* that . . .

A chorus of Clouds enters singing.

Chorus.

     Virgins of rain,
     look on Pallas' shining earth,
     this oil-anointed land,
     country of Kekrops'
     hero-breeding plain!
     Holiness is here,
     home of the mysteries,
     whose unrevealable rites
     sanctify the soul.
     And here the gods have gifts.
     Below the splendid gables go
     processions of the blest,
     and every season sees
     its festivals, its crowns.
     And early every Spring
     Dionysos brings his joy,
     the weaving of the dance,
     the Muses and the flutes.

Strepsiades.
Holy Zeus, Sokrates, who were those ladies that sang
that solemn hymn? Were they heroines of mythology?

Sokrates.

        No, old man.
Those were the Clouds of heaven, goddesses of men of leisure

and philosophers. To them we owe our repertoire of verbal talents:
our eloquence, intellect, fustian, casuistry, force, wit,
prodigious vocabulary, circumlocutory skill—. . . .

Strepsiades.

                                                By Zeus, it's news to me.
I always used to think they were just fog and drizzle and mist.

Sokrates.

Clearly then you must also be ignorant of the fact that the Clouds
are also patrons of a varied group of gentlemen, comprising:
chiropractors, prophets, longhairs, quacks, fops, charlatans,
fairies, dithyrambic poets, scientists, dandies, astrologers,
and other men of leisure. And because all alike, without exception,
walk with their heads among the clouds and base their inspiration
on the murky Muse, the Clouds support them and feed them. . . .

A great burst of thunder.
Strepsiades cowers with fright.

Koryphaios.

                                        Hail, superannuated man!
Hail, old birddog of culture!

To Sokrates.

                                        And hail to you, O Sokrates,
high priest of poppycock!
                                        Inform us what your wishes are.
For of all the polymaths on earth, it's you we most prefer—
you and Prodikos. Him we love for wisdom's sake, but you, sir,
for your swivel-eyes, your barefoot swagger down the street,
because you're poor on our account and terribly affected.

Strepsiades.

Name of Earth, what a voice! Solemn and holy and awful!

Sokrates.

These are the only gods there are. The rest are but figments.

Strepsiades.

Holy name of Earth! Olympian Zeus is a figment?

Sokrates.
Zeus?
        What Zeus?
                        Nonsense.
                                There is no Zeus.

Strepsiades.

                                        No Zeus?
Then *who* makes it rain? Answer me that.

Sokrates.

                                        Why, the Clouds,
of course.

What's more, the proof is incontrovertible.

For instance,
have you ever yet seen rain when you didn't see a cloud?
But if your hypothesis were correct, Zeus could drizzle from an empty
   sky
while the clouds were on vacation.

Strepsiades.

By Apollo, you're right. A pretty
   proof.
And to think I always used to believe the rain was just Zeus
pissing through a sieve.

All right, *who* makes it thunder?
Brrr. I get goosebumps just saying it.

Sokrates.

The Clouds again,
of course. A simple process of Convection.

Strepsiades.

I admire you,
but I don't follow you.

Sokrates.

Listen. The Clouds are a saturate water-solution.
Tumescence in motion, of necessity, produces precipitation.
When those distended masses collide—*boom!*

Fulmination.

Strepsiades.
But who makes them move before they collide? Isn't that Zeus?

Sokrates.
Not Zeus, idiot. The Convection-principle!

Strepsiades.

Convection? That's a
   new one.
Just think. So Zeus is out and convection-principle's in.
Tch, tch.

But wait: you haven't told me who makes it thunder.

Sokrates.
But I just *finished* telling you! The Clouds are water-packed;
they collide with each other and explode because of the pressure.

Strepsiades.

Yeah?

And what's your proof for *that?*

Sokrates.

Why, take yourself as example.
You know that meat-stew the vendors sell at the Panathenaia?
How it gives you the cramps and your stomach starts to rumble?

Strepsiades.

Yes.

by Apollo! I remember. What an awful feeling! You feel sick
and your belly churns and the fart rips loose like thunder.
First just a gurgle, *pappapax;* then louder, *pappaPAPAXapaX,*
and finally like thunder, *PAPAPAPAXAPAXAPPAPAXapap!*

Sokrates.
Precisely.
First think of the tiny fart that your intestines make.
Then consider the heavens: their infinite farting is thunder.
For thunder and farting are, in principle, one and the same. . . .

Chorus.
—Ah, how he hungers after learning!

To Strepsiades.

—Sir, if you can pass our test,
we guarantee that you shall be
—the cynosure of Hellas.
—Our requirements are these:
—First, is your memory keen?
—Do you hanker for researching?
—Are you subject to fatigue
from standing up or walking?
—Does winter weather daunt you?
—Can you go without a meal?
—Abstain from wine and exercise?
—And keep away from girls?
—Last, do you solemnly swear
adherence to our code?
—*To wrangle*
—*niggle*
—*haggle*
—*battle*
—*a loyal soldier of the Tongue, conducting yourself always
like a true philosopher.*

Strepsiades.

Ladies, if all you require
is hard work, insomnia, worry, endurance, and a stomach
that eats anything, why, have no fear. For I'm your man
and as hard as nails.

Sokrates.

And you promise to follow faithfully in my path,
acknowledging no other gods but mine, to wit, the Trinity—
GREAT CHAOS, THE CLOUDS, and BAMBOOZLE?

Strepsiades.

If I met
another god,
I'd cut him dead, so help me. Here and now I swear off sacrifice and
prayer forever.

At the opposite extreme from Aristophanes' mockery is the grave and reverent account by Plato of Socrates' last conversation with his friends and his death.

From *Phaedo*

But do you mean to take away your thoughts with you, Socrates? said Simmias. Will you not impart them to us?—for they are a benefit in which we too are entitled to share. Moreover, if you succeed in convincing us, that will be an answer to the charge against yourself.

I will do my best, replied Socrates. But you must first let me hear what Crito wants; he has long been wishing to say something to me.

Only this, Socrates, replied Crito:—the attendant who is to give you the poison has been telling me, and he wants me to tell you, that you are not to talk much; talking, he says, increases heat, and this is apt to interfere with the action of the poison; persons who excite themselves are sometimes obliged to take a second or even a third dose.

Then, said Socrates, let him mind his business and be prepared to give the poison twice or even thrice if necessary; that is all.

I knew quite well what you would say, replied Crito; but I was obliged to satisfy him.

Never mind him, he said.

And now, O my judges, I desire to prove to you that the real philosopher has reason to be of good cheer when he is about to die, and that after death he may hope to obtain the greatest good in the other world . . . let us discuss the matter among ourselves. Do we believe that there is such a thing as death?

To be sure, replied Simmias.

Is it not the separation of soul and body? And to be dead is the completion of this; when the soul exists in herself, and is released from the body and the body is released from the soul, what is this but death?

Just so, he replied.

There is another question, which will probably throw light on our present enquiry if you and I can agree about it:—Ought the philosopher to care about the pleasures—if they are to be called pleasures—of eating and drinking?

Certainly not, answered Simmias.

And what about the pleasures of love—should he care for them?

By no means.

And will he think much of the other ways of indulging the body, for example, the acquisition of costly raiment, or sandals, or other adornments of the body? Instead of caring about them, does he not rather despise anything more than nature needs? What do you say?

I should say that the true philosopher would despise them.

From Plato, *Phaedo*, B. Jowett, trans. in *The Dialogues of Plato*, 3rd ed. (Oxford: Oxford University Press, 1892, reprinted 1924), Vol. 2, pp. 202–206, 264–266.

Would you not say that he is entirely concerned with the soul and not with the body? He would like, as far as he can, to get away from the body and to turn to the soul.

Quite true.

In matters of this sort philosophers, above all other men, may be observed in every sort of way to dissever the soul from the communion of the body.

Very true.

Whereas, Simmias, the rest of the world are of opinion that to him who has no sense of pleasure and no part in bodily pleasure, life is not worth having; and that he who is indifferent about them is as good as dead.

That is also true.

What again shall we say of the actual acquirement of knowledge?— is the body, if invited to share in the enquiry, a hinderer or a helper? I mean to say, have sight and hearing any truth in them? Are they not, as the poets are always telling us, inaccurate witnesses? and yet, if even they are inaccurate and indistinct, what is to be said of the other senses?—for you will allow that they are the best of them?

Certainly, he replied.

Then when does the soul attain truth?—for in attempting to consider anything in company with the body she is obviously deceived.

True.

Then must not true existence be revealed to her in thought, if at all?

Yes.

And thought is best when the mind is gathered into herself and none of these things trouble her—neither sounds nor sights nor pain nor any pleasure,—when she takes leave of the body, and has as little as possible to do with it, when she has no bodily sense or desire, but is aspiring after true being?

Certainly.

And in this the philosopher dishonours the body; his soul runs away from his body and desires to be alone and by herself?

That is true.

Well, but there is another thing, Simmias: Is there or is there not an absolute justice?

Assuredly there is.

And an absolute beauty and absolute good?

Of course.

But did you ever behold any of them with your eyes?

Certainly not.

Or did you ever reach them with any other bodily sense?—and I speak not of these alone, but of absolute greatness, and health, and strength, and of the essence or true nature of everything. Has the reality of them ever been perceived by you through the bodily organs? or rather, is not the nearest approach to the knowledge of their several natures made by him who so orders his intellectual vision as to have the most exact conception of the essence of each thing which he considers?

Certainly.

And he attains to the purest knowledge of them who goes to each with the mind alone, not introducing or intruding in the act of thought sight or any other sense together with reason, but with the very light of the mind in her own clearness searches into the very truth of each; he who has got rid, as far as he can, of eyes and ears and, so to speak, of the whole body, these being in his opinion distracting elements which when they infect the soul hinder her from acquiring truth and knowledge—who, if not he, is likely to attain to the knowledge of true being?

What you say has a wonderful truth in it, Socrates, replied Simmias.

And when real philosophers consider all these things, will they not be led to make a reflection which they will express in words something like the following? 'Have we not found,' they will say, 'a path of thought which seems to bring us and our argument to the conclusion, that while we are in the body, and while the soul is infected with the evils of the body, our desire will not be satisfied? and our desire is of the truth. For the body is a source of endless trouble to us by reason of the mere requirement of food; and is liable also to diseases which overtake and impede us in the search after true being: it fills us full of loves, and lusts, and fears, and fancies of all kinds, and endless foolery, and in fact, as men say, takes away from us the power of thinking at all. Whence come wars, and fightings, and factions? whence but from the body and the lusts of the body? Wars are occasioned by the love of money, and money has to be acquired for the sake and in the service of the body; and by reason of all these impediments we have no time to give to philosophy; and, last and worst of all, even if we are at leisure and betake ourselves to some speculation, the body is always breaking in upon us, causing turmoil and confusion in our enquiries, and so amazing us that we are prevented from seeing the truth. It has been proved to us by experience that if we would have pure knowledge of anything we must be quit of the body—the soul in herself must behold things in themselves: and then we shall attain the wisdom which we desire, and of which we say that we are lovers; not while we live, but after death; for if while in company with the body, the soul cannot have pure knowledge, one of two things follows—either knowledge is not to be attained at all, or, if at all, after death. For then, and not till then, the soul will be parted from the body and exist in herself alone. In this present life, I reckon that we make the nearest approach to knowledge when we have the least possible intercourse or communion with the body, and are not surfeited with the bodily nature, but keep ourselves pure until the hour when God himself is pleased to release us. And thus having got rid of the foolishness of the body we shall be pure and hold converse with the pure, and know of ourselves the clear light everywhere, which is no other than the light of truth.' For the impure are not permitted to approach the pure. These are the sort of words, Simmias, which the true lovers of knowledge cannot help saying to one another, and thinking. You would agree; would you not?

Undoubtedly, Socrates.

But, O my friend, if this be true, there is great reason to hope that, going whither I go, when I have come to the end of my journey, I shall attain that which has been the pursuit of my life. And therefore I go on my way rejoicing, and not I only, but every other man who believes that his mind has been made ready and that he is in a manner purified. . . .

When he had spoken these words, he arose and went into a chamber to bathe; Crito followed him and told us to wait. So we remained behind, talking and thinking of the subject of discourse, and also of the greatness of our sorrow; he was like a father of whom we were being bereaved, and we were about to pass the rest of our lives as orphans. When he had taken the bath his children were brought to him—(he had two young sons and an elder one); and the women of his family also came, and he talked to them and gave them a few directions in the presence of Crito; then he dismissed them and returned to us.

Now the hour of sunset was near, for a good deal of time had passed while he was within. When he came out, he sat down with us again after his bath, but not much was said. Soon the jailer, who was the servant of the Eleven, entered and stood by him, saying:—To you, Socrates, whom I know to be the noblest and gentlest and best of all who ever came to this place, I will not impute the angry feelings of other men, who rage and swear at me, when, in obedience to the authorities, I bid them drink the poison—indeed, I am sure that you will not be angry with me; for others, as you are aware, and not I, are to blame. And so fare you well, and try to bear lightly what must needs be—you know my errand. Then bursting into tears he turned away and went out.

Socrates looked at him and said: I return your good wishes, and will do as you bid. Then turning to us, he said, How charming the man is: since I have been in prison he has always been coming to see me, and at times he would talk to me, and was as good to me as could be, and now see how generously he sorrows on my account. We must do as he says, Crito; and therefore let the cup be brought, if the poison is prepared: if not, let the attendant prepare some.

Yet, said Crito, the sun is still upon the hill-tops, and I know that many a one has taken the draught late, and after the announcement has been made to him, he has eaten and drunk, and enjoyed the society of his beloved; do not hurry—there is time enough.

Socrates said: Yes, Crito, and they of whom you speak are right in so acting, for they think that they will be gainers by the delay; but I am right in not following their example, for I do not think that I should gain anything by drinking the poison a little later; I should only be ridiculous in my own eyes for sparing and saving a life which is already forfeit. Please then to do as I say, and not to refuse me.

Crito made a sign to the servant, who was standing by; and he went out, and having been absent for some time, returned with the jailer carrying the cup of poison. Socrates said: You, my good friend, who are experienced in these matters, shall give me directions how I am to proceed. The man answered: You have only to walk about until your legs are heavy, and then to lie down, and the poison will act. At the same time he handed the cup to Socrates, who in the easiest and gentlest manner, without the least fear or change of colour or feature, looking at the man with all his eyes, Echecrates, as his manner was, took the cup and said: What do you say about making a libation out of this cup to any god? May I, or not? The man answered: We only prepare, Socrates, just so much as we deem enough. I understand, he said: but I may and must ask the gods to prosper my journey from this to the other world—even so—and so be it according to my prayer. Then raising the cup to his lips, quite readily and cheerfully he drank off the poison. And hitherto most of us had been able to control our sorrow; but now when we saw him drinking, and saw too that he had finished the draught, we could no longer forbear, and in spite of myself my own tears were flowing fast; so that I covered my face and wept, not for him, but at the thought of my own calamity in having to part from such a friend. Nor was I the first; for Crito, when he found himself unable to restrain his tears, had got up, and I followed; and at that moment, Apollodorus, who had been weeping all the time, broke out in a loud and passionate cry which made cowards of us all. Socrates alone retained his calmness: What is this strange outcry? he said. I sent away the women mainly in order that they might not misbehave in this way, for I have been told that a man should die in peace. Be quiet then, and have patience. When we heard his words we were ashamed, and refrained our tears; and he walked about until, as he said, his legs began to fail, and then he lay on his back, according to the directions, and the man who gave him the poison now and then looked at his feet and legs; and after a while he pressed his foot hard, and asked him if he could feel; and he said, No; and then his leg, and so upwards and upwards, and showed us that he was cold and stiff. And he felt them himself, and said: When the poison reaches the heart, that will be the end. He was beginning to grow cold about the groin, when he uncovered his face, for he had covered himself up, and said—they were his last words—he said: Crito, I owe a cock to Asclepius; will you remember to pay the debt? The debt shall be paid, said Crito; is there anything else? There was no answer to this question; but in a minute or two a movement was heard, and the attendants uncovered him; his eyes were set, and Crito closed his eyes and mouth.

Such was the end, Echecrates, of our friend; concerning whom I may truly say, that of all the men of his time whom I have known, he was the wisest and justest and best.

Plato's Cave

Socrates affirmed the existence of "absolute beauty and absolute good." In his famous allegory of the cave, Plato explained how a philosopher could ascend from the world of sense experience to a contemplation of these ultimate realities.

From *The Republic*

And now, I said, let me show in a figure how far our nature is enlightened or unenlightened:—Behold! human beings living in an underground den, which has a mouth open towards the light and reaching all along the den; here they have been from their childhood, and have their legs and necks chained so that they cannot move, and can only see before them [facing inward], being prevented by the chains from turning round their heads. Above and behind them a fire is blazing at a distance, and between the fire and the prisoners there is a raised way; and you will see, if you look, a low wall built along the way, like the screen which marionette players have in front of them, over which they show the puppets.

I see.

And do you see, I said, men passing along the wall carrying all sorts of vessels, and statues and figures of animals made of wood and stone and various materials, which appear over the wall? Some of them are talking, others silent.

You have shown me a strange image, and they are strange prisoners.

Like ourselves, I replied; and they see only their own shadows, or the shadows of one another, which the fire throws on the opposite wall of the cave?

True, he said; how could they see anything but the shadows if they were never allowed to move their heads?

And of the objects which are being carried in like manner they would only see the shadows?

Yes, he said.

And if they were able to converse with one another, would they not suppose that they were naming what was actually before them?

Very true.

And suppose further that the prison had an echo which came from the other side, would they not be sure to fancy when one of the passers-by spoke that the voice which they heard came from the passing shadow?

No question, he replied.

To them, I said, the truth would be literally nothing but the shadows of the images.

From Plato, *The Republic*, B. Jowett, trans. in *The Dialogues of Plato,* 3rd ed. (Oxford: Oxford University Press, 1895, reprinted 1924), Vol. 3, pp. 214–217.

That is certain.

And now look again, and see what will naturally follow if the prisoners are released and disabused of their error. At first, when any of them is liberated and compelled suddenly to stand up and turn his neck round and walk and look towards the light, he will suffer sharp pains; the glare will distress him, and he will be unable to see the realities of which in his former state he had seen the shadows; and then conceive some one saying to him, that what he saw before was an illusion, but that now, when he is approaching nearer to being and his eye is turned towards more real existence, he has a clearer vision,—what will be his reply? And you may further imagine that his instructor is pointing to the objects as they pass and requiring him to name them,— will he not be perplexed? Will he not fancy that the shadows which he formerly saw are truer than the objects which are now shown to him?

Far truer.

And if he is compelled to look straight at the light, will he not have a pain in his eyes which will make him turn away to take refuge in the objects of vision which he can see, and which he will conceive to be in reality clearer than the things which are now being shown to him?

True, he said.

And suppose once more, that he is reluctantly dragged up a steep and rugged ascent, and held fast until he is forced into the presence of the sun himself, is he not likely to be pained and irritated? When he approaches the light his eyes will be dazzled, and he will not be able to see anything at all of what are now called realities.

Not all in a moment, he said.

He will require to grow accustomed to the sight of the upper world. And first he will see the shadows best, next the reflections of men and other objects in the water, and then the objects themselves; then he will gaze upon the light of the moon and the stars and the spangled heaven; and he will see the sky and the stars by night better than the sun or the light of the sun by day?

Certainly.

Last of all he will be able to see the sun, and not mere reflections of him in the water, but he will see him in his own proper place, and not in another; and he will contemplate him as he is.

Certainly.

He will then proceed to argue that this is he who gives the season and the years, and is the guardian of all that is in the visible world, and in a certain way the cause of all things which he and his fellows have been accustomed to behold?

Clearly, he said, he would first see the sun and then reason about him.

And when he remembered his old habitation, and the wisdom of the den and his fellow-prisoners, do you not suppose that he would felicitate himself on the change, and pity them?

Certainly, he would.

And if they were in the habit of conferring honours among themselves on those who were quickest to observe the passing shadows and to remark which of them went before, and which followed after, and which were together; and who were therefore best able to draw conclusions as to the future, do you think that he would care for such honours and glories, or envy the possessors of them? Would he not say with Homer,

'Better to be the poor servant of a poor master,'

and to endure anything, rather than think as they do and live after their manner?

Yes, he said, I think that he would rather suffer anything than entertain these false notions and live in this miserable manner.

Imagine once more, I said, such an one coming suddenly out of the sun to be replaced in his old situation; would he not be certain to have his eyes full of darkness?

To be sure, he said.

And if there were a contest, and he had to compete in measuring the shadows with the prisoners who had never moved out of the den, while his sight was still weak, and before his eyes had become steady (and the time which would be needed to acquire this new habit of sight might be very considerable), would he not be ridiculous? Men would say of him that up he went and down he came without his eyes; and that it was better not even to think of ascending; and if any one tried to loose another and lead him up to the light, let them only catch the offender, and they would put him to death.

No question, he said.

This entire allegory, I said, you may now append, dear Glaucon, to the previous argument; the prison-house is the world of sight, the light of the fire is the sun, and you will not misapprehend me if you interpret the journey upwards to be the ascent of the soul into the intellectual world according to my poor belief, which, at your desire, I have expressed—whether rightly or wrongly God knows. But, whether true or false, my opinion is that in the world of knowledge the idea of good appears last of all, and is seen only with an effort; and, when seen, is also inferred to be the universal author of all things beautiful and right, parent of light and of the lord of light in this visible world, and the immediate source of reason and truth in the intellectual; and that this is the power upon which he who would act rationally either in public or private life must have his eye fixed.

FAMILY AND STATE—IDEALISM

Platonic Utopianism

Plato's Republic *deals with the ideal of justice as embodied in the individual and the state. In the course of his argument Plato expressed some radical views on community of property and roles of women.*

From *The Republic*

Is not the love of learning the love of wisdom, which is philosophy?

They are the same, he replied.

And may we not say confidently of man also, that he who is likely to be gentle to his friends and acquaintances, must by nature be a lover of wisdom and knowledge?

That we may safely affirm.

Then he who is to be a really good and noble guardian of the State will require to unite in himself philosophy and spirit and swiftness and strength?

Undoubtedly.

Then we have found the desired natures; and now that we have found them, how are they to be reared and educated? Is not this an enquiry which may be expected to throw light on the greater enquiry which is our final end—How do justice and injustice grow up in States?

Adeimantus thought that the enquiry would be of great service to us. . . .

Come then, and let us pass a leisure hour in story-telling, and our story shall be the education of our heroes.

By all means.

And what shall be their education? Can we find a better than the traditional sort?—and this has two divisions, gymnastic for the body, and music for the soul.

True. . . .

Very good, I said; then what is the next question? Must we not ask who are to be rulers and who subjects?

From Plato, *The Republic*, B. Jowett, trans. in *The Dialogues of Plato*, 3rd ed. (Oxford: Oxford University Press, 1895, reprinted 1924), Vol. 3, pp. 58, 100–101, 103, 106, 142–144, 147–149, 150–151, 159, 170–171.

Certainly.

There can be no doubt that the elder must rule the younger.

Clearly.

And that the best of these must rule.

That is also clear.

Now, are not the best husbandmen those who are most devoted to husbandry?

Yes.

And as we are to have the best of guardians for our city, must they not be those who have most the character of guardians?

Yes. . . .

Then there must be a selection. Let us note among the guardians those who in their whole life show the greatest eagerness to do what is for the good of their country, and the greatest repugnance to do what is against her interests.

Those are the right men.

And they will have to be watched at every age, in order that we may see whether they preserve their resolution, and never, under the influence either of force or enchantment, forget or cast off their sense of duty to the State. . . . And he who at every age, as boy and youth and in mature life, has come out of the trial victorious and pure, shall be appointed a ruler and guardian of the State; he shall be honoured in life and death, and shall receive sepulture and other memorials of honour, the greatest that we have to give. But him who fails, we must reject. I am inclined to think that this is the sort of way in which our rulers and guardians should be chosen and appointed. I speak generally, and not with any pretension to exactness.

And, speaking generally, I agree with you, he said. . . .

Then let us consider what will be their way of life, if they are to realize our idea of them. In the first place, none of them should have any property of his own beyond what is absolutely necessary; neither should they have a private house or store closed against any one who has a mind to enter; their provisions should be only such as are required by trained warriors, who are men of temperance and courage; they should agree to receive from the citizens a fixed rate of pay, enough to meet the expenses of the year and no more; and they will go to mess and live together like soldiers in a camp. Gold and silver we will tell them that they have from God; the diviner metal is within them, and they have therefore no need of the dross which is current among men, and ought not to pollute the divine by any such earthly admixture; for that commoner metal has been the source of many unholy deeds, but their own is undefiled. And they alone of all the citizens may not touch or handle silver or gold, or be under the same roof with them, or wear them, or drink from them. And this will be their salvation, and they will be the saviours of the State. But should they ever acquire homes or lands or moneys of their own, they will become

housekeepers and husbandmen instead of guardians, enemies and tyrants instead of allies of the other citizens; hating and being hated,
plotting and being plotted against, they will pass their whole life in
much greater terror of internal than of external enemies, and the hour
of ruin, both to themselves and to the rest of the State, will be at hand.
For all which reasons may we not say that thus shall our State be ordered, and that these shall be the regulations appointed by us for our
guardians concerning their houses and all other matters?

Yes, said Glaucon. . . .

The part of the men has been played out, and now properly enough
comes the turn of the women. Of them I will proceed to speak, and
the more readily since I am invited by you.

For men born and educated like our citizens, the only way, in my
opinion, of arriving at a right conclusion about the possession and use
of women and children is to follow the path on which we originally
started, when we said that the men were to be the guardians and
watchdogs of the herd.

True.

Let us further suppose the birth and education of our women to be
subject to similar or nearly similar regulations; then we shall see
whether the result accords with our design.

What do you mean?

What I mean may be put into the form of a question, I said: Are
dogs divided into hes and shes, or do they both share equally in hunting and in keeping watch and in the other duties of dogs? or do we
entrust to the males the entire and exclusive care of the flocks, while
we leave the females at home, under the idea that the bearing and
suckling their puppies is labour enough for them?

No, he said, they share alike; the only difference between them is
that the males are stronger and the females weaker.

But can you use different animals for the same purpose, unless they
are bred and fed in the same way?

You cannot.

Then, if women are to have the same duties as men, they must have
the same nurture and education?

Yes.

The education which was assigned to the men was music and
gymnastic.

Yes.

Then women must be taught music and gymnastic and also the art
of war, which they must practise like the men?

That is the inference, I suppose.

I should rather expect, I said, that several of our proposals, if they
are carried out, being unusual, may appear ridiculous.

No doubt of it.

Yes, and the most ridiculous thing of all will be the sight of women naked in the palaestra, exercising with the men, especially when they are no longer young; they certainly will not be a vision of beauty, any more than the enthusiastic old men who in spite of wrinkles and ugliness continue to frequent the gymnasia.

Yes, indeed, he said: according to present notions the proposal would be thought ridiculous.

But then, I said, as we have determined to speak our minds, we must not fear the jests of the wits which will be directed against this sort of innovation; how they will talk of women's attainments both in music and gymnastic, and above all about their wearing armour and riding upon horseback!

Very true, he replied. . . .

My friend, I said, there is no special faculty of administration in a state which a woman has because she is a woman, or which a man has by virtue of his sex, but the gifts of nature are alike diffused in both; all the pursuits of men are the pursuits of women also, but in all of them a woman is inferior to a man.

Very true.

Then are we to impose all our enactments on men and none of them on women?

That will never do.

One woman has a gift of healing, another not; one is a musician, and another has no music in her nature?

Very true.

And one woman has a turn for gymnastic and military exercises, and another is unwarlike and hates gymnastics?

Certainly.

And one woman is a philosopher, and another is an enemy of philosophy; one has spirit, and another is without spirit?

That is also true.

Then one woman will have the temper of a guardian, and another not. Was not the selection of the male guardians determined by differences of this sort?

Yes.

Men and women alike possess the qualities which make a guardian; they differ only in their comparative strength or weakness.

Obviously.

And those women who have such qualities are to be selected as the companions and colleagues of men who have similar qualities and whom they resemble in capacity and in character?

Very true.

And ought not the same natures to have the same pursuits?

They ought.

Then, as we were saying before, there is nothing unnatural in assigning music and gymnastic to the wives of the guardians—to that point we come round again.

Certainly not.

The law which we then enacted was agreeable to nature, and therefore not an impossibility or mere aspiration; and the contrary practice, which prevails at present, is in reality a violation of nature.

That appears to be true. . . .

Then let the wives of our guardians strip, for their virtue will be their robe, and let them share in the toils of war and the defence of their country; only in the distribution of labours the lighter are to be assigned to the women, who are the weaker natures, but in other respects their duties are to be the same. . . .

Very true.

Here, then, is one difficulty in our law about women, which we may say that we have now escaped; the wave has not swallowed us up alive for enacting that the guardians of either sex should have all their pursuits in common; to the utility and also to the possibility of this arrangement the consistency of the argument with itself bears witness.

Yes, that was a mighty wave which you have escaped.

Yes, I said, but a greater is coming; you will not think much of this when you see the next.

Go on; let me see.

The law, I said, which is the sequel of this and of all that has preceded, is to the following effect,—'that the wives of our guardians are to be common, and their children are to be common, and no parent is to know his own child, nor any child his parent.'

Yes, he said, that is a much greater wave than the other; and the possibility as well as the utility of such a law are far more questionable. . . .

Both the community of property and the community of families, as I am saying, tend to make them more truly guardians; they will not tear the city in pieces by differing about 'mine' and 'not mine;' each man dragging any acquisition which he has made into a separate house of his own, where he has a separate wife and children and private pleasures and pains; but all will be affected as far as may be by the same pleasures and pains because they are all of one opinion about what is near and dear to them, and therefore they all tend towards a common end.

Certainly, he replied. . . .

Let me next endeavour to show what is that fault in States which is the cause of their present maladministration, and what is the least change which will enable a State to pass into the truer form; and let the change, if possible, be of one thing only, or, if not, of two; at any rate, let the changes be as few and slight as possible.

Certainly, he replied.

I think, I said, that there might be a reform of the State if only one change were made, which is not a slight or easy though still a possible one.

What is it? he said.

Now then, I said, I go to meet that which I liken to the greatest of the waves; yet shall the word be spoken, even though the wave break and drown me in laughter and dishonour; and do you mark my words.

Proceed.

I said: *Until philosophers are kings, or the kings and princes of this world have the spirit and power of philosophy, and political greatness and wisdom meet in one, and those commoner natures who pursue either to the exclusion of the other are compelled to stand aside, cities will never have rest from their evils,—no, nor the human race, as I believe,—and then only will this our State have a possibility of life and behold the light of day.*

FAMILY AND STATE—REALISM

An Athenian Household

The everyday life of an upper-class Athenian housewife was very different from that of Plato's imaginary female guardians. In his treatise on household management, Xenophon gives a more realistic picture.

From Xenophon. *Household Management*

"Ischomachus," said I, "I would like to ask you whether you instructed your wife yourself, so that she might be qualified as she ought to be, or whether, when you received her from her father and mother, she was possessed of sufficient knowledge to manage what belongs to her." "And how," said he, "could she have had sufficient knowledge when I took her, since she came to my house when she was not fifteen years old, and had spent the preceding part of her life under the strictest restraint, in order that she might see as little, hear as little, and ask as few questions as possible? Does it not appear to you to be quite sufficient, if she did but know, when she came, how to take wool and make a garment, and had seen how to apportion the tasks of spinning among the maid-servants? for as to what concerns the appetite,[1]" added he, "which seems to me a most important part of instruction both for a man and for a woman, she came to me extremely well instructed." "But as to other things, Ischomachus," said I, "did you yourself instruct your wife, so that she should be qualified to attend to the affairs belonging to her?" . . .

"Well," returned Ischomachus, "when she grew familiarized and domesticated with me, so that we conversed freely together, I began to question her in some such was as this: 'Tell, me, my dear wife, have you ever considered with what view I married you, and with what object your parents gave you to me? For that there was no want of other persons with whom we might have shared our respective beds must, I

[1]I.e., as regards temperance.

From Xenophon, *Oeconomicus*, translation based on J. S. Watson, *Xenophon's Minor Works* (London: George Bell and Sons, 1882), pp. 97–103.

am sure, be evident to you as well as to me. But when I considered for myself, and your parents for you, whom we might select as the best partner for a house and children, I preferred you, and your parents, as it appears, preferred me, out of those who were possible objects of choice. If, then, the gods should ever grant children to be born to us, we shall then consult together, with regard to them, how we may bring them up as well as possible; for it will be a common advantage to both of us to find them of the utmost service as supporters and maintainers of our old age. At present, however, this is our common household; for I deposit all that I have as in common between us, and you put everything that you have brought into our common stock. Nor is it necessary to consider which of the two has contributed the greater share; but we ought to feel assured that whichsoever of us is the better manager of our common fortune will give the more valuable service.' To these remarks, my wife replied, 'In what respect could I coöperate with you? What power have I? Everything lies with you. My duty, my mother told me, was to conduct myself discreetly.' 'Yes, by Jupiter, my dear wife,' replied I, 'and my father told me the same. But it is the part of discreet people, as well husbands as wives, to act in such a manner that their property may be in the best possible condition, and that as large additions as possible may be made to it by honourable and just means.' 'And, what do you see,' said my wife, 'that I can do to assist in increasing our property?' . . .

" 'The gods, as it seems to me,' said I, 'have plainly adapted the nature of the woman for works and duties within doors, and that of the man for works and duties without doors. For the divinity has fitted the body and mind of the man to be better able to bear cold, and heat, and travelling, and military exercises, so that he has imposed upon him the work without doors; and by having formed the body of the woman to be less able to bear such exertions, he appears to me to have laid upon her,' said I, 'the duties within doors. But knowing that he had given the woman by nature, and laid upon her, the office of rearing young children, he has also bestowed upon her a greater portion of love for her newly-born offspring than on the man. Since, too, the divinity has laid upon the woman the duty of guarding what is brought into the house, he, knowing that the mind, by being timid, is not less adapted for guarding, has given a larger share of timidity to the woman than to the man; and knowing also that if any one injures him who is engaged in the occupations without, he must defend himself, he has on that account given a greater portion of boldness to the man. But as it is necessary for both alike to give and to receive, he has bestowed memory and the power of attention upon both impartially, so that you cannot distinguish whether the female or the male has the larger portion of them. The power of being temperate also in what is necessary he has conferred in equal measure upon both, and has allowed that whichsoever of the two is superior in this virtue, whether the man or the woman, shall receive a greater portion of the benefit arising from it. But as the nature of both is not fully adapted for all these requirements, they in consequence stand in greater need of aid from one another, and the pair are of greater service to each other, when the one is able to do those things in which the other is deficient. As we know, then, my dear wife,' continued I, 'what is appointed to each of us by Providence, it is incumbent on us to discharge as well as we can that which each of us has to do.'. . .

" 'Will it then be necessary for me,' said my wife, 'to do such things?' 'It will certainly be necessary for you,' said I, 'to remain at home, and to send out such of the labourers as have to work abroad, to their duties; and over such as have business to do in the house you must exercise a watchful superintendence. Whatever is brought into the house, you must take charge of it; whatever portion of it is required for use you must give out; and whatever should be laid by, you must take account of it and keep it safe, so that the provision stored up for a year, for example, may not be expended in a month. Whenever wool is brought home to you, you must take care that garments be made for those who want them. You must also be careful that the dried provisions may be in a proper condition for eating. One of your duties, however,' I added, 'will perhaps appear somewhat disagreeable, namely that whoever of all the servants may fall sick, you must take charge of him, that he may be recovered.' 'Nay, assuredly,' returned my wife, 'that will be a most agreeable office, if such as receive good treatment are likely to make a grateful return, and to become more attached to me than before.'. . .

" 'Some other of your occupations, my dear wife,' continued I, 'will be pleasing to you. For instance, when you take a young woman who does not know how to spin, and make her skilful at it, and she thus becomes of twice as much value to you. Or when you take one who is ignorant of the duties of a housekeeper or servant, and, having made her accomplished, trustworthy, and handy, render her of the highest value. Or when it is in your power to do services to such of your attendants as are steady and useful, while, if any one is found transgressing, you can inflict punishment. But you will experience the greatest of pleasures, if you show yourself superior to me, and render me your servant, and have no cause to fear that, as life advances, you may become less respected in your household, but may trust that, while you grow older, the better consort you prove to me, and the more faithful guardian of your house for your children, so much the more will you be esteemed by your family. For what is good and honourable,' I added, 'gains increase of respect, not from beauty of person, but from merits directed to the benefit of human life.' Such were the subjects on which, as far as I remember, I first conversed seriously with my wife."

State Finances

*Like women, resident aliens and slaves were excluded from Athenian political
life. Xenophon gave some practical advice about how they could be used to
enhance the revenues of the state.*

From Xenophon. *On the Revenues*

All these advantages [of Athens] may, I believe, be traced primarily to
the soil and position of Attica itself. But these natural blessings may be
added to: in the first place, by a careful handling of our resident alien
population. And, for my part, I can hardly conceive of a more splendid source of revenue than lies open in this direction. Here you have
a self-supporting class of residents conferring large benefits upon the
state, and instead of receiving payment themselves, contributing on the
contrary to the gain of the exchequer by the sojourners' tax. Nor, under the term careful handling, do I demand more than the removal of
obligations which, whilst they confer no benefit on the state, have an
air of inflicting various disabilities on the resident aliens. And I would
further relieve them from the obligation of serving as hoplites [sol-
diers] side by side with the citizen proper; since, beside the personal
risk, which is great, the trouble of quitting trades and homesteads is no
trifle. Incidentally the state itself would be benefited by this exemption,
if the citizens were more in the habit of campaigning with one another,
rather than shoulder to shoulder with Lydians, Phrygians, Syrians, and
barbarians from all quarters of the world, who form the staple of our
resident alien class. . . .

In the next place, seeing that there are at present numerous building sites within the city walls as yet devoid of houses, supposing the
state were to make free grants of such land to foreigners for building
purposes in cases where there could be no doubt as to the respectabil-
ity of the applicant, if I am not mistaken, the result of such a measure
will be that a larger number of persons, and of a better class, will be
attracted to Athens as a place of residence.

Lastly, if we could bring ourselves to appoint, as a new government
office, a board of guardians of foreign residents like our Guardians of
Orphans, with special privileges assigned to those guardians who
should show on their books the greatest number of resident aliens,—
such a measure would tend to improve the goodwill of the class in
question, and in all probability all people without a city of their own
would aspire to the status of foreign residents in Athens, and so further increase the revenues of the city.

From Xenophon, *On the Revenues*, in H. G. Dakyns, trans., *The Works of Xenophon* (London: Macmillan, 1892), Vol. 2, pp. 329–330, 334–341.

I come to a new topic. I am persuaded that the establishment of the silver mines on the proper footing would be followed by a large increase of wealth apart from the other sources of revenue. And I would like, for the benefit of those who may be ignorant, to point out what the capacity of these mines really is. You will then be in a position to decide how to turn them to better account. It is clear, I presume, to every one that these mines have for a very long time been in active operation; at any rate no one will venture to fix the date at which they first began to be worked. Now in spite of the fact that the silver ore has been dug and carried out for so long a time, I would ask you to note that the mounds of rubbish so shovelled out are but a fractional portion of the series of hillocks containing veins of silver, and as yet unquarried. Nor is the silver-bearing region gradually becoming circumscribed. On the contrary it is evidently extending in wider area from year to year. That is to say, during the period in which thousands of workers have been employed within the mines no hand was ever stopped for want of work to do. Rather, at any given moment, the work to be done was more than enough for the hands employed. And so it is to-day with the owners of slaves working in the mines: no one dreams of reducing the number of his hands. On the contrary, the object is perpetually to acquire as many additional hands as the owner possibly can. The fact is that with few hands to dig and search, the find of treasure will be small, but with an increase of labour the discovery of the ore itself is more than proportionally increased. So much so, that of all operations with which I am acquainted, this is the only one in which no sort of jealousy is felt at a further development of the industry. . . .

It is an old story, trite enough to those of us who have cared to attend to it, how once on a time Nicias, the son of Niceratus, owned a thousand men in the silver mines, whom he let out to Sosias, a Thracian, on the following terms. Sosias was to pay him a net obol a day, without charge or deduction, for every slave of the thousand, and be responsible for keeping up the number perpetually at that figure. So again Hipponicus had six hundred slaves let out on the same principle, which brought him in a net mina a day without charge or deduction. Then there was Philemonides, with three hundred, bringing him in half a mina, and others, I make no doubt there were, making profits in proportion to their respective resources and capital. But there is no need to revert to ancient history. At the present moment there are hundreds of human beings in the mines let out on the same principle. And given that my proposal were carried into effect, the only novelty in it is that, just as the individual in acquiring the ownership of a gang of slaves finds himself at once provided with a permanent source of income, so the state, in like fashion should possess herself of a body of public slaves, to the number, say, of three for every Athenian citizen.

As to the feasibility of our proposals, I challenge any one whom it may concern to test the scheme point by point and to give his verdict. . . .

Let it be granted, however, that at first a nucleus of twelve hundred slaves is formed. It is hardly too sanguine a supposition that out of the profits alone, within five or six years this number may be increased to at least six thousand. Again, out of that number of six thousand—supposing each slave to bring in an obol a day clear of all expenses—we get a revenue of sixty talents a year. And supposing twenty talents out of this sum laid out on the purchase of more slaves, there will be forty talents left for the state to apply to any other purpose it may find advisable. By the time the round number of ten thousand is reached the yearly income will amount to a hundred talents. . . .

The citizens of Athens are divided, as we all know, into ten tribes. Let the state then assign to each of these ten tribes an equal number of slaves, and let the tribes agree to associate their fortunes and proceed to open new cuttings. What will happen? Any single tribe hitting upon a productive lode will be the means of discovering what is advantageous to all. Or, supposing two or three, or possibly the half of them, hit upon a lode, clearly these several operations will proportionately be more remunerative still. That the whole ten will fail is not at all in accordance with what we should expect from the history of the past. It is possible, of course, for private persons to combine in the same way, and share their fortunes and minimise their risks. Nor need you apprehend, sirs, that a state mining company, established on this principle, will prove a thorn in the side of the private owner, or the private owner prove injurious to the state. But rather like allies who render each other stronger the more they combine, so in these silver mines, the greater number of companies at work the larger the riches they will discover and disinter.

This then is a statement, as far as I can make it clear, of the method by which, with the proper state organisation, every Athenian may be supplied with ample maintenance at the public expense.

ARISTOTLE—NATURAL SCIENCE AND SOCIAL SCIENCE

Scientific Method

Aristotle believed that everything in the universe serves an appropriate end or purpose, just as each part of the human body serves a purpose in the functioning of the whole. The way to a full scientific understanding of any phenomenon was an inquiry into this end or purpose, which Aristotle called the "Final Cause." (This approach remained influential until the scientific revolution of the seventeenth century.)

From *Parts of Animals*

. . . Whatever Nature makes she makes to serve some purpose; for it is evident that, even as art is present in the objects produced by art, so in things themselves there is some principle or cause of a like sort, which came to us from the universe around us, just as our material constituents (the hot, the cold, etc.) did. Wherefore there is better reason for holding that the Heaven was brought into being by some such cause—if we may assume that it came into being at all—and that through that cause it continues to be, than for holding the same about the mortal things it contains—the animals; at any rate, there is much clearer evidence of definite ordering in the heavenly bodies than there is in us; for what is mortal bears the marks of change and chance. . . .

Furthermore, we see that there are more causes than one concerned in the formation of natural things: there is the Cause *for the sake of which* the thing is formed, and the Cause to which *the beginning of the motion* is due. Therefore another point for us to decide is which of these two Causes stands first and which comes second. Clearly the first is that which we call the "Final" Cause—that for the sake of which the thing is formed. . . . The physician or the builder sets before himself something quite definite—the one, health, apprehensible by the mind, the other, a house, apprehensible by the senses; and once he has got this, each of them can tell you the causes and the rational grounds for

From Aristotle, *Parts of Animals*, A. L. Peck, trans. (Cambridge, Mass.: Harvard University Press, 1937), pp. 55–61, 99–103. Reprinted by permission of the publishers and Loeb Classical Library.

everything he does, and why it must be done as he does it. Yet the Final Cause (purpose) and the Good is more fully present in the works of Nature than in the works of Art. . . . If a house, or any other End, is to be realized, it is necessary that such and such material shall be available; one thing must first be formed, and set in motion, and then another thing; and so on continually in the same manner up to the End, which is the Final Cause, for the sake of which every one of those things is formed and for which it exists. The things which are formed in Nature are in like case. . . .

Of "things divine" we have already treated and have set down our views concerning them; so it now remains to speak of animals and their Nature. So far as in us lies, we will not leave out any one of them, be it never so mean; for though there are animals which have no attractiveness for the senses, yet for the eye of science, for the student who is naturally of a philosophic spirit and can discern the causes of things, Nature which fashioned them provides joys which cannot be measured. If we study mere likenesses of these things and take pleasure in so doing, because then we are contemplating the painter's or the carver's Art which fasioned them, and yet fail to delight much more in studying the works of Nature themselves, though we have the ability to discern the actual causes—that would be a strange absurdity indeed. . . . We ought not to hesitate nor to be abashed, but boldly to enter upon our researches concerning animals of every sort and kind, knowing that in not one of them is Nature or Beauty lacking.

I add "Beauty," because in the works of Nature purpose and not accident is predominant; and the purpose or end for the sake of which those works have been constructed or formed has its place among what is beautiful. If, however, there is anyone who holds that the study of the animals is an unworthy pursuit, he ought to go further and hold the same opinion about the study of himself, for it is not possible without considerable disgust to look upon the blood, flesh, bones, bloodvessels, and suchlike parts of which the human body is constructed. In the same way, when the discussion turns upon any one of the parts or structures, we must not suppose that the lecturer is speaking of the material of them in itself and for its own sake; he is speaking of the whole conformation. Just as in discussing a house, it is the whole figure and form of the house which concerns us, not merely the bricks and mortar and timber; so in Natural science, it is the composite thing, the thing as a whole, which primarily concerns us, not the materials of it, which are not found apart from the thing itself whose materials they are.

Now, as each of the parts of the body, like every other instrument, is for the sake of some purpose, viz. some action, it is evident that the body as a whole must exist for the sake of some complex action. Just as the saw is there for the sake of sawing and not sawing for the sake of the saw, because sawing is the using of the instrument, so in some way the body exists for the sake of the soul, and the parts of the body for the sake of those functions to which they are naturally adapted.

Ethics and Politics

In his Ethics, *Aristotle applied the concept of end or purpose to the study of human personality.*

From *The Nichomachean Ethics*

Every art and every scientific inquiry, and similarly every action and purpose, may be said to aim at some good. Hence the good has been well defined as that at which all things aim. . . . As there are various actions, arts, and sciences, it follows that the ends are also various. Thus health is the end of medicine, a vessel of shipbuilding, victory of strategy, and wealth of domestic economy.

As it appears that there are more ends than one and some of these, e.g. wealth, flutes, and instruments generally we desire as means to something else, it is evident that they are not all final ends. But the highest good is clearly something final. Hence if there is only one final end, this will be the object of which we are in search, and if there are more than one, it will be the most final of them. We speak of that which is sought after for its own sake as more final than that which is sought after as a means to something else; we speak of that which is never desired as a means to something else as more final than the things which are desired both in themselves and as means to something else; and we speak of a thing as absolutely final, if it is always desired in itself and never as a means to something else.

It seems that happiness preeminently answers to this description, as we always desire happiness for its own sake and never as a means to something else, whereas we desire honour, pleasure, intellect, and every virtue, partly for their own sakes (for we should desire them independently of what might result from them) but partly also as being means to happiness, because we suppose they will prove the instruments of happiness. Happiness, on the other hand, nobody desires for the sake of these things, nor indeed as a means to anything else at all. . . .

Perhaps, however, it seems a truth which is generally admitted, that happiness is the supreme good; what is wanted is to define its nature a little more clearly. The best way of arriving at such a definition will probably be to ascertain the function of Man. For, as with a flute-

From Aristotle, *The Nichomachean Ethics*, J. E. C. Welldon, trans. (London: Macmillan, 1897), pp. 1, 13–14, 15–16.

player, a statuary, or any artisan, or in fact anybody who has a definite function and action, his goodness, or excellence seems to lie in his function, so it would seem to be with Man, if indeed he has a definite function. Can it be said then that, while a carpenter and a cobbler have definite functions and actions, Man, unlike them, is naturally functionless? The reasonable view is that, as the eye, the hand, the foot, and similarly each several part of the body has a definite function, so Man may be regarded as having a definite function apart from all these. What then, can this function be? It is not life; for life is apparently something which man shares with the plants; and it is something peculiar to him that we are looking for. We must exclude therefore the life of nutrition and increase. There is next what may be called the life of sensation. But this too, is apparently shared by Man with horses, cattle, and all other animals. There remains what I may call the practical life of the reason, part of Man's very being.

The function of Man then is an activity of soul in accordance with reason, or not independently of reason. Again the functions of a person of a certain kind, and of such a person who is good of his kind e.g. of a harpist and a good harpist, are in our view generically the same, and this view is true of people of all kinds without exception, the superior excellence being only an addition to the function; for it is the function of a harpist to play the harp, and of a good harpist to play the harp well. This being so, if we define the function of Man as a kind of life, and this life as an activity of soul, or a course of action in conformity with reason, if the function of a good man is such activity or action of a good and noble kind, and if everything is successfully performed when it is performed in accordance with its proper excellence, it follows that the good of Man is an activity of soul in accordance with virtue or, if there are more virtues than one, in accordance with the best and most complete virtue. But it is necessary to add the words "in a complete life." For as one swallow or one day does not make a spring, so one day or a short time does not make a fortunate or happy man.

In discussing political theory, Aristotle argued that the state was natural to mankind since it was the only form of association in which all the resources of human personality could reach their full development. Hence lesser association grew "naturally" into states.

From *The Politics*

Every state is a community of some kind, and every community is established with a view to some good; for mankind always act in order to

From Aristotle, *The Politics*, in B. Jowett, trans., *The Works of Aristotle*, x, rev. ed. (Oxford: Clarendon Press, 1921), I. 1–2; III. 7; IV. 1; II. 4; III. 11; IV. 11.

obtain that which they think good. But, if all communities aim at some good, the state or political community, which is the highest of all, and which embraces all the rest, aims at good in a greater degree than any other, and at the highest good. . . . He who thus considers things in their first growth and origin, whether a state or anything else, will obtain the clearest view of them. In the first place there must be a union of those who cannot exist without each other; namely, of male and female, that the race may continue (and this is a union which is formed, not of deliberate purpose, but because, in common with other animals and with plants, mankind have a natural desire to leave behind them an image of themselves), and of natural ruler and subject, that both may be preserved. For that which can foresee by the exercise of mind is by nature intended to be lord and master, and that which can with its body give effect to such foresight is a subject, and by nature a slave; hence master and slave have the same interest. Now nature has distinguished between the female and the slave. For she is not niggardly, like the smith who fashions the Delphian knife for many uses; she makes each thing for a single use, and every instrument is best made when intended for one and not for many uses. But among barbarians no distinction is made between women and slaves, because there is no natural ruler among them: they are a community of slaves, male and female. Wherefore the poets say,—

'It is meet that Hellenes should rule over barbarians';

as if they thought that the barbarian and the slave were by nature one.

Out of these two relationships between man and woman, master and slave, the first thing to arise is the family, and Hesiod is right when he says,—

'First house and wife and an ox for the plough',

for the ox is the poor man's slave. The family is the association established by nature for the supply of men's everyday wants, and the members of it are called by Charondas 'companions of the cupboard', and by Epimenides the Cretan, 'companions of the manger'. But when several families are united, and the association aims at something more than the supply of daily needs, the first society to be formed is the village. And the most natural form of the village appears to be that of a colony from the family, composed of the children and grandchildren, who are said to be 'suckled with the same milk'. And this is the reason why Hellenic states were originally governed by kings; because the Hellenes were under royal rule before they came together, as the barbarians still are. Every family is ruled by the eldest, and therefore in the colonies of the family the kingly form of government prevailed because they were of the same blood. As Homer says:

'Each one gives law to his children and to his wives.'

For they lived dispersedly, as was the manner in ancient times. Wherefore men say that the Gods have a king, because they themselves either are or were in ancient times under the rule of a king. For they imagine, not only the forms of the Gods, but their ways of life to be like their own.

When several villages are united in a single complete community, large enough to be nearly or quite self-sufficing, the state comes into existence, originating in the bare needs of life, and continuing in existence for the sake of a good life. And therefore, if the earlier forms of society are natural, so is the state, for it is the end of them, and the nature of a thing is its end. For what each thing is when fully developed, we call its nature, whether we are speaking of a man, a horse, or a family. Besides, the final cause and end of a thing is the best, and to be self-sufficing is the end and the best.

Hence it is evident that the state is a creation of nature, and that man is by nature a political animal. And he who by nature and not by mere accident is without a state, is either a bad man or above humanity; he is like the

'Tribeless, lawless, hearthless one,'

whom Homer denounces—the natural outcast is forthwith a lover of war; he may be compared to an isolated piece at draughts.

Now, that man is more of a political animal than bees or any other gregarious animals is evident. Nature, as we often say, makes nothing in vain, and man is the only animal whom she has endowed with the gift of speech. And whereas mere voice is but an indication of pleasure or pain, and is therefore found in other animals (for their nature attains to the perception of pleasure and pain and the intimation of them to one another, and no further), the power of speech is intended to set forth the expedient and inexpedient, and therefore likewise the just and the unjust. And it is a characteristic of man that he alone has any sense of good and evil, of just and unjust, and the like, and the association of living beings who have this sense makes a family and a state.

Further, the state is by nature clearly prior to the family and to the individual, since the whole is of necessity prior to the part; for example, if the whole body be destroyed, there will be no foot or hand, except in an equivocal sense, as we might speak of a stone hand; for when destroyed the hand will be no better than that. But things are defined by their working and power; and we ought not to say that they are the same when they no longer have their proper quality, but only that they have the same name. The proof that the state is a creation of nature and prior to the individual is that the individual, when isolated, is not self-sufficing; and therefore he is like a part in relation to the whole. But he who is unable to live in society, or who has no need because he is sufficient for himself, must be either a beast or a god: he is no part of a state. A social instinct is implanted in all men by nature, and yet he who first founded the state was the greatest of benefactors. For man, when perfected, is the best of animals, but, when separated from law and justice, he is the worst of all; since armed injustice is the more dangerous, and he is equipped at birth with arms, meant to be used by intelligence and virtue, which he may use for the worst ends. Wherefore, if he have not virtue, he is the most unholy and the most savage of animals, and the most full of lust and gluttony. But justice is the bond of men in states, for the administration of justice, which is the determination of what is just, is the principle of order in political society.

Having determined these points, we have next to consider how many forms of government there are, and what they are; and in the first place what are the true forms, for when they are determined the perversions of them will at once be apparent. The words constitution and government have the same meaning, and the government, which is the supreme authority in states, must be in the hands of one, or of a few, or of the many. The true forms of government, therefore, are those in which the one, or the few, or the many, govern with a view to the common interest; but governments which rule with a view to the private interest, whether of the one, or of the few, or of the many, are perversions. For the members of a state, if they are truly citizens, ought to participate in its advantages. Of forms of government in which one rules, we call that which regards the common interests, kingship or royalty; that in which more than one, but not many, rule, aristocracy; and it is so called, either because the rulers are the best men, or because they have at heart the best interests of the state and of the citizens. But when the citizens at large administer the state for the common interest, the government is called by the generic name,— a constitution. . . .

Of the above-mentioned forms, the perversions are as follows:—of royalty, tyranny; of aristocracy, oligarchy; of constitutional government, democracy. For tyranny is a kind of monarchy which has in view the interest of the monarch only; oligarchy has in view the interest of the wealthy; democracy, of the needy: none of them the common good of all.

It is obvious which of the three perversions is the worst, and which is the next in badness. That which is the perversion of the first and most divine is necessarily the worst. And just as a royal rule, if not a mere name, must exist by virtue of some great personal superiority in the king, so tyranny, which is the worst of governments, is necessarily the farthest removed from a well-constituted form; oligarchy is little better, for it is a long way from aristocracy, and democracy is the most tolerable of the three.

Thus it is manifest that the best political community is formed by citizens of the middle class, and that those states are likely to be well-administered, in which the middle class is large, and stronger if possible than both the other classes, or at any rate than either singly; for the addition of the middle class turns the scale, and prevents either of the extremes from being dominant. Great then is the good fortune of a state in which the citizens have a moderate and sufficient property; for where some possess much, and the others nothing, there may arise an extreme democracy, or a pure oligarchy; or a tyranny may grow out of either extreme,—either out of the most rampant democracy, or out of an oligarchy; but it is not so likely to arise out of the middle constitutions and those akin to them. . . . And democracies are safer and more permanent than oligarchies, because they have a middle class which is more numerous and has a greater share in the government; for when there is no middle class, and the poor greatly exceed in number, troubles arise, and the state soon comes to an end.

IV

RELIGION AND NATURE
The Mother-Goddess
  From Apuleius. *Metamorphoses*
Paganism
  From Vergil. *The Georgics*
Epicureanism
  From Lucretius. *On the Nature of
    the Universe*
Stoicism
  From *Works of Epictetus*

**ROME—REPUBLIC AND
  REVOLUTION**
Republican Institutions
  From *The Histories of Polybius*
  From *The Roman History of Appian*
The Roman Revolution
  From *The Roman History of Appian*
  From *Writings of Cicero*
  From *The Annals of Tacitus*

ROMAN FAMILIES
Patriarchal Tradition
  From *Roman Antiquities*
  From *The Histories of Polybius*
  From Plutarch. *Life of Cato*
Legislation of Augustus
  From *Dio's Roman History*
  From *The Institutes of Gaius*
  From *Opinions of Julius Paulus*
Roman Wives
  From *Juvenal's Sixth Satire*
  From *Praise of Turia*

**THE EMPIRE—AUGUSTUS TO
  TRAJAN**
Imperial Mission
  From Vergil. *Eclogue IV*
  From Vergil. *The Aeneid*
Provincial Administration
  From *Letters of Pliny*

112

HELLENISM AND ROME—FROM REPUBLIC TO EMPIRE

ALEXANDER THE GREAT (356–323 B.C.) absorbed the world of Greek city states into a vast empire; but when he died the Mediterranean world again divided into independent city-states and kingdoms. In spite of the political fragmentation, a common "Hellenistic" culture permeated the life of the upper classes. It was characterized by a growth of new philosophies and a spread of oriental religious cults. The two major philosophical systems, Epicureanism and Stoicism, both tried in different ways to show how the individual person could live a satisfying life in a troubled, disordered world. The old Greek gods of Olympus continued to be acknowledged (under Latin names at Rome—e.g., Jupiter, Mars, Venus), but their worship became mainly a matter of formalistic observance. The spreading oriental "mystery religions" offered colorful secret ceremonies, redemption from sin, and often a promise of life after death. Perhaps the most popular of them all was the cult of the great mother-goddess, Isis.

The rise of Roman power created a new political unity in the Mediterranean world. The Romans were a practical people. They built good roads; they deployed disciplined armies; they made enduring laws. By the end of the first century B.C., the Romans dominated the whole Mediterranean basin and their conquests had extended northward to the Rhine and the Danube. This was a most formidable aggregation of power and territory; but tensions existed even at the height of Roman power. Class disputes arose between aristocratic and "middle-class" Romans; major problems were encountered in adapting the institutions of the original Roman city-state to the rule of a great empire; and the old ideal of a stable family ruled by a stern patriarch—the traditional foundation of Roman morality—was more and more seen to conflict with the practical realities of Roman social life.

RELIGION AND NATURE

The Mother-Goddess

Lucius, a dissolute young man, is turned into an ass at the beginning of Apuleius's story. After many ribald adventures he repents of his follies and is restored to human form through the merciful intercession of the goddess Isis.

From Apuleius. *Metamorphoses*

Scarcely had I closed my eyes, when behold! a divine form emerged from the middle of the sea, and disclosed features that even the gods themselves might venerate. After this, by degrees, the vision, resplendent throughout the whole body, seemed gradually to take its stand before me, rising above the surface of the sea. I will even make an attempt to describe to you its wondrous appearance, if, indeed, the poverty of human language will afford me the power of appropriately setting it forth; or, if the Divinity herself will supply me with a sufficient stock of eloquent diction.

In the first place, then, her hair, long and hanging in tapered ringlets, fell luxuriantly on her divine neck; a crown of varied form encircled the summit of her head, with a diversity of flowers, and in the middle of it, just over her forehead, there was a flat circlet, which resembled a mirror, or rather emitted a white refulgent light, thus indicating that she was the moon. Vipers rising from furrows of the earth, supported this on the right hand and on the left, while ears of corn projected on either side. Her garment was of many colours, woven of fine flax; in one part it was resplendent with a clear white colour, in another it was yellow like the blooming crocus, and in another flaming with a rosy redness. And then, what riveted my gaze far more than all, was her mantle of the deepest black, that shone with a glossy lustre. It was wrapped around her, and passing from below her right side over the left shoulder, was fastened in a knot that resembled the boss of a shield, while a part of the robe fell down in many folds, and gracefully floated with its little knots of fringe that edged its extremities. Glitter-

From *The Works of Apuleius* (London: George Bell and Sons, 1881), pp. 222–226.

ing stars were dispersed along the embroidered extremities of the robe, and over its whole surface; and in the middle of them a moon of two weeks old breathed forth its flaming fires. Besides this, a garland, wholly consisting of flowers and fruits of every kind, adhered naturally to the border of this beautiful mantle, in whatever direction it was wafted by the breeze. . . .

Such was the appearance of the mighty goddess, as, breathing forth the fragrant perfumes of Arabia the happy, she deigned with her divine voice thus to address me: "Behold me, Lucius; moved by thy prayers, I appear to thee; I, who am Nature, the parent of all things, the mistress of all the elements, the primordial offspring of time, the supreme among Divinities, the queen of departed spirits, the first of the celestials, and the uniform manifestation of the Gods and Goddesses; who govern by my nod the luminous heights of heaven, the salubrious breezes of the ocean, and the anguished silent realms of the shades below: whose one sole divinity the whole orb of the earth venerates under a manifold form, with different rites, and under a variety of appellations. Hence the Phrygians, that primaeval race, call me Pessinuntica, the Mother of the Gods; the Aborigines of Attica, Cecropian Minerva; the Cyprians, in their sea-girt isle, Paphian Venus; the arrow-bearing Cretans, Diana Dictynna; the three-tongued Sicilians, Stygian Proserpine; and the Eleusinians, the ancient Goddess Ceres. Some call me Juno, others Bellona, others Hecate, and others Rhamnusia. But those who are illumined by the earliest rays of that divinity, the Sun, when he rises, the Aethiopians, the Arii, and the Egyptians, so skilled in ancient learning, worshipping me with ceremonies quite appropriate, call me by my true name, Queen Isis. Behold then, commiserating your calamities, I am come to thy assistance; favouring and propitious I am come. Away, then, with tears; leave your lamentations; cast off all sorrow. . . .

"Only remember, and always keep it fast in the very depths of your heart, that the remaining period of your life must be dedicated to me, even to the moment of your latest breath. Nor is it unjust that you should devote your whole life to that goddess, by whose assistance you will have been restored to human form. But under my protection you will live happy, you will live glorious: and when, having passed through the allotted period of your life, you shall descend to the realms beneath, there, also, in the subterranean hemisphere, you, dwelling in the Elysian fields, shall frequently adore me whom you now behold thus propitious to you, and shall there see me shining amidst the darkness of Acheron, and reigning in the Stygian realms. And further, if you shall be found to deserve the protection of my divinity by sedulous obedience, religious devotion, and inviolable chastity, you shall be sensible that it is possible for me, and me alone, to extend your life beyond the limits that have been appointed to it by your destiny."

Paganism

Popular attitudes to the natural environment among the Greeks and Romans were shaped by their belief in a host of lesser deities—nymphs and fauns and dryads—who inhabited the countryside and could help or hinder human activities.

From Vergil. *The Georgics*

What makes the cornfields glad, beneath what star,
Maecenas, it is well to turn the soil,
And wed the vine to the elm, how to tend oxen,
For nurturing flocks and herds what care is needful,
For keeping thrifty bees what knowledge, now
Shall I essay to sing. O ye most glorious
Lights of the universe, that lead along
Through heaven the gliding years; and you, Liber
And kindly Ceres, by whose bounty earth exchanged
Chaonian acorns for the rich ear of corn,
And blended with pure water from the stream
The new-found grape; and you Fauns, present deities
Of country folk (draw near together, Fauns
And Dryad maidens), it is your gifts to men
I sing. And thou, O Neptune, for whom earth,
Smitten by thy mighty trident, first sent forth
The neighing horse; and thou too, Genius of the groves,[1]
For whom three hundred snow-white steers roam grazing
Through Cea's fertile woodlands; and thou, Pan,
Guardian of flocks, leaving thy native forests
And the glades of Lycaeus, come, O Lord
Of Tegea, as thou lovest thine own Maenalus,[2]
Come hither of thy grace; Minerva too,
Inventress of the olive, and that youth[3]
Who showed to men the use of the bent plough;
And thou, Silvanus,[4] bearing in thy hand
A young uprooted cypress; and all you Gods
And Goddesses, who lovingly protect our fields,

[1]Aristaeus, a bucolic demigod, whose story is told in the fourth Georgic.
[2]Lycaeus and Maenalus are mountains in Arcadia.
[3]Triptolemus.
[4]The Latin forest-god.

From *The Eclogues and Georgics*, R. C. Trevelyan, trans. (Cambridge: Cambridge University Press, 1944), pp. 38–39. Reprinted by permission of the publisher.

Foster the unsown saplings, or send down
From heaven plenteous rain-showers on our crops. . . .

Epicureanism

The Epicureans derived a skeptical view of the universe from earlier Greek atomism. They recommended a life of quiet enjoyment, spent away from the troubles of the world.

From Lucretius. *On the Nature of the Universe*

What joy it is, when out at sea the stormwinds are lashing the waters, to gaze from the shore at the heavy stress some other man is enduring! Not that anyone's afflictions are in themselves a source of delight; but to realize from what troubles you yourself are free is joy indeed. What joy, again, to watch opposing hosts marshalled on the field of battle when you have yourself no part in their peril! But this is the greatest joy of all: to stand aloof in a quiet citadel, stoutly fortified by the teaching of the wise, and to gaze down from that elevation on others wandering aimlessly in a vain search for the way of life, pitting their wits one against another, disputing for precedence, struggling night and day with unstinted effort to scale the pinnacles of wealth and power. O joyless hearts of men! O minds without vision! How dark and dangerous the life in which this tiny span is lived away! Do you not see that nature is clamouring for two things only, a body free from pain, a mind released from worry and fear for the enjoyment of pleasurable sensations?

And now to business. I will explain *the motion by which the generative bodies of matter give birth to various things,* and, after they are born, dissolve them once more; the force that compels them to do this; and the power of movement through the boundless void with which they are endowed. . . . Since the atoms are moving freely through the void, they must all be kept in motion either by their own weight or on occasion by the impact of another atom. For it must often happen that two of them in their course knock together and immediately bounce apart in opposite directions, a natural consequence of their hardness and solidity and the absence of anything behind to stop them.

As a further indication that all particles of matter are on the move, remember that the universe is bottomless: there is no place where the atoms could come to rest. As I have already shown by various arguments and proved conclusively, space is without end or limit and spreads out immeasurably in all directions alike.

It clearly follows that no rest is given to the atoms in their course through the depths of space. Driven along in an incessant but variable movement, some of them bounce far apart after a collision while others recoil only a short distance from the impact. From those that do not recoil far, being driven into a closer union and held there by the entanglement of their own interlocking shapes, are composed firmly rooted rock, the stubborn strength of steel and the like. Those others that move freely through larger tracts of space, springing far apart and carried far by the rebound—these provide for us thin air and blazing sunlight. Besides these, there are many other atoms at large in empty space which have been thrown out of compound bodies and have nowhere even been granted admittance so as to bring their motions into harmony.

Next, the theory that the gods deliberately created the world in all its natural splendour for the sake of man, so that we ought to praise this eminently praiseworthy piece of divine workmanship and believe it eternal and immortal and think it a sin to unsettle by violence the everlasting abode established for mankind by the ancient purpose of the gods and to worry it with words and turn it topsy-turvy—this theory, Memmius, with all its attendant fictions is sheer nonsense. For what benefit could immortal and blessed beings reap from our gratitude, that they should undertake any task on our behalf? Or what could tempt those who had been at peace so long to change their old life for a new? The revolutionary is one who is dissatisfied with the old order. But one who has known no trouble in the past, but spent his days joyfully—what could prick such a being with the itch for novelty? Or again, what harm would it have done us to have remained uncreated? Are we to suppose that our life was sunk in gloom and grief till the light of creation blazed forth? True that, once a man is born, he must will to remain alive so long as beguiling pleasure holds him. But one who has never tasted the love of life, or been enrolled among the living, what odds is it to him if he is never created?

Even if I knew nothing of the atoms, I would venture to assert on the evidence of the celestial phenomena themselves, supported by many other arguments, that the universe was certainly not created for us by divine power: it is so full of imperfections. In the first place, of all that is covered by the wide sweep of the sky, part has been greedily seized by mountains and the woodland haunts of wild beasts. Part is usurped by crags and desolate bogs and the sea that holds far asunder the shores of the lands. Almost two-thirds are withheld from mankind by torrid heat and perennial deposits of frost. The little that is left of cultivable soil, if the force of nature had its way, would be choked with briars, did not the force of man oppose it. It is man's way, for the sake of life, to groan over the stout mattock and cleave the earth with down-pressed plough. Unless we turn the fruitful clods with the coulter and break up the soil to stimulate the growth of the crops, they cannot emerge of their own accord into the open air. Even so, when by dint of hard work all the fields at last burst forth into leaf and flower, then either the fiery sun withers them with intemperate heat, or sudden showers and icy frosts destroy them and gales of wind batter them with hurricane force. Again, why does nature feed and breed the fearsome brood of wild beasts, a menace to the human race by land and sea? Why do the changing seasons bring pestilence in their train? Why does untimely death roam abroad?

Certainly the atoms did not post themselves purposefully in due order by an act of intelligence, nor did they stipulate what movements each should perform. But multitudinous atoms, swept along in multitudinous courses through infinite time by mutual clashes and their own weight, have come together in every possible way and realized everything that could be formed by their combinations. So it comes about that a voyage of immense duration, in which they have experienced every variety of movement and conjunction, has at length brought together those whose sudden encounter normally forms the starting-point of substantial fabrics—earth and sea and sky and the races of living creatures.

First of all, the earth girdled its hills with a green glow of herbage, and over every plain the meadows gleamed with verdure and with bloom. Then trees of every sort were given free rein to join in an eager race for growth into the gusty air. As feathers, fur and bristles are generated at the outset from the bodies of winged and four-footed creatures, so then *the new-born earth first flung up herbs and shrubs. Next in order it engendered the various breeds of mortal creatures,* manifold in mode of origin as in form. The animals cannot have fallen from the sky, and those that live on land cannot have emerged from the briny gulfs. We are left with the conclusion that the name of mother has rightly been bestowed on the earth, since out of the earth everything is born.

Stoicism

*Stoics believed in a universal, divinely ordained natural law. Epictetus
(c. A.D. 60–c. 120) lived at Rome as the slave of a rich freedman.*

From *Works of Epictetus*

... What else can I do, a lame old man, but sing hymns to God? Were
I a nightingale, I would act the part of a nightingale; were I a swan,
the part of a swan. But since I am a reasonable creature, it is my duty
to praise God. This is my business. I do it. Nor will I ever desert this
post, so long as it is permitted me; and I call on you to join in the same
song.

From every event that happens in the world it is easy to celebrate
Providence, if a person hath but these two qualities in himself; a faculty of considering what happens to each individual, and a grateful
temper. Without the first, he will not perceive the usefulness of things
which happen; and without the other, he will not be thankful for them.
If God had made colors, and had not made the faculty of seeing them,
what would have been their use? None. On the other hand, if he had
made the faculty of observation, without objects to observe, what
would have been the use of that? None. Again; if he had formed both
the faculty and the objects, but had not made light? Neither in that
case would they have been of any use.

Who is it then that hath fitted each of these to the other? Who is it
that hath fitted the sword to the scabbard, and the scabbard to the
sword? Is there no such Being? From the very construction of a complete work, we are used to declare positively, that it must be the operation of some artificer, and not the effect of mere chance. Doth every
such work, then, demonstrate an artificer; and do not visible objects,
and the sense of seeing, and light, demonstrate one? Do not the difference of the sexes, and their inclination to each other, and the use of
their several powers; do not these things demonstrate an artificer?
Most certainly they do.

All things serve and obey the laws of the universe; the earth, the sea,
the sun, the stars, and the plants and animals of the earth. Our body
likewise obeys the same laws, in being sick and well, young and old,
and passing through the other changes they decree. It is therefore reasonable that what depends on ourselves, that is, our own understanding, should not be the only rebel against natural law. For the universe
is powerful and superior, and consults the best for us by governing us
in conjunction with the whole. And further; opposition, besides that it

From T. W. Higginson, *The Works of Epictetus* (Boston, Mass.: Little, Brown and
Co., 1886).

is unreasonable, and produces nothing except a vain struggle, throws us into pain and sorrows.

If what philosophers say of the kinship between God and men be true, what has any one to do, but, like Socrates, when he is asked what countryman he is, never to say that he is a citizen of Athens, or of Corinth, but of the universe? ... Men alone are qualified to partake of a communication with the Deity, being connected with him by reason; why may not such a one call himself a citizen of the universe? Why not a son of God?

You, O man are God's principal work. You are a distinct portion of the essence of God; and contain a certain part of him in yourself. Why then are you ignorant of your noble birth? Why do not you consider whence you came? You carry a God about with you, poor wretch, and know nothing of it. Do you suppose I mean some god without you of gold or silver? It is within yourself that you carry him; and you do not observe that you profane him by impure thoughts and unclean actions. If the mere external image of God were present, you would not dare to act as you do; and when God himself is within you, and hears and sees all, are not you ashamed to think and act thus; insensible of your own nature, and at enmity with God?

When we are children, our parents deliver us to the care of a tutor; who is continually to watch over us that we get no hurt. When we are become men, God delivers us to the guardianship of an implanted conscience. We ought by no means, then, to despise this guardian; for it will both displease God, and we shall be enemies to our own conscience.

Why should any one person envy another? Why should he be impressed with awe by those who have great possessions, or are placed in high rank? especially, if they are powerful and passionate? For what will they do to us? The things which they can do, we do not regard: the things about which we are concerned, they cannot reach. Who then, after all, shall hold sway over a person thus disposed?

Women from fourteen years old are flattered by men with the title of mistresses. Therefore, perceiving that they are regarded only as qualified to give men pleasure, they begin to adorn themselves, and in that to place all their hopes. It is worth while, therefore, to take care that they may perceive themselves honored only so far as they appear beautiful in their demeanor, and modestly virtuous.

Sickness is an impediment to the body, but not to the will, unless itself pleases. Lameness is an impediment to the leg, but not to the will[1];

[1]The Christian author Origen handed down a story that Epictetus was lamed by his master. The master tortured Epictetus by twisting his leg. Epictetus remarked calmly, "You are going to break it." When the leg broke he added in the same tone, "There, I told you so."

and say this to yourself with regard to everything that happens. For you will find it to be an impediment to something else, but not truly to yourself.

I must die: if instantly, I will die instantly; if in a short time, I will dine first; and when the hour comes, then I will die. How? As becomes one who restores what is not his own.

Do not you know that both sickness and death must overtake us? At what employment? The husbandman at his plough; the sailor on his voyage. At what employment would you be taken? For my own part, I would be found engaged in nothing but in the regulation of my own Will; how to render it undisturbed, unrestrained, uncompelled, free. I would be found studying this, that I may be able to say to God, "Have I transgressed Thy commands? Have I perverted the powers, the senses, the instincts, which Thou hast given me? Have I ever accused Thee, or censured Thy dispensations? I have been sick, because it was Thy pleasure, like others; but I willingly. I have been poor, it being Thy will; but with joy. I have not been in power, because it was not Thy will; and power I have never desired. Hast Thou ever seen me saddened because of this? Have I not always approached Thee with a cheerful countenance; prepared to execute Thy commands and the indications of Thy will? Is it Thy pleasure that I should depart from this assembly? I depart. I give Thee all thanks that Thou hast thought me worthy to have a share in it with Thee; to behold Thy works, and to join with Thee in comprehending Thy administration." Let death overtake me while I am thinking, while I am writing, while I am reading such things as these.

ROME—REPUBLIC AND REVOLUTION

Republican Institutions

The Greek historian Polybius (205–125 B.C.), like many ancient authors, believed in a cyclical theory of history. But he thought the Roman constitution was so perfectly balanced that it might avoid the usual process of decay.

From *The Histories of Polybius*

What is the origin then of a constitution, and whence is it produced? Suppose that from floods, pestilences, failure of crops, or some such causes the race of man is reduced almost to extinction. Such things we are told have happened, and it is reasonable to think will happen again. Suppose accordingly all knowledge of social habits and arts to have been lost. Suppose that from the survivors, as from seeds, the race of man to have again multiplied. In that case I presume they would, like the animals, herd together; for it is but reasonable to suppose that bodily weakness would induce them to seek those of their own kind to herd with. And in that case too, as with the animals, he who was superior to the rest in strength of body or courage of soul would lead and rule them. . . . The limit of this authority would be physical strength, and the name we should give it would be despotism. . . .

When the leading and most powerful man among his people . . . assumes in the eyes of his subject the appearance of being the distributor to each man according to his deserts, they no longer obey him and support his rule from fear of violence, but rather from conviction of its utility, however old he may be, rallying round him with one heart and soul, and fighting against all who form designs against his government. In this way he becomes a *king* instead of a *despot* by imperceptible degrees, reason having ousted brute courage and bodily strength from their supremacy. . . .

But when royal power became hereditary in their family, and they found every necessary for security ready to their hands, as well as more than was necessary for their personal support, then they gave the

From E. S. Shuckburgh, trans., *The Histories of Polybius* (London: Macmillan, 1889), pp. 461–474.

rein to their appetites; imagined that rulers must needs wear different clothes from those of subjects; have different and elaborate luxuries of the table; and must even seek sensual indulgence, however unlawful the source, without fear of denial. These things having given rise in the one case to jealousy and offence, in the other to outburst of hatred and passionate resentment, the kingship became a tyranny: the first step in disintegration was taken; and plots began to be formed against the government, which did not now proceed from the worst men but from the noblest, most high-minded, and most courageous, because these are the men who can least submit to the tyrannical acts of their rulers.

But as soon as the people got leaders, they cooperated with them against the dynasty for the reasons I have mentioned; and then *kingship* and *despotism* were alike entirely abolished, and *aristocracy* once more began to revive and start afresh. For in their immediate gratitude to those who had deposed the despots, the people employed them as leaders, and entrusted their interests to them; who, looking upon this charge at first as a great privilege, made the public advantage their chief concern, and conducted all kinds of business, public or private, with diligence and caution. But when the sons of these men received the same position of authority from their fathers,—having had no experience of misfortunes, and none at all of civil equality and freedom of speech, but having been bred up from the first under the shadow of their fathers' authority and lofty position,—some of them gave themselves up with passion to avarice and unscrupulous love of money, others to drinking and the boundless debaucheries which accompanies it, and others to the violation of women or the forcible appropriation of boys; and so they turned an *aristocracy* into an *oligarchy*. But it was not long before they roused in the minds of the people the same feelings as before; and their fall therefore was very like the disaster which befel the tyrants.

For no sooner had the knowledge of the jealousy and hatred existing in the citizens against them emboldened some one to oppose the government by word or deed, than he was sure to find the whole people ready and prepared to take his side. Having then got rid of these rulers by assassination or exile, they do not venture to set up a king again, being still in terror of the injustice to which this led before; nor dare they intrust the common interests again to more than one, considering the recent example of their misconduct: and therefore, as the only sound hope left them is that which depends upon themselves, they are driven to take refuge in that; and so changed the constitution from an oligarchy to a *democracy,* and took upon themselves the superintendence and charge of the state. And as long as any survive who have had experience of oligarchical supremacy and domination, they regard their present constitution as a blessing, and hold equality and freedom as of the utmost value. But as soon as a new generation has arisen, and the democracy has descended to their children's children, long association weakens their value for equality and freedom, and some seek to become more powerful than the ordinary citizens; and the most liable to this temptation are the rich. So when they begin to be fond of office, and find themselves unable to obtain it by their own unassisted efforts and their own merits, they ruin their estates, while enticing and corrupting the common people in every possible way. By which means when, in their senseless mania for reputation, they have made the populace ready and greedy to receive bribes, the virtue of democracy is destroyed, and it is transformed into a government of violence and the strong hand. For the mob, habituated to feed at the expense of others, and to have its hopes of a livelihood in the property of its neighbours, as soon as it has got a leader sufficiently ambitious and daring, being excluded by poverty from the sweets of civil honours, produces a reign of mere violence. Then come tumultuous assemblies, massacres, banishments, redivisions of land; until, after losing all trace of civilisation, it has once more found a master and a despot.

This is the regular cycle of constitutional revolutions, and the natural order in which constitutions change, are transformed, and return again to their original stage.

As for the Roman constitution, it had three elements, each of them possessing sovereign powers: and their respective share of power in the whole state had been regulated with such a scrupulous regard to equality and equilibrium, that no one could say for certain, not even a native, whether the constitution as a whole were an aristocracy or democracy or despotism. And no wonder: for if we confine our observation to the power of the Consuls we should be inclined to regard it as despotic; if on that of the Senate, as aristocratic; and if finally one looks at the power possessed by the people it would seem a clear case of a democracy. . . .

The result of this power of the several estates for mutual help or harm is a union sufficiently firm for all emergencies, and a constitution than which it is impossible to find a better. For whenever any danger from without compels them to unite and work together, the strength which is developed by the State is so extraordinary, that everything required is unfailingly carried out by the eager rivalry shown by all classes to devote their whole minds to the need of the hour, and to secure that any determination come to should not fail for want of promptitude; while each individual works, privately and publicly alike, for the accomplishment of the business in hand. Accordingly, the peculiar constitution of the State makes it irresistible, and certain of obtaining whatever it determines to attempt. Nay, even when these external alarms are past, and the people are enjoying their good fortune and the fruits of their victories, and, as usually happens, growing corrupted by flattery and idleness, show a tendency to violence and arrogance,—it is in these circumstances, more than ever, that the constitution is seen to possess within itself the power of correcting abuses. For when any one of the three classes becomes puffed up, and manifests an inclination to be contentious and unduly encroaching, the mutual interdependency of all the three, and the possibility of the pretensions of any one being checked and thwarted by the others, must plainly check this tendency: and so the proper equilibrium is maintained by the impulsiveness of the one part being checked by its fear of the other. . . .

Polybius's idealized version of the constitution masked real social stresses. The underlying tensions—between rich and poor and between freemen and slaves—gave rise to open conflict in the time of Tiberius Gracchus, who became tribune in 133 B.C.

From *The Roman History of Appian*

The Romans, as they subdued the Italian nations successively in war, seized a part of their lands and built towns there, or established their own colonies in those already existing, and used them in place of garrisons. Of the land acquired by war they assigned the cultivated part forthwith to settlers, or leased or sold it. Since they had no leisure as yet to allot the part which then lay desolated by war (this was generally the greater part), they made proclamation that in the meantime those who were willing to work it might do so for a share of the yearly crops—a tenth of the grain and a fifth of the fruit. From those who kept flocks was required a share of the animals, both oxen and small cattle. They did these things in order to multiply the Italian race, which they considered the most laborious of peoples, so that they might have plenty of allies at home. But the very opposite thing happened; for the rich, getting possession of the greater part of the undistributed lands, and being emboldened by the lapse of time to believe that they would never be dispossessed, and adding to their holdings the small farms of their poor neighbors, partly by purchase and partly by force, came to cultivate vast tracts instead of single estates, using for this purpose slaves as laborers and herdsmen, lest free laborers should be drawn from agriculture into the army. The ownership of slaves itself brought them great gain from the multitude of their progeny, who increased because they were exempt from military service. Thus the powerful ones became enormously rich and the race of slaves multiplied throughout the country, while the Italian people dwindled in numbers and strength, being oppressed by penury, taxes, and military service. If they had any respite from these evils they passed their time

From H. White, trans. *The Roman History of Appian* (New York: Macmillan, 1899), Vol. 2, pp. 5–14.

in idleness, because the land was held by the rich, who employed slaves instead of freemen as cultivators.

For these reasons the people became troubled lest they should no longer have sufficient allies of the Italian stock, and lest the government itself should be endangered by such a vast number of slaves. Not perceiving any remedy, as it was not easy, nor exactly just, to deprive men of so many possessions they had held so long, including their own trees, buildings, and fixtures, a law was once passed with difficulty at the instance of the tribunes, that nobody should hold more than 500 jugera of this land, or pasture on it more than 100 cattle or 500 sheep. To ensure the observance of this law it was provided also that there should be a certain number of freemen employed on the farms, whose business it should be to watch and report what was going on. Those who held possession of lands under the law were required to take an oath to obey the law, and penalties were fixed for violating it, and it was supposed that the remaining land would soon be divided among the poor in small parcels. But there was not the smallest consideration shown for the law or the oaths. The few who seemed to pay some respect to them conveyed their lands to their relations fraudulently, but the greater part disregarded it altogether.

At length Tiberius Sempronius Gracchus, an illustrious man, eager for glory, a most powerful speaker, and for these reasons well know to all, delivered an eloquent discourse, while serving as tribune, concerning the Italian race, lamenting that a people so valiant in war, and blood relations to the Romans, were declining little by little in pauperism and paucity of numbers without any hope of remedy. He inveighed against the multitude of slaves as useless in war and never faithful to their masters, and adduced the recent calamity brought upon the masters by their slaves in Sicily, where the demands of agriculture had greatly increased the number of the latter; recalling also the war waged against them by the Romans, which was neither easy nor short, but long-protracted and full of vicissitudes and dangers. After speaking thus he again brought forward the law, providing that nobody should hold more than 500 jugera of the public domain. But he added a provision to the former law, that the sons of the present occupiers might each hold one-half of that amount, and that the remainder should be divided among the poor by triumvirs, who should be changed annually.

This was extremely disturbing to the rich because, on account of the triumvirs, they could no longer disregard the law as they had done before; nor could they buy the allotments of others, because Gracchus had provided against this by forbidding sales. They collected together in groups, and made lamentation, and accused the poor of appropriating the results of their tillage, their vineyards, and their dwellings. Some said that they had paid the price of the land to their neighbors. Were they to lose the money with the land? Others said that the graves of their ancestors were in the ground, which had been allotted to them in the division of their fathers' estates. Others said that their wives' dowries had been expended on the estates, or that the land had been given to their own daughters as dowry. Money-lenders could show loans made on this security. All kinds of wailing and expressions of indignation were heard at once. On the other side were heard the lamentations of the poor—that they had been reduced from competence to extreme penury, and from that to childlessness, because they were unable to rear their offspring. They recounted the military services they had rendered, by which this very land had been acquired, and were angry that they should be robbed of their share of the common property. They reproached the rich for employing slaves, who were always faithless and ill-tempered and for that reason unserviceable in war, instead of freemen, citizens, and soldiers. While these classes were lamenting and indulging in mutual accusations, a great number of others, composed of colonists, or inhabitants of the free towns, or persons otherwise interested in the lands and who were under like apprehensions, flocked in and took sides with their respective factions. Emboldened by numbers and exasperated against each other they attached themselves to turbulent crowds, and waited for the voting on the new law, some trying to prevent its enactment by all means, and others supporting it in every possible way. In addition to personal interest the spirit of rivalry spurred both sides in the preparations they were making against each other for the day of the comitia.

What Gracchus had in his mind in proposing the measure was not wealth, but an increase of efficient population. Inspired greatly by the usefulness of the work, and believing that nothing more advantageous or admirable could ever happen to Italy, he took no account of the difficulties surrounding it. When the time for voting came he advanced many other arguments at considerable length and also asked them whether it was not just to divide among the common people what belonged to them in common; whether a citizen was not worthy of more consideration at all times than a slave; whether a man who served in the army was not more useful than one who did not; and whether one who had a share in the country was not more likely to be devoted to the public interests. He did not dwell long on this comparison between freemen and slaves, which he considered degrading, but proceeded at once to a review of their hopes and fears for the country, saying that the Romans had acquired most of their territory by conquest, and that they had hopes of occupying the rest of the habitable world, but now the question of greatest hazard was, whether they should gain the rest by having plenty of brave men, or whether, through their weakness and mutual jealousy, their enemies should take away what they already possessed. After exaggerating the glory and riches on the one side and the danger and fear on the other, he admonished the rich to take heed, and said that for the realization of these hopes they ought to bestow this very land as a free gift, if necessary, on men who would rear children, and not, by contending about small things, overlook larger ones; especially since they were receiving an ample compensation for labor expended in the undisputed title to 500 jugera each of free land, in a high state of cultivation, without cost, and half as much more for each son of those who had sons. After saying much more to the same purport and exciting the poor, as well as others who were moved by reason rather than by the desire for gain, he ordered the scribe to read the proposed law.

Gracchus succeeded in having his law passed but only by persuading the people to depose (unconstitutionally) another tribune who opposed it. The following year Gracchus was assassinated by partisans of the wealthy senatorial class.

The Roman Revolution

Internal dissensions in the republic created opportunities for ambitious generals to seize absolute power. The sequence of events leading to the "Roman revolution" was succinctly described by Appian.

From *The Roman History of Appian*

No unseemly deed was wanting until, about fifty years after the death of Gracchus, Cornelius Sulla, one of these chiefs of factions, doctoring one evil with another, made himself the absolute master of the state for an indefinite period. Such officials were formerly called dictators—an office created in the most perilous emergencies for six months only, and long since fallen into disuse. Sulla, although nominally elected, became dictator for life by force and compulsion. Nevertheless, he became satiated with power and was the first man, so far as I know, holding supreme power, who had the courage to lay it down voluntarily and to declare that he would render an account of his stewardship to any who were dissatisfied with it. And so, for a considerable period, he walked to the forum as a private citizen in the sight of all and returned home unmolested, so great was the awe of his government still remaining in the minds of the onlookers, or their amazement at his laying it down. Perhaps they were ashamed to call for an accounting, or entertained other good feeling toward him, or a belief that his despotism had been beneficial to the state. Thus there was a cessation of factions for a short time while Sulla lived, and a compensation for the evils which Sulla had wrought.

From H. White, trans., *The Roman History of Appian* (New York: Macmillan, 1899), Vol. 2, pp. 2–4.

After his death the troubles broke out afresh and continued until Gaius Caesar, who had held the command in Gaul by election for some years, was ordered by the Senate to lay down his command. He charged that it was not the wish of the Senate, but of Pompey, his enemy, who had command of an army in Italy, and was scheming to depose him. So he sent a proposal that both should retain their armies, so that neither need fear the other's enmity, or that Pompey should dismiss his forces also and live as a private citizen under the laws in like manner with himself. Both requests being refused, he marched from Gaul against Pompey in the Roman territory, entered it, put him to flight, pursued him into Thessaly, won a brilliant victory over him in a great battle, and followed him to Egypt. After Pompey had been slain by the Egyptians Caesar set to work on the affairs of Egypt and remained there until he had settled the dynasty of that country. Then he returned to Rome. Having overpowered by war his principal rival, who had been surnamed the Great on account of his brilliant military exploits, he now ruled without disguise, nobody daring any longer to dispute him about anything, and was chosen, next after Sulla, dictator for life. Again all civil dissensions ceased until Brutus and Cassius, envious of his great power and desiring to restore the government of their fathers, slew in the Senate this most popular man, who was also the one most experienced in the art of government. The people mourned for him greatly. They scoured the city in pursuit of his murderers. They buried him in the middle of the forum and built a temple on the place of his funeral pile, and offered sacrifice to him as a god.

And now civil discord broke out again worse than ever and increased enormously. Massacres, banishments, and proscriptions of both senators and the so-called knights took place straightway, including great numbers of both classes, the chief of factions surrendering their enemies to each other, and for this purpose not sparing even their friends and brothers; so much does animosity toward rivals overpower the love of kindred. So in the course of events the Roman empire was partitioned, as though it had been their private property, by these three men: Antony, Lepidus, and the one who was first called Octavius, but afterward Caesar from his relationship to the other Caesar and adoption in his will. Shortly after this division they fell to quarrelling among themselves, as was natural, and Octavius, who was the superior in understanding and skill, first deprived Lepidus of Africa, which had fallen to his lot, and afterward, as the result of the battle of Actium, took from Antony all the provinces lying between Syria and the Adriatic gulf. Thereupon, while all the world was filled with astonishment at these wonderful displays of power, he sailed to Egypt and took that country, which was the oldest and at that time the strongest possession of the successors of Alexander, and the only one wanting to complete the Roman empire as it now stands. In consequence of these exploits he was at once elevated to the rank of a deity while still living, and was the first to be thus distinguished by the Romans, and was called by them Augustus. He assumed to himself an authority like Caesar's over the country and the subject nations, and even greater than Caesar's, not needing any form of election, or authorization, or even the pretence of it. His government being strengthened by time and mastery, and himself successful in all things and revered by all, he left a lineage and succession that held the supreme power in like manner after him.

Thus, out of multifarious civil commotions, the Roman state passed into solidarity and monarchy.

Cicero, a great master of Latin eloquence, was an outstanding defender of the republic in its last days. In his treatise On the Laws, *he identified the Roman magistracies with a rule of universal justice.*

From *Writings of Cicero*

This is the duty of magistrates, to superintend and prescribe all things which are just and useful, and in accordance with the law. For as the law is set over the magistrate, even so are the magistrates set over the people. And, therefore, it may be truly said, "that the magistrate is a speaking law, and the law a silent magistrate."

Moreover, nothing is so conformable to justice and to the condition of nature (and when I use that expression, I wish it to be understood that I mean the law, and nothing else,) as sovereign power; without which, neither house, nor commonwealth, nor nation, nor mankind itself, nor the entire nature of things, nor the universe itself, could exist. For this universe is obedient to God, and land and sea are submissive to the universe; and human life depends on the just administration of the laws of order.

But to come to considerations nearer home. . . . Magistrates are absolutely necessary; since, without their prudence and diligence, a state cannot exist; and since it is by their regulations that the whole commonwealth is kept within the bounds of moderation. But it is not enough to prescribe them a rule of domination, unless we likewise prescribe the citizens a rule of obedience. For he who commands well, must at some time or other have obeyed; and he who obeys with modesty appears worthy of some day or other being allowed to command. It is desirable, therefore, that he who obeys should expect that some day he will come to command, and that he who commands should bear in mind that ere long he may be called to the duty of submission.

We would not, however, limit ourselves to requiring from the citizens submission and obedience towards their magistrates; we would

From C. D. Yonge, trans., *The Treatises of Cicero: On the Laws* (London: George Bell and Sons, 1878), pp. 411–412, 417, 461–463, 466. E. S. Shuckburgh, trans., *The Letters of Cicero* (London: George Bell and Sons, 1904), Vol. 1, pp. 47–48. A. P. Peabody, *Cicero De Officiis* (Boston, Mass.: Little, Brown and Co., 1883), pp. 219–221.

also enjoin them by all means to honour and love their rulers, as Charondas prescribes in his code. Our Plato likewise held that those who
oppose their magistrates are like the race of Titans who in like manner
rebelled against the heavenly deities.... For you may take it for
granted that it is the establishment of magistrates that gives its form to
a commonwealth, and it is exactly by this distribution and subordination that we must determine the nature of the constitution. Which establishment being very wisely and discreetly settled by our ancestors,
there is nothing, or at all events very little alteration that I think necessary in the laws.

*In a letter of 61 B.C. Cicero described the disputes between senatorial aristo-
crats and well-to-do middle-class Romans ("equites") that were undermining
Roman stability. (By this time Pompey and Caesar had both emerged as successful generals.)*

At Rome I find politics in a shaky condition; everything is unsatisfactory and foreboding change. For I have no doubt you have been
told that our friends, the equites, are all but alienated from the senate.
Their first grievance was the promulgation of a bill on the authority of
the senate for the trial of such as had taken bribes for giving a verdict.
I happened not to be in the house when that decree was passed, but
when I found that the equestrian order was indignant at it, and yet
refrained from openly saying so, I remonstrated with the senate, as I
thought, in very impressive language, and was very weighty and eloquent considering the unsatisfactory nature of my cause. But here is
another piece of almost intolerable coolness on the part of the equites,
which I have not only submitted to, but have even put in as good a
light as possible! The companies which had contracted with the censors
[to collect the taxes from the province of Asia] complained that in the
heat of the competition they had taken the contract at an excessive
price; they demanded that the contract should be annulled. I led in
their support, or rather, I was second, for it was Crassus who induced
them to venture on this demand. The case is scandalous, the demand
a disgraceful one, and a confession of rash speculation. Yet there was
a very great risk that, if they got no concession, they would be completely alienated from the senate. Here again I came to the rescue
more than anyone else, and secured them a full and very friendly
house, in which I, on the 1st and 2nd of December, delivered long
speeches on the dignity and harmony of the two orders. The business
is not yet settled, but the favourable feeling of the senate has been
made manifest: for no one had spoken against it except the consul-des-
ignate, Metellus; while our hero Cato had still to speak, the shortness
of the day having prevented his turn being reached. Thus I, in the
maintenance of my steady policy, preserve to the best of my ability that
harmony of the orders which was originally my joiner's work; but since
it all now seems in such a crazy condition, I am constructing what
I may call a road towards the maintenance of our power, a safe one I

hope, which I cannot fully describe to you in a letter, but of which I will nevertheless give you a hint. *I cultivate close intimacy with Pompey.*

In his book On Moral Duties, *Cicero condemned Julius Caesar as a tyrant who destroyed Roman liberty.*

Caesar himself had always on his lips the Greek verses from the Phoenissae, which I will render as I can, awkwardly it may be, but still so as to be intelligible:—

> "Transcend the right in quest of power alone;
> In all things else hold fast the bond of kindred."

It was criminal . . . to except that one thing which was the most wicked of all. . . . Here you have a man who desired to be king of the Roman people, and who accomplished his purpose. Whoever says that this desire was right, is mad; for he approves of the destruction of laws and of liberty, and deems their foul and detestable suppression glorious. But as for him who acknowledges that it is not right to usurp sovereign power in a state which was and which ought to be free, yet that it is expedient for him who can do so, by what remonstrance, or rather by what reproach, can I strive to draw him back from so grave an error? For (ye immortal gods!) can the basest and foulest parricide—murder of the fatherland—be expedient for any man, even though he who has made himself thus guilty be called father by the citizens whom he has brought under the yoke? Expediency, then, ought to be measured by the right, . . . I do not accord with the opinion of the multitude who ask what can be more expedient than the possession of sovereign power; on the other hand, I find nothing more inexpedient for him who has obtained this power unjustly, when I begin to recall reason to things as they really are. For can anxieties, solicitudes, terrors by day and by night, a life crowded full of snares and of perils, be expedient for any one?

After Julius Caesar's assassination and a period of civil wars, Augustus, Caesar's great-nephew and adopted son, emerged as sole ruler. He maintained a facade of republican institutions, but really established a new system of monarchical power, often called "the principate." Tacitus, a contemporary writer, described his way of ruling.

From *The Annals of Tacitus*

When the last army of the Republic had fallen with Brutus and Cassius on the field; when Sextus Pompeius had been crushed in Sicily; and when the deposition of Lepidus, followed by the death of Antonius,

From G. G. Ramsey, trans., *The Annals of Tacitus* (London: John Murray, 1904), pp. 3–5, 8.

had left Augustus sole leader of the Julian party, he laid aside the title of Triumvir, assumed the Consulship, and professed himself content with the Tribunitian Power for the protection of the plebs. But when he had won the soldiery by bounties, the populace by cheap corn, and all classes alike by the sweets of peace, he rose higher and higher by degrees, and drew into his own hands all the functions of the Senate, the magistrates and the laws. And there was no one to oppose; for the most ardent patriots had fallen on the field, or in the proscriptions; and the rest of the nobles, advanced in wealth and place in proportion to their servility, and drawing profit out of the new order of affairs, preferred the security of the present to the hazards of the past.

Nor did the provinces resent the change; for the rule of the Senate and the People had become odious to them from the contests between great leaders, and the greed of magistrates, against whom the law, upset by force, by favour, and, in fine, by bribery, were powerless to protect them. . . .

Thus a revolution had been accomplished. The old order had passed away; everything had suffered change. The days of equality were gone: men looked to the Prince for his commands, having no anxiety for the present, so long as Augustus was of the age, and had the strength, to keep himself, his house and the public peace secure. But when he advanced in years, when his health and strength failed, and his approaching end gave birth to new hopes, some few discoursed idly on the blessings of liberty; many dreaded war; some longed for it.

ROMAN FAMILIES

Patriarchal Tradition

*Early Roman society was strictly patriarchal in structure. The Greek histo-
rian Dionysius of Halicarnassus preserved a tradition of the first laws established by Romulus, legendary founder of Rome.*

From *Roman Antiquities*

The law was to this effect, that a woman joined to her husband by a
holy marriage should share in all his possessions and sacred
rites. . . . This law obliged both the married women, as having no other
refuge, to conform themselves entirely to the temper of their husbands, and the husbands to rule their wives as necessary and inseparable possessions. Accordingly, if a wife was virtuous and in all things
obedient to her husband, she was mistress of the house to the same
degree as her husband was master of it, and after the death of her husband she was heir to his property in the same manner as a daughter
was to that of her father; that is, if he died without children and intes-
tate, she was mistress of all that he left, and if he had children, she
shared equally with them. But if she did any wrong, the injured party
was her judge and determined the degree of her punishment. Other
offences, however, were judged by her relations together with her husband; among them was adultery, or where it was found she had drunk
wine—a thing which the Greeks would look upon as the least of all
faults. For Romulus permitted them to punish both these acts with
death, as being the gravest offences women could be guilty of, since he
looked upon adultery as the source of reckless folly, and drunkenness
as the source of adultery. And both these offences continued for a long
time to be punished by the Romans with merciless severity. . . .

Mild punishments are not sufficient to restrain the folly of youth
and its stubborn ways or to give self-control to those who have been
heedless of all that is honourable; and accordingly among the Greeks
many unseemly deeds are committed by children against their parents.
But the lawgiver of the Romans gave virtually full power to the father

From E. Cary, *The Roman Antiquities of Dionysius of Halicarnassus* (Cambridge,
Mass.: Harvard University Press, 1937), Vol. 1, pp. 381, 383, 385, 387, 389.

over his son, even during his whole life, whether he thought proper to imprison him, to scourge him, to put him in chains and keep him at work in the fields, or to put him to death, and this even though the son were already engaged in public affairs, though he were numbered among the highest magistrates, and though he were celebrated for his zeal for the commonwealth. Indeed, in virtue of this law men of distinction, while delivering speeches from the rostra hostile to the senate and pleasing to the people, and enjoying great popularity on that account, have been dragged down from thence and carried away by their fathers to undergo such punishment as these thought fit; and while they were being led away through the Forum, none present, neither consul, tribune, nor the very populace, which was flattered by them and thought all power inferior to its own, could rescue them.

Upper-class Romans cherished intense family loyalties. One way of express-ing them was to cultivate the memory of ancestors.

From *The Histories of Polybius*

Whenever one of their illustrious men dies, in the course of his fu-neral, the body with all its paraphernalia is carried into the forum to the Rostra, as a raised platform there is called, and sometimes is propped upright upon it so as to be conspicuous, or, more rarely, is laid upon it. Then with all the people standing round, his son, if he has left one of full age and he is there, or, failing him, one of his re-lations, mounts the Rostra and delivers a speech concerning the virtues of the deceased, and the successful exploits performed by him in his lifetime. By these means the people are reminded of what has been done, and made to see it with their own eyes,—not only such as were engaged in the actual transactions but those also who were not;—and their sympathies are so deeply moved, that the loss appears not to be confined to the actual mourners, but to be a public one affecting the whole people. After the burial and all the usual ceremonies have been performed, they place the likeness of the deceased in the most con-spicuous spot in his house, surmounted by a wooden canopy or shrine. This likeness consists of a mask made to represent the deceased with extraordinary fidelity both in shape and colour. These likenesses they display at public sacrifices adorned with much care. And when any il-lustrious member of the family dies, they carry these masks to the fu-neral, putting them on men whom they thought as like the originals as possible in height and other personal peculiarities. And these substi-tutes assume clothes according to the rank of the person represented: if he was a consul or praetor, a toga with purple stripes; if a censor, whole purple; if he had also celebrated a triumph or performed any exploit of that kind, a toga embroidered with gold. These representa-

From E. S. Shuckburgh, *The Histories of Polybius* (London: Macmillan, 1889), pp. 503–504.

tives also ride themselves in chariots, while the fasces and axes, and all the other customary insignia of the particular offices, lead the way, according to the dignity of the rank in the state enjoyed by the deceased in his lifetime; and on arriving at the Rostra they all take their seats on ivory chairs in their order. There could not easily be a more inspiring spectacle than this for a young man of noble ambitions and virtuous aspirations. For can we conceive any one to be unmoved at the sight of all the likenesses collected together of the men who have earned glory, all as it were living and breathing? Or what could be a more glorious spectacle?

The elder Cato (239–149 B.C.) was remembered as a paragon of stern republican virtue. This is how he managed his household.

From Plutarch. *Life of Cato*

He married a wife more noble than rich; being of opinion, that the rich and the high-born are equally haughty and proud; but that those of noble blood, would be more ashamed of base things, and consequently more obedient to their husbands in all that was fit and right. A man who beat his wife or child, laid violent hands, he said, on what was most sacred; and a good husband he reckoned worthy of more praise than a great senator; and he admired the ancient Socrates for nothing so much, as for having lived a temperate and contented life with a wife who was a scold, and children who were half-witted.

As soon as he had a son born, though he had never such urgent business upon his hands, unless it were some public matter, he would be by when his wife washed it, and dressed it in its swaddling clothes. For she herself suckled it, nay, she often too gave her breast to her servants' children, to produce, by sucking the same milk, a kind of natural love in them to her son. When he began to come to years of discretion, Cato himself would teach him to read, although he had a servant, a very good grammarian, called Chilo, who taught many others; but he thought not fit, as he himself said, to have his son reprimanded by a slave, or pulled, it may be, by the ears when found tardy in his lesson: nor would he have him owe to a servant the obligation of so great a thing as his learning; he himself, therefore, (as we were saying,) taught him his grammar, law, and his gymnastic exercises. Nor did he only show him, too, how to throw a spear, to fight in armor, and to ride, but to box also and to endure both heat and cold, and to swim over the most rapid and rough rivers. He says, likewise, that he wrote histories, in large characters, with his own hand, that so his son, without stirring out of the house, might learn to know about his countrymen and forefathers: nor did he less abstain from speaking any thing

From *Plutarch's Lives*, The Translation Called Dryden's, rev. A. H. Clough (Boston, Mass.: Little, Brown and Co., 1872), Vol. 2, pp. 341–344.

obscene before his son, than if it had been in the presence of the sacred virgins, called vestals. Nor would he ever go into the bath with him; which seems indeed to have been the common custom of the Romans. Sons-in-law used to avoid bathing with fathers-in-law, disliking to see one another naked: but having, in time, learned of the Greeks to strip before men, they have since taught the Greeks to do it even with the women themselves.

Thus, like an excellent work, Cato formed and fashioned his son to virtue. . . .

He purchased a great many slaves out of the captives taken in war, but chiefly bought up the young ones, who were capable to be, as it were, broken and taught like whelps and colts. None of these ever entered another man's house, except sent either by Cato himself or his wife. If any one of them were asked what Cato did, they answered merely, that they did not know. When a servant was at home, he was obliged either to do some work or sleep; for indeed Cato loved those most who used to lie down often to sleep, accounting them more docile than those who were wakeful, and more fit for any thing when they were refreshed with a little slumber. Being also of opinion, that the great cause of the laziness and misbehavior of slaves was their running after their pleasures, he fixed a certain price for them to pay for permission amongst themselves, but would suffer no connections out of the house. At first, when he was but a poor soldier, he would not be difficult in any thing which related to his eating, but looked upon it as a pitiful thing to quarrel with a servant for the belly's sake; but afterwards, when he grew richer, and made any feasts for his friends and colleagues in office, as soon as supper was over he used to go with a leathern thong and scourge those who had waited or dressed the meat carelessly. He always contrived, too, that his servants should have some difference one among another, always suspecting and fearing a good understanding between them. Those who had committed any thing worthy of death, he punished, if they were found guilty by the verdict of their fellow-servants. But being after all much given to the desire of gain, he looked upon agriculture rather as a pleasure than profit; resolving, therefore, to lay out his money in safe and solid things, he purchased ponds, hot baths, grounds full of fuller's earth, remunerative lands, pastures, and woods; from all which he drew large returns, nor could Jupiter himself, he used to say, do him much damage.

Legislation of Augustus

The emperor Augustus was concerned about a growing instability of marriages and a low birth rate among the free Roman population. Because the old death penalty for adultery was hard to enforce in practice, he devised a new one. He also introduced incentives to increase the size of families, including one providing that a woman with three children could be freed from guardianship. (Normally every Roman woman was under the care of some man—father, husband, or legally appointed guardian.)

In the following reading the emperor is addressing Roman fathers of the equestrian class.

From *Dio's Roman History*

Surely the best of all things is a woman who is temperate, domestic, a good housekeeper, a rearer of children; one to gladden you when in health, to tend you when sick; to be your partner in good fortune, to console you in misfortune; to restrain the frenzied nature of the youth and to temper the superannuated severity of the old man. Is it not a delight to acknowledge a child bearing the nature of both, to nurture and educate it, a physical image and a spiritual image, so that in its growth you yourself live again? Is it not most blessed on departing from life to leave behind a successor to and inheritor of one's substance and family, something that is one's own, sprung from one's self? . . . These are the private advantages that accrue to those who marry and beget children: but for the State, for whose sake we ought to do many things that are even distasteful to us, how excellent and how necessary it is, if cities and peoples are to exist, if you are to rule others and others are to obey you, that there should be a multitude of men to till the earth in peace and quiet, to make voyages, practice arts, follow handicrafts, men who in war will protect what we already have with the greater zeal because of family ties and will replace those that fall by others. Therefore, men,—for you alone may properly be called men,—and fathers,—for you are worthy to hold this title like myself,— I love you and I praise you for this, I am glad of the prizes I have already offered and I will glorify you still more besides by honors and offices. Thus you may yourselves reap great benefits and leave them to your children undiminished.

From H. B. Foster, trans., *Dio's Roman History* (Troy: Pafraets Book Co., 1905), Vol. 4, pp. 206–207.

The texts of Augustus's marriage laws (known as the Julian and Pappian laws) have not survived. But later jurists described their content and commented on them. The following texts date from the second century A.D.

From *The Institutes of Gaius*

Parents are permitted to appoint guardians . . . for male children under the age of puberty and for females who are beyond it, even if they are married; for the ancients thought it right that women should be

From T. Muirhead, ed., *Institutes of Gaius* (Edinburgh: T. and T. Clark, 1880), Vol. 1, pp. 144–145, 194, 190.

under guardianship, even when of full age, because of their fickleness of mind.

Therefore, if anyone appoints a guardian for his son and daughter and both reach the age of puberty, the son will cease to have a guardian but the daughter will still be under guardianship; for according to the Julian and Pappian Laws women are freed from guardianship only by the birth of children.

Moreover, a freeborn woman is freed from guardianship by the birth of three children, a freedwoman by the birth of four. . . .

There does not seem to be any good reason though why women of full age should be under guardianship. The one commonly assigned— that owing to their fickleness of mind they are easily misled and so it is only just that they be under the authority of guardians—seems more specious than real. For women of full age manage their own business affairs. In some cases the guardian interposes his authority merely as a matter of form; and not infrequently he is compelled to do so by the praetor even though he may be unwilling.

From *Opinions of Julius Paulus*

It was enacted (under Augustus) that women convicted of adultery should be punished by the confiscation of half of their dowry and a third of their property and by relegation to an island. Also that male adulterers be punished by confiscation of half of their property and relegation to an island—provided that the parties were relegated to different islands.

From R. Gneist, ed., *Opinions of Julius Paulus* (Leipzig: B. G. Teubner, 1880), II.26.4.

Roman Wives

Toward the end of the first century A.D. *Juvenal was still complaining about the fickleness of Roman ladies and their unwillingness to bear children.*

From *Juvenal's Sixth Satire*

> The bed holds more than a bride; you lie with bicker and
>   quarrel
> Always, all night long, and sleep is the last thing you get there.

From Rolfe Humphries, trans., *The Satires of Juvenal* (Bloomington, Ind.: Indiana University Press, 1958), pp. 73, 74, 87. Reprinted by permission of the publisher.

There she can really throw her weight around, like a tigress
Robbed of her young; or else, to atone for her own bad
    conscience,
She fakes the outraged sigh, and hates the boys whom her
    husband
Has, or she says he has, or sheds tears over a mistress
Purely fictitious, of course. Her tears come down like the
    raindrops,
With plenty more where they came from, ready to flow at her
    bidding.
Abject slug that you are, you think this proves that she loves you.
Aren't you pleased with yourself, as your lips go seeking those
    lashes
Wet with her pitiful tears? But what if you happened to open
The drawers of her desk, and found those notes, those fervent
    epistles,

Saved by your green-eyed wife, the hypocritical cheater?
You may catch her in bed with a slave or a knight. What
    happens?
All she can do in that case is invoke the art of Quintilian,
"Master of Rhetoric, help! Come to my aid, I implore you."
"Sorry," Quintilian replies, "I'm stuck; get yourself out of this
    one."
This does not bother her much; her explanation is ready.
"Long ago," she says, "it was understood between us
Perfectly well, you could do what you pleased, and no double
    standard
Kept me from having my fun. So howl as much as you want to,
I am human, too." Can you beat their nerve when you catch
    them?
That's when their very guilt supplies them anger and spirit.

Where, you ask, do they come from, such monsters as these? In
    the old days
Latin women were chaste by dint of their lowly fortunes.
Toil and short hours for sleep kept cottages free from contagion,
Hands were hard from working the wool, and husbands were
    watching,
Standing to arms at the Colline Gate, and the shadow of
    Hannibal's looming.
Now we suffer the evils of long peace. Luxury hatches
Terrors worse than the wars, avenging a world beaten down.
Every crime is here, and every lust, as they have been
Since the day, long since, when Roman poverty perished. . . .
(Poor) women at least endure the perils of childbirth,
Suffer the nuisance of nursing—but when did you ever discover

Labor pains in a golden bed? There are potent prescriptions,
Fine professional skill, to be hired for inducing abortions,
Killing mankind in the womb. Rejoice, unfortunate husband,
Give her the dose yourself, whatever it is; never let her
Carry till quickening time, or go on to full term and deliver
Something whose hue would seem to prove you a blackamoor
     father,
Sire of an off-color heir you'd prefer not to meet in the daylight.

A funeral oration from the time of Augustus describes a different sort of wife. (Her husband, who delivered the eulogy, was proscribed in the political troubles of 43 B.C.)

From *Praise of Turia*

Marriages of such long duration, not dissolved by divorce, but terminated by death alone, are indeed rare. For our union was prolonged in unclouded happiness for forty-one years. Would that our long marriage had come to its final end by *my* death, and that *I* as the older— which was more just—had yielded to fate.

Why recall your natural qualities, your modesty, deference, affability, your amiable disposition, your faithful attendance to household duties, your enlightened religion, your unassuming elegance, the modest simplicity of your attire? Need I speak of your attachment to your kindred, your affection for your family—when you cherished my mother as you did your own parents—you who share countless other virtues with Roman matrons who cherish their fair name? These qualities which I claim for you are your own; few have possessed the like and been able to hold on to and maintain them; the experience of men teaches us how rare they are.

With joint zeal we have preserved all the patrimony which you received from your parents. Entrusting it all to me, you were not troubled with the care of increasing it; thus did we share the task of administering it, that I undertook to protect your fortune, and you to guard mine. On this point I pass by many things in silence, for fear of attributing to myself a portion of your desserts. . . .

You helped my escape by selling your jewels and turning over to me all your gold and the pearls removed from your person; and thereupon the household furnished money; and deceiving the guards of our opponents, you made my absence comfortable. . . . Why should I now conjure up the memory of the hidden counsels, concealed plans, and secret talks? How, aroused by the sudden arrival of messages from you to a realization of the present and imminent perils, I was saved by

From Naphtali Lewis and Meyer Reinhold, eds., *Roman Civilization* (New York: Columbia University Press, 1951), Vol. 1, pp. 485–487. Reprinted courtesy of the publisher.

your counsel. How you did not allow me recklessly through excessively bold plans to face danger, and how, bent on more discreet plans, you provided for me a safe retreat, choosing as sharers in your plans for my safety—fraught with danger as they were for you all—your sister and her husband, Gaius Cluvius. Were I to attempt to touch on all these matters, it would be an endless task. Suffice it for me and for you that the retreat provided by you ensured my safety.

I should confess, however, that on this occasion I suffered one of the bitterest experiences of my life, in the fate that befell you. When the favor and decision of Caesar Augustus, then absent [from Rome], had restored me to my country, still a useful citizen perhaps, Marcus Lepidus, his colleague, then present in the city, interposed objections to my pardon. Then, when you prostrated yourself at his feet, he not only did not raise you up—but, dragged along and abused, as though a common slave, your body all covered with bruises, yet with unflinching steadfastness of purpose you recalled to him Caesar's edict and the letter of felicitation on my pardon. Braving his taunts and suffering the most brutal insults and wounds, you denounced these cruelties publicly so that he became known as the author of all my perils. And his punishment for this was not long delayed.

When all the world was again at peace and the Republic reestablished, peaceful and happy days followed for us. We longed for children, which an envious fate denied us for some time. Had Fortune permitted herself to smile on us in the ordinary fashion, what had been lacking to complete our happiness? But advancing age put an end to our hopes. . . . Despairing of your fertility and disconsolate to see me without children . . . you spoke of divorce because of my unhappiness on this account, offering to yield our home to another spouse more fertile, with no other intention than that of yourself searching for and providing for me a spouse worthy of our well-known mutual affection, whose children you assured me you would have treated as though your own. . . . Nothing would have been changed, only that you would have rendered to me henceforth the services and devotion of a sister or mother-in-law.

I must admit that I was so angry that I was deprived of my mind, and that I was so horrified at your proposal that I scarcely regained control of myself. That you should have spoken of divorce between us before the decree of fate had been given; that you should have conceived of any reason why you, while you were still alive, should cease to be my wife, you who when I was almost an exile from life remained most faithful. . . .

Would that our time of life had permitted our union to endure until I, the older, had passed away—which was more just—and that you might perform for me the last rites, and that I might have departed, leaving you behind, with a daughter to replace me in your widowhood.

By fate's decree your course was run before mine. You left me the grief, the longing for you, the sad fate to live alone. . . .

THE EMPIRE—AUGUSTUS TO TRAJAN

Imperial Mission

Under Augustus's successors the Roman empire reached the height of its power. Vergil, the greatest poet of the era, anticipated a coming golden age. It is not certain who was the "blessed boy" of the following poem. Pollio, to whom the verses are addressed, was consul in 40 B.C. and it is possible that Vergil was writing of the child expected by Augustus and his wife in that same year. (However, the child turned out to be a girl.) Later on, Christians could not resist seeing an allusion to the coming of Christ.

From Vergil. *Eclogue IV*

Muses
Muses of Sicily
Now let us sing a serious song
There are taller trees than the apple and the crouching tamerisk
If we sing of the woods, let our forest be stately.

Now the last age is coming
As it was written in the Sybil's book
The great circle of the centuries begins again
Justice, the Virgin, has returned to earth
With all of Saturn's court
A new line is sent down to us from the skies
And thou, Lucina, must smile
Smile for the birth of the boy, the blessed boy
For whom they will beat their swords into ploughshares
For whom the golden race will rise, the whole world new

Smile, pure Lucina, smile
Thine own Apollo will reign
And thou, Pollio
It is in thy term this glorious age begins
And the great months begin their march
When we shall lose all trace of the old guilt

From G. Howe and G. A. Harrer, eds., *Roman Literature in Translation* (New York: Harper & Row, 1959), p. 387.

And the world learn to forget fear
For the boy will become divine
He will see gods and heroes
And will himself be seen by them as god and hero
As he rules over a world of peace
A world made peaceful by his father's wisdom. . . .

In the Aeneid, *Vergil expressed succinctly his understanding of Rome's special genius.*

From Vergil. *The Aeneid*

Let others better mould the running mass
Of metals, and inform the breathing brass,
And soften into flesh a marble face;
Plead better at the bar; describe the skies,
And when the stars descend, and when they rise.
But, Rome! 'tis thine alone, with awful sway,
To rule mankind, and make the world obey:
Disposing peace and war thy own majestic way.
To tame the proud, the fettered slave to free,
These are imperial arts, and worthy thee.

From Vergil, *The Aeneid*, John Dryden, trans. (London: F. Warne, 1877), p. 166.

Provincial Administration

Pliny the Younger was appointed governor of Bithynia (in modern Turkey) about A.D. *111. His correspondence with the emperor Trajan illustrates many aspects of Roman imperial administration, especially the relationship between central and local authority.*

From *Letters of Pliny*

Letter XVI. To the Emperor Trajan

As I had a very favorable voyage to Ephesus, so in travelling post from thence I was extremely incommoded by the heats, which threw me into a fever, and kept me some time at Pergamum. From thence,

From W. Melmoth, trans., *The Letters of Pliny the Consul* (London: J. Dodsley, 1770), Vol. 2, pp. 595–598, 610–614, 620–624.

Sir, I took ship again; but being detained by contrary winds, I did not arrive at Bithynia so soon as I hoped. However I have no reason to complain of this delay, since (which indeed was the most auspicious circumstance that could attend me) I reached the province in time to celebrate your birth-day. I am at present engaged in examining into the finances of the Prusenses, their disbursements and credits; and the farther I proceed in this affair, the more I am convinced of the necessity of my enquiry. Several large sums of money are owing to the city from private persons, which they neglect to pay upon various pretences; as on the other hand, I find the public funds are, in some instances, very unwarrantly applied. This, Sir, I write to you immediately on my arrival. I entered this province on the 17th of September, and found it in those sentiments of obedience and loyalty, which you justly merit from all mankind. You will consider, Sir, whether it would not be proper to send hither a surveyor; for I am inclined to think, much might be deducted from what is charged by those who have the conduct of the public works, if a faithful admeasurement were to be taken: at least I am of that opinion from what I have already seen of the accounts of this city, which I am now examining, with the assistance of Maximus.

Letter XVII. Trajan to Pliny

I should have rejoiced to have hear'd that you arrived at Bithynia without inconvenience to yourself or any of your train; and that your journey from Ephesus had been as easy, as your voyage to that place was favorable. For the rest, your letter informs me, my dear Pliny, what day you reached Bithynia. The people of that province will be convinced, I persuade myself, that I am attentive to their interest; as your conduct towards them will make it manifest, that I could have chosen no person more proper to supply my place. Your first inquiry ought, no doubt, to turn upon the state of the public finances; for that they have been abused, is but too evident. I have scarce surveyors enough to inspect those works which I am carrying on at Rome, and in the neighbourhood: but persons of integrity and skill in this art may be found, most certainly, in every province; so that you cannot be at a loss in that point, if you will make due enquiry.

Letter XXX. To the Emperor Trajan

I beg your determination, Sir, in a point wherein I am greatly doubtful: it is, whether I should place the public slaves as sentinels round the prisons of the several cities in this province (as has been hitherto the practice) or employ a party of soldiers for that purpose? On the one hand, I am afraid the public slaves will not attend this duty with the fidelity they ought; and on the other, that it will engage too large a body of the soldiery: in the mean while I have joined a few of the latter with the former. I suspect however, there may be some danger that this method will occasion a general neglect of duty, as it will afford them a mutual pretence of throwing the blame upon each other.

Letter XXXI. Trajan to Pliny

There is no occasion, my dear Pliny, to draw off any soldiers in order to guard the prisons. Let us rather persevere in the ancient customs observed by this province, of employing the public slaves for that purpose: and the fidelity with which they shall execute their duty will depend much upon your care and strict discipline. It is greatly to be feared, as you observe, if the soldiers should be mixed with the public slaves, they will mutually trust to each other, and by that means grow so much the more negligent. But the principal objection I have, is, that as few soldiers as possible should be called off from their colors.

Letter XXXIV. To the Emperor Trajan

The Prusenses, Sir, have an ancient and ruinous bath, which they desire your leave to repair. Upon examining into the condition of it, I find it ought to be rebuilt. I think therefore you may indulge them in this request, as there will be a sufficient fund for that purpose, partly from those debts which are due from private persons to the public, which I am now calling in; and partly from what they raise among themselves towards furnishing the bath with oil, which they are willing to apply to the carrying on of this building: a work which the dignity of the city, and the splendor of your times seems to demand.

Letter XXXV. Trajan to Pliny

If the erecting a public bath will not be too great a charge upon the Prusenses, we may comply with their request: provided, however, that no new tax be levied for this purpose, nor any of those taken off which are applied for necessary services.

Letter XLII. To the Emperor Trajan

While I was making a progress in a different part of the province, a prodigious fire broke out at Nicomedia, which not only consumed several private houses, but also two public buildings; the town-house and the temple of Isis, tho' they stood on contrary sides of the street. The occasion of its spreading thus far, was partly owing to the violence of the wind, and partly to the indolence of the people, who I am well assured, stood fixed and idle spectators of this terrible calamity. The truth is, the city was not provided either with engines, buckets, or any one single instrument proper to extinguish fires; which I have now however given directions to have prepared. You will consider, Sir, whether it may not be advisable to institute a company of fire-men, consisting only of one hundred and fifty members. I will take care none but those of that business shall be admitted into it; and that the privileges granted them shall not be extended to any other purpose. As this incorporated body will consist of so small a number, it will be easy enough to keep them under proper regulation.

Letter XLIII. Trajan to Pliny

You are of opinion it would be proper to constitute a company of fire-men in Nicomedia, agreeably to what has been practised in several other cities. But it is to be remember'd, that this sort of societies have greatly disturb'd the peace of that province in general, and of those cities in particular. Whatever name we give them, and for whatever purposes they may be founded, they will not fail to form themselves into assemblies, however short their meetings may be. It will therefore be safer, to provide such machines as are of service in extinguishing fires, enjoining the owners of houses to assist upon such occasions; and if it shall be necessary, to call in the help of the populace.

Letter XLVI. To the Emperor Trajan

The city of Nicomedia, Sir, have expended three millions three hundred and twenty nine sesterces building an aquaeduct; but, not being able to finish it, the works are entirely falling to ruin. They made a second attempt in another place, where they laid out two millions. But this likewise is discontinued; so that after having been at an immense charge to no purpose, they must still be at a farther expence, in order to be accommodated with water. I have examined a fine spring from whence the water may be conveyed over arches (as was done in their first design) in such a manner that the higher, as well as level and low parts of the city may be supplied. There are but very few of the old arches remaining; the square stones, however, employed in the former building, may be used in turning the new ones. I am of opinion part should be raised with brick, as that will be the easier and cheaper method. But that this work may not be carried on with the same ill success as the former, it will be necessary to send here an architect and an engineer. And I will venture to say, from the beauty and usefulness of the design, it will be a work worthy the splendor of your times.

Letter XLVII. Trajan to Pliny

Care must be taken to supply the city of Nicomedia with water; and you will do so, I am well persuaded, with all the diligence you ought. But it is most certainly no less incumbent upon you to examine, by whose misconduct it has happened, that such large sums have been thrown away upon this work, lest by applying the money to private purposes, this aquaeduct should likewise be left unfinished. You will let me know the result of your enquiry.

V

ORIGINS OF CHRISTIANITY
Judaism
From *The Jewish War*
The Coming of Jesus
From *The Gospel According to Luke*
From *The Gospel According to John*
Life and Teaching
From *The Gospel According to Matthew*
From *The Gospel According to Matthew*
From *The Gospel According to Mark*

THE EARLY CHURCH
Christian and Pagan
From *Paul's First Epistle to the Corinthians*
From Minucius Felix. *Octavius*
From Hippolytus. *Apostolic Tradition*
The Nicene Creed
Church and State
From *The Annals of Tacitus*
From *Letters of Pliny*
From *The "Edict of Milan"*
From Eusebius. *Life of Constantine*
From *The Theodosian Code*
Christian Women: Marriage and Celibacy
From *Paul's Epistle to the Ephesians*
From *Paul's First Epistle to the Corinthians*
From *The Acts of the Christian Martyrs*
From Jerome. *Against Helvidius*
From *Letter of Pope Damasus on Celibacy*

DECLINE AND FALL
Imperial Centralization
From J. W. Thompson. *The Middle Ages*

From *The Death of the Persecutors*
From *The Theodosian Code*
Christian Reactions
Salvianus. *The Burden of Taxation*
Jerome. *The Barbarian Invasions*
Augustine. *The Two Cities*
Augustine. *The Six Ages of the World*
Epilogue
From Edward Gibbon. *The Decline and Fall of the Roman Empire*

CHRISTIANITY AND THE FALL OF ROME

AS THE ROMAN state approached the height of its power in the second century, a new religion was spreading from the eastern Mediterranean through the provinces of the empire. Christianity resembled the various mystery religions in offering secret ceremonies, redemption from sin, and a promise of life after death. But its founder was not just a mythical figure. He was a real person who had taught on earth and commissioned disciples to carry his message to all nations. Christians believed in the resurrection of Jesus as an actual historical event that justified their hope of everlasting life. Their teachings appealed mainly to humble and illiterate people at first, but eventually they came to fascinate the most subtle minds of the late classical world. The new religion influenced every level of life and thought—philosophy, politics, morality, attitudes towards marriage and sexuality.

Christianity preserved the Judaic tradition of monotheism. A Christian could not worship any other god or even join in the state ceremonies honoring the emperor as a divine being. The imperial authorities responded with fierce persecutions of the Christians, but the persecutions were never sustained long enough to wipe out the whole church and the martyrs they created inspired new generations of Christians by their heroic examples. The last great persecution was launched by Diocletian in 303. A dramatic change came under Constantine, the next emperor. Constantine first proclaimed tolerance for Christianity in 313, then himself embraced the Christian faith. Under his successors Christianity became the official religion of the empire.

Between 400 and 500 the empire experienced repeated invasions by barbarian peoples who had been settled along its borders. Under these attacks the institutions of the Roman state crumbled away, but the Christian church survived and helped to shape the new world of early medieval Europe.

ORIGINS OF CHRISTIANITY

Judaism

The Jewish historian Josephus, writing in the first century A.D.*, described several "sects" of Judaism that existed in the time of Jesus.*

From *The Jewish War*

There are three philosophical sects among the Jews. The followers of the first of which are the Pharisees, of the second the Sadducees, and the third sect, which pretends to a severe discipline, are called Essens. These last are Jews by birth, and seem to have a greater affection for one another than the other sects have. These Essens reject pleasures as an evil, but esteem continence and the conquest over our passions to be virtue. They neglect wedlock, but choose out other persons' children while they are pliable and fit for learning, and esteem them to be of their kindred, and form them according to their own manners. They do not absolutely deny the fitness of marriage, and the succession of mankind thereby continued; but they guard against the lascivious behaviour of women, and are persuaded that none of them preserve their fidelity to one man.

These men are despisers of riches, and their communism raises our admiration. Nor is there any one to be found among them who hath more than another; for it is a law among them, that those who come to them must let what they have be common to the whole order, insomuch that among them all there is no appearance of poverty, or excess of riches, but everyone's possessions are intermingled with every other's possessions, and so there is, as it were, one patrimony among all the brethren. They think that oil is a defilement, and if anyone of them be anointed, without his own intention, he wipes his body; for they think to be unwashed is a good thing, as they do also to be clothed in white garments. They also have stewards appointed by vote to take care of their common affairs, who every one of them have no separate business for any, but what is for the uses of them all. . . .

They contemn the miseries of life, and are above pain, by the gen-

From Flavius Josephus, *The Jewish War*, W. Whiston and D. S. Margoliouth, trans. (London: George Routledge and Sons, 1906), pp. 76, 79–80.

erosity of their mind. And as for death, if it will come with glory, they esteem it better than immortality; and indeed our war with the Romans gave abundant evidence what great souls they had in their trials wherein, although they were tortured and distorted, burnt and torn to pieces, and went through all kinds of instruments of torment, that they might be forced either to blaspheme their legislator, or to eat what was forbidden them, yet could they not be made to do either of them, no nor once to flatter their tormentors, or to shed a tear; but they smiled in their very pains, and laughed those to scorn who inflicted the torments upon them, and resigned up their souls with great alacrity, as expecting to receive them again.

For the opinion is strongly held among them, that bodies are corruptible, and that the matter they are made of is not permanent; but that the souls are immortal, and continue forever, and that they come out of the most subtile air, and are united to their bodies as to prisons, into which they are drawn by a certain natural enticement; but that when they are set free from the bonds of the flesh, they then, as released from a long bondage, rejoice and mount upward. And their opinion is like that of the Greeks, that good souls have their habitations beyond the ocean, in a region that is neither oppressed with storms of rain or snow, or with intense heat, but that this place is such as is refreshed by the gentle breathing of a west wind, that is perpetually blowing from the ocean; while they allot to bad souls a dark and tempestuous den, full of never-ceasing punishments. . . . These are the divine doctrines of the Essens about the soul, whereby they lay an unavoidable bait for such as have once had a taste of their philosophy. . . .

But then as to the two other orders at first mentioned, the Pharisees are those who are esteemed most skilful in the exact explication of their laws, and are regarded the first sect. These ascribe all to fate, and to God, and yet allow, that to act as is right, or the contrary, is principally in the power of men: although fate does co-operate in every action. They say, that all souls are incorruptible, but that the souls of good men only are removed into other bodies, but that the souls of bad men are subject to eternal punishment. But the Sadducees are those that compose the second order, and take away fate entirely, and suppose that God is not concerned in our doing or not doing what is evil; and they say, that to act what is good or what is evil, is at men's own choice, and each man attaches himself to the one or the other as he will. They also take away the belief of the immortal duration of the soul, and the punishments and rewards in Hades. Moreover, the Pharisees are friendly to one another, and are for the exercise of concord, and regard for the public; but the behaviour of the Sadducees one towards another is in some degree wild, and their conversation with those that are of their own party is as barbarous as if they were strangers to them. And this is what I had to say concerning the philosophic sects among the Jews.

The Coming of Jesus

The four Gospels (written c. 50–c. 100) record the story of Jesus as it was handed down to the early Christian communities. Luke gives the familiar "Christmas story" of Jesus' birth at Bethlehem.

From *The Gospel According to Luke*

In the sixth month the angel Gabriel was sent from God to a city of Galilee named Nazareth, to a virgin betrothed to a man whose name was Joseph, of the house of David; and the virgin's name was Mary. And he came to her and said, "Hail, O favored one, the Lord is with you!" But she was greatly troubled at the saying, and considered in her mind what sort of greeting this might be. And the angel said to her, "Do not be afraid, Mary, for you have found favor with God. And behold, you will conceive in your womb and bear a son, and you shall call his name Jesus.

> He will be great, and will be called
>   the Son of the Most High;
> and the Lord God will give to him
>   the throne of his father David,
> and he will reign over the house of
>   Jacob for ever;
> and of his kingdom there will be no
>   end."

And Mary said to the angel, "How shall this be, since I have no husband?" And the angel said to her,

> "The Holy Spirit will come upon
>   you,
> and the power of the Most High
>   will overshadow you;
> therefore the child to be born
>   will be called holy,
> the Son of God. . . ."

And Mary said, "Behold, I am the handmaid of the Lord; let it be to me according to your word." And the angel departed from her.

In those days a decree went out from Caesar Augustus that all the world should be enrolled. This was the first enrollment, when Quirinius was governor of Syria. And all went to be enrolled, each to his own city. And Joseph also went up from Galilee, from the city of Nazareth, to Judea, to the city of David, which is called Bethlehem, because he was of the house and lineage of David, to be enrolled with Mary, his betrothed, who was with child. And while they were there, the time came for her to be delivered. And she gave birth to her first-born son and wrapped him in swaddling cloths, and laid him in a manger, because there was no place for them in the inn.

And in that region there were shepherds out in the field, keeping watch over their flock by night. And an angel of the Lord appeared to them, and the glory of the Lord shone around them, and they were filled with fear. And the angel said to them, "Be not afraid; for behold, I bring you good news of a great joy which will come to all the people; for to you is born this day in the city of David a Savior, who is Christ the Lord. And this will be a sign for you: you will find a babe wrapped in swaddling cloths and lying in a manger." And suddenly there was with the angel a multitude of the heavenly host praising God and saying,

> "Glory to God in the highest,
> and on earth peace among men with
>   whom he is pleased!"

When the angels went away from them into heaven, the shepherds said to one another, "Let us go over to Bethlehem and see this thing that has happened, which the Lord has made known to us." And they went with haste, and found Mary and Joseph, and the babe lying in a manger. And when they saw it they made known the saying which had been told them concerning this child; and all who heard it wondered at what the shepherds told them. But Mary kept all these things, pondering them in her heart. And the shepherds returned, glorifying and praising God for all they had heard and seen, as it had been told them.

John's later account is more abstract and philosophical. The idea of a divine creative "Word" (logos) existed in early Hellenistic philosophy.

From *The Gospel According to John*

In the beginning was the Word, and the Word was with God, and the Word was God. He was in the beginning with God; all things were made through him, and without him was not anything made that was made. In him was life, and the life was the light of men. The light shines in the darkness, and the darkness has not overcome it.

There was a man sent from God, whose name was John. He came

for testimony, to bear witness to the light, that all might believe through him. He was not the light, but came to bear witness to the light.

The true light that enlightens every man was coming into the world. He was in the world, and the world was made through him, yet the world knew him not. He came to his own home, and his own people received him not. But to all who received him, who believed in his name, he gave power to become children of God; who were born, not of blood nor of the will of the flesh nor of the will of man, but of God.

And the Word became flesh and dwelt among us, full of grace and truth; we have beheld his glory, glory as of the only Son from the Father. (John bore witness to him, and cried, "This was he of whom I said, 'He who comes after me ranks before me, for he was before me.' ") And from his fulness have we all received, grace upon grace. For the law was given through Moses; grace and truth came through Jesus Christ. No one has ever seen God; the only Son, who is in the bosom of the Father, he has made him known.

Life and Teaching

Jesus' moral teaching is summarized in this collection of his sayings known as the Sermon on the Mount.

From *The Gospel According to Matthew*

Seeing the crowds, he went up on the mountain, and when he sat down his disciples came to him. And he opened his mouth and taught them, saying:

"Blessed are the poor in spirit, for theirs is the kingdom of heaven.

"Blessed are those who mourn, for they shall be comforted.

"Blessed are the meek, for they shall inherit the earth.

"Blessed are those who hunger and thirst for righteousness, for they shall be satisfied.

"Blessed are the merciful, for they shall obtain mercy.

"Blessed are the pure in heart, for they shall see God.

"Blessed are the peacemakers, for they shall be called sons of God.

"Blessed are those who are persecuted for righteousness' sake, for theirs is the kingdom of heaven.

From the *Revised Standard Version Bible* (New York: Oxford University Press, 1973). The Gospel According to Matthew 5:1–18, 38–48; 6:1, 7–14, 24–33. Copyright 1946, 1952, © 1971, 1973 by the National Council of the Churches of Christ. Reprinted by permission.

"Blessed are you when men revile you and persecute you and utter all kinds of evil against you falsely on my account. Rejoice and be glad, for your reward is great in heaven, for so men persecuted the prophets who were before you.

"You are the salt of the earth; but if salt has lost its taste, how shall its saltness be restored? It is no longer good for anything except to be thrown out and trodden under foot by men.

"You are the light of the world. A city set on a hill cannot be hid. Nor do men light a lamp and put it under a bushel, but on a stand, and it gives light to all in the house. Let your light so shine before men, that they may see your good works and give glory to your Father who is in heaven.

"Think not that I have come to abolish the law and the prophets; I have come not to abolish them but to fulfill them. For truly, I say to you, till heaven and earth pass away, not an iota, not a dot, will pass from the law until all is accomplished. . . .

"You have heard that it was said, 'An eye for an eye and a tooth for a tooth.' But I say to you, Do not resist one who is evil. But if any one strikes you on the right cheek, turn to him the other also; and if any one would sue you and take your coat, let him have your cloak as well; and if any one forces you to go one mile, go with him two miles. Give to him who begs from you, and do not refuse him who would borrow from you.

"You have heard that it was said, 'You shall love your neighbor and hate your enemy.' But I say to you, Love your enemies and pray for those who persecute you, so that you may be sons of your Father who is in heaven; for he makes the sun rise on the evil and on the good, and sends rain on the just and on the unjust. For if you love those who love you, what reward have you? Do not even the tax collectors do the same? And if you salute only your brethren, what more are you doing than others? Do not even the Gentiles do the same? You, therefore, must be perfect, as your heavenly Father is perfect.

"Beware of practicing your piety before men in order to be seen by them; for then you will have no reward from your Father who is in heaven. . . .

"And in praying do not heap up empty phrases as the Gentiles do; for they think that they will be heard for their many words. Do not be like them, for your Father knows what you need before you ask him. Pray then like this:

> Our Father who art in heaven,
> Hallowed by thy name.
> Thy kingdom come.
> Thy will be done,
>   On earth as it is in heaven.
> Give us this day our daily bread;
> And forgive us our debts,

> As we also have forgiven our
>   debtors;
> And lead us not into temptation,
>   But deliver us from evil.

For if you forgive men their trespasses, your heavenly Father also will forgive you; but if you do not forgive men their trespasses, neither will your Father forgive your trespasses. . . .

"No one can serve two masters; for either he will hate the one and love the other, or he will be devoted to the one and despise the other. You cannot serve God and mammon.

"Therefore I tell you, do not be anxious about your life, what you shall eat or what you shall drink, nor about your body, what you shall put on. Is not life more than food, and the body more than clothing? Look at the birds of the air: they neither sow nor reap nor gather into barns, and yet your heavenly Father feeds them. Are you not of more value than they? And which of you by being anxious can add one cubit to his span of life? And why are you anxious about clothing? Consider the lilies of the field, how they grow; they neither toil nor spin; yet I tell you, even Solomon in all his glory was not arrayed like one of these. But if God so clothes the grass of the field, which today is alive and tomorrow is thrown into the oven, will he not much more clothe you, O men of little faith? Therefore do not be anxious, saying, 'What shall we eat?' or 'What shall we drink?' or 'What shall we wear?' For the Gentiles seek all these things; and your heavenly Father knows that you need them all. But seek first his kingdom and his righteousness, and all these things shall be yours as well."

Some texts identified Jesus with the "Messiah" promised by God to Israel.

From *The Gospel According to Matthew*

Now when Jesus came into the district of Caesarea Philippi, he asked his disciples, "Who do men say that the Son of man is?" And they said, "Some say John the Baptist, others say Elijah, and others Jeremiah or one of the prophets." He said to them, "But who do you say that I am?" Simon Peter replied, "You are the Christ, the Son of the living God." And Jesus answered him, "Blessed are you, Simon Bar-Jona! For flesh and blood has not revealed this to you, but my Father who is in heaven. And I tell you, you are Peter, and on this rock I will build my church, and the powers of death shall not prevail against it. I will give you the keys to the kingdom of heaven, and whatever you bind on earth shall be bound in heaven, and whatever you loose on earth shall be loosed in heaven." Then he strictly charged the disciples to tell no one that he was the Christ.

From that time Jesus began to show his disciples that he must go to Jerusalem and suffer many things from the elders and chief priests and scribes, and be killed, and on the third day be raised.

Each of the four Gospels tells of Jesus' death and resurrection. The earliest account is from Mark.

From *The Gospel According to Mark*

And on the first day of Unleavened Bread, when they sacrificed the passover lamb, his disciples said to him, "Where will you have us go and prepare for you to eat the passover?" And he sent two of his disciples, and said to them, "Go into the city, and a man carrying a jar of water will meet you; follow him, and wherever he enters, say to the householder, 'The Teacher says, Where is my guest room, where I am to eat the passover with my disciples?' And he will show you a large upper room furnished and ready; there prepare for us." And the disciples set out and went to the city, and found it as he had told them; and they prepared the passover.

And when it was evening he came with the twelve. And as they were at table eating, Jesus said, "Truly, I say to you, one of you will betray me, one who is eating with me." They began to be sorrowful, and to say to him one after another, "Is it I?" He said to them, "It is one of the twelve, one who is dipping bread into the dish with me. For the Son of man goes as it is written of him, but woe to that man by whom the Son of man is betrayed! It would have been better for that man if he had not been born."

And as they were eating, he took bread, and blessed, and broke it, and gave it to them, and said, "Take; this is my body." And he took a cup, and when he had given thanks he gave it to them, and they all drank of it. And he said to them, "This is my blood of the covenant, which is poured out for many. Truly, I say to you, I shall not drink again of the fruit of the vine until that day when I drink it new in the kingdom of God.". . .

And as soon as it was morning the chief priests, with the elders and scribes, and the whole council held a consultation; and they bound Jesus and led him away and delivered him to Pilate. And Pilate asked him, "Are you the King of the Jews?" And he answered him, "You

From the *Revised Standard Version Bible* (New York: Oxford University Press, 1973). The Gospel According to Mark 14:12–25; 15:1–15, 33–47; 16:1–20. Copyright 1946, 1952, © 1971, 1973 by the National Council of the Churches of Christ. Reprinted by permission.

have said so." And the chief priests accused him of many things. And Pilate again asked him, "Have you no answer to make? See how many charges they bring against you." But Jesus made no further answer, so that Pilate wondered.

Now at the feast he used to release for them one prisoner for whom they asked. And among the rebels in prison, who had committed murder in the insurrection, there was a man called Barabbas. And the crowd came up and began to ask Pilate to do as he was wont to do for them. And he answered them, "Do you want me to release for you the King of the Jews?" For he perceived that it was out of envy that the chief priests had delivered him up. But the chief priests stirred up the crowd to have him release for them Barabbas instead. And Pilate again said to them, "Then what shall I do with the man whom you call the King of the Jews?" And they cried out again, "Crucify him." And Pilate said to them, "Why, what evil has he done?" But they shouted all the more, "Crucify him." So Pilate, wishing to satisfy the crowd, released for them Barabbas; and having scourged Jesus, he delivered him to be crucified. . . .

And when the sixth hour had come, there was darkness over the whole land until the ninth hour. And at the ninth hour Jesus cried with a loud voice, "Elo-i, Elo-i, lama sabach-thani?" which means, "My God, my God, why hast thou forsaken me?" And some of the bystanders hearing it said, "Behold, he is calling Elijah." And one ran and, filling a sponge full of vinegar, put it on a reed and gave it to him to drink, saying, "Wait, let us see whether Elijah will come to take him down." And Jesus uttered a loud cry, and breathed his last. And the curtain of the temple was torn in two, from top to bottom. And when the centurion, who stood facing him, saw that he thus breathed his last, he said, "Truly this man was the Son of God!"

There were also women looking on from afar, among whom were Mary Magdalene, and Mary, the mother of James the younger and of Joses, and Salome, who, when he was in Galilee, followed him and ministered to him; and also many other women who came up with him to Jerusalem.

And when evening had come, since it was the day of Preparation, that is, the day before the sabbath, Joseph of Arimathea, a respected member of the council, who was also himself looking for the kingdom of God, took courage and went to Pilate, and asked for the body of Jesus. And Pilate wondered if he were already dead; and summoning the centurion, he asked him whether he was already dead. And when he learned from the centurion that he was dead, he granted the body to Joseph. And he bought a linen shroud, and taking him down, wrapped him in the linen shroud, and laid him in a tomb which had been hewn out of the rock; and he rolled a stone against the door of the tomb. Mary Magdalene and Mary the mother of Joseph saw where he was laid.

And when the sabbath was past, Mary Magdalene, and Mary the mother of James, and Salome, bought spices, so that they might go and anoint him. And very early on the first day of the week they went to the tomb when the sun had risen. And they were saying to one another, "Who will roll away the stone for us from the door of the tomb?" And looking up, they saw that the stone was rolled back—it was very large. And entering the tomb, they saw a young man sitting on the right side, dressed in a white robe; and they were amazed. And he said to them, "Do not be amazed; you seek Jesus of Nazareth, who was crucified. He has risen, he is not here; see the place where they laid him. But go, tell his disciples and Peter that he is going before you to Galilee; there you will see him, as he told you." And they went out and fled from the tomb; for trembling and astonishment had come upon them; and they said nothing to any one, for they were afraid.

Now when he rose early on the first day of the week, he appeared first to Mary Magdalene, from whom he had cast out seven demons. She went and told those who had been with him, as they mourned and wept. But when they heard that he was alive and had been seen by her, they would not believe it.

After this he appeared in another form to two of them, as they were walking into the country. And they went back and told the rest, but they did not believe them.

Afterward he appeared to the eleven themselves as they sat at the table; and he upbraided them for their unbelief and hardness of heart, because they had not believed those who saw him after he had risen. And he said to them, "Go into all the world and preach the gospel to the whole creation. He who believes and is baptized will be saved; but he who does not believe will be condemned." . . .

So then the Lord Jesus, after he had spoken to them, was taken up into heaven, and sat down at the right hand of God. And they went forth and preached everywhere, while the Lord worked with them and confirmed the message by the signs that attended it. Amen.

THE EARLY CHURCH

Christian and Pagan

Paul emphasized the Christian message of love in his letter to the church at Corinth, probably written in A.D. 57.

From *Paul's First Epistle to the Corinthians*

If I speak in the tongues of men and of angels, but have not love, I am a noisy gong or a clanging cymbal. And if I have prophetic powers, and understand all mysteries and all knowledge, and if I have all faith, so as to remove mountains, but have not love, I am nothing. If I give away all I have, and if I deliver my body to be burned, but have not love, I gain nothing.

Love is patient and kind; love is not jealous or boastful; it is not arrogant or rude. Love does not insist on its own way; it is not irritable or resentful; it does not rejoice at wrong, but rejoices in the right. Love bears all things, believes all things, hopes all things, endures all things.

Love never ends; as for prophecies, they will pass away; as for tongues, they will cease; as for knowledge, it will pass away. For our knowledge is imperfect and our prophecy is imperfect; but when the perfect comes, the imperfect will pass away. When I was a child, I spoke like a child, I thought like a child, I reasoned like a child; when I became a man, I gave up childish ways. For now we see in a mirror dimly, but then face to face. Now I know in part; then I shall understand fully, even as I have been fully understood. So faith, hope, love abide, these three; but the greatest of these is love.

To many educated pagans the new religion seemed a vicious, superstitious cult. Minucius Felix (c. 200), a Christian himself, attributed the following views to a pagan, Caecilius.

From the *Revised Standard Version Bible* (New York: Oxford University Press, 1973). I Corinthians 13:1–13. Copyright 1946, 1952, © 1971, 1973 by the National Council of the Churches of Christ. Reprinted by permission.

From Minucius Felix. *Octavius*

And now, as wickeder things advance more fruitfully, and abandoned manners creep on day by day, those abominable shrines of an impious assembly are maturing themselves throughout the whole world. Assuredly this confederacy ought to be rooted out and execrated. They know one another by secret marks and insignia, and they love one another almost before they know one another; everywhere also there is mingled among them a certain religion of lust, and they call one another promiscuously brothers and sisters, that even a not unusual debauchery may by the intervention of that sacred name become incestuous: it is thus that their vain and senseless superstition glories in crimes.

Nor, concerning these things, would intelligent report speak of things so great and various, and requiring to be prefaced by an apology, unless truth were at the bottom of it. I hear that they adore the head of an ass, that basest of creatures, consecrated by I know not what silly persuasion,—a worthy and appropriate religion for such manners. Some say that they worship the genitals of their pontiff and priest, and adore the nature, as it were, of their common parent. I know not whether these things are false; certainly suspicion is applicable to secret and nocturnal rites; and he who explains their ceremonies by reference to a man punished by extreme suffering for his wickedness, and to the deadly wood of the cross, appropriates fitting altars for reprobate and wicked men, that they may worship what they deserve.

Now the story about the initiation of young novices is as much to be detested as it is well known. An infant covered over with meal, that it may deceive the unwary, is placed before him who is to be stained with their rites: this infant is slain by the young pupil, who has been urged on as if to harmless blows on the surface of the meal, with dark and secret wounds. Thirstily—O horror!—they lick up its blood; eagerly they divide its limbs. By this victim they are pledged together; with this consciousness of wickedness they are covenanted to mutual silence.

The charge of ritual cannibalism was probably based on confused accounts of the Christian eucharist. Hippolytus of Rome tells us what actually went on at a Christian service. This early eucharistic prayer—still used in some churches—dates from the beginning of the third century.

From Minucius Felix, *Octavius*, R. E. Wallis, trans. in *The Ante–Nicene Fathers* (Buffalo, N. Y.: The Christian Literature Publishing Co., 1887), Vol. 4, pp. 177–178.

From Hippolytus. *Apostolic Tradition*

When one has been consecrated bishop all give him the kiss of peace . . . and the deacons bring him the offering . . . he lays hands upon it with all the priests and gives thanks, saying, "The Lord be with you." And all answer, "And with your spirit." "Lift up your hearts." "We have lifted them up to the Lord." "Let us give thanks to the Lord." "It is right and just."

And he thus continues, "We give thanks to you O God through your beloved son Jesus Christ whom in these last times you have sent to us as the redeemer and saviour and messenger of your will. He is your inseparable Word, through whom you created all things and who was acceptable to you. You sent him from heaven into the Virgin's womb and in her womb he was made man and was manifested your son, born of the Holy Spirit and of the Virgin. Fulfilling your will and buying for you a holy people, he stretched forth his hands when he suffered, that by his Passion he might deliver those who believed in you. When he was delivered over to his Passion of his own will, to destroy death, to break the bonds of the devil, to trample upon Hell, to enlighten the just, and to manifest his resurrection, taking bread and giving thanks to you, he said: *Take and eat, this is my body which shall be broken for you.* And taking likewise the cup, he said: *This is my blood which shall be shed for you; when you do this, do it in memory of me.*

"Mindful therefore of his death and resurrection, we offer you this bread and cup, giving thanks to you because you have found us worthy to stand before you and serve you. And we beg you to send the Holy Spirit upon the offering of the holy church and gather into one all who have received it . . . that we may praise and glorify you through your son Jesus Christ, through whom is glory and honor to the Father and the Son and the Holy Spirit, in your holy church both now and forever. Amen."

From H. Achelis, *Die Canones Hippolyti* (Leipzig, 1881), pp. 48–55.

Around A.D. 300, the Egyptian priest Arius raised new problems concerning the divinity of Christ. He denied that Christ was "eternally begotten" of the Father. The first general council of the church, meeting at Nicea in 325, rejected his doctrine. The Nicene Creed became a touchstone of orthodoxy in later disputes.

The Nicene Creed

We believe in one God the Father All-sovereign, maker of heaven and earth, and of all things visible and invisible;

From Henry Bettenson, ed., *Documents of the Christian Church*, 2nd ed. (London: Oxford University Press, 1963), pp. 36–37. Copyright © 1963 by Oxford University Press. Reprinted by permission of Oxford University Press.

And in one Lord Jesus Christ, the only-begotten Son of God, Begotten of the Father before all ages, Light of Light, true God of true God, begotten not made, of one substance with the Father, through whom all things were made; who for us men and for our salvation came down from the heavens, and was made flesh of the Holy Spirit and the Virgin Mary, and became man, and was crucified for us under Pontius Pilate, and suffered and was buried, and rose again on the third day according to the Scriptures, and ascended into the heavens, and sitteth on the right hand of the Father, and cometh again with glory to judge living and dead, of whose kingdom there shall be no end:

And in the Holy Spirit, the Lord and the Life-giver, that proceedeth from the Father, who with Father and Son is worshipped together and glorified together, who spake through the prophets:

In one holy Catholic and Apostolic Church:

We acknowledge one baptism unto remission of sins. We look for a resurrection of the dead, and the life of the age to come.

Church and State

Roman rulers often regarded the Christian church as a dangerous, subversive organization—and a convenient scapegoat in times of trouble. A major persecution was launched by the emperor Nero after the great fire of Rome in A.D. *64.*

From *The Annals of Tacitus*

Neither human aid, nor imperial bounty, nor atoning-offerings to the Gods, could remove the sinister suspicion that the fire had been brought about by Nero's order. To put an end therefore to this rumour, he shifted the charge on to others, and inflicted the most cruel tortures upon a body of men detested for their abominations, and popularly known by the name of Christians. This name came from one Christus, who was put to death in the reign of Tiberius by the Procurator Pontius Pilate; but though checked for the time, the detestable superstition broke out again, not in Judaea only, where the mischief began, but even in Rome, where every horrible and shameful iniquity, from every quarter of the world, pours in and finds a welcome.

First those who acknowledged themselves of this persuasion were arrested; and upon their testimony a vast number were condemned, not so much on the charge of incendiarism as for their hatred of the human race. Their death was turned into a diversion. They were clothed

From G. G. Ramsay, trans., *The Annals of Tacitus* (London: J. Murray, 1904), Vol. 2, pp. 280–282.

in the skins of wild beasts, and torn to pieces by dogs; they were fastened to crosses, or set up to be burned, so as to serve the purpose of lamps when daylight failed. Nero gave up his own gardens for this spectacle; he provided also Circensian games, during which he mingled with the populace, or took his stand upon a chariot, in the garb of a charioteer. But guilty as these men were and worthy of direst punishment, the fact that they were being sacrificed for no public good, but only to glut the cruelty of one man, aroused a feeling of pity on their behalf.

The emperor Trajan (98–117) advised a more temperate approach to the Christian problem.

From *Letters of Pliny*

Letter XCVII. To the Emperor Trajan

It is a rule, Sir, which I inviolably observe, to refer myself to you in all my doubts; for who is more capable of removing my scruples, or informing my ignorance? Having never been present at any trials concerning those who profess Christianity, I am unacquainted not only with the nature of their crimes, or the measure of their punishment, but how far it is proper to enter into an examination concerning them. Whether therefore any difference is usually made with respect to the ages of the guilty, or no distinction is to be observed between the young and the adult; whether repentance intitles them to a pardon; or if a man has been once a Christian, it avails nothing to desist from his error; whether the very profession of Christianity, unattended with any criminal act, or only the crimes themselves inherent in the profession are punishable; in all these points I am greatly doubtful. In the mean while the method I have observed towards those who have been brought before me as Christians, is this: I interrogated them whether they were Christians; if they confessed I repeated the question twice again, adding threats at the same time; when, if they still persevered, I ordered them to be immediately punished: for I was persuaded, whatever the nature of their opinions might be, a contumacious and inflexible obstinacy certainly deserved correction. There were others also brought before me possessed with the same infatuation, but being citizens of Rome, I directed them to be carried thither. But this crime spreading (as is usually the case) while it was actually under prosecution, several instances of the same nature occurred. An information was presented to me without any name subscribed, containing a charge against several persons, who upon examination denied they were Christians, or had ever been so. They repeated after me an invocation

From W. Melmoth, trans., *The Letters of Pliny the Consul* (London: J. Dodsley, 1770), Vol. 2, pp. 671–677.

to the gods, and offered religious rites with wine and frankincense before your statue; (which for the purpose I had ordered to be brought together with those of the gods) and even reviled the name of Christ: whereas there is no forcing, it is said, those who are really Christians, into a compliance with any of these articles: I thought proper therefore to discharge them. Some among those who were accused by a witness in person, at first confessed themselves Christians, but immediately after denied it; while the rest own'd indeed that they had been of that number formerly, but had now (some above three, others more, and a few above twenty years ago) forsaken that error. They all worshipped your statue and the images of the gods, throwing out imprecations at the same time against the name of Christ. They affirmed, the whole of their guilt, or their error, was, that they met on a certain stated day before it was light, and addressed themselves in a form of prayer to Christ, as to some God, binding themselves by a solemn oath, not for the purposes of any wicked design, but never to commit any fraud, theft, or adultery, never to falsify their word, nor deny a trust when they should be called upon to deliver it up; after which, it was their custom to separate, and then reassemble, to eat in common a harmless meal. From this custom, however, they desisted after the publication of my edict, by which, according to your orders, I forbade the meeting of any assemblies. After receiving this account, I judged it so much the more necessary to endeavor to extort the real truth, by putting two female slaves to the torture, who were said to administer in their religious functions: but I could discover nothing more than an absurd and excessive superstition. I thought proper therefore to adjourn all farther proceedings in this affair, in order to consult with you. For it appears to be a matter highly deserving your consideration; more especially as great numbers must be involved in the danger of these prosecutions, this enquiry having already extended, and being still likely to extend, to persons of all ranks and ages, and even of both sexes. For this contagious superstition is not confined to the cities only, but has spread its infection among the country villages. Nevertheless, it still seems possible to remedy this evil and restrain its progress. The temples, at least, which were once almost deserted, begin now to be frequented; and the sacred solemnities, after a long intermission, are again revived; while there is a general demand for the victims, which for some time past have met with but few purchasers. From hence it is easy to imagine, what numbers might be reclaimed from this error, if a pardon were granted to those who shall repent.

Letter XCVIII. Trajan to Pliny

The method you have pursued, my dear Pliny, in the proceedings against those Christians which were brought before you, is extremely proper; as it is not possible to lay down any fixed plan by which to act in all cases of this nature. But I would not have you officiously enter into any enquiries concerning them. If indeed they should be brought before you, and the crime is proved, they must be punished; with the restriction however that where the party denies himself to be a Christian, and shall make it evident that he is not, by invoking our Gods, let him (notwithstanding any former suspicion) be pardoned upon his repentance. Information without the accuser's name subscribed, ought not to be received in prosecutions of any sort, as it is introducing a very dangerous precedent, and by no means agreeable to the equity of my government.

Constantine proclaimed a new policy of toleration for Christianity in 313. Later he himself became a Christian and took an active part in directing the affairs of the church.

From The "Edict of Milan"

When we, Constantine and Licinius, Emperors, met at Milan in conference concerning the welfare and security of the realm, we decided that of the things that are of profit to all mankind, the worship of God ought rightly to be our first and chiefest care, and that it was right that Christians and all others should have freedom to follow the kind of religion they favoured; so that the God who dwells in heaven might be propitious to us and to all under our rule. We therefore announce that, notwithstanding any provisions concerning the Christians in our former instructions, all who choose that religion are to be permitted to continue therein, without any let or hindrance, and are not to be in any way troubled or molested. Note that at the same time all others are to be allowed the free and unrestricted practice of their religions; for it accords with the good order of the realm and the peacefulness of our times that each should have freedom to worship God after his own choice; and we do not intend to detract from the honour due to any religion or its followers. Moreover, concerning the Christians, we before gave orders with respect to the places set apart for their worship. It is now our pleasure that all who have bought such places should restore them to the Christians, without any demand for payment.

From Henry Bettenson, ed., *Documents of the Christian Church*, 2nd ed. (London: Oxford University Press, 1963), pp. 22–23. Copyright © 1963 by Oxford University Press. Reprinted by permission of Oxford University Press.

From Eusebius. *Life of Constantine*

He [Constantine] exercised a peculiar care over the church of God: and whereas, in the several provinces there were some who differed

From Eusebius, *The Life of Constantine*, E. C. Richardson, trans. in *A Select Library of Nicene and Post–Nicene Fathers*, Second Series (New York: The Christian Literature Co., 1890), Vol. 1, pp. 494–495.

from each other in judgment, he, like some general bishop constituted by God, convened synods of his ministers. Nor did he disdain to be present and sit with them in their assembly, but bore a share in their deliberations, ministering to all that pertained to the peace of God. He took his seat, too, in the midst of them, as an individual amongst many, dismissing his guards and soldiers, and all whose duty it was to defend his person; but protected by the fear of God, and surrounded by the guardianship of his faithful friends. Those whom he saw inclined to a sound judgment, and exhibiting a calm and conciliatory temper, received his high approbation, for he evidently delighted in a general harmony of sentiment; while he regarded the unyielding with aversion.

In 380 the emperor Theodosius established orthodox Christianity as the official religion of the empire.

From *The Theodosian Code*

It is our desire that all the various nations which are subject to our Clemency and Moderation, should continue in the profession of that religion which was delivered to the Romans by the divine Apostle Peter, as it hath been preserved by faithful tradition; and which is now professed by the Pontiff Damasus and by Peter, Bishop of Alexandria, a man of apostolic holiness. According to the apostolic teaching and the doctrine of the Gospel, let us believe the one deity of the Father, the Son and the Holy Spirit, in equal majesty and in a holy Trinity. We authorize the followers of this law to assume the title of Catholic Christians; but as for the others, since, in our judgment, they are foolish madmen, we decree that they shall be branded with the ignominious name of heretics, and shall not presume to give to their conventicles the name of churches. They will suffer in the first place the chastisement of the divine condemnation, and in the second the punishment which our authority, in accordance with the will of Heaven, shall de-

Christian Women: Marriage and Celibacy

From the beginning, the Christian church displayed an ambivalent attitude toward human sexuality. In some contexts, the love between husband and wife was praised as a symbol of the love between Christ and the church. In others, virginity was presented as a higher state than marriage. Both attitudes appear in Paul's writings.

From Henry Bettenson, ed., *Documents of the Christian Church*, 2nd ed. (London: Oxford University Press, 1963), p. 31. Copyright © 1963 by Oxford University Press. Reprinted by permission of Oxford University Press.

From *Paul's Epistle to the Ephesians*

Be subject to one another out of reverence for Christ. Wives, be subject to your husbands, as to the Lord. For the husband is the head of the wife as Christ is the head of the church, his body, and is himself its Savior. As the church is subject to Christ, so let wives also be subject in everything to their husbands. Husbands, love your wives, as Christ loved the church and gave himself up for her, that he might sanctify her, having cleansed her by the washing of water with the word, that he might present the church to himself in splendor, without spot or wrinkle or any such thing, that she might be holy and without blemish. Even so husbands should love their wives as their own bodies. He who loves his wife loves himself. For no man ever hates his own flesh, but nourishes and cherishes it, as Christ does the church, because we are members of his body. "For this reason a man shall leave his father and mother and be joined to his wife, and the two shall become one flesh." This mystery is a profound one, and I am saying that it refers to Christ and the church; however, let each one of you love his wife as himself, and let the wife see that she respects her husband.

From *Paul's First Epistle to the Corinthians*

Now concerning the matters about which you wrote. It is well for a man not to touch a woman. But because of the temptation to immorality, each man should have his own wife and each woman her own husband. The husband should give to his wife her conjugal rights, and likewise the wife to her husband. For the wife does not rule over her own body, but the husband does; likewise the husband does not rule over his own body, but the wife does. Do not refuse one another except perhaps by agreement for a season, that you may devote yourselves to prayer; but then come together again, lest Satan tempt you through lack of self-control. I say this by way of concession, not of command. I wish that all were as I myself am. But each has his own special gift from God, one of one kind and one of another.

To the unmarried and the widows I say that it is well for them to remain single as I do. But if they cannot exercise self-control, they should marry. For it is better to marry than to be aflame with passion. . . .

I think that in view of the present distress it is well for a person to remain as he is. Are you bound to a wife? Do not seek to be free. Are you free from a wife? Do not seek marriage. But if you marry, you do not sin, and if a girl marries she does not sin. Yet those who marry will have worldly troubles, and I would spare you that. I mean, brethren, the appointed time has grown very short; from now on, let those who have wives live as though they had none, and those who mourn as though they were not mourning, and those who rejoice as though they were not rejoicing, and those who buy as though they had no goods, and those who deal with the world as though they had no dealings with it. For the form of this world is passing away.

I want you to be free from anxieties. The unmarried man is anxious about the affairs of the Lord, how to please the Lord; but the married man is anxious about worldly affairs, how to please his wife, and his interests are divided. And the unmarried woman or girl is anxious about the affairs of the Lord, how to be holy in body and spirit; but the married woman is anxious about worldly affairs, how to please her husband. I say this for your own benefit, not to lay any restraint upon you, but to promote good order and to secure your undivided devotion to the Lord.

If any one thinks that he is not behaving properly toward his betrothed, if his passions are strong, and it has to be, let him do as he wishes: let them marry—it is no sin. But whoever is firmly established in his heart, being under no necessity but having his desire under control, and has determined this in his heart, to keep her as his betrothed, he will do well. So that he who marries his betrothed does well; and he who refrains from marriage will do better.

Many of the martyrs whose memories were cherished in the early church were women. Irene was one of three sisters put to death in Diocletian's persecution.

From *The Acts of the Christian Martyrs*

Dulcitius the prefect said: "Your sisters, in accordance with my commands in their regard, have received their sentence. Now you were guilty even before you ran away and before you concealed these writings and parchments, and hence I do not wish you to die immediately in the same way. Instead I sentence you to be placed naked in the brothel with the help of the public notaries of this city and of Zosimus the executioner; and you will receive merely one loaf of bread from our residence, and the notaries will not allow you to leave."

And so, after the notaries and the slave Zosimus, the executioner, were brought in, the prefect said: "Be it known to you that if ever I

From Herbert Musurillo, trans., *The Acts of the Christian Martyrs* (Oxford: Clarendon Press, 1972), pp. 291–292. Copyright © 1972 by Oxford University Press. Reprinted by permission of Oxford University Press.

find out from the troops that this girl was removed from the spot where I have ordered her to be even for a single instant, you will immediately be punished with the most extreme penalties. The writings we have referred to, in the cabinets and chests belonging to Irene, are to be publicly burned."

After those who were put in charge had taken the girl off to the public brothel in accordance with the prefect's order, by the grace of the Holy Spirit which preserved and guarded her pure and inviolate for the God who is the lord of all things, no man dared to approach her or so much as tried to insult her in speech. Hence the prefect Dulcitius called back this most saintly girl, had her stand before the tribunal, and said to her: "Do you still persist in the same folly?"

But Irene said to him: "It is not folly, but piety."

"It was abundantly clear from your earlier testimony," said the prefect Dulcitius, "that you did not wish to submit religiously to the bidding of the emperors; and now I perceive that you are persisting in the same foolishness. Therefore you shall pay the appropriate penalty."

He then asked for a sheet of papyrus and wrote the sentence against her as follows: "Whereas Irene has refused to obey the command of the emperors and to offer sacrifice, and still adheres to a sect called the Christians, I therefore sentence her to be burned alive, as I did her two sisters before her."

After this sentence had been pronounced by the prefect, the soldiers took the girl and brought her to a high place, where her sisters had been martyred before her. They ignited a huge pyre and ordered her to climb up on it. And the holy woman Irene, singing and praising God, threw herself upon it and so died. It was in the ninth consulship of Diocletian Augustus, in the eighth of Maximian Augustus, on the first day of April, in the kingship of our Lord Christ Jesus, who reigns for ever, with whom there is glory to the Father with the Holy Spirit for ever. Amen.

Jerome (c. 340–420) developed Paul's argument for virginity as a higher state than marriage.

From Jerome. *Against Helvidius*

A virgin is defined as she that is holy in body and in spirit, for it is no good to have virgin flesh if a woman be married in mind.

"But she that is married is careful for the things of the world, how

From Jerome, *Against Helvidius*, W. H. Fremantle, trans. in *A Select Library of Nicene and Post–Nicene Fathers*, Second Series (New York: The Christian Literature Co., 1893), Vol. 6, pp. 344–345.

she may please her husband."[1] Do you think there is no difference between one who spends her time in prayer and fasting, and one who must, at her husband's approach, make up her countenance, walk with mincing gait, and feign a shew of endearment? The virgin's aim is to appear less comely; she will wrong herself so as to hide her natural attractions. The married woman has the paint laid on before her mirror, and, to the insult of her Maker, strives to acquire something more than her natural beauty. Then come the prattling of infants, the noisy household, children watching for her word and waiting for her kiss, the reckoning up of expenses, the preparation to meet the outlay. On one side you will see a company of cooks, girded for the onslaught and attacking the meat: there you may hear the hum of a multitude of weavers. Meanwhile a message is delivered that the husband and friends have arrived. The wife, like a swallow, flies all over the house. She has to see to everything. Is the sofa smooth? Is the pavement swept? Are the flowers in the cups? Is dinner ready? Tell me, pray, where amid all this is there room for the thought of God? Are these happy homes? Where there is the beating of drums, the noise and clatter of pipe and lute, the clanging of cymbals, can any fear of God be found? Enter next the half-naked victims of the passions, a mark for every lustful eye. The unhappy wife must either take pleasure in them, and perish, or be displeased, and provoke her husband. Hence arises discord, the seed-plot of divorce. Or suppose you find me a house where these things are unknown, which is rare indeed! yet even there the very management of the household, the education of the children, the wants of the husband, the correction of the servants, cannot fail to call away the mind from the thought of God. "It had ceased to be with Sarah after the manner of women"[2]: so the Scripture says, and afterwards Abraham received the command, "In all that Sarah saith unto thee, hearken unto her voice."[3] She who is not subject to the anxiety and pain of child-bearing and having passed the change of life has ceased to perform the functions of a woman, is freed from the curse of God: nor is her desire to her husband, but on the contrary her husband becomes subject to her, and the voice of the Lord commands him, "In all that Sarah saith unto thee, hearken unto her voice." Thus they begin to have time for prayer. For so long as conjugal rights are used, earnest prayer is neglected.

[1] I Corinthians 7:34.
[2] Genesis 18:11.
[3] Genesis 21:12.

Toward the end of the fourth century a Roman synod required celibacy of all higher clergy. Its decision was announced in this letter, probably written by Pope Damasus in 384.

From *Letter of Pope Damasus on Celibacy*

This is what has been decided, about bishops in the first place, but also about priests and deacons, whose duty it is to take part in the divine sacrifice (of the Eucharist) and whose hands confer the grace of baptism and make present the body of Christ. It is not only us but divine Scripture that binds them to be perfectly chaste. . . . How could a bishop or priest dare to preach continence to a widow or virgin, or urge anyone to keep his bed pure, if he himself were more concerned to have children for this world than for God? Why did Paul say "You are not in the flesh but in the spirit" and "Let those who have wives live as though they had none"? Would he, who so exhorted the people, complaisantly allow carnal activity to priests?—he who also said "Make no provision for the flesh, to gratify its desires" and "I wish that all were as I myself am." One who is in the service of Christ, who sits in the chair of the master, can he not observe the rule of service. . . . Those who offered sacrifices in the Temple remained the whole year in the Temple so that they should be pure and did not enter their own homes. . . . Even idolaters, in order to celebrate their impious cult and sacrifice to demons, imposed continence on themselves as regards women and abstained from certain foods so as to remain pure. And you ask me if the priest of the living God, who is to offer spiritual sacrifices, should live always in a state of purity or if, wholly involved in the flesh he should give himself to the cares of the flesh. If intercourse is defilement . . . that is why the mystery of God may not be entrusted to men of that sort, defiled and faithless. . . . They doubtless know that "flesh and blood cannot inherit the kingdom of God, nor does the corrupt inherit the incorruptible"; shall a priest or deacon dare then to lower himself to act as the animals do?

From H. T. Bruns, *Canones apostolorum et conciliorum saeculorum IV–VII*, (Berlin, 1839), Vol. 2, p. 276. Translated by B. Tierney.

DECLINE AND FALL

Imperial Centralization

During the third century, new civil wars threatened to tear apart the Roman world. The emperor Diocletian (284–305) succeeded in restoring order but only by imposing a more despotic form of government on the empire. A modern historian gives this picture of Diocletian's court.

From J. W. Thompson. *The Middle Ages*

The emperor was a god and moved as an absolute sovereign reigning by divine right. On state occasions he was attired in silken robes of blue and gold symbolizing the sky and the sun; his hair was dressed to imitate the sun and sprinkled with gold; upon his head rested a jeweled tiara; a collar of pearls was around his neck; over his breast flowed necklaces of rubies and emeralds; his hands were encrusted with rings flashing with precious stones; his finger-nails were gilded; his shoes were of red Persian leather with golden soles. Over all he wore a mantle of such immense length that the train was borne by eight lackeys. In his hand he carried a scepter that terminated in a gold ball typifying the globe and was tipped with a gold eagle in whose talons was a splendid blue sapphire, again symbolic of the blue of heaven. The throne was an exquisite piece of workmanship in carved precious wood, inlaid with mother of pearl and lapis lazuli—again the color of blue—standing upon a dais covered with rare rugs and carpets and having suspended over it a great blue silk canopy representative of heaven. The throne-room befitted in its adornment the magnificence of the imperial Presence. But no person in the audience there assembled on state occasions was suffered to sit down; indeed, there was no furniture in the room except the throne. When the emperor entered, preceded by lackeys perfuming the air with attar of roses and other perfumes, by fan-bearers carrying ostrich- and peacock-feather fans, and the usher of the gold rod, every person in the throne-room sank to the floor in true Oriental obeisance and remained prostrate until the Sacred Presence was seated. One may imagine the tremendously impressive effect

From J. W. Thompson, *The Middle Ages 300–1500* (New York: Alfred A. Knopf, 1932).

of such magnificence. It would be almost true to say that from the Tigris to the Pillars of Hercules and from the cataracts of the Nile to the Wall of Antoninus in Britain, the Roman world trembled at the emperor's nod.

This criticism of Diocletian's policies by the Christian author Lactantius was influenced by Diocletian's persecution of the church.

From *The Death of the Persecutors*

While Diocletian, that author of ill, and deviser of misery, was ruining all things, he could not withhold his insults, not even against God. This man, by avarice partly, and partly by timid counsels, overturned the Roman empire: for he made choice of three persons to share the government with him; and thus, the empire having been quartered, armies were multiplied, and each of the four princes strove to maintain a much more considerable military force than any sole emperor had done in times past. There began to be fewer men who paid taxes than there were who received wages from the state; so that the means of the husbandmen being exhausted by enormous impositions, the farms were abandoned, cultivated grounds became woodland, and universal dismay prevailed. Besides, the provinces were divided into minute portions, and many presidents and a multitude of inferior officers lay heavy on each territory, and almost on each city. There were also many stewards of different degrees, and deputies of presidents. Very few civil causes came before them: but there were condemnations daily, and forfeitures frequently inflicted; taxes on numberless commodities, and those not only often repeated, but perpetual, and, in exacting them, intolerable wrongs.

Whatever was laid on for the maintenance of the soldiery might have been endured; but Diocletian, through his insatiable avarice, would never allow the sums of money in his treasury to be diminished: he was constantly heaping together extraordinary aids and free gifts, that his original hoards might remain untouched and inviolable. He also, when by various extortions he had made all things exceedingly dear, attempted by an ordinance to limit their prices.[1] Then much blood was shed for the veriest trifles; men were afraid to expose aught to sale, and the scarcity became more excessive and grievous than ever,

---

[1]Lactantius refers to a price control edict issued in 301.

From Lactantius, *On the Manner in Which the Persecutors Died*, W. Fletcher, trans. in *The Ante–Nicene Fathers VII* (New York: The Christian Literature Co., 1888), p. 303.

until, in the end, the ordinance, after having proved destructive to multitudes, was from mere necessity abrogated.

Under Diocletian's successors many occupations considered useful to the state were made compulsory and hereditary. (Coloni were dependent peasants forbidden to leave the land they cultivated. Decurions were members of municipal councils, responsible for local government and tax collection; in earlier centuries the position had been much sought after as one of high honor.)

From *The Theodosian Code*

I, 5, 11. All persons who govern provinces shall exact payment of the delinquent taxes for their term of office when they have laid aside their administration. Those landholders whom no sense of shame can move to fulfill their public obligations shall be notified three times within a year, and if they do not complete all such public obligations, they shall pay double the amount of the debt through the office of Your Magnificence.

V, 17, 1. Any person in whose possession a colonus that belongs to another is found not only shall restore the aforesaid colonus to his birth status but also shall assume the capitation tax for this man for the time that he was with him.

1. Coloni also who meditate flight must be bound with chains and reduced to a servile condition, so that by virtue of their condemnation to slavery, they shall be compelled to fulfill the duties that befit freemen.

VI, 2, 14. We order that exemption from the payment of the glebal tax shall be granted to all those persons from Macedonia . . . who have been added to the Most August Order of the City of Constantinople [the Senate], according to the precedent of the Senators who were chosen from Thrace.

XI, 2, 4. Whenever, in accordance with custom, payment is demanded in the case of regular taxes or of taxes due, not the prices of natural products demanded shall be paid, but the natural products themselves. . . .

XII, 1, 13. Since we have learned that the municipal councils are being left desolate by those persons who are obligated to them through

From Clyde Pharr, trans., *The Theodosian Code and Novels and the Sirmondian Constitutions* (Princeton, N.J.: Princeton University Press, 1952), pp. 17, 115, 119, 296, 344, 351, 406, 407, 408. Copyright 1952 by Clyde Pharr, copyright © renewed 1980 by Roy Pharr. Reprinted by permission of Princeton University Press.

birth status and who are requesting imperial service for themselves through supplications to the Emperor and are running away to the legions and various governmental offices, We order all municipal councils to be admonished that if they should apprehend any persons with less than twenty terms of service in governmental offices . . . they shall drag such persons back to the municipal councils. . . .

XII, 1, 18. It is our will, indeed, that the sons of military men, according to the former regulation, either shall pursue the aforesaid service of their fathers, or, if they refuse to perform military service and had reached the age of thirty-five years, they shall be assigned to the municipal councils.

XII, 1, 62. If a decurion should steal into a guild of artisans for the purpose of evading other duties, he shall be restored to his pristine status, and in the future no person who derives his birth status from decurions shall dare to aspire to the duties of such a guild.

XIV, 2, 4. If any guild members of the City of Rome have illegally passed into foreign parts, they shall be forced to return by the administrative action of the governors of the provinces, in order that they may perform the compulsory public services which ancient custom has imposed upon them.

XIV, 3, 8. The office of Your Sincerity shall be on guard that if any man should once and for all be assigned to the guild of breadmakers, he shall not be granted the opportunity and power in any way to withdraw, even if the assent of all the breadmakers should strive to obtain his release and their assembly should appear to have agreed. Not even this privilege shall be granted to any breadmaker, namely, that he may pass from one breadmaking establishment to another.

XIV, 3, 14. If a daughter of a breadmaker should marry any man and afterward, when her fortune had been squandered, he should suppose that she may be released from the guild, We command that he shall be bound to the compulsory duties and guild of breadmaking by the same law and reason as if he were held by the bond of birth service to such compulsory status.

Christian Reactions

According to Salvianus (c. 400–480) the oppressive burden of taxation had undermined loyalty to the Roman state at the time of the barbarian invasions.

Salvianus. *The Burden of Taxation*

But what else can these wretched people wish for, they who suffer the incessant and even continuous destruction of public tax levies. To them there is always imminent a heavy and relentless proscription. They desert their homes, lest they be tortured in their very homes. They seek exile, lest they suffer torture. The enemy is more lenient to them than the tax collectors. This is proved by this very fact, that they flee to the enemy in order to avoid the full force of the heavy tax levy. This very tax levying, although hard and inhuman, would nevertheless be less heavy and harsh if all would bear it equally and in common. Taxation is made more shameful and burdensome because all do not bear the burden of all. They extort tribute from the poor man for the taxes of the rich, and the weaker carry the load for the stronger. There is no other reason that they cannot bear all the taxation except that the burden imposed on the wretched is greater than their resources.

They suffer from envy and want, which are misfortunes most diverse and unlike. Envy is bound up with payment of the tax; need, with the ability to pay. If you look at what they pay, you will think them abundant in riches, but if you look at what they actually possess, you will find them poverty stricken. Who can judge an affair of this wretchedness? They bear the payment of the rich and endure the poverty of beggars.

Do we think we are unworthy of the punishment of divine severity when we thus constantly punish the poor? Do we think, when we are constantly wicked, that God should not exercise His justice against all of us? Where or in whom are evils so great, except among the Romans? Whose injustice so great except our own? The Franks are ignorant of this crime of injustice. The Huns are immune to these crimes. There are no wrongs among the Vandals and none among the Goths. So far are the barbarians from tolerating these injustices among the Goths, that not even the Romans who live among them suffer them.

Therefore, in the districts taken over by the barbarians, there is one desire among all the Romans, that they should never again find it necessary to pass under Roman jurisdiction. In those regions, it is the one and general prayer of the Roman people that they be allowed to carry on the life they lead with the barbarians. And we wonder why the Goths are not conquered by our portion of the population, when the Romans prefer to live among them rather than with us. Our brothers, therefore, are not only altogether unwilling to flee to us from them, but they even cast us aside in order to flee to them.

From J. F. O'Sullivan, trans., *The Writings of Salvian the Presbyter*, Fathers of the Church Series (Washington, D.C.: The Catholic University of America Press, 1947), Vol. 3, pp. 138, 141. Reprinted by permission of the publisher.

During the fifth century all the provinces of the Western empire were occupied by barbarians. Jerome, living far away in Bethlehem, heard the news with dismay.

Jerome. *The Barbarian Invasions*

Innumerable and most ferocious people have overrun the whole of Gaul. The entire area bounded by the Alps, the Pyrenees, the ocean and the Rhine is occupied by the Quadi, Vandals, Sarmatians, Alanni, Gepides, Saxons, Burgundians, Alammani—oh weep for the empire—and the hostile Pannonians. . . . Mainz, once a noble city, is captured and razed, and thousands have been massacred in the church. Worms has succumbed to a long siege. Rheims, the impregnable, Amiens, Artois . . . Tours, Nimes and Strasburg are in the hands of the Germans. The provinces of Aquitaine, of the land of the nine peoples, of Lyons and Narbonne are completely occupied and devastated either by the sword from without or famine within. I cannot mention Toulouse without tears, for until now it has been spared, due to the merits of its saintly bishop Exuperus. The Spaniards tremble, expecting daily the invasion and recalling the horrors of the incursion of the Cimbri. What others are going through the Spaniards suffer in continual anticipation.

Who would believe that Rome, victor over all the world, would fall, that she would be to her people both the womb and the tomb. Once all the East, Egypt and Africa acknowledged her sway and were counted among her men servants and her maid servants. Who would believe that holy Bethlehem would receive as beggars nobles, both men and women, once abounding in riches? Where we cannot help we mourn and mingle with theirs our tears. . . . There is not an hour, not even a moment, when we are not occupied with crowds of refugees, when the peace of the monastery is not invaded by a horde of guests so that we shall either have to shut the gates or neglect the Scriptures for which the gates were opened. Consequently I have to snatch furtively the hours of the night, which now with winter approaching are growing longer, and try to dictate by candle light and thus through the labor of exegesis relieve a mind distraught. I am not boasting of our hospitality, as some may suspect, but simply explaining to you the delay.

The most profound Christian reflections on the fall of Rome came from Augustine (354–430). He began writing The City of God *to refute the charge that abandonment of the old pagan gods had brought about Rome's disasters; but the work turned onto a far-ranging meditation on human history and destiny.*

From R. H. Bainton, *The Medieval Church* (Princeton, N.J.: D. Van Nostrand, 1962), pp. 89–90.

Augustine. *The Two Cities*

God, desiring not only that the human race might be able by their similarity of nature to associate with one another, but also that they might be bound together in harmony and peace by the ties of relationship, was pleased to derive all men from one individual, and created man with such a nature that the members of the race should not have died, had not the two first (of whom the one was created out of nothing, and the other out of him) merited this by their disobedience; for by them so great a sin was committed, that by it the human nature was altered for the worse, and was transmitted also to their posterity, liable to sin and subject to death. And the kingdom of death so reigned over men, that the deserved penalty of sin would have hurled all headlong even into the second death, of which there is no end, had not the undeserved grace of God saved some therefrom. And thus it has come to pass, that though there are very many and great nations all over the earth, whose rites and customs, speech, arms, and dress, are distinguished by marked differences, yet there are no more than two kinds of human society, which we may justly call two cities, according to the language of our Scriptures. The one consists of those who wish to live after the flesh, the other of those who wish to live after the spirit; and when they severally achieve what they wish, they live in peace, each after their kind.

Of these two first parents of the human race, then, Cain was the first-born, and he belonged to the city of man; after him was born Abel, who belonged to the city of God. . . . Accordingly, it is recorded of Cain that he built a city, but Abel, being a sojourner, built none. For the city of the saints is above, although here below it begets citizens, in whom it sojourns till the time of its reign arrives, when it shall gather together all in the day of the resurrection; and then shall the promised kingdom be given to them, in which they shall reign with their Prince, the King of the ages, time without end.

But the earthly city, which shall not be everlasting (for it will no longer be a city when it has been committed to the extreme penalty), has its good in this world, and rejoices in it with such joy as such things can afford. But as this is not a good which can discharge its devotees of all distresses, this city is often divided against itself by litigations, wars, quarrels, and such victories as are either life-destroying or short-lived.

Thus the founder of the earthly city was a fratricide [Cain]. Overcome with envy, he slew his own brother, a citizen of the eternal city,

From Augustine, *The City of God*, M. Dods, trans. in *A Select Library of the Nicene and Post–Nicene Fathers* (Buffalo, N.Y.: The Christian Literature Co., 1887), Vol. 2, pp. 262, 284–285, 286–287, 412–413, 504.

and a sojourner on earth. So that we cannot be surprised that this first specimen, or, as the Greeks say, archetype of crime, should, long afterwards, find a corresponding crime at the foundation of that city which was destined to reign over so many nations, and be the head of this earthly city of which we speak. For of that city also, as one of their poets has mentioned, "the first walls were stained with a brother's blood," or, as Roman history records, Remus was slain by his brother Romulus. And thus there is no difference between the foundation of this city and of the earthly city, unless it be that Romulus and Remus were both citizens of the earthly city.

But the families which do not live by faith seek their peace in the earthly advantages of this life; while the families which live by faith look for those eternal blessings which are promised, and use as pilgrims such advantages of time and of earth as do not fascinate and divert them from God. . . . The earthly city, which does not live by faith, seeks an earthly peace, and the end it proposes, in the well-ordered concord of civic obedience and rule, is the combination of men's wills to attain the things which are helpful to this life. The heavenly city, or rather the part of it which sojourns on earth and lives by faith, makes use of this peace only because it must, until this mortal condition which necessitates it shall pass away. Consequently, so long as it lives like a captive and a stranger in the earthly city, though it has already received the promise of redemption, and the gift of the Spirit as the earnest of it, it makes no scruple to obey the laws of the earthly city, whereby the things necessary for the maintenance of this mortal life are administered; and thus, as this life is common to both cities, so there is a harmony between them in regard to what belongs to it. But, as the earthly city has had some philosophers whose doctrine is condemned by the divine teaching . . . it has come to pass that the two cities could not have common laws of religion, and that the heavenly city has been compelled in this matter to dissent, and to become obnoxious to those who think differently, and to stand the brunt of their anger and hatred and persecutions, except in so far as the minds of their enemies have been alarmed by the multitude of the Christians and quelled by the manifest protection of God accorded to them. This heavenly city, then, while it sojourns on earth, calls citizens out of all nations, and gathers together a society of pilgrims of all languages, not scrupling about diversities in the manners, laws, and institutions whereby earthly peace is secured and maintained, but recognizing that, however various these are, they all tend to one and the same end of earthly peace. It therefore is so far from rescinding and abolishing these diversities, that it even preserves and adopts them, so long only as no hindrance to the worship of the one supreme and true God is thus introduced. Even the heavenly city, therefore, while in its state of pilgrimage, avails itself of the peace of earth, and, so far as it can without injuring faith and godliness, desires and maintains a common agreement among men regarding the acquisition of the necessaries of life, and makes this earthly peace bear upon the peace of heaven; for this alone can be truly called and esteemed the peace of the reasonable creatures, consisting as it does in the perfectly ordered and harmonious enjoyment of God and of one another in God. When we shall have reached that peace, this mortal life shall give place to one that is eternal, and our body shall be no more this animal body which by its corruption weighs down the soul, but a spiritual body feeling no want.

Augustine's emphasis on the afterlife did not make him insensitive to the natural beauties of the earthly environment. He regarded them as gifts of God to man.

How can I tell of the rest of creation, with all its beauty and utility, which the divine goodness has given to man to please his eye and serve his purposes, condemned though he is, and hurled into these labors and miseries? Shall I speak of the manifold and various loveliness of sky, and earth, and sea; of the plentiful supply and wonderful qualities of the light; of sun, moon, and stars; of the shade of trees; of the colors and perfume of flowers; of the multitude of birds, all differing in plumage and in song; of the variety of animals, of which the smallest in size are often the most wonderful,—the works of ants and bees astonishing us more than the huge bodies of whales? Shall I speak of the sea, which itself is so grand a spectacle, when it arrays itself as it were in vestures of various colors, now running through every shade of green, and again becoming purple or blue? . . . How grateful is the alternation of day and night! how pleasant the breezes that cool the air! how abundant the supply of clothing furnished us by trees and animals! Who can enumerate all the blessings we enjoy?

In another work Augustine, departing from earlier cylical theories of time, saw all history as a progression of ages culminating in the Christian era.

Augustine. *The Six Ages of the World*

Five ages of the world, accordingly, having been now completed (there has entered the sixth). Of these ages the first is from the beginning of the human race, that is, from Adam, who was the first man that was made, down to Noah, who constructed the ark at the time of the flood. Then the second extends from that period on to Abraham, who was called the father indeed of all nations which should follow the example of his faith, but who at the same time in the way of natural descent from his own flesh was the father of the destined people of the Jews;

From Augustine, *On Catechizing the Uninstructed*, S. D. F. Salmond, trans. in *A Select Library of the Nicene and Post–Nicene Fathers* (Buffalo, N.Y.: The Christian Literature Publishing Co., 1887), p. 307.

which people, previous to the entrance of the Gentiles into the Christian faith, was the one people among all the nations of all lands that worshipped the one true God: from which people also Christ the Saviour was decreed to come according to the flesh. . . . the third age extends from Abraham on to David the king; the fourth from David on to that captivity whereby the people of God passed over into Babylonia; and the fifth from that transmigration down to the advent of our Lord Jesus Christ. With His coming the sixth age has entered on its process; so that now the spiritual grace, which in previous times was known to a few patriarchs and prophets, may be made manifest to all nations. . . . in order that in this sixth age the mind of man may be renewed after the image of God, even as on the sixth day man was made after the image of God.

Epilogue

From Edward Gibbon. *The Decline and Fall of the Roman Empire*

As the happiness of a *future* life is the great object of religion, we may hear, without surprise or scandal, that the introduction, or at least the abuse, of Christianity had some influence on the decline and fall of the Roman empire. The clergy successfully preached the doctrines of patience and pusillanimity; the active virtues of society were discouraged; and the last remains of the military spirit were buried in the cloister; a large portion of public and private wealth was consecrated to the specious demands of charity and devotion; and the soldiers' pay was lavished on the useless multitudes of both sexes, who could only plead the merits of abstinence and chastity. Faith, zeal, curiosity, and the more earthly passions of malice and ambition kindled the flame of theological discord; the church, and even the state, were distracted by religious factions, whose conflicts were sometimes bloody, and always implacable; the attention of the emperors was diverted from camps to synods; the Roman world was oppressed by a new species of tyranny; and the persecuted sects became the secret enemies of their country. Yet party-spirit, however pernicious or absurd, is a principle of union as well as of dissension. The bishops, from eighteen hundred pulpits, inculcated the duty of passive obedience to a lawful and orthodox sovereign; their frequent assemblies, and perpetual correspondence, maintained the communion of distant churches: and the benevolent temper of the gos-

From Edward Gibbon, *The History of the Decline and Fall of the Roman Empire*, J. B. Bury, ed. (London, 1901), Vol. 4, 162–163.

pel was strengthened, though confined, by the spiritual alliance of the Catholics. The sacred indolence of the monks was devoutly embraced by a servile and effeminate age; but, if superstition had not afforded a decent retreat, the same vices would have tempted the unworthy Romans to desert, from baser motives, the standard of the republic. Religious precepts are easily obeyed, which indulge and sanctify the natural inclinations of their votaries; but the pure and genuine influence of Christianity may be traced in its beneficial, though imperfect, effects on the Barbarian proselytes of the North. If the decline of the Roman empire was hastened by the conversion of Constantine, his victorious religion broke the violence of the fall, and mollified the ferocious temper of the conquerors.

VI

THE EARLY GERMANS—
SOCIETY AND CULTURE
A Roman Account
From Tacitus. *On Germany*
Laws and Customs
From *Laws of the Salian Franks*
From *Laws of the Burgundians*
A Germanic Hero-King
From *Beowulf*

CHRISTIAN INSTITUTIONS
The Papacy
From *Sermon of Leo I*
From Gelasius I. *Letter to Emperor Anastasius*
Monasticism
From *The Rule of St. Benedict*

ROMAN CHRISTIANITY AND
NORTHERN EUROPE
Gregory the Great as Teacher
From *Homily of Gregory I*
From *Pastoral Care*
Mission to England
Gregory I. *Letter to Mellitus*
From Bede. *Ecclesiastical History*
From Bede. *Ecclesiastical History*
Germany. Wilderness and Monasteries
Oath of Boniface
From *Life of Boniface*
From *Life of Sturmi*
Walafrid Strabo. *A Monastic Garden*

CHARLEMAGNE
Charlemagne and His Family
From Einhard. *Life of Charlemagne*
Economic Foundations
From *Capitulary De Villis*
Carolingian Government
From *General Capitulary for the Missi*

The Imperial Coronation
From Einhard. *Life of Charlemagne*
From *Annals of Lorsch*
From *Frankish Royal Annals*

A NEW EUROPE—BARBARIANS AND CHRISTIANS

*F*OR EDWARD GIBBON *the end of the Roman empire was simply a story of "decline and fall," a "triumph of barbarism and superstition." But, from another point of view, the settlement of the western provinces of the empire by barbarian invaders and their conversion to Christianity can be seen as the beginning of a new European civilization.*

The barbarians brought their own values—ideas about honor and law and family structure—that helped to shape the growth of Western society in the following centuries. The Christian church, surviving the fall of the empire, had enough vitality to assimilate these new peoples. For a time the genius for government that had characterized the Roman state in its best days seemed to pass to the Roman church. Great pontiffs like Leo I (440–461) and Gregory I (590–604) played major roles in civil as well as religious affairs. Christian monasteries, standing as islands of peaceful life through all the violence and disorders of the age, preserved in their libraries not only the writings of the Christian church fathers, but also much of the classical literature of ancient Rome.

The Anglo-Saxon peoples were converted to Christianity during the seventh century. Subsequently they sent out missionaries who carried their new religion to regions of central and eastern Germany that had never formed part of the old Roman empire. A new cultural entity was being formed that would later be called "Western Christendom." Its emergence was symbolized by the coronation of a great Germanic warrior king, Charlemagne, as head of a new Western empire in St. Peter's church, Rome, on Christmas Day in the year 800.

THE EARLY GERMANS—SOCIETY AND CULTURE

A Roman Account

The first detailed account of the German peoples was written by Tacitus in A.D. *98.*

From Tacitus. *On Germany*

Physical Characteristics For my own part, I agree with those who think that the tribes of Germany are free from all taint of intermarriages with foreign nations, and that they appear as a distinct, unmixed race, like none but themselves. Hence, too, the same physical peculiarities throughout so vast a population. All have fierce blue eyes, red hair, huge frames, fit only for a sudden exertion. They are less able to bear laborious work. Heat and thirst they cannot in the least endure; to cold and hunger their climate and their soil inure them. . . .

Government. Influence of Women They choose their kings by birth, their generals for merit. These kings have not unlimited or arbitrary power, and the generals do more by example than by authority. If they are energetic, if they are conspicuous, if they fight in the front, they lead because they are admired. But to reprimand, to imprison, even to flog, is permitted to the priests alone, and that not as a punishment, or at the general's bidding, but, as it were, by the mandate of the god whom they believe to inspire the warrior. They also carry with them into battle certain figures and images taken from their sacred groves. And what most stimulates their courage is, that their squadrons or battalions, instead of being formed by chance or by a fortuitous gathering, are composed of families and clans. Close by them, too, are those dearest to them, so that they hear the shrieks of women, the cries of infants. *They* are to every man the most sacred witnesses of his bravery—*they* are his most generous applauders. The soldier brings his wounds to mother and wife, who shrink not from counting or even de-

From Tacitus, *The Agricola and Germany*, A. J. Church and W. J. Brodribb, trans. (London: Macmillan, 1877), pp. 87–107.

manding them and who administer both food and encouragement to the combatants.

Councils About minor matters the chiefs deliberate, about the more important the whole tribe. Yet even when the final decision rests with the people, the affair is always thoroughly discussed by the chiefs. They assemble, except in the case of a sudden emergency, on certain fixed days, either at new or at full moon. . . . Then the king or the chief, according to age, birth, distinction in war, or eloquence, is heard, more because he has influence to persuade than because he has power to command. If his sentiments displease them, they reject them with murmurs; if they are satisfied, they brandish their spears. The most complimentary form of assent is to express approbation with their weapons. . . .

Punishments. Administration of Justice In their councils an accusation may be preferred or a capital crime prosecuted. Penalties are distinguished according to the offence. Traitors and deserters are hanged on trees; the coward, the unwarlike, the man stained with abominable vices, is plunged into the mire of the morass with a hurdle put over him. This distinction in punishment means that crime, they think, ought, in being punished, to be exposed, while infamy ought to be buried out of sight. Lighter offences, too, have penalties proportioned to them; he who is convicted, is fined in a certain number of horses or of cattle. Half of the fine is paid to the king or to the state, half to the person whose wrongs are avenged and to his relatives. In these same councils they also elect the chief magistrates, who administer law in the cantons and the towns. Each of these has a hundred associates chosen from the people, who support him with their advice and influence. . . .

Warlike Ardour of the People When they go into battle, it is a disgrace for the chief to be surpassed in valour, a disgrace for his followers not to equal the valour of the chief. And it is an infamy and a reproach for life to have survived the chief, and returned from the field. To defend, to protect him, to ascribe one's own brave deeds to his renown, is the height of loyalty. The chief fights for victory; his vassals fight for their chief. If their native state sinks into the sloth of prolonged peace and repose, many of its noble youths voluntarily seek those tribes which are waging some war, both because inaction is odious to their race, and because they win renown more readily in the midst of peril, and cannot maintain a numerous following except by violence and war. Indeed, men look to the liberality of their chief for their war-horse and their bloodstained and victorious lance. Feasts and entertainments, which, though inelegant, are plentifully furnished, are their only pay. The means of this bounty come from war and rapine. Nor are they as easily persuaded to plough the earth and to wait for the year's produce as to challenge an enemy and earn the honour of wounds. Nay, they actually think it tame and stupid to acquire by the sweat of toil what they might win by their blood.

Habits in Time of Peace   Whenever they are not fighting, they pass much of their time in the chase, and still more in idleness, giving themselves up to sleep and to feasting, the bravest and the most warlike doing nothing, and surrendering the management of the household, of the home, and of the land, to the woman, the old men, and all the weakest members of the family. They themselves lie buried in sloth, a strange combination in their nature that the same men should be so fond of idleness, so averse to peace. . . .

Marriage Laws   Their marriage code, however, is strict, and indeed no part of their manners is more praiseworthy. Almost alone among barbarians they are content with one wife, except a very few among them, and these not from sensuality, but because their noble birth procures for them many offers of alliance. The wife does not bring a dower to the husband, but the husband to the wife. The parents and relatives are present, and pass judgment on the marriage-gifts, gifts not meant to suit a woman's taste, nor such as a bride would deck herself with, but oxen, a caparisoned steed, a shield, a lance, and a sword. With these presents the wife is espoused, and she herself in her turn brings her husband a gift of arms. This they count their strongest bond of union, these their sacred mysteries, these their gods of marriage. Lest the woman should think herself to stand apart from aspirations after noble deeds and from the perils of war, she is reminded by the ceremony which inaugurates marriage that she is her husband's partner in toil and danger, destined to suffer and to dare with him alike both in peace and in war. The yoked oxen, the harnessed steed, the gift of arms, proclaim this fact. She must live and die with the feeling that she is receiving what she must hand down to her children neither tarnished nor depreciated, what future daughters-in-law may receive, and may be so passed on to her grandchildren.

Thus with their virtue protected they live uncorrupted by the allurements of public shows or the stimulant of feastings. Clandestine correspondence is equally unknown to men and women. Very rare for so numerous a population is adultery, the punishment for which is prompt, and in the husband's power. Having cut off the hair of the adulteress and stripped her naked, he expels her from the house in the presence of her kinsfolk, and then flogs her through the whole village. The loss of chastity meets with no indulgence; neither beauty, youth, nor wealth will procure the culprit a husband. No one in Germany laughs at vice, nor do they call it the fashion to corrupt and to be corrupted. . . .

Hereditary Feuds. Fines for Homicide. Hospitality It is a duty among them to adopt the feuds as well as the friendships of a father or a kinsman. These feuds are not implacable; even homicide is expiated by the payment of a certain number of cattle and of sheep, and the satisfaction is accepted by the entire family, greatly to the advantage of the state, since feuds are dangerous in proportion to a people's freedom.

No nation indulges more profusely in entertainments and hospitality. To exclude any human being from their roof is thought impious; every German, according to his means, receives his guest with a well-furnished table.

Laws and Customs

Surviving codes of customary law provide much evidence about the structure of early Germanic society.

From *Laws of the Salian Franks*

Title I. Concerning Summonses.

1. If any one be summoned before the "Thing"[1] by the king's law, and do not come, he shall be sentenced to 600 denars, which make 15 shillings (solidi).

Title III. Concerning Thefts of Cattle.

4. If any one steal that bull which rules the herd and never has been yoked, he shall be sentenced to 1800 denars, which make 45 shillings.

5. But if that bull is used for the cows of three villages in common, he who stole him shall be sentenced to three times 45 shillings.

6. If any one steal a bull belonging to the king he shall be sentenced to 3600 denars, which make 90 shillings.

Title XIII. Concerning Rape Committed by Freemen.

1. If three men carry off a free born girl, they shall be compelled to pay 30 shillings.

2. If there are more than three, each one shall pay 5 shillings.

[1] The folk assembly.

From E. F. Henderson, trans. in *Select Historical Documents of the Middle Ages* (London: George Bell and Sons, 1892), pp. 176–189.

3. Those who shall have been present with boats shall be sentenced to three shillings.

4. But those who commit rape shall be compelled to pay 2500 denars, which make 63 shillings.

Title XVII. Concerning Wounds.

1. If any one have wished to kill another person, and the blow have missed, he on whom it was proved shall be sentenced to 2500 denars, which make 63 shillings.

2. If any person have wished to strike another with a poisoned arrow, and the arrow have glanced aside, and it shall be proved on him: he shall be sentenced to 2500 denars, which make 63 shillings.

3. If any person strike another on the head so that the brain appears, and the three bones which lie above the brain shall project, he shall be sentenced to 1200 denars, which make 30 shillings.

4. But if it shall have been between the ribs or in the stomach, so that the wound appears and reaches to the entrails, he shall be sentenced to 1200 denars—which make 30 shillings—besides five shillings for the physician's pay.

Title XXIV. Concerning the Killing of Little Children and Women.

1. If any one have slain a boy under 10 years—up to the end of the tenth—and it shall have been proved on him, he shall be sentenced to 24000 denars, which make 600 shillings.

3. If any one have hit a free woman who is pregnant, and she dies, he shall be sentenced to 28000 denars, which makes 700 shillings.

6. If any one have killed a free woman after she has begun bearing children, he shall be sentenced to 24000 denars, which make 600 shillings.

7. After she can have no more children, he who kills her shall be sentenced to 8000 denars, which make 200 shillings.

Title XXX. Concerning Insults.

3. If any one, man or woman, shall have called a woman harlot, and shall not have been able to prove it, he shall be sentenced to 1800 denars, which make 45 shillings.

4. If any person shall have called another "fox," he shall be sentenced to 3 shillings.

5. If any man shall have called another "hare," he shall be sentenced to 3 shillings.

Title XLI. Concerning the Murder of Freemen.

1. If any one shall have killed a free Frank, or a barbarian living under the Salic law, and it have been proved on him, he shall be sentenced to 8000 denars.

2. But if he shall have thrown him into a well or into the water, or shall have covered him with branches or anything else, to conceal him, he shall be sentenced to 24000 denars, which make 600 shillings.

3. But if any one has slain a man who is in the service of the king, he shall be sentenced to 24000 denars, which make 600 shillings.

4. But if he have put him in the water or in a well, and covered him with anything to conceal him, he shall be sentenced to 72000 denars, which make 1800 shillings.

5. If any one have slain a Roman who eats in the king's palace, and it have been proved on him, he shall be sentenced to 12000 denars, which make 300 shillings.

6. But if the Roman shall not have been a landed proprietor and table companion of the king, he who killed him shall be sentenced to 4000 denars, which make 100 shillings.

Title LIX. Concerning Private Property.

1. If any man die and leave no sons, if the father and mother survive, they shall inherit.

2. If the father and mother do not survive, and he leave brothers or sisters, they shall inherit.

3. But if there are none, the sisters of the father shall inherit.

4. But if there are no sisters of the father, the sisters of the mother shall claim that inheritance.

5. If there are none of these, the nearest relatives on the father's side shall succeed to that inheritance.

6. But of Salic land no portion of the inheritance shall come to a woman: but the whole inheritance of the land shall come to the male sex.

Title LXII. Concerning Wergeld.

1. If any one's father have been killed, the sons shall have half the compounding money (wergeld); and the other half the nearest relatives, as well on the mother's as on the father's side, shall divide among themselves.

2. But if there are no relatives, paternal or maternal, that portion shall go to the fisc.

The laws of other German peoples contain parallel provisions regulating family affairs and inheritances, with variations of detail from people to people.

From *Laws of the Burgundians*

Of the Stealing of Girls.

1. If anyone shall steal a girl, let him be compelled to pay the price set for such a girl ninefold, and let him pay a fine to the amount of twelve solidi.

Of Succession.

1. Among Burgundians we wish it to be observed that if anyone does not leave a son, let a daughter succeed to the inheritance of the father and mother in place of the son.

Of Burgundian Women Entering a Second or Third Marriage.

1. If any Burgundian woman, as is the custom, enters a second or third marriage after the death of her husband, and she has children by each husband, let her possess the marriage gift (*donatio nuptialis*) in usufruct while she lives; after her death, let what his father gave her be given to each son, with the further provision that the mother has the power neither of giving, selling, or transferring any of the things which she received in the marriage gift.

2. If by chance the woman has no children, after her death let her relatives receive half of whatever has come to her by way of marriage gift, and let the relatives of the dead husband who was the donor receive half.

3. But if perchance children shall have been born and they shall have died after the death of their father, we command that the inheritance of the husband or children belong wholly to the mother.

Of Women Violated.

1. Whatever native freeman does violence to a maidservant, and force can be proved, let him pay twelve solidi to him to whom the maidservant belongs.

2. If a slave does this, let him receive a hundred fifty blows.

Of Divorces.

1. If any woman leaves (puts aside) her husband to whom she is legally married, let her be smothered in mire.

From *The Burgundian Code*, Katherine Fischer, trans. (Philadelphia, Pa.: University of Pennsylvania Press, 1949), pp. 31, 32, 40, 45, 46, 85. Reprinted by permission of the publisher.

2. If anyone wishes to put away his wife without cause, let him give her another payment such as he gave for her marriage price, and let the amount of the fine be twelve solidi.

3. If by chance a man wishes to put away his wife, and is able to prove one of these three crimes against her, that is, adultery, witchcraft, or violation of graves, let him have full right to put her away: and let the judge pronounce the sentence of the law against her, just as should be done against criminals.

4. But if she admits none of these three crimes, let no man be permitted to put away his wife for any other crime. But if he chooses, he may go away from the home, leaving all household property behind, and his wife with their children may possess the property of her husband.

Of Women Who Go to Their Husbands Voluntarily.

If any woman, Burgundian or Roman, gives herself voluntarily in marriage to a husband, we order that the husband have the property of that woman; just as he has power over her, so also over her property and all her possessions.

A Germanic Hero-King

At the end of the Anglo-Saxon epic Beowulf, *the hero ("lord of the Geats") fights to the death with a monstrous fire-breathing dragon who guards a great treasure-hoard. The story of* Beowulf *illustrates early Germanic ideals of conduct with vivid force.*

From *Beowulf*

Stout-hearted he shouted; his voice went roaring, clear in battle, in under the gray stone. Hate was stirred up, the hoard's guard knew the voice of a man. No more time was there to ask for peace. First the monster's breath came out of the stone, the hot war-steam. The earth resounded. The man below the barrow, the lord of the Geats, swung his shield against the dreadful visitor. Then the heart of the coiled thing was aroused to seek combat. The good war-king had drawn his sword, the old heirloom, not blunt of edge. To each of them as they threatened destruction there was terror of the other. Firm-hearted he stood with his shield high, the lord of friends, while quickly the worm coiled itself; he waited in his armor. Then, coiling in flames, he came gliding on, hastening to his fate. The good shield protected the life and body of the famous prince, but for a shorter while than his wish was. There for the first time, the first day in his life, he might not prevail, since fate did not assign him such glory in battle. The lord of the Geats raised his hand, struck the shining horror so with his forged blade that the edge failed, bright on the bone, bit less surely than its folk-king had need, hard-pressed in perils. Then because of the battle-stroke the barrow-ward's heart was savage, he exhaled death-fire—the war-flames sprang wide. The gold-friend of the Geats boasted of no great victories: the war blade had failed, naked at need, as it ought not to have done, iron good from old times. That was no pleasant journey, not one on which the famous son of Ecgtheow would wish to leave his land; against his will he must take up a dwelling-place elsewhere—as every man must give up the days that are lent him.

It was not long until they came together again, dreadful foes. The hoard-guard took heart, once more his breast swelled with his breathing. Encircled with flames, he who before had ruled a folk felt harsh pain. Nor did his companions, sons of nobles, take up their stand in a troop about him with the courage of fighting men, but they crept to the wood, protected their lives. In only one of them the heart surged with sorrows: nothing can ever set aside kinship in him who means well.

He was called Wiglaf, son of Weohstan, a rare shield-warrior, a man of the Scylfings, kinsman of Aelfhere. He saw his liege lord under his war-mask suffer the heat. Then he was mindful of the honors he had given him before, the rich dwelling-place of the Waegmundings, every folk-right such as his father possessed. He might not then hold back, his hand seized his shield, the yellow linden-wood; he drew his ancient sword. . . .

Wiglaf spoke, said many fit words to his companions—his mind was mournful: "I remember that time we drank mead, when we promised our lord in the beer-hall—him who gave us these rings—that we would repay him for the war-arms if a need like this befell him—the helmets and the hard swords. Of his own will he chose us among the host for this venture, thought us worthy of fame—and gave me these treasures—because he counted us good war-makers, brave helm-bearers, though our lord intended to do this work of courage alone, as keeper of the folk, because among men he had performed the greatest deeds of glory, daring actions. Now the day has come that our liege lord has need of the strength of good fighters. Let us go to him, help our war-chief while the grim terrible fire persists. God knows of me that I should rather that the flame enfold my body with my gold-giver. It does not seem right to me for us to bear our shields home again unless we can first fell the foe, defend the life of the prince of the Weather-Geats. I know well that it would be no recompense for past deeds that he alone of the company of the Geats should suffer pain, fall in the fight. For us both shall there be a part in the work of sword and helmet, of battle-shirt and war-clothing."

Then he waded through the deadly smoke, bore his war-helmet to the aid of his king, spoke in few words: "Beloved Beowulf, do all well, for, long since in your youth, you said that you would not let your glory fail while you lived. Now, great-spirited noble, brave of deeds, you must protect your life with all your might. I shall help you."

After these words, the worm came on, angry, the terrible malice-filled foe, shining with surging flames, to seek for the second time his enemies, hated men. Fire advanced in waves; shield burned to the boss; mail-shirt might give no help to the young spear-warrior; but the young man went quickly under his kinsman's shield when his own was consumed with flames. Then the war-king was again mindful of fame, struck with his war-sword with great strength so that it stuck in the head-bone, driven with force: Naegling broke, the sword of Beowulf failed in the fight, old and steel-gray. It was not ordained for him that iron edges might help in the combat. Too strong was the hand that I have heard strained every sword with its stroke, when he bore wound-hardened weapon to battle: he was none the better for it.

Then for the third time the folk-harmer, the fearful fire-dragon, was mindful of feuds, set upon the brave one when the chance came, hot and battle-grim seized all his neck with his sharp fangs: he was smeared with life-blood, gore welled out in waves. . . .

Then the wound that the earth-dragon had caused began to burn and to swell; at once he felt dire evil boil in his breast, poison within him. Then the prince, wise of thought, went to where he might sit on a seat near the wall. He looked on the work of giants, how the timeless earth-hall held within it stone-arches fast on pillars. Then with his hands the thane, good without limit, washed him with water, blood-besmeared, the famous prince, his beloved lord, sated with battle; and he unfastened his helmet.

Beowulf spoke—despite his wounds spoke, his mortal hurts. He knew well he had lived out his days' time, joy on earth; all passed was the number of his days, death very near. "Now I would wish to give my son my war-clothing, if any heir after me, part of my flesh, were granted. I held this people fifty winters. There was no folk-king of those dwelling about who dared approach me with swords, threaten me with fears. In my land I awaited what fate brought me, held my own well, sought no treacherous quarrels, nor did I swear many oaths unrightfully. Sick with life-wounds, I may have joy of all this, for the Ruler of Men need not blame me for the slaughter of kinsmen when life goes from my body. Now quickly go to look at the hoard under the gray stone, beloved Wiglaf, now that the worm lies sleeping from sore wounds, bereft of his treasure. Be quick now, so that I may see the ancient wealth, the golden things, may clearly look on the bright curious gems, so that for that, because of the treasure's richness, I may the more easily leave life and nation I have long held."

Then sorrow came to the young man that he saw him whom he most loved on the earth, at the end of his life, suffering piteously. His slayer likewise lay dead, the awful earth-dragon bereft of life, overtaken by evil. No longer should the coiled worm rule the ring-hoard, for iron edges had taken him, hard and battle-sharp work of the hammers, so that the wide-flier, stilled by wounds, had fallen on the earth near the treasure-house. He did not go flying through the air at midnight, proud of his property, showing his aspect, but he fell to earth through the work of the chief's hands. Yet I have heard of no man of might on land, though he was bold of every deed, whom it should prosper to rush against the breath of the venomous foe or disturb with hands the ring-hall, if he found the guard awake who lived in the barrow. The share of the rich treasures became Beowulf's, paid for by death: each of the two had journeyed to the end of life's loan.

Then it was not long before the battle-slack ones left the woods, ten weak troth-breakers together, who had not dared fight with their spears in their liege lord's great need. But they bore their shields, ashamed, their war-clothes, to where the old man lay, looked on Wiglaf. He sat wearied, the foot-soldier near the shoulders of his lord, would waken him with water: it gained him nothing. He might not, though he much wished it, hold life in his chieftain on earth nor change anything of the Ruler's: the judgment of God would control the deeds of every man, just as it still does now. Then it was easy to get from the young man a grim answer to him who before had lost courage. Wiglaf spoke, the son of Weohstan, a man sad at heart, looked on the unloved ones:

"Yes, he who will speak truth may say that the liege lord who gave you treasure, the war-gear that you stand in there, when he used often to hand out to hall-sitters on the ale-benches, a prince to his thanes, helmets and war-shirts such as he could find mightiest anywhere, both far and near—that he quite threw away the war-gear, to his distress when war came upon him. The folk-king had no need to boast of his war-comrades. Yet God, Ruler of Victories, granted him that he might avenge himself, alone with his sword, when there was need for his courage. I was able to give him little life-protection in the fight, and yet beyond my power I did begin to help my kinsman. The deadly foe was ever the weaker after I struck him with my sword, fire poured less strongly from his head. Too few defenders thronged about the prince when the hard time came upon him. Now there shall cease for your race the receiving of treasure and the giving of swords, all enjoyment of pleasant homes, comfort. Each man of your kindred must go deprived of his land-right when nobles from afar learn of your flight, your inglorious deed. Death is better for any earl than a life of blame."

Then the people of the Geats made ready for him a funeral pyre on the earth, no small one, hung with helmets, battle-shields, bright mail-shirts, just as he had asked. Then in the midst they laid the great prince, lamenting their hero, their beloved lord. Then warriors began to awaken on the barrow the greatest of funeral-fires; the wood-smoke climbed, black over the fire; the roaring flame mixed with weeping—the wind-surge died down—until it had broken the bone-house, hot at its heart. Sad in spirit they lamented their heart-care, the death of their liege lord. And the Geatish woman, wavy-haired, sang a sorrowful song about Beowulf, said again and again that she sorely feared for herself invasions of armies, many slaughters, terror of troops, humiliation, and captivity. Heaven swallowed the smoke.

Then the people of the Weather-Geats built a mound on the promontory, one that was high and broad, wide-seen by seafarers, and in ten days completed a monument for the bold in battle, surrounded the remains of the fire with a wall, the most splendid that men most skilled might devise. In the barrow they placed rings and jewels, all such ornaments as troubled men had earlier taken from the hoard. They let the earth hold the wealth of earls, gold in the ground, where now it still dwells, as useless to men as it was before. Then the brave in battle rode round the mound, children of nobles, twelve in all, would bewail their sorrow and mourn their king, recite dirges and speak of the man. They praised his great deeds and his acts of courage, judged well of his powers. So it is fitting that man honor his liege lord with words, love him in heart when he must be led forth from the body. Thus the people of the Geats, his hearth-companions, lamented the death of their lord. They said that he was of world-kings the mildest of men and the gentlest, kindest to his people, and most eager for fame.

CHRISTIAN INSTITUTIONS

The Papacy

From early days the church of Rome was respected as the see of Peter and as the church of the imperial capital. Leo I (440–461) emphasized a doctrine of Roman primacy based on the pope's role as successor of St. Peter.

From *Sermon of Leo I*

For the solidity of that faith which was praised in the chief of the Apostles is perpetual: and as that remains which Peter believed in Christ, so that remains which Christ instituted in Peter. For when, as has been read in the Gospel lesson, the Lord had asked the disciples whom they believed Him to be amid the various opinions that were held, and the blessed Peter had replied, saying, "Thou art the Christ, the Son of the living God," the Lord says, "Blessed art thou, Simon Bar-Jona, because flesh and blood hath not revealed it to thee, but My Father, which is in heaven. And I say to thee, that thou art Peter, and upon this rock will I build My church, and the gates of Hades shall not prevail against it. And I will give unto thee the keys of the kingdom of heaven. And whatsoever thou shalt bind on earth, shall be bound in heaven; and whatsoever thou shalt loose on earth, shall be loosed also in heaven."

The dispensation of Truth therefore abides, and the blessed Peter persevering in the strength of the Rock, which he has received, has not abandoned the helm of the Church, which he undertook. For he was ordained before the rest in such a way that from his being called the Rock, from his being pronounced the Foundation, from his being constituted the Doorkeeper on the kingdom of heaven, from his being set as the Umpire to bind and to loose, whose judgments shall retain their validity in heaven, from all these mystical titles we might know the nature of his association with Christ. And still to-day he more fully and effectually performs what is entrusted to him, and carries out every part of his duty and charge in Him and with Him, through Whom he

From *Sermon of Leo the Great*, C. L. Feltoe, trans. in *Library of Nicene and Post–Nicene Fathers,* Second Series, (New York: Christian Literature Co., 1895), Vol. 12, p. 117.

has been glorified. And so if anything is rightly done and rightly decreed by us, if anything is won from the mercy of God by our daily supplications, it is of his work and merits whose power lives and whose authority prevails in his See.

Pope Gelasius I (492–496) made an important declaration on the right relationship between papal and imperial government.

From Gelasius I. *Letter to Emperor Anastasius*

... Two there are, august emperor, by which this world is chiefly ruled, the sacred authority [*auctoritas*] of the priesthood and the royal power [*potestas*]. Of these the responsibility of the priests is more weighty in so far as they will answer for the kings of men themselves at the divine judgement. You know, most clement son, that, although you take precedence over all mankind in dignity, nevertheless you piously bow the neck to those who have charge of divine affairs and seek from them the means of your salvation, and hence you realize that, in the order of religion, in matters concerning the reception and right administration of the heavenly sacraments, you ought to submit yourself rather than rule, and that in these matters you should depend on their judgement rather than seek to bend them to your will. For if the bishops themselves, recognizing that the imperial office was conferred on you by divine disposition, obey your laws so far as the sphere of public order is concerned lest they seem to obstruct your decrees in mundane matters, with what zeal, I ask you, ought you to obey those who have been charged with administering the sacred mysteries? Moreover, just as no light risk attends pontiffs who keep silent in matters concerning the service of God, so too no little danger threatens those who show scorn—which God forbid—when they ought to obey. And if the hearts of the faithful should be submitted to all priests in general who rightly administer divine things, how much more should assent be given to the bishop of that see which the Most High wished to be preeminent over all priests, and which the devotion of the whole church has honored ever since. As Your Piety is certainly well aware, no one can ever raise himself by purely human means to the privilege and place of him whom the voice of Christ has set before all, whom the church has always venerated and held in devotion as its primate. The things which are established by divine judgement can be assailed by human presumption; they cannot be overthrown by anyone's power.

Monasticism

The most enduring pattern of western monasticism was established by Benedict of Nursia (c. 480–543).

From *The Rule of St. Benedict*

Prologue ... we are about to found, therefore, a school for the Lord's service; in the organization of which we trust that we shall ordain nothing severe and nothing burdensome. But even if, the demands of justice dictating it, something a little irksome shall be the result, for the purpose of amending vices or preserving charity;—thou shalt not therefore, struck by fear, flee the way of salvation, which can not be entered upon except through a narrow entrance. But as one's way of life and one's faith progresses, the heart becomes broadened, and, with the unutterable sweetness of love, the way of the mandates of the Lord is traversed. Thus, never departing from His guidance, continuing in the monastery in His teaching until death, through patience we are made partakers in Christ's passion, in order that we may merit to be companions in His kingdom. ...

What the Abbot Should Be Like   An abbot who is worthy to preside over a monastery ought always to remember what he is called, and carry out with his deeds the name of a Superior. For he is believed to be Christ's representative, since he is called by His name, the apostle saying: "Ye have received the spirit of adoption of sons, whereby we call Abba, Father." And so the abbot should not—grant that he may not—teach, or decree, or order, any thing apart from the precept of the Lord; but his order or teaching should be sprinkled with the ferment of divine justice in the minds of his disciples. Let the abbot always be mindful that, at the tremendous judgment of God, both things will be weighed in the balance: his teaching and the obedience of his disciples. And let the abbot know that whatever the father of the family finds of less utility among the sheep is laid to the fault of the shepherd. ... Therefore, when any one receives the name of abbot, he ought to rule over his disciples with a double teaching; that is, let him show forth all good and holy things by deeds more than by words. ... He shall make no distinction of persons in the monastery. One shall not be more cherished than another, unless it be the one whom he finds excelling in good works or in obedience. A free-born man shall

From E. F. Henderson, trans. in *Select Historical Documents of the Middle Ages* (London: George Bell and Sons, 1892), pp. 176–189.

not be preferred to one coming from servitude, unless there be some other reasonable cause. . . . for whether we be bond or free we are one in Christ; and, under one God, we perform an equal service of subjection; for God is no respecter of persons. . . . In his teaching indeed the abbot ought always to observe that form laid down by the apostle when he says: "reprove, rebuke, exhort." That is, mixing seasons with seasons, blandishments with terrors, let him display the feeling of a severe yet devoted master. He should, namely, rebuke more severely the unruly and the turbulent. The obedient, moreover, and the gentle and the patient, he should exhort, that they may progress to higher things. But the negligent and scorners, we warn him to admonish and reprove. . . .

About Calling in the Brethren to Take Council   As often as anything especial is to be done in the monastery, the abbot shall call together the whole congregation, and shall himself explain the question at issue. And, having heard the advice of the brethren, he shall think it over by himself, and shall do what he considers most advantageous.

Concerning Obedience   The first grade of humility is obedience without delay. This becomes those who, on account of the holy service which they have professed, or on account of the fear of hell or the glory of eternal life, consider nothing dearer to them than Christ: so that, so soon as anything is commanded by their superior, they may not know how to suffer delay in doing it, even as if it were a divine command. Concerning whom the Lord said: "As soon as he heard of me he obeyed me."

Concerning Humility . . . The sixth grade of humility is, that a monk be contented with all lowliness or extremity, and consider himself, with regard to everything which is enjoined on him, as a poor and unworthy workman; saying to himself with the prophet: "I was reduced to nothing and was ignorant; I was made as the cattle before thee, and I am always with thee." The seventh grade of humility is, not only that he, with his tongue, pronounce himself viler and more worthless than all; but that he also believe it in the innermost workings of his heart; humbling himself and saying with the prophet, etc. . . . The eighth degree of humility is that a monk do nothing except what the common rule of the monastery, or the example of his elders, urges him to do. . . .

How Divine Service Shall Be Held Through the Day   As the prophet says: "Seven times in the day do I praise Thee." Which sacred number of seven will thus be fulfilled by us if, at matins, at the first, third, sixth, ninth hours, at vesper time and at "completorium" we perform the duties of our service; for it is of these hours of the day that he said: "Seven times in the day do I praise Thee."[1] For, concerning nocturnal vigils, the same prophet says: "At midnight I arose to confess unto thee." Therefore, at these times, let us give thanks to our Creator concerning the judgments of his righteousness; that is, at matins, etc. . . . , and at night we will rise and confess to him. . . .

How the Monks Shall Sleep   They shall sleep separately in separate beds. They shall receive positions for their beds, after the manner of their characters, according to the dispensation of their abbot. If it can be done, they shall all sleep in one place. If, however, their number do not permit it, they shall rest by tens or twenties, with elders who will concern themselves about them. A candle shall always be burning in that same cell until early in the morning. They shall sleep clothed, and girt with belts or with ropes; and they shall not have their knives at their sides while they sleep, lest perchance in a dream they should wound the sleepers. And let the monks be always on the alert; and, when the signal is given, rising without delay, let them hasten to mutually prepare themselves for the service of God—with all gravity and modesty, however. The younger brothers shall not have beds by themselves, but interspersed among those of the elder ones. And when they rise for the service of God, they shall exhort each other mutually with moderation on account of the excuses that those who are sleepy are inclined to make.

Whether the Monks Should Have Anything of Their Own   More than anything else is this special vice to be cut off root and branch from the monastery, that one should presume to give or receive anything without the order of the abbot, or should have anything of his own. He should have absolutely not anything: neither a book, nor tablets, nor a pen—nothing at all.—For indeed it is not allowed to the monks to have their own bodies or wills in their own power. But all things necessary they must expect from the Father of the monastery; nor is it allowable to have anything which the abbot did not give or permit. All things shall be common to all, as it is written: "Let not any man presume or call anything his own." But if any one shall have been discovered delighting in this most evil vice: being warned once and again, if he do not amend, let him be subjected to punishment. . . .

[1] "Completorium" or "compline" was the last prayer of the evening before the monks went to bed. Then they rose during the night for "Vigils."

Concerning Old Age and Infancy ... Although human nature it-self is prone to have pity for these ages—that is, old age and infancy—nevertheless the authority of the Rule also has regard for them. Their weakness shall always be considered, and in the matter of food, the strict tenor of the Rule shall by no means be observed, as far as they are concerned; but they shall be treated with pious consideration, and may anticipate the canonical hours. ...

Concerning the Amount of Food ... We believe, moreover, that, for the daily refection of the sixth as well as of the ninth hour, two cooked dishes, on account of the infirmities of the different ones, are enough for all tables: so that whoever, perchance, can not eat of one may par-take of the other. Therefore let two cooked dishes suffice for all the brothers: and, if it is possible to obtain apples or growing vegetables, a third may be added. One full pound of bread shall suffice for a day, whether there be one refection, or a breakfast and a supper. ... But to younger boys the same quantity shall not be served, but less than that to the older ones; moderation being observed in all things. But the eating of the flesh of quadrupeds shall be abstained from altogether by every one, excepting alone the weak and the sick.

Concerning the Amount of Drink Each one has his own gift from God, the one in this way, the other in that. Therefore it is with some hesitation that the amount of daily sustenance for others is fixed by us. Nevertheless, in view of the weakness of the infirm we believe that a hemina of wine a day is enough for each one. Those moreover to whom God gives the ability of bearing abstinence shall know that they will have their own reward. But the prior shall judge if either the needs of the place, or labour or the heat of summer, requires more; considering in all things lest satiety or drunkenness creep in. Indeed we read that wine is not suitable for monks at all. But because, in our day, it is not possible to persuade the monks of this, let us agree at least as to the fact that we should not drink till we are sated, but sparingly. For wine can make even the wise to go astray. Where, moreover, the necessities of the place are such that the amount written above can not be found—but much less or nothing at all—those who live there shall bless God and shall not murmur. And we admonish them to this above all: that they be without murmuring. ...

Concerning the Daily Manual Labour Idleness is the enemy of the soul. And therefore, at fixed times, the brothers ought to be occupied in manual labour; and again, at fixed times, in sacred reading. ... Above all there shall certainly be appointed one or two elders, who shall go round the monastery at the hours in which the brothers are engaged in reading, and see to it that no troublesome brother chance to be found who is open to idleness and trifling, and is not intent on his reading; being not only of no use to himself, but also stirring up others.

Concerning Clothes and Shoes ... Vestments shall be given to the brothers according to the quality of the places where they dwell, or the temperature of the air. For in cold regions more is required; but in warm, less. This, therefore, is a matter for the abbot to decide. We nevertheless consider that for ordinary places there suffices for the monks a cowl and gown apiece—the cowl, in winter hairy, in summer plain or old—and a working garment, on account of their labours. As clothing for the feet, shoes and boots. . . .

Concerning the Manner of Receiving Brothers When any new comer applies for conversion, an easy entrance shall not be granted him: but, as the apostle says, "Try the spirits if they be of God." Therefore, if he who comes perseveres in knocking, and is seen after four or five days to patiently endure the insults inflicted upon him, and the difficulty of ingress, and to persist in his demand: entrance shall be allowed him, and he shall remain for a few days in the cell of the guests. After this, moreover, he shall be in the cell of the novices, where he shall meditate and eat and sleep. . . . If he promise perseverance in his steadfastness, after the lapse of two months this Rule shall be read to him in order, and it shall be said to him: Behold the law under which thou dost wish to serve; if thou canst observe it, enter; but if thou canst not, depart freely. And, after the lapse of six months, the Rule shall be read to him; that he may know upon what he is entering. And, if he stand firm thus far, after four months the same Rule shall again be re-read to him. And if, having deliberated with himself, he shall promise to keep everything, and to obey all the commands that are laid upon him: then he shall be received in the congregation; knowing that it is decreed, by the law of the Rule, that from that day he shall not be allowed to depart from the monastery, nor to shake free his neck from the yoke of the Rule, which, after such tardy deliberation, he was at liberty either to refuse or receive. . . .

Concerning the Ordination of An Abbot In ordaining an abbot this consideration shall always be observed: that such a one shall be put into office as the whole congregation, according to the fear of God, with one heart—or even a part, however small, of the congregation with more prudent counsel—shall have chosen. He who is to be ordained, moreover, shall be elected for merit of life and learnedness in wisdom; even though he be the lowest in rank in the congregation. But even if the whole congregation with one consent shall have elected a person consenting to their vices—which God forbid;—and those vices shall in any way come clearly to the knowledge of the bishop to whose diocese that place pertains, or to the neighbouring abbots or Christians: the latter shall not allow the consent of the wicked to prevail, but shall set up a dispenser worthy of the house of God; knowing that they will receive a good reward for this, if they do it chastely and with zeal for God. Just so they shall know, on the contrary, that they have sinned if they neglect it.

ROMAN CHRISTIANITY AND NORTHERN EUROPE

Gregory the Great as Teacher

The greatest of the early medieval popes, Pope Gregory I (590–604), living in the ruins of the Roman empire, was convinced that the last days of the world were at hand.

From *Homily of Gregory I*

[Of all the signs described by our Lord as presaging the end of the world], some we see already accomplished; the others we dread as close upon us. For we now see that nation rises against nation, and that they press and weigh upon the land in our own times as never before in the annals of the past. Earthquakes overwhelm countless cities, as we often hear from other parts of the world. Pestilence we endure without interruption. It is true that as yet we do not behold signs in the sun and moon and stars; but that these are not far off we may infer from the changes in the atmosphere. Before Italy was given over to be desolated by the sword of a heathen foe, we beheld fiery ranks in heaven, and even the streaming blood of the human race as it was afterwards spilt.

From J. H. Robinson, trans. in *Readings in European History* (Boston, Mass.: Ginn and Co., 1904), Vol. 1, pp. 75–76.

Although he thought the world was coming to an end, Gregory labored to spread Christianity in the time that remained. His Pastoral Care, *a book of guidance for bishops, was translated into several languages, including Anglo-Saxon.*

From *Pastoral Care*

The conduct of a prelate should so far surpass the conduct of the people, as the life of a pastor sets him apart from his flock. For one who is so regarded that the people are called his flock, must carefully consider how necessary it is for him to maintain a life of rectitude. It is

From *St. Gregory the Great, Pastoral Care*, trans. and annot. by Henry Davis, S. J. in *The Ancient Christian Writers* Series (Westminster, Md.: The Newman Press, 1950), pp. 45, 61, 64, 77, 79. Reprinted by permission of Paulist Press.

necessary, therefore, that he should be pure in thought, exemplary in conduct, discreet in keeping silence, profitable in speech, in sympathy a near neighbour to everyone, in contemplation exalted above all others, a humble companion to those who lead good lives, erect in his zeal for righteousness against the vices of sinners. He must not be remiss in his care for the inner life by preoccupation with the external; nor must he in his solicitude for what is internal, fail to give attention to the external.

Often, however, a ruler by the very fact of his preeminence over others becomes conceited; and because everything is at his service, because his orders are quickly executed to suit his wishes, because all his subjects praise him for what he has done well, but have no authority to criticise what he has done amiss and because they usually praise even what they ought to blame, his mind, led astray by those below him, is lifted above itself. While he is outwardly surrounded by abounding favours, the truth within him is made void.

Consequently, humility must be preserved in the heart, and discipline in action. Between these two, we must diligently beware not to relax the rights of government by immoderate adherence to the virtue of humility, for if the superior depreciates himself unduly, he may be unable to restrain the lives of subjects under the bond of discipline. Let rulers, therefore, uphold externally what they undertake for the service of others, and internally retain their fear in their estimate of themselves. Nevertheless, let the subjects themselves perceive, by signs becomingly manifested, that their rulers are humble in their own estimation. They should thus apprehend both what they ought to fear from authority, and what to imitate in the sphere of humility.

It should also be observed that at times the faults of subjects must be prudently overlooked, but they should be given to understand that they are being overlooked. Sometimes even what is openly known should be judiciously tolerated, while in other cases even hidden faults must be subjected to a close scrutiny; and, as the case may be, they should be either gently reproved or sharply censured.

It is also to be observed that good rulers should wish to please men, but so as to draw their neighbours to the love of truth by the fair esteem they have of their rulers, not that these long to be loved themselves, but wish that this love should be a road, as it were, whereby they lead the hearts of the hearers to the love of the Creator. It is difficult for one who is not loved, however well he preaches, to find a sympathetic hearing. Wherefore, he who rules ought to aim at being loved, that he may be listened to, and yet not seek to be loved on his own account, lest he be discovered to rebel in the tyranny of his thought against Him whom he ostensibly serves in his office.

Mission to England

In 596 Gregory sent a group of monks led by Augustine—the first archbishop of Canterbury—to convert the pagan English. Later (601) he sent instructions about the conduct of the mission.

From Gregory I. *Letter to Mellitus*

When Almighty God shall have brought you to our most reverend brother the bishop Augustine, tell him that I have long been considering with myself about the case of the Angli; to wit, that the temples of idols in that nation should not be destroyed, but that the idols themselves that are in them should be. Let blessed water be prepared, and sprinkled in these temples, and altars constructed, and relics deposited, since, if these same temples are well built, it is needful that they should be transferred from the worship of idols to the service of the true God; that, when the people themselves see that these temples are not destroyed, they may put away error from their heart and, knowing and adoring the true God, may have recourse with the more familiarity to the places they have been accustomed to. And, since they are wont to kill many oxen in sacrifice to demons, they should have also some solemnity of this kind in a changed form, so that on the day of dedication, or on the anniversaries of the holy martyrs whose relics are deposited there, they may make for themselves tents of the branches of trees around these temples that have been changed into churches, and celebrate the solemnity with religious feasts. Nor let them any longer sacrifice animals to the devil, but slay animals to the praise of God for their own eating, and return thanks to the Giver of all for their fulness, so that, while some joys are reserved to them outwardly, they may be able the more easily to incline their minds to inward joys. For it is undoubtedly impossible to cut away everything at once from hard hearts, since one who strives to ascend to the highest place must needs rise by steps or paces, and not by leaps.

From *Selected Epistles of Gregory the Great,* J. Barmby, trans. in *Library of Nicene and Post–Nicene Fathers,* Second Series (New York: Christian Literature Co., 1895), Vol. 13, pp. 84–85.

The Roman missionary Paulinus preached before King Edwin of Northumbria in 627. This story suggests something of the appeal of the new religion.

From Bede. *Ecclesiastical History*

Paulinus consenting, the king did as he said; for, holding a council with the wise men, he asked of every one in particular what he thought

From *Bede's Ecclesiastical History of England,* A. M. Sellar, trans. (London: George Bell and Sons, 1907), pp. 116–117.

of this doctrine hitherto unknown to them, and the new worship of God that was preached? . . . [One of the chief men replied] "The present life of man upon earth, O king, seems to me, in comparison with that time which is unknown to us, like to the swift flight of a sparrow through the house wherein you sit at supper in winter, with your ealdormen and thegns, while the fire blazes in the midst, and the hall is warmed, but the wintry storms of rain or snow are raging abroad. The sparrow, flying in at one door and immediately out of another, whilst he is within, is safe from the wintry tempest; but after a short space of fair weather, he immediately vanishes out of your sight, passing from winter into winter again. So this life of man appears for a little while, but of what is to follow or what went before we know nothing at all. If, therefore, this new doctrine tells us something more certain, it seems justly to deserve to be followed." The other elders and king's counsellors, by Divine prompting, spoke to the same effect.

But Coifi added, that he wished more attentively to hear Paulinus discourse concerning the God Whom he preached. When he did so, at the king's command, Coifi, hearing his words, cried out, "This long time I have perceived that what we worshipped was naught; because the more diligently I sought after truth in that worship, the less I found it. But now I freely confess, that such truth evidently appears in this preaching as can confer on us the gifts of life, of salvation, and of eternal happiness. For which reason my counsel is, O king, that we instantly give up to ban and fire those temples and altars which we have consecrated without reaping any benefit from them." In brief, the king openly assented to the preaching of the Gospel by Paulinus, and renouncing idolatry, declared that he received the faith of Christ.

In the north of England Roman missionaries encountered Irish monks who had begun to preach there. In 664 King Oswy of Northumbria had to choose between the two groups. (They disagreed about the date of Easter and other points of church usage.)

From Bede. *Ecclesiastical History*

Then Colman said, "The Easter which I keep, I received from my elders, who sent me hither as bishop; all our forefathers, men beloved of God, are known to have celebrated it after the same manner; and that it may not seem to any contemptible and worthy to be rejected, it is the same which the blessed John the Evangelist, the disciple specially beloved of our Lord, with all the churches over which he presided, is recorded to have celebrated."

Then Wilfrid, being ordered by the king to speak, began thus:—

From *Bede's Ecclesiastical History of England*, A. M. Sellar, trans. (London: George Bell and Sons, 1907), pp. 195–196, 200–201.

"The Easter which we keep, we saw celebrated by all at Rome, where the blessed Apostles, Peter and Paul, lived, taught, suffered, and were buried; we saw the same done by all in Italy and in Gaul, when we travelled through those countries for the purpose of study and prayer. We found it observed in Africa, Asia, Egypt, Greece, and all the world, wherever the Church of Christ is spread abroad, among divers nations and tongues, at one and the same time; save only among these and their accomplices in obstinacy, I mean the Picts and the Britons, who foolishly, in these two remote islands of the ocean, and only in part even of them, strive to oppose all the rest of the world.

"But as for you and your companions, you certainly sin, if, having heard the decrees of the Apostolic see, nay, of the universal Church, confirmed, as they are, by Holy Scripture, you scorn to follow them; for, though your fathers were holy, do you think that those few men, in a corner of the remotest island, are to be preferred before the universal Church of Christ throughout the world? And if that Columba of yours, (and, I may say, ours also, if he was Christ's servant,) was a holy man and powerful in miracles, yet could he be preferred before the most blessed chief of the Apostles, to whom our Lord said, 'Thou art Peter, and upon this rock I will build my Church, and the gates of hell shall not prevail against it, and I will give unto thee the keys of the kingdom of Heaven?' "

When Wilfrid had ended thus, the king said, "Is it true, Colman, that these words were spoken to Peter by our Lord?" He answered, "It is true, O king!" Then said he, "Can you show any such power given to your Columba?" Colman answered, "None." Then again the king asked, "Do you both agree in this, without any controversy, that these words were said above all to Peter, and that the keys of the kingdom of Heaven were given to him by our Lord?" They both answered, "Yes." Then the king concluded, "And I also say unto you, that he is the door-keeper, and I will not gainsay him, but I desire, as far as I know and am able, in all things to obey his laws, lest haply when I come to the gates of the kingdom of Heaven, there should be none to open them, he being my adversary who is proved to have the keys." The king having said this, all who were seated there or standing by, both great and small, gave their assent, and renouncing the less perfect custom, hastened to conform to that which they had found to be better.

Germany. Wilderness and Monasteries

In the eighth century the English church sent out missionaries to Germany. The greatest of them, St. Boniface, worked in close contact with the papacy.

Oath of Boniface

I, Boniface, bishop by the grace of God, promise to you, the blessed Peter, chief of the apostles, and to thy vicar, the blessed Pope Gregory, and to his successors, by the Father and the Son and the Holy Ghost, the indivisible Trinity, and by this thy most holy body, that, God helping me, I will maintain all the belief and the purity of the holy Catholic faith, and I will remain steadfast in the unity of this faith in which the whole salvation of Christians lies, as is established without doubt.

I will in no wise oppose the unity of the one universal Church, no matter who may seek to persuade me. But as I have said, I will maintain my faith and purity and union with thee and the benefits of thy Church, to whom God has given the power to loose and to bind, and with thy vicar and his successors, in all things. And if it comes to my knowledge that priests have turned from the ancient practices of the holy fathers, I will have no intercourse nor connection with them; but rather, if I can restrain them, I will. If I cannot, I will at once faithfully make known the whole matter to my apostolic lord.

From J. H. Robinson, trans. in *Readings in European History* (Boston, Mass.: Ginn and Co., 1904), Vol. 1, p. 106.

Some Christian attitudes to the natural world were colored by hostility to the old pagan deities of the countryside. (Christians thought of them as demons.) To win converts to Christianity Boniface had first to overcome the heathen gods.

From *Life of Boniface*

Many of the people of Hesse were converted [by Boniface] to the Catholic faith and confirmed by the grace of the spirit: and they received the laying on of hands. But some there were, not yet strong of soul, who refused to accept wholly the teachings of the true faith. Some men sacrificed secretly, some even openly, to trees and springs. Some secretly practiced divining, soothsaying, and incantations, and some openly. But others, who were of sounder mind, cast aside all heathen profanation and did none of these things; and it was with the advice and consent of these men that Boniface sought to fell a certain tree of great size, at Geismar, and called, in the ancient speech of the region, the oak of Thor.

The man of God was surrounded by the servants of God. When he would cut down the tree, behold a great throng of pagans who were there cursed him bitterly among themselves because he was the enemy of their gods. And when he had cut into the trunk a little way, a breeze sent by God stirred overhead, and suddenly the branching top of the

From *Willibald's Life of Boniface*, J. H. Robinson, trans. in *Readings in European History* (Boston, Mass.: Ginn and Co., 1904), Vol. 1, pp. 106–107.

tree was broken off, and the oak in all its huge bulk fell to the ground. And it was broken into four parts, as if by the divine will, so that the trunk was divided into four huge sections without any effort of the brethren who stood by. When the pagans who had cursed did see this, they left off cursing and, believing, blessed God. Then the most holy priest took counsel with the brethren: and he built from the wood of the tree an oratory, and dedicated it to the holy apostle Peter.

The German forest was a forbidding wilderness to the first missionaries who explored it.

From *Life of Sturmi*

For almost three years [Sturmi] fulfilled the duties of the priesthood, preaching and baptizing among the people. Then by the inspiration of God the purpose came into his soul to chasten himself by the straiter life and the hardships of the wilderness. He sought counsel thereupon from Boniface,—his master in the spirit,—who, when he understood Sturmi, knew that this purpose was inspired of God and rejoiced that God had designed to lead him by his grace. He gave Sturmi two companions, and when he had prayed and blessed them all he said: "Go forth into that solitude which is called Bochonia and seek a place meet for the servants of God to dwell in. For God is able to prepare for his servants a place in the wilderness."

And so those three went forth into the wilderness and entered into places solitary and rough, and saw almost nothing but heaven and earth and great trees; and they prayed Christ fervently that he would direct their feet in the path of peace. On the third day they came to the place which even to this day is called Hersfeld; and when they had seen and explored the region round about, they asked Christ that the place might be blest to the dwellers therein. . . .

Then after some time spent in holy meditation Sturmi returned to the bishop, and described the lay of the land and the course of the streams, and the hills and valleys. . . . Boniface heard him attentively, and answered: "I fear to have you dwell in this place which ye have found because a barbarous race lives close by, for, as thou knowest, the fell Saxons are near at hand. Wherefore seek a dwelling in the wilderness farther away and higher up the stream, where ye may remain without danger."

Then the holy man Sturmi returned to his companions. With two

From *Eigil's Life of Sturmi,* J. H. Robinson, trans. in *Readings in European History* (Boston, Mass.: Ginn and Co., 1904), Vol. 1, pp. 107–111.

brethren he entered a boat and traveled along the river Fulda, spying out the land, but they found no place which pleased them. So Sturmi went again to Boniface and said, "For many days did we sail along the river Fulda, but we found nothing that we would dare to praise to you." And the holy bishop saw that God had not yet revealed the place which he had chosen.

Sturmi returned to the cell which had now been built in a place above Hersfeld. Here he saluted the brethren and reported to them what the holy bishop had counseled. Then after resting a little he mounted his ass and set forth alone, commending his journey to Christ, who is the way, the truth, and the life. All alone, sitting upon his ass, he began his journey through the vast places of the wilderness. He eagerly explored the region and observed with quick eye the mountains and the hills and the plains, the springs and torrents and rivers. With psalms always upon his lips, he prayed to God with groaning, his soul lifted up to heaven. And wherever night found him, there he rested; and he hewed wood with the sword which he bore in his hand, and laid it in a circle, and set it on fire to protect his ass, lest the wild beasts which were there in great numbers might devour him. For himself, he made on his forehead the sign of the cross of Christ, in the name of God, and rested in safety. . . .

And then he went back a little way and came to the place already made ready and blessed by God, even the place where the holy monastery [of Fulda] now stands. When he had come thither straightway the holy man Sturmi was filled with exceeding great joy, for he knew that through the merits and prayers of the holy bishop Boniface the place had been revealed to him by God.

Then on the second day the man of God came again to Hersfeld and found his brethren there calling upon God with fervent prayers. He told them of the place he had found and bade them make ready to go thither with him. But Sturmi went straightway to the holy bishop Boniface to tell him how he had found a place for the brethren to dwell in. Together they rejoiced and gave God thanks and held sweet converse about the life and conversation of monks. Then did the bishop let Sturmi go back to his wilderness, while he went to the palace of Carloman, the king, to gain from him a grant of the place Sturmi had chosen. . . .

And the brethren decided to follow the rule of the holy father Benedict. They spent many years in holy pursuits; and the number of brethren in the monastery grew greater, for many men gave themselves and all that they had to serve God there. And the holy bishop was zealous to visit them from time to time; and he had compassion upon their poverty, and gave them some lands to furnish them necessary food.

In contrast to the wilderness, the monastic enclosure seemed a haven of beauty and tranquillity.

Walafrid Strabo. *A Monastic Garden*

To Grimold, Abbot of St. Gall, with his book "Of Gardening"

A very paltry gift, of no account,
My father, for a scholar like to thee,
But Strabo sends it to thee with his heart.
So might you sit in the small garden close
In the green darkness of the apple trees
Just where the peach tree casts its broken shade,
And they would gather you the shining fruit
With the soft down upon it; all your boys,
Your little laughing boys, your happy school,
And bring huge apples clasped in their two hands.
Something the book may have of use to thee.
Read it, my father, prune it of its faults,
And strengthen with thy praise what pleases thee.
And may God give thee in thy hands the green
Unwithering palm of everlasting life.

From Helen Waddell, trans., *Medieval Latin Lyrics* (London: Constable, 1933), p. 115. Copyright © 1978 by Stanbrook Abbey, England. Reprinted by permission of Constable Publishers and by permission of W. W. Norton & Company, Inc.

CHARLEMAGNE

The Frankish King Charles, a great conqueror, made himself ruler of nearly all western Europe. Then, in association with the pope, he created a new medieval empire—later known as the Holy Roman Empire.

Charlemagne and His Family

From Einhard. *Life of Charlemagne*

Charles was large and strong, and of lofty stature, though not disproportionately tall (his height is well known to have been seven times the length of his foot); the upper part of his head was round, his eyes very large and animated, nose a little long, hair fair, and face laughing and merry. Thus his appearance was always stately and dignified, whether he was standing or sitting; although his neck was thick and somewhat short, and his belly rather prominent; but the symmetry of the rest of his body concealed these defects. His gait was firm, his whole carriage manly, and his voice clear, but not so strong as his size led one to expect. His health was excellent, except during the four years preceding his death, when he was subject to frequent fevers; at the last he even limped a little with one foot. . . .

Charles was temperate in eating, and particularly so in drinking, for he abominated drunkenness in anybody, much more in himself and those of his household; but he could not easily abstain from food, and often complained that fasts injured his health. He very rarely gave entertainments, only on great feast-days, and then to large numbers of people. His meals ordinarily consisted of four courses, not counting the roast, which his huntsmen used to bring in on the spit; he was more fond of this than of any other dish. While at table, he listened to reading or music. The subjects of the readings were the stories and deeds of olden time: he was fond, too, of St. Augustine's books, and especially of the one entitled "The City of God." He was so moderate in the use of wine and all sorts of drink that he rarely allowed himself more than three cups in the course of a meal. In summer, after the midday meal, he would eat some fruit, drain a single cup, put off his clothes and shoes, just as he did for the night, and rest for two or three

From Einhard, *The Life of Charlemagne*, S. E. Turner, trans. (New York: American Book Co., 1880), pp. 47–62. Foreword copyright © 1960 by The University of Michigan. Reprinted by permission of University of Michigan Press.

217

hours. He was in the habit of awaking and rising from bed four or five times during the night. While he was dressing and putting on his shoes, he not only gave audience to his friends, but if the Count of the Palace told him of any suit in which his judgment was necessary, he had the parties brought before him forthwith, took cognizance of the case, and gave his decision, just as if he were sitting on the judgment-seat. This was not the only business that he transacted at this time, but he performed any duty of the day whatever, whether he had to attend to the matter himself, or to give commands concerning it to his officers.

Charles had the gift of ready and fluent speech, and could express whatever he had to say with the utmost clearness. He was not satisfied with command of his native language merely, but gave attention to the study of foreign ones, and in particular was such a master of Latin that he could speak it as well as his native tongue; but he could understand Greek better than he could speak it. He was so eloquent, indeed, that he might have passed for a teacher of eloquence. . . . He also tried to write, and used to keep tablets and blanks in bed under his pillow, that at leisure hours he might accustom his hand to form the letters; however, as he did not begin his efforts in due season, but late in life, they met with ill success.

He married a daughter of Desiderius, King of the Lombards, at the instance of his mother; but he repudiated her at the end of a year for some reason unknown, and married Hildegard, a woman of high birth, of Suabian origin. He had three sons by her—Charles, Pepin, and Lewis—and as many daughters—Hruodrud, Bertha, and Gisela. He had three other daughters besides these—Theoderada, Hiltrud, and Ruodhaid—two by his third wife, Fastrada, a woman of East Frankish (that is to say, of German) origin, and the third by a concubine, whose name for the moment escapes me. At the death of Fastrada, he married Liutgard, an Alemannic woman, who bore him no children. After her death he had three concubines—Gersuinda, a Saxon, by whom he had Adaltrud; Regina, who was the mother of Drogo and Hugh; and Ethelind, by whom he had Theodoric. Charles's mother, Berthrada, passed her old age with him in great honour; he entertained the greatest veneration for her; and there was never any disagreement between them except when he divorced the daughter of King Desiderius, whom he had married to please her. She died soon after Hildegard, after living to see three grandsons and as many granddaughters in her son's house, and he buried her with great pomp in the Basilica of St. Denis, where his father lay. He had an only sister, Gisela, who had consecrated herself to a religious life from girlhood, and he cherished as much affection for her as for his mother. She also died a few years before him in the nunnery where she had passed her life.

The plan that he adopted for his children's education was, first of all, to have both boys and girls instructed in the liberal arts, to which he also turned his own attention. As soon as their years admitted, in accordance with the custom of the Franks, the boys had to learn horsemanship, and to practise war and the chase, and the girls to familiarize themselves with cloth-making, and to handle distaff and spindle, that they might not grow indolent through idleness, and he fostered in them every virtuous sentiment. He only lost three of all his children before his death, two sons and one daughter, Charles, who was the eldest, Pepin, whom he had made King of Italy, and Hruodrud, his oldest daughter, whom he had betrothed to Constantine, Emperor of the Greeks. . . . When his sons and his daughter died, he was not so calm as might have been expected from his remarkably strong mind, for his affections were no less strong, and moved him to tears. Again, when he was told of the death of Hadrian, the Roman Pontiff, whom he had loved most of all of his friends, he wept as much as if he had lost a brother, or a very dear son. He was by nature most ready to contract friendships, and not only made friends easily, but clung to them persistently, and cherished most fondly those with whom he had formed such ties. He was so careful of the training of his sons and daughters that he never took his meals without them when he was at home, and never made a journey without them; his sons would ride at this side, and his daughters follow him, while a number of his body-guard, detailed for their protection, brought up the rear. Strange to say, although they were very handsome women, and he loved them very dearly, he was never willing to marry any of them to a man of their own nation or to a foreigner, but kept them all at home until his death, saying that he could not dispense with their society. Hence, though otherwise happy, he experienced the malignity of fortune as far as they were concerned: yet he concealed his knowledge of the rumours current in regard to them, and of the suspicions entertained of their honour.[1]

Economic Foundations

Charlemagne's revenues came mainly from great agricultural estates scattered throughout his domains. This letter illustrates the material basis of early medieval society.

[1]Bertha had a notorious affair with a Frankish noble, Angilbert, and had two children by him.

From *Capitulary De Villis*

We desire that each steward shall make an annual statement of all our income, giving an account of our lands cultivated by the oxen which our own plowmen drive and of our lands which the tenants of farms ought to plow; of the pigs, of the rents, of the obligations and fines; of the game taken in our forests without our permission; of the various compositions; of the mills, of the forest, of the fields, of the bridges and ships; of the free men and the districts under obligations to our treasury; of markets, vineyards, and those who owe wine to us; of the hay, firewood, torches, planks, and other kinds of lumber; of the waste lands; of the vegetables, millet, panic; of the wool, flax, and hemp; of the fruits of the trees; of the nut trees, larger and smaller; of the grafted trees of all kinds; of the gardens; of the turnips; of the fish ponds; of the hides, skins, and horns; of the honey and wax; of the fat, tallow, and soap; of the mulberry wine, cooked wine, mead, vinegar, beer, and wine, new and old, of the new grain and the old; of the hens and eggs; of the geese; of the number of fishermen, workers in metal, sword makers, and shoemakers; of the bins and boxes; of the turners and saddlers; of the forges and mines—that is, of iron, lead, or other substances; of the colts and fillies. They shall make all these known to us, set forth separately and in order, at Christmas, so that we may know what and how much of each thing we have.

The greatest care must be taken that whatever is prepared or made with the hands—that is, bacon, smoked meat, sausage, partially salted meat, wine, vinegar, mulberry wine, cooked wine, garum, mustard, cheese, butter, malt, beer, mead, honey, wax, flour—all should be prepared and made with the greatest cleanliness.

Each steward on each of our domains shall always have, for the sake of ornament, peacocks, pheasants, ducks, pigeons, partridges, and turtle-doves.

In each of our estates the chambers shall be provided with counterpanes, cushions, pillows, bedclothes, coverings for the tables and benches; vessels of brass, lead, iron, and wood; andirons, chains, pothooks, adzes, axes, augers, cutlasses, and all other kinds of tools, so that it shall never be necessary to go elsewhere for them, or to borrow them. And the weapons which are carried against the enemy shall be well cared for, so as to keep them in good condition; and when they are brought back they shall be placed in the chamber.

For our women's work they are to give at the proper time, as has been ordered, the materials—that is, the linen, wool, woad, vermilion, madder, wool combs, teasels, soap, grease, vessels, and the other objects which are necessary.

From J. H. Robinson, trans. in *Readings in European History* (Boston, Mass.: Ginn and Co., 1904), Vol. 1, pp. 137–139.

Of the kinds of food not forbidden on fast days, two thirds shall be sent each year for our own use—that is, of the vegetables, fish, cheese, butter, honey, mustard, vinegar, millet, panic, dried and green herbs, radishes, and, in addition, of the wax, soap, and other small products; and let it be reported to us, by a statement, how much is left, as we have said above; and this statement must not be omitted as in the past, because after those two thirds we wish to know how much remains.

Each steward shall have in his district good workmen, namely, blacksmiths, a goldsmith, a silversmith, shoemakers, turners, carpenters, sword makers, fishermen, foilers, soap makers, men who know how to make beer, cider, perry, or other kind of liquor good to drink, bakers to make pastry for our table, net makers who know how to make nets for hunting, fishing, and fowling, and other sorts of workmen too numerous to be designated.

Carolingian Government

Charlemagne imposed on his empire an unusual degree of peace and order (for those days). This capitulary of 902 described the aims of his government.

From *General Capitulary for the Missi*

Concerning the embassy sent out by the lord emperor. Therefore, the most serene and most Christian lord emperor Charles has chosen from his nobles the wisest and most prudent men, both archbishops and some of the other bishops also, and venerable abbots and pious laymen, and has sent them throughout his whole kingdom, and through them by all the following chapters has allowed men to live in accordance with the correct law. Moreover, where anything which is not right and just has been enacted in the law, he has ordered them to inquire into this most diligently and to inform him of it; he desires, God granting, to reform it. And let no one, through his cleverness or astuteness, dare to oppose or thwart the written law, as many are wont to do, or the judicial sentence passed upon him, or to do injury to the churches of God or the poor or the widows or the wards or any Christian. But all shall live entirely in accordance with God's precept, justly and under a just rule, and each one shall be admonished to live in harmony with his fellows in his business or profession; the canonical clergy ought to

From D. C. Munro, trans. in *University of Pennsylvania Translations and Reprints* (Philadelphia, Pa.: University of Pennsylvania, 1900), Vol. 4, No. 5, pp. 16.

observe in every respect a canonical life without heeding base gain, nuns ought to keep diligent watch over their lives, laymen and the secular clergy ought rightly to observe their laws without malicious fraud, and all ought to live in mutual charity and perfect peace. And let the *missi* themselves make a diligent investigation whenever any man claims that an injustice has been done to him by any one, just as they desire to deserve the grace of omnipotent God and to keep their fidelity promised to Him, so that entirely in all cases everywhere, in accordance with the will and fear of God, they shall administer the law fully and justly in the case of the holy churches of God and of the poor, of wards and widows and of the whole people. And if there shall be anything of such a nature that they, together with the provincial counts, are not able of themselves to correct it and to do justice concerning it, they shall, without any ambiguity, refer this, together with their reports, to the judgment of the emperor; and the straight path of justice shall not be impeded by any one on account of flattery or gifts from any one, or on account of any relationship, or from fear of the powerful. . . .

The Imperial Coronation

There are several accounts of Charlemagne's imperial coronation from ninth-century sources. Each tells a slightly different story.

From Einhard. *Life of Charlemagne*

The Romans had inflicted many injuries upon the Pontiff Leo, tearing out his eyes and cutting out his tongue, so that he had been compelled to call upon the King for help. Charles accordingly went to Rome, to set in order the affairs of the Church, which were in great confusion, and passed the whole winter there. It was then that he received the titles of Emperor and Augustus, to which he at first had such an aversion that he declared that he would not have set foot in the Church the day that they were conferred, although it was a great feast-day, if he could have foreseen the design of the Pope. He bore very patiently with the jealousy which the [East] Roman emperors showed upon his assuming these titles, for they took this step very ill; and by dint of frequent embassies and letters, in which he addressed them as brothers, he made their haughtiness yield to his magnanimity, a quality in which he was unquestionably much their superior.

From Einhard, *The Life of Charlemagne*, S. E. Turner, trans. (New York: American Book Co.), pp. 65–66. Foreword copyright © 1960 by The University of Michigan. Reprinted by permission of University of Michigan Press.

From *Annals of Lorsch*

Now since the title of emperor had become extinct among the Greeks and a woman claimed the imperial authority it seemed to the apostle Leo and to all the holy fathers who were present at the council and to the rest of the Christian people that Charles, king of the Franks, ought to be named emperor, for he held Rome itself where the Caesars were always wont to reside and also other cities in Italy, Gaul, and Germany. Since almighty God had put all these places in his power it seemed to them that, with the help of God, and in accordance with the request of all the Christian people, he should hold this title. King Charles did not wish to refuse their petition, and, humbly submitting himself to God and to the petition of all the Christian priests and people, he accepted the title of emperor on the day of the nativity of our Lord Jesus Christ and was consecrated by the lord Pope Leo.

From *Annals of Lorsch*, G. H. Pertz, *Monumenta Germaniae Historica, Scriptores I* (Hanover, 1826), p. 38, Brian Tierney, trans. in *Great Issues in Western Civilization*, 3rd ed., Brian Tierney, Donald Kagan, and L. Pearce Williams, eds. (New York: Random House, 1976), p. 337. Copyright © 1967, 1972, 1976 by Random House, Inc. Reprinted by permission of the publisher.

From *Frankish Royal Annals*

On the most holy day of the nativity of the Lord, as the king rose from praying at Mass before the tomb of the blessed apostle Peter, pope Leo placed a crown on his head and all the Roman people cried out, "To Charles Augustus, crowned by God, great and peace-giving emperor of the Romans, life and victory." And after the laudation he was adored by the pope in the manner of the ancient princes and, the title of patrician being set aside, he was called emperor and Augustus. A few days later he commanded the men who had deposed the pope the year before to be brought before him. They were examined according to Roman law on a charge of treason and condemned to death. However, the pope interceded for them with the emperor and they were spared in life and limb. Subsequently they were sent into exile for so great a crime.

From *Frankish Royal Annals*, G. H. Pertz, *Monumenta Germaniae Historica, Scriptores I* (Hanover, 1826), p. 188, Brian Tierney, trans. in *Great Issues in Western Civilization*, 3rd ed., Brian Tierney, Donald Kagan, and L. Pearce Williams, eds. (New York: Random House, 1976), p. 338. Copyright © 1967, 1972, 1976 by Random House, Inc. Reprinted by permission of the publisher.

VII

FEUDAL INSTITUTIONS
Lords and Vassals
From *Annals of Xanten*
Capitulary of Mersen
Oaths of Allegiance
From *Chronicle of Galbert of Bruges*
Liege Homage
The Fief
Capitulary of Lestinnes (747)
Grant of Fief with Immunity (815)
*Foundation of the Duchy of
Normandy (911)*
Feudal Obligations
From *Fulbert of Chartres*
Feudal Aids
Knight Service
Court Service
Wardship and Marriage
Violence and Restraint
From *Suger's Life of Louis VI*
Truce of God (1063)

REFORM OF THE CHURCH
Beginnings of Reform
Parishes in Italy
Simony in France
Foundation Charter of Cluny
Papal Reform Decrees (1074–1075)
Dictatus Papae (1075)
Empire and Papacy
*Henry IV to Gregory VII (January
24, 1076)*
*Deposition of Henry IV (February 22,
1076)*
*Gregory VII to the Princes of
Germany (1077)*
*Gregory VII to Hermann of Metz
(1081)*
Concordat of Worms

THE FIRST CRUSADERS
Western Views
From *The Song of Roland*
Pope Urban's Speech at Clermont
An Arab View
From *Autobiography of Ousama*

MEDIEVAL FOUNDATIONS—FEUDALISM, CHURCH REFORM, AND CRUSADE

CHARLEMANGE'S EMPIRE SOON disintegrated. His descendants established separate kingdoms and waged frequent wars against one another. At the same time Europe was invaded by Vikings from the north and Magyars from the east. The forces of Islam, which had occupied Spain during the eighth century, took Sicily and attacked southern Italy. The very survival of Christian Europe seemed threatened for a time.

But slowly the foundations for a new growth of civilization in the West were established. Most important were the development of feudal institutions and the emergence of a revitalized church. Feudalism, based on a relationship of personal loyalty between a vassal and a lord, evolved as a response to the near-anarchy of the times. In the difficult conditions of the ninth century, kings were often unable to govern effectively all their territories. Sometimes they would grant a whole province as a fief to a great lord. Such a lord would usually divide his lands into lesser fiefs, each held by a vassal who owed him military service. Europe came to be dominated by a warrior aristocracy. Government was decentralized. Such order as existed was provided by personal bonds of loyalty, not by the allegiance of citizens to a state. Marriages were commonly arranged to serve feudal ends—to create family alliances or consolidate existing fiefs.

The church suffered in the general disorder of the times. Great monasteries and cathedral churches fell under the control of lay lords. The old discipline of celibacy for clergy was forgotten and priests commonly married or lived with concubines. From the early tenth century, movements of reform grew up, at first in monastic centers. Then, from the mid-eleventh century onward, a revitalized papacy began to carry through a general reform of the whole Western church. The claims of the popes, and especially their attempts to free churches from lay control, led on to the first great conflict of empire and papacy. After fifty years of strife, it was ended by a compromise agreement in 1122.

By that time the combination of feudal force and religious enthusiasm had made possible a new movement of expansion. Crusading armies first pushed back the Saracens in Spain, then launched an attack on Palestine to establish a Christian kingdom in the Holy Land.

225

FEUDAL INSTITUTIONS

Lords and Vassals

The records of the abbey of Xanten in Germany describe the chaotic conditions from which feudal institutions emerged.

From *Annals of Xanten*

846

According to their custom the Northmen plundered Eastern and Western Frisia and burned the town of Dordrecht, with two other villages, before the eyes of Lothaire, who was then in the castle of Nimwegen, but could not punish the crime. The Northmen, with their boats filled with immense booty, including both men and goods, returned to their own country.

In the same year Louis sent an expedition from Saxony against the Wends across the Elbe. He personally, however, went with his army against the Bohemians, whom we called Beu-winitha, but with great risk. . . . Charles advanced against the Britons, but accomplished nothing.

At this same time, as no one can mention or hear without great sadness, the mother of all churches, the basilica of the apostle Peter, was taken and plundered by the Moors, or Saracens, who had already occupied the region of Beneventum. The Saracens, moreover, slaughtered all the Christians whom they found outside the walls of Rome, either within or without this church. They also carried men and women away prisoners. They tore down, among many others, the altar of the blessed Peter, and their crimes from day to day bring sorrow to Christians. Pope Sergius departed life this year.

847

After the death of Sergius no mention of the apostolic see has come in any way to our ears. Rabanus [Maurus], master and abbot of Fulda, was solemnly chosen archbishop as the successor of Bishop Otger, who

From *Annals of Xanten, 845–854,* J. H. Robinson, trans. in *Readings in European History* (Boston, Mass.: Ginn and Co., 1904), Vol. 1, pp. 158–162.

had died. Moreover the Northmen here and there plundered the Christians and engaged in a battle with the counts Sigir and Liuthar. They continued up the Rhine as far as Dordrecht, and nine miles farther to Meginhard, when they turned back, having taken their booty.

849

While King Louis was ill his army of Bavaria took its way against the Bohemians. Many of these were killed and the remainder withdrew, much humiliated, into their own country. The heathen from the North wrought havoc in Christendom as usual and grew greater in strength; but it is revolting to say more of this matter.

850

On January 1st of that season, in the octave of the Lord, towards evening, a great deal of thunder was heard and a mighty flash of lightning seen; and an overflow of water afflicted the human race during this winter. In the following summer an all too great heat of the sun burned the earth. Leo, pope of the apostolic see, an extraordinary man, built a fortification round the church of St. Peter the apostle. The Moors, however, devastated here and there the coast towns in Italy. The Norman Rorik, brother of the above-mentioned younger Heriold, who earlier had fled dishonored from Lothaire, again took Dordrecht and did much evil treacherously to the Christians. In the same year so great a peace existed between the two brothers—Emperor Lothaire and King Louis—that they spent many days together in Osning [Westphalia] and there hunted, so that many were astonished thereat; and they went each his way in peace.

851

The bodies of certain saints were sent from Rome to Saxony,—that of Alexander, one of seven brethren, and those of Romanus and Emerentiana. In the same year the very noble empress, Irmingard by name, wife of the emperor Lothaire, departed this world. The Normans inflicted much harm in Frisia and about the Rhine. A mighty army of them collected by the river Elbe against the Saxons, and some of the Saxon towns were besieged, others burned, and most terribly did they oppress the Christians. A meeting of our kings took place on the Maas.

852

The steel of the heathen glistened; excessive heat; a famine followed. There was not fodder enough for the animals. The pasturage for the swine was more than sufficient.

The protection of a local lord seemed to offer the best chance of survival.

Capitulary of Mersen (Kings Lothar, Lewis, and Charles, 847)

We will moreover that each free man in our kingdom shall choose a lord, from us or our faithful, such a one as he wishes.

We command moreover that no man shall leave his lord without just cause, nor should any one receive him, except in such a way as was customary in the time of our predecessors.

And we wish you to know that we want to grant right to our faithful subjects and we do not wish to do anything to them against reason. Similarly we admonish you and the rest of our faithful subjects that you grant right to your men and do not act against reason toward them.

And we will that the man of each one of us in whosoever kingdom he is, shall go with his lord against the enemy, or in his other needs unless there shall have been (as may there not be) such an invasion of the kingdom as is called a *landwer,* so that the whole people of that kingdom shall go together to repel it.

The relationship of loyalty between a warrior and his chosen lord goes back to early Teutonic practices. From the seventh century onward we have set formulas of commendation. These early examples are from England and France respectively.

Oaths of Allegiance

Thus shall one take the oath of fidelity:

By the Lord before whom this sanctuary is holy, I will to N. be true and faithful, and love all which he loves and shun all which he shuns, according to the laws of God and the order of the world. Nor will I ever with will or action, through word or deed, do anything which is unpleasing to him, on condition that he will hold to me as I shall deserve it, and that he will perform everything as it was in our agreement when I submitted myself to him and chose his will.

It is right that those who offer to us unbroken fidelity should be protected by our aid. And since *such and such* a faithful one of ours, by the favor of God, coming here in our palace with his arms, has seen fit to swear trust and fidelity to us in our hand, therefore we decree and command by the present precept that for the future *such and such* above mentioned be counted with the number of antrustions. And if

From E. P. Cheyney, trans. in *University of Pennsylvania Translations and Reprints* (Philadelphia, Pa.: University of Pennsylvania Press, 1898), Vol. 4, No. 3, pp. 3–15, 18.

anyone perchance should presume to kill him, let him know that he will be judged guilty of his wergild of 600 shillings.

The following ceremony took place in Flanders in 1127.

From *Chronical of Galbert of Bruges*

Through the whole remaining part of the day those who had been previously enfeoffed by the most pious count Charles, did homage to the count, taking up now again their fiefs and offices and whatever they had before rightfully and legitimately obtained. On Thursday the seventh of April, homages were again made to the count being completed in the following order of faith and security.

First they did their homage thus, the count asked if he was willing to become completely his man, and the other replied, "I am willing"; and with clasped hands, surrounded by the hands of the count, they were bound together by a kiss. Secondly, he who had done homage gave his fealty to the representative of the count in these words, "I promise on my faith that I will in future be faithful to count William, and will observe my homage to him completely against all persons in good faith and without deceit," and thirdly, he took his oath to this upon the relics of the saints. Afterward, with a little rod which the count held in his hand, he gave investitures to all who by this agreement had given their security and homage and accompanying oath.

Sometimes a vassal held fiefs from several lords. This oath illustrates the complexities that could arise.

Liege Homage

I, John of Toul, make known that I am the liege man of the lady Beatrice, countess of Troyes, and of her son, Theobald, count of Champagne, against every creature, living or dead, saving my allegiance to lord Enjorand of Coucy, lord John of Arcis, and the count of Grandpré. If it should happen that the count of Grandpré should be at war with the countess and count of Champagne on his own quarrel, I will aid the count of Grandpré in my own person, and will send to the count and the countess of Champagne the knights whose service I owe to them for the fief which I hold of them. But if the count of Grandpré shall make war on the countess and the count of Champagne on behalf of his friends and not in his own quarrel, I will aid in my own person the countess and count of Champagne, and will send one knight to the count of Grandpré for the service which I owe him

From O. J. Thatcher and E. H. McNeal, trans., *A Source Book for Mediaeval History* (New York: Charles Scribner's, 1905), pp. 364–365.

for the fief which I hold of him, but I will not go myself into the territory of the count of Grandpré to make war on him.

The Fief

A form of land tenure (precarium) *similar to the later fief existed already in the eighth century. In 747, churches were required to grant out lands as pre-caria to support Frankish warriors.*

Capitulary of Lestinnes (747)

Because of the threats of war and the attacks of certain tribes on our borders, we have determined, with the consent of God and by the advice of our clergy and people, to appropriate for a time part of the ecclesiastical property for the support of our army. The lands are to be held as *precaria* for a fixed rent; one solidus, or twelve denarii, shall be paid annually to the church or monastery for each *casata* [farm]. When the holder dies the whole possession shall return to the church. If, however, the exigency of the time makes it necessary, the prince may require the *precarium* to be renewed and given out again. Care shall be taken, however, that the churches and monasteries do not incur suffering or poverty through the granting of *precaria*. If the poverty of the church makes it necessary, the whole possession shall be restored to the church.

The grant of a fief often included immunity from royal jurisdiction, leaving the lord free to govern his own lands.

Grant of Fief with Immunity (815)

In the name of our Lord and Savior Jesus Christ. Louis, by divine providence emperor, Augustus. Be it known to all our subjects, present and future, that our faithful subject, John, has come to us and commended himself to us, and has besought us to confirm to him the possession of lands [described] which he and his sons and their men have cleared and occupied. He has shown us the charter which he received from our father Charles the Great. We have consented to do this and have done even more; we have given him certain villas [named] with their extent and dependencies . . . granting that he and his sons and his posterity may hold them in peace and security. No count, *vicarius*, or their subordinates, or any other public official shall presume to

From O. J. Thatcher and E. H. McNeal, trans., *A Source Book for Mediaeval History* (New York: Charles Scribner's, 1905), pp. 357, 353.

judge or constrain any persons living on those lands, but John and his sons and their posterity shall judge and constrain them. . . .

Sometimes the "gift" of a fief merely recognized a seizure of lands that the king could not defend. Thus King Charles of France founded the Duchy of Normandy by conferring on a Viking, Rollo, territories that Rollo had already conquered.

Foundation of the Duchy of Normandy (911)

At the agreed time Charles and Rollo came together at the place that had been decided on. . . . Looking on Rollo, the invader of France, the Franks said to one another, "This duke who has fought such battles against the warriors of this realm is a man of great power and great courage and prowess and good counsel and of great energy too." Then, persuaded by the words of the Franks, Rollo put his hands between the hands of the king, a thing which his father and grandfather and great-grandfather had never done; and so the king gave his daughter Gisela in marriage to the duke and conferred on him the agreed lands from the River Epte to the sea as his property in hereditary right, together with all Brittany from which he could live.

Rollo was not willing to kiss the foot of the king. The bishops said, "Anyone who receives such a gift ought to be eager to kiss the king's foot." He replied, "I have never bent my knees at anyone's knees, nor will I kiss anyone's foot." But, urged by the entreaties of the Franks, he commanded one of his warriors to kiss the foot of the king. The warrior promptly seized the king's foot, carried it to his mouth and kissed it standing up while the king was thrown flat on his back. At that there was a great outburst of laughter and great excitement among the people. Nevertheless King Charles, Duke Robert, the counts and nobles, the bishops and abbots swore by the Catholic faith and by their lives, limbs and the honor of the whole kingdom to the noble Rollo that he should hold and possess the land described above and pass it on to his heirs.

Feudal Obligations

Bishop Fulbert of Chartres gave a somewhat idealized description of feudal relationships.

From *De Moribus et Actis Primorum Normanniae Ducum, Mémoires de la Société des Antiquaires de Normandie*, 3e Série, III (1858), pp. 165–169, trans. Brian Tierney in *Great Issues in Western Civilization*, 3rd ed., Brian Tierney, Donald Kagan, and L. Pearce Williams, eds. (New York: Random House, 1976). Copyright © 1967, 1972, 1976 by Random House, Inc. Reprinted by permission of the publisher.

From *Fulbert of Chartres*

To William most glorious duke of the Aquitanians, bishop Fulbert the favor of his prayers.

Asked to write something concerning the form of fealty, I have noted briefly for you on the authority of the books the things which follow. He who swears fealty to his lord ought always to have these six things in memory; what is harmless, safe, honorable, useful, easy, practicable. Harmless, that is to say that he should not be injurious to his lord in his body; safe, that he should not be injurious to him in his secrets or in the defenses through which he is able to be secure; honorable, that he should not be injurious to him in his justice or in other matters that pertain to his honor; useful, that he should not be injurious to him in his possessions; easy or practicable, that that good which his lord is able to do easily, he make not difficult, nor that which is practicable he make impossible to him.

However, that the faithful vassal should avoid these injuries is proper, but not for this does he deserve his holding; for it is not sufficient to abstain from evil, unless what is good is done also. It remains, therefore, that in the same six things mentioned above he should faithfully counsel and aid his lord, if he wishes to be looked upon as worthy of his benefice and to be safe concerning the fealty which he has sworn.

The lord also ought to act toward his faithful vassal reciprocally in all these things. And if he does not do this he will be justly considered guilty of bad faith, just as the former, if he should be detected in the avoidance of or the doing of or the consenting to them, would be perfidious and perjured.

I would have written to you at greater length, if I had not been occupied with many other things, including the rebuilding of our city and church which was lately entirely consumed in a great fire; from which loss though we could not for a while be diverted, yet by the hope of the comfort of God and of you we breathe again.

From E. P. Cheyney, *University of Pennsylvania Translations and Reprints* (Philadelphia, Pa.: University of Pennsylvania Press, 1898), Vol. 4, No. 3, pp. 23–24.

The next three readings define feudal obligations more specifically.

Feudal Aids

Next it is proper to see the chief aids of Normandy, which are called chief because they should be paid to the chief lords.

In Normandy there are three chief aids. One is to make the oldest

From *Le Grand Coutumier de Normandie, Les Etablissements de St. Louis, Leges Henrici Primi*, E. P. Cheyney, trans. in *University of Pennsylvania Translations and Reprints* (Philadelphia, Pa.: University of Pennsylvania Press, 1898), Vol. 4, No. 3, pp. 28–33.

son of his lord a knight; the second, to marry his oldest daughter; the third to ransom the body of his lord from prison when he is taken in the Duke's war.

Knight Service

The baron and all vassals of the king are bound to appear before him when he shall summon them, and to serve him at their own expense for forty days and forty nights, with as many knights as each one owes; and he is able to exact from them these services when he wishes and when he has need of them. And if the king wishes to keep them more than forty days at their own expense, they are not bound to remain if they do not wish it. And if the king wishes to keep them at his expense for the defence of the realm, they are bound to remain. And if the king wishes to lead them outside of the kingdom, they need not go unless they wish to, for they have already served their forty days and forty nights.

Court Service

To every lord it is allowed to summon his man that he may be at right to him in his court; and even if he is resident at the most distant manor of that honor from which he holds, he shall go to the plea if his lord summons him. If his lord holds different fiefs the man of one honor is not compelled by law to go to another plea, unless the cause belongs to the other to which his lord has summoned him.

When a vassal died leaving a widow with dependent children they fell under the lord's control. Thus marriages and family relationships were greatly influenced by feudal ties.

Wardship and Marriage

Alice, countess of Warwick, renders account of £1000 and 10 palfreys to be allowed to remain a widow as long as she pleases, and not to be forced to marry by the king. And if perchance she should wish to marry, she shall not marry except with the assent and on the grant of the king, where the king shall be satisfied; and to have the custody of her sons whom she has from the earl of Warwick her late husband.

Hawisa, who was wife of William Fitz Robert renders account of 130 marks and 4 palfreys that she may have peace from Peter of Borough to whom the king has given permission to marry her; and that she may not be compelled to marry.

From *English Exchequer Rolls,* E. P. Cheyney, trans. in *University of Pennsylvania Translations and Reprints* (Philadelphia, Pa.: University of Pennsylvania Press, 1898), Vol. 4, No. 3, p. 27.

Geoffrey de Mandeville owes 20,000 marks to have as his wife Isabella, countess of Gloucester, with all the lands and tenements and fiefs which fall to her.

Thomas de Colville renders an account of 100 marks for having the custody of the sons of Roger Torpel and their land until they come of age.

William, bishop of Ely, owes 220 marks for having the custody of Stephen de Beauchamp with his inheritance and for marrying him where he wishes.

William of St. Mary's church, renders an account of 500 marks for having the custody of the heir of Robert Young, son of Robert Fitzharding, with all his inheritance and all its appurtenances and franchises; that is to say with the services of knights and gifts of churches and marriages of women, and to be allowed to marry him to whatever one of his relatives he wishes; and that all his land is to revert to him freely when he comes of age.

Bartholomew de Muleton renders an account of 100 marks for having the custody of the land and the heiress of Lambert of Ibtoft, and for marrying the wife of the same Lambert to whomsoever he wishes where she shall not be disparaged and that he may be able to confer her (the heiress) upon whom he wishes.

Violence and Restraint

Louis VI (1108–1137) began to rebuild royal power in France by waging endless campaigns against the "robber barons" around Paris.

From *Suger's Life of Louis VI*

A king, when he takes the royal power, vows to put down with his strong right arm insolent tyrants whensoever he sees them vex the state with endless wars, rejoice in rapine, oppress the poor, destroy the churches, give themselves over to lawlessness which, and it be not checked, would flame out into ever greater madness; for the evil spirits who instigate them are wont cruelly to strike down those whom they fear to lose, but give free rein to those whom they hope to hold, while they add fuel to the flames which are to devour their victims to all eternity.

Such an utterly abandoned man was Thomas of Marle. While King Louis was busied with many wars, he laid waste the territories of Laon, Rheims, and Amiens, devouring like a raging wolf. He spared not the

From J. H. Robinson, trans. in *Readings in European History* (Boston, Mass.: Ginn and Co., 1904), Vol. 1, pp. 202–204.

clergy—fearing not the vengeance of the Church—nor the people for humanity's sake. And the devil aided him, for the success of the foolish does ever lead them to perdition. Slaying all men, spoiling all things, he seized two manors, exceeding rich, from the abbey of the nuns of St. John of Laon. He fortified the two exceeding strong castles, Crécy and Nogent, with a marvelous wall and very high towers, as if they had been his own; and made them like to a den of dragons and a cave of robbers, whence he did waste almost the whole country with fire and pillage; and he had no pity.

The Church of France could no longer bear this great evil; wherefore the clergy, who had met together in a general synod at Beauvais, proceeded to pass sentence of condemnation upon the enemy of the Church's true spouse, Jesus Christ. The venerable Cono, bishop of Praeneste and legate of the holy Roman Church, troubled past endurance by the plaints of churches, of the orphans, of the poor, did smite this ruthless tyrant with the sword of the blessed Peter, which is general anathema. He did also ungird the knightly sword belt from him, though he was absent, and by the judgment of all declared him infamous, a scoundrel, unworthy the name of Christian.

And the king was moved by the plaints of this great council and led an army against him right quickly. He had the clergy, to whom he was ever humbly devoted, in his company, and marched straight against the castle of Crécy. Well fortified was it; yet he took it unprepared because his soldiers smote with an exceeding strong hand; or rather, because the hand of the Lord fought for him. He stormed the strongest tower as if it were the hut of a peasant, and put to confusion the wicked men and piously destroyed the impious. Because they had no pity upon other men, he cut them down without mercy. None could behold the castle tower flaming like the fires of hell and not exclaim, "The whole universe will fight for him against these madmen."

After he had won this victory, the king, who was ever swift to follow up his advantage, pushed forward toward the other castle, called Nogent. There came to him a man who said: "Oh, my lord king, it should be known to thy Serenity that in that wicked castle dwell exceeding wicked men who are worthy to lie in hell, and there only. Those are they who, when thou didst issue commands to destroy the commune of Laon, did burn with fire not only the city of Laon, but the noble church of the Mother of God, and many others beside. And well-nigh all the noble men of the city suffered martyrdom because they were true to their faith and defended their lord the bishop. And these evil men feared not to raise their hands against thy venerable Bishop Gaudin, the anointed of the Lord, defender of the church, but did him most cruelly to death, and exposed his naked body on the open road for beasts and birds of prey to feed upon; but first they cut off his finger with the pontifical ring. And they have agreed together, persuaded by the wicked Thomas, to attack and hold your tower."

The king was doubly animated by these words, and he attacked the wicked castle, broke open the abominable places of confinement, like prisons of hell, and set free the innocent; the guilty he punished with very heavy punishment. He alone avenged the injuries of many. Athirst for justice, he ordained that whatsoever murderous wretches he came upon should be fastened to a gibbet, and left as common food for the greed of kites, crows, and vultures. And this they deserved who had not feared to raise their hand against the Lord's anointed.

When he had taken these two adulterine castles and given back to the monastery of St. John the domains that had been seized, he returned to the city of Amiens and laid seige to a tower of that city which was held by a certain Adam, a cruel tyrant who was laying waste the churches and all the regions round about. He held the place besieged for hard upon two years, and at last forced those who defended it to give themselves up. When he had taken it he destroyed it utterly, and thus brought peace to the realm. He fulfilled most worthily the duty of a king who beareth not the sword in vain, and he deprived the wicked Thomas and his heirs forever of the lordship over that city.

Bishops tried to restrain feudal violence by using spiritual sanctions.

Truce of God (1063)

Drogo, bishop of Terouanne, and count Baldwin [of Hainault] have established this peace with the cooperation of the clergy and people of the land.

Dearest brothers in the Lord, these are the conditions which you must observe during the time of the peace which is commonly called the truce of God, and which begins with sunset on Wednesday and lasts until sunrise on Monday.

1. During those four days and five nights no man or woman shall assault, wound, or slay another, or attack, seize, or destroy a castle, burg, or villa, by craft or by violence.

2. If anyone violates this peace and disobeys these commands of ours, he shall be exiled for thirty years as a penance, and before he leaves the bishopric he shall make compensation for the injury which he committed. Otherwise he shall be excommunicated by the Lord God and excluded from all Christian fellowship.

3. All who associate with him in any way, who give him advice or aid, or hold converse with him, unless it be to advise him to do penance and to leave the bishopric, shall be under excommunication until they have made satisfaction.

4. If any violator of the peace shall fall sick and die before he com-

From O. J. Thatcher and E. H. McNeal, trans., *A Source Book for Mediaeval History* (New York: Charles Scribner's, 1905), pp. 417–418.

pletes his penance, no Christian shall visit him or move his body from the place where it lay, or receive any of his possessions.

5. In addition, brethren, you should observe the peace in regard to lands and animals and all things that can be possessed. If anyone takes from another an animal, a coin, or a garment, during the days of the truce, he shall be excommunicated unless he makes satisfaction. If he desires to make satisfaction for his crime he shall first restore the thing which he stole or its value in money, and shall do penance for seven years within the bishopric. If he should die before he makes satisfaction and completes his penance, his body shall not be buried or removed from the place where it lay, unless his family shall make satisfaction for him to the person whom he injured.

6. During the days of the peace, no one shall make a hostile expedition on horseback, except when summoned by the count; and all who go with the count shall take for their support only as much as is necessary for themselves and their horses.

7. All merchants and other men who pass through your territory from other lands shall have peace from you.

8. You shall also keep this peace every day of the week from the beginning of Advent to the octave of Epiphany and from the beginning of Lent to the octave of Easter, and from the feast of Rogations [the Monday before Ascension Day] to the octave of Pentecost.

9. We command all priests on feast days and Sunday to pray for all who keep the peace, and to curse all who violate it or support its violators.

10. If anyone has been accused of violating the peace and denies the charge, he shall take the communion and undergo the ordeal of hot iron. If he is found guilty, he shall do penance within the bishopric for seven years.

REFORM OF THE CHURCH

Beginnings of Reform

The influence of the church on early feudal society was limited because the churches themselves often fell under the control of kings or local nobles. The next reading describes the kind of abuses that could arise.

Parishes in Italy

Marquis Boniface of Tuscany at one time held thirteen parish churches from the bishop of Reggio, who shared the revenues of fourteen others with the local knights. In the Piedmontese bishoprics numerous churches and tithes were held by laymen, although here, to a greater extent than elsewhere in Italy, the tithe was annexed to manorial churches without parochial rights. Ulric-Manfred, count of Turin, and his daughter Adelaide had in their possession many churches and their revenues. When a reformer in the eleventh century used the term "simony," he had before his eyes this whole complex of mercenary transactions which resulted from the growth of the proprietary system of churches and the extension of the proprietary idea to the parishes. It will be noted that the clergy as well as the laity exercised proprietary rights over the lower churches, treating them as if they were their private property and disposing of their revenues as if they were private income.

Abuses of a moral order were undoubtedly fostered by these practices. Clerical marriage was of course widespread in Italy, as well as less legitimate relations. Rathier of Verona, late in the tenth century, stated that if he tried to enforce clerical celibacy in his diocese, he would be left without a clergy. In Milan the clergy married according to the forms of civil law and claimed that marriage was a custom permitted to the church of St. Ambrose. Clerical marriage became doubly dangerous to ecclesiastical order when combined with the leasing of churches to the clergy under tenurial forms which gave them complete control of church property; there was a real possibility that church offices and property might become hereditary.

From Catherine E. Boyd, *Tithes and Parishes in Medieval Italy* (Ithaca, N.Y.: Cornell University Press, 1952), pp. 104–105.

The plaintiff in the following incident, Count Berengar of Narbonne, was addressing a church council in 1056.

Simony in France

The archbishopric of Narbonne used to belong to my uncle, Archbishop Ermengaud, and in his day it was one of the best bishoprics between Rome and Spain, richly endowed with manors and castles, with estates and allodial lands. The church, filled with books and adorned with gilded pictures, caskets and crucifixes, was resplendent with golden crowns and precious stones. The voices of many canons were heard at regular hours, prayers were offered, and all good works increased. . . .

But, when the aforementioned archbishop of holy memory died, Count Wifred of Cerdana, to whom my wife was a kinswoman, came to Narbonne and approached both my parents and myself to obtain the archbishopric for his son, our bishop mentioned above, who was only ten years old at the time; and he offered a great gift of a hundred thousand *solidi* to my father and the count of Rodez. But my father and mother would not agree. I, however, moved by regard for his kinship and deceived by his pretence of friendship, broke with my parents over this matter and declared that I would destroy them if they did not give way to me. My father, seeing me so moved and so hostile to him acceded to my wishes and to the requests of Wifred, and, having received a hundred thousand *solidi* for ourselves and the count of Rodez as the price of the bishopric, we gave it to Wifred's son, our bishop. Calling God to witness and swearing an oath, he gave his firm word and pledged his faith that if he was to be our bishop, as he was and is, no injury would be done to us or ours or to the bishopric. I was confident that when he was enthroned in the cathedral and grew in years and honor he would be a protection to me and a shield against the spears of all my enemies, that he would remember his kinship to my wife and how I had helped to place him in a position of such honor, and that, as he had declared, he would help me to have and to hold my honor. But then, arrogant as a devil, he unexpectedly provoked me to anger and harassed me and built castles against me and made cruel war on me with a vast army, so that on account of him almost a thousand men were slaughtered on both sides. Then he snatched away from God and his ministers the castles and manors, estates and possessions of the aforesaid church, together with the revenues and possessions of the canons and what they held in common, and gave them to the devil and his servants. . . .

From Brian Tierney, trans., *The Crises of Church and State, 1050–1300* (New York: Prentice–Hall, 1964), pp. 29–30. Copyright © 1964 by Prentice–Hall, Inc. Reprinted courtesy of the publisher.

The abbey of Cluny, founded in 911, became the center of a great, reformed monastic order.

Foundation Charter of Cluny

To all right thinkers it is clear that the providence of God has so provided for certain rich men that, by means of their transitory possessions, if they use them well, they may be able to merit everlasting rewards. As to which thing, indeed, the divine word, showing it to be possible and altogether advising it, says: "The riches of a man are the redemption of his soul." (Prov. xiii.) I, William, count and duke by the grace of God, diligently pondering this, and desiring to provide for my own safety while I am still able, have considered it advisable—nay, most necessary, that from the temporal goods which have been conferred upon me I should give some little portion for the gain of my soul. . . . Therefore be it known to all who live in the unity of the faith and who await the mercy of Christ, and to those who shall succeed them and who shall continue to exist until the end of the world, that, for the love of God and of our Saviour Jesus Christ, I hand over from my own rule to the holy apostles, Peter, namely, and Paul, the possessions over which I hold sway, the town of Cluny, namely, with the court of demesne manor, and the church in honour of St. Mary the mother of God and of St. Peter the prince of the apostles, together with all the things pertaining to it, the vills, indeed, the chapels, the serfs of both sexes, the vines, the fields, the meadows, the woods, the waters and their outlets, the mills, the incomes and revenues, what is cultivated and what is not, all in their entirety. Which things are situated in or about the country of Macon, each one surrounded by its own bounds. . . .

I give these things, moreover, with this understanding, that in Cluny a regular monastery shall be constructed in honour of the holy apostles Peter and Paul, and that there the monks shall congregate and live according to the rule of St. Benedict, and that they shall possess, hold, have and order these same things unto all time. In such wise, however, that the venerable house of prayer which is there shall be faithfully frequented with vows and supplications, and that celestial converse shall be sought and striven after with all desire and with the deepest ardour; and also that there shall be sedulously directed to God prayers, beseechings and exhortations as well for me as for all, according to the order in which mention has been made of them above. And let the monks themselves, together with all the aforesaid possessions, be under the power and dominion of the abbot Berno, who, as long as he shall live, shall preside over them regularly according to his knowledge

From "Charter of Abbey of Cluny," in E. F. Henderson, ed., *Select Historical Documents of the Middle Ages* (London: George Bell and Sons, 1892), pp. 329–332.

and ability. But after his death, those same monks shall have power and permission to elect any one of their order whom they please as abbot and rector, following the will of God and the rule promulgated by St. Benedict—in such wise that neither by the intervention of our own or of any other power may they be impeded from making a purely canonical election. Every five years, moreover, the aforesaid monks shall pay to the church of the apostles at Rome ten shillings to supply them with lights; and they shall have the protection of those same apostles and the defence of the Roman pontiff; and those monks may, with their whole heart and soul, according to their ability and knowledge, build up the aforesaid place. We will, further, that in our times and in those of our successors, according as the opportunities and possibilities of that place shall allow, there shall daily, with the greatest zeal be performed there works of mercy towards the poor, the needy, strangers and pilgrims. It has pleased us also to insert in this document that, from this day, those same monks there congregated shall be subject neither to our yoke, nor to that of our relatives, nor to the sway of the royal might, nor to that of any earthly power. And, through God and all his saints, and by the awful day of judgment, I warn and abjure that no one of the secular princes, no count, no bishop whatever, not the pontiff of the aforesaid Roman see, shall invade the property of these servants of God, or alienate it, or diminish it, or exchange it, or give it as a benefice to any one, or constitute any prelate over them against their will.

In mid-eleventh century Emperor Henry III of Germany established a line of reforming popes in Rome. After his death, Pope Gregory VII (1073–1085) carried on the reform program in a radical fashion.

Papal Reform Decrees (1074–1075)

Those who have been advanced to any grade of holy orders, or to any office, through simony, that is, by the payment of money, shall hereafter have no right to officiate in the holy church. Those also who have secured churches by giving money shall certainly be deprived of them.

If there are any priests, deacons, or subdeacons who are married, by the power of omnipotent God and the authority of St. Peter we forbid them to enter a church until they repent and mend their ways. But if any remain with their wives, no one shall dare hear them [when they officiate in the church], because their benediction is turned into a curse, and their prayer into a sin. For the Lord says through the prophet, "I will curse your blessings" [Mal. 2:2]. Whoever shall refuse to obey this most salutary command shall be guilty of the sin of idola-

From O. J. Thatcher and E. H. McNeal, trans., *A Source Book for Mediaeval History* (New York: Charles Scribner's, 1905), pp. 135–136.

try. For Samuel says: "For rebellion is as the sin of witchcraft, and stubbornness is as iniquity and idolatry" [1 Sam. 15:23]. Whoever therefore asserts that he is a Christian but refuses to obey the apostolic see, is guilty of paganism.

Since we know that investitures have been made by laymen in many places, contrary to the decrees of the holy fathers, and that very many disturbances injurious to the Christian religion have thereby arisen in the church, we therefore decree: that no clergyman shall receive investiture of a bishopric, monastery, or church from the hand of the emperor, or the king, or any lay person, man or woman. And if anyone has ventured to receive such investiture, let him know that it is annulled by apostolic authority, and that he is subject to excommunication until he has made due reparation.

Gregory VII also put forward very high claims for the papal office in his Dictatus Papae—*"Assertions of the Pope."*

Dictatus Papae (1075)

1. That the Roman church was founded by God alone.
2. That the Roman pontiff alone can with right be called universal.
3. That he alone can depose or reinstate bishops.
4. That, in a council, his legate, even if a lower grade, is above all bishops, and can pass sentence of deposition against them.
5. That the pope may depose the absent.
6. That, among other things, we ought not to remain in the same house with those excommunicated by him.
7. That for him alone is it lawful, according to the needs of the time, to make new laws, to assemble together new congregations, to make an abbey of a canonry; and, on the other hand, to divide a rich bishopric and unite the poor ones.
8. That he alone may use the imperial insignia.
9. That of the pope alone all princes shall kiss the feet.
10. That his name alone shall be spoken in the churches.
11. That this is the only name in the world.
12. That it may be permitted to him to depose emperors.
13. That he may be permitted to transfer bishops if need be.
14. That he has power to ordain a clerk of any church he may wish.
15. That he who is ordained by him may *preside* over another. church, but may not hold a subordinate position; and that such a one may not receive a higher grade from any bishop.
16. That no synod shall be called a general one without his order.

From E. F. Henderson, ed., *Select Historical Documents of the Middle Ages* (London: George Bell and Sons, 1892), pp. 366–367.

17. That no chapter and no book shall be considered canonical without his authority.

18. That a sentence passed by him may be retracted by no one; and that he himself, alone of all, may retract it.

19. That he himself may be judged by no one.

20. That no one shall dare to condemn one who appeals to the apostolic chair.

21. That to the latter should be referred the more important cases of every church.

22. That the Roman church has never erred; nor will it err to all eternity, the Scripture bearing witness.

23. That the Roman pontiff, if he have been canonically ordained, is undoubtedly made a saint by the merits of St. Peter; St. Ennodius, bishop of Pavia, bearing witness, and many holy fathers agreeing with him. As is contained in the decrees of St. Symmachus the pope.

24. That, by his command and consent, it may be lawful for subordinates to bring accusations.

25. That he may depose and reinstate bishops without assembling a synod.

26. That he who is not at peace with the Roman church shall not be considered catholic.

27. That he may absolve subjects from their fealty to wicked men.

Empire and Papacy

King Henry IV of Germany (son of Henry III) refused to obey the pope's decrees. The particular point at issue was "lay investiture," the king's claim to appoint bishops and invest them with ring and staff, the symbols of sacred office. When Gregory threatened to depose Henry, the king denounced the pope as a usurper.

Henry IV to Gregory VII (January 24, 1076)

Henry, king not through usurpation but through the holy ordination of God, to Hildebrand, at present not pope but false monk. Such greeting as this hast thou merited through thy disturbances, inasmuch as there is no grade in the church which thou hast omitted to make a partaker not of honour but of confusion, not of benediction but of malediction. For, to mention few and especial cases out of many, not

From E. F. Henderson, ed., *Select Historical Documents of the Middle Ages* (London: George Bell and Sons, 1892), pp. 372–373.

only hast thou not feared to lay hands upon the rulers of the holy church, the anointed of the Lord—the archbishops, namely, bishops and priests—but thou hast trodden them under foot like slaves ignorant of what their master is doing. Thou hast won favour from the common herd by crushing them; thou hast looked upon all of them as knowing nothing, upon thy sole self, moreover, as knowing all things. This knowledge, however, thou hast used not for edification but for destruction; so that with reason we believe that St. Gregory, whose name thou hast usurped for thyself, was prophesying concerning thee when he said: "The pride of him who is in power increases the more, the greater the number of those subject to him; and he thinks that he himself can do more than all." And we, indeed, have endured all this, being eager to guard the honour of the apostolic see; thou, however, hast understood our humility to be fear, and hast not, accordingly, shunned to rise up against the royal power conferred upon us by God, daring to threaten to divest us of it. As if we had received our kingdom from thee! As if the kingdom and the empire were in thine and not in God's hand! And this although our Lord Jesus Christ did call us to the kingdom, did not, however, call thee to the priesthood. For thou has ascended by the following steps. By wiles, namely, which the profession of monk abhors, thou hast achieved money; by money, favour; by the sword, the throne of peace. And from the throne of peace thou hast disturbed peace, inasmuch as thou hast armed subjects against those in authority over them; inasmuch as thou, who wert not called, hast taught that our bishops called of God are to be despised; inasmuch as thou hast usurped for laymen the ministry over their priests, allowing them to depose or condemn those whom they themselves had received as teachers from the hand of God through the laying on of hands of the bishops. On me also who, although unworthy to be among the anointed, have nevertheless been anointed to the kingdom, thou hast lain thy hand; me who—as the tradition of the holy Fathers teaches, declaring that I am not to be deposed for any crime unless, which God forbid, I should have strayed from the faith—am subject to the judgment of God alone. For the wisdom of the holy fathers committed even Julian the apostate not to themselves, but to God alone, to be judged and to be deposed. For himself the true pope, Peter, also exclaims: "Fear God, honour the king." But thou who dost not fear God, dost dishonour in me his appointed one. Wherefore St. Paul, when he has not spared an angel of Heaven if he shall have preached otherwise, has not excepted thee also who dost teach otherwise upon earth. For he says: "If any one, either I or an angel from Heaven, should preach a gospel other than that which has been preached to you, he shall be damned." Thou, therefore, damned by this curse and by the judgment of all our bishops and by our own, descend and relinquish the apostolic chair which thou hast usurped. Let another ascend the throne of St.

Peter, who shall not practise violence under the cloak of religion, but shall teach the sound doctrine of St. Peter. I Henry, king by the grace of God, do say unto thee, together with all our bishops: Descend, descend, to be damned throughout the ages.

Gregory responded with a sentence of deposition.

Deposition of Henry IV (February 22, 1076)

O St. Peter, chief of the apostles, incline to us, I beg, thy holy ears, and hear me thy servant whom thou hast nourished from infancy, and whom, until this day, thou hast freed from the hand of the wicked, who have hated and do hate me for my faithfulness to thee. Thou, and my mistress the mother of God, and thy brother St. Paul are witnesses for me among all the saints that thy holy Roman church drew me to its helm against my will; that I had no thought of ascending thy chair through force, and that I would rather have ended my life as a pilgrim than, by secular means, to have seized thy throne for the sake of earthly glory. And therefore I believe it to be through thy grace and not through my own deeds that it has pleased and does please thee that the Christian people, who have been especially committed to thee, should obey me. And especially to me, as thy representative and by thy favour, has the power been granted by God of binding and loosing in Heaven and on earth. On the strength of this belief therefore, for the honour and security of thy church, in the name of Almighty God, Father, Son and Holy Ghost, I withdraw, through thy power and authority, from Henry the king, son of Henry the emperor, who has risen against thy church with unheard of insolence, the rule over the whole kingdom of the Germans and over Italy. And I absolve all Christians from the bonds of the oath which they have made or shall make to him; and I forbid any one to serve him as king. For it is fitting that he who strives to lessen the honour of thy church should himself lose the honour which belongs to him. And since he has scorned to obey as a Christian, and has not returned to God whom he had deserted—holding intercourse with the excommunicated; practising manifold iniquities; spurning my commands which, as thou dost bear witness, I issued to him for his own salvation; separating himself from thy church and striving to rend it—I bind him in thy stead with the chain of the anathema. And, leaning on thee, I so bind him that the people may know and have proof that thou art Peter, and above thy rock the Son of the living God hath built His church, and the gates of Hell shall not prevail against it.

From E. F. Henderson, ed., *Select Historical Documents of the Middle Ages* (London: George Bell and Sons, 1892), pp. 376–377.

After a rebellion in Germany Henry sought absolution from Gregory. The two rulers met at the castle of Canossa in northern Italy. Afterward Gregory sent this account to his allies, the German princes.

Gregory VII to the Princes of Germany (1077)

Bishop Gregory, servant of the servants of God, to all the archbishops, bishops, dukes, counts and other princes of the realm of the Germans who defend the Christian faith, greeting and apostolic benediction.

Inasmuch as for love of justice ye assumed common cause and danger with us in the struggle of Christian warfare, we have taken care to indicate to you, beloved, with sincere affection, how the king, humbled to penance, obtained the pardon of absolution and how the whole affair has progressed since his entry into Italy up to the present time.

As had been agreed with the legates who had been sent to us on your part, we came into Lombardy about twenty days before the date on which one of the commanders was to come over the pass to meet us, awaiting his advent that we might cross over to the other side. But when the term fixed upon had already passed, and we were told that at this time on account of many difficulties—as we can readily believe—an escort could not be sent to meet us, we were involved in no little care as to what would be best for us to do, having no other means of crossing to you.

Meanwhile, however, we learned for certain that the king was approaching. He also, before entering Italy, sent on to us suppliant legates, offering in all things to render satisfaction to God, to St. Peter and to us. And he renewed his promise that, besides amending his life, he would observe all obedience if only he might merit to obtain from us the favour of absolution and the apostolic benediction. When, after long deferring this and holding frequent consultations, we had, through all the envoys who passed, severely taken him to task for his excesses: he came at length of his own accord, with a few followers, showing nothing of hostility or boldness, to the town of Canossa where we were tarrying. And there, having laid aside all the belongings of royalty, wretchedly, with bare feet and clad in wool, he continued for three days to stand before the gate of the castle. Nor did he desist from imploring with many tears the aid and consolation of the apostolic mercy until he had moved all of those who were present there, and whom the report of it reached, to such pity and depth of compassion that, interceding for him with many prayers and tears, all wondered indeed at the unaccustomed hardness of our heart, while some actually cried out that we were exercising, not the gravity of apostolic severity, but the cruelty, as it were, of a tyrannical ferocity.

From E. F. Henderson, ed., *Select Historical Documents of the Middle Ages* (London: George Bell and Sons, 1892), pp. 385–387.

Finally, conquered by the persistency of his compunction and by the constant supplications of all those who were present, we loosed the chain of the anathema and at length received him into the favour of communion and into the lap of the holy mother church, those being accepted as sponsors for him whose names are written below. And of this transaction we also received a confirmation at the hands of the abbot of Cluny, of our daughters Matilda and the countess Adelaide, and of such princes, episcopal and lay, as seemed to us useful for this purpose.

Having thus accomplished these matters, we desire at the first opportunity to cross over to your parts in order that, by God's aid, we may more fully arrange all things for the peace of the church and the concord of the kingdom, as has long been our wish. For we desire, beloved, that ye should know beyond a doubt that the whole question at issue is as yet so little cleared up—as ye can learn from the sponsors mentioned—that both our coming and the unanimity of your counsels are extremely necessary. Wherefore strive ye all to continue in the faith in which ye have begun and in the love of justice; and know that we are not otherwise bound to the king save that, by word alone as is our custom, we have said that he might have hopes from us in those matters in which, without danger to his soul or to our own, we might be able to help him to his salvation and honour either through justice or through mercy.

Bishop Hermann of Metz questioned the pope's right to depose a king. Gregory sent him a detailed explanation of the papal claim.

Gregory VII to Hermann of Metz (1081)

Thy demand to be aided, as it were, by our writings and fortified against the madness of those who babble forth with unhallowed mouth that the authority of the holy and apostolic see had no right to excommunicate Henry—a man who despises the Christian law; a destroyer, namely, of the churches and of the empire; a favourer of heretics and a partaker with them—or to absolve any one from the oath of fealty to him, does not seem to us to be altogether necessary when so many and such absolutely certain proofs are to be found in the pages of Holy Scripture . . .

For, to cite a few passages from among many, who does not know the words of our Lord and Saviour Jesus Christ who says in the gospel: "Thou art Peter and upon this rock will I build my church, and the gates of hell shall not prevail against it; and I will give unto thee the

From E. F. Henderson, ed., *Select Historical Documents of the Middle Ages* (London: George Bell and Sons, 1892), pp. 394–395.

keys of the kingdom of Heaven; and whatsoever thou shalt bind upon earth shall be bound also in Heaven, and whatsoever thou shalt loose upon earth shall be loosed also in Heaven"? Are kings excepted here, or do they not belong to the sheep which the Son of God committed to St. Peter? Who, I ask, in this universal concession of the power of binding and loosing, can think that he is withdrawn from the authority of St. Peter, unless, perhaps, that unfortunate man who is unwilling to bear the yoke of the Lord and subjects himself to the burden of the devil, refusing to be among the number of Christ's sheep? It will help him little to his wretched liberty, indeed, that he shake from his proud neck the divinely granted power of Peter. For the more any one, through pride, refuses to bear it, the more heavily shall it press upon him unto damnation at the judgment. . . .

Who does not know that kings and leaders are sprung from those who—ignorant of God—by pride, plunder, perfidy, murders—in a word by almost every crime, the devil, who is the prince of this world, urging them on as it were—have striven with blind cupidity and intolerable presumption to dominate over their equals; namely, over men? To whom, indeed, can we better compare them, when they seek to make the priests of God bend to their footprints, than to him who is head over all the sons of pride and who, tempting the Highest Pontiff Himself, the Head of priests, the Son of the Most High, and promising to Him all the kingdoms of the world, said: "All these I will give unto Thee if Thou wilt fall down and worship me"? Who can doubt but that the priests of Christ are to be considered the fathers and masters of kings and princes and of all the faithful? . . .

In the different kingdoms of the earth, from the beginning of the world, very few of the innumerable multitude of kings are found to have been holy: whereas in one see alone—the Roman one, namely—almost a hundred of the successive pontiffs since the time of St. Peter the apostle are counted among the most holy. Why, then, is this—except that the kings and princes of the earth, enticed by vain glory, prefer, as has been said, the things that are their own to the things that are spiritual; but the pontiffs of the church, despising vain glory, prefer to carnal things the things that are of God? The former readily punish those who sin against themselves and are indifferent to those who sin against God; the latter quickly pardon those who sin against themselves and do not lightly spare those who sin against God. The former, too much bent on earthly deeds, think slightingly of spiritual ones; the latter, sedulously meditating on heavenly things, despise the things which are of earth.

Therefore all Christians who desire to reign with Christ should be warned not to strive to rule through ambition of worldly power. . . . Let them always prefer the honour of God to their own; let them cherish and guard justice by observing the rights of every man; let them not walk in the counsel of the ungodly but, with an assenting heart, always consort with good men. Let them not seek to subject to themselves or to subjugate the holy church as a handmaid; but chiefly let them strive, by recognizing the teachers and fathers, to honour in due form her eyes—namely the priests of God. For if we are ordered to honour our carnal fathers and mothers—how much more our spiritual ones!

The dispute over lay investiture was never settled in the lifetimes of Gregory VII and Henry IV. A compromise was finally reached in 1122.

Concordat of Worms

Privilege of Pope Calixtus II

I, bishop Calixtus, servant of the servants of God, do grant to thee beloved son, Henry—by the grace of God august emperor of the Romans—that the elections of the bishops and abbots of the German kingdom, who belong to the kingdom, shall take place in thy presence, without simony and without any violence; so that if any discord shall arise between the parties concerned, thou, by the counsel or judgment of the metropolitan and the co-provincials, may'st give consent and aid to the party which has the more right. The one elected, moreover, without any exaction may receive the regalia from thee through the lance, and shall do unto thee for these what he rightfully should. But he who is consecrated in the other parts of thy empire (*i.e.* Burgundy and Italy) shall, within six months, and without any exaction, receive the regalia from thee through the lance, and shall do unto thee for these what he rightfully should. Excepting all things which are known to belong to the Roman church. Concerning matters, however, in which thou dost make complaint to me, and dost demand aid,—I, according to the duty of my office, will furnish aid to thee. I give unto thee true peace.

Edict of the Emperor Henry V

In the name of the holy and indivisible Trinity, I, Henry, by the grace of God august emperor of the Romans, for the love of God and of the holy Roman church and of our master pope Calixtus, and for the healing of my soul, do remit to God, and to the holy apostles of God, Peter and Paul, and to the holy catholic church, all investiture through ring and staff; and do grant that in all the churches that are in my kingdom or empire there may be canonical election and free consecration. All the possessions and regalia of St. Peter which, from

From E. F. Henderson, ed., *Select Historical Documents of the Middle Ages* (London: George Bell and Sons, 1892), pp. 397–398, 403–404.

the beginning of this discord unto his day, whether in the time of my father or also in mine, have been abstracted, and which I hold: I restore to that same holy Roman church. As to those things, moreover, which I do not hold, I will faithfully aid in their restoration. As to the possessions also of all other churches and princes, and of all others lay and clerical persons which have been lost in that war: according to the counsel of the princes, or according to justice, I will restore the things that I hold; and of those things which I do not hold I will faithfully aid in the restoration. And I grant true peace to our master pope Calixtus, and to the holy Roman church, and to all those who are or have been on its side. And in matters where the holy Roman church shall demand aid I will grant it; and in matters concerning which it shall make complaint to me I will duly grant to it justice.

THE FIRST CRUSADERS

Western Views

The mixture of feudal warrior ethics and religious enthusiasm that inspired the crusades is captured perfectly in the Song of Roland *(written toward 1100). The story is set in the days of Charlemagne but it reflects the ideals of the eleventh-century crusaders against the Saracens of Spain. (The hero, Roland, commanding Charlemagne's rear guard, refuses out of pride to sound his horn in order to recall the main army when he is attacked by a host of Saracens.)*

From *The Song of Roland*

The pagans put Saracen hauberks on,
Most of them reinforced with triple mail;
They lace the splendid Saragossan helms,
Gird on their swords wrought of Viana steel,
Take their fine shields and their spears from Valence
With gonfalons of crimson, blue and white.
Then they forsake their palfreys and their mules,
Mount on their steeds, and ride in close array.
Bright was the day and radiant the sun;
All their equipment glitters in its rays.
A thousand bugles sound a flourish forth:
Great is the clamour, and the Frenchmen hear.
Said Oliver: 'Sir comrade, I believe
We may do battle with the Saracens.'
Roland replies: 'And may God grant it so!
Our duty bids us stand firm for our king:
A man should suffer hardship for his lord,
Endure great heat and bear with bitter cold,
And be prepared to lose both hair and skin.
Now let each man take care to deal great blows,

From *The Song of Roland*, D. D. R. Owen, trans. (London: George Allen and Unwin, 1972), pp. 51–55 (*ll.* 994–1016, 1049–1069, 1082–1109, 1124–1138). Reprinted by permission of D. D. R. Owen.

So that no song of shame be sung of us!
Pagans are wrong and Christians in the right;
No bad example shall be set by me.'

Said Oliver: 'The pagans have vast strength,
And our Frenchmen beside them seem so few.
Friend Roland, I beseech you, sound your horn!
Then Charles will hear; the army will turn back.'
Roland replies; 'Should I act like a fool
And lose my fame and honour in fair France?
No! I shall strike great blows with Durendal,
Stain it with gore up to its golden hilt.
The pagan knaves shall rue their coming here,
For this I pledge: each one is doomed to die.'

'Companion Roland, sound your oliphant!
The king will hear, and turn the army back;
Charles and his barons will come to our aid.'
Roland replies: 'May it never please God
That blame should fall on my kinsfolk through me,
Or fair France ever lapse in infamy!
Rather I'll strike amain with Durendal
My trusty sword that hangs here at my side;
And you will see its blade all stained with gore.
Those pagan knaves shall rue their gathering.
I pledge you this: they are all marked for death.'

Said Oliver: 'I see no blame in it;
For I have seen the Saracens from Spain:
They cover both the mountains and the vales,
Swarming on hillsides and throughout the plains.
Huge are the armies of the foreign folk,
While we have but a puny company,'
Roland replies: 'I like it better so.
May God Himself and His angels forbid
That through me France's worth should ever wane!
I'd rather die than suffer such a shame.
Stout blows endear us to the emperor.'

Roland is valiant, Oliver is wise,
And both are matchless in their chivalry.
When they are armed and mounted on their steeds,
For fear of death neither will shun the fray.
Excellent are the counts, lofty their speech.
The wicked pagans wrathfully ride on.
Oliver said: 'Roland, just see them all!

How close they are, with Charles so far away!
You did not deign to sound your oliphant,
Yet if the king were here, we'd have no harm.
Look up towards the passes into Spain!
Now you can see what plight the rearguard's in:
Its men will never form another one.'
Roland replies: 'Tell no such tale to me!
Cursed be the heart that quakes within the breast!
We shall stand fast and firm to hold our ground,
Hewing and hacking there as best we may.'

Archbishop Turpin is not far away.
Spurring his horse, he gallops up a hill,
Summons the French, and speaks these solemn words:
'My lords and barons, Charles has left us here,
And for our king we should in duty die.
Lend aid now to maintain the Christian faith!
You'll join in battle, as you know full well:
Before your eyes you see the Saracens.
Say your confessions, for God's mercy pray!
I will absolve you to secure your souls.
If you die, blessed martyrs you will be
And have your place on high in Paradise.'
The French dismount and to the ground they fall,
And God's archbishop gives the benison.
As penance he commands that they strike hard.

The first crusade directed against the eastern Mediterranean was proclaimed in 1095.

Pope Urban's Speech at Clermont

Now that you, O sons of God, have consecrated yourselves to God to maintain peace among yourselves more vigorously and to uphold the laws of the Church faithfully, there is work to do, for you must turn the strength of your sincerity, now that you are aroused by divine correction, to another affair that concerns you and God. Hastening to the way, you must help your brothers living in the Orient, who need your aid for which they have already cried out many times.

For, as most of you have been told, the Turks, a race of Persians, who have penetrated within the boundaries of Romania even to the

From Fulcher of Chartres, *Chronicle of the First Crusade*, M. E. McGinty, trans. (Philadelphia, Pa.: University of Pennsylvania Press, 1941), pp. 15–17.

Mediterranean to that point which they call the Arm of Saint George, in occupying more and more of the lands of the Christians, have overcome them, already victims of seven battles, and have killed and captured them, have overthrown churches, and have laid waste God's kingdom. If you permit this supinely for very long, God's faithful ones will be still further subjected.

Concerning this affair, I, with suppliant prayer—not I, but the Lord—exhort you, heralds of Christ, to persuade all of whatever class, both knights and footmen, both rich and poor, in numerous edicts, to strive to help expel that wicked race from our Christian lands before it is too late.

I speak to those present, I send word to those not here; moreover, Christ commands it. Remission of sins will be granted for those going thither, if they end a shackled life either on land or in crossing the sea, or in struggling against the heathen. I, being vested with that gift from God, grant this to those who go.

O what a shame, if a people, so despised, degenerate, and enslaved by demons would thus overcome a people endowed with the trust of almighty God, and shining in the name of Christ! O how many evils will be imputed to you by the Lord Himself, if you do not help those who, like you, profess Christianity!

Let those who are accustomed to wage private wars wastefully even against Believers, go forth against the Infidels in a battle worthy to be undertaken now and to be finished in victory. Now, let those, who until recently existed as plunderers, be soldiers of Christ; now, let those, who formerly contended against brothers and relations, rightly fight barbarians; now, let those, who recently were hired for a few pieces of silver, win their eternal reward. Let those, who wearied themselves to the detriment of body and soul, labor for a twofold honor. Nay, more, the sorrowful here will be glad there, the poor here will be rich there, and the enemies of the Lord here will be His friends there.

Let no delay postpone the journey of those about to go, but when they have collected the money owed to them and the expenses for the journey, and when winter has ended and spring has come, let them enter the crossroads courageously with the Lord going on before.

An Arab View

Ousama Ibn Mounkidh, an Arab chieftain, left an account of the Frankish settlers in the Levant. From his Muslim viewpoint they seemed coarse and uncivilized and their women oddly liberated.

From *Autobiography of Ousama*

It is always those who have recently come to live in Frankish territory who show themselves more inhuman than their predecessors who have been established amongst us and become familiarised with the Mohammedans.

A proof of the harshness of the Franks (the scourge of Allah upon them!) is to be seen in what happened to me when I visited Jerusalem. I went into the mosque Al-Aksa. By the side of this was a little mosque which the Franks had converted into a church. When I went into the mosque Al-Aksa, which was occupied by the Templars, who were my friends, they assigned me this little mosque in which to say my prayers. One day I went into it and glorified Allah. I was engrossed in my praying when one of the Franks rushed at me, seized me and turned my face to the East, saying, "That is how to pray!" A party of Templars made for him, seized his person and ejected him. I returned to my prayers. The same man, escaping their attention, made for me again and turned my face round to the East, repeating, "That is how to pray!" The Templars again made for him and ejected him, then they apologised to me and said to me, "He is a stranger who has only recently arrived from Frankish lands. He has never seen anyone praying without turning to the East." I answered, "I have prayed sufficiently for to-day."

The Franks understand neither the feeling of honour nor the nature of jealousy. If one of them is walking with his wife and he meets another man, the latter takes the woman's hand and goes and talks to her while the husband stands aside waiting for the end of the interview. If the woman prolongs it unreasonably, the husband leaves her alone with her companion and goes back.

Here is a fact of the same nature of which I was witness. When I was in Neapolis, I lived at the house of a man named Mou'izz at whose house Mohammedans used to stay. Our windows opened on to the street. Opposite, on the other side, there lived a Frank who sold wine to merchants. . . . One day, going to his bedroom, the wine-merchant found a man in bed with his wife. "What has induced you to come in to my wife?" he asked. "I was tired," the other said, "and I came in to rest myself." "But how," said the Frank, "did you dare to go in to my bed?" "I found a couch smoothed over like a rug and I went to sleep on it." "But my wife was sleeping by your side." "The bed belonged to her, could I turn her away from it?" "By the truth of my religion," the husband answered, "I swear to you that if you do it again we shall see

The Autobiography of Ousama (1095–1188), G. R. Potter, trans. (London: George Routledge, 1929), pp. 176–179, 181–182. Reprinted by permission of Routledge & Kegan Paul Ltd.

an estrangement between us." That is what discontent is with a Frank and that is the measure of his jealousy.

Another fact of the same nature: We had with us a bath-attendant named Salim, who came from Ma'arrat an-No'man, and who was employed in my father's service (may Allah have mercy upon him!). Salim told us one day, "I set up some baths at Ma'arrat an-No'man to make a living by them. A Frankish knight came to them. Now they dislike our custom of bathing with a costume. My customer reached out his hand and pulled my costume off. He then saw that I had a little previously shaved my body. He called to me, 'Salim!' I came to him. He touched me and said, 'Salim is magnificent *(salim)*! By the truth of my religion, do to me likewise.' He lay on his back and I shaved the hair from his body. He passed his hand over his skin and felt how smooth it was. He then said to me, 'Salim, by your religion, I conjure you, do likewise to madame *(dama)*.' Now in their language, 'madame' *(dama)* is the wife. He was thinking of his wife. He sent one of his servants to tell his wife to come. The servant went to her and brought her. At his orders a similar operation was performed on her, while her husband sat by her and watched it done. He then thanked me and gave me my fee for my pains."

Consider this absolute contradiction. Here are men without jealousy and without a feeling of honour. On the other hand they are endowed with great courage. Generally speaking, courage originates solely in feelings of honour and the care people take to avoid any slur on their reputation.

At Neapolis, I was once present at a curious sight. They brought in two men for trial by battle, the cause being the following. Some Mohammedan brigands had raided some property in the neighbourhood of Neapolis. A farmer was suspected of having guided the brigands to this spot. The farmer took flight but soon returned, the king having had his children imprisoned. "Treat me with equity," said the accused, "and allow me to fight with him who has named me as the person who brought the brigands into the village." The king then said to the lord who had received the village as a fief: "Send for his opponent." The lord returned to his village, picked out a blacksmith who was working there, and said to him, "You must go and fight a duel." For the owner of the fief was primarily anxious to see that none of his labourers got himself killed, for fear his crops should suffer.

I saw this blacksmith. He was a strong young man, but one who, walking or sitting, was always wanting something to drink. As for the other, the challenger to single combat, he was an old man of great courage, who snapped his fingers as a token of defiance and prepared for the fight without perturbation. The sheriff *(al-biskound)*, governor *(schihna)* of the town, appeared, gave each of the two fighers a cudgel and shield and made the crowd form a ring round them.

The fight started. The old man forced the blacksmith backwards, throwing him on to the edge of the crowd, and then returned to the middle of the ring. The exchange of blows was so violent that the rivals, who remained standing, seemed to make up one pillar of blood.

The fight continued, while the sheriff urged them to force a conclusion. "Quicker," he shouted to them. The blacksmith profited by his experience at wielding a hammer. When the old man was exhausted, the blacksmith aimed a blow at him which overthrew him, making the cudgel, which he was holding in his hand, fall behind him. The blacksmith crouched over the old man so as to put his fingers into his eyes, but he could not reach them because of the streams of blood which were flowing from them; he got up and struck his head so violently with his cudgel that he finished him off.

VIII

RURAL LIFE
The Medieval Manor
From *A Manor of the Hundred Rolls*
(1279)
From *Select Pleas in Manorial Courts*
Peasant Daily Fare
From *Piers Plowman*

TOWNS AND TRADE
City Life
From *Otto of Freising's Chronicle*
From *A Description of London*
Economic Activities
Rules of a Merchant Guild
(Southampton)
Silk Spinners at Paris
Advice to Merchants

MEDIEVAL MONARCHIES
England
From *Magna Carta*
Summons of Representatives to
Parliament (1295)
From *Rolls of Parliament*
From *Flowers of History*
France
From *Joinville. Life of St. Louis*
The Empire
From *Otto of Freising's Chronicle*

CHURCH AND STATE
**Innocent III—Papal Power at Its
Zenith**
From *Letters of Innocent III*
Innocent IV and Frederick II
Frederick II According to Salimbene
Deposition of Frederick II (1245)
**Boniface VIII—The Crisis of Papal
Power**
Unum Sanctam
Accusations Against Boniface VIII
Decree of Clement V (1306)
Decree of Clement V (1311)

Reflections on Government
From Innocent IV. *Commentary on
the Decretals*
From John of Paris. *On Royal and
Papal Power (1303)*
From Giles of Rome. *On the Rule
of Princes*

THE MEDIEVAL WORLD—ECONOMY AND GOVERNMENT

MEDIEVAL CIVILIZATION WAS *built on an agrarian foundation—rural manors worked by peasant labor. Then, from the eleventh century onward, an increasing volume of international commerce stimulated the growth of trading cities, which came to play a major role in economic and political life. In the cities new guilds of craftsmen and merchants grew up. They sought to regulate production and exchange while providing fellowship and mutual support for the members.*

The slowly expanding medieval economy made possible a growth of more sophisticated institutions of government. National monarchies were consolidated in England and France and in other regions of Europe. Important experiments in constitutional government occurred. The kings of Germany, who also claimed the title emperor, tried to extend their rule over Italy, but they were defeated by the combined opposition of the northern Italian cities and the papacy.

Throughout the thirteenth century the papacy was the greatest center of organized government in western Europe. While dominating Rome and central Italy as temporal princes, the popes controlled the ecclesiastical affairs of all Europe as heads of the church. Under Innocent III (1198–1217) they claimed a kind of universal jurisdiction over all the kings of Europe, and under Boniface VIII (1298–1305) such claims were put forward in an extreme form. Boniface, however, was defeated in a struggle with the king of France. At the beginning of the fourteenth century various political philosophers were seeking to discriminate between the proper spheres of action of the church and the state.

RURAL LIFE

The Medieval Manor

From *A Manor of the Hundred Rolls (1279)*

The abbot of Peterborough holds the manor of Alwalton and vill from the lord king directly; which manor and vill with its appurtenances the lord Edward, formerly king of England gave to the said abbot and convent of that place in free, pure, and perpetual alms. And the court of the said manor with its garden contains one half an acre. And to the whole of the said vill of Alwalton belong 5 hides and a half and 1 virgate of land and a half; of which each hide contains 5 virgates of land and each virgate contains 25 acres. Of these hides the said abbot has in demesne 1 hide and a half of land and half a virgate, which contain as above. Likewise he has there 8 acres of meadow. Also he has there separable pasture which contains 1 acre. Likewise he has there three water mills. Likewise he has there a common fish pond with a fish-weir on the bank of the Nene, which begins at Wildlake and extends to the mill of Newton and contains in length 2 leagues. Likewise he has there a ferry with a boat.

Free Tenants Thomas le Boteler holds a messuage with a court yard which contains 1 rood, and 3 acres of land, by charter, paying thence yearly to the said abbot 14s.

Likewise the rector of the church of Alwalton holds 1 virgate of land with its appurtenances, with which the said church was anciently endowed. Likewise the said rector has a holding the tenant of which holds 1 rood of ground by paying to the said rector yearly 12d.

And the abbot of Peterboro is patron of the church.

Villeins Hugh Miller holds 1 virgate of land in villenage by paying thence to the said abbot 3s. 1d. Likewise the same Hugh works through the whole year except 1 week at Christmas, 1 week at Easter, and 1 at Whitsuntide, that is in each week 3 days, each day with 1 man, and in

From "A Manor of the Hundred Rolls: Alwalton," in J. H. Robinson, *University of Pennsylvania Translations and Reprints* (Philadelphia, Pa.: University of Pennsylvania Press, 1897), Vol. 3, No. 5, pp. 4–8.

autumn each day with 2 men, performing the said works at the will of the said abbot as in plowing and other work. Likewise he gives 1 bushel of wheat for benseed and 18 sheaves of oats for fodder-corn. Likewise he gives 3 hens and 1 cock yearly and 5 eggs at Easter. Likewise he does carrying to Peterborough and to Jakele and no where else, at the will of the said abbot. Likewise if he sells a brood mare in his court yard for 10s. or more, he shall give to the said abbot 4d., and if for less he shall give nothing to the aforesaid. He gives also merchet and heriot, and is tallaged at the feast of St. Michael, at the will of the said abbot. There are also there 17 other villeins, viz. John of Ganesoupe, Robert son of Walter, Ralph son of the reeve, Emma ate Pertre, William son of Reginald, Thomas son of Gunnilda, Eda widow of Ralph, Ralph Reeve, William Reeve, William son of William Reeve, Thomas Flegg, Henry Abbott, William Hereward, Serle son of William Reeve, Walter Palmer, William Abbot, Henry Serle; each of whom holds 1 virgate of land in villenage, paying and doing in all things, each for himself, to the said abbot yearly just as the said Hugh Miller. There are also 5 other villeins, viz. Simon Mariot, Robert of Hastone, Thomas Smith, John Mustard, and William Carter, each of whom holds half a virgate of land by paying and doing in all things half of the whole service which Hugh Miller pays and does.

Cotters   Henry, son of the miller, holds a cottage with a croft which contains 1 rood, paying thence yearly to the said abbot 2s. Likewise he works for 3 days in carrying hay and in other works at the will of the said abbot, each day with 1 man and in autumn 1 day in cutting grain with 1 man.

Likewise Ralph Miller holds a cottage with a croft which contains a rood, paying to the said abbot 2s.; and he works just as the said Henry.

Likewise William Arnold holds a cottage with a croft which contains half a rood, paying to the abbot 2d.; and he works just as the said Henry.

Likewise Hugh Day holds a cottage with a croft which contains 1 rood, paying to the abbot 8d.; and he works just as the said Henry.

Likewise Sara, widow of Matthew Miller, holds a cottage and a croft which contains half a rood, paying to the said abbot 4d.; and she works just as the said Henry.

Likewise William Drake holds a cottage with a croft which contains half a rood, paying to the abbot 6d.; and he works just as the said Henry.

There are there also 6 other cotters, viz. William Drake Jr., Amycia the widow, Alice the widow, Robert son of Eda, William Pepper, William Coleman, each of whom holds a cottage with a croft which contains half a rood, paying and doing in all things, each for himself, just as the said William Drake.

Likewise William Russel holds a cottage with a croft which contains half a rood, paying to the abbot 8d.; and he works in all things just as the said Henry Miller.

There are moreover there 5 other cotters, viz. Walter Pestel, Ralph Shepherd, Henry Abbot, Matilda Tut, Jordan Mustard, each of whom holds a cottage with a croft which contains half a rood, paying thence and doing in all things to the said abbot just as the said William Russel.

Likewise Beatrice of Hampton holds a cottage and croft which contains 1 rood, paying to the abbot 12d.; and she works in all things just as the said Henry.

Likewise Hugh Miller holds 3 acres of land paying to the abbot 42d.

Likewise Thomas, son of Richard, holds a cottage with a croft which contains half a rood, and 3 acres of land, paying to the abbot 4s. and he works just as the said Henry.

Likewise Ralph Reeve holds a cottage with a croft which contains 1 rood, and 1 acre of land, paying to the abbot 2s.; and he works just as the said Henry.

Likewise each of the said cottagers, except the widows, gives yearly after Christmas a penny which is called head-penny.

Many details of day-to-day village life survive in the records of manorial courts. These examples are from the years 1246 to 1249.

From *Select Pleas in Manorial Courts*

John Sperling complains that Richard of Newmere on the Sunday next before S. Bartholomew's day last past with his cattle, horses, and pigs wrongfully destroyed the corn on his [John's] land to his damage to the extent of one thrave of wheat, and to his dishonour to the extent of two shillings; and of this he produces suit. And Richard comes and defends all of it. Therefore let him go to the law six handed.[1] His pledges, Simon Combe and Hugh Frith.

Hugh Free in mercy for his beast caught in the lord's garden. Pledges, Walter Hill and William Slipper. Fine 6d.

[The] twelve jurors say that Hugh Cross has right in the bank and hedge about which there was a dispute between him and William White. Therefore let him hold in peace and let William be distrained for his many trespasses. (Afterwards he made fine for 12d.)

From the whole township of Little Ogbourne, except seven, for not coming to wash the lord's sheep, 6s. 8d.

Gilbert Richard's son gives 5s. for licence to marry a wife. Pledge, Seaman. Term [for payment,] the Purification.

[1]I.e., he must appear with six companions who will swear to his innocence.

From F. W. Maitland, ed., "Select Pleas in Manorial Courts," in G. G. Coulton, ed., *Social Life in Britain from the Conquest to the Reformation* (London: Cambridge University Press, 1918), pp. 306–308.

William Jordan in mercy for bad ploughing on the lord's land. Pledge, Arthur. Fine, 6d.

The parson of the Church is in mercy for his cow caught in the lord's meadow. Pledges, Thomas Ymer and William Coke.

From Martin Shepherd 6d. for the wound that he gave Pekin.

Ragenhilda of Bec gives 2s. for having married without licence. Pledge, William of Primer.

The Court presented that William Noah's son is the born bondman of the lord and a fugitive and dwells at Dodford. Therefore he must be sought. They say also that William Askil, John Parsons and Godfrey Green have furtively carried off four geese from the vill of Horepoll.

It was presented that Robert Carter's son by night invaded the house of Peter Burgess and in felony threw stones at his door so that the said Peter raised the hue. Therefore let the said Robert be committed to prison. Afterwards he made fine with 2s.

All the ploughmen of Great Ogbourne are convicted by the oath of twelve men . . . because by reason of their default [the land] of the lord was ill-ploughed whereby the lord is damaged to the amount of 9s. . . . And Walter Reaper is in mercy for concealing [i.e. not giving information as to] the said bad ploughing. Afterwards he made fine with the lord with 1 mark.

Peasant Daily Fare

A medieval peasant's diet was barely adequate at best. The poorest ones often went hungry.

From *Piers Plowman*

"I have no penny," said Piers, "to buy pullets,
Nor geese nor pigs, but two green cheeses,
A few curds of cream, a cake of oatmeal,
Two loaves of beans and bran, baked for my children;
And, by my soul, I swear I have no salt bacon,
Nor cook to make collops, I take Christ to witness!
But I have parsley and pot herbs and a plenty of cab-
     bages,
And a cow and a calf, and a cart mare
To draw my dung afield till the drought is over.
This is the little we must live on till the Lammas season.

From *The Vision of Piers Plowman*, H. W. Wells, trans. (New York: Sheed and Ward, 1935), pp. 86, 92. Copyright 1935 by Sheed and Ward. Reprinted by permission of Andrews and McMeel, Inc.

And then I hope to have my harvest in the garner.
And then I may spread your supper to my soul's con-
　　tent."
So all the poor people fetched peascods,
And brought him beans and baked apples by the lapful,
Ripe cherries, chervils and many small onions,
And offered Piers the present to please Hunger.

The needy are our neighbours, if we note rightly;
As prisoners in cells, or poor folk in hovels,
Charged with children and overcharged by landlords.
What they may spare in spinning they spend on rental,
On milk, or on meal to make porridge
To still the sobbing of the children at meal time.
Also they themselves suffer much hunger.
They have woe in winter time, and wake at midnight
To rise and to rock the cradle at the bedside,
To card and to comb, to darn clouts and to wash them,
To rub and to reel and to put rushes on the paving.
The woe of these women who dwell in hovels
Is too sad to speak of or to say in rhyme.
And many other men have much to suffer
From hunger and from thirst; they turn the fair side
　　outward,
For they are abashed to beg, lest it should be acknowl-
　　edged
At their neighbours what they need at noon and even.
I know all this well; for the world has taught me
What befalls another who has many children,
With no claim but his craft to clothe and feed them,
When the mouths are many and the money scarce.
They have bread and penny ale in place of a pittance,
And cold flesh and cold fish for venison from the
　　butcher.
On Fridays and fast days a farthing worth of mussels
Would be a feast for such folk, with a few cockles.
It were an alms to help all with such burdens,
And to comfort such cottagers and crooked men and
　　blind folk.

TOWNS AND TRADE

City Life

This account of the northern Italian cities was written by a German bishop who accompanied Frederick Barbarossa during his invasion of Italy in 1154.

From *Otto of Freising's Chronicle*

In the governing of their cities and in the conduct of public affairs, [the Lombards] still imitate the wisdom of the ancient Romans. Finally, they are so desirous of liberty that, avoiding the insolence of power, they are governed by the will of consuls rather than rulers. There are known to be three orders among them: captains, vavasors, and commoners. And in order to suppress arrogance, the aforesaid consuls are chosen not from one but from each of the classes. And lest they should exceed bounds by lust for power, they are changed almost every year. The consequence is that, as practically that entire land is divided among the cities, each of them requires its bishops to live in the cities, and scarcely any noble or great man can be found in all the surrounding territory who does not acknowledge the authority of his city. And from this power to force all elements together they are wont to call the several lands of each [noble, or magnate] their contado *(comitatus)*. . . .

Also, that they may not lack the means of subduing their neighbors, they do not disdain to give the girdle of knighthood or the grades of distinction to young men of inferior station and even some workers of the vile mechanical arts, whom other peoples bar like the pest from the more respected and honorable pursuits. From this it has resulted that they far surpass all other states of the world in riches and in power. They are aided in this not only, as has been said, by their characteristic industry, but also by the absence of their princes, who are accustomed to remain on the far side of the Alps. In this, however, forgetful of their ancient nobility, they retain traces of their barbaric imperfection, because while boasting that they live in accordance with law, they are

From Otto of Freising and his continuator, Rahewin, *The Deeds of Frederick Barbarossa,* C. C. Mierow, trans. (New York: Columbia University Press, 1953), pp. 127–128. Reprinted courtesy of Columbia University Press.

not obedient to the laws. For they scarcely if ever respect the prince to whom they should display the voluntary deference of obedience or willingly perform that which they have sworn by the integrity of their laws, unless they sense his authority in the power of his great army. Therefore it often happens that although a citizen must be humbled by the laws and an adversary subdued by arms in accordance with the laws, yet they very frequently receive in hostile fashion him whom they ought to accept as their own gentle prince, when he demands what is rightfully his own.

An English chronicler, William FitzStephen, wrote this description of London in the late twelfth century.

From *A Description of London*

Amongst the noble and celebrated cities of the world, that of London, the capital of the kingdom of England, is one of the most renowned, possessing above all others abundant wealth, extensive commerce, great grandeur and magnificence. It is happy in the salubrity of its climate, in the profession of the Christian religion, in the strength of its fortresses, the nature of its situation, the honour of its citizens, and the chastity of its matrons; in its sports too it is most pleasant, and in the production of illustrous men most fortunate. All which things I wish separately to consider.

There then

"Men's minds are soft'ned by a temp'rate clime,"

not so however that they are addicted to licentiousness, but so that they are not savage and brutal, but rather kind and generous.

There is in St. Paul's church an episcopal see. . . . As regards divine worship, there are also in London and in the suburbs thirteen larger conventional churches, besides one hundred and thirty-six parochial ones.

On the east stands the Palatine tower, a fortress of great size and strength, the court and walls of which are erected upon a very deep foundation, the mortar used in the building being tempered with the blood of beasts. On the west are two castles strongly fortified; the wall of the city is high and thick, with seven double gates, having on the north side towers placed at proper intervals. London formerly had walls and towers in like manner on the south, but that most excellent

From William Fitz Stephen, "A Description of the Most Noble City of London," *The Survey of London by John Stow* (London: Everyman's Library, 1912), pp. 504–506. Reprinted courtesy of J. M. Dent & Sons Ltd.

river the Thames, which abounds with fish, and in which the tide ebbs
and flows, runs on that side, and has in a long space of time washed
down, undermined, and subverted the walls in that part. On the west
also, higher up on the bank of the river, the royal palace rears its head,
an incomparable structure, furnished with a breastwork and bastions,
situated in a populous suburb, at a distance of two miles from the city.

Adjoining to the houses on all sides lie the gardens of those citizens
that dwell in the suburbs, which are well furnished with trees, spacious
and beautiful.

On the north side too are fields for pasture, and a delightful plain
of meadow land, interspersed with flowing streams, on which stand
mills, whose clack is very pleasing to the ear. Close by lies an immense
forest, in which are densely wooded thickets, the coverts of game,
stags, fallow-deer, boars, and wild bulls. The tillage lands of the city
are not barren gravelly soils, but like the fertile plains of Asia, which
produce abundant crops, and fill the barns of their cultivators with

"Ceres' plenteous sheaf."

There are also round London, on the northern side, in the suburbs,
excellent springs; the water of which is sweet, clear, and salubrious,

"Mid glistening pebbles gliding playfully:"

amongst which, Holywell, Clerkenwell, and St. Clement's well, are of
most note, and most frequently visited, as well by the scholars from the
schools, as by the youth of the city when they go out to take the air in
the summer evenings. The city is delightful indeed, when it has a good
governor. . . .

The artizans of the several crafts, the vendors of the various commodities, and the labourers of every kind, have each their separate station, which they take every morning. There is also in London, on the
bank of the river, amongst the wine-shops which are kept in ships and
cellars, a public eating-house: there every day, according to the season,
may be found viands of all kinds, roast, fried, and boiled, fish large
and small, coarser meat for the poor, and more delicate for the rich,
such as venison, fowls, and small birds. . . . There is, without one of the
gates, immediately in the suburb, a certain smooth field in name and
in reality [Smithfield]. There every Friday, unless it be one of the more
solemn festivals, is a noted show of well-bred horses exposed for sale.
The earls, barons, and knights, who are at the time resident in the city,
as well as most of the citizens, flock thither either to look on or buy. It
is pleasant to see the nags, with their sleek and shining coats, smoothly
ambling along, raising and setting down alternately, as it were, their
feet on either side: in one part are horses better adapted to esquires;
these, whose pace is rougher but yet expeditious, lift up and set down,

as it were, the two opposite fore and hind feet together; in another the young blood colts, not yet accustomed to the bridle,

"Which upright walk on pasterns firm and straight,
Their motions easy, prancing in their gait."

In a third are the horses for burden, strong and stout-limbed; and in a fourth, the more valuable chargers, of an elegant shape and noble height, with nimbly moving ears, erect necks, and plump haunches. . . . In another quarter, apart from the rest, stand the goods of the peasants, implements of husbandry, swine with their long sides, cows and distended udders,

"Oxen of bulk immense, and woolly flocks."

There, too, stand the mares fitted for the plough, the dray, and the cart, of which some are big with foal, others have their frolicsome colts running close by their sides. To this city, from every nation under heaven, merchants bring their commodities by sea,

"Arabia's gold, Sabaea's spice and incense,
Scythia's keen weapons, and the oil of palms
From Babylon's rich soil, Nile's precious gems,
Norway's warm peltries, Russia's costly sables,
Sera's rich vestures, and the wines of Gaul,
Hither are sent."

According to the evidence of chroniclers London is more ancient than Rome: for, as both derive their origin from the same Trojan ancestors, this was founded by Brutus before that by Romulus and Remus. Hence it is that, even to this day, both cities use the same ancient laws and ordinances. This, like Rome, is divided into wards; it has annual sheriffs instead of consuls; it has an order of senators and inferior magistrates, and also sewers and aqueducts in its streets; each class of suits, whether of the deliberative, demonstrative, or judicial kind, has its appropriate place and proper court; on stated days it has its assemblies. I think that there is no city in which more approved customs are observed—in attending churches, honouring God's ordinances, keeping festivals, giving alms, receiving strangers, confirming espousals, contracting marriages, celebrating weddings, preparing entertainments, welcoming guests, and also in the arrangement of the funeral ceremonies and the burial of the dead. The only inconveniences of London are, the immoderate drinking of foolish persons, and the frequent fires. Moreover, almost all the bishops, abbots, and great men of England, are, in a manner, citizens and freemen of London; as they have magnificent houses there, to which they resort, spending large sums of money, whenever they are summoned thither to councils and assemblies by the king or their metropolitan, or are compelled to go there by their own business.

Economic Activities

Each major city had a merchant guild and numerous craft guilds. They combined economic, religious, and charitable functions.

Rules of a Merchant Guild (Southampton)

In the first place, there shall be elected from the gild merchant, and established, an alderman, a steward, a chaplain, four skevins, and an usher. And it is to be known that whosoever shall be alderman shall receive from each one entering into the gild fourpence; the steward, twopence; the chaplain, twopence; and the usher, one penny. And the gild shall meet twice a year: that is to say, on the Sunday next after St. John the Baptist's day, and on the Sunday next after St. Mary's day.

And when the gild shall be sitting no one of the gild is to bring in any stranger, except when required by the alderman or steward. And the alderman shall have a sergeant to serve before him, the steward another sergeant, and the chaplain shall have his clerk.

And when the gild shall sit, the alderman is to have, each night, so long as the gild sits, two gallons of wine and two candles, and the steward the same; and the four skevins and the chaplain, each of them one gallon of wine and one candle, and the usher one gallon of wine.

And when the gild shall sit, the lepers of La Madeleine shall have of the alms of the gild, two sesters (approximately eight gallons) of ale, and the sick of God's House and of St. Julian shall have two sesters of ale. And the Friars Minors shall have two sesters of ale and one sester of wine. And four sesters of ale shall be given to the poor wherever the gild shall meet.

And when the gild is sitting, no one who is of the gild shall go outside the town for any business, without the permission of the steward. And if any does so, let him be fined two shillings, and pay them.

And when the gild sits, and any gildsman is outside of the city so that he does not know when it will happen, he shall have a gallon of wine, if his servants come to get it. And if a gildsman is ill and is in the city, wine shall be sent to him, two loaves of bread and a gallon of wine and a dish from the kitchen; and two approved men of the gild shall go to visit him and look after his condition.

And when a gildsman dies, all those who are of the gild and are in the city shall attend the service of the dead, and the gildsmen shall bear the body and bring it to the place of burial. And whoever will not do this shall pay according to his oath, two pence, to be given to the poor. And those of the ward where the dead man shall be ought to

From E. P. Cheyney, trans., *University of Pennsylvania Translations and Reprints* (Philadelphia, Pa.: University of Pennsylvania Press, 1897), Vol. 2, No. 1, pp. 12–17.

find a man to watch over the body the night that the dead shall lie in his house. And so long as the service of the dead shall last, that is to say the vigil and the mass, there ought to burn four candles of the gild, each candle of two pounds weight or more, until the body is buried. And these four candles shall remain in the keeping of the steward of the gild.

And when a gildsman dies, his eldest son or his next heir shall have the seat of his father, or of his uncle, if his father was not a gildsman, and of no other one; and he shall give nothing for his seat. No husband can have a seat in the gild by right of his wife, nor demand a seat by right of his wife's ancestors.

And no one of the city of Southampton shall buy anything to sell again in the same city, unless he is of the gild merchant or of the franchise. And if anyone shall do so and is convicted of it, all which he has so bought shall be forfeited to the king; and no one shall be quit of custom unless he proves that he is in the gild or in the franchise, and this from year to year.

And no one shall buy honey, fat, salt herrings, or any kind of oil, or millstones, or fresh hides, or any kind of fresh skins, unless he is a gildsman: nor keep a tavern for wine, nor sell cloth at retail, except in market or fair days; nor keep grain in his granary beyond five quarters, to sell at retail, if he is not a gildsman; and whoever shall do this and be convicted, shall forfeit all to the king.

If any gildsman falls into poverty and has not the wherewithal to live, and is not able to work or to provide for himself, he shall have one mark from the gild to relieve his condition when the gild shall sit. No one of the gild nor of the franchise shall avow another's goods for his by which the custom of the city shall be injured. And if any one does so and is convicted, he shall lose the gild and the franchise; and the merchandise so avowed shall be forfeited to the king.

And no private man nor stranger shall bargain for or buy any kind of merchandise coming into the city before a burgess of the gild merchant, so long as the gildsman is present and wishes to bargain for and buy this merchandise; and if anyone does so and is convicted, that which he buys shall be forfeited to the king.

The common chest shall be in the house of the chief alderman or of the steward, and the three keys of it shall be lodged with three discreet men of the aforesaid twelve sworn men, or with three of the skevins, who shall loyally take care of the common seal, and the charters and of the treasure of the town, and the standards, and other muniments of the town; and no letter shall be sealed with the common seal, nor any charter taken out of the common-chest but in the presence of six or twelve sworn men, and of the alderman or steward; and nobody shall sell by any kind of measure or weight that is not sealed, under forfeiture of two shillings.

No one shall go out to meet a ship bringing wine or other merchandise coming to the town, in order to buy anything, before the ship be arrived and come to anchor for unlading; and if any one does so and is convicted, the merchandise which he shall have bought shall be forfeited to the king.

Some medieval crafts were dominated by women. The spinners' guild of Paris provides an example.

Silk Spinners at Paris

Any woman who wishes to be a silk spinster on large spindles in the city of Paris—i.e., reeling, spinning, doubling and retwisting—may freely do so, provided she observe the following customs and usages of the craft:

No spinster on large spindles may have more than three apprentices, unless they be her own or her husband's children born in true wedlock; nor may she contract with them for an apprenticeship of less than seven years or for a fee of less than 20 Parisian sols to be paid to her, their mistress. The apprenticeship shall be for eight years if there is no fee, but she may accept more years and money if she can get them. . . .

No woman of the said craft may hire an apprentice or workgirl who has not completed her years of service with the mistress to whom she was apprenticed. If a spinster has assumed an apprentice, she may not take on another before the first has completed her seven years unless the apprentice die or forswear the craft forever. If an apprentice spinster buy her freedom before serving the said seven years, she may not herself take on an apprentice until she has practiced the craft for seven years. If any spinster sell her apprentice, she shall owe six deniers to the guardians appointed in the King's name to guard the [standards of the] craft. The buyer shall also owe six deniers. . . .

If a working woman comes from outside Paris and wishes to practice the said craft in the city, she must swear before two guardians of the craft that she will practice it well and loyally and conform to its customs and usages.

If anyone give a woman of the said craft silk to be spun and the woman pawn it and the owner complain, the fine shall be 5 sols.

No workwoman shall farm out another's silk to be worked upon outside her own house.

The said craft has as guardians two men of integrity sworn in the King's name but appointed and changed at the will of the provost of Paris. Taking an oath in the provost's presence, they shall swear to

From Etienne Boileau, *Livres des Métiers* in J. D. O'Faolain and L. Martines, *Not in God's Image* (New York: Harper & Row, 1973), pp. 155–156. Reprinted courtesy of the publisher.

guard the craft truly, loyally, and to their utmost, and to inform him or his agents of all malpractices discovered therein.

This is the advice of a thirteenth-century Norwegian father to his son.

Advice to Merchants

The man who is to be a trader will have to brave many perils, sometimes at sea and sometimes in heathen lands, but nearly always among alien peoples; and it must be his constant purpose to act discreetly wherever he happens to be. On the sea he must be alert and fearless.

When you are in the market town, or wherever you are, be polite and agreeable; then you will secure the friendship of all good men. Make it a habit to rise early in the morning, and go first and immediately to church wherever it seems most convenient to hear the canonical hours, and hear all the hours and mass from matins on. Join in the worship, repeating such psalms and prayers as you have learned. When the services are over, go out to look after your business affairs. If you are unacquainted with the traffic of the town, observe carefully how those who are reputed the best and most prominent merchants conduct their business. You must also be careful to examine the wares that you buy before the purchase is finally made to make sure that they are sound and flawless. And whenever you make a purchase, call in a few trusty men to serve as witnesses as to how the bargain was made.

You should keep occupied with your business till breakfast or, if necessity demands it, till midday; after that you should eat your meal. Keep your table well provided and set with a white cloth, clean victuals, and good drinks. Serve enjoyable meals, if you can afford it. After the meal you may either take a nap or stroll about a little while for pastime and to see what other good merchants are employed with, or whether any new wares have come to the borough which you ought to buy. On returning to your lodgings examine your wares, lest they suffer damage after coming into your hands. If they are found to be injured and you are about to dispose of them, do not conceal the flaws from the purchaser: show him what the defects are and make such a bargain as you can; then you cannot be called a deceiver. Also put a good price on your wares, though not too high, and yet very near what you see can be obtained; then you cannot be called a foister.

Finally, remember this, that whenever you have an hour to spare you should give thought to your studies, especially to the law books. . . . But although I have most to say about laws, I regard no man perfect in knowledge unless he has thoroughly learned and mas-

From *The King's Mirror*, L. M. Larson, trans. (New York: The American–Scandinavian Foundation, 1917), pp. 79–81, 83–86. Reprinted courtesy of the American–Scandinavian Foundation.

tered the customs of the place where he is sojourning. And if you wish to become perfect in knowledge, you must learn all the languages, first of all Latin and French, for these idioms are most widely used; and yet do not neglect your native tongue or speech. . . .

And further, there are certain things which you must beware of and shun like the devil himself: these are drinking, chess, harlots, quarrelling, and throwing dice for stakes. For upon such foundations the greatest calamities are built; and unless they strive to avoid these things, few only are able to live long without blame or sin.

Observe carefully how the sky is lighted, the course of the heavenly bodies, the grouping of the hours, and the points of the horizon. Learn also how to mark the movements of the ocean and to discern how its turmoil ebbs and swells; for that is knowledge which all must possess who wish to trade abroad. Learn arithmetic thoroughly, for merchants have great need of that.

If you come to a place where the king or some other chief who is in authority has his officials, seek to win their friendship; and if they demand any necessary fees on the ruler's behalf, be prompt to render all such payments, lest by holding too tightly to little things you lose the greater. Also beware lest the king's belongings find their way into your purse; for you cannot know but that he may be covetous who has those things in charge, and it is easier to be cautious beforehand than to crave pardon afterwards. If you can dispose of your wares at suitable prices, do not hold them long; for it is the wont of merchants to buy constantly and to sell rapidly.

If you are preparing to carry on trade beyond the seas and you sail your own ship, have it thoroughly coated with tar in the autumn and, if possible, keep it tarred all winter. But if the ship is placed on timbers too late to be coated in the fall, tar it when spring opens and let it dry thoroughly afterwards. Always buy shares in good vessels or in none at all. Keep your ship attractive, for then capable men will join you and it will be well manned. Be sure to have your ship ready when summer begins and do your traveling while the season is best. Keep reliable tackle on shipboard at all times, and never remain out at sea in late autumn, if you can avoid it. If you attend carefully to all these things, with God's mercy you may hope for success. This, too, you must keep constantly in mind, if you wish to be counted a wise man, that you ought never to let a day pass without learning something that will profit you. . . .

If your wealth takes on rapid growth, divide it and invest it in a partnership trade in fields where you do not yourself travel; but be cautious in selecting partners. Always let Almighty God, the holy Virgin Mary, and the saint whom you have most frequently called upon to intercede for you be counted among your partners. Watch with care over the property which the saints are to share with you and always bring it faithfully to the place to which it was originally promised.

If you have much capital invested in trade, divide it into three parts: put one-third into partnerships with men who are permanently located in market boroughs, are trustworthy, and are experienced in business. Place the other two parts in various business ventures; for if your capital is invested in different places, it is not likely that you will suffer losses in all your wealth at one time; more likely it will be secure in some localities, though frequent losses be suffered. But if you find that the profits of trade bring a decided increase to your funds, draw out the two-thirds and invest them in good farm land, for such property is generally thought the most secure, whether the enjoyment of it falls to one's self or to one's kinsmen. With the remaining third you may do as seems best—continue to keep it in business or place it all in land. However, though you decide to keep your funds invested in trade, discontinue your own journeys at sea or as a trader in foreign fields, as soon as your means have attained sufficient growth and you have studied foreign customs as much as you like. Keep all that you see in careful memory, the evil with the good; remember evil practices as a warning, and the good customs as useful to yourself and to others who may wish to learn from you.

MEDIEVAL MONARCHIES

England

Magna Carta (1215) described a system of government based on cooperation between king and barons. Some of the clauses dealt with technical feudal matters. Others defined English rights and liberties in more general terms.

From *Magna Carta*

John, by the grace of God, king of England, lord of Ireland, duke of Normandy and Aquitaine, count of Anjou, to the archbishops, bishops, abbots, earls, barons, justiciars, foresters, sheriffs, reeves, servants, and all bailiffs and his faithful people greeting.

1. In the first place we have granted to God, and by this our present charter confirmed, for us and our heirs forever, that the English church shall be free, and shall hold its rights entire and its liberties uninjured; and we will that it thus be observed; which is shown by this, that the freedom of elections, which is considered to be most important and especially necessary to the English church, we, of our pure and spontaneous will, granted, and by our charter confirmed, before the contest between us and our barons had arisen; and obtained a confirmation of it by the lord Pope Innocent III.; which we will observe and which we will shall be observed in good faith by our heirs forever.

We have granted moreover to all free men of our kingdom for us and our heirs forever all the liberties written below, to be had and holden by themselves and their heirs from us and our heirs.

2. If any of our earls or barons, or others holding from us in chief by military service shall have died, and when he has died his heir shall be of full age and owe relief, he shall have his inheritance by the ancient relief; that is to say, the heir or heirs of an earl for the whole barony of an earl a hundred pounds; the heir or heirs of a baron for a whole barony a hundred pounds; the heir or heirs of a knight, for a whole knight's fee, a hundred shillings at most; and who owes less let him give less according to the ancient custom of fiefs.

From "Magna Carta," in E. P. Cheyney, trans., *University of Pennsylvania Translations and Reprints* (Philadelphia, Pa.: University of Pennsylvania Press, 1897), Vol. 1, No. 6, pp. 6–16.

3. If moreover the heir of any one of such shall be under age, and shall be in wardship, when he comes of age he shall have his inheritance without relief and without a fine.

4. The custodian of the land of such a minor heir shall not take from the land of the heir any except reasonable products, reasonable customary payments, and reasonable services, and this without destruction or waste of men or of property. . . .

6. Heirs shall be married without disparity, so nevertheless that before the marriage is contracted, it shall be announced to the relatives by blood of the heir himself.

7. A widow, after the death of her husband, shall have her marriage portion and her inheritance immediately. . . .

8. No widow shall be compelled to marry so long as she prefers to live without a husband, provided she gives security that she will not marry without our consent, if she holds from us, or without the consent of her lord from whom she holds, if she holds from another.

12. No scutage or aid shall be imposed in our kingdom except by the common council of our kingdom, except for the ransoming of our body, for the making of our oldest son a knight, and for once marrying our oldest daughter, and for these purposes it shall be only a reasonable aid; in the same way it shall be done concerning the aids of the city of London.

13. And the city of London shall have all its ancient liberties and free customs, as well by land as by water. Moreover, we will and grant that all other cities and boroughs and villages and ports shall have all their liberties and free customs.

14. And for holding a common council of the kingdom concerning the assessment of an aid otherwise than in the three cases mentioned above, or concerning the assessment of a scutage we shall cause to be summoned the archbishops, bishops, abbots, earls, and greater barons by our letters under seal; and besides we shall cause to be summoned generally, by our sheriffs and bailiffs all those who hold from us in chief, for a certain day, that is at the end of forty days at least, and for a certain place; and in all the letters of that summons, we will express the cause of the summons, and when the summons has thus been given the business shall proceed on the appointed day, on the advice of those who shall be present, even if not all of those who were summoned have come.

15. We will not grant to any one, moreover, that he shall take an aid from his free men, except for ransoming his body, for making his oldest son a knight, and for once marrying his oldest daughter; and for these purposes only a reasonable aid shall be taken.

16. No one shall be compelled to perform any greater service for a knight's fee, or for any other free tenement than is owed from it.

17. The common pleas shall not follow our court, but shall be held in some certain place.

20. A free man shall not be fined for a small offence, except in proportion to the measure of the offence; and for a great offence he shall be fined in proportion to the magnitude of the offence, saving his freehold; and a merchant in the same way, saving his merchandise; and the villain shall be fined in the same way, saving his wainage, if he shall be at our mercy; and none of the above fines shall be imposed except by the oaths of honest men of the neighborhood.

21. Earls and barons shall only be fined by their peers, and only in proportion to their offence.

28. No constable or other bailiff of ours shall take anyone's grain or other chattels, without immediately paying for them in money, unless he is able to obtain a postponement at the good-will of the seller.

39. No free man shall be taken or imprisoned or dispossessed, or outlawed, or banished, or in any way destroyed, nor will we go upon him, nor send upon him, except by the legal judgment of his peers or by the law of the land.

40. To no one will we sell, to no one will we deny, or delay right or justice.

41. All merchants shall be safe and secure in going out from England and coming into England and in remaining and going through England, as well by land as by water, for buying and selling, free from all evil tolls, by the ancient and rightful customs, except in time of war, and if they are of a land at war with us; and if such are found in our land at the beginning of war, they shall be attached without injury to their bodies or goods, until it shall be known from us or from our principal justiciar in what way the merchants of our land are treated who shall be then found in the country which is at war with us; and if ours are safe there, the others shall be safe in our land.

60. Moreover, all those customs and franchises mentioned above which we have conceded in our kingdom, and which are to be fulfilled, as far as pertains to us, in respect to our men; all men of our kingdom as well clergy as laymen, shall observe as far as pertains to them, in respect to their men.

61. Since, moreover, for the sake of God, and for the improvement of our kingdom, and for the better quieting of the hostility sprung up lately between us and our barons, we have made all these concessions; wishing them to enjoy these in a complete and firm stability forever, we make and concede to them the security described below; that is to say, that they shall elect twenty-five barons of the kingdom, whom they will, who ought with all their power to observe, hold, and cause to be observed, the peace and liberties which we have conceded to them, and by this our present charter confirmed to them; in this manner, that if we or our justiciar, or our bailiffs, or any one of our servants shall have done wrong in any way toward any one, or shall have transgressed any of the articles of peace or security; and the wrong shall have been shown to four barons of the aforesaid twenty-five barons, let those four

barons come to us or to our justiciar, if we are out of the kingdom, laying before us the transgression, and let them ask that we cause that transgression to be corrected without delay. And if we shall not have corrected the transgression or, if we shall be out of the kingdom, if our justiciar shall not have corrected it within a period of forty days, counting from the time in which it has been shown to us or to our justiciar, if we are out of the kingdom; the aforesaid four barons shall refer the matter to the remainder of the twenty-five barons, and let these twenty-five barons with the whole community of the country distress and injure us in every way they can; that is to say by the seizure of our castles, lands, possessions, and in such other ways as they can until it shall have been corrected according to their judgment, saving our person and that of our queen, and those of our children; and when the correction has been made, let them devote themselves to us as they did before.

Around 1300 the English parliament began to develop as a representative assembly. Along with the great prelates and barons who traditionally advised the king, elected representatives of towns and counties were often summoned to its meetings.

Summons of Representatives to Parliament (1295)

The king to the sheriff of Northamptonshire. Since we intend to have a consultation and meeting with the earls, barons and other principal men of our kingdom with regard to providing remedies against the dangers which are in these days threatening the same kingdom; and on that account have commanded them to be with us on the Lord's day next after the feast of St. Martin in the approaching winter, at Westminster, to consider, ordain, and do as may be necessary for the avoidance of these dangers; we strictly require you to cause two knights from the aforesaid county, two citizens from each city in the same county, and two burgesses from each borough, of those who are especially discreet and capable of laboring, to be elected without delay, and to cause them to come to us at the aforesaid time and place.

Moreover, the said knights are to have full and sufficient power for themselves and for the community of the aforesaid county, and the said citizens and burgesses for themselves and the communities of the aforesaid cities and boroughs separately, then and there for doing what shall then be ordained according to the common counsel in the premises; so that the aforesaid business shall not remain unfinished in any way for defect of this power. And you shall have there the names of the knights, citizens and burgesses and this writ.

Witness the king at Canterbury on the third day of October.

From E. P. Cheyney, trans., *University of Pennsylvania Translations and Reprints* (Philadelphia, Pa.: University of Pennsylvania Press, 1897), Vol. 1, No. 6, p. 35.

A major function of the representatives was to present petitions to the king and his council on behalf of individuals and communities.

From *Rolls of Parliament*

County of Hertford, 1290

The men of the county of Hertford beg that they may build a prison in the town of Hertford, from doing which William of Valence [Earl of Pembroke] hinders them, as it is said, to the King's loss and the county's vexation.

[Answer] The King granted it.

County of Cumberland, 1305

To the petition of the community of Cumberland, seeking redress for that when the lord King by his writ commanded the sheriff of the county to provide the Kings' larder against the King's arrival in Scotland in the twenty-second year of his reign, the sheriff on pretext of the order took from the community a certain number of oats, and though he had an appropriation for them in his account, he paid nothing to the community:—

It is answered thus: Let suit be brought at the Exchequer, and if the sheriff has received an appropriation but has not paid, let him be punished by the established penalty and let him pay. But if otherwise let the treasurer ordain what is proper.

Merchants of England, 1290

The merchants of England sought £2000 damages from the Count of Flanders, by virtue of the convention made with the king at Mustrel, which damages they suffered by the seizure and detention in Flanders of their chattels valued at £10,000.

[Answer] The King can do nothing except to ask him [the Count] by a letter (which he granted) to satisfy them and cause them to be indemnified; because it is not recorded that any convention was made or discussed for paying damages, and because the Count can seek his damages from the English in the same way.

Hospital of St. Katherine, 1290

The brothers and sisters of the hospital of St. Katherine petition that the King grant them the fifty shillings which King Henry, father of the

From F. Palgrave, ed., *Parliamentary Writs* (London: Record Commission, 1827) in B. D. Henning, A. S. Foord, and B. L. Mathias, *Crises in English History* (New York: Holt, Rinehart and Winston, 1949), pp. 62–64. Copyright © 1949 by Holt, Rinehart and Winston, CBS College Publishing. Reprinted courtesy of the publisher.

present lord King, gave them annually, which they received for the soul of Sanchia, formerly Queen of Germany, that they might maintain a chapel in the Tower of London where they celebrate [masses] for her soul; and the arrears of the same for ten years back.

[Answer] It is not found at the Exchequer that they received any of the said fifty shillings either in the time of King Henry or in the time of the present King, . . . and nothing is to be done in the matter.

Countess of Cornwall, 1298

Touching the lands of the Countess of Cornwall, which were assigned to her for her sustenance by her lord, and from which she claims that she was ejected: it seemed to the council that the *Curia Regis* can not interfere in any arrangement made between the Countess and her husband the Earl.

Poor Alice, 1302

Alice de la Chapele of the Isle of Guernsey begs the magnanimity, grace, and compassion of our lord the King: for that she has taken thirty-five sheaves of various kinds of grain from the sharecrop of our lord the King, which sheaves were of little value, . . . so she begs in charity and compassion that grace be granted her upon her oath that she took them because of her poverty and to nourish her child.

[Answer] Let her have grace. Let the bailiffs certify the King concerning the cause and manner [of the theft], and if they find it as stated, the King concedes that it be done as is petitioned.

Other activities of parliament were described in a contemporary chronicle written by a monk of Westminster abbey.

From *Flowers of History*

A.D. 1275   The king commanded all the nobles of his kingdom to assemble in a parliament at Westminster; in which parliament many statutes for the benefit of the kingdom were published, and among them one which bridled the usurious extortions of the Jews.

From C. D. Yonge, trans. *The Flowers of History* (London: Henry G. Bohn, 1853), Vol. 2, pp. 468–469, 481, 501, 513.

A.D. 1285 . . .   About the same time, the king, having convoked the principal nobles of his land to meet him at Westminster, promulgated some statutes, which are called the Second Statutes of Westminster; by some of which he curtailed the jurisdiction of the ecclesiastical judges. . . . Afterwards, at Winchester, about the time of the festival of the Nativity of the blessed Mary, he caused some statutes to be published, for the purpose of checking the truculent fury of robbers and banditti.

A.D. 1294   Edward, king of England, held his parliament at Westminster, after the feast of Pentecost, which was attended by John, king of Scotland, and by all the nobles of England; and at this parliament were recited, in the hearing of all those then present, the reasons for the commencement and continuance of this war, and the reports of the ambassadors; and also the promises which had been made of re-establishing peace in England. At which statement each of the ambassadors of the lord the king showed his hand in all good faith, to the utmost of his power. At last, every one agreed to recover Guienne by force of arms. Then the king of Scotland granted to the king of England, for three years, the revenues of all his estates, which belonged to him by hereditary right, in the kingdom of England, as a subsidy towards the recovery of Guienne, contenting himself with those of Scotland alone. And the other earls and nobles promised him aid from their resources. . . .

A.D. 1295   On the eve of the feast of Saint Andrew, the clergy, nobles, and laity having been summoned to Westminster, the king again requested that they would grant him a subsidy out of their substance, for the defence of the kingdom. And an eleventh was granted him from those who had paid a tenth the year before; and those who had paid a sixth that year, were now to contribute a seventh. Moreover, the archbishop of Canterbury having been indulged with permission to confer with his suffragans on this subject, with their unanimous consent offered the king a tenth of all ecclesiastical property; which having been offered, but not accepted, the bishops returned a second time to consider of this matter. Therefore, the king seeing their firmness, sent to them a great man, fifty years of age, namely, the chief justice of the king's bench, and his subordinate officers, who said, "O bishop, the king says, I neither accept, nor will I accept your offering, but descend speedily and fulfil his will, granting him at least a fourth part, or a third." . . . The body of the clergy was not moved from their resolution, but as they had previously granted a tenth, they now repeated the offer. Therefore, the king seeing that his demand was beyond the ability of the clergy to grant, not wishing to afflict them, on the day after the feast of the Conception of the blessed Mary, he received their offering as if welcome. And the clergy received this as a good omen, and so Israel returned to their tents.

France

King Louis IX (1226–1270), later canonized as Saint Louis, seemed to many of his contemporaries the ideal feudal king.

From Joinville. *Life of St. Louis*

The Virtues of St. Louis

St. Louis loved God with his whole heart and it was on Him that he modelled his actions. This could be seen in that, as God died for the love of His people, so did the King more than once put his own body in danger of death for the love he bore his people; and this although, had he wished it, he might well have been excused. Of this I will tell you more later.

The great love that he had for his people was shown by what he said, when he lay very sick at Fontainebleau, to his eldest son, my Lord Louis. "Dear son," he said, "I pray you to win the love of the people of your Kingdom. In truth, I would rather that a Scotsman came from Scotland and governed them, so long as his rule was good and fair, than that you should be seen by the world to govern it ill." The holy King so loved truth that not even to the Saracens would he break his word when he had once made an agreement with them, as I shall tell you later.

In eating he was so temperate that never once in my life did I hear him order any dish for his table, as many rich men do. He was content to eat what his cook prepared for him and what was set before him. In his speech he was restrained. Never in my life did I hear him speak ill of any man, nor name the devil—whose name is much heard in the Kingdom now, a thing which I think can hardly be pleasing to God.

He mixed his wine with water, measuring the water according to the amount that he saw the wine could stand. Once in Cyprus he asked me why I put no water in my wine. I told him that the doctors were re-

From John of Joinville, *The Life of St. Louis*, Rene Hague, trans. from the text edited by Natalis De Wailly (New York: Sheed & Ward, 1955), pp. 26–27, 37–38, 203–207. Copyright 1955 by Sheed & Ward, Inc. Reprinted by permission of Andrews and McMeel, Inc.

sponsible for this; they told me that I had a large head and a cold stomach and that it was impossible for me to get drunk. The King told me that they were deluding me, for if I did not learn to water my wine in my youth and tried to do so when I was old, I should be attacked by gout and diseases of the stomach, so that I should never enjoy my health; and if I drank my wine neat when I was an old man I should be drunk every evening; and it was a mighty ugly thing for a good man to get drunk.

St. Louis' Justice

Often in the summer he went after Mass to the wood of Vincennes and sat down with his back against an oak tree, and made us sit all around him. Everyone who had an affair to settle could come and speak to him without the interference of any usher or other official. The King would speak himself and ask, "Is there any one here who has a case to settle?" All those who had would then stand up and he would say, "Quiet, all of you, and your cases shall be dealt with in turn." Then he would call my Lord Peter of Fontaines and my Lord Geoffrey of Villette and say to one of them, "Now give me your judgment in this case."

Decree for the Reform of the Realm, 1256

We, Louis, by the grace of God King of France, do ordain that all our judges, viscounts, provosts, mayors, and all other officers, in whatever matter it may be, and whatever office they may hold, shall take oath that so long as they hold their office or judgeship, they shall do justice to all men, without exception of person, to poor as well as to rich, to strangers as well as to natives, and shall keep the usages and customs that are good and proved.

And should it happen that the judges or viscounts or others, as officers or forest rangers, should violate their oaths, and should so be convicted, it is our wish that they be punished in their goods, or in their persons should the misdeed require it; the judges shall be punished by us, and the others by the judges.

Again, the other provosts, judges and officers, shall swear that they will loyally guard our revenues and our rights, and that they will not allow our rights to be stolen or taken away or diminished; with this they shall swear that they will not take or receive, either themselves or through others, gold nor silver nor any indirect benefits, nor anything else, other than fruit, or bread, or wine, or other such present up to the value of ten *sous*, which sum shall not be exceeded. . . .

We will and ordain that all our provosts and judges shall refrain from any speech which is disrespectful to God, Our Lady or any of the saints, and that they shall abstain from dicing and taverns. We will that the manufacture of dice be forbidden throughout our Kingdom and that loose women be expelled from their houses, and that whoever lets a house to a loose woman, shall pay to the provost or judge one year's rent of the house. . . .

We order that neither judges nor provosts nor any others shall maintain too many sergeants or beadles, so that the people may not be over-burdened. . . .

We order that neither judge nor provost in our service shall oppress honest folk in his jurisdiction by excessive sentences, beyond what is right; and that no subjects of ours shall be imprisoned for debt, except the debt be owed to us.

We ordain that none of our judges shall impose any fine for a debt owed by our subjects, nor for any misdemeanour, except in open court, where the fine can be judged and assessed, and with the advice of honest men. . . .

We forbid our judges and provosts to burden our subjects who have brought cases before them by moving from one place to another; they are to hear the business brought to them in the place where they have customarily sat, so that our subjects may not be forced by trouble and expense to abandon their search for justice.

Again, we order that they shall not dispossess any man of seisin he holds, without a full examination of the matter or without our special order; nor shall they burden our people with new impositions or taxes or new tolls; nor shall they summon them to ride to arms in order to obtain money from them; for it is our wish that no man from whom military service is due be summoned to the army without necessary cause, and those who are willing to join the army in person shall not be obliged to compound in money for their service. . . .

Again, it is our wish that all former judges, viscounts, provosts, and mayors, shall, after they are out of office, remain for forty days either in person or by proxy in the district in which they held office, that they may answer to the new judges for any injustice they may have done against those who wish to bring complaints against them.

In all these things which we have ordained for the well-being of our subjects and our Kingdom, we reserve to ourselves the power to explain, amend, add, or diminish, as we shall be advised.

The Empire

Frederick Barbarossa (1152–1190) expressed his imperial claims vigorously in this address to the representatives of the commune of Rome (1155).

From *Otto of Freising's Chronicle*

We have heard much heretofore concerning the wisdom and the valor of the Romans, yet more concerning their wisdom. Wherefore we cannot wonder enough at finding your words insipid with swollen pride rather than seasoned with the salt of wisdom. You set forth the ancient renown of your city. You extoll to the very stars the ancient status of your sacred republic. Granted, granted! To use the words of your own writer, "There was, *there was once* virtue in this republic." "Once," I say. And O that we might truthfully and freely say "now"! Your Rome—nay, ours also—has experienced the vicissitudes of time. She could not be the only one to escape a fate ordained by the Author of all things for all that dwell beneath the orb of the moon. What shall I say? It is clear how first the strength of your nobility was transferred from this city of ours to the royal city of the East, and how for the course of many years the thirsty Greekling sucked the breasts of your delight. Then came the Frank, truly noble, in deed as in name, and forcibly possessed himself of whatever freedom was still left to you. Do you wish to know the ancient glory of your Rome? The worth of the senatorial dignity? The impregnable disposition of the camp? The virtue and the discipline of the equestrian order, its unmarred and unconquerable boldness when advancing to a conflict? Behold our state. All these things are to be found with us. All these have descended to us, together with the empire. Not in utter nakedness did the empire come to us. It came clad in its virtue. It brought its adornments with it. With us are your consuls. With us is your senate. With us is your soldiery. These very leaders of the Franks must rule you by their counsel, these very knights of the Franks must avert harm from you with the sword. You boastfully declare that by you I have been summoned, that by you I have been made first a citizen and then the prince, that from you I have received what was yours. How lacking in reason, how void of truth this novel utterance is, may be left to your own judgment and to the decision of men of wisdom! Let us ponder over the exploits of modern emperors, to see whether it was not our divine princes Charles [Charlemagne] and Otto [I] who, by their valor and not by anyone's bounty, wrested the City along with Italy from the Greeks and the Lombards and added it to the realms of the Franks. Desiderius and Berengar teach you this, your tyrants, of whom you boasted, on whom you relied as your princes. We have learned from reliable accounts that they were not only subjugated and taken captive by our Franks, but grew old and ended their lives in their servitude. Their ashes, buried among us, constitute the clearest evidence of this fact. But, you say: "You came on my invitation," I admit it; I was invited. Give me the

From Otto of Freising and his continuator, Rahewin, *The Deeds of Frederick Barbarossa* (New York: Columbia University Press, 1953), pp. 146–148, 183–184. Reprinted courtesy of Columbia University Press.

reason why I was invited! You were being assailed by enemies and could not be freed by your own hand or by the effeminate Greeks. The power of the Franks was invoked by invitation. I would call it entreaty rather than invitation. In your misery you besought the happy, in your frailty the valiant, in your weakness the strong, in your anxiety the carefree. Invited after that fashion—if it may be called an invitation—I have come. I have made your prince my vassal and from that time until the present have transferred you to my jurisdiction. I am the lawful possessor. Let him who can, snatch the club from the hand of Hercules. . . .

CHURCH AND STATE

Innocent III—Papal Power at Its Zenith

Innocent III (1198–1216) claimed a role of leadership for the papacy in all the spiritual and temporal affairs of Christendom.

From *Letters of Innocent III*

To the Nobles of Tuscany

Just as the founder of the universe established two great lights in the firmament of heaven, a greater one to preside over the day and a lesser to preside over the night, so too in the firmament of the universal church, which is signified by the word heaven, he instituted two great dignities, a greater one to preside over souls as if over day and a lesser one to preside over bodies as if over night. These are the pontifical authority and the royal power. Now just as the moon derives its light from the sun and is indeed lower than it in quantity and quality, in position and in power, so too the royal power derives the spendor of its dignity from the pontifical authority. . . .

To the Princes of Germany

. . . Just as we do not want our justice to be usurped by others, so too we do not want to claim for ourselves the rights of the princes. We do indeed acknowledge, as we should, that the princes, to whom this belongs by right and ancient custom, have the right and power to elect a king who is afterwards to be promoted emperor; and especially so since this right and power came to them from the apostolic see which transferred the Roman empire from the Greeks to the Germans in the person of the great Charles. But the princes should acknowledge, and indeed they do acknowledge, that right and authority to examine the person elected as king, who is to be promoted to the imperial dignity, belong to us who anoint, consecrate and crown him; for it is regularly

From *Letters of Innocent III*, Brian Tierney, trans. in *The Crisis of Church and State 1050–1300* (New York: Prentice–Hall, 1964), pp. 132–137. Copyright © 1964 by Prentice–Hall, Inc. Reprinted courtesy of Prentice–Hall, Inc., Englewood Cliffs, N. J.

and generally observed that the examination of a person pertains to the one to whom the laying-on of hands belongs. If the princes elected as king a sacrilegious man or an excommunicate, a tyrant, a fool or a heretic, and that not just by a divided vote but unanimously, ought we to anoint, consecrate and crown such a man? Of course not.

It is clear from law and precedent that, if the votes of the princes are divided in an election, we can favor one of the parties after due warning and a reasonable delay, especially after the unction, consecration and coronation are demanded of us, for it has often happened that both parties demanded them. For if the princes after due warning and delay cannot or will not agree, shall the apostolic see then lack an advocate and defender and be penalized for their fault? . . .

To the Bishops of France

. . . Let no one suppose that we wish to diminish or disturb the jurisdiction and power of the king when he ought not to impede or restrict our jurisdiction and power. Since we are insufficient to exercise all our own jurisdiction why should we want to usurp another's? But the Lord says in the Gospel, "If thy brother shall offend against thee, go, and rebuke him between thee and him alone. If he shall hear thee thou shalt gain thy brother. And if he will not hear thee, take with thee one or two more, that in the mouth of two or three witnesses every word may stand. And if he will not hear them, tell the church. And if he will not hear the church let him be to thee as the heathen and the publican" (Matthew 18:15); and the king of England is ready, so he asserts, to prove fully that the king of the French is offending against him and that he has proceeded according to the evangelical rule in rebuking him and, having achieved nothing, is at last telling it to the church. How then can we, who have been called to the rule of the universal church by divine providence, obey the divine command if we do not proceed as it lays down, unless perhaps [King Philip] shows sufficient reason to the contrary before us or our legate. For we do not intend to judge concerning a fief, judgement on which belongs to him—except when some special privilege or contrary custom detracts from the common law—but to decide concerning a sin, of which the judgement undoubtedly belongs to us, and we can and should exercise it against any-one. . . . But it may be said that kings are to be treated differently from others. We, however, know that it is written in the divine law, "You shall judge the great as well as the little and there shall be no difference of persons" (*cf.* Deuteronomy 1:17). . . . Although we are empowered to proceed in this fashion against any criminal sin in order to recall the sinner from error to truth and from vice to virtue, this is especially so when it is a sin against peace, peace which is the bond of love. . . . Finally, when a treaty of peace was made between the kings and confirmed on both sides by oaths which, however, were not kept for the agreed period, can we not take cognizance of such a sworn oath, which certainly belongs to the judgement of the church, in order to re-establish the broken treaty of peace? . . .

To King John of England

The king of kings and lord of lords, Jesus Christ, a priest for ever after the order of Melchisedech, has so established the priesthood and kingship in the church that the kingship is priestly and the priesthood is royal, as Peter in his Epistle and Moses in the Law bear witness, and he has set over all one whom he appointed to be his vicar on earth so that, just as every knee on earth and in heaven and even under the earth is bowed to him, so all should obey his vicar and strive that there be one fold and one shepherd. The kings of the world so venerate this vicar for the sake of God that they do not regard themselves as reigning properly unless they take care to serve him devotedly. Prudently heeding this, beloved son, and mercifully inspired by him in whose hand are the hearts of kings and who sways them as he wishes, you have decreed that your person and your kingdom should be temporally subject to the one to whom you knew them to be spiritually subject, so that kingship and priesthood, like body and soul, should be united in the one person of the vicar of Christ to the great advantage and profit of both. He has deigned to bring this about who, being alpha and omega, related the end to the beginning and revealed the beginning in the end, so that those provinces which formerly had the holy Roman church as their proper teacher in spiritual matters now have her as their special lord in temporal affairs also. . . .

Innocent IV and Frederick II

The somewhat colorful personality of Emperor Frederick II (1215–1250) was described by a thirteenth-century Franciscan. His account is paraphrased below.

Frederick II According to Salimbene

To Salimbene, as to Dante, Frederick was a man of heroic proportions in his very sins. "Of faith in God he had none; he was crafty, wily, avaricious, lustful, malicious, wrathful; and yet a gallant man at times, when he would show his kindness or courtesy; full of solace, jocund, delightful, fertile in devices. He knew to read, write, and sing, and to make songs and music. He was a comely man, and well-formed, but of

From G. G. Coulton, *St. Francis to Dante* (London: David Nutt, 1906), pp. 242–243.

middle stature. I have seen him, and once I loved him, for on my behalf he wrote to Bro. Elias, Minister-General of the Friars Minor, to send me back to my father. Moreover, he knew to speak with many and varied tongues, and, to be brief, if he had been rightly Catholic, and had loved God and His Church, he would have had few emperors his equals in the world." [Salimbene] goes on to enumerate several specimens of the Emperor's "curiosities" or "excesses," though for sheer weariness he will not tell them all. Frederick cut off a notary's thumb who had spelt his hame *Fredericus* instead of *Fridericus*. Like Psammetichus in Herodotus, he made linguistic experiments on the vile bodies of hapless infants, "bidding foster-mothers and nurses to suckle and bathe and wash the children, but in no wise to prattle or speak with them; for he would have learnt whether they would speak the Hebrew language (which had been the first), or Greek, or Latin, or Arabic, or perchance the tongue of their parents of whom they had been born. But he laboured in vain, for the children could not live without clappings of the hands, and gestures, and gladness of countenance, and blandishments." Again, "when he saw the Holy Land, (which God had so oft-times commended as a land flowing with milk and honey and most excellent above all lands,) it pleased him not, and he said that if the God of the Jews had seen *his* lands of Terra di Lavoro, Calabria, Sicily, and Apulia, then He would not so have commended the land which He promised to the Jews." Again, he compelled "Nicholas the Fish," whom his mother's curse had condemned to an amphibious life, to dive and fetch his golden cup a second time from the very bottom of Charybdis: in which repeated attempt the poor man knew that he must perish. Fifthly, "he enclosed a living man in a cask that he might die there, wishing thereby to show that the soul perished utterly, as if he might say the word of Isaiah 'Let us eat and drink, for to-morrow we die.' For he was an Epicurean; wherefore, partly of himself and partly through his wise men, he sought out all that he could find in Holy Scripture which might make for the proof that there was no other life after death, as for instance 'Thou shalt destroy them, and not build them up': and again 'Their sepulchres shall be their houses for ever.' "

Pope Innocent IV (1243–1254) struggled for several years—in the end successfully—against Frederick's plans to dominate Italy.

Deposition of Frederick II (1245)

[Frederick] has committed four very grave offences, which can not be covered up by any subterfuge (we say nothing for the moment about his other crimes); he has abjured God on many occasions; he has wan-

From Innocent IV, in S. Z. Ehler and J. B. Morrall, eds. and trans., *Church and State Through the Centuries* (Westminster, Md.: Newman Press, 1954), pp. 80, 86.

tonly broken the peace which had been re-established between the Church and the Empire; he has also committed sacrilege by causing to be imprisoned the Cardinals of the holy Roman Church and the prelates and clerics, regular and secular, of other churches, coming to the Council which our predecessor had summoned; he is also accused of heresy not by doubtful and flimsy but by formidable and clear proofs. . . .

We therefore, who are the vicar, though unworthy, of Jesus Christ on earth and to whom it was said in the person of blessed Peter the Apostle: "Whatsoever thou shalt bind on earth," etc., show and declare an account of the above-mentioned shameful crimes and of many others, having held careful consultation with our brethren and the holy Council, that the aforesaid prince—who has rendered himself so unworthy of all the honor and dignity of the Empire and the kingdom and who, because of his wickedness, has been rejected by God from acting as king or Emperor—is bound by his sins and cast out and deprived of all honor and dignity by God, to which we add our sentence of deprivation also. We absolve for ever all who owe him allegiance in virtue of an oath of fealty from any oath of this kind; and we strictly forbid by Apostolic authority that any one should obey him or look upon him henceforth as king or Emperor, and we decree that whoever shall in the future afford him advice, help or goodwill as if he were Emperor or king, shall fall "ipso facto" under the binding force of excommunication. But let those in the same Empire whose duty it is to look to the election of an Emperor, elect a successor freely. We shall make it our business to provide for the aforesaid kingdom of Sicily as seems best to us with the advice of our brethren.

Boniface VIII—The Crisis of Papal Power

In the course of a conflict with King Philip IV of France, Pope Boniface VIII (1294–1303) promulgated a definitive statement of papal claims.

Unam Sanctam

That there is one holy, Catholic and apostolic church we are bound to believe and to hold, our faith urging us, and this we do firmly believe and simply confess; and that outside this church there is no salvation or remission of sins, as her spouse proclaims in the Canticles, "One is my dove, my perfect one. She is the only one of her mother, the cho-

From Brian Tierney, *The Crisis of Church and State 1050 to 1300* (New York: Prentice–Hall, 1964), pp. 188–189. Copyright © 1964 by Prentice–Hall, Inc. Reprinted courtesy of Prentice–Hall, Inc., Englewood Cliffs, N. J.

sen of her that bore her" (Canticles 6:8); which represents one mystical body whose head is Christ, while the head of Christ is God. In this church there is our Lord, one faith, one baptism. At the time of the Flood there was one ark, symbolizing the one church. It was finished in one cubit and had one helmsman and captain, namely Noah, and we read that all things on earth outside of it were destroyed. This church we venerate and this alone, the Lord saying through his prophet, "Deliver, O God, my soul from the sword, my only one from the power of the dog" (Psalm 21:21). He prayed for the soul, that is himself, the head, and at the same time for the body, which he called the one church on account of the promised unity of faith, sacraments and charity of the church. This is that seamless garment of the Lord which was not cut but fell by lot. Therefore there is one body and one head of this one and only church, not two heads as though it were a monster, namely Christ and Christ's vicar, Peter and Peter's successor, for the Lord said to this Peter, "Feed my sheep" (John 21:17). He said "My sheep" in general, not these or those, whence he is understood to have committed them all to Peter. Hence, if the Greeks or any others say that they were not committed to Peter and his successors, they necessarily admit that they are not of Christ's flock, for the Lord says in John that there is one sheepfold and one shepherd.

We are taught by the words of the Gospel that in this church and in her power there are two swords, a spiritual one and a temporal one. For when the apostles said "Here are two swords" (Luke 22:38), meaning in the church since it was the apostles who spoke, the Lord did not reply that it was too many but enough. Certainly anyone who denies that the temporal sword is in the power of Peter has not paid heed to the words of the Lord when he said, "Put up thy sword into its sheath" (Matthew 26:52). Both then are in the power of the church, the material sword and the spiritual. But the one is exercised for the church, the other by the church, the one by the hand of the priest, the other by the hand of kings and soldiers, though at the will and suffrance of the priest. One sword ought to be under the other and the temporal authority subject to the spiritual power. For, while the apostle says, "There is no power but from God and those that are ordained of God" (Romans 13:1), they would not be ordained unless one sword was under the other and, being inferior, was led by the other to the highest things. For, according to the blessed Dionysius, it is the law of divinity for the lowest to be led to the highest through intermediaries. In the order of the universe all things are not kept in order in the same fashion and immediately but the lowest are ordered by the intermediate and inferiors by superiors. But that the spiritual power excels any earthly one in dignity and nobility we ought the more openly to confess in proportion as spiritual things excel temporal ones. Moreover we clearly perceive this from the giving of tithes, from benediction and sanctification, from the acceptance of this power and from the very government of things. For, the truth bearing witness, the spiritual power has to institute the earthly power and to judge it if it has not been good. So is verified the prophecy of Jeremias [1.10] concerning the church and the power of the church, "Lo, I have set thee this day over the nations and over kingdoms" etc.

Therefore, if the earthly power errs, it shall be judged by the spiritual power, if a lesser spiritual power errs it shall be judged by its superior, but if the supreme spiritual power errs it can be judged only by God not by man, as the apostle witnesses, "The spiritual man judgeth all things and he himself is judged of no man" (1 Corinthians 2:15). Although this authority was given to a man and is exercised by a man it is not human but rather divine, being given to Peter at God's mouth, and confirmed to him and to his successors in him, the rock whom the Lord acknowledged when he said to Peter himself "Whatsoever thou shalt bind" etc. (Matthew 16:19). Whoever therefore resists this power so ordained by God resists the ordinance of God unless, like the Manicheans, he imagines that there are two beginnings, which we judge to be false and heretical, as Moses witnesses, for not "in the beginnings" but "in the beginning" God created heaven and earth (Genesis 1:1). Therefore we declare, state, define and pronounce that it is altogether necessary to salvation for every human creature to be subject to the Roman Pontiff.

In June 1303, King Philip launched an extraordinary series of charges against Boniface. The accusations were presented by the king's minister, Guillaume de Plaisans, to a royal council in Paris.

Accusations Against Boniface VIII

He does not believe in the immortality or incorruptibility of the rational soul but believes that the rational soul undergoes corruption with the body. He does not believe in an eternal life to come . . . and he was not ashamed to declare that he would rather be a dog or an ass or any brute animal than a Frenchman, which he would not have said if he believed that a Frenchman had an immortal soul. . . . He does not faithfully believe that, through the words instituted by Christ, spoken by a faithful and properly ordained priest in the manner prescribed by the chuch over a Host, it becomes the true body of Christ. . . . He is reported to say that fornication is not a sin any more than rubbing the hands together is . . . He has often said that he would ruin himself and the whole world and the whole church to lay low the king and the French people if he could not do it otherwise. . . . He has had silver images of himself erected in churches to perpetuate his damnable

From P. Dupony, *Histoire du différend d'entre le pape Boniface VIII et Philippe le Bel* (Paris, 1655), Brian Tierney, trans. in *Crisis of Church and State 1050–1300* (New York: Prentice–Hall, 1964), p. 190. Copyright © 1964 by Prentice–Hall, Inc. Reprinted courtesy of Prentice–Hall, Inc., Englewood Cliffs, N. J.

memory, so leading men into idolatry. . . . He has a private demon whose advice he takes in all matters. . . . He has publicly preached that the Roman pope cannot commit simony, which is heresy. . . . He is guilty of the crime of sodomy. . . . He has caused many clerics to be murdered in his presence, rejoicing in their deaths. . . . He has compelled certain priests to reveal men's confessions and then, without the consent of those who confessed, has made them public to their shame and confusion. . . . He does not fast on fast days or in Lent. . . . He has depressed and debased the rank and status of the cardinals. . . . He is openly called a simonist or rather the fount and origin of simony. . . . He is publicly accused of treating inhumanly his predecessor Celestine—a man of holy memory and holy life who perhaps did not know that he could not resign and that accordingly Boniface could not legitimately enter upon his see—imprisoning him in a dungeon and causing him to die there swiftly and secretly, and this is notorious throughout the whole world. . . . He does not seek the salvation of souls but their perdition.

Philip succeeded in rallying French support against the claims of Boniface. A later pope, Clement V (1305–1314), put forward a conciliatory explanation of Unam Sanctam *and commended the actions of the French king.*

Decree of Clement V (1306)

The full and sincere affection that our son Philip, illustrious king of the French, bears toward us and the Roman church has merited—and the outstanding merits of his forefathers, together with the sincerity and purity of the devotion of the people of his kingdom have also merited—that we show benevolent favor to both king and kingdom. Hence it is that we do not wish or intend that anything prejudicial to that king or kingdom should arise from the declaration of our predecessor of happy memory Pope Boniface VIII, which began with the words "Unam sanctam"; nor that the aforementioned king, kingdom and people should be any more subject to the Roman church on account of it than they were before. But everything is understood to be in the same state as it was before the said definition, both as regards the church and as regards the aforementioned king, kingdom and people.

Decree of Clement V (1311)

. . . Finally, having inquired diligently into the matter we find that the said assertors, objectors and denouncers [of Boniface] . . . and the said

From *Regestum Clementi Papae*, Brian Tierney, trans. in *Crisis of Church and State 1050–1300* (New York: Prentice–Hall, 1964), p. 192. Copyright © 1964 by Prentice–Hall, Inc. Reprinted courtesy of Prentice–Hall, Inc., Englewood Cliffs, N. J.

king ... were not impelled by any preconceived malice but were actuated by an estimable, just and sincere zeal ... and by apostolic authority we pronounce and with the council of our brothers we decree and by these presents declare that they were and are guiltless of malicious accusation and that they acted out of an estimable, just and sincere zeal and from the fervor of their Catholic faith.

Reflections on Government

Innocent IV was not only a pope but also a great jurist. In his Commentary on the Decretals *he presented a doctrine of universal papal authority against a background of the whole history of human government. His comments also remind us of the medieval background from which later ideas of natural rights and natural law emerged.*

From Innocent IV. *Commentary on the Decretals*

Is it licit to invade the lands of infidels? ... In truth the earth belongs to God ... for God is the creator of all things, and he subjected everything to the rational creature for whom he had made all these things as in Genesis, 1. In the beginning therefore all things were common until, by the usage of our first parents, it was introduced that lands should be divided and delimited and appropriated. ... Now this was not bad but good, for common ownership gives rise to discord and common possessions are often neglected. Thus in the beginning all things and possessions belonged to no one except God and they were conceded to the first occupier. ... But once they had been occupied it was not licit for anyone else to occupy them. This was forbidden by the law of nature which tells everyone not to do to another what he does not want done to himself. ... No one had ownership of men as slaves before the introduction of the Law of Nations, because by nature all men are free.

... I read of just and lawful jurisdiction where the sword given for vengeance is mentioned above at *Decretales* 1.33.6. But how this jurisdiction first began I do not know unless perhaps God assigned some person or persons to do justice to criminals or unless in the beginning the father of a family had complete jurisdiction over his family by the law of nature, though now he has it only in a few minor matters. ... This at any rate is certain, that God himself exercised jurisdiction from the beginning as is noted above at *Decretales* 2.2.10, *Licet*.

From Innocent IV, *Commentaria Super Libros Quinque Decretalium* (Frankfurt, 1570), III. 34.8. Brian Tierney, trans. in *Crisis of Church and State 1050 to 1300* (New York: Prentice–Hall, 1964), p. 155. Copyright © 1964 by Prentice–Hall, Inc. Reprinted courtesy of Prentice–Hall, Inc., Englewood Cliffs, N.J.

Again the people could have princes by election as they had Saul and many others. . . . I maintain, therefore, that lordship, possession and jurisdiction can belong to infidels licitly and without sin, for these things were made not only for the faithful but for every rational creature as has been said. For he makes his sun to rise on the just and the wicked and he feeds the birds of the air, Matthew c.5, c.6. Accordingly we say that it is not licit for the pope or the faithful to take away from infidels their belongings or their lordships or jurisdictions because they possess them without sin. Nevertheless we do certainly believe that the pope, who is vicar of Jesus Christ, has power not only over Christians but also over all infidels, for Christ had power over all, whence it is said in the psalm, "Give to the king thy judgment O God" (Psalm 71:2), and he would not seem to have been a careful father unless he had committed full power over all to his vicar whom he left on earth. Again he gave the keys of the kingdom of heaven to Peter and his successors and said, "Whatsoever you shall bind, etc." (Matthew 16:19). And again, elsewhere, "Feed my sheep, etc." (John 21:17). . . . But all men, faithful and infidels, are Christ's sheep by creation even though they are not of the fold of the church and thus from the foregoing it is clear that the pope has jurisdiction and power over all *de iure* though not *de facto.*

John of Paris sought to discriminate carefully between the roles of king and pope.

From John of Paris. *On Royal and Papal Power* (1303)

First it should be known that kingship, properly understood, can be defined as the rule of one man over a perfect multitude so ordered as to promote the public good. . . . Such a government is based on natural law and the law of nations. For, since man is naturally a civil or political creature as is said in Book I of the *Politics*—and the Philosopher proves this from food, clothing and defense in which a solitary man is not self-sufficient as also from speech which is addressed to another, these things being necessary only for men—it is essential for a man to live in a multitude and in such a multitude as is self-sufficient for life. The community of a household or village is not of this sort, but the community of a city or kingdom is, for in a household or village there is not found everything necessary for food, clothing and defense through a whole life as there is in a city or kingdom. But every multitude scatters and disintegrates as each man pursues his own ends un-

From *De potestate regia et papali*, J. Leclereq, ed. in *Jean de Paris et l'ecclesiologie du XIIIe siècle* (Paris: J. Vrin, 1942), pp. 176–178, 199, 214, 236.

less it is ordered to the common good by some one man who has charge of this common good. . . .

Next it must be borne in mind that man is not ordered only to such a good as can be acquired by nature, which is to live virtuously, but is further ordered to a supernatural end which is eternal life, and the whole multitude of men living virtuously is ordered to this. Therefore it is necessary that there be some one man to direct the multitude to this end. If indeed this end could be attained by the power of human nature, it would necessarily pertain to the office of the human king to direct men to this end, for we call a human king him to whom is committed the highest duty of government in human affairs. But since man does not come to eternal life by human power but by divine . . . this kind of rule pertains to a king who is not only man but also God, namely Jesus Christ . . . and because Christ was to withdraw his corporal presence from the church it was necessary for him to institute others as ministers who would administer the sacraments to men, and these are called priests. . . . Hence priesthood may be defined in this fashion. Priesthood is a spiritual power of administering sacraments to the faithful conferred by Christ on ministers of the church.

The royal power both existed and was exercised before the papal, and there were kings in France before there were Christians. Therefore neither the royal power nor its exercise is from the pope but from God and from the people, who elect a king by choosing either a person or a royal house. . . . It would seem that the power of inferior pontiffs and ministers is derived from the pope more than the royal power, for ecclesiastical prelates are more immediately dependent on the pope than secular princes. But the power of prelates is not from God through the pope but immediately from God and from the people who elect or consent.

Concerning the ecclesiastical power of censure or correction it should be known that, directly, it is only spiritual, for it can impose no penalty in the external court but a spiritual one, except conditionally and incidentally. For though the ecclesiastical judge has to lead men back to God and draw them away from sin and correct them, he has to do this only in the way laid down for him by God, which is to say by cutting them off from the sacraments and from the company of the faithful and by similar measures which are proper to ecclesiastical censure. I said "conditionally" in reference to one who is willing to repent and accept a pecuniary penalty, for the ecclesiastical judge cannot impose any corporal or pecuniary penalty for a crime as a secular judge can, except only on one who is willing to accept it. . . . I said "incidentally" because if a prince was a heretic and incorrigible and contemptuous of ecclesiastical censures, the pope might so move the people that he would be deprived of his secular dignity and deposed by the people. The pope might do this in the case of an ecclesiastical crime, of which cognizance belonged to him, by excommunicating all who obeyed such a man as a lord, and thus the people would depose him, and the pope "incidentally." So too, if the pope on the other hand behaved criminally and brought scandal on the church and was incorrigible, the prince might indirectly excommunicate him and "incidentally" bring about his deposition by warning him personally or through the cardinals. And if the pope were unwilling to yield the emperor might so move the people as to compel him to resign or be deposed by the people, for the emperor could, by taking securities or imposing corporal penalties, prevent each and everyone from obeying him or serving him as pope. So each can act toward the other, for both pope and emperor have jurisdiction universally and everywhere, but the one has spiritual jurisdiction, the other temporal.

... Although a form of government in which one man simply rules according to virtue is better than any other simple government, as the Philosopher proves in Book III of the *Politics*, nevertheless if it is mixed with aristocracy and democracy it is better than a simple form in that, in a mixed constitution, all have some part in the government. Through this the peace of the people is maintained and all of them love such a government and preserve it.

In Western political theory, ideas about the family often influenced ideas about the state. (All paternalistic theories of government were based implicitly or explicitly on a father's supposedly "natural" rule over his family.) Giles of Rome interpolated a lengthy discussion of the family into his treatise On the Rule of Princes.

From Giles of Rome. *On the Rule of Princes*

We shall next discuss the rule of families. It is not enough that kings and princes are good in themselves unless they are also good as regards others and know how to govern others. Nor does it suffice that kings know how to rule themselves unless they know how to rule a household, a city, and a realm. . . .

Someone may be doubtful and think we are ignoring the limits of our subject, because the community or society which is sufficient to provide food and clothing and the other necessities of life is not the household but the civic community, since, according to the Philosopher (Aristotle), the household does not suffice for the whole of life. . . . But all other communities presuppose the household. Hence, if any community is necessary to provide all that is sufficient for human life, the household is necessary. . . .

The Philosopher holds that at the first establishment of a household it consists of two associations—man and wife and master and servants

From Giles of Rome, *De regimine principum* (Rome, 1556), pp. 128–141, 173–174, Brian Tierney, trans.

. . but if the household is to be complete a third kind of association is needed—father and sons. . . . Hence there are three kinds of governance: conjugal, whereby a husband rules his wife; paternal, whereby a father rules his sons; dominative or despotic, whereby a master rules his servants. . . .

For anyone who rules others either rules them according to certain laws and agreements, and this kind of rule is called "political" or "civil"; or he rules them according to his own will. This again can be in one of two ways. Either the ruler intends his own good and then his rule is called "despotic" or "dominative" or he intends the good of his subjects, and then his rule is called "regal." Now these three ways of ruling, in accordance with which we see cities and castles governed, can be compared with the three ways of ruling found in a household. For conjugal rule is like a "political" regime, because no one ought to rule his wife simply by his own will but rather as the laws of matrimony require and in accordance with the fitting and honorable engagements that man and wife enter into. Paternal rule is like a "regal" regime. For a father rules his sons by his own will, not according to compacts and agreements. Agreements and compacts have no place between subject and lord, unless it is in the power of the subjects to choose for themselves a ruler. But it is not in the power of sons to choose their fathers, for sons take a natural origin from their parents. Sons do not choose their fathers as wives their husbands. Hence, since sons are ruled by will and for their own good, this kind of rule is not like a "political" regime but like a "regal" one. . . . The third kind of rule in a household, by which servants are ruled, is like a "dominative" regime. . . . From this it is clearly shown that sons of the king ought not to be ruled by the same regime as servants. For a lord rules his servants for his own good, not for the good of the servants and, according to the Philosopher, this is to rule others dominatively . . . but a father ought to rule his sons for the good of the sons. From this distinction therefore it is clear that paternal rule is not the same as dominative; rather it takes its origin from love.

IX

REASON, FAITH, AND LOVE
Abelard and Bernard: Reason and Faith
  From Abelard. *Sic et Non*
  From Bernard. *Letter to Pope Innocent II*
  From Abelard. *Dialectica*
  From Bernard. *The Love of God*
Abelard and Heloise: Learning and Love
  From Abelard. *A Story of Calamities*
  From Heloise. *Letter to Abelard*
  From Peter the Venerable. *Letter to Heloise*

LORDS AND LADIES: EVE AND MARY
Troubadour Songs
  Jaufré Rudel. *To His Love Afar*
  Walther Von Der Vogelweide. *A Spring Song*
  Countess de Dia. *A Distressed Lover*
Love and Marriage
  From *The Art of Courtly Love*
Eve and Mary
  Adam Lay Y-Bounden
  From *Liber Exemplorum*

GOD AND NATURE—THE WAY OF THE HEART
Franciscan Ideals
  Francis's Testament
Creator and Creatures
  From *Thomas of Celano*
  The Canticle of the Sun

GOD AND NATURE—THE WAY OF THE MIND
Chance and Necessity—Maimonides
  From *The Guide for the Perplexed*

Nature and Law—Aquinas
  From *Summa Theologiae*
Heaven and Earth—Dante
  From *The Banquet*

GOD AND NATURE—THE WAY OF DISSENT
Albigensians and Patarins
  From Raynaldus. *Annales Decree of Emperor Frederick II (c. 1235)*
  From *Montaillou*
Beguins
  From *The Inquisitor's Manual of Bernard Gui*

THE MEDIEVAL WORLD—RELIGION AND CULTURE

*T*HE TWELFTH CENTURY *was a time of vivid new life in many areas of human conduct and intellectual activity. The people of the age often reveal themselves to us as living personalities—for instance, a Peter Abelard, Heloise, or Bernard of Clairvaux. A fresh, more confident attitude to nature inspired poets, religious mystics, and philosophers. Devotion to the Virgin Mary led to an emphasis on the "feminine" virtues of tenderness and compassion in medieval religion. At the same time the cult of courtly love provided for the lay aristocracy a new conception of the ideal relationship between women and men.*

In the sphere of thought, the rediscovery of Aristotle's philosophy and science opened up a new world to medieval intellectuals. The great problem that emerged for them was to fit all the new knowledge into a framework of generally accepted religion. Peter Abelard pointed to the need for using critical reason in interpreting old texts. The outstanding philosophers of the next century, like Moses Maimonides and Thomas Aquinas, sought to combine Aristotle's philosophy with biblical revelation in great syntheses of universal knowledge. For a time it seemed that they might succeed; but eventually it proved that the "medieval synthesis," for all its richness and depth, would not persist as the permanent pattern of Western culture. (Medieval people themselves often looked forward to a coming new age when the achievements of their own day would be transcended.)

REASON, FAITH, AND LOVE

Abelard and Bernard: Reason and Faith

Peter Abelard, a brilliant teacher in the schools of Paris at the beginning of the twelfth century, was renowned for his critical approach to sacred authorities. In his Sic et Non (Yes and No) *he showed that, superficially at least, the great church fathers often seemed to contradict one another. Part of the Introduction and the first Question are given below.*

From Abelard. *Sic et Non*

In order that the way be not blocked and posterity deprived of the healthy labor of treating and debating difficult questions of language and style, a distinction must be drawn between the work of later authors and the supreme canonical authority of the Old and New Testaments. If, in Scripture, anything seems absurd you are not permitted to say, "The author of this book did not hold to the truth"—but rather that the codex is defective or that the interpreter erred or that you do not understand. But if anything seems contrary to truth in the works of later authors, which are contained in innumerable books, the reader or auditor is free to judge, so that he may approve what is pleasing and reject what gives offense, unless the matter is established by certain reason or by canonical authority (of the Scriptures). . . .

In view of these considerations we have undertaken to collect various sayings of the Fathers that give rise to questioning because of their apparent contradictions as they occur to our memory. This questioning excites young readers to the maximum of effort in inquiring into the truth, and such inquiry sharpens their minds. Assiduous and frequent questioning is indeed the first key to wisdom. Aristotle, that most perspicacious of all philosophers, exhorted the studious to practice it eagerly, saying, "Perhaps it is difficult to express oneself with confidence on such matters if they have not been much discussed. To entertain doubts on particular points will not be unprofitable." For by doubting we come to inquiry; through inquiring we perceive the truth,

From Brian Tierney, trans. in *Great Issues in Western Civilization*, Brian Tierney, Donald Kagan, and L. Pearce Williams, eds. (New York: Random House, 1976), pp. 397–400. Copyright © 1967, 1972, 1976 by Random House, Inc. Reprinted by permission of the publisher.

according to the Truth Himself. "Seek and you shall find," He says, "Knock and it shall be opened to you."

That Faith Should Be Based on Human Reason—And the Contrary

Gregory in Homily XXVI.

We know that the works of the Lord would not excite wonder if they were understood by reason; nor is there any merit in faith where human reason offers proof.

Idem in Homily V.

At one word of command Peter and Andrew left their nets and followed the Redeemer. They had seen him work no miracles; they had heard nothing from him about eternal retribution; and nevertheless, at one command of the Lord, they forgot what they had seemed to possess. . . .

From the First Book of Augustine against Faustus.

Faustus: It is a weak profession of faith if one does not believe in Christ without evidence and argument.

From the Life of St. Sylvester,

where, disputing with the Jews, he said to the Rabbi Roasus, "Faith is not submitted to human reason, and faith teaches us that this God, whom you confess to be one God, is Father, Son, and Holy Spirit."

Augustine, on the Morals of the Church Against the Manicheans.

The order of nature is such that, when we state anything, authority precedes reason for a reason might seem weak if, after it has been presented, authority is cited to confirm it. . . .

Ambrose.

If I am convinced by reason I give up faith. . . .

Gregory to Bishop Dominicus.

Although these things are so I wish that all heretics be held in check by Catholic priests vigorously and always by reasoning.

Idem in Pastoral Care.

The wise of this world and the dull are to be admonished differently. The former are for the most part converted by the arguments of reason, the latter sometimes better by examples. . . .

Hilary, on the Trinity, Book XII.

It is fitting that those who preach Christ to the world should refute the irreligious and unsound doctrines of the world through their knowledge of omnipotent wisdom, according as the Apostle says. . . .

Augustine to Count Valerian.

The Apostle Peter commanded us to be always ready to give satisfaction to anyone asking us the reason for our faith and hope. . . . We should give an account of our faith and hope to enquirers in a two-fold fashion. We should always explain the just grounds of our faith and hope to questioners, whether they ask honestly or dishonestly, and we should hold fast to the pure profession of our faith and hope even amid the pressures of our adversaries.

(Abelard then considered in the same fashion, giving authorities for and against each proposition, some of the central teachings of the church—e.g., "That there is one God—and the contrary"; "That the Son is without beginning—and the contrary"; "That God can do all things—and the contrary"; "That without baptism of water no one can be saved—and the contrary"; "That saintly works do not justify man—and the contrary.")

Bernard of Clairvaux, a great spiritual teacher and a leader of the Cistercian Order of monks, was outraged by Abelard's approach to sacred learning.

From Bernard. *Letter to Pope Innocent II*

To his most loving Father and Lord, Innocent, Supreme Pontiff Brother Bernard, called Abbot of Clairvaux, sends humble greeting. . . .

We have in France an old teacher turned into a new theologian, who is his early days amused himself with dialectics, and now gives utterance to wild imaginations upon the Holy Scriptures. He is endeavouring again to quicken false opinions, long ago condemned and put to rest, not only his own, but those of others; and is adding fresh ones as well. I know not what there is in heaven above and in the earth beneath which he deigns to confess ignorance of: he raises his eyes to Heaven, and searches the deep things of God, and then returning to us, he brings back unspeakable words which it is not lawful for a man to utter, while he is presumptuously prepared to give a reason for

From S. J. Eales, trans., *Life and Works of St. Bernard* (London: John Hodges, 1889), Vol. 2, pp. 565, 574–575.

everything, even of those things which are above reason; he presumes against reason and against faith. For what is more against reason than by reason to attempt to transcend reason? And what is more against faith than to be unwilling to believe what reason cannot attain?

But on the other hand our theologian says: "What is the use of speaking of doctrine unless what we wish to teach can be explained so as to be intelligible?" And so he promises understanding to his hearers, even on those most sublime and sacred truths which are hidden in the very bosom of our holy faith. . . . It is no wonder if a man who is careless of what he says should, when rushing into the mysteries of the Faith, so irreverently assail and tear asunder the hidden treasures of godliness, since he has neither piety nor faith in his notions about the piety of faith. For instance, on the very threshold of his theology (I should rather say his stultology) he defines faith as private judgment; as though in these mysteries it is to be allowed to each person to think and speak as he pleases, or as though the mysteries of our faith are to hang in uncertainty amongst shifting and varying opinions, when on the contrary they rest on the solid and unshakable foundation of truth. Is not our hope baseless if our faith is subject to change? Fools then were our martyrs for bearing so cruel tortures for an uncertainty, and for entering, without hesitation, on an everlasting exile, through a bitter death, when there was a doubt as to the recompense of their reward. But far be it from us to think that in our faith or hope anything, as he supposes, depends on the fluctuating judgment of the individual, and that the whole of it does not rest on sure and solid truth, having been commended by miracles and revelations from above, founded and consecrated by the Son of the Virgin, by the Blood of the Redeemer, by the glory of the risen Christ. These infallible proofs have been given us in superabundance. But if not, the Spirit itself, lastly, bears witness with our spirit that we are the sons of God. How, then, can any one dare to call faith opinion, unless it be that he has not yet received that Spirit, or unless he either knows not the Gospel or thinks it to be a fable? *I know in whom I have believed, and I am confident* (2 Tim. i. 12), cries the Apostle, and you mutter in my ears that faith is only an opinion. . . . Faith is not an opinion, but a certitude.

Abelard insisted in his Dialectica *that a Christian philosopher should pursue all available knowledge.*

From Abelard. *Dialectica*

A new calumny against me, have my rivals lately devised, because I write upon the dialectic art; affirming that it is not lawful for a Christian to treat of things which do not pertain to the Faith. Not only they

From H. O. Taylor, trans., *The Mediaeval Mind*, 4th ed. (Cambridge, Mass.: Harvard University Press, 1962), Vol. 2, p. 379. Reprinted by permission of the publisher.

say that this science does not prepare us for the Faith, but that it destroys faith by the implications of its arguments. But it is wonderful if I must not discuss what is permitted them to read. If they allow that the art militates against faith, surely they deem it not to be science (*scientia*). For the science of truth is the comprehension of things, whose *species* is the wisdom in which faith consists. Truth is not opposed to truth. For not as falsehood may be opposed to falsity, or evil to evil, can the true be opposed to the true, or the good to the good; but rather all good things are in accord. All knowledge is good, even that which relates to evil, because a righteous man must have it. Since he may guard against evil, it is necessary that he should know it beforehand: otherwise he could not shun it. Though an act be evil, knowledge regarding it is good; though it be evil to sin, it is good to know the sin, which otherwise we could not shun. Nor is the science *mathematica* to be deemed evil, whose practice (astrology) is evil. Nor is it a crime to know with what services and immolations the demons may be compelled to do our will, but to use such knowledge. For if it were evil to know this, how could God be absolved, who knows the desires and cogitations of all His creatures, and how the concurrence of demons may be obtained? If therefore it is not wrong to know, but to do, the evil is to be referred to the act and not to the knowledge. Hence we are convinced that all knowledge, which indeed comes from God alone and from His bounty, is good. Wherefore the study of every science should be conceded to be good, because that which is good comes from it; and especially one must insist upon the study of that *doctrina* by which the greater truth is known. This is dialectic, whose function is to distinguish between every truth and falsity; as leader in all knowledge, it holds the primary and rule of all philosophy. The same also is shown to be needful to the Catholic Faith, which cannot without its aid resist the sophistries of schismatics.

For Bernard, the way to approach God was through love, not through logical argumentation. He taught that through love the soul could attain a mystical union with Christ. To express his vision of divine love Bernard turned to the passionate language of the biblical Song of Solomon.

From Bernard. *The Love of God*

You would hear from me, then, why and how God is to be loved? I answer: The cause of loving God is God; the manner is to love without measure. Is this enough? Yes, perhaps, for the wise. But I am debtor to the unwise as well; where enough is said for the wise, we must comply with the others also. Therefore I will not refuse to repeat it, more

From Bernard of Clairvaux, *On the Love of God*, E. G. Gardner, trans. (London: J. M. Dent, 1916), pp. 27, 39, 71. Reprinted by permission of J. M. Dent & Sons Ltd.

fully rather than more deeply, for the sake of the slower in apprehension. I may say that God is to be loved for His own sake for a double reason: because nothing can be loved more justly, nothing more fruitfully. The question, why God is to be loved, bears a double meaning. For it can be asked what is especially asked; whether for what desert of His, or for what advantage of ours, God is to be loved. But I will give the same answer to either: assuredly I find no other worthy cause of loving Him, save Himself. And first with respect to desert. Verily He has deserved much of us, who gave Himself to us for no deserts of ours. For what better than Himself could even He have given? Therefore, if the desert of God is sought, when the cause of loving Him is sought, it is this above all: that *He hath first loved us.* Worthy, indeed, is He to be loved in return, especially if we consider who loved, whom He loved, and how much. For who? Is it not He to whom every spirit confesses: *Thou art my God, for thou has no need of my goods?* It is the true charity of this Majesty who seeketh not His own. But to whom is love so unalloyed shown? *When we were yet enemies,* it is said, *we were reconciled to God.* God loved then, both freely, and His enemies. But how much? As much as John says: *God so loved the world, that he gave his only begotten Son;* and Paul says: *He spared not his own Son, but delivered him up for us all.* That very Son, too, of Himself saith: *Greater love hath no man than this, that a man lay down his life for his friends. . . .*

. . . The Pagan is in no wise stirred by such prickings of love as the Church feels, who says: *I am wounded with charity;* and again: *Stay me with flowers, comfort me with apples; for I am sick of love.* She beholds king Solomon *with the crown wherewith his mother crowned him*; she beholds the Only Begotten of the Father, bearing His cross; she beholds the Lord of Majesty buffeted and spat upon; she beholds the Author of life and of glory fastened by nails, pierced by the lance, overwhelmed with reproaches, and at last laying down that dear life of His for His friends. She beholds these things, and the more the sword of love pierces her own soul, and she says: *Stay me with flowers, comfort me with apples; for I am sick of love.* These indeed are the pomegranates, which the bride, brought into the garden of her Beloved, gathers from the tree of life, which have borrowed their taste from the heavenly bread, their colour from the blood of Christ. Then she sees death dead, and the author of death led in triumph. She sees captivity led captive from hell to earth, from earth to heaven, *that at the name of Jesus every knee should bow, of things in heaven, and things in earth, and things under the earth.* She perceives the earth, which had brought forth thorns and thistles under the ancient curse, renewed and flowering again at the grace of a new blessing. And, in all this, she remembers that verse: *And my flesh hath flourished again, and with my will I will give praise to him*; she desires to wax strong on the apples of the Passion, which she has plucked from the tree of the Cross, and on the flowers of the Resurrection, whose fragrance especially invites the Bridegroom to visit her more often. . . . *Now,* He saith, *the winter is past, the rain is over and gone, the flowers have appeared on the earth;* meaning that the time of summer is come with Him who was loosed from the cold of death into a spring mildness of new life. *Behold,* He saith, *I make all things new;* whose flesh was sown in death, and flowered again in the Resurrection, at the fragrance whereof straightway in the field of our valley the dry becomes green, the cold grows warm, the dead return to life.

... Lo, I remember what I said in the beginning, that the manner of loving God is to love without measure. And since the object of the love of God is immeasurable and infinite (for God is infinite and immeasurable), what, I ask, should be the limit or measure of our love? Our very love is not rendered as a free gift, but repaid as a debt. Immeasurableness loves, eternity loves, *charity which passeth knowledge* loves; God loves, whose greatness is unsearchable, whose wisdom is infinite, whose peace passeth all understanding; and do we pay back again with measure? *I will love thee, O Lord, my strength, my rock, my refuge, and my deliverer;* and my sum of all that is desirable and worthy of love. My God, my helper, I love thee according to Thy gift, and in my measure, less indeed than just, but surely not less than my power; I, who cannot as much as I ought, and yet cannot beyond what I can. I shall, indeed, be able to love more, when Thou shalt deign to give more; though never in proportion to Thy worth. *Thine eyes did see my imperfect being;* but, nevertheless, *in thy book all shall be written,* they who do what they can, albeit they cannot what they should. It is clear enough, methinks, both in what measure God is to be loved, and by what desert of His own. By what desert of His, I say; for the greatness of it, who may fully see? Who may tell? Who may know?

Abelard and Heloise: Learning and Love

Abelard was remembered at Paris not only for his teachings but also for his role in one of the most famous love stories of the Middle Ages. Each of the lovers, Abelard and Heloise, wrote an account of their relationship and, fortunately, both accounts have survived. Abelard told the story in an autobiography called A Story of Calamities.

From Abelard. *A Story of Calamities*

How having fallen in love with Heloise he was thereby wounded as well in body as in mind.

From Peter Abelard and Heloise, *The Letters of Abelard and Heloise,* C. K. Scott, trans. (New York: Alfred A. Knopf, 1942), pp. 10–13. Copyright 1926 and renewed 1954 by Alfred A. Knopf, Inc. Reprinted by permission of the publisher.

Now there was in this city of Paris a certain young maiden by the name of Heloise, the niece of a certain Canon who was called Fulbert, who, so great was his love for her, was all the more diligent in his zeal to instruct her, so far as was in his power, in the knowledge of letters. Who, while in face she was not inferior to other women, in the abundance of her learning was supreme. For inasmuch as this advantage, namely literary knowledge, is rare in women, so much the more did it commend the girl and had won her the greatest renown throughout the realm. Seeing in her, therefore, all those things which are wont to attract lovers, I thought it suitable to join her with myself in love, and believed that I could effect this most easily. For such renown had I then, and so excelled in grace of youth and form, that I feared no refusal from whatever woman I might deem worthy of my love.

So, being wholly inflamed with love for this girl, I sought an opportunity whereby I might make her familiar with me in intimate and daily conversation, and so the more easily lead her to consent. With which object in view, I came to terms with the aforesaid uncle of the girl, certain of his friends intervening, that he should take me into his house, which was hard by our school, at whatever price he might ask. . . .

What more need I say? First in one house we are united, then in one mind. So, under the pretext of discipline, we abandoned ourselves utterly to love, and those secret retreats which love demands, the study of our texts afforded us. And so, our books lying open before us, more words of love rose to our lips than of literature, kisses were more frequent than speech. Oftener went our hands to each other's bosom than to the pages; love turned our eyes more frequently to itself than it directed them to the study of the texts. That we might be the less suspected, blows were given at times, by love, not by anger, affection, not indignation, which surpassed all ointments in their sweetness. What more shall I say? No stage of love was omitted by us in our cupidity, and, if love could elaborate anything new, that we took in addition. The less experienced we were in these joys, the more ardently we persisted in them and the less satiety did they bring us. And the more this pleasure occupied me the less leisure could I find for my philosophy and to attend to my school. Most tedious was it for me to go to the school or to stay there; laborious likewise when I was keeping nightly vigils of love and daily of study. Which also so negligently and tepidly I now performed that I produced nothing from my mind but everything from memory; nor was I anything now save a reciter of things learned in the past, and if I found time to compose a few verses, they were amorous, and not secret hymns of philosophy. Of which songs the greater part are to this day, as thou knowest, repeated and sung in many parts, principally by those to whom a like manner of life appeals. . . .

[Heloise had a child and Abelard married her. He tried, however, to keep the marriage secret and sent Heloise to stay at the convent of Argenteuil, where she had been brought up as a young girl.]

Hearing which, the uncle and his kinsmen and associates were of the opinion that I had played a trick on them, and had taken an easy way to rid myself of Heloise, making her a nun. Whereat vehemently indignant, and conspiring together against me, on a certain night while I slumbered and slept in an inner room of my lodging, having corrupted a servant of mine with money, they punished me with a most cruel and shameful vengeance, and one that the world received with the utmost amazement: amputating, to wit, those parts of my body wherewith I had committed that of which they complained. Who presently taking flight, two of them who could be caught were deprived of their eyes and genitals. One of whom was the servant afore-mentioned, who while he remained with me in my service was by cupidity led to my betrayal.

Of the injury to his body. He becomes a monk in the Monastery of Saint Denis: Heloise a nun at Argenteuil.

But day coming the whole town congregating round about me, with what amazement they were transfixed, with what an outcry they lamented. . . . It occurred to my mind with what glory I had but recently shone, how easily and in a moment this had been brought low, nay, utterly extinguished. By how just a judgment of God was I stricken in that portion of my body wherein I had sinned. With how just a betrayal had the man repaid me for my former betrayal of him. With what shouts of praise would my rivals extol so manifest an equity. What contrition of perpetual grief would this stroke bring to my family and friends. With what expansion would this matchless infamy occupy the minds of the whole world. What way would lie open to me thereafter, with what face would I appear in public, to be pointed out by every finger, scarified by every tongue, doomed to be a monstrous spectacle to all. . . .

. . . Plunged in so wretched a contrition, it was the confusion of shame, I confess, rather than the devotion of conversion that drove me to the retirement of a monastic cloister. She, moreover, had already at my command willingly taken the veil and entered a convent. And so both the two of us at one time put on the sacred habit, I in the Abbey of Saint Denis and she in the Convent of Argenteuil aforesaid. Who indeed, I remember, when divers in compassion of her tried vainly to deter so young a woman from the yoke of the monastic rule, as from an intolerable burden, breaking out, as best she could amid her tears and sobs, into that famous complaint of Cornelia, answered:

> Great husband, undeserving of my bed!
> What right had I to bow so lofty a head?
> Why, impious female, did I marry thee,
> To cause thy hurt? Accept the penalty
> That of my own free will I'll undergo . . .

And with these words she hastened to the altar and straightway, before the Bishop, took the blessed veil from the altar and publicly bound herself to the monastic profession.

When Heloise read the Story of Calamities, *she sent a letter to Abelard, asking him to write to her.*

From Heloise. *Letter to Abelard*

To her master, rather to a father, to her husband, rather to a brother, his maid or rather daughter, his wife or rather sister, to Abaelard, Heloise.

Dearest, thou knowest—who knows not?—how much I lost in thee, and that an infamous act of treachery robbed me of thee and of myself at once. The greater my grief, the greater need of consolation, not from another but from thee, that thou who art alone my cause of grief may be alone my consolation It is thou alone that canst sadden me or gladden me or comfort me. And thou alone owest this to me, especially since I have done thy will so utterly that, unable to offend thee, I endured to wreck myself at thy command. Nay, more than this, love turned to madness and cut itself off from hope of that which alone it sought, when I obediently changed my garb and my heart too in order that I might prove thee sole owner of my body as well as of my spirit. God knows, I have ever sought in thee only thyself, desiring simply thee and not what was thine. I asked no matrimonial contract, I looked for no dowry; not my pleasure, not my will, but thine have I striven to fulfil. And if the name of wife seemed holier or more potent, the word mistress *(amica)* was always sweeter to me, or even—be not angry!—concubine or harlot; for the more I lowered myself before thee, the more I hoped to gain thy favour, and the less I should hurt the glory of thy renown. This thou didst graciously remember, when condescending to point out in that letter to a friend some of the reasons (but not all!) why I preferred love to wedlock and liberty to a chain. I call God to witness that if Augustus, the master of the world, would honour me with marriage and invest me with equal rule, it would still seem to me dearer and more honourable to be called thy strumpet than his empress. . . .

What country, what city does not thirst to see you? Who, I ask, did not hurry to see you appearing in public and crane his neck to catch a last glimpse as you departed? What wife, what maid did not yearn for you absent, and burn when you were present? What queen did not envy me my joys and couch? There were in you two qualities by which

From H. O. Taylor, trans. *The Mediaeval Mind*, 4th ed. (Cambridge, Mass.: Harvard University Press, 1962), Vol. 2, pp. 38–40. Reprinted by permission of the publisher.

you could draw the soul of any woman, the gift of poetry and the gift of singing, gifts which other philosophers have lacked. As a distraction from labour, you composed love-songs both in metre and in rhyme, which for their sweet sentiment and music have been sung and resung and have kept your name in every mouth. Your sweet melodies do not permit even the illiterate to forget you. Because of these gifts women sighed for your love. And, as these songs sung of our loves, they quickly spread my name in many lands, and made me the envy of my sex. What excellence of mind or body did not adorn your youth? No woman, then envious, but now would pity me bereft of such delights. What enemy even would not now be softened by the compassion due me? . . .

God knows, at your command I would have followed or preceded you to fiery places. For my heart is not with me, but with thee; and now more than ever, if not with thee it is nowhere, for it cannot exist without thee. That my heart may be well with thee, see to it, I beg; and it will be well if it finds thee kind, rendering grace for grace—a little for much. Beloved, would that thy love were less sure of me so that it might be more solicitous; I have made you so secure that you are negligent. Remember all I have done and think what you owe. While I enjoyed carnal joy with you, many people were uncertain whether I acted from love or lust. Now the end makes clear the beginning; I have cut myself off from pleasure to obey thy will. I have kept nothing, save to be more than ever thine. Think how wicked it were in thee where all the more is due to render less, nothing almost; especially when little is asked, and that so easy for you. In the name of God to whom you have vowed yourself, give me that of thee which is possible, the consolation of a letter. I promise, thus refreshed, to serve God more readily. When of old you would call me to pleasures, you sought me with frequent letters, and never failed with thy songs to keep thy Heloise on every tongue; the streets, the houses re-echoed me. How much fitter that you should now incite me to God than then to lust? Bethink thee what thou owest; heed what I ask; and a long letter I will conclude with a brief ending: farewell only one!

After Bernard's attack, Abelard's theology was condemned by a church council in France. Abelard set off for Rome to appeal the sentence but fell ill on the way and spent the last months of his life in a priory of Cluny. When he died, the abbot of Cluny, Peter the Venerable, wrote to Heloise.

From Peter the Venerable. *Letter to Heloise*

To his venerable and dearly loved sister in Christ, the abbess Heloise.
    . . . I rejoice in your renowned learning; your piety, of which many

From H. O. Taylor, trans., *The Mediaeval Mind*, 4th ed. (Cambridge, Mass.: Harvard University Press, 1962), Vol. 2, pp. 52–53. Reprinted by permission of the publisher.

have spoken to me, is still more attractive. Would that our order of
Cluny had you! Would that our convent of Marcigny held you . . . I
would prefer your gifts of learning and religion to the greatest treasures of any kings. . . .

But although God's providence denied us this, it was granted us to
enjoy the presence of him—who was yours—Master Peter Abaelard, a
man always to be spoken of with honour as a true servant of Christ
and a philosopher. The divine dispensation placed him in Cluny for
his last years, and through him enriched our monastery with treasure
richer than gold. No brief writing could do justice to his holy, humble,
and devoted life among us. I have not seen his equal in humility of
garb and manner. When in the crowd of our brethren I forced him to
take a first place, in meanness of clothing he appeared as the last of all.
Often I marvelled, as the monks walked past me, to see a man so great
and famous thus despise and abase himself. He was abstemious in food
and drink, refusing and condemning everything beyond the bare necessities. He was assiduous in study, frequent in prayer, always silent
unless compelled to answer the question of some brother or expound
sacred themes before us. He partook of the sacrament as often as possible. Truly his mind, his tongue, his act, taught and exemplified religion, philosophy, and learning. So he dwelt with us, a man simple and
righteous, fearing God, turning from evil, consecrating to God the latter days of his life. At last, because of his bodily infirmities, I sent him
to a quiet and salubrious retreat on the banks of the Saone. There he
bent over his books, as long as his strength lasted, always praying,
reading, writing, or dictating. . . . When he came to pay humanity's last
debt, his illness was brief. With holy devotion he made confession of
the Catholic Faith, then of his sins. The brothers who were with him
can testify how devoutly he received the viaticum of that last journey,
and with what fervent faith he commended his body and soul to his
Redeemer. Thus this master, Peter, completed his days. He who was
known throughout the world by the fame of his teaching, entered the
school of Him who said, "Learn of me, for I am meek and lowly of
heart"; and continuing meek and lowly he passed to Him, as we may
believe.

Venerable and dearest sister in the Lord, the man who was once
joined to thee in the flesh, and then by the stronger chain of divine
love, him in thy stead, or as another thee, the Lord holds in His
bosom; and at the day of His coming, His grace will restore him to
thee.

LORDS AND LADIES: EVE AND MARY

Troubadour Songs

During the twelfth century a new fashion for songs of courtly love spread from Provence through most of Europe.

Jaufré Rudel. *To His Love Afar*

When the days lengthen in the month of May,
Well pleased am I to hear the birds
      Sing far away.
And when from that place I am gone,
I hang my head and make dull moan,
Since she my heart is set upon
      Is far away.

So far, that song of birds, flower o' the thorn,
Please me no more than winter morn,
      With ice and sleet.
Ah, would I were a pilgrim over sea,
With staff and scrip and cloak to cover me,
That some day I might kneel me on one knee
      Before her feet.

Most sad, most joyous shall I go away,
Let me have seen her for a single day,
      My love afar.
I shall not see her, for her land and mine
Are sundered, and the ways are hard to find,
So many ways, and I shall lose my way,
      So wills it God.

Yet shall I know no other love but hers,
And if not hers, no other love at all.
      She hath surpassed all.
So fair she is, so noble, I would be

From Jaufré Rudel, "To His Love Afar," in Helen Waddell, trans., *The Wandering Scholars*, 7th ed. (London: Constable, 1934), pp. 205–206. Reprinted by permission of the publisher.

A captive with the hosts of paynimrie
In a far land, if so be upon me
      Her eyes might fall.

God, who hath made all things in earth that are,
That made my love, and set her thus afar,
      Grant me this grace,
That I may some day come within a room,
Or is some garden gloom
      Look on her face.

It will not be, for at my birth they said
That one had set this doom upon my head,
      —God curse him among men!—
That I should love, and not till I be dead,
      Be loved again.

Walther Von Der Vogelweide. *A Spring Song*

When from the sod the flow'rets spring,
    And smile to meet the sun's bright ray,
When birds their sweetest carols sing
    In all the morning pride of May,
What lovelier than the prospect there?
Can earth boast anything more fair?
To me it seems an almost heaven,
So beauteous to my eyes that vision bright is given.

But when a lady, chaste and fair,
    Noble and clad in rich attire,
Walks through the throng with gracious air,
    As sun that bids the stars retire—
Then, where are all thy boastings, May?
What hast thou beautiful and gay
Compared with that supreme delight?
We leave thy loveliest flowers, and watch that lady bright.

Wouldst thou believe me—come and place
    Before thee all this pride of May;
Then look but on my lady's face,
    And, which is best and brightest? say:
For me, how soon (if choice were mine)
This would I take, and that resign!
And say, "Though sweet thy beauties, May,
I'd rather forfeit all than lose my lady gay."

From J. H. Robinson, trans., *Readings in European History* (Boston, Mass.: Ginn and Co., 1904), pp. 437–438.

Some troubadour songs were written by ladies. This one is by the Countess de Dia.

Countess de Dia. *A Distressed Lover*

I've lately been in great distress
over a knight who once was mine,
and I want it known for all eternity
how I loved him to excess.
Now I see I've been betrayed
because I wouldn't sleep with him;
night and day my mind won't rest
to think of the mistake I made.

How I wish just once I could caress
that chevalier with my bare arms,
for he would be in ecstasy
if I'd just let him lean his head against my breast.
I'm sure I'm happier with him
than Blancaflor with Floris.
My heart and love I offer him,
my mind, my eyes, my life.

Handsome friend, charming and kind
when shall I have you in my power?
If only I could lie beside you for an hour
and embrace you lovingly—
know this, that I'd give almost anything
to have you in my husband's place,
but only under the condition
that you swear to do my bidding.

From Meg Bogin, trans. in *The Women Troubadours* (New York: Paddington Press Ltd., 1976), p. 89. Reprinted by permission of the author.

Love and Marriage

A much debated question was whether true love could exist between a man and his wife.

From *The Art of Courtly Love*

What the Effect of Love Is   Now it is the effect of love that a true lover cannot be degraded with any avarice. Love causes a rough and

From Andreas Capellanus, *The Art of Courtly Love* (Milestone of Thought Series), J. J. Parry, trans., edited and abridged by Frederick W. Locke (New York: Frederick Ungar, 1954), pp. 4, 15–19, 24. Copyright © 1957 by Frederick Ungar Publishing Co. Reprinted by permission of the publisher.

uncouth man to be distinguished for his handsomeness; it can endow a man even of the humblest birth with nobility of character; it blesses the proud with humility; and the man in love becomes accustomed to performing many services gracefully for everyone. O what a wonderful thing is love, which makes a man shine with so many virtues and teaches everyone, no matter who he is, so many good traits of character! There is another thing about love that we should not praise in few words: it adorns a man, so to speak, with the virtue of chastity, because he who shines with the light of one love can hardly think of embracing another woman, even a beautiful one. For when he thinks deeply of his beloved the sight of any other women seems to his mind rough and rude.

A man of the higher nobility speaks with a woman of the simple nobility   THE WOMAN SAYS: "We are separated by too wide and too rough an expanse of country to be able to offer each other love's solaces or to find proper opportunities for meeting. . . . Besides there is another fact, by no means trivial, which keeps me from loving you. I have a husband who is greatly distinguished by his nobility, his good breeding, and his good character, and it would be wicked for me to violate his bed or submit to the embraces of any other man, since I know that he loves me with his whole heart and I am bound to him with all the devotion of mine. The laws themselves bid me refrain from loving another man when I am blessed with such a reward for my love."

THE MAN SAYS: "I admit it is true that your husband is a very worthy man and that he is more blest than any man in the world because he has been worthy to have the joy of embracing Your Highness. But I am greatly surprised that you wish to misapply the term 'love' to that marital affection which husband and wife are expected to feel for each other after marriage, since everybody knows that love can have no place between husband and wife. They may be bound to each other by a great and immoderate affection, but their feeling cannot take the place of love, because it cannot fit under the true definition of love. For what is love but an inordinate desire to receive passionately a furtive and hidden embrace? But what embrace between husband and wife can be furtive, I ask you, since they may be said to belong to each other and may satisfy each other's desires without fear that anybody will object.

"But there is another reason why husband and wife cannot love each other and that is that the very substance of love, without which true love cannot exist—I mean jealousy—is in such a case very much frowned upon and they should avoid it like the pestilence; but lovers should always welcome it as the mother and the nurse of love. From this you may see clearly that love cannot possibly flourish between you and your husband. Therefore, since every woman of character ought to love, prudently, you can without doing yourself any harm accept the prayers of a suppliant and endow your suitor with your love."

THE WOMAN SAYS: "You are trying to take under your protection what all men from early times down have agreed to consider very reprehensible and to reject as hateful. For who can rightly commend envious jealousy or speak in favor of it, since jealousy is nothing but a shameful and evil suspicion of a woman? God forbid, therefore, that any worthy man should feel jealous about anyone, since this proves hostile to every prudent person and throughout the world is hated by everybody good. You are trying also, under cover of defining love, to condemn love between husband and wife, saying that their embraces cannot be furtive, since without fear that anyone may object they can fulfill each other's desires. But if you understood the definition correctly it could not interfere with love between husband and wife, for the expression 'hidden embraces' is simply an explanation in different words of the preceding one, and there seems to be no impossibility in husband and wife giving each other hidden embraces, even though they can do so without the least fear that anybody may raise an objection. Everyone should choose that love which may be fostered by security for continual embraces and, what is more, can be practiced every day without any sin. I ought therefore to choose a man to enjoy my embraces who can be to me both husband and lover, because, no matter what the definition of love may say, love seems to be nothing but a great desire to enjoy carnal pleasure with someone, and nothing prevents this feeling existing between husband and wife."

THE MAN SAYS: "If the theory of love were perfectly clear to you and Love's dart had ever touched you, your own feelings would have shown you that love cannot exist without jealousy, because, as I have already told you in more detail, jealousy between lovers is commended by every man who is experienced in love, while between husband and wife it is condemned throughout the world; the reason for this will be perfectly clear from a description of jealousy. Now jealousy is a true emotion whereby we greatly fear that the substance of our love may be weakened by some defect in serving the desires of our beloved, and it is an anxiety lest our love may not be returned. . . .

"As for what you tried to prove by your answer—that the love which can be practiced without sin is far preferable—that, apparently, cannot stand. For whatever solaces married people extend to each other beyond what are inspired by the desire for offspring or the payment of the marriage debt, cannot be free from sin, and the punishment is always greater when the use of a holy thing is perverted by misuse than if we practice the ordinary abuses. It is a more serious offense in a wife than in another woman, for the too ardent lover, as we are taught by the apostolic law, is considered an adulterer with his own wife."

The Love of Peasants   If you should, by some chance, fall in love with a peasant woman, be careful to puff her up with lots of praise and then, when you find a convenient place, do not hesitate to take what you seek and to embrace her by force. For you can hardly soften their outward inflexibility so far that they will grant you their embraces quietly or permit you to have the solaces you desire unless first you use a little compulsion as a convenient cure for their shyness. We do not say these things, however, because we want to persuade you to love such women, but only so that, if through lack of caution you should be driven to love them, you may know, in brief compass, what to do.

Eve and Mary

The church was torn between the image of woman as Eve—the temptress who led Adam to sin, and Mary—the virgin mother of the Redeemer.

Adam Lay Y-Bounden

> Adam lay y-bounden
>   Bounden in a bond;
> Four thousand winter
>   Thought he not too long;
> And all was for an apple
>   An apple that he took,
> As clerkes finden written
>   In theire book.
>
> Ne had the apple taken been,
>   The apple taken been,
> Ne hadde never our Lady
>   A been heaven's queen.
> Blessed be the time
>   That apple taken was!
> Therefore we may singen
>   'Deo Gratias!'

From Helen Gardner, ed., *The New Oxford Book of English Verse* (Oxford: Oxford University Press, 1972), pp. 12–13.

Endless stories were told of Mary's "miracles."

From *Liber Exemplorum*

One more instance of the loving kindness of the glorious Virgin I found in an ancient sermon, and certainly it should not be despised. A certain poor woman loved the Blessed Virgin, decking her image with

From A. G. Little, ed., *Liber Exemplorum*, G. G. Coulton, trans. in *Life in the Middle Ages* (Cambridge: Cambridge University Press, 1928–1930, Vol. 1, p. 152.

roses and lilies and such ornaments as she could find. It befell that her son was taken and hanged. The woman, in the bitterness of her soul, went to the image of the Blessed Virgin and besought her to restore her son; and, seeing that she recovered not her son as soon as she wished, she said: "Is this then the price of service to thee, that thou succorest me not in my need?" Then, as though maddened by the excess of her grief, she said: "If thou restore me not my son, I will take away thy Son." And, as she reached out her hand impetuously to bear away the image of the little Babe, behold! her son stood by her and seized her cloak and cried, "What dost thou, Mother? Hast thou lost thy senses? Behold, the Mother of God hath restored me to thee." So the mother rejoiced to recover her son.

GOD AND NATURE—THE WAY OF THE HEART

Franciscan Ideals

Francis of Assisi (1182–1226) inspired a great new religious order by striving to follow simply and literally the teachings of Jesus.

Francis's Testament

The Lord gave to me, Brother Francis, thus to begin to do penance; for when I was in sin it seemed to me very bitter to see lepers, and the Lord Himself led me amongst them and I showed mercy to them. And when I left them, that which had seemed to me bitter was changed for me into sweetness of body and soul. And afterwards I remained a little and I left the world. And the Lord gave me so much faith in churches that I would simply pray and say thus: "We adore Thee Lord Jesus Christ here and in all Thy churches which are in the whole world, and we bless Thee because by Thy holy cross Thou hast redeemed the world."

After that the Lord gave me, and gives me, so much faith in priests who live according to the form of the holy Roman Church, on account of their order, that if they should persecute me, I would have recourse to them. And if I had as much wisdom as Solomon had, and if I should find poor priests of this world, I would not preach against their will in the parishes in which they live. And I desire to fear, love, and honor them and all others as my masters; and I do not wish to consider sin in them, for in them I see the Son of God and they are my masters. And I do this because in this world, I see nothing corporally of the most high Son of God himself except His most holy Body and Blood, which they receive and they alone administer to others. And I will that these most holy mysteries be honored and revered above all things and that they be placed in precious places. Wheresoever I find His most holy Names and written words in unseemly places, I wish to collect them, and I ask that they may be collected and put in a becoming place. And we ought to honor and venerate all theologians and those who minister

From *The Writings of Saint Francis of Assisi,* Paschal Robinson, trans. (Philadelphia: Dolphin Press, 1906), pp. 81–86.

to us the most holy Divine Words as those who minister to us spirit and life.

And when the Lord gave me some brothers, no one showed me what I ought to do, but the Most High Himself revealed to me that I should live according to the form of the holy Gospel. And I caused it to be written in few words and simply, and the Lord Pope confirmed it for me. And those who came to take this life upon themselves gave to the poor all that they might have and they were content with one tunic, patched within and without, by those who wished, with a cord and breeches, and we wished for no more.

We clerics said the Office like other clerics; the laics said the *Paternoster,* and we remained in the churches willingly enough. And we were simple and subject to all. And I worked with my hands and I wish to work and I wish firmly that all the other brothers should work at some labor which is compatible with honesty. Let those who know not [how to work] learn, not through desire to receive the price of labor but for the sake of example and to repel idleness. And when the price of labor is not given to us, let us have recourse to the table of the Lord, begging alms from door to door.

The Lord revealed to me this salutation, that we should say: "The Lord give thee peace." Let the brothers take care not to receive on any account churches, poor dwelling-places, and all other things that are constructed for them, unless they are as is becoming the holy poverty which we have promised in the Rule, always dwelling there as strangers and pilgrims.

I strictly enjoin by obedience on all the brothers that, wherever they may be, they should not dare, either themselves or by means of some interposed person, to ask any letter in the Roman curia either for a church or for any other place, nor under pretext of preaching, nor on account of their bodily persecution; but, wherever they are not received let them flee to another land to do penance, with the blessing of God. And I wish to obey the minister general of this brotherhood strictly and the guardian whom it may please him to give me. And I wish to be so captive in his hands that I cannot go or act beyond his obedience and his will because he is my master. And although I am simple and infirm, I desire withal always to have a cleric who will perform the office with me as it is contained in the Rule.

And let all the other brothers be found to obey their guardian and to perform the office according to the Rule. And those who may be found not performing the office according to the Rule and wishing to change it in some way, or who are not Catholics, let all the brothers wherever they may be, if they find one of these, be bound by obedience to present him to the custos who is nearest to the place where they have found him. And the custos shall be strictly bound, by obedience, to guard him strongly day and night as a prisoner so that he cannot be snatched from his hands until he shall personally place him in the hands of his minister. And the minister shall be firmly bound by obedience to send him by such brothers as shall watch him day and night like a prisoner until they shall present him to the Lord of Ostia, who is master protector, and corrector of this brotherhood.

And let not the brothers say: This is another Rule; for this is a remembrance, a warning, and an exhortation and my Testament which I, little Brother Francis, make for you, my blessed brothers, in order that we may observe in a more Catholic way the Rule which we have promised to the Lord. And let the minister general and all the other ministers and custodes be bound by obedience not to add to these words or to take from them. And let them always have this writing with them beside the Rule. And in all the Chapter they hold, when they read the Rule let them read these words also. And I strictly enjoin on all my brothers, clerics and laics, by obedience, not to put glosses on the Rule or on these words saying: Thus they ought to be understood; but as the Lord has given me to speak and to write the Rule and these words simply and purely, so shall you understand them simply and purely and with holy operation observe them until the end.

And whoever shall observe these things may he be filled in heaven with the blessing of the Most High Father and may he be filled on earth with blessing of His Beloved Son together with the Holy Ghost, the Paraclete, and all the Powers of heaven and all the saints. And I, Brother Francis, your little one and servant, in so far as I am able, I confirm to you within and without this most holy blessing. Amen.

Creator and Creatures

Francis brought something new to medieval religion—a rare delight in natural beauty and an extraordinary love and reverence for all created beings. Later on, many fanciful legends grew up about Francis and the animals. These passages are from Thomas of Celano, who knew Francis personally and wrote the first biography of him.

From *Thomas of Celano*

Francis was filled with the spirit of love. He cared not only for men in need but for dumb animals, reptiles, birds and all other creatures, an-

From *Thomas of Celano* in *Great Issues in Western Civilization*, 3rd ed., Brian Tierney, Donald Kagan, and L. Pearce Williams, eds. (New York: Random House, 1976), pp. 421–422. Copyright © 1967, 1972, 1976 by Random House, Inc. Reprinted by permission of the publisher.

imate and inanimate. Among all other animals, he loved little lambs with a special affection and regard, because in the sacred scriptures the humility of our Lord Jesus Christ is most often likened to that of a Lamb.

Who can tell the joy he felt when he contemplated in created things the wisdom and power and goodness of the Creator? He was often filled with a wonderful and indescribable rejoicing because of this when he looked at the sun and the moon and gazed on the stars and the heavens.

All the creatures tried to love the saint in return. . . . Near his cell at the Portiuncula a cicada used to perch on a fig tree and chirp all day long. Sometimes the blessed father would hold out his hand and call to it saying, "Sister cicada, come to me." And it flew straight to his hand as if endowed with reason. Then Francis would say, "Sister cicada, sing and praise your Creator with a joyful song."

He told his brothers not to chop down the whole tree when they were cutting wood, so that it could grow again. He told the gardeners not to dig up the border round the garden so that in due season the green grass and beauty of wild flowers would proclaim the beauty of the Father of all things. . . . He picked up worms from the road so that they would not be trampled on, and he ordered that honey and good wine be set out for the bees in the cold of winter lest they perish from want. He called all animals by the name of *brother,* though he cared most of all for the gentle ones.

When he came upon a great field of flowers he preached to them and invited them to praise God as though they could understand him. In the same way he exhorted cornfields and vineyards, stones and woodlands, all the beautiful things of the fields, springs of water and the green plants of gardens, earth and fire, air and wind, to love God and serve him willingly. Finally, he called all creatures *brothers* and in a most excellent manner, unknown to others, he saw into the hidden nature of things with his discerning heart, like one who had already escaped into the glorious freedom of the sons of God.

Often, without moving his lips, he would meditate inwardly and, drawing external things into himself, would raise his spirit on high. Then he directed all his regard and affection to the *one thing he asked of the Lord,* becoming not so much like a man praying as himself a prayer. What sweetness of heart pervaded a man used to such things? He knows; I can only wonder. It is given to one who has experienced such things to know, not to those without experience. And so, his whole soul and his whole appearance melted by a glowing fervor of spirit, he dwelt already in the highest realms of the Kingdom of Heaven.

Francis gave vivid expression to his vision of creator and creation in this song.

The Canticle of the Sun

Most high, omnipotent, good Lord,
Praise, glory and honor and benediction
    all, are Thine.
To Thee alone do they belong, most High,
And there is no man fit to mention Thee.

Praise be to Thee, my Lord, with all Thy crea-
    tures,
Especially to my worshipful brother sun,
The which lights up the day, and through him
    dost Thou brightness give;
And beautiful is he and radiant with splendor
    great;
Of Thee, most High, signification gives.

Praised be my Lord, for sister moon and for the
    stars,
In heaven Thou has formed them clear and
    precious and fair.
Praised be my Lord for brother wind
And for the air and clouds and fair and every
    kind of weather,
By the which Thou givest to Thy creatures
    nourishment.
Praised be my Lord for sister water,
The which is greatly helpful and humble and
    precious and pure.

Praised be my Lord for brother fire,
By the which Thou lightest up the dark.
And fair is he and gay and mighty and strong.

Praised be my Lord for our sister, mother earth,
The which sustains and keeps us
And brings forth diverse fruits with grass and
    flowers bright.

Praised be my Lord for those who for Thy love
    forgive
And weakness bear and tribulation.
Blessed those who shall in peace endure,
For by Thee, most High, shall they be crowned.

From *The Writings of Saint Francis of Assisi*, Paschal Robinson, trans. (Philadelphia: Dolphin Press, 1906), pp. 81–86.

Praised be my Lord for our sister, the bodily
    death,
From the which no living man can flee.
Woe to them who die in mortal sin;
Blessed those who shall find themselves in Thy
    most holy will,
For the second death shall do them no ill

Praise ye and bless ye my Lord and give Him
    thanks,
And be subject unto him with great humility.

GOD AND NATURE—THE WAY OF THE MIND

A major task for thirteenth-century Jewish and Christian thinkers was to reconcile Aristotle's natural philosophy with scriptural revelation.

Chance and Necessity—Maimonides

Moses Maimonides considered a problem that modern scientists and philosophers still discuss. How far is the universe governed by sheer chance and how far by some underlying law or Providence?

From *The Guide for the Perplexed*

There are five different theories concerning Divine Providence; they are all ancient, known since the time of the Prophets, when the true Law was revealed to enlighten these dark regions.

First Theory—There is no Providence at all for anything in the Universe; all parts of the Universe, the heavens and what they contain, owe their origin to accident and chance; there exists no being that rules and governs them or provides for them. This is the theory of Epicurus, who assumes also that the Universe consists of atoms, that these have combined by chance, and have received their various forms by mere accident. . . .

Second Theory—Whilst one part of the Universe owes its existence to Providence, and is under the control of a ruler and governor, another part is abandoned and left to chance. This is the view of Aristotle about Providence, and I will now explain to you his theory. He holds that God controls the spheres and what they contain: therefore the individual beings in the spheres remain permanently in the same form. Alexander has also expressed it in his writings that Divine Providence extends down to, and ends with, the sphere of the moon. [According to Aristotle, Providence endows each species on earth with a capacity to preserve itself, but does not control all the particular actions of individuals.] All other movements, however, which are made by the individual members of each species are due to accident; they are not, according to Aristotle, the result of rule and management; e.g., when a

From M. Friedlander, trans., *The Guide for the Perplexed*, 2nd ed. (London: George Routledge and Sons Ltd., 1910), pp. 282–287. Reprinted by permission of Routledge & Kegan Paul Ltd.

storm or gale blows, it causes undoubtedly some leaves of a tree to drop, breaks off some branches of another tree, tears away a stone from a heap of stones, raises dust over herbs and spoils them, and stirs up the sea so that a ship goes down with the whole or part of her contents. Aristotle sees no difference between the falling of a leaf or a stone and the death of the good and noble people in the ship; nor does he distinguish between the destruction of a multitude of ants caused by an ox depositing on them his excrement and the death of worshippers killed by the fall of the house when its foundations give way; nor does he discriminate between the case of a cat killing a mouse that happens to come in her way, or that of a spider catching a fly, and that of a hungry lion meeting a prophet and tearing him.... This view is closely connected with his theory of the Eternity of the Universe, and with his opinion that everything different from the existing order of things in Nature is impossible. It is the belief of those who turned away from our Law, and said: "God hath forsaken the earth" (Ezek. ix. 9).

Third Theory—This theory is the reverse of the second. According to this theory, there is nothing in the whole Universe, neither a class nor an individual being, that is due to chance; everything is the result of will, intention, and rule. It is a matter of course that he who rules must know [that which is under his control]. The Mohammedan Ashariyah adhere to this theory, notwithstanding evident absurdities implied in it; for they admit that Aristotle is correct in assuming one and the same cause [viz., the wind] for the fall of leaves [from the tree] and for the death of a man [drowned in the sea]. But they hold at the same time that the wind did not blow by chance; it is God that caused it to move; it is not therefore the wind that caused the leaves to fall; each leaf falls according to the Divine decree; it is God who caused it to fall at a certain time and in a certain place; it could not have fallen before or after that time or in another place, as this has previously been decreed. The Ashariyah were therefore compelled to assume that motion and rest of living beings are predestined, and that it is not in the power of man to do a certain thing or to leave it undone.... It follows also from this theory, that precepts are perfectly useless, since the people to whom any law is given are unable to do anything: they can neither do what they are commanded nor abstain from what they are forbidden....

When we see a person born blind or leprous, who could not have merited a punishment for previous sins, they say, It is the will of God; when a pious worshipper is tortured and slain, it is likewise the will of God; and no injustice can be asserted to Him for that, for according to their opinion it is proper that God should afflict the innocent and do good to the sinner. Their views on these matters are well known.

Fourth Theory—Man has free will; it is therefore intelligible that the Law contains commands and prohibitions, with announcements of reward and punishment. All acts of God are due to wisdom; no injustice is found in Him, and He does not afflict the good. The Mu'tazila profess this theory, although they do not believe in man's absolute free will. They hold also that God takes notice of the falling of the leaf and the destruction of the ant, and that His Providence extends over all things. This theory likewise implies contradictions and absurdities. The absurdities are these: The fact that some persons are born with defects, although they have not sinned previously, is ascribed to the wisdom of God, it being better for those persons to be in such a condition than to be in a normal state, though we do not see why it is better; and they do not suffer thereby any punishment at all, but, on the contrary, enjoy God's goodness. In a similar manner the slaughter of the pious is explained as being for them the source of an increase of reward in future life. They go even further in their absurdities. We ask them why is God only just to man and not to other beings, and how has the irrational animal sinned, that it is condemned to be slaughtered? and they reply it is good for the animal, for it will receive reward for it in the world to come; also the flea and the louse will there receive compensation for their untimely death: the same reasoning they apply to the mouse torn by a cat or vulture; the wisdom of God decreed this for the mouse, in order to reward it after death for the mishap.

Fifth Theory—This is our theory, or that of our Law. . . . The theory of man's perfectly free will is one of the fundamental principles of the Law of our Teacher Moses, and of those who follow the Law. According to this principle man does what is in his power to do, by his nature, his choice, and his will; and his action is not due to any faculty created for the purpose. All species of irrational animals likewise move by their own free will. This is the Will of God; that is to say, it is due to the eternal divine will that all living beings should move freely, and that man should have power to act according to his will or choice within the limits of his capacity. Against this principle we hear, thank God, no opposition on the part of our nation. Another fundamental principle taught by the Law of Moses is this: Wrong cannot be ascribed to God in any way whatever; all evils and afflictions as well as all kinds of happiness of man, whether they concern one individual person or a community, are distributed according to justice; they are the result of strict judgment that admits no wrong whatever.

My opinion on this principle of Divine Providence I will now explain to you. In the principle which I now proceed to expound I do not rely on demonstrative proof, but on my conception of the spirit of the Divine Law, and the writings of the Prophets. The principle which I accept is far less open to objections, and is more reasonable than the opinions mentioned before. It is this: In the lower or sublunary portion of the Universe Divine Providence does not extend to the individual members of species except in the case of mankind. It is only in this species that the incidents in the existence of the individual beings, their good and evil fortunes, are the result of justice, in accordance with the words, "For all His ways are judgment." But I agree with Aristotle as regards all other living beings, and *a fortiori* as regards plants and all the rest of earthly creatures. For I do not believe that it is through the interference of Divine Providence that a certain leaf drops [from a tree], nor do I hold that when a certain spider catches a certain fly, that this is the direct result of a special decree and will of God in that moment; it is not by a particular Divine decree that the spittle of a certain person moved, fell on a certain gnat in a certain place, and killed it; nor is it by the direct will of God that a certain fish catches and swallows a certain worm on the surface of the water. In all these cases the action is, according to my opinion, entirely due to chance, as taught by Aristotle. Divine Providence is connected with Divine intellectual influence, and the same beings which are benefited by the latter so as to become intellectual, and to comprehend things comprehensible to rational beings, are also under the control of Divine Providence, which examines all their deeds in order to reward or punish them. It may be by mere chance that a ship goes down with all her contents, as in the abovementioned instance, or the roof of a house falls upon those within; but it is not due to chance, according to our view, that in the one instance the men went into the ship, or remained in the house in the other instance; it is due to the will of God, and is in accordance with the justice of His judgments, the method of which our mind is incapable of understanding. . . .

Nature and Law—Aquinas

Thomas Aquinas (1225–1274) was much concerned with problems of reason and faith, nature and grace. One of his characteristic sayings was "Grace does not destroy nature but perfects it; hence natural reason should minister to the faith" (Summa Theologiae, I.1.8). This attitude is reflected in his teaching on the varieties of law, illustrated in the readings below.

From *Summa Theologiae*

Whether There Is an Eternal Law?

Law is nothing other than a decree of practical reason from a sovereign who governs a perfect community. But it is evident, granted that the world is governed by divine providence (as we have shown in

From *Summa Theologiae*, I–IIae.91.1–4, Brian Tierney, trans. in *Great Issues in Western Civilization*, 3rd ed. (New York: Random House, 1976), pp. 414–415. Copyright © 1967, 1972, 1976 by Random House Inc. Reprinted by permission of the publisher.

the *First Book*), that the whole community of the universe is governed by divine reason. Moreover, this reason that rules all things exists in God as the sovereign of the universe; hence it has the nature of law. And since the divine reason conceives nothing in time but has an eternal concept as is said in *Proverbs 8.23 (I was set up from eternity and of old before the earth was made)*, it follows that this law should be called eternal.

Whether There Is in Us a Natural Law?

Since all things subject to divine providence are regulated and measured by eternal law as we have seen, it is evident that all things participate in some way in eternal law, in that they have from its impress their tendencies toward their own proper acts and ends.

But, among all the rest, intelligent creatures are subject to divine Providence in a more noble way in that they participate in Providence by taking thought for themselves and others. Thus they share in the eternal reason through which they have a natural inclination to their proper acts and ends. And such a sharing in the eternal law by an intelligent creature is called natural law.

Whether There Is a Human Law?

Just as speculative reason draws the conclusions of various sciences from first principles that are indemonstrable but naturally recognized ... so too it is necessary for the human reason to make more detailed arrangements, derived from the principles of natural law as indemonstrable and commonly-held principles. And these detailed arrangements made by human reason are called human law.

Whether There Was Any Need for a Divine Law?

The direction of human life requires a divine law besides natural law and human law ... because law directs man to the acts proper for the achievement of his final end. If man was destined for an end that did not exceed the measure of his natural abilities he would not need any directive of reason apart from natural law and the human law derived from it. But since man is destined to achieve an eternal happiness which is beyond the measure of natural human ability, it is necessary that he be directed to this end by a divinely given law above natural law and human law.

Whether Human Law Binds a Man in Conscience?

Laws framed by man are either just or unjust. If they be just, they have the power of binding in conscience, from the eternal law whence they are derived. . . .

On the other hand laws may be unjust in two ways: first, by being contrary to human good, through being opposed to the things mentioned above:—either in respect of the end, as when an authority imposes on his subjects burdensome laws, conducive, not to the common good, but rather to his own cupidity or vainglory;—or in respect of the author, as when a man makes a law that goes beyond the power committed to him;—or in respect of the form, as when burdens are imposed unequally on the community, although with a view to the common good. The like are acts of violence rather than laws; because, as Augustine says *(De Lib. Arb.*i.), *a law that is not just, seems to be no law at all.* Wherefore such laws do not bind in conscience, except perhaps in order to avoid scandal or disturbance, for which cause a man should even yield his right, according to Matth. v. 40, 41: *If a man . . . take away thy coat, let go thy cloak also unto him; and whosoever will force thee one mile, go with him other two.*

Secondly, laws may be unjust through being opposed to the Divine good: such are the laws of tyrants inducing to idolatry, or to anything else contrary to the Divine law: and laws of this kind must nowise be observed, because, as stated in Acts v. 29, *we ought to obey God rather than men.*

Whether Matrimony Is of Natural Law?

It would seem that matrimony is not natural. Because the natural law is what nature has taught all animals. But in other animals the sexes are united without matrimony. Therefore matrimony is not of natural law. . . .

I answer that, A thing is said to be natural in two ways. First, as resulting of necessity from the principles of nature; thus upward movement is natural to fire. In this way matrimony is not natural, nor are any of those things that come to pass at the intervention or motion of the free-will. Secondly, that is said to be natural to which nature inclines, although it comes to pass through the intervention of the free-will; thus acts of virtue and the virtues themselves are called natural; and in this way matrimony is natural, because natural reason inclines thereto in two ways. First, in relation to the principal end of matrimony, namely the good of the offspring. For nature intends not only the begetting of offspring, but also its education and development until it reach the perfect state of man as man, and that is the state of virtue. Hence, according to the Philosopher (*Ethic.* viii. 11, 12), we derive three things from our parents, namely *existence, nourishment,* and *education.* Now a child cannot be brought up and instructed unless it have certain and definite parents, and this would not be the case unless

From *Summa Theologiae,* III.41.1, I–IIae.96.4, The Fathers of the English Dominican Province (New York: Benziger Brothers, 1947), Vol. 20, pp. 76–78, Vol. 7, pp. 69–70.

there were a tie between the man and a definite woman, and it is in this that matrimony consists. Secondly, in relation to the secondary end of matrimony, which is the mutual services which married persons render one another in household matters. For just as natural reason dictates that men should live together, since one is not self-sufficient in all things concerning life, for which reason man is described as being naturally inclined to political society, so too among those works that are necessary for human life some are becoming to men, others to women. Wherefore nature inculcates that society of man and woman which consists in matrimony. These two reasons are given by the Philosopher (*Ethic.* viii., *loc. cit.*).

Heaven and Earth—Dante

Medieval people, like ancient ones, believed that the earth was at the center of the universe and that the planets and stars revolved about it in fixed spheres or "heavens."

From *The Banquet*

Plato . . . wrote in one of his books, called *Timaeus*, that the earth, with the sea, was actually the centre of all [the universe] but that its circumference revolved round its centre, following the first movement of the heavens; but very slowly, owing to the grossness of its matter, and its exceeding distance from the *Primum Mobile*.[1]

These opinions are reproved as false in the second *Of Heaven and Earth*, by that glorious Philosopher to whom Nature has most completely revealed her secrets; and by him it is there proved that this world, that is, our earth, stands still and fixed to all eternity. And the reasons Aristotle gives to controvert these opinions, and to affirm the truth, it is not my intention to relate here; because it is quite enough for those to whom I speak, to know on his great authority that this earth is immovable, and does not revolve, and that, with the sea, it is the centre of the heavens.

The heavens revolve continually around this centre. . . .

And the order of position [of the heavens] is this, that the first one enumerated is that where the Moon is; the second that where Mercury is; the third that where Venus is; the fourth that where the Sun is; the fifth that where Mars is; the sixth that where Jupiter is; the seventh that where Saturn is; the eighth that where the Fixed Stars are; the

[1]The First Mover that imparted motion to the rest of the universe.
From Katherine Hillard, trans., *The Banquet of Dante Alighieri* (London: Kegan Paul, Trench and Co., 1889), pp. 155, 66–67.

ninth is that which is not perceptible to sense (except by the motion spoken of above), and which is called by many the Crystalline, that is, the diaphanous, or wholly transparent. However, beyond all these, the Catholics place the Empyrean Heaven, which is as much as to say the Heaven of *Flame* or *Luminous* Heaven; and they hold it to be immovable, because it has within itself, in every part, that which its matter demands. And this is the reason that the *Primum Mobile* moves with immense velocity; because the fervent longing of all its parts to be united to those of this [tenth and] most divine and quiet heaven, makes it revolve with so much desire that its velocity is almost incomprehensible. And this quiet and peaceful heaven is the abode of that Supreme Deity who alone doth perfectly behold Himself. This is the abode of the beatified spirits, according to the holy Church, who cannot lie; and Aristotle also seems to think so, if rightly understood, in the first of *The Heavens and Earth*. This is the supreme edifice of the universe. . . . This is that magnificence of which the Psalmist spake, when he says to God, "Thy magnificence is exalted above the heavens."

GOD AND NATURE—THE WAY OF DISSENT

Albigensians and Patarins

Some medieval dissidents rejected the whole concept of a material universe created by a good God.

From Raynaldus. *Annales*

First it is to be known that the heretics held that there are two Creators; viz. one of invisible things, whom they called the benevolent God, and another of visible things, whom they named the malevolent God. The New Testament they attributed to the benevolent God; but the Old Testament to the malevolent God, and rejected it altogether.... They affirmed also, that all the fathers of the Old Testament were damned; that John the Baptist was one of the greater demons. They said also, in their secret doctrine, *(in secreto suo)* that that Christ who was born in the visible, and terrestrial Bethlehem, and crucified in Jerusalem, was a bad man, and that Mary Magdalene was his concubine; and that she was the woman taken in adultery, of whom we read in the gospel. For the good Christ, as they said, never ate, nor drank, nor took upon him true flesh, nor ever was in this world, except spiritually in the body of Paul....

They said that almost all the Church of Rome was a den of thieves; and that it was the harlot of which we read in the Apocalypse. They so far annulled the sacraments of the Church, as publicly to teach that the water of holy Baptism was just the same as river water, and that the Host of the most holy body of Christ did not differ from common bread; instilling into the ears of the simple this blasphemy, that the body of Christ, even though it had been as great as the Alps, would have been long ago consumed, and annihilated by those who had eaten of it. Confirmation and Confession, they considered as altogether vain and frivolous. They preached that Holy Matrimony was meretricious, and that none could be saved in it, if they should beget children. Denying also the Resurrection of the flesh, they invented some unheard of notions, saying, that our souls are those of angelic spirits who, being cast down from heaven by the apostasy of pride, left their glorified bodies in the air; and that these souls themselves, after successively in-

From Raynaldus, "Annales," in S. R. Maitland, trans., *History of the Albigenses and Waldenses* (London: C. J. G. and F. Rivington, 1832), pp. 392–394.

335

habiting seven terrene bodies, or one sort or another, having at length fulfilled their penance, return to those deserted bodies.

It is also to be known that some among the heretics were called "perfect" or "good men;" others "believers" of the heretics. Those who were called perfect, wore a black dress, falsely pretended to chastity, abhorred the eating of flesh, eggs and cheese, wished to appear not liars, when they were continually telling lies, chiefly respecting God. They said also that they ought not on any account to swear.

Those were called *believers* of the heretics, who lived after the manner of the world, and who though they did not attain so far as to imitate the life of the perfect, nevertheless hoped to be saved in their faith; and though they differed as to their mode of life, they were one with them in belief and unbelief. Those who were called believers of the heretics were given to usury, rapine, homicide, lust, perjury and every vice; and they, in fact, sinned with more security, and less restraint, because they believed that without restitution, without confession and penance, they should be saved, if only, when on the point of death, they could say a *Pater noster,* and receive imposition of hands from the teachers.

Decree of Emperor Frederick II (c. 1235)

We decree, in the first place, that the crime of heresy and of reprehensible teaching, of whatever kind, by whatever name its adherents may be known, shall, as provided by the older laws, be included among the recognized crimes. (For should not what is recognized to be an offense against the Divine Majesty be judged more terrible than the crime of leze majesty directed against ourself, although in the eyes of the law one is not graver than the other?) As the crime of treason deprives the guilty of life and property, and even blackens the memory of the dead, so in the aforesaid crimes of which the Patarins[1] are guilty, we wish the same rules to be observed in all respects.

And in order that the wickedness of those who walk in darkness, since they do not follow God, should be thoroughly exterminated, we desire that those who practice this class of crimes should, like other malefactors, be diligently sought for and hunted out by our officers. If such be discovered, even if there be only the slightest suspicion of their guilt, we command that they shall be examined by churchmen and prelates. If they shall be found by these to have deviated from the Catholic faith, even in a single respect, and if, when admonished by such churchmen in their function of pastors, they refuse by leaving the wiles of the devil to recognize the God of light, and stubbornly adhere to their error, we command, by this our present edict, that such con-

[1] The Patarins were an Italian sect accused of holding views like those of the French Albigensians.

demned Patarins shall suffer the death they court; that, condemned to the sentence of the flames, they shall be burned alive in the sight of the people.

In spite of persecution, some Albigensian communities survived. This picture of an Albigensian family was constructed from the records of the inquisitor Jacques Fournier, Bishop of Pamiers (1318–1325). (Words in italics are direct quotations from the medieval record.)

From *Montaillou*

The difference there might be between a father's and a mother's love is shown in the story of the Pierre family, an episode which has the additional interest of dealing with a little girl less than one year old. Despite the infant's extreme youth, it was undoubtedly the object of emotion. Raymond Pierre was a sheep-farmer in the village of Arques, a terminus on the migration route used by the people of Montaillou. He had one daughter, Jacotte, by Sybille his wife (iii.414–15). Jacotte, not yet a year old, was seriously ill, and her parents decided, so much did they love the child, against all the rules of heresy, to have her hereticated before she died. In theory it was not right to hereticate anyone so young: Jacotte *did not have the understanding of good.* But Prades Tavernier, the *parfait* who undertook the ceremony, was laxer than the Authiés and thought there was nothing to be lost by it.[1] So he started to administer the *consolamentum: He performed a lot of bows and elevations,* and placed that rare object, a book, on the child's head. Once these rites were accomplished, Raymond Pierre could say to his wife, *'If Jacotte dies, she will be an angel of God. Neither you nor I, wife, could give our daughter as much as this heretic has given her.'*

Full of joy and disinterested love, Raymond Pierre left the house to see Prades Tavernier on his way. Before going, the *parfait* told Sybille not to give the baby any milk or meat. If Jacotte lived, all she was to have was fish and vegetables (ii.414). For a child of that age, and in the dietetic conditions of the period, this was risky. In fact, what it amounted to was that after the father and the *parfait* left, Jacotte would be doomed to imminent death by a process similar to the *endura,* or final fast.

But there was a hitch. Sybille Pierre's love for her little girl was essentially warm and physical, not spiritual and sublime like that of Ray-

[1]An Albigensian was "hereticated" by receiving a sacrament called the *consolamentum*—usually when close to death. Afterwards he or she was expected to live as one of the "perfect" *(parfait)* and abstain from animal foods.

From E. LeRoy Ladurie, *Montaillou: The Promised Land of Error* (New York: George Braziller, 1978), pp. 211–212. Copyright © 1980 by Editions du Soleil. English translation copyright © 1982 by George Braziller, Inc. and Scholars Press. Reprinted by permission of George Braziller, Inc.

mond. So, relates Sybille, *when my husband and Prades Tavernier had left the house, I could not bear it any longer. I couldn't let my daughter die before my very eyes. So I put her to the breast. When my husband came back, I told him I had fed my daughter. He was very grieved and troubled, and lamented. Pierre Maury* [Raymond Pierre's shepherd] *tried to console his master. He said to my husband, 'It is not your fault.'*

And Pierre said to my baby, 'You have a wicked mother.'

And he said to me, 'You are a wicked mother. Women are demons.'

My husband wept. He insulted and threatened me. After this scene, he stopped loving [diligere] *the child; and he also stopped loving me for a long while, until later, when he admitted that he had been wrong.* (Raymond Pierre's change of heart occurred at the same time as all the inhabitants of Arques decided collectively to renounce Catharism). *My daughter Jacotte,* Sybille concluded (ii.415), *survived this episode for a year; and then she died.*

Beguins

A different heresy grew up among some radical followers of Francis of Assisi. They believed that Francis had come to inaugurate a new age of the world—a sort of future utopia in which the existing institutions of the church would cease to exist.

From *The Inquisitor's Manual of Bernard Gui*

They distinguish as it were two churches: the carnal Church, which is the Roman Church, with its reprobate multitude, and the spiritual Church, composed of people whom they call spiritual and evangelical, who follow the life of Christ and the apostles. The latter, they claim, is their Church.

Also, they teach that at the end of the sixth era of the Church, the era in which they say we now are, which began with St. Francis, the carnal Church, Babylon, the great harlot, shall be rejected by Christ, just as the synagogue of the Jews was rejected for crucifying Christ. For the carnal Church crucifies and persecutes the life of Christ in those brethren whom they call the Poor and the Spirituals of the order of St. Francis.

Also, they teach that, just as Christ chose from the synagogue of the Jews, after it had been rejected, a few poor men through whom the primitive Church of Christ was founded in the first era of the Church, so, after the rejection and destruction of the carnal Church of Rome

From W. L. Wakefield and A. P. Evans, *Heresies of the High Middle Ages* (New York: Columbia University Press), pp. 425–426.

in the sixth or present era, there will remain a few chosen men, spiritual, poor, and evangelical. The majority of these, they say, will be drawn from both the orders of St. Francis, the first and the third, and through them will be founded the spiritual Church, which will be humble and good, in the seventh and last era of the Church, which begins with the death of Antichrist. . . .

Also, they teach that the Antichrist is dual; that is, there is one who is spiritual or mystical, and another, the real, greater Antichrist. The first prepares the way for the second. They say, too, that the first Antichrist is that pope under whom will occur and, in their opinion, is now occurring the persecution and condemnation of their sect.

Also, they fix the time within which the greater Antichrist will come, begin to preach, and run his course. This Antichrist, they say, has already been born and will run his course, according to some of them, in the year of our Lord 1325. Others say it will be in the year 1330; while still others put it later, in the year 1335. . . .

Also, drawing further upon their imaginations, they teach that the destruction of the carnal Church will occur amid mighty wars and great destruction of Christian peoples. Large numbers of men will fall in the war they wage in defense of the carnal Church. Then, when almost all the men are dead, the surviving Christian women will embrace trees out of love and longing for men. On this subject they tell a number of other fabulous tales. . . . Then the Church will be reduced to the same number of persons as founded the primitive Church; scarcely twelve shall survive. In them the Church will be established and upon them the Holy Spirit will be poured in equal or greater abundance than when He came upon the apostles in the primitive Church, as is recounted above.

Also, they say that after the death of Antichrist, the said Spirituals will convert the whole world to the faith of Christ and the whole world will be good and merciful, so that there will be no malice or sin in the people of that era, with the possible exception of venial sin in some. Everything will be for use in common and there will be no one to offend another or tempt him to sin, for great love will there be among them. There will then be one flock and one shepherd. This state and condition of men will last, some of them think, for a hundred years. Then, as love wanes, malice will creep in little by little and gradually spread so far that Christ will be forced by the excesses of wickedness, as it were, to come to the universal judgment of all.

X

THE "WANING" OF THE
MIDDLE AGES
**Pestilence, Persecution, and
Flagellants**
From *Jean de Venette's Chronicle*
Peasant Rebellion
From *Froissart's Chronicle*
The Great Schism
Manifesto of the Cardinals (1378)
*Opinion of the University of Paris
(1393)*
The Decree Haec Sancta (1415)
The Decree Execrabilis (1459)
Joan and Her Judges
From *The Trial of Jeanne d'Arc*

NEW LIGHT IN ITALY
The Dignity of Man
From Pico della Mirandola.
Oration on the Dignity of Man
Nature and Art
From Giorgio Vasari. *Lives of the
Most Eminent Painters (1550)*
**Renaissance Types—Man of Letters,
Courtier, Artist and Patron**
From *Petrarch's Letters*
From Baldassare Castiglione. *The
Book of the Courtier (1518)*
From Benvenuto Cellini.
Autobiography

RENAISSANCE FAMILIES
A Modern Description
From *The Western Experience*
Family and Fortune
From Alberti. *I Libri Della Famiglia*
A Florentine Family—Fact
From Landucci. *A Florentine Diary*
A Florentine Family—Fiction
From Machiavelli. *La Mandragola*

RENAISSANCE STATECRAFT
Italy: Prince and State
From Machiavelli. *The Prince*
France: Louis XI
From *Memoirs of Commynes*
England: Henry VII
From *Bacon's Life of Henry VII*

AN AGE OF RENAISSANCE—DECLINE AND RENEWAL, 1300–1500

THE FOURTEENTH CENTURY has been called an "age of adversity." Certainly the people of that time had to endure many disasters—plague, war, peasant rebellions, schism in the church. But society did not disintegrate under all these stresses. Instead people found the resilience to resist them and move on to a new era of expansion and exploration.

In Italy, the generation that survived the great plague of 1347 displayed an extraordinary vitality. Many intellectuals felt a sense of alienation from late medieval culture and a new devotion to the ancient civilizations of Greece and Rome. The rebirth of classical studies led on to an era of brilliant achievement in art and literature. Writers expressed a new sense of the dignity and worth of the human personality; artists found new ways of celebrating natural beauty—especially the beauty of the human body.

The "humanism" of the new age took many forms. Sometimes it stimulated a secularist, skeptical attitude to the traditional teachings of religion and morality. But many leaders of Renaissance thought saw no conflict between the old doctrines of Christianity and their new quest for beauty and truth.

THE "WANING" OF THE MIDDLE AGES

Pestilence, Persecution, and Flagellants

From *Jean de Venette's Chronicle*

In A.D. 1348, the people of France and of almost the whole world were struck by a blow other than war. For in addition to the famine which I described in the beginning and to the wars which I described in the course of this narrative, pestilence and its attendant tribulations appeared again in various parts of the world. . . .

All this year and the next, the mortality of men and women, of the young even more than of the old, in Paris and in the kingdom of France, and also, it is said, in other parts of the world, was so great that it was almost impossible to bury the dead. People lay ill little more than two or three days and died suddenly, as it were in full health. He who was well one day was dead the next and being carried to his grave. Swellings appeared suddenly in the armpit or in the groin—in many cases both—and they were infallible signs of death. This sickness or pestilence was called an epidemic by the doctors. Nothing like the great numbers who died in the years 1348 and 1349 has been heard of or seen or read of in times past. This plague and disease came from *ymaginatione* or association and contagion, for if a well man visited the sick he only rarely evaded the risk of death. Wherefore in many towns timid priests withdrew, leaving the exercise of their ministry to such of the religious as were more daring. In many places not two out of twenty remained alive. So high was the mortality at the Hôtel-Dieu in Paris that for a long time, more than five hundred dead were carried daily with great devotion in carts to the cemetery of the Holy Innocents in Paris for burial. A very great number of the saintly sisters of the Hôtel-Dieu who, not fearing to die, nursed the sick in all sweetness and humility, with no thought of honor, a number too often renewed by death, rest in peace with Christ, as we may piously believe.

This plague, it is said, began among the unbelievers, came to Italy, and then crossing the Alps reached Avignon, where it attacked several cardinals and took from them their whole household. Then it spread,

From Richard Newhall, ed., *The Chronicle of Jean de Venette*, Jean Birdsall, trans. (New York: Columbia University Press, 1953), pp. 48–52.

unforeseen, to France, through Gascony and Spain, little by little, from town to town, from village to village, from house to house, and finally from person to person. It even crossed over to Germany, though it was not so bad there as with us. . . .

In the year 1349, while the plague was still active and spreading from town to town, men in Germany, Flanders, Hainaut, and Lorraine uprose and began a new sect on their own authority. Stripped to the waist, they gathered in large groups and bands and marched in procession through the crossroads and squares of cities and good towns. There they formed circles and beat upon their backs with weighted scourges, rejoicing as they did so in loud voices and singing hymns suitable to their rite and newly composed for it. Thus for thirty-three days they marched through many towns doing their penance and affording a great spectacle to the wondering people. They flogged their shoulders and arms with scourges tipped with iron points so zealously as to draw blood. But they did not come to Paris nor to any part of France, for they were forbidden to do so by the king of France, who did not want them. He acted on the advice of the masters of theology of the University of Paris, who said that this new sect had been formed contrary to the will of God, to the rites of Holy Mother Church, and to the salvation of all their souls. That indeed this was and is true appeared shortly. For Pope Clement VI was fully informed concerning this fatuous new rite by the masters of Paris through emissaries reverently sent to him and, on the grounds that it had been damnably formed, contrary to law, he forbade the Flagellants under threat of anathema to practise in the future the public penance which they had so presumptuously undertaken. His prohibition was just, for the Flagellants, supported by certain fatuous priests and monks, were enunciating doctrines and opinions which were beyond measure evil, erroneous, and fallacious. For example, they said that their blood thus drawn by the scourge and poured out was mingled with the blood of Christ. Their many errors showed how little they knew of the Catholic faith. Wherefore, as they had begun fatuously of themselves and not of God, so in a short time they were reduced to nothing. On being warned, they desisted and humbly received absolution and penance at the hands of their prelates as the pope's representatives. Many honorable women and devout matrons, it must be added, had done this penance with scourges marching and singing through towns and churches like the men, but after a little like the others they desisted.

Some said that this pestilence was caused by infection of the air and waters, since there was at this time no famine nor lack of food supplies, but on the contrary great abundance. As a result of this theory of infected water and air as the source of the plague the Jews were suddenly and violently charged with infecting wells and water and corrupting the air. The whole world rose up against them cruelly on this account. In Germany and other parts of the world where Jews lived, they were massacred and slaughtered by Christians, and many thousands were burned everywhere, indiscriminately. The unshaken, if fatuous, constancy of the men and their wives was remarkable. For mothers hurled their children first into the fire that they might not be baptized and then leaped in after them to burn with their husbands and children. It is said that many bad Christians were found who in a like manner put poison into wells. But in truth, such poisonings, granted that they actually were perpetrated, could not have caused so great a plague nor have infected so many people. There were other causes; for example, the will of God and the corrupt humors and evil inherent in air and earth. Perhaps the poisonings, if they actually took place in some localities, reenforced these causes. The plague lasted in France for the greater part of the years 1348 and 1349 and then ceased. Many country villages and many houses in good towns remained empty and deserted. Many houses, including some splendid dwellings, very soon fell into ruins. Even in Paris several houses were thus ruined, though fewer here than elsewhere.

After the cessation of the epidemic, pestilence, or plague, the men and women who survived married each other. There was no sterility among the women, but on the contrary fertility beyond the ordinary. Pregnant women were seen on every side. Many twins were born and even three children at once. . . .

But woe is me! the world was not changed for the better but for the worse by this renewal of population. For men were more avaricious and grasping than before, even though they had far greater possessions. They were more covetous and disturbed each other more frequently with suits, brawls, disputes, and pleas. Nor by the mortality resulting from this terrible plague inflicted by God was peace between kings and lords established. On the contrary, the enemies of the king of France and of the Church were stronger and wickeder than before and stirred up wars on sea and on land. Greater evils than before pullulated everywhere in the world. . . .

Peasant Rebellion

From *Froissart's Chronicle*

Anon after the deliverance of the king of Navarre [1358] there began a marvellous tribulation in the realm of France, as in Beauvoisin, in Brie, on the river of Marne, in Laonnois, and about Soissons. For certain people of the common villages, without any head or ruler, assem-

From G. C. Macaulty, ed., *The Chronicles of Froissart,* Lord Berners, trans. (London: Macmillan, 1904), pp. 136–137.

bled together in Beauvoisin. In the beginning they passed not a hundred in number; they said how the noblemen of the realm of France, knights and squires, shamed the realm, and that it should be a great wealth to destroy them all; and each of them said it was true, and said all with one voice: "Shame have he that doth not his power to destroy all the gentlemen of the realm!"

Thus they gathered together without any other counsel, and without any armour saving with staves and knives, and so went to the house of a knight dwelling thereby, and brake up his house and slew the knight and the lady and all his children great and small and burnt his house. And then they went to another castle, and took the knight thereof and bound him fast to a stake, and then violated his wife and his daughter before his face and then slew the lady and his daughter and all his other children, and then slew the knight by great torment and burnt and beat down the castle. And so they did to divers other castles and good houses; and they multiplied so that they were a six thousand, and ever as they went forward they increased, for such like as they were fell ever to them, so that every gentleman fled from them and took their wives and children with them, and fled ten or twenty leagues off to be in surety, and left their houses void and their goods therein.

These mischievous people thus assembled without captain or armour robbed, brent and slew all gentlemen that they could lay hands on, and forced and ravished ladies and damosels, and did such shameful deeds that no human creature ought to think on any such, and he that did most mischief was most praised with them and greatest master. I dare not write the horrible deeds that they did to ladies and damosels: among other they slew a knight and after did put him on a broach and roasted him at the fire in the sight of the lady his wife and his children; and after the lady had been enforced and ravished with a ten or twelve, they made her perforce to eat of her husband and after made her to die an evil death and all her children. They made among them a king, one of Clermont in Beauvoisin: they chose him that was the most ungraciousest of all other and they called him king Jaques Goodman, and so thereby they were called companions of the Jaquery. They destroyed and burnt in the country of Beauvoisin about Corbie, Amiens and Montdidier more than threescore good houses and strong castles. In like manner these unhappy people were in Brie and Artois, so that all the ladies, knights and squires of that country were fain to fly away to Meaux in Brie, as well the duchess of Normandy and the duchess of Orleans as divers other ladies and damosels, or else they had been violated and after murdered. Also there were a certain of the same ungracious people between Paris and Noyon and between Paris and Soissons, and all about the land of Coucy, in the county of Valois, in the bishopric of Laon, Nyon and Soissons. There were burnt and destroyed more than a hundred castles and good houses of knights and squires in that country.

The Great Schism

In 1378 the cardinals elected Urban VI pope; then they claimed that the election had been made under duress and chose another candidate, Clement VII. This led to a schism that divided Europe for forty years.

Manifesto of the Cardinals (1378)

. . . After the apostolic seat was made vacant by the death of our lord, pope Gregory XI, who died in March, we assembled in conclave for the election of a pope, as is the law and custom, in the papal palace, in which Gregory had died. . . . Officials of the city with a great multitude of the people, for the most part armed and called together for this purpose by the ringing of bells, surrounded the palace in a threatening manner and even entered it and almost filled it. To the terror caused by their presence they added threats that unless we should at once elect a Roman or an Italian they would kill us. They gave us no time to deliberate, but compelled us unwillingly, through violence and fear, to elect an Italian without delay. In order to escape the danger which threatened us from such a mob, we elected Bartholomew, archbishop of Bari, thinking that he would have enough conscience not to accept the election, since every one knew that it was made under such wicked threats. But he was unmindful of his own salvation and burning with ambition, and so, to the great scandal of the clergy and of the Christian people, and contrary to the laws of the church, he accepted this election which was offered him, although not all the cardinals were present at the election, and it was extorted from us by the threats and demands of the officials and people of the city. And although such an election is null and void, and the danger from the people still threatened us, he was enthroned and crowned, and called himself pope and apostolic. But according to the holy fathers and to the law of the church, he should be called apostate, anathema, Antichrist, and the mocker and destroyer of Christianity. . . .

From Baluzius, *Vitae paparum Avenionsiensium*, trans. in O. J. Thatcher and E. H. McNeal, *A Source Book for Mediaeval History* (New York: Charles Scribner's, 1905), p. 325.

During the schism many theologians suggested that a general council could judge between the rival "popes."

Opinion of the University of Paris (1393)

The First Way   Now the first way to end the schism is that both parties should entirely renounce and resign all rights which they may have or claim to have to the papal office. . . .

From D'Achéry, *Spicilegium*, trans. in O. J. Thatcher and E. H. McNeal, *A Source Book for Mediaeval History* (New York: Charles Scribner's, 1905), pp. 326–327.

The Second Way   But if both cling tenaciously to their rights and refuse to resign, as they have done up to now, we would propose the way of arbitration. That is, that they should together choose worthy and suitable men, or permit such to be chosen in a regular and canonical way, and these shall have the full power and authority to discuss the case and decide it, and if necessary and expedient, and approved by those who according to the canon law have the authority [that is, the cardinals], they may also have the right to proceed to the election of a pope.

The Third Way   If the rival popes, after being urged in a brotherly and friendly manner, will not accept either of the above ways, there is a third way which we propose as an excellent remedy for this sacrilegious schism. We mean that the matter shall be left to a general council. This general council might be composed, according to canon law, only of prelates, or, since many of them are very illiterate, and many of them are bitter partisans of one or the other pope, there might be joined with the prelates an equal number of masters and doctors of theology and law from the faculties of approved universities. Or if this does not seem sufficient to anyone, there might be added besides one or more representatives from cathedral chapters and the chief monastic orders, in order that all decisions might be rendered only after most careful examination and mature deliberation.

In 1415 the general council of Constance claimed supreme authority over the church and subsequently removed all the contending "popes". (By then there were three would-be pontiffs.)

The Decree Haec Sancta (1415)

This holy synod of Constance, being a general council, and legally assembled in the Holy Spirit for the praise of God and for ending the present schism, and for the union and reformation of the church of God in its head and in its members, in order more easily, more securely, more completely, and more fully to bring about the union and reformation of the church of God, ordains, declares, and decrees as follows: And first it declares that this synod, legally assembled, is a general council, and represents the catholic church militant and has its authority directly from Christ; and everybody, of whatever rank or dignity, including also the pope, is bound to obey this council in those things which pertain to the faith, to the ending of this schism, and to a general reformation of the church in its head and members. Likewise

From Von der Hardt, *Concilium Constanciense* and Denziger, *Enchiridion*, in O. J. Thatcher and E. H. McNeal, *A Source Book for Mediaeval History* (New York: Charles Scribner's 1905), pp. 328–329, 332.

it declares that if anyone, of whatever rank, condition, or dignity, including also the pope, shall refuse to obey the commands, statutes, ordinances, or orders of this holy council, or of any other holy council properly assembled, in regard to the ending of the schism and to the reformation of the church, he shall be subject to the proper punishment; and unless he repents, he shall be duly punished; and if necessary, recourse shall be had to other aids of justice.

The new line of popes established at Constance later repudiated the doctrine of conciliar supremacy and reestablished a system of papal monarchy.

The Decree Execrabilis (1459)

The execrable and hitherto unknown abuse has grown up in our day, that certain persons, imbued with the spirit of rebellion, and not from a desire to secure a better judgment, but to escape the punishment of some offence which they have committed, presume to appeal from the pope to a future council, in spite of the fact that the pope is the vicar of Jesus Christ and to him, in the person of St. Peter, the following was said: "Feed my sheep" [John 21:16] and "Whatsoever thou shalt bind on earth shall be bound in heaven" [Matt. 16:18]. Wishing therefore to expel this pestiferous poison from the church of Christ and to care for the salvation of the flock entrusted to us, and to remove every cause of offence from the fold of our Saviour, with the advice and consent of our brothers, the cardinals of the holy Roman church, and of all the prelates, and of those who have been trained in the canon and civil law, who are at our court, and with our own sure knowledge, we condemn all such appeals and prohibit them as erroneous and detestable.

Joan and Her Judges

The trial of Joan of Arc brought into dramatic focus many themes of fifteenth-century culture—Joan's simple faith, new stirrings of nationalist feeling, abuse of religious authority . . .

From The Trial of Jeanne d'Arc

(This letter of Joan was introduced as evidence at her trial.)

JHESUS MARIA

King of England, and you Duke of Bedford, calling yourself regent of France, you William Pole, Count of Suffolk John Talbot, and you Thomas Lord Scales, calling yourselves lieutenants of the said Duke of

From W. P. Barrett, trans., *The Trial of Jeanne d'Arc* (London: George Routledge, 1931), pp. 165–166. Reprinted by permission of Routledge & Kegan Paul Ltd.

Bedford, do right in the King of Heaven's sight. Surrender to *The Maid* sent hither by God the King of Heaven, the keys of all the good towns you have taken and laid waste in France. She comes in God's name to establish the Blood Royal, ready to make peace if you agree to abandon France and repay what you have taken. And you, archers, comrades in arms, gentles and others, who are before the town of Orleans, retire in God's name to your own country. If you do not, expect to hear tidings from *The Maid* who will shortly come upon you to your very great hurt. And to you, King of England, if you do not thus, I am a chieftain of war, and whenever I meet your followers in France, I will drive them out; if they will not obey, I will put them all to death. I am sent here in God's name, the King of Heaven, to drive you body for body out of all France. If they obey, I will show them mercy. Do not think otherwise; you will not withhold the kingdom of France from God, the King of Kings, Blessed Mary's Son. The King Charles, the true inheritor, will possess it, for God wills it, and has revealed it to him through *The Maid*, and he will enter Paris with a good company. If you do not believe these tidings from God and *The Maid*, wherever we find you we shall strike you and make a greater tumult than France has heard for a thousand years. Know well that the King of Heaven will send a greater force to *The Maid* and her good people than you in all your assaults can overcome: and by blows shall the favour of the God of Heaven be seen. You Duke of Bedford, *The Maid* prays and beseeches not to bring yourself to destruction. If you obey her, you may join her company, where the French shall do the fairest deed ever done for Christendom. Answer, if you desire peace in the city of Orleans; if not, bethink you of your great hurt soon. Written this Tuesday of Holy Week.

[*The following excerpts are from the record of Joan's interrogations.*]

Asked how old she was, she replied she thought nineteen. She said moreover that her mother taught her the Paternoster, Ave Maria, and Credo; and that no one but her mother had taught her her Credo. . . . Afterwards she declared that at the age of thirteen she had a voice from God to help her and guide her. And the first time she was much afraid. And this voice came towards noon, in summer, in her father's garden: and the said Jeanne had [not] fasted on the preceding day. She heard the voice on her right, in the direction of the church; and she seldom heard it without a light. This light came from the same side as the voice, and generally there was a great light. When she came to France she often heard the voice. . . .

From W. P. Barrett, trans., *The Trial of Jeanne d'Arc*, (London: George Routledge, 1931), pp. 51, 54–57, 70, 78–79, 124, 126. Reprinted by permission of Routledge & Kegan Paul Ltd.

Asked what instruction this voice gave her for the salvation of her soul: she said it taught her to be good and to go to church often; and it told her that she must come to France. And, Jeanne added, Beaupère would not learn from her, this time, in what form that voice appeared to her. She further said that this voice told her once or twice a week that she should leave and come to France, and that her father knew nothing of her leaving. She said that the voice told her to come, and she could no longer stay where she was; and the voice told her again that she should raise the siege of the city of Orleans. She said moreover that the voice told her that she, Jeanne, should go to Robert de Baudricourt, in the town of Vaucouleurs of which he was captain, and he would provide an escort for her. And the said Jeanne answered that she was a poor maid, knowing nothing of riding or fighting. . . .

She said that she sent to the English at Orleans letters telling them to depart, as shown in the copy of the letters which had been read to her in this town of Rouen, except two or three words in the copy: for example, where in this copy it read *Surrender to the Maid* it should read *Surrender to the King.* There are also these words, *body for body* and *chieftain of war,* which were not in the original letters.

After this the said Jeanne told that she went without hindrance to him whom she calls her king. And when she had arrived at Ste. Catherine de Fierbois, then she sent first to Chinon, where he who she calls her king was. She reached Chinon towards noon and lodged at an inn; and after dinner she went to him whom she calls king, who was at the castle. She said that when she entered her king's room she recognized him among many others by the counsel of her voice, which revealed him to her. She told him she wanted to make war on the English.

Asked whether, when the voice showed her her king, there was no light, she answered: "Pass on to the next question." Asked if she saw no angel above the king, she answered: "Spare me that. Continue." She said also that before the king put her to work he had several apparitions and beautiful revelations.

Asked what revelations and apparitions the king had, she answered: "I will not tell you. It is not now the time to tell you; but send to the king and he will tell you.". . .

Asked if God ordered her to wear a man's dress, she answered that the dress is a small, nay, the least thing. Nor did she put on man's dress by the advice of any man whatsoever; she did not put it on, nor did she do aught, but by the command of God and the angels.

Asked whether it seemed to her that this command to assume male attire was lawful, she answered: "Everything I have done is at God's command; and if He had ordered me to assume a different habit, I should have done it, because it would have been His command."

Asked if she did it at the order of Robert de Baudricourt she said no. . . .

Asked if the saints which appeared to her had hair, she answered: "It is well to know that they have."

Asked if there were anything between their crowns and their hair, she answered no.

Asked if their hair were long and hung down, she answered: "I do not know." She added that she did not know whether they appeared to have arms or other members. She saw they spoke very well and beautifully; and she understood them very well.

Asked how they spoke if they had no other members, she answered: "I leave that to God." She said the voice was gentle, soft and low, and spoke in French.

Asked if St. Margaret spoke in the English tongue, she answered: "Why should she speak English when she is not on the English side?". . .

Asked how she knew that St. Catherine and St. Margaret hated the English, she answered: "They love those whom God loves, and hate whom He hates."

Asked if God hated the English, she answered that of God's love or His hatred for the English, or of what He would do to their souls, she knew nothing, but she was certain that, excepting those who died there, they would be driven out of France, and God would send victory to the French and against the English.

Asked if God was for the English when they were prospering in France, she answered that she knew not whether God hated the French, but she believed it was His will to suffer them to be beaten for their sins, if they were in a state of sin.

Asked what warrant and what help she expected to have from Our Lord by the fact that she wore man's dress, she answered that in this as in other things she sought only the salvation of her soul. . . .

Asked if she wished to submit all her acts or sayings, either good or evil, to the decision of Our Mother the Church, she answered that she loved the Church and would support it with all her might for the Christian Faith: and she was not a person to be forbidden to go to church or hear Mass. As for the good works she did, and her coming, she must commit herself to the King of Heaven who sent her to Charles, son of Charles, King of France, who should be King of France. "And you will see," she said, "that the people of France will soon win a great undertaking which God will send, and which will shake almost the whole kingdom of France." And she said this so that when it should happen men might recall that she had foretold it.

Required to give the date of this event, she answered: "I refer to Our Lord."

NEW LIGHT IN ITALY

The readings in this section illustrate Renaissance attitudes to the human personality, to art and nature, and to classical learnings.

The Dignity of Man

Pico della Mirandola lived from 1463 to 1494.

From Pico della Mirandola. *Oration on the Dignity of Man*

At last it seems to me I have come to understand why man is the most fortunate of creatures and consequently worthy of all admiration and what precisely is that rank which is his lot in the universal chain of Being—a rank to be envied not only by brutes but even by the stars and by minds beyond this world. It is a matter past faith and a wondrous one. Why should it not be? For it is on this very account that man is rightly called and judged a great miracle and a wonderful creature indeed. But hear, Fathers, exactly what this rank is and, as friendly auditors, conformably to your kindness, do me this favor. God the Father, the supreme Architect, had already built this cosmic home we behold, the most sacred temple of His godhead, by the laws of His mysterious wisdom. The region above the heavens He had adorned with Intelligences, the heavenly spheres He had quickened with eternal souls, and the excrementary and filthy parts of the lower world He had filled with a multitude of animals of every kind. But, when the work was finished, the Craftsman kept wishing that there were someone to ponder the plan of so great a work, to love its beauty, and to wonder at its vastness. Therefore, when everything was done (as Moses and Timaeus bear witness), He finally took thought concerning the creation of man. But there was not among His archetypes that from which He could fashion a new offspring, nor was there in His treasurehouses anything which He might bestow on His new son as an inheritance, nor was there in the seats of all the world a place where the latter might sit to contemplate the universe. All was now complete; all things had been assigned to the highest, the middle, and the lowest orders. But in its final creation it was not the part of the Father's power to fail as though exhausted. It was not the part of His wisdom to waver in a needful

From E. Cassirer, P. O. Kristeller, and J. H. Randall, Jr., eds., *The Renaissance Philosophy of Man* (Chicago, Ill.: University of Chicago Press, 1948), pp. 223–225. Reprinted by permission of The University of Chicago Press.

matter through poverty of counsel. It was not the part of His kindly love that he who was to praise God's divine generosity in regard to others should be compelled to condemn it in regard to himself. At last the best of artisans ordained that the creature to whom He had been able to give nothing proper to himself should have joint possession of whatever had been peculiar to each of the different kinds of being. He therefore took man as a creature of indeterminate nature and, assigning him a place in the middle of the world, addressed him thus: "Neither a fixed abode nor a form that is thine alone nor any function peculiar to thyself have we given thee, Adam, to the end that according to thy longing and according to thy judgment thou mayest have and possess what abode, what form, and what functions thou thyself shalt desire. The nature of all other beings is limited and constrained within the bounds of laws prescribed by Us. Thou, constrained by no limits, in accordance with thine own free will, in whose hand We have placed thee, shalt ordain for thyself the limits of thy nature. We have set thee at the world's center that thou mayest from thence more easily observe whatever is in the world. We have made thee neither of heaven nor of earth, neither mortal nor immortal, so that with freedom of choice and with honor, as though the maker and molder of thyself, thou mayest fashion thyself in whatever shape thou shalt prefer. Thou shalt have the power to degenerate into the lower forms of life, which are brutish. Thou shalt have the power, out of thy soul's judgment, to be reborn into the higher forms, which are divine." O supreme generosity of God the Father, O highest and most marvelous felicity of man! To him it is granted to have whatever he chooses, to be whatever he wills.

Nature and Art

From Giorgio Vasari. *Lives of the Most Eminent Painters* (1550)

It is without doubt a fixed opinion, common to almost all writers, that the arts of sculpture and painting were first discovered by the nations of Egypt, although there are some who attribute the first rude attempts in marble, and the first statues and relievi, to the Chaldeans, while they accord the invention of the pencil, and of colouring, to the Greeks. But I am myself convinced, that design, which is the foundation of both these arts, nay, rather the very soul of each, comprising and nourish-

From Giorgi Vasari, *Lives of the Most Eminent Painters, Sculptors and Architects*, Mrs. J. Foster, trans. (London: H. G. Bohn, 1850), pp. 9–16, 20–22, 35, 43, 94.

ing within itself all the essential parts of both, existed in its highest perfection from the first moment of creation, when the Most High having formed the great body of the world, and adorned the heavens with their resplendent lights, descended by his spirit, through the limpidity of the air, and penetrating the solid mass of earth, created man; and thus unveiled, with the beauties of creation, the first form of sculpture and painting. For from this man, as from a true model, were copied by slow degrees (we may not venture to affirm the contrary), statues and sculptures: the difficulties of varied attitude,—the flowing lines of contour—and in the first paintings, whatever these may have been, the softness, harmony, and that concord in discord, whence result light and shade. The first model, therefore, from which the first image of man arose, was a mass of earth; and not without significance, since the Divine Architect of time and nature, Himself all-perfect, designed to instruct us by the imperfection of the material, in the true method of attaining perfection, by repeatedly diminishing and adding to; as the best sculptors and painters are wont to do, for by perpetually taking from or adding to their models they conduct their work, from its first imperfect sketch, to that finish of perfection which they desire to attain. The Creator further adorned his model with the most vivid colours, and these same colours, being afterwards drawn by the painter from the mines of earth, enable him to imitate whatsoever object he may require for his picture. . . .

We find, then, that the art of sculpture was zealously cultivated by the Greeks, among whom many excellent artists appeared; those great masters, the Athenian Phidias, with Praxiteles and Polycletus, were of the number, while Lysippus and Pyrgoteles, worked successfully in intaglio, and Pygmalion produced admirable reliefs in ivory—nay, of him it was affirmed, that his prayers obtained life and soul for the statue of a virgin which he had formed. Painting was in like manner honoured, and those who practised it successfully were rewarded among the ancient Greeks and Romans; this is proved by their according the rights of citizenship, and the most exalted dignities, to such as attained high distinction in these arts. . . .

I suggested above that the origin of these arts was Nature herself—the first image or model, the most beautiful fabric of the world—and the master, the divine light infused into us by special grace, and which has made us not only superior to all other animals, but has exalted us, if it be permitted so to speak, to the similitude of God Himself. This is my belief, and I think that every man who shall maturely consider the question, will be of my opinion. And if it has been seen in our times— as I hope to demonstrate presently by various examples—that simple children, rudely reared in the woods, have begun to practise the arts of design with no other model than those beautiful pictures and sculptures furnished by Nature, and no other teaching than their own genius—how much more easily may we believe that the first of mankind, in whom nature and intellect were all the more perfect in proportion as they were less removed from their first origin and divine parentage,— that these men, I say, having Nature for their guide, and the unsullied purity of their fresh intelligence for their master, with the beautiful model of the world for an exemplar, should have given birth to these most noble arts, and from a small beginning, ameliorating them by slow degrees, should have conducted them finally to perfection? . . .

But as fortune, when she has raised either persons or things to the summit of her wheel, very frequently casts them to the lowest point, whether in repentance or for her sport, so it chanced that, after these things, the barbarous nations of the world arose, in divers places, in rebellion against the Romans; whence there ensued, in no long time, not only the decline of that great empire, but the utter ruin of the whole and more especially of Rome herself, when all the best artists, sculptors, painters, and architects, were in like manner totally ruined, being submerged and buried, together with the arts themselves, beneath the miserable slaughters and ruins of that much renowned city. . . .

But infinitely more ruinous than all other enemies to the arts above named, was the fervent zeal of the new Christian religion, which, after long and sanguinary combats, had finally overcome and annihilated the ancient creeds of the pagan world, by the frequency of miracles exhibited, and by the earnest sincerity of the means adopted; and ardently devoted, with all diligence, to the extirpation of error, nay, to the removal of even the slightest temptation to heresy, it not only destroyed all the wondrous statues, paintings, sculptures, mosaics, and other ornaments of the false pagan deities, but at the same time extinguished the very memory, in casting down the honours, of numberless excellent ancients, to whom statues and other monuments had been erected, in public places, for their virtues, by the most virtuous times of antiquity. Nay, more than this, to build the churches of the Christian faith, this zeal not only destroyed the most renowned temples of the heathens, but, for the richer ornament of St. Peter's, and in addition to the many spoils previously bestowed on that building, the tomb of Adrian, now called the castle of St. Angelo, was deprived of its marble columns, to employ them for this church, many other buildings being in like manner despoiled, and which we now see wholly devastated. And although the Christian religion did not effect this from hatred to these works of art, but solely for the purpose of abasing and bringing into contempt the gods of the Gentiles, yet the result of this too ardent zeal did not fail to bring such total ruin over the noble arts, that their very form and existence was lost. . . .

The overwhelming flood of evils by which unhappy Italy had been submerged and devastated, had not only destroyed whatever could properly be called buildings, but, a still more deplorable consequence, had totally exterminated the artists themselves, when, by the will of God, in the year 1240, Giovanni Cimabue, of the noble family of that name, was born, in the city of Florence, to give the first light to the art of painting. . . .

I will not omit to observe, that if the greatness of Giotto, his disciple, had not diminished the glory of Cimabue, his fame would have risen still higher. . . . Giotto certainly did obscure his fame, as a great light diminishes the splendour of a lesser one; so that, although Cimabue may be considered, perhaps, the first cause of the restoration of the art of painting, yet Giotto, his disciple, impelled by laudable ambition, and well aided by heaven and nature, was the man who, attaining to superior elevation of thought, threw open the gates of the true way to those who afterwards exalted the art to that perfection and greatness which it displays in our age; when, accustomed as men are, daily, to see the prodigies and miracles, nay, the impossibilities, now performed by artists, they have arrived at such a point that they no longer marvel at anything accomplished by men, even though it be more divine than human. . . . And it was in truth a great marvel, that from so rude and inapt an age, Giotto should have had strength to elicit so much, that the art of design, of which the men of those days had little, if any, knowledge, was, by his means, effectually recalled into life. The birth of this great man took place in the hamlet of Vespignano, fourteen miles from the city of Florence, in the year 1276. His father's name was Bondone, a simple husbandman, who reared the child, to whom he had given the name of Giotto, with such decency as his condition permitted. The boy was early remarked for extreme vivacity in all his childish proceedings, and for extraordinary promptitude of intelligence; so that he became endeared, not only to his father, but to all who knew him in the village and around it. When he was about ten years old, Bondone gave him a few sheep to watch, and with these he wandered about the vicinity—now here and now there. But, induced by Nature herself to the arts of design, he was perpetually drawing on the stones, the earth, or the sand, some natural object that came before him, or some fantasy that presented itself to his thoughts. It chanced one day that the affairs of Cimabue took him from Florence to Vespignano, when he perceived the young Giotto, who, while his sheep fed around him, was occupied in drawing one of them from the life, with a stone slightly pointed, upon a smooth clean piece of rock,—and that without any teaching whatever, but such as Nature herself had imparted. Halting in astonishment, Cimabue inquired of the boy if he would accompany him to his home, and the child replied, he would go willingly, if his father were content to permit it. Cimabue therefore requesting the consent of Bondone, the latter granted it readily, and suffered the artist to conduct his son to Florence, where, in a short time, instructed by Cimabue and aided by Nature, the boy not only equalled his master in his own manner, but became so good an imitator of Nature, that he totally banished the rude Greek manner,—restoring art to the better path adhered to in modern times, and introducing the custom of accurately drawing living persons from nature, which had not been used for more than two hundred years.

Renaissance Types—Man of Letters, Courtier, Artist and Patron

Petrarch (1304–1374) helped to revive the study of classical literature in Italy.

From *Petrarch's Letters*

Your Cicero has been in my possession four years and more. There is a good reason, though, for so long a delay; namely, the great scarcity of copyists who understand such work. It is a state of affairs that has resulted in an incredible loss to scholarship. Books that by their nature are a little hard to understand are no longer multiplied, and have ceased to be generally intelligible, and so have sunk into utter neglect, and in the end have perished. This age of ours consequently has let fall, bit by bit, some of the richest and sweetest fruits that the tree of knowledge has yielded; has thrown away the results of the vigils and labours of the most illustrious men of genius, things of more value, I am almost tempted to say, than anything else in the whole world. . . .

But I must return to your Cicero. I could not do without it, and the incompetence of the copyists would not let me possess it. What was left for me but to rely upon my own resources, and press these weary fingers and this worn and ragged pen into the service? The plan that I followed was this. I want you to know it, in case you should ever have to grapple with a similar task. Not a single word did I read except as I wrote. But how is that, I hear someone say; did you write without knowing what it was that you were writing? Ah! but from the very first it was enough for me to know that it was a work of Tullius, and an extremely rare one too. And then as soon as I was fairly started I found at every step so much sweetness and charm, and felt so strong a desire to advance, that the only difficulty which I experienced in reading and writing at the same time came from the fact that my pen could not cover the ground so rapidly as I wanted it to, whereas my

From J. H. Robinson and H. W. Rolfe, trans., *Petrarch: The First Modern Scholar and Man of Letters* (New York: Putnam, 1898), pp. 275–278.

expectation had been rather that it would outstrip my eyes, and that my ardour for writing would be chilled by the slowness of my reading. So the pen held back the eye, and the eye drove on the pen, and I covered page after page, delighting in my task, and committing many and many a passage to memory as I wrote. For just in proportion as the writing is slower than the reading does the passage make a deep impression and cling to the mind.

And yet I must confess that I did finally reach a point in my copying where I was overcome by weariness; not mental, for how unlikely that would be where Cicero was concerned, but the sort of fatigue that springs from excessive manual labour. I began to feel doubtful about this plan that I was following, and to regret having undertaken a task for which I had not been trained; when suddenly I came across a place where Cicero tells how he himself copied the orations of—someone or other; just who it was I do not know, but certainly no Tullius, for there is but one such man, one such voice, one such mind. These are his words: "You say that you have been in the habit of reading the orations of Cassius in your idle moments. But I," he jestingly adds, with his customary disregard of his adversary's feelings, "have made a practice of *copying* them, so that I might *have* no idle moments." As I read this passage I grew hot with shame, like a modest young soldier who hears the voice of his beloved leader rebuking him. I said to myself, "So Cicero copied orations that another wrote, and you are not ready to copy his? What ardour! what scholarly devotion! what reverence for a man of godlike genius!" These thoughts were a spur to me, and I pushed on, with all my doubts dispelled. If ever from my darkness there shall come a single ray that can enhance the splendour of the reputation which his heavenly eloquence has won for him, it will proceed in no slight measure from the fact that I was so captivated by his ineffable sweetness that I did a thing in itself most irksome with such delight and eagerness that I scarcely knew I was doing it at all.

So then at last your Cicero has the happiness of returning to you, bearing you my thanks. And yet he also stays, very willingly, with me; a dear friend, to whom I give the credit of being almost the only man of letters for whose sake I would go to the length of spending my time, when the difficulties of life are pressing on me so sharply and inexorably and the cares pertaining to my literary labours make the longest life seem far too short, in transcribing compositions not my own. I may have done such things in former days, when I thought myself rich in time, and had not learned how stealthily it slips away: but I now know that this is of all our riches the most uncertain and fleeting; the years are closing in upon me now, and there is no longer any room for deviation from the beaten path. I am forced to practice strict economy; I only hope that I have not begun too late. But Cicero! he assuredly is worthy of a part of even the little that I still have left. Farewell.

From Baldassare Castiglione. *The Book of the Courtier (1518)*

I wish, then, that this Courtier of ours should be nobly born and of gentle race . . . for noble birth is like a bright lamp that manifests and makes visible good and evil deeds, and kindles and stimulates to virtue both by fear of shame and by hope of praise. . . .

But to come to some details, I am of opinion that the principal and true profession of the Courtier ought to be that of arms; which I would have him follow actively above all else, and be known among others as bold and strong, and loyal to whomsoever he serves. And he will win a reputation for these good qualities by exercising them at all times and in all places, since one may never fail in this without severest censure. And just as among women, their fair fame once sullied never recovers its first lustre, so the reputation of a gentleman who bears arms, if once it be in the least tarnished with cowardice or other disgrace, remains forever infamous before the world and full of ignominy. . . .

Not that we would have him look so fierce, or go about blustering, or say that he has taken his cuirass to wife, or threaten with those grim scowls that we have often seen in Berto, because to such men as this, one might justly say that which a brave lady jestingly said in gentle company to one whom I will not name at present; who, being invited by her out of compliment to dance, refused not only that, but to listen to the music, and many other entertainments proposed to him,—saying always that such silly trifles were not his business; so that at last the lady said, "What is your business, then?" He replied with a sour look, "To fight." Then the lady at once said, "Now that you are in no war and out of fighting trim, I should think it were a good thing to have yourself well oiled, and to stow yourself with all your battle harness in a closet until you be needed, lest you grow more rusty than you are"; and so, amid much laughter from the bystanders, she left the discomfited fellow to his silly presumption.

Therefore let the man we are seeking, be very bold, stern, and always among the first, where the enemy are to be seen; and in every other place, gentle, modest, reserved, above all things avoiding ostentation and that impudent self-praise by which men ever excite hatred and disgust in all who hear them. . . . I say, however, that he, who in praising himself runs into no errour and incurs no annoyance or envy at the hands of those that hear him, is a very discreet man indeed and merits praise from others in addition to that which he bestows upon himself; because it is a very difficult matter. . . .

I would have our Courtier's aspect; not so soft and effeminate as is sought by many, who not only curl their hair and pluck their brows, but gloss their faces with all those arts employed by the most wanton

From Baldassare Castiglione, *The Book of the Courtier*, L. E. Opdycke, trans. (New York: Charles Scribner's Sons, 1903), pp. 22, 25–31, 59, 62–66, 93–95.

and unchaste women in the world; and in their walk, posture and every act, they seem so limp and languid that their limbs are like to fall apart; and they pronounce their words so mournfully that they appear about to expire upon the spot: and the more they find themselves with men of rank, the more they affect such tricks. Since nature has not made them women, as they seem to wish to appear and be, they should be treated not as good women but as public harlots, and driven not merely from the courts of great lords but from the society of honest men. . . . And so I would have him well built and shapely of limb, and would have him show strength and lightness and suppleness, and know all bodily exercises that befit a man of war: whereof I think the first should be to handle every sort of weapon well on foot and on horse, to understand the advantages of each, and especially to be familiar with those weapons that are ordinarily used among gentlemen; for besides the use of them in war, where such subtlety in contrivance is perhaps not needful, there frequently arise differences between one gentleman and another, which afterwards result in duels often fought with such weapons as happen at the moment to be within reach: thus knowledge of this kind is a very safe thing.

There are also many other exercises, which although not immediately dependent upon arms, yet are closely connected therewith, and greatly foster manly sturdiness; and one of the chief among these seems to me to be the chase, because it bears a certain likeness to war: and truly it is an amusement for great lords and befitting a man at court, and furthermore it is seen to have been much cultivated among the ancients. It is fitting also to know how to swim, to leap, to run, to throw stones, for besides the use that may be made of this in war, a man often has occasion to show what he can do in such matters; whence good esteem is to be won, especially with the multitude, who must be taken into account withal. Another admirable exercise, and one very befitting a man at court, is the game of tennis, in which are well shown the disposition of the body, the quickness and suppleness of every member, and all those qualities that are seen in nearly every other exercise. Nor less highly do I esteem vaulting on horse, which although it be fatiguing and difficult, makes a man very light and dexterous more than any other thing; and besides its utility, if this lightness is accompanied by grace, it is to my thinking a finer show than any of the others.

I think that the conversation which the Courtier ought most to try in every way to make acceptable, is that which he holds with his prince; and although this word "conversation" implies a certain equality that seems impossible between a lord and his inferior, yet we will call it so for the present. Therefore, besides daily showing everyone that he possesses the worth we have already described, I would have the Courtier strive, with all the thoughts and forces of his mind, to love and almost to adore the prince whom he serves, above every other thing, and mould his wishes, habits and all his ways to his prince's liking. . . .

Moreover it is possible without flattery to obey and further the wishes of him we serve, for I am speaking of those wishes that are reasonable and right, or of those that in themselves are neither good nor evil, such as would be a liking for play or a devotion to one kind of exercise above another. And I would have the Courtier bend himself to this even if he be by nature alien to it, so that on seeing him his lord shall always feel that he will have something agreeable to say; which will come about if he has the good judgment to perceive what his prince likes, and the wit and prudence to bend himself thereto, and a deliberate purpose to like that which perhaps he by nature dislikes. . . .

He will very rarely or almost never ask anything of his lord for himself, lest his lord, being reluctant to deny it to him directly, may sometimes grant it with an ill grace, which is much worse. Even in asking for others he will choose his time discreetly and ask proper and reasonable things; and he will so frame his request, by omitting what he knows may displease and by skilfully doing away with difficulties, that his lord shall always grant it, or shall not think him offended by refusal even if it be denied; for when lords have denied a favour to an importunate suitor, they often reflect that he who asked it with such eagerness, must have desired it greatly, and so having failed to obtain it, must feel ill will towards him who denied it; and believing this, they begin to hate the man and can never more look upon him with favour.

Pope Clement VII employed the artist Cellini (1500–1571) to design an ornament incorporating a splendid diamond.

From Benvenuto Cellini. *Autobiography*

While we were waiting for the money, the Pope turned once more to gaze at leisure on the dexterous device I had employed for combining the diamond with the figure of God the Father. I had put the diamond exactly in the centre of the piece; and above it God the Father was shown seated, leaning nobly in a sideways attitude, which made a perfect composition, and did not interfere with the stone's effect. Lifting his right hand, he was in the act of giving the benediction. Below the diamond I had placed three children, who, with their arms upraised, were supporting the jewel. One of them, in the middle, was in full relief, the other two in half-relief. All round I set a crowd of cherubs, in divers attitudes, adapted to the other gems. A mantle undulated to the wind around the figure of the Father, from the folds of which cherubs peeped out; and there were other ornaments besides which made a

From J. Symonds, trans., *The Life of Benvenuto Cellini* (London: J. C. Nimmo, 1893), pp. 102, 114–116.

very beautiful effect. The work was executed in white stucco on a black stone. When the money came, the Pope gave it me with his own hand, and begged me in the most winning terms to let him have it finished in his own days, adding that this should be to my advantage.

[Cellini's brother was murdered about this time.]

I went on applying myself with the utmost diligence upon the gold-work for Pope Clement's button. He was very eager to have it, and used to send for me two or three times a week, in order to inspect it; and his delight in the work always increased. Often would he rebuke and scold me, as it were, for the great grief in which my brother's loss had plunged me; and one day, observing me more downcast and out of trim than was proper, he cried aloud: "Benvenuto, oh! I did not know that you were mad. Have you only just learned that there is no remedy against death? One would think that you were trying to run after him." When I left the presence, I continued working at the jewel and the dies for the Mint; but I also took to watching the arquebusier who shot my brother, as though he had been a girl I was in love with. The man had formerly been in the light cavalry, but afterwards had joined the arquebusiers as one of the Bargello's corporals; and what increased my rage was that he had used these boastful words: "If it had not been for me, who killed that brave young man, the least trifle of delay would have resulted in his putting us all to flight with great disaster." When I saw that the fever caused by always seeing him about was depriving me of sleep and appetite, and was bringing me by degrees to sorry plight, I overcame my repugnance to so low and not quite praiseworthy an enterprise, and made my mind up one evening to rid myself of the torment. The fellow lived in a house near a place called Torre Sanguigna, next door to the lodging of one of the most fashionable courtesans in Rome, named Signora Antea. It had just struck twenty-four, and he was standing at the house-door, with his sword in hand, having risen from supper. With great address I stole up to him, holding a large Pistojan dagger, and dealt him a back-handed stroke, with which I meant to cut his head clean off; but as he turned round very suddenly, the blow fell upon the point of his left shoulder and broke the bone. He sprang up, dropped his sword, half-stunned with the great pain, and took to flight. I followed after, and in four steps caught him up, when I lifted my dagger above his head, which he was holding very low, and hit him in the back exactly at the junction of the nape-bone and the neck. The poniard entered this point so deep into the bone, that, though I used all my strength to pull it out, I was not able. For just at that moment four soldiers with drawn swords sprang out from Antea's lodging, and obliged me to set hand to my own sword to defend my life. Leaving the poniard then, I made off, and fearing I might be recognised, I took refuge in the palace of Duke Alessandro, which was between Piazza Navona and the Rotunda.

On my arrival, I asked to see the Duke, who told me that, if I was alone, I need only keep quiet and have no further anxiety, but go on working at the jewel which the Pope had set his heart on, and stay eight days indoors. . . .

More than eight days elapsed, and the Pope did not send for me according to his custom. Afterwards he summoned me through his chamberlain, the Bolognese nobleman I have already mentioned, who let me, in his own modest manner, understand that his Holiness knew all, but was very well inclined toward me, and that I had only to mind my work and keep quiet. When we reached the presence, the Pope cast so menacing a glance towards me that the mere look of his eyes made me tremble. Afterwards, upon examining my work, his countenance cleared, and he began to praise me beyond measure, saying that I had done a vast amount in a short time. Then, looking me straight in the face, he added: "Now that you are cured, Benvenuto, take heed how you live." I, who understood his meaning, promised that I would. Immediately upon this, I opened a very fine shop in the Banchi, opposite Raffaello, and there I finished the jewel after the lapse of a few months.

RENAISSANCE FAMILIES

A Modern Description

From *The Western Experience*

The cities were populous, but the households within them were small, the average size in Florence in 1427 being only 3.8 persons; in Bologna in 1395, 3.5 persons; in Verona in 1425, 3.7 persons. Average household size tended to increase over the fifteenth century, perhaps reflecting the return of better economic times, but it still remained distinctly small. This was primarily due to the late age at which men married. At Florence in 1427 most men postponed marriage until their early thirties. Economic pressures such as the need for prolonged training to master a profession or the fear of dividing a patrimony excessively were the primary reasons for the delay. Late marriage for men seems to have resulted in a younger marriage age for women. Inevitably, some men died before they reached age thirty. Therefore, there were fewer men of thirty than of twenty-five; consequently, if men married at thirty, there would be fewer marriages. Many girls of marriageable age were thus deprived of all statistical chance of finding a husband. The shortage of older grooms spread panic among the fathers of daughters and led them to increase dowries and lower the age at which they gave the girls in marriage. The most common age of marriage for girls at Florence in 1427 was fifteen. Those who were not married before they were twenty had no alternative but to enter convents.

Obviously, late marriage for men limited the duration of the marital union, and many husbands died while their wives were still quite young. The combination of girls placed in convents and numerous young widows in the population seems to account for another characteristic of the city—its relative infertility. It appears that for some periods the cities were not even able to maintain their own numbers through reproduction. In the countryside men characteristically married in their middle twenties and took as brides girls nearer in age to

From Mortimer Chambers, Raymond Grew, David Herlihy, Theodore K. Rabb, and Isser Woloch, *The Western Experience* (New York: Alfred A. Knopf, 1974), p. 395. Copyright © 1974 by Alfred A. Knopf, Inc. Reprinted by permission of the publisher.

themselves; thus relatively more rural girls married, and the duration of marriage was longer. Rural areas were therefore more successful than the cities in producing children.

The cities were thus forced to replenish their numbers by encouraging large-scale immigration from the countryside and small towns. This promoted social mobility as the cities recruited and rewarded the most skilled and energetic persons from these areas. Many of the leaders of the cultural Renaissance—Boccaccio, Leonardo Bruni, Poggio Bracciolini, Leonardo da Vinci, and others—were of rural or small-town origin and came to the city in response to its constant need for men.

The urban household was small and fairly unstable, but these factors seem to have intensified the emotional ties binding together its members, especially parents and children. In general the age witnesses a true discovery of childhood and of the contribution which children can make to the contentment of the household. Renaissance educational tracts show a new awareness of the psychology of children, and Renaissance art for the first time in the West represents children, even the infant Jesus, not as diminutive adults, but authentically, looking and acting as children do. The playful baby angels known as putti appear in even the most solemn religious paintings. The very fragility of the Italian urban family seems to have made men more appreciative of the values of family life.

Family and Fortune

Leon Battista Alberti, distinguished both as an artist and a writer, lived from 1404 to 1472.

From Alberti. *I Libri Della Famiglia*

In our discussion we may establish four general precepts as sound and firm foundation for all the other points to be developed or added. I shall name them. In the family the number of men must not diminish but augment; possessions must not grow less, but more; all forms of disgrace are to be shunned—a good name and fine reputation is precious and worth pursuing; hatreds, enmities, rancor must be carefully avoided, while good will, numerous acquaintances, and friendships are something to look for, augment, and cultivate. . . .

From Leon Battista Alberti, *I Libri della Famiglia* in Renée N. Watkins, trans., *The Family in Renaissance Florence* (Columbia, S.C.: University of South Carolina Press, 1969), pp. 110–120. Copyright © 1969 by Renée Watkins. Reprinted by permission of the University of South Carolina Press.

Families increase in population no differently than do countries, regions, and the whole world. As anyone who uses his imagination will quickly realize, the number of mortal men has grown from a small number to the present almost infinite multitude through the procreation and rearing of children. And, for the procreation of children, no one can deny that man requires woman. Since a child comes into the world as a tender and delicate creature, he needs someone to whose care and devotion he comes as a cherished trust. This person must nourish him with diligence and love and must defend him from harm. Too much cold or too much sun, rain, and the wild blowing of a storm are harmful to children. Woman, therefore, did first find a roof under which to nourish and protect herself and her offspring. There she remained, busy in the shadow, nourishing and caring for her children. And since woman was busy guarding and taking care of the heir, she was not in a position to go out and find what she and her children required for the maintenance of their life. Man, however, was by nature more energetic and industrious, and he went out to find things and bring what seemed to him necessary.

Nature showed, further, that this relationship could not be permitted with more than one wife at a time, since man was by no means able to provide and bring home more than was needed for himself and one wife and children. . . . To satisfy nature, then, a man need only choose a woman with whom he can dwell in tranquillity under one roof all his life.

Young people, however, very often do not cherish the good of the family enough to do this. Marriage, perhaps, seems to them to take away their present liberty and freedom. It may be, as the comic poets like to tell us, that they are held back and dissuaded by some mistress. Sometimes, too, young men find it hard enough to manage one life, and fear as an excessive and undesirable burden the task of supporting a wife and children besides. They may doubt their capacity to maintain in honorable estate a family which grows in needs from day to day. Viewing the conjugal bed as a troublesome responsibility, they then avoid the legitimate and honorable path to the increase of a family.

If a family is not to fall for these reasons into what we have described as the most unfortunate condition of decline, but is to grow, instead, in fame and in the prosperous multitude of its youth, we must persuade our young men to take wives. We must use every argument for this purpose, offer incentive, promise reward, employ all our wit, persistence, and cunning. A most appropriate reason for taking a wife may be found in what we were saying before, about the evil of sensual indulgence, for the condemnation of such things may lead young men to desire honorable satisfactions. As other incentives, we may also speak to them of the delights of this primary and natural companionship of marriage. Children act as pledges and securities of marital love and kindness. At the same time they offer a focus for all a man's hopes and desires. Sad, indeed, is the man who has labored to get wealth and power and lands, and then has no true heir and perpetuator of his memory. No one can be more suited than a man's true and legitimate sons to gain advantages by virtue of his character, position, and authority, and to enjoy the fruits and rewards of his labor. If a man leaves such heirs, furthermore, he need not consider himself wholly dead and gone. His children keep his own position and his true image in the family. . . .

When, by the urging and counsel of their elders and of the whole family, young men have arrived at the point of marriage, their mothers and other female relatives and friends, who have known the virgins of the neighborhood from earliest childhood and know the way their upbringing has formed them, should select all the well-born and well-brought-up girls and present that list to the new groom-to-be. He can then choose the one who suits him best. The elders of the house and all of the family shall reject no daughter-in-law unless she is tainted with the breath of scandal or bad reputation. Aside from that, let the man who will have to satisfy her satisfy himself. He should act as do wise heads of families before they acquire some property—they like to look it over several times before they actually sign a contract. . . . The man who has decided to marry must be still more cautious. I recommend that he examine and anticipate in every way, and consider for many days, what sort of person it is he is to live with for all his years as husband and companion. Let him be minded to marry for two purposes: first to perpetuate himself in his children, and second to have a steady and constant companion all his life. A woman is needed, therefore, who is likely to bear children and who is desirable as a perpetual mate.

They say that in choosing a wife one looks for beauty, parentage, and riches. . . . Among the most essential criteria of beauty in a woman is an honorable manner. Even a wild, prodigal, greasy, drunken woman may be beautiful of feature, but no one would call her a beautiful wife. A woman worthy of praise must show first of all in her conduct, modesty, and purity. Marius, the illustrious Roman, said in that first speech of his to the Roman people: "Of women we require purity, of men labor." And I certainly agree. There is nothing more disgusting than a coarse and dirty woman. Who is stupid enough not to see clearly that a woman who does not care for neatness and cleanliness in her appearance, not only in her dress and body but in all her behavior and language, is by no means well mannered? How can it be anything but obvious that a bad mannered woman is also rarely virtuous? We shall consider elsewhere the harm that comes to a family from women who lack virtue, for I myself do not know which is the worse fate for a family, total celibacy or a single dishonored woman. In a bride, therefore, a man must first seek beauty of mind, that is, good conduct and virtue.

In her body he must seek not only loveliness, grace, and charm but must also choose a woman who is well made for bearing children, with the kind of constitution that promises to make them strong and big. There's an old proverb, "When you pick your wife, you choose your children." All her virtues will in fact shine brighter still in beautiful children. It is a well-known saying among poets: "Beautiful character dwells in a beautiful body." The natural philosophers require that a woman be neither thin nor very fat. Those laden with fat are subject to coldness and constipation and slow to conceive. They say that a woman should have a joyful nature, fresh and lively in her blood and her whole being. They have no objections to a dark girl. They do reject girls with a frowning black visage, however. They have no liking for either the undersized or the overlarge and lean. They find that a woman is most suited to bear children if she is fairly big and has limbs of ample length. They always have a preference for youth, based on a number of arguments which I need not expound here, but particularly on the point that a young girl has a more adaptable mind. Young girls are pure by virtue of their age and have not developed any spitefulness. They are by nature modest and free of vice. They quickly learn to accept affectionately and unresistingly the habits and wishes of their husbands. . . .

The matter of dowry is next, which I would like to see middling in size, certain and prompt rather than large, vague, or promised for an indefinite future. I know not why everyone, as if corrupted by a common vice, takes advantage of delay to grow lazy in paying debts. Sometimes, in cases of marriage, people are further tempted because they hope to evade payment altogether. As your wife spends her first year in your house, it seems impossible not to reinforce the new bonds of kinship by frequent visiting and parties. But it will be thought rude if, in the middle of a gathering of kinsmen, you put yourself forward to insist and complain. If, as new husbands usually do, you don't want to lose their still precarious favor, you may ask your in-laws in restrained and casual words. Then you are forced to accept any little excuse they may offer. If you make a more forthright demand for what is your own, they will explain to you their many obligations, will complain of fortune, blame the conditions of the time, complain of other men, and say that they hope to be able to ask much of you in greater difficulties. As long as they can, in fact, they will promise you bounteous repayment at an ever-receding date. . . . This is why the dowry should be precisely set, promptly paid, and not too high. The larger the payments are to be and the longer they are to be carried, the more discussion you will be forced into, the more reluctantly you will be paid, and the more obliged you will feel to spend inordinate sums for all sorts of things. There will be indescribable bitterness and often totally ruinous results in setting dowries very high. . . .

When you have chosen your wife and decided on the girl you like best, when you have received the advice and permission of all your elders, and when she is highly pleasing to you and to your family for her ways and her beauty, then the first thing you ought to do is as Xenophon has the good husband say to Socrates: pray to God that he graciously grant that your bride will be fertile, and that you may always have peace and honor in your house. Address God with abundant piety, for these are the things essential to a wife and without which suffering abounds. With them, on the other hand, a man is happy and grateful for what are truly the gifts of God. Not every man who seeks finds a good wife. Not every man who would like a faithful wife has one, though some perhaps think they have. On the contrary, it has always been a rare and singular favor of God to settle a man with a wholly peaceable wife whose character is above reproach. One may consider oneself lucky if one's wife never gives rise to scandal or disgrace. Blessed is he who is not afflicted with grief through having a bad wife. Many should be the prayers addressed to God, therefore, that he may grant the young husband a wife who will prove good, peaceful, honorable, and, as we have said, prolific. This I repeat: one should never cease praying to God that he may keep one's wife faithful, tranquil, and loving.

A Florentine Family—Fact

A Florentine merchant, Luca Landucci, left this brief account of his marriage in a diary that he kept over many years.

From Landucci. *A Florentine Diary*

1466. 24th May. A Saturday and the eve of the *Spirito Santo,* I was wedded to a daughter of Domenico, son of Domenico Pagni, whose name was Salvestra. She had a dowry of 400 florins, in the state funds, praise God!

5th July. A Sunday evening, I gave her the ring, the contract being made before Ser Giovanni, son of Francesco di Neri. (Should be 6*th* July. [Trans.])

27th July. A Sunday evening, I took my wife to *Casa Domenico.* She had as bridal outfit the following:

A pale blue sack-garment, with narrow sleeves, embroidered with pearls.

A purple gown, with sleeves of *brocatello.*[1]

[1]A thin brocade. [Trans.]

From *A Florentine Diary from 1450 to 1516,* A. de Rosen Jervis, trans. (London: J. M. Dent & Sons, 1927), pp. 5–8.

A white under-gown.
Twenty-four kerchiefs of hand-woven linen.
Six linen towels.
Twenty-four *benducci da lato*.[2]
Eight shifts, woven in lozenge-pattern; new.
Twelve coifs.
A girdle of white silk webbing, with silver threads.
Three caps of various kinds.
A green reticule, with silver ornaments.
A pincushion, with pearls.
They were estimated by two dealers at the value of thirty-eight florins *di suggello*.[3] . . .

My above-mentioned wife and dear companion, who had not her equal for kindness and virtue, died after living with me for forty-eight years, and never once having given me cause for anger. She had twelve children; and at her death left me four boys and three girls, one of the latter a nun at Foligno, and the two others at home. God be praised!

A Florentine Family—Fiction

From Machiavelli. *La Mandragola*

Nowadays Machiavelli is remembered mainly for his political writings. In his own day he was famous as the author of a play, La Mandragola (The Mandrake).

The plot goes like this. Young Callimaco wants to seduce Lucrezia, who is married to Nicia, a foolish, rich old man. Lucrezia is beautiful, virtuous, and intelligent; her only failing as a wife is that she has no children. Callimaco presents himself as a doctor and assures Nicia that a potion made from the mandrake plant will cure Lucrezia's infertility. The only problem, Callimaco says, is that, when a lady has taken the mandrake potion, the first man who sleeps with her afterwards will inevitably die within eight days. Callimaco suggests that Nicia give his wife the potion, then kidnap some youth off the streets and send him to bed with Lucrezia. The youth will naturally make love to Lucrezia and then conveniently die. The problem is to persuade Lucrezia to go along with the plan. Callimaco achieves this by bribing Lucrezia's confessor, Friar Timoteo . . .

[2] Strips of stuff fastened to the shoulder to be used as a handkerchief. [Trans.]
[3] Sealed florins: that is, weighed, tested, and then sealed up in cardboard-boxes or purses. [Trans.]

From Niccolo Machiavelli, *La Mandragola*, Stark Young, trans. (New York: Macaulay Company, 1927), pp. 149–155. Reprinted by permission of the Estate of Stark Young.

SCENE IX

(Timoteo alone)

> . . . Messer Nicia and Callimaco are both rich and each for diverse reasons can be well plucked. The thing must be kept dark, that's as important to them as it is to me. Be it as they wish, I'll not repent me of it. Forsooth I doubt not we shall find it hard, for Donna Lucrezia is sensible and good. But I'll work on her kindness, all women have little brains, and if one of them knows enough to say two words, there must be a sermon about it: for in the realm of the blind the one-eyed is king. And here she is with her mother, who is a very beast and will be of great use in bringing her around to my wishes.

SCENE X

(Sostrata *and* Lucrezia)

Sostrata. I'm sure you believe, daughter, that I set as much store by your honor as anybody in the world, and that I should never advise you to do anything that was not good. I have told you and I tell you again that if Brother Timoteo says that there's nothing in it to trouble your conscience, you may do it without another thought.

Lucrezia. I have never had a doubt that the longing Messer Nicia has for children would sooner or later make us do something foolish; and just on this account, whenever he has come to me with some notion, have I been jealous and suspicious of it. But of all the things that we have tried, this last seems to me the strangest; to have to submit my body to this outrage, and to cause a man to die for outraging me; I'd never have believed, no not if I were the last woman left in the world and the human race had to start all over again from me, that such a thing could have fallen to my lot.

Sostrata. I can't explain such matters, daughter; you'll talk to the friar and you'll see what he tells you, and then do as you are advised by him, by us and by those who wish you well.

Lucrezia. I'm sweating with rage.

SCENE XI

(Timoteo, Lucrezia *and* Sostrata)

Timoteo. You are welcome both. I know what you wish to know from me, Messer Nicia has told me. Truly I have been in my books more than two hours studying this case; and after much question, I find many things both in general and in particular that are in our favor.

Lucrezia. Are you serious or jesting?

Timoteo. Ah! Donna Lucrezia, are these matters for jesting? Is that what you think of me?

Lucrezia. Father, no; but this seems to me the strangest business I ever heard of.

Timoteo. Madam, I believe you: but I would not have you say any more in this vein. There are many things which seen at a distance appear terrible, unbearable, strange; but when you come nearer to them they prove to be human, bearable, familiar; wherefore it is said that the fear is worse than the evil. And this is one of them.

Lucrezia. It's the will of God.

Timoteo. I'll go back to what I was saying at first. For the sake of your conscience you must go on this general principle: where there is a certain good and an uncertain evil, we must not forsake that good for fear of that evil. Here is a certain good, you will be with child. You will donate a soul to the Lord God. The uncertain evil is that he who lies with you after you've taken the potion, dies: but he will also find himself among those who will never die. But since the thing is dubious, it's right that Messer Nicia should run no risk. And if the act is sinful, it's only in a manner of speaking so after all, for the will is what sins, not the body: it's a sin on the grounds that it displeases your husband, and you please him: it's a sin on the grounds of taking pleasure in it, and you take no pleasure in it. Moreover the end is what you must consider in every case. Your end is to fill a seat in Paradise, to make your husband happy. The Bible says that the daughters of Lot, believing that they alone were left in the world, consorted with their father; and since their intention was good they did not sin.

Lucrezia. What would you persuade me to?

Sostrata. Let yourself be persuaded, daughter. Don't you see that a woman who has no children has no home? When her husband is dead she remains, like a beast, deserted by everyone.

Timoteo. I swear to you, Madam, by the holy sacrament, that your duty in this case is to obey your husband, though it were to eat meat on Wednesdays; which is a sin that no holy water can wash away.

Lucrezia. Where are you pushing me, father?

Timoteo.   I'm urging you to things that you'll ask God to bless me for, and that next year you'll value more than now.

Sostrata.   She'll do what you wish. I'll put her to bed myself to-night. What are you afraid of, idiot? There are fifty women in this land who would lift their hands to heaven for this that you'll be getting.

Lucrezia.   I consent; but I don't expect to be alive tomorrow morning.

Timoteo.   Have no fear, my daughter: I will pray God for you; I will say a prayer to the angel Rafael to be at your side. Go quickly and prepare for this mystery that the night will bring.

Sostrata.   Rest in peace, father.

Lucrezia.   God and Our Lady keep me from harm.

Everything ends happily for everyone. Callimaco arranges that he is the young man who is kidnapped and put to bed with Lucrezia. He suffers no ill effect from the mandrake, and he pleases Lucrezia so much that she decides to take him as a permanent lover. Nicia remains contentedly ignorant of the affair. One is left with a reasonable hope that Lucrezia's infertility will be overcome.

RENAISSANCE STATECRAFT

Machiavelli (1469–1527) presented an amoral science of politics—the end proposed was simply to win and hold power by any effective means. Toward 1500 monarchs in various parts of Europe practiced a calculating statecraft in consolidating their kingdoms.

Italy: Prince and State

From Machiavelli. *The Prince*

It now remains for us to consider what ought to be the conduct and bearing of a Prince in relation to his subjects and friends. And since I know that many have written on this subject, I fear it may be thought presumptuous in me to write of it also: the more so, because in my treatment of it I depart from the views that others have taken.

But since it is my object to write what shall be useful to whosoever understands it, it seems to me better to follow the real truth of things than an imaginary view of them. For many Republics and Princedoms have been imagined that were never seen or known to exist in reality. And the manner in which we live, and that in which we ought to live, are things so wide asunder, that he who quits the one to betake himself to the other is more likely to destroy than to save himself; since any one who would act up to a perfect standard of goodness in everything, must be ruined among so many who are not good. It is essential, therefore, for a Prince who desires to maintain his position, to have learned how to be other than good, and to use or not to use his goodness as necessity requires.

Beginning, then, with the first of the qualities above noticed, I say that it may be a good thing to be reputed liberal, but, nevertheless, that liberality without the reputation of it is hurtful; because, though it be worthily and rightly used, still if it be not known, you escape not the reproach of its opposite vice. Hence, to have credit for liberality with the world at large, you must neglect no circumstance of sumptuous display; the result being, that a Prince of a liberal disposition will consume his whole substance in things of this sort, and, after all, be obliged, if he would maintain his reputation for liberality, to burden his subjects with extraordinary taxes, and to resort to confiscations and all the other shifts whereby money is raised. But in this way he becomes hateful to his subjects, and growing impoverished is held in little esteem by

From Niccolo Machiavelli, *The Prince*, N. Thompson, trans. (Oxford: Oxford University Press, 1897), pp. 109–110, 113–115, 118–119, 125–130.

any. So that in the end, having by his liberality offended many and obliged few, he is worse off than when he began, and is exposed to all his original dangers. Recognizing this, and endeavouring to retrace his steps, he at once incurs the infamy of miserliness.

A Prince, therefore, since he cannot without injury to himself practise the virtue of liberality so that it may be known, will not, if he be wise, greatly concern himself though he be called miserly. Because in time he will come to be regarded as more and more liberal, when it is seen that through his parsimony his revenues are sufficient; that he is able to defend himself against any who make war on him; that he can engage in enterprises against others without burdening his subjects; and thus exercise liberality towards all from whom he does not take, whose number is infinite, while he is miserly in respect of those only to whom he does not give, whose number is few.

Passing to the other qualities above referred to, I say that every Prince should desire to be accounted merciful and not cruel. Nevertheless, he should be on his guard against the abuse of this quality of mercy. Cesare Borgia was reputed cruel, yet his cruelty restored Romagna, united it, and brought it to order and obedience; so that if we look at things in their true light, it will be seen that he was in reality far more merciful than the people of Florence, who, to avoid the imputation of cruelty, suffered Pistoja to be torn to pieces by factions.

A Prince should therefore disregard the reproach of being thought cruel where it enables him to keep his subjects united and obedient. For he who quells disorder by a very few signal examples will in the end be more merciful than he who from too great leniency permits things to take their course and so to result in rapine and bloodshed; for these hurt the whole State, whereas the severities of the Prince injure individuals only.

A Prince should, therefore, understand how to use well both the man and the beast. And this lesson has been covertly taught by the ancient writers, who relate how Achilles and many others of these old Princes were given over to be brought up and trained by Chiron the Centaur; since the only meaning of their having for instructor one who was half man and half beast is, that it is necessary for a Prince to know how to use both natures, and that the one without the other has no stability.

But since a Prince should know how to use the beast's nature wisely, he ought of beasts to choose both the lion and the fox; for the lion cannot guard himself from the toils, nor the fox from wolves. He must therefore be a fox to discern toils, and a lion to drive off wolves.

To rely wholly on the lion is unwise; and for this reason a prudent Prince neither can nor ought to keep his word when to keep it is hurtful to him and the causes which led him to pledge it are removed. If all men were good, this would not be good advice, but since they are dishonest, and do not keep faith with you, you, in return, need not keep faith with them; and no Prince was ever at a loss for plausible reasons to cloak a breach of faith. Of this numberless recent instances could be given, and it might be shown how many solemn treaties and engagements have been rendered inoperative and idle through want of faith in Princes, and that he who has best known to play the fox has had the best success.

It is necessary, indeed, to put a good colour on this nature, and to be skilful in simulating and dissembling. But men are so simple, and governed so absolutely by their present needs, that he who wishes to deceive will never fail in finding willing dupes. One recent example I will not omit. Pope Alexander VI had no care or thought but how to deceive, and always found material to work on. No man ever had a more effective manner of asseverating, or made promises with more solemn protestations, or observed them less. And yet, because he understood this side of human nature, his frauds always succeeded.

It is not essential, then, that a Prince should have all the good qualities which I have enumerated above, but it is most essential that he should seem to have them; I will even venture to affirm that if he has and invariably practises them all, they are hurtful, whereas the appearance of having them is useful. Thus, it is well to seem merciful, faithful, humane, religious, and upright, and also to be so; but the mind should remain so balanced that were it needful not to be so, you should be able and know how to change to the contrary.

And you are to understand that a Prince, and most of all a new Prince, cannot observe all those rules of conduct in respect whereof men are accounted good, being often forced, in order to preserve his Princedom, to act in opposition to good faith, charity, humanity, and religion. He must therefore keep his mind ready to shift as the winds and tides of Fortune turn, and, as I have already said, he ought not to quit good courses if he can help it, but should know how to follow evil courses if he must.

A Prince should therefore be very careful that nothing ever escapes his lips which is not replete with the five qualities above named, so that to see and hear him, one would think him the embodiment of mercy, good faith, integrity, humanity, and religion. And there is no virtue which it is more necessary for him to seem to possess than this last; because men in general judge rather by the eye than by the hand, for every one can see but few can touch. Every one sees what you seem, but few know what you are, and these few dare not oppose themselves to the opinion of the many who have the majesty of the State to back them up.

Moreover, in the actions of all men, and most of all of Princes, where there is no tribunal to which we can appeal, we look to results. Wherefore if a prince succeeds in establishing and maintaining his authority, the means will always be judged honourable and be approved by every one. For the vulgar are always taken by appearances and by results, and the world is made up of the vulgar, the few only finding room when the many have no longer ground to stand on.

France: Louis XI

From *Memoirs of Commynes*

It may be urged that other princes have been more given to suspicion than he, but it was not in our time; and, perhaps, their wisdom was not so eminent, nor were their subjects so good. They might too, probably, have been tyrants, and bloody-minded; but our king never did any person a mischief who had not offended him first, though I do not say all who offended him deserved death. I have not recorded these things merely to represent our master as a suspicious and mistrustful prince; but . . . that those princes who may be his successors, may learn by his example to be more tender and indulgent to their subjects, and less severe in their punishments than our master had been: although I will not censure him, or say I ever saw a better prince; for though he oppressed his subjects himself, he would never see them injured by anybody else. . . .

I knew him, and was entertained in his service in the flower of his age, and at the height of his prosperity, yet I never saw him free from labour and care. Of all diversions he loved hunting and hawking in their seasons; but his chief delight was in dogs. As for ladies, he never meddled with any in my time; for about the time of my coming to his court he lost a son, at whose death he was extremely afflicted, and he made a vow to God in my presence never to have intercourse with any other woman but the queen; and though this was no more than what he was bound to do by the canons of the church, yet it was much that his self-command should be so great, that he should be able to persevere in his resolution so firmly, considering that the queen (though an excellent princess in other respects) was not a person in whom a man could take any great delight. . . .

When his body was at rest his mind was at work, for he had affairs in several places at once, and would concern himself as much in those of his neighbours as in his own, putting officers of his own over all the great families, and endeavouring to divide their authority as much as possible. When he was at war he laboured for a peace or a truce, and when he had obtained it, he was impatient for war again. He troubled

From A. R. Scoble, ed., *The Memoirs of Philip de Commynes* (London: Henry G. Bohn, 1856), pp. 79–82.

himself with many trifles in his government, which he had better have let alone: but it was his temper, and he could not help it; besides, he had a prodigious memory, and he forgot nothing, but knew everybody, as well in other countries as in his own.

And, in truth, he seemed better fitted to rule a world than to govern a single kingdom.

England: Henry VII

From *Bacon's Life of Henry VII*

With his justice, he was also a merciful prince: as in whose time, there were but three of the nobility that suffered; the earl of Warwick, the lord chamberlain, and the lord Audley: . . . there were never so great rebellions, expiated with so little blood, drawn by the hand of justice, as the two rebellions of Blackheath and Exeter. As for the severity used upon those which were taken in Kent, it was but upon a scum of people. His pardons went ever both before and after his sword. But then he had withal a strange kind of interchanging of large and inexpected pardons, with severe executions: which, his wisdom considered, could not be imputed to any inconstancy or inequality; but either to some reason which we do not now know, or to a principle he had set unto himself, that he would vary, and try both ways in turn. But the less blood he drew, the more he took of treasure. And, as some construed it, he was the more sparing in the one, that he might be the more pressing in the other; for both would have been intolerable. Of nature assuredly he coveted to accumulate treasure. . . . This excess of his had at that time many glosses and interpretations. Some thought the continual rebellions wherewith he had been vexed, had made him grow to hate his people: some thought it was done to pull down their stomachs, and to keep them low: some, for that he would leave his son a golden fleece: some suspected he had some high design upon foreign parts: but those perhaps shall come nearest the truth, that fetch not their reasons so far off; but rather impute it to nature, age, peace, and a mind fixed upon no other ambition or pursuit. Whereunto I should add, that having every day occasion to take notice of the necessities and shifts for money of other great Princes abroad, it did the better, by comparison, set off to him the felicity of full coffers. As to his expending of treasure, he never spared charge which his affairs required; and in his buildings was magnificent, but his rewards were very limited: so

From J. R. Lumby, ed., *Bacon's Life of Henry VII* (Cambridge: Cambridge University Press, 1889), pp. 213–218.

that his liberality was rather upon his own state and memory than upon the deserts of others.

He was of an high mind, and loved his own will and his own way: as one that revered himself and would reign indeed. Had he been a private man, he would have been termed proud. But in a wise Prince, it was but keeping of distance, which indeed he did towards all; not admitting any near or full approach, either to his power, or to his secrets: for he was governed by none. His Queen, notwithstanding she had presented him with divers children, and with a crown also, though he would not acknowledge it, could do nothing with him. His mother he reverenced much, heard little. . . .

To his council he did refer much, and sat oft in person; knowing it to be the way to assist his power, and inform his judgment. In which respect also he was fairly patient of liberty, both of advice, and of vote, till himself were declared. He kept a strait hand on his nobility, and chose rather to advance clergymen and lawyers, which were more obsequious to him, but had less interest in the people; which made for his absoluteness, but not for his safety. Insomuch as, I am persuaded, it was one of the causes of his troublesome reign; for that his nobles, though they were loyal and obedient, yet did not co-operate with him, but let every man go his own way. He was not afraid of an able man, as Lewis the eleventh was: but contrariwise, he was served by the ablest men that were to be found; without which his affairs could not have prospered as they did. . . . Neither did he care how cunning they were that he did employ; for he thought himself to have the master-reach. And as he chose well, so he held them up well; for it is a strange thing, that though he were a dark prince, and infinitely suspicious, and his times full of secret conspiracies and troubles; yet in twenty-four years' reign, he never put down, or discomposed counsellor, or near servant, save only Stanley the lord chamberlain. As for the disposition of his subjects in general towards him, it stood thus with him; that of the three affections which naturally tie the hearts of the subjects to their sovereigns, love, fear, and reverence; he had the last in height, the second in good measure, and so little of the first, as he was beholden to the other two.

He was a Prince, sad, serious, and full of thoughts, and secret observations, and full of notes and memorials of his own hand, especially touching persons. As, whom to employ, whom to reward, whom to inquire of, whom to beware of, what were the dependencies, what were the factions, and the like; keeping, as it were, a journal of his thoughts. There is to this day a merry tale; that his monkey, set on as it was thought by one of his chamber, tore his principal notebook all to pieces, when by chance it lay forth: whereat the court, which liked not those pensive accounts, was almost tickled with sport.

XI

NORTHERN HUMANISTS
Papal Failings
From Erasmus. *In Praise of Folly*
Religion in Utopia
From Thomas More. *Utopia*
Germany and Rome
From *Wimpheling's Response*

MARTIN LUTHER
Luther as Monk
From *Luther's Table Talk*
The Break With Rome
From *Tetzel's Sermon*
From *The Ninety-Five Theses (1517)*
From *Disputation Against Scholastic
    Theology*
From *Address to the Christian
    Nobility of the German Nation*
From *Luther's Speech at Worms*
Celibacy and Marriage
From *What Luther Says*

DEVELOPMENTS OF
PROTESTANT THOUGHT
Switzerland and France
Zwingli on the Eucharist
From John Calvin. *Institutes of the
    Christian Religion*
Scotland and England
From John Knox. *The Book of
    Discipline*
From *The Thirty-Nine Articles*

THE CATHOLIC
REFORMATION
Doctrine Reaffirmed
From *Decrees of the Council of Trent*
Religious Reformers
From Ignatius Loyola. *The Spiritual
    Exercises*
From Teresa of Avila. *The Way of
    Perfection*

REFORMATION AND
POLITICS
Germany
From *Twelve Articles of the Peasants*
From Charles V. *Abdication Speech*
Peace of Augsburg (1555)
France
*St. Bartholomew's Day Massacre
Edict of Nantes*

REFORMATIONS—PROTESTANT AND CATHOLIC

MANY ELEMENTS CONTRIBUTED to the religious upheavals of the sixteenth century. As the peoples of Europe grew into self-conscious nations, it became more difficult for them to remain united in a single religious organization. Resentment against Rome's taxation and jurisdiction increased. The papacy itself became worldly and corrupt.

Perhaps a reform movement would have arisen in any case. But the particular kind of "Reformation" that occurred was shaped by the religious experience of a particular individual, a German monk, Martin Luther (1483–1546). Luther strove to be a good monk but he became convinced that he could not find salvation through his own "good works." After a period of near-despair he came to believe that he was saved, not through any merit of his own, but through the freely given grace of Christ. On the basis of this insight Luther built a whole structure of Lutheran theology, opposed at many points to Catholic doctrine (which emphasized the mediating role of priests and sacraments in man's salvation). Other Protestant reformers assimilated elements of Luther's teaching into their own systems of thought.

The Protestant Reformation in the north was matched by a surge of religious vitality in the Catholic lands of central and southern Europe. The Council of Trent (1545–1563) reformed long-standing abuses; Ignatius Loyola founded the immensely influential new order of Jesuits; great saints like Teresa of Avila led reform movements in the old monastic orders. Although all the reformers intended to revitalize the church, not to divide it, one effect of their work was to create permanent religious cleavages that profoundly influenced the subsequent cultural and political history of Europe.

NORTHERN HUMANISTS

Papal Failings

Many writers who never chose to become Protestants criticized the state of the church on the eve of the Reformation.

From Erasmus. *In Praise of Folly*

Now as to the popes of Rome, who pretend themselves Christ's vicars, if they would but imitate his exemplary life, in the being employed in an unintermitted course of preaching; in the being attended with poverty, nakedness, hunger, and a contempt of this world; if they did but consider the import of the word pope, which signifies a father; or if they did but practice their surname of most holy, what order or degrees of men would be in a worse condition? There would be then no such vigorous making of parties, and buying of votes, in the conclave upon a vacancy of that see: and those who by bribery, or other indirect courses, should get themselves elected, would never secure their sitting firm in the chair by pistol, poison, force, and violence.

How much of their pleasure would be abated if they were but endowed with one dram of wisdom? Wisdom, did I say? Nay, with one grain of that salt which our Saviour bid them not lose the savour of. All their riches, all their honour, their jurisdictions, their Peter's patrimony, their offices, their dispensations, their licences, their indulgences, their long train and attendants (see in how short a compass I have abbreviated all their marketing of religion); in a word, all their perquisites would be forfeited and lost; and in their room would succeed watchings, fastings, tears, prayers, sermons, hard studies, repenting sighs, and a thousand such like severe penalties: nay, what's yet more deplorable, it would then follow, that all their clerks, amanuenses, notaries, advocates, proctors, secretaries, the offices of grooms, ostlers, serving-men, pimps (and somewhat else, which for modesty's sake I shall not mention); in short, all these troops of attendants, which depend on his holiness, would all lose their several employments. This indeed would be hard, but what yet remains would be more dreadful: the very Head of the Church, the spiritual prince, would then be brought from all his splendour to the poor equipage of a scrip and

From Erasmus, *In Praise of Folly* (London: Reeves and Turner, 1876), pp. 156–160.

staff. But all this is upon the supposition only that they understood what circumstances they are placed in; whereas now, by a wholesome neglect of thinking, they live as well as heart can wish. . . .

They think to satisfy that Master they pretend to serve, our Lord and Saviour, with their great state and magnificence, with the ceremonies of instalments, with the titles of reverence and holiness, and with exercising their episcopal function only in blessing and cursing. The working of miracles is old and out-dated; to teach the people is too laborious; to interpret scripture is to invade the prerogative of the schoolmen; to pray is too idle; to shed tears is cowardly and unmanly; to fast is too mean and sordid; to be easy and familiar is beneath the grandeur of him, who, without being sued to and intreated, will scarce give princes the honour of kissing his toe; finally, to die for religion is too self-denying; and to be crucified as their Lord of Life, is base and ignominious.

[They claim as Peter's] inheritance, fields, towns, treasures, and large dominions; for the defending whereof, inflamed with a holy zeal, they fight with fire and sword, to the great loss and effusion of Christian blood, thinking they are apostolical maintainers of Christ's spouse, the church, when they have murdered all such as they call her enemies; though indeed the church has no enemies more bloody and tyrannical than such impious popes, who give dispensations for the not preaching of Christ; evacuate the main effect and design of our redemption by their pecuniary bribes and sales; adulterate the gospel by their forced interpretations, and undermining traditions; and lastly, by their lusts and wickedness grieve the Holy Spirit, and make their Saviour's wounds to bleed anew.

Religion in Utopia

From Thomas More. *Utopia*

There are several sorts of religions, not only in different parts of the island, but even in every town; some worshipping the sun, others the moon, or one of the planets: some worship such men as have been eminent in former times for virtue, or glory, not only as ordinary deities, but as the supreme God: Yet the greater and wiser sort of them worship none of these, but adore one eternal, invisible, infinite, and incomprehensible Deity; as a Being that is far above all our apprehensions, that is spread over the whole universe, not by his bulk, but by his power and virtue: him they call the Father of all, and acknowledge

From Thomas More, *Utopia*, Gilbert Burnett, trans. (London: R. Chiswell, 1684).

that the beginnings, the encrease, the progress, the vicissitudes, and the end of all things come only from him; nor do they offer divine honors to any but to him alone. And indeed, though they differ concerning other things, yet all agree in this; that they think there is one Supreme Being that made and governs the world, whom they call in the language of their country, Mithras. They differ in this, that one thinks the God whom he worships is this Supreme Being, and another thinks that his idol is that God; but they all agree in one principle that whoever is this Supreme Being, he is also that great essence, to whose glory and majesty all honors are ascribed by the consent of all nations. . . .

After they had heard from us, an account of the doctrine, the course of life, and the miracles of Christ, and of the wonderful constancy of so many martyrs, whose blood, so willingly offered up by them, was the chief occasion of spreading their religion over a vast number of nations, it is not to be imagined how inclined they were to receive it. I shall not determine whether this proceeded from any secret inspiration of God, or whether it was because it seemed so favorable to that community of goods, which is an opinion so particular, as well as so dear to them; since they perceived that Christ and his followers lived by that rule: and that it was still kept up in some communities among the sincerest sort of Christians. From whichsoever of these motives it might be, true it is that many of them came over to our religion, and were initiated into it by baptism. But as two of our number were dead, so none of the four that survived, were in priests orders; we therefore could only baptize them; so that to our great regret, they could not partake of the other sacraments, that can only be administered by priests: But they are instructed concerning them, and long most vehemently for them. They have had great disputes among themselves, whether one chosen by them to be a priest would not be thereby qualified to do all the things that belong to that character, even though he had no authority derived from the pope; and they seemed to be resolved to choose some for that employment, but they had not done it when I left them.

Those among them that have not received our religion, do not fright any from it, and use none ill that goes over to it; so that all the while I was there, one man was only punished on this occasion. He being newly baptized, did, notwithstanding all that we could say to the contrary, dispute publickly concerning the Christian religion, with more zeal than discretion; and with so much heat, that he not only preferred our worship to theirs, but condemned all their rights as profane; and cried out against all that adhered to them, as impious and sacrilegious persons, that were to be damned to everlasting burnings. Upon his having frequently preached in this manner, he was seized, and after trial, he was condemned to banishment, not for having disparaged their religion, but for his inflaming the people to sedition: for this is one of their most ancient laws, that no man ought to be punished for his religion. At the first constitution of their government, Utopus having understood that, before his coming among them, the old inhabitants had been engaged in great quarrels concerning religion, by which they were so divided among themselves that he found it an easy thing to conquer them, since instead of uniting their forces against him, every different party in religion fought by themselves: after he had subdued them, he made a law that every man might be of what religion he pleased, and might endeavor to draw others to it by the force of argument, and by amicable and modest ways, but without bitterness against those of other opinions; but that he ought to use no other force but that of persuasion; and was neither to mix with it reproaches nor violence; and such as did otherwise were to be condemned to banishment or slavery.

This law was made by Utopus, not only for preserving the public peace, which he saw suffered much by daily contentions and irreconcilable heats, but because he thought the interest of religion itself required it. He judged it not fit to determine any thing rashly; and seemed to doubt whether those different forms of religion might not all come from God, who might inspire men in a different manner, and be pleased with this variety; he therefore thought it indecent and foolish for any man to threaten and terrify another to make him believe what did not appear to him to be true. And supposing that only one religion was really true, and the rest false, he imagined that the native force of truth would at last break forth and shine bright, if supported only by the strength of argument, and attended to with a gentle and unprejudiced mind; while, on the other hand, if such debates were carried on with violence and tumults, as the most wicked are always the most obstinate, so the best and most holy religion, might be choked with superstition, as corn is with briars and thorns; he therefore left men wholly to their liberty, that they might be free to believe as they should see cause. . . .

Germany and Rome

In 1515, Jacob Wimpheling, a German humanist, wrote this "Response" to a treatise on Germany by Enea Silvio Piccolomini (who became Pope Pius II).

From *Wimpheling's Response*

Enea makes much of the fact that we Germans received our Christian faith from his compatriots. "Rome," he writes, "preached Christ to

From Gerald Strauss, trans., *Manifestations of Discontent in Germany on the Eve of the Reformation* (Bloomington, Ind.: Indiana University Press, 1971), pp. 42–43. Reprinted by permission of the publisher.

you; it was faith in Christ, received from Rome, that extinguished barbarism in you." We concede, of course, that missionaries from Rome brought the saving message of Christ to our land. But by the same token Rome herself was, like Germany, converted to the Christian faith, and Rome should therefore show no less gratitude than Germany for the reception of her faith. For was it not Peter, a Jew from Palestine, who preached the Gospel of Christ in Rome? If Enea's argument were applied to the Romans themselves, they would now be obliged to send annual tributes of gold and silver to Syria. . . .

It is not that we deny our debt to Rome. But we ask: Is Rome not also indebted to us? Have not two of our compatriots, clever and skillful men hailing from Strassburg and Mainz, invented the noble art of printing, which makes it possible to propagate the correct doctrines of faith and morals throughout the world and in all languages? . . . Do we, who have been true and industrious in our service to religion and to the Holy Roman Church, who are steadfast in our faith and even—as Enea admits—prepared to shed our blood for it, who willingly obey orders, buy indulgences, travel to Rome, and send money—do we who perform all these duties deserve to be called barbarians? . . . Despite this slanderous label, Enea speaks with lavish praise of our fatherland, of our cities and buildings. For what purpose? For one only: to make our ears more receptive to the demands coming from Rome dressed in Christian garb but serving Italian interests; in other words, to put us in the mood for wasting our fortunes on foreigners. . . . As it is, our compatriots crowd the road to Rome. They pay for papal reservations and dispensations. They appear before papal courts—and not always because they have appealed a case to Rome, but rather because their cases have been arbitrarily transferred there. Is there a nation more patient and willing to receive indulgences, though we well know that the income from them is divided between the Holy See and its officialdom? Have we not paid dearly for the confirmation of every bishop and abbot? . . .

Thus we are done out of fortune, and for no purpose other than to support the innumerable retainers and hangers-on that populate the papal court. Enea himself gives us a list of these papal lackeys, the number of which increases daily. True, if the pope must furnish court rooms for all the legal business in Christendom, he requires a huge staff. But there is no need for this. Apart from imperial courts, there exist in our German cities learned and honorable judges to whom appeals from lower episcopal courts could be directed. It is in the highest degree objectionable that Rome bypasses courts of higher resort—often on trivial pretexts or out of pique—and compels our compatriots, laymen included, to appear in Rome.

MARTIN LUTHER

Luther as Monk

In casual conversations—recorded by his friends—Luther often referred to the stages of his religious development.

From *Luther's Table Talk*

I, Martin Luther, entered the monastery against the will of my father and lost favor with him, for he saw through the knavery of the monks very well. On the day on which I sang my first mass he said to me, "Son, don't you know that you ought to honor your father?" . . . Later when I stood there during the mass and began the canon, I was so frightened that I would have fled if I hadn't been admonished by the prior. For when I read the words, "Thee, therefore, most merciful Father," etc., and thought I had to speak to God without a Mediator, I felt like fleeing from the world like Judas. Who can bear the majesty of God without Christ as Mediator? In short, as a monk I experienced such horrors; I had to experience them before I could fight them.

When I was a monk I was unwilling to omit any of the prayers, but when I was busy with public lecturing and writing I often accumulated my appointed prayers for a whole week, or even two or three weeks. Then I would take a Saturday off, or shut myself in for as long as three days without food and drink, until I had said the prescribed prayers. This made my head split, and as a consequence I couldn't close my eyes for five nights, lay sick unto death, and went out of my senses. Even after I had quickly recovered and I tried again to read, my head went 'round and 'round. Thus our Lord God drew me, as if by force, from that torment of prayers. . . .

I almost fasted myself to death, for again and again I went for three days without taking a drop of water or a morsel of food. I was very serious about it. I really crucified the Lord Christ. I wasn't simply an observer but helped to carry him and pierce [his hands and feet]. God forgive me for it, for I have confessed it openly! This is the truth: the

From *Luther's Works*, J. Pelikan and H. T. Lehmann, eds. (Philadelphia: Fortress Press, 1967), Vol. 54, pp. 85, 193–194, 234, 264–265, 339–340. Copyright © 1967 by Fortress Press. Reprinted by permission of Fortress Press.

most pious monk is the worst scoundrel. He denies that Christ is the mediator and highpriest and turns him into a judge.

The words "righteous" and "righteousness of God" struck my conscience like lightning. When I heard them I was exceedingly terrified. If God is righteous [I thought], he must punish. But when by God's grace I pondered, in the tower and heated room of this building, over the words, "He who through faith is righteous shall live" [Rom. 1:17] and "the righteousness of God" [Rom. 3:21], I soon came to the conclusion that if we, as righteous men, ought to live from faith and if the righteousness of God should contribute to the salvation of all who believe, then salvation won't be our merit but God's mercy. My spirit was thereby cheered. For it's by the righteousness of God that we're justified and saved through Christ. These words [which had before terrified me] now became more pleasing to me. The Holy Spirit unveiled the Scriptures for me in this tower.

God led us away from all this in a wonderful way; without my quite being aware of it he took me away from that game more than twenty years ago. How difficult it was at first when we journeyed toward Kemberg after All Saints' Day in the year 1517, when I first made up my mind to write against the crass errors of indulgences! Dr. Jerome Schurff advised against this: "You wish to write against the pope? What are you trying to do? It won't be tolerated!" I replied, "And if they have to tolerate it?" Presently Sylvester, master of the sacred palace, entered the arena, fulminating against me with this syllogism: "Whoever questions what the Roman church says and does is heretical. Luther questions what the Roman church says and does, and therefore [he is a heretic]." So it all began.

The Break With Rome

Luther was outraged by the preaching of the Dominican friar Tetzel.

From *Tetzel's Sermon*

You may obtain letters of safe conduct from the vicar of our Lord Jesus Christ, by means of which you are able to liberate your soul from the hands of the enemy, and convey it by means of contrition and

From J. H. Robinson and M. Whitcomb, eds., *University of Pennsylvania Translations and Reprints* (Philadelphia: University of Pennsylvania Press, 1902), Vol. 2, No. 6, pp. 9–10.

confession, safe and secure from all pains of Purgatory, into the happy kingdom. For know that in these letters are stamped and engraven all the merits of Christ's passion there laid bare. Consider, that for each and every mortal sin it is necessary to undergo seven years of penitence after confession and contrition, either in this life or in Purgatory.

How many mortal sins are committed in a day, how many in a week, how many in a month, how many in a year, how many in the whole course of life! They are well-nigh numberless, and those that commit them must needs suffer endless punishment in the burning pains of Purgatory.

But with these confessional letters you will be able at any time in life to obtain full indulgence for all penalties imposed upon you, in all cases except the four reserved to the Apostolic See. Therefore throughout your whole life, whenever you wish to make confession, you may receive the same remission, except in cases reserved to the Pope, and afterwards, at the hour of death, a full indulgence as to all penalties and sins, and your share of all spiritual blessings that exist in the church militant and all its members.

Do you not know that when it is necessary for anyone to go to Rome or undertake any other dangerous journey, he takes his money to a broker and gives a certain per cent—five or six or ten—in order that at Rome or elsewhere he may receive again his funds intact, by means of the letter of this same broker? Are you not willing, then, for the fourth part of a florin, to obtain these letters, by virtue of which you may bring, not your money, but your divine and immortal soul safe and sound into the land of Paradise?

From *The Ninety-Five Theses (1517)*

Out of love and zeal for truth and the desire to bring it to light, the following theses will be publicly discussed at Wittenberg under the chairmanship of the reverend father Martin Luther, Master of Arts and Sacred Theology and regularly appointed Lecturer on these subjects at that place. He requests that those who cannot be present to debate orally with us will do so by letter.

In the Name of Our Lord Jesus Christ. Amen.

1. When our Lord and Master Jesus Christ said, "Repent" [Matt. 4:17], he willed the entire life of believers to be one of repentance.

2. This word cannot be understood as referring to the sacrament of penance, that is, confession and satisfaction, as administered by the clergy.

From *Luther's Works*, J. Pelikan and H. T. Lehmann, eds. (Philadelphia: Fortress Press, 1957), Vol. 31, pp. 25–33. Copyright © 1957 by Fortress Press. Reprinted by permission of Fortress Press.

5. The pope neither desires nor is able to remit any penalties except those imposed by his own authority or that of the canons.

20. Therefore the pope, when he uses the words "plenary remission of all penalties," does not actually mean "all penalties," but only those imposed by himself.

21. Thus those indulgence preachers are in error who say that a man is absolved from every penalty and saved by papal indulgences.

27. They preach only human doctrines who say that as soon as the money clinks into the money chest, the soul flies out of purgatory.

50. Christians are to be taught that if the pope knew the exactions of the indulgence preachers, he would rather that the basilica of St. Peter were burned to ashes than built up with the skin, flesh, and bones of his sheep.

81. This unbridled preaching of indulgences makes it difficult even for learned men to rescue the reverence which is due the pope from slander or from the shrewd questions of the laity.

82. Such as: "Why does not the pope empty purgatory for the sake of holy love and the dire need of the souls that are there if he redeems an infinite number of souls for the sake of miserable money with which to build a church? The former reasons would be most just; the latter is most trivial."

94. Christians should be exhorted to be diligent in following Christ, their head, through penalties, death, and hell;

95. And thus be confident of entering into heaven through many tribulations rather than through the false security of peace.

In the same year that he wrote the Ninety-Five Theses, Luther was developing his doctrine of salvation by grace.

From *Disputation Against Scholastic Theology*

4. It is true that man, being a bad tree, can only will and do evil [Cf. Matt. 7:17–18].

5. It is false to state that man's inclination is free to choose between either of two opposites. Indeed, the inclination is not free, but captive. This is said in opposition to common opinion.

6. It is false to state that the will can by nature conform to correct precept.

7. As a matter of fact, without the grace of God the will produces an act that is perverse and evil.

From *Luther's Works*, J. Pelikan and H. T. Lehmann, eds. (Philadelphia: Fortress Press, 1957), Vol. 31, pp. 9–14. Copyright © 1957 by Fortress Press. Reprinted by permission of Fortress Press.

21. No act is done according to nature that is not an act of concupiscence against God.

22. Every act of concupiscence against God is evil and a fornication of the spirit.

29. The best and infallible preparation for grace and the sole means of obtaining grace is the eternal election and predestination of God.

30. On the part of man, however, nothing precedes grace except ill will and even rebellion against grace.

40. We do not become righteous by doing righteous deeds but, having been made righteous, we do righteous deeds. This in opposition to the philosophers.

41. Virtually the entire *Ethics* of Aristotle is the worst enemy of grace. This in opposition to the scholastics.

42. It is an error to maintain that Aristotle's statement concerning happiness does not contradict Catholic doctrine. This in opposition to the doctrine on morals.

50. Briefly, the whole Aristotle is to theology as darkness is to light. This in opposition to the scholastics.

67. It is by the grace of God that one does not lust or become enraged.

68. Therefore it is impossible to fulfil the law in any way without the grace of God.

69. As a matter of fact, it is more accurate to say that the law is destroyed by nature without the grace of God.

At first Luther hoped that the papacy would support his reform efforts. By 1520 he was moving toward an open break with Rome.

From *Address to the Christian Nobility of the German Nation*

The Romanists have very cleverly built three walls around themselves. Hitherto they have protected themselves by these walls in such a way that no one has been able to reform them. As a result, the whole of Christendom has fallen abominably.

In the first place, when pressed by the temporal power they have made decrees and declared that the temporal power had no jurisdiction over them, but that, on the contrary, the spiritual power is above the temporal. In the second place, when the attempt is made to reprove them with the Scriptures, they raise the objection that only the pope may interpret the Scriptures. In the third place, if threatened

From *Luther's Works*, J. Pelikan and H. T. Lehmann, eds. (Philadelphia: Fortress Press, 1966), Vol. 44, pp. 126–127, 129–130, 133–134, 136. Copyright © 1966 by Fortress Press. Reprinted by permission of Fortress Press.

with a council, their story is that no one may summon a council but the pope. . . .

May God help us, and give us just one of those trumpets with which the walls of Jericho were overthrown to blast down these walls of straw and paper in the same way and set free the Christian rods for the punishment of sin, [and] bring to light the craft and deceit of the devil, to the end that through punishment we may reform ourselves and once more attain God's favor.

Let us begin by attacking the first wall. It is pure invention that pope, bishop, priests, and monks are called the spiritual estate while princes, lords, artisans, and farmers are called the temporal estate. This is indeed a piece of deceit and hypocrisy. Yet no one need be intimidated by it, and for this reason: all Christians are truly of the spiritual estate, and there is no difference among them except that of office. Paul says in I Corinthians 12 [:12–13] that we are all one body, yet every member has its own work by which it serves the others. This is because we all have one baptism, one gospel, one faith, and are all Christians alike; for baptism, gospel, and faith alone make us spiritual and a Christian people. . . .

It follows from this argument that there is no true, basic difference between laymen and priests, princes and bishops, between religious and secular, except for the sake of office and work, but not for the sake of status. They are all of the spiritual estate, all are truly priests, bishops, and popes. But they do not all have the same work to do. Just as all priests and monks do not have the same work. This is the teaching of St. Paul in Romans 12 [:4–5] and I Corinthians 12 [:12] and in I Peter 2 [:9], as I have said above, namely, that we are all one body of Christ the Head, and all members one of another. Christ does not have two different bodies, one temporal, the other spiritual. There is but one Head and one body. . . .

The second wall is still more loosely built and less substantial. The Romanists want to be the only masters of Holy Scripture, although they never learn a thing from the Bible all their life long. They assume the sole authority for themselves, and, quite unashamed, they play about with words before our very eyes, trying to persuade us that the pope cannot err in matters of faith, regardless of whether he is righteous or wicked. Yet they cannot point to a single letter.[1] This is why so many heretical and un-Christian, even unnatural, ordinances stand in the canon law. But there is no need to talk about these ordinances at present. Since these Romanists think the Holy Spirit never leaves them, no matter how ignorant and wicked they are, they become bold and decree only what they want. And if what they claim were true, why have Holy Scripture at all? Of what use is Scripture? Let us burn the

[1]I.e., a single letter of Scripture to support their claim.

Scripture and be satisfied with the unlearned gentlemen at Rome who possess the Holy Spirit! And yet the Holy Spirit can be possessed only by pious hearts. If I had not read the words with my own eyes, I would not have believed it possible for the devil to have made such stupid claims at Rome, and to have won supporters for them. . . .

The third wall falls of itself when the first two are down. When the pope acts contrary to the Scriptures, it is our duty to stand by the Scriptures, to reprove him and to constrain him, according to the word of Christ, Matthew 18 [:15–17], "If your brother sins against you, go and tell it to him, between you and him alone; if he does not listen to you, then take one or two others with you; if he does not listen to them, tell it to the church; if he does not listen to the church, consider him a heathen." Here every member is commanded to care for every other. How much more should we do this when the member that does evil is responsible for the government of the church, and by his evil-doing is the cause of much harm and offense to the rest! But if I am to accuse him before the church, I must naturally call the church together.

The Romanists have no basis in Scripture for their claim that the pope alone has the right to call or confirm a council. This is just their own ruling, and it is only valid as long as it is not harmful to Christendom or contrary to the laws of God. Now when the pope deserves punishment, this ruling no longer obtains, for not to punish him by authority of a council is harmful to Christendom.

At the Council of Worms (1521), held in the presence of Emperor Charles V, Luther was ordered to renounce his "heresies."

From *Luther's Speech at Worms*

". . . Because I am a man and not God, I am not able to shield my books with any other protection than that which my Lord Jesus Christ himself offered for his teaching. When questioned before Annas about his teaching and struck by a servant, he said: 'If I have spoken wrongly, bear witness to the wrong' [John 18:19–23]. If the Lord himself, who knew that he could not err, did not refuse to hear testimony against his teaching, even from the lowliest servant, how much more ought I, who am the lowest scum and able to do nothing except err, desire and expect that somebody should want to offer testimony against my teaching! Therefore, I ask by the mercy of God, may your most serene majesty, most illustrious lordships, or anyone at all who is

From *Luther's Works*, J. Pelikan and H. T. Lehmann, eds. (Philadelphia: Fortress Press, 1958), Vol. 32, pp. 111–113. Copyright © 1958 by Fortress Press. Reprinted by permission of Fortress Press.

able, either high or low, bear witness, expose my errors, overthrowing them by the writings of the prophets and the evangelists. Once I have been taught I shall be quite ready to renounce every error, and I shall be the first to cast my books into the fire.

"From these remarks I think it is clear that I have sufficiently considered and weighed the hazards and dangers, as well as the excitement and dissensions aroused in the world as a result of my teachings, things about which I was gravely and forcefully warned yesterday. To see excitement and dissension arise because of the Word of God is to me clearly the most joyful aspect of all in these matters. For this is the way, the opportunity, and the result of the Word of God, just as He [Christ] said, 'I have not come to bring peace, but a sword. For I have come to set a man against his father, etc.' [Matt. 10:34–35]. Therefore, we ought to think how marvelous and terrible is our God in his counsels, lest by chance what is attempted for settling strife grows rather into an intolerable deluge of evils, if we begin by condemning the Word of God. And concern must be shown lest the reign of this most noble youth, Prince Charles (in whom after God is our great hope), become unhappy and inauspicious. I could illustrate this with abundant examples from Scripture—like Pharaoh, the king of Babylon, and the kings of Israel who, when they endeavored to pacify and strengthen their kingdoms by the wisest counsels, most surely destroyed themselves. For it is He who takes the wise in their own craftiness [Job 5:13] and overturns mountains before they know it [Job 9:5]. Therefore we must fear God. I do not say these things because there is a need of either my teachings or my warnings for such leaders as you, but because I must not withhold the allegiance which I owe my Germany. With these words I commend myself to your most serene majesty and to your lordships, humbly asking that I not be allowed through the agitation of my enemies, without cause, to be made hateful to you. I have finished."

When I had finished, the speaker for the emperor said, as if in reproach, that I had not answered the question, that I ought not call into question those things which had been condemned and defined in councils; therefore what was sought from me was not a horned response, but a simple one, whether or not I wished to retract.

Here I answered:

"Since then your serene majesty and your lordships seek a simple answer, I will give it in this manner, neither horned nor toothed: Unless I am convinced by the testimony of the Scriptures or by clear reason (for I do not trust either in the pope or in councils alone, since it is well known that they have often erred and contradicted themselves), I am bound by the Scriptures I have quoted and my conscience is captive to the Word of God. I cannot and I will not retract anything, since it is neither safe nor right to go against conscience.

"I cannot do otherwise, here I stand, may God help me, Amen."

Celibacy and Marriage

In several of his works Luther condemned the Catholic teaching on clerical celibacy. (He himself married a former nun who left her convent to become a Protestant.)

From *What Luther Says*

First, not every priest can do without a woman, not only on account of the weakness of the flesh but much more because of the needs of the household. If, then, he is to keep a woman, and the pope grants him permission to do so, but he may not have her in marriage, what is this but leaving a man and a woman alone and forbidding them to fall? It is like putting fire and straw together and commanding that there shall be neither smoke nor fire. Secondly, the pope has as little power to give this command as he has to forbid eating, drinking, the natural process of bodily elimination, or becoming fat. No one, therefore, is in duty bound to keep this commandment, and the pope is responsible for all the sins that are committed against this ordinance, for all the souls lost thereby, and for all the consciences thereby confused and tortured. Consequently, he undoubtedly has deserved long ago that someone should drive him out of the world, so many souls has he strangled with this devilish snare; although I hope that God has been more gracious to many of them at their end than the pope had been during their life. Nothing good has ever come out of the papacy and its laws, nor ever will.

Listen! In all my days I have not heard the confession of a nun, but in the light of Scripture I shall hit upon how matters fare with her and know I shall not be lying. If a girl is not sustained by great and exceptional grace, she can live without a man as little as she can without eating, drinking, sleeping, and other natural necessities. Nor, on the other hand, can a man dispense with a wife. The reason for this is that procreating children is an urge planted as deeply in human nature as eating and drinking. That is why God has given and put into the body the organs, arteries, fluxes, and everything that serves it. Therefore what is he doing who would check this process and keep nature from running its desired and intended course? He is attempting to keep nature from being nature, fire from burning, water from wetting, and a man from eating, drinking, and sleeping.

Whoever intends to enter married life should do so in faith and in God's name. He should pray God that it may prosper according to His

From *What Luther Says*, E. M. Plass, ed. (Saint Louis, Mo.: Concordia Publishing House, 1959), Vol. 2, pp. 888–889, 891. Copyright © 1959 by Concordia Publishing House. Reprinted by permission of the publisher.

will and that marriage may not be treated as a matter of fun and folly. It is a hazardous matter and as serious as anything on earth can be. Therefore we should not rush into it as the world does, in keeping with its frivolousness and wantonness and in pursuit of its pleasure; but before taking this step we should consult God, so that we may lead our married life to His glory. Those who do not go about it in this way may certainly thank God if it turns out well. If it turns out badly, they should not be surprised; for they did not begin it in the name of God and did not ask for His blessing.

DEVELOPMENTS OF PROTESTANT THOUGHT

Switzerland and France

Although they differed among themselves, all the Protestant reformers rejected the Catholic doctrine of transubstantiation in the Eucharist. Zwingli (1484–1531) was especially concerned with this question.

Zwingli on the Eucharist

I believe that in the holy Eucharist—i.e., the supper of thanksgiving— the true body of Christ is present by the contemplation of faith; i.e., that they who thank the Lord for the kindness conferred on us in His Son acknowledge that He assumed true flesh, in it truly suffered, truly washed away our sins in His own blood; and thus everything done by Christ becomes present to them by the contemplation of faith. But that the body of Christ in essence and really—i.e., the natural body itself— is either present in the supper or masticated with our mouth or teeth, as the Papists and some who long for the flesh-pots of Egypt assert, we not only deny, but firmly maintain is an error opposed to God's Word.

From S. M. Jackson, *Huldreich Zwingli* (New York: G. P. Putnam's Sons, 1900), p. 471.

John Calvin (1509–1564) emphasized especially predestination, vocation, and the need for rigorous church discipline.

From John Calvin. *Institutes of the Christian Religion*

If it be evidently the result of the Divine will, that salvation is freely offered to some, and others are prevented from attaining it; this immediately gives rise to important and difficult questions, which are incapable of any other explication, than by the establishment of pious minds in what ought to be received concerning election and predestination:—a question, in the opinion of many, full of perplexity; for they consider nothing more unreasonable, than that of the common mass of mankind some should be predestinated to salvation, and others to de-

From John Calvin, *Institutes of the Christian Religion*, J. Allen, trans. (London: T. Tegg and Son, 1838), Vol. 2, pp. 120–121, 128–129, 154–155, 365.

struction. But how unreasonably they perplex themselves will afterwards appear from the sequel of our discourse. Besides, the very obscurity which excites such dread, not only displays the utility of this doctrine, but shews it to be productive of the most delightful benefit. We shall never be clearly convinced as we ought to be, that our salvation flows from the fountain of God's free mercy, till we are acquainted with his eternal election, which illustrates the grace of God by this comparison, that he adopts not all promiscuously to the hope of salvation, but gives to some what he refuses to others. Ignorance of this principle evidently detracts from the Divine glory, and diminishes real humility. But according to Paul, what is so necessary to be known, never can be known, unless God, without any regard to works, chooses those whom he has decreed. "At this present time also, there is a remnant according to the election of grace. And if by grace, then it is no more of works: otherwise, grace is no more grace. . . ." [Romans 11:5–6]

In conformity, therefore, to the clear doctrine of the Scripture, we assert, that by an eternal and immutable counsel, God hath once for all determined, both whom he would admit to salvation, and whom he would condemn to destruction. We affirm that this counsel, as far as concerns the elect, is founded on his gratuitous mercy, totally irrespective of human merit: but that to those whom he devotes to condemnation, the gate of life is closed by a just and irreprehensible, but incomprehensible, judgment. In the elect, we consider calling as an evidence of election, and justification as another token of its manifestation, till they arrive in glory, which constitutes its completion. As God seals his elect by vocation and justification, so by excluding the reprobate from the knowledge of his name and the sanctification of his Spirit, he affords an indication of the judgment that awaits them. Here I shall pass over many fictions fabricated by foolish men to overthrow predestination. It is unnecessary to refute things which, as soon as they are advanced, sufficiently prove the falsehood.

But, in order to a further elucidation of the subject, it is necessary to treat of the calling of the elect, and of the blinding and hardening of the impious. On the former I have already made a few observations, with a view to refute the error of those who suppose the generality of the promises to belong equally to all mankind. But the discriminating election of God, which is otherwise concealed within himself, he manifests only by his calling, which may therefore with propriety be termed the testification or evidence of it. "For whom he did foreknow, he also did predestinate to the image of his Son. Moreover, whom he did predestinate, them he also called: and whom he called, them he also justified," in order to their essential glorification. [Romans 8:29–30] Though by choosing his people, the Lord hath adopted them as his children, yet we see that they enter not on the possession of so great a blessing till they are called; on the other hand, as soon as they are called, they immediately enjoy some communication of his election. On this account Paul calls the Spirit received by them both "the Spirit of adoption, and the seal and earnest of the future inheritance;" [Romans 8:15–16] because, by his testimony, he confirms and seals to their hearts the certainty of their future adoption. . . . Those whom God hath chosen, therefore, he designates as his children, and determines himself to be their Father. By calling, he introduces them into his family, and unites them to himself, that they may be one. By connecting calling with election, the Scripture evidently suggests, that nothing is requisite to it but the free mercy of God. For if we inquire whom he calls, and for what reason, the answer is, those whom he had elected. But when we come to election, we see nothing but mercy on every side.

If no society, and even no house, though containing only a small family, can be preserved in a proper state without discipline, this is far more necessary in the Church, the state of which ought to be the most orderly of all. As the saving doctrine of Christ is the soul of the Church, so discipline forms the ligaments which connect the members together, and keep each in its proper place. Whoever, therefore, either desire the abolition of all discipline, or obstruct its restoration, whether they act from design or inadvertency, they certainly promote the entire dissolution of the Church. For what will be the consequence, if every man be at liberty to follow his own inclinations? But such would be the case, unless the preaching of the doctrine were accompanied with private admonitions, reproofs, and other means to enforce the doctrine, and prevent it from being altogether ineffectual. Discipline, therefore, serves as a bridle to curb and restrain the refractory, who resist the doctrine of Christ; or as a spur to stimulate the inactive; and sometimes as a father's rod, with which those who have grievously fallen may be chastised in mercy with the gentleness of the Spirit of Christ.

Scotland and England

John Knox described the practice of church discipline in the Calvinist churches of Scotland.

From John Knox. *The Book of Discipline*

As that no Commonwealth can flourish or long endure without good laws, and sharp execution of the same, so neither can the Church of God be brought to purity, neither yet be retained in the same, without the order of Ecclesiastical Discipline, which stands in reproving and

From John Knox, *History of the Reformation in Scotland* (London: Thomas Nelson and Sons, 1949), Vol. 2, pp. 306–309. Reprinted courtesy of Thomas Nelson and Sons Ltd.

correcting of those faults which the civil sword doth either neglect, either may not punish. Blasphemy, adultery, murder, perjury, and other crimes capital, worthy of death, ought not properly to fall under censure of the Church; because all such open transgressors of God's laws ought to be taken away by the civil sword. But drunkenness, excess (be it in apparel, or be it in eating and drinking), fornication, oppression of the poor by exactions, deceiving of them in buying or selling by wrong mete or measure, wanton words and licencious living tending to slander, do properly appertain to the Church of God, to punish the same as God's word commandeth.

But because this accursed Papistry hath brought in such confusion in the world, that neither was virtue rightly praised, neither vice severely punished, the Church of God is compelled to draw the sword, which of God she hath received, against such open and manifest offenders, cursing and excommunicating all such, as well those whom the civil sword ought to punish as the others, from all participation with her in prayers and sacraments, till open repentance manifestly appear in them. As the order of Excommunication and proceeding to the same ought to be grave and slow, so, being once pronounced against any person, of what estate and condition that ever they be, it must be kept with all severity. For laws made and not kept engendereth contempt of virtue and brings in confusion and liberty to sin. And therefore this order we think expedient to be observed before and after excommunication.

First, if the offence be secret and known to few, and rather stands in suspicion than in manifest probation, the offender ought to be privately admonished to abstain from all appearance of evil; which, if he promises to do, and to declare himself sober, honest, and one that feareth God, and feareth to offend his brethren, then may the secret admonition suffice for his correction. But if he either contemn the admonition, or, after promise made, do show himself no more circumspect than he was before, then must the Minister admonish him; to whom if he be found inobedient, they must proceed according to the rule of Christ, as after shall be declared.

If the crime be public, and such as is heinous, as fornication, drunkenness, fighting, common swearing, or execration, then ought the offender to be called in the presence of the Minister, Elders, and Deacons, where his sin and offence ought to be declared and agredged, so that his conscience may feel how far he hath offended God, and what slander he hath raised in the Church. If signs of unfeigned repentance appear to him, and if he require to be admitted to public repentance, the Ministry may appoint unto him a day when the whole Church conveneth together, that in presence of all he may testify the repentance which before them he professed. Which, if he accept, and with reverence do, confessing his sin, and damning the same, and earnestly desiring the Congregation to pray to God with him for mercy, and to accept him in their society, notwithstanding his former offence, then the

Church may, and ought [to] receive him as a penitent. [If the sinner did not repent he was to be excommunicated.]

After which sentence may no person (his wife and family only excepted) have any kind of conversation with him, be it in eating and drinking, buying or selling, yea, in saluting or talking with him, except that it be at the commandment or licence of the Ministry for his conversion; that he by such means confounded, seeing himself abhorred of the faithful and godly, may have occasion to repent and be so saved. The sentence of his Excommunication must be published universally throughout the Realm, lest that any man should pretend ignorance.

His children begotten or born after that sentence and before his repentance, may not be admitted to baptism, till either they be of age to require the same, or else that the mother, or some of his especial friends, members of the Church, offer and present the child, abhorring and damning the iniquity and obstinate contempt of the impenitent. If any think it severe that the child should be punished for the iniquity of the father, let them understand that the sacraments appertain only to the faithful and to their seed: But such as stubbornly contemn all godly admonition, and obstinately remain in their iniquity, cannot be accounted amongst the faithful.

The Church of England, although it adopted some central Protestant doctrines, retained more Catholic usages than the other reformed churches. The Thirty-Nine Articles (1562) emphasized the right of each church to choose its own practices and the role of the queen as head of the Church of England.

From *The Thirty-Nine Articles*

Of the Authority of the Church

The Church hath power to decree Rites or Ceremonies, and authority in Controversies of Faith: And yet it is not lawful for the Church to ordain any thing that is contrary to God's Word written, neither may it so expound one place of Scripture, that it be repugnant to another. Wherefore, although the Church be a witness and a keeper of holy Writ, yet, as it ought not to decree any thing against the same, so besides the same ought it not to enforce any thing to be believed for necessity of Salvation.

Of the Traditions of the Church

It is not necessary that Traditions and Ceremonies be in all places one, or utterly like; for at all times they have been divers, and may be

From *Articles Agreed Upon by the Archbishops and Bishops, 1562* (London: R. Barker, 1631).

changed according to the diversities of countries, times, and men's manners, so that nothing be ordained against God's Word. Whosoever through his private judgment, willingly and purposely, doth openly break the traditions and ceremonies of the Church, which be not repugnant to the Word of God, and be ordained and approved by common authority, ought to be rebuked openly (that others may fear to do the like) as he that offendeth against the common order of the Church, and hurteth the authority of the Magistrate, and woundeth the consciences of the weak brethren.

Every particular or national Church hath authority to ordain, change, and abolish, ceremonies or rites of the Church ordained only by man's authority, so that all things be done to edifying.

Of the Civil Magistrates

The Queen's Majesty hath the chief power in this Realm of England and other her Dominious, unto whom the chief Government of all Estates of this Realm, whether they be Ecclesiastical or Civil, in all causes doth appertain, and is not, nor ought to be, subject to any foreign Jurisdiction.

Where we attribute to the Queen's Majesty the chief government, by which Titles we understand the minds of some slanderous folks to be offended; we give not to our Princes the ministering either of God's Word, or of the Sacraments, the which thing the Injunctions also lately set forth by Elizabeth our Queen do most plainly testify; but that only prerogative, which we see to have been given always to all godly Princes in holy Scriptures, by God himself; that is, that they should rule all estates and degrees committed to their charge by God, whether they be Ecclesiastical or Temporal, and restrain with the civil sword the stubborn and evildoers.

The Bishop of Rome hath no jurisdiction in this Realm of England.

The Laws of the Realm may punish Christian men with death, for heinous and grievous offences.

It is lawful for Christian men, at the commandment of the Magistrate, to wear weapons, and serve in the wars.

THE CATHOLIC REFORMATION

Doctrine Reaffirmed

The Council of Trent enacted much reform legislation but also reaffirmed the doctrines that Protestant reformers had attacked.

From *Decrees of the Council of Trent*

Profession of Faith

I, *N,* with steadfast faith believe and profess each and all the things contained in the Symbol of faith which the holy Roman Church uses namely "I believe in One God," etc. [The Nicene Creed].

I most firmly acknowledge and embrace the Apostolical and ecclesiastical traditions and other observances and constitutions of the same Church. I acknowledge the sacred Scripture according to that sense which Holy Mother Church has held and holds, to whom it belongs to decide upon the true sense and interpretation of the holy Scriptures, nor will I ever receive and interpret the Scripture except according to the unanimous consent of the Fathers.

I profess likewise that true God is offered in the Mass, a proper and propitiatory sacrifice for the living and the dead, and that in the most Holy Eucharist there are truly, really and substantially the body and blood, together with the soul and divinity of Our Lord Jesus Christ, and that a conversion is made of the whole substance of bread into his body and of the whole substance of wine into his blood, which conversion the Catholic Church calls transubstantiation. I also confess that the whole and entire Christ and the true sacrament is taken under the one species alone.

I hold unswervingly that there is a purgatory and that the souls there detained are helped by the intercessions of the faithful; likewise also that the Saints who reign with Christ are to be venerated and invoked; that they offer prayers to God for us and that their relics are to be venerated. I firmly assert that the images of Christ and of the ever-

From Henry Bettenson, ed., *Documents of the Christian Church,* 2nd ed. (London: Oxford University Press, 1963), pp. 375–377. Copyright © 1963 by Oxford University Press. Reprinted by permission of Oxford University Press.

Virgin Mother of God, as also those of other Saints, are to be kept and retained, and that due honour and veneration is to be accorded them; and I affirm that the power of indulgences has been left by Christ in the Church, and that their use is very salutary for Christian people.

I recognize the Holy Catholic and Apostolic Roman Church as the Mother and mistress of all churches; and I vow and swear true obedience to the Roman Pontiff, the successor of blessed Peter, the chief of the Apostles and the representative [*vicarius*] of Jesus Christ.

I accept and profess, without doubting the traditions, definitions and declarations of the sacred Canons and Oecumenical Councils and especially those of the holy Council of Trent; and at the same time I condemn, reject and anathematize all things contrary thereto, and all heresies condemned, rejected and anathematized by the Church. This true Catholic Faith (without which no one can be in a state of salvation), which at this time I of my own will profess and truly hold, I, *N*, vow and swear, God helping me, most constantly to keep and confess entire and undefiled to my life's last breath, and that I will endeavour, as far as in me shall lie, that it be held, taught and preached by my subordinates or by those who shall be placed under my care: so help me God and these Holy Gospels of God.

On Justification

[*The following propositions were condemned.*]

1. That man can be justified before God by his own works, which are done either in the strength of human nature or through the teaching of the law, apart from the divine grace through Jesus Christ.

3. That without the prevenient inspiration of the Holy Spirit and his aid a man can believe, hope and love, or can repent, as he should, so that on him the grace of justification may be conferred.

4. That the free will of man, moved and aroused by God, does not cooperate at all by responding to the awakening call of God, so as to dispose and prepare itself for the acquisition of the grace of justification, nor can it refuse that grace, if it so will, but it does nothing at all, like some inanimate thing, and is completely passive.

5. That man's free will has been wholly lost and destroyed after Adam's sin.

6. That it is not in the power of man to make his ways evil, but that evil works as well as good are wrought by God, not just by ways of permission but even by his own personal activity; so that the betrayal of Judas is no less his work than the calling of Paul.

7. That all works before justification, for whatever reason they were done, are in truth sins and deserve the hatred of God, or that the more strongly a man strives to dispose himself to receive Grace, the more grievously he sins.

9. That the impious is justified by faith alone—if this means that nothing else is required by way of co-operation in the acquisition of the grace of justification, and that it is in no way necessary for a man to be prepared and disposed by the motion of his own will.

15. That a man reborn and justified is bound by faith to believe that he is assuredly in the number of the predestinate.

24. That justification once received is not preserved and even increased in the sight of God through good works; but that these same works are only fruits and signs of justification, not causes of its increase.

Religious Reformers

Ignatius Loyola (1491–1556) designed his "Exercises" for the spiritual formation of his followers in the Jesuit order. They emphasized personal devotion to Christ and loyalty to the institutions of the Catholic church.

From Ignatius Loyola. *The Spiritual Exercises*

The Nativity

The usual preparatory prayer.

First Preliminary   The story. Our Lady, in the ninth month of her pregnancy, sets out for Nazareth riding, as we may devoutly picture her, on a donkey, accompanied by Joseph and a servant-girl, leading an ox. They are going to Bethlehem to pay the tax which Caesar had levied on all this territory.

Second Preliminary   The picture. Represent to yourself in imagination the road from Bethlehem, in its length and breadth. Is it level or through valleys or over hillsides?

In the same way, study the place of the Nativity. Is the cave spacious or cramped, low or high? How is it furnished?

Third Preliminary   The same as in the preceding contemplation and in the same form.

First Heading   Look at the persons, our Lady, St Joseph, the servant-girl and, after He is born, the Infant Jesus. I must see myself as an

From *The Spiritual Exercises of Saint Ignatius,* Thomas Corbishley, trans. (New York: P. J. Kennedy and Sons, 1963), pp. 42–44, 47–48, 120–122. Reprinted by permission of Burns & Oates Ltd.

impoverished attendant, not fit to be there, but watching and studying them, looking after all their wants as if I were actually present, in a spirit of complete and respectful subservience.

Then I should think of myself to derive some benefit.

Second Heading   See, observe and study what they are saying. Then think of myself, to derive some benefit.

Third Heading   See and reflect on what they are doing. Here it is the journey they have to make, the hardships they have to put up with, before our Lord is born in utter destitution. After all His labours, after suffering from hunger and thirst, heat and cold, being treated with injustice and insulted, He is to die on the Cross—and all for me. Thinking of all this, I will derive some benefit for my soul.

End with a colloquy as in the preceding contemplation, and with an *Our Father*.

The King

The Call of the Earthly King Helps in the Contemplation of the Life of the Eternal King

The preparatory prayer will be as usual.

First Preliminary   A picture of the scene. Here it will be to see in imagination the synagogues, towns and hamlets through which Christ our Lord went preaching.

Second Preliminary   To ask the grace I want. Here I ask our Lord the grace not to be deaf to His summons, but ready and enthusiastic to carry out His holy purpose.

First Heading   I imagine a temporal king, chosen by our Lord God, revered and obeyed by the rulers and all the common men of Christendom.

Second Heading   See how this king addresses all his followers, saying: I am determined to bring under my control the entire land of the unbeliever. Anyone, then, who wishes to join me must be satisfied to eat the food I eat, to drink what I drink, to dress as I dress; by day he will have to work alongside me, and take his turn with me at keeping a look-out by night; there will be other things. But his share in my triumph will be proportionate to his share in my hardships.

Third Heading   Think what response loyal subjects must make to a king so generous and so understanding: equally, were one to refuse the appeal of such a king, how he would incur the reprobation of all mankind and be regarded as a disgraceful coward.

The second part of this exercise consists in relating this illustration of the earthly king to Christ our Lord, point for point.

First Heading If we cannot ignore such a challenge, issued to his followers by an earthly king, how much more worthy of our attention is that of Christ our Lord, the Eternal King, as He confronts the whole world: to each and all He issues His summons in these words: I am determined to bring under my control the whole world and all my enemies, and so to come to the glory of my Father. To anyone, then, who chooses to join me, I offer nothing but a share in my hardships; but if he follows me in suffering he will assuredly follow me in glory.

Second Heading We realize that anyone possessed of right reason will offer himself totally for the task.

Third Heading Those who are anxious to show greater enthusiasm still and distinguish themselves in unstinted service of their eternal King and Lord of the universe, will not be content to offer themselves without reservation for the enterprise. Going against their natural weakness and their love of the world and of the flesh, thcy will make their dedication of themselves still more valuable and worthwhile, in these terms:

Eternal Lord of the Universe, in the presence of Your own infinite goodness, of Your glorious Mother and all the saints of Heaven's court, by Your grace and help, I make this my offering: I intend and desire, and it is my deliberate resolve, granted it be for the more perfect service and greater praise of Your Majesty, to imitate You in putting up with all injustice, all abuse, all poverty in reality no less than in the spirit, should Your Most Sacred Majesty be willing to choose and admit me to this state of life.

The Mind of the Church

The following rules are to be observed in order that we may hold the opinions we should hold in the Church militant.

(1) We should put away completely our own opinion and keep our minds ready and eager to give our entire obedience to our holy Mother the hierarchical Church, Christ our Lord's undoubted Spouse.

(2) We should speak with approval of confession to a priest, of the reception of Holy Communion once a year, still more once a month, most of all once a week, the requisite conditions being duly fulfilled.

(3) We should openly approve of the frequent hearing of Mass, and also of hymns, psalms and lengthy prayers both inside and outside the church, as well as the set times for the divine office as a whole, for prayer in general and for all the canonical hours.

(4) We should speak with particular approval of religious orders, and the states of virginity and celibacy, not rating matrimony as high as any of these.

(6) We should approve of relics of the saints, showing reverence for them and praying to the saints themselves; visits to Station churches, pilgrimages, indulgences, jubilees, Crusade bulls, the lighting of candles in churches should all be commended.

(7) We should approve of the laws of fasting and abstinence in Lent, on Ember Days, vigils, Fridays and Saturdays, as well as mortifications both interior and exterior.

(8) We should praise church decoration and architecture, as well as statues, which we should venerate in view of what they portray.

(9) Finally, all the Church's commandments should be spoken of favourably, our minds being always eager to find arguments in her defence, never in criticism.

(13) To arrive at complete certainty, this is the attitude of mind we should maintain: I will believe that the white object I see is black if that should be the decision of the hierarchical Church, for I believe that linking Christ our Lord the Bridegroom and His Bride the Church, there is one and the same Spirit, ruling and guiding us for our souls' good. For our Holy Mother the Church is guided and ruled by the same Spirit, the Lord who gave the Ten Commandments.

Teresa of Avila (1515–1582), a great writer on the spiritual life, was also a practical church reformer. Here she reflects on the role of women in religious orders and their relationship to God.

From Teresa of Avila. *The Way of Perfection*

This convent was founded for the reasons already given in the work above mentioned, also on account of certain favours that God showed me, in which He revealed that He would be served with great fervour in this house. I did not at first intend that such rigorous bodily mortifications should be practised in it, nor that it should possess no income; on the contrary, I wished it to have sufficient means to prevent the possibility of want, though weak and wicked as I am, I meant rather to do what was right than to seek for self-indulgence.

Just at this time I heard of the miseries France was suffering, of the havoc the Lutherans were making there, and how this wretched sect was increasing. It grieved me bitterly, and as if I could have done anything, or have been of any consequence, I cried to God and begged Him to cure this terrible evil. I felt that I would have laid down a thousand lives to save one of the many souls perishing there. Yet, as I am but a woman, feeble and faulty, it was impossible for me to serve God in the way I wished—indeed, all I cared for then, as I do now, was that,

From Teresa of Avila, *The Way of Perfection,* "A Benedictine of Stanbrook," trans., B. Zimmerman, ed. (London: Burns & Oates, 1961), pp. 4–5, 17–19. Reprinted by permission of Search Press/Burns & Oates Ltd.

as the enemies of God are so many and His friends so few, these latter might at least be good ones. Therefore I determined to do what little was in my power, which was to follow the Evangelical counsels as perfectly as I could and to see that the few nuns here should do the same. Trusting in the great mercy of God which never fails those who resolve to leave all things for His sake, I hoped that, as my sisters here are all that I ever wished them to be, their virtues would be strong enough to resist the influence of my defects and that I might be able to bring some comfort to our Lord. Thus, being all of us employed in interceding for the champions of the Church, and the preachers and theologians who defend her, we might, to our utmost, aid this Lord of mine who is attacked with such cruelty by those on whom He has conferred great benefits that it seems as though they would fasten Him to the Cross again leaving Him no place to lay His head. . . .

It seems presumption in me to imagine that I have any power to obtain this—I place all my confidence, O my God, in these servants of Thine, who are with me and who, I know, neither desire nor seek to do aught but please Thee. For Thee they left the little they possessed, only wishing they owned more to offer Thee. Thou art not ungrateful, O my Creator, that I need think Thou wilt refuse them what they ask, nor, O Lord of my soul, didst Thou hate women whilst Thou wert in the world, but didst ever favour them and show them tender love and pitiful compassion! Thou didst put greater trust in them than in men, for among them was Thy most holy Mother whose merits we share, and whose habit we wear, unworthy as we are by reason of our sins. We can do nothing for Thee in public, nor do we dare to tell the truths over which we weep in secret, lest Thou shouldst not hear our most right petition. Just and good as Thou art, O Lord, I will not believe that Thou wilt reject us. Thou art a just Judge, not like earthly judges who, being sons of Adam and stern men, have no faith in women's virtue. The day will come, my King, when all will be known. I speak not for myself, for all men know of my wickedness and I rejoice that it is made public, but seeing in what manner of times we are living, it is not right to repulse the good and valiant though they are but women. When we beg of Thee honours, income, riches, any wordly things, do not listen to us, but how shouldst Thou not hear us when we ask for what concerns the honour of Thy Son? Why, O Eternal Father, shouldst Thou refuse those who would forfeit a thousand honours and a thousand lives for Thee? Not for our sakes, O God, for we deserve it not, but for the sake of Thy Son and of His merits! O Eternal Father, such stripes and insults and such bitter torments should not be forgotten! How can a heart so loving as Thine, my Creator, endure that what was instituted with such ardent love by Thy Son for the sake of pleasing Thee (for Thou didst bid Him love us) should be held of so little value as is the Blessed Sacrament in these days by heretics? For they drive It from Its dwelling-place when they destroy the churches. It is not as if He had left undone aught that could please Thee. No, He consummated everything! Was it not enough, O Eternal Father, for Him to have no place in which to lay His head whilst He lived amid incessant toils, that now they must deprive Him of the place to which He invites His friends, seeing that they are fainting and knowing that those who labour need to be supported by such meat? Has He not paid in overwhelming excess for the sin of Adam? Must this most meek and loving Lamb atone anew for every fresh sin we commit? Do not suffer it, my Sovereign King; let Thy Majesty be appeased; look not on our faults but on Thy most holy Son who has redeemed us; reflect on His merits, on those of His glorious Mother and on how many Saints and Martyrs have died for Thee! But alas, O my God, who am I who have dared to offer Thee this petition in the name of all? My daughters, what a wretched advocate you have to gain a hearing and to present your petition for you! What if my presumption should anger this supreme Judge, as would be only right and just? But remember, O my Sovereign and my Lord, that Thou art the God of mercy; do Thou prove it to this poor sinner and worm who is thus bold with Thee! Look, O my God, upon my desires and on the tears with which I beg this of Thee, and forgetting my evil actions for Thine own sake, take pity on the many perishing souls and have mercy on Thy Church! Do not permit these evils to increase in Christendom, O Lord, but illuminate its darkness!

REFORMATION AND POLITICS

Germany

Economic and religious grievances inspired the great Peasants' Rebellion (1524) in Germany. Some of the peasants' demands echoed Lutheran principles.

From *Twelve Articles of the Peasants*

The First Article   First, it is our humble petition and desire, as also our will and resolution, that in the future we should have power and authority so that each community should choose and appoint a pastor, and that we should have the right to depose him should he conduct himself improperly. The pastor thus chosen should teach us the Gospel pure and simple, without any addition, doctrine or ordinance of man.

The Second Article   According as the just tithe is established by the Old Testament and fulfilled in the New, we are ready and willing to pay the fair tithe of grain.

The Third Article   It has been the custom hitherto for men to hold us as their own property, which is pitiable enough, considering that Christ has delivered and redeemed us all, without exception by the shedding of his precious blood, the lowly as well as the great. Accordingly, it is consistent with Scripture that we should be free and wish to be so. Not that we would wish to be absolutely free and under no authority.... We are thus ready to yield obedience according to God's law to our elected and regular authorities in all proper things becoming to a Christian. We, therefore, take it for granted that you will release us from serfdom, as true Christians, unless it should be shown us from the Gospel that we are serfs.

The Fourth Article   In the fourth place it has been the custom heretofore, that no poor man should be allowed to touch venison or wild fowl, or fish in flowing water, which seems to us quite unseemly and unbrotherly, as well as selfish and not agreeable to the word of God.

From J. H. Robinson, trans., *Readings in European History* (Boston, Mass.: Ginn and Co., 1906), Vol. 2, pp. 95–99.

The Fifth Article   In the fifth place we are aggrieved in the matter of woodcutting, for the noble folk have appropriated all the woods to themselves alone.

The Sixth Article   Our sixth complaint is in regard to the excessive services demanded of us, which are increased from day to day. We ask that this matter be properly looked into so that we shall not continue to be oppressed in this way, and that some gracious consideration be given us, since our forefathers were required only to serve according to the word of God.

The Seventh Article   Seventh, we will not hereafter allow ourselves to be farther oppressed by our lords, but will let them demand only what is just and proper according to the word of the agreement between the lord and the peasant.

The Eighth Article   In the eighth place, we are greatly burdened by holdings which cannot support the rent exacted from them. The peasants suffer loss in this way and are ruined; and we ask that the lords may appoint persons of honor to inspect these holdings, and fix a rent in accordance with justice, so that the peasant shall not work for nothing, since the laborer is worthy of his hire.

The Ninth Article   In the ninth place, we are burdened with a great evil in the constant making of new laws. We are not judged according to the offence, but sometimes with great ill will, and sometimes much too leniently. In our opinion we should be judged according to the old written law, so that the case shall be decided according to its merits, and not with partiality.

The Tenth Article   In the tenth place, we are aggrieved by the appropriation by individuals of meadows and fields which at one time belonged to a community. These we will take again into our own hands.

The Eleventh Article   In the eleventh place we will entirely abolish the due called *Todfall* [i.e., heriot], and will no longer endure it, nor allow widows and orphans to be thus shamefully robbed against God's will, and in violation of justice and right, as has been done in many places, and by those who should shield and protect them. These have disgraced and despoiled us, and although they had little authority they assumed it. God will suffer this no more, but it shall be wholly done away with, and for the future no man shall be bound to give little or much.

Conclusion   In the twelfth place it is our conclusion and final resolution, that if one or more of the articles here set forth should not be in agreement with the word of God, as we think they are, such article we will willingly recede from, when it is proved really to be against the word of God by a clear explanation of the Scripture.

[*Luther regarded the peasants' secular demands as a distortion of his spiritual teaching and was dismayed at the destructiveness of their rebellion. He called on the German princes to repress it without mercy.*]

Emperor Charles V, ruler of Spain, Flanders, and extensive territories in Germany, reflected on some political consequences of the Reformation in his abdication speech (Brussels, 1556).

From Charles V. *Abdication Speech*

... Soon came the death of my grandfather Maximilian, in my nineteenth year, and although I was still young, they conferred upon me in his stead the imperial dignity. I had no inordinate ambition to rule a multitude of kingdoms, but merely sought to secure the welfare of Germany, to provide for the defence of Flanders, to consecrate my forces to the safety of Christianity against the Turk and to labor for the extention of the Christian religion. But although such zeal was mine, I was unable to show so much of it as I might have wished, on account of the troubles raised by the heresies of Luther and the other innovators of Germany and on account of serious war into which the hostility and envy of neighboring princes had driven me, and from which I have safely emerged, thanks to the favor of God.

This is the fourth time that I go to Spain, there to bury myself. I wish to say to you that nothing I have ever experienced has given me so much pain or rested so heavily upon my soul as that which I experience in parting from you today, without leaving behind me that peace and quiet which I so much desired. ... I am no longer able to attend to my affairs without great bodily fatigue and consequent detriment to the affairs of the state. The cares which so great a responsibility involves; the extreme dejection it causes; my health already ruined; all these leave me no longer the strength sufficient for governing the states which God has confided to me. The little strength that remains to me is rapidly disappearing. So I should long ago have put down the burden if my son's immaturity and my mother's incapacity had not forced both my spirit and my body to sustain its weight until this hour.

The last time that I went to Germany I had determined to do what you see me do today, but I could not bring myself to do it when I saw the wretched condition of the Christian state, a prey to such a multitude of disturbances, of innovations, of singular opinions as to faith, of worse than civil wars, and fallen finally into so many lamentable disorders. I was turned from my purpose because my ills were not yet so great, and I hoped to make an end of all these things and restore the

From J. H. Robinson, trans., *Readings in European History* (Boston, Mass.: Ginn and Co., 1906), Vol. 2, pp. 165–167.

peace. In order that I might not be wanting in my duty I risked my strength, my goods, my repose and my life for the safety of Christianity and the defence of my subjects. From this struggle I emerged with a portion of the things I desired. But the king of France and certain Germans, failing to preserve the peace and amity they had sworn, marched against me and were upon the point of seizing my person. The king of France took the city of Metz, and I, in the dead of winter, exposed to intense cold, in the midst of snow and blood, advanced with a powerful army raised at my own expense to retake the city and restore the Empire. The Germans saw that I had not yet laid aside the imperial crown and had no disposition to allow its majesty to be diminished.

I have carried out what God has permitted, since the outcome of our efforts depends upon the will of God. We human beings act according to our powers, our strength, our spirit, and God awards the victory and permits defeat. I have ever done as I was able, and God has aided me. I return to Him boundless thanks for having succored me in my greatest trials and in all my dangers.

I am determined then to retire to Spain, to yield to my son Philip the possession of all my states, and to my brother, the king of the Romans, the Empire. I particularly commend to you my son, and I ask of you in remembrance of me, that you extend to him the love which you have always borne towards me; moreover I ask you to preserve among yourselves the same affection and harmony. Be obedient towards justice, zealous in the observance of the laws, preserve respect for all that merits it, and do not refuse to grant to authority the support of which it stands in need.

Above all, beware of infection from the sects of neighboring lands. Extirpate at once the germs, if they appear in your midst, for fear lest they may spread abroad and utterly overthrow your state, and lest you may fall into the direst calamities.

A civil war between Protestant and Catholic princes of Germany ended with an acceptance of a permanent religious division of the country. (The agreement did not prevent the outbreak of further savage religious wars in the next century.)

Peace of Augsburg (1555)

In order to bring peace into the holy empire of the Germanic Nation, between the Roman Imperial Majesty and the Electors, Princes, and Estates: let neither his Imperial Majesty nor the Electors, Princes, etc., do any violence or harm to any estate of the Empire on account of the Augsburg Confession,[1] but let them enjoy their religious belief, liturgy and ceremonies as well as their estates and other rights and privileges in peace; and complete religious peace shall be obtained only by Christian means of amity, or under threat of the punishment of the imperial ban.

Likewise the Estates espousing the Augsburg Confession shall let all the Estates and Princes who cling to the old religion live in absolute peace and in the enjoyment of all their estates, rights and privileges.

However all such as do not belong to the two above-mentioned religions shall not be included in the present peace but be totally excluded from it.

. . . Where an archbishop, bishop, or prelate or any other priest of our old religion shall abandon the same, his archbishopric, bishopric, prelacy, and other benefices, together with all their income and revenues which he has so far possessed, shall be abandoned by him without any further objection or delay. The chapters and such as are entitled to it by common law or the custom of the place shall elect a person espousing the old religion, who may enter on the possession and enjoyment of all the rights and incomes of the place without any further hindrance and without prejudging any ultimate amicable settlement of religion. . . .

In case our subjects, whether belonging to the old religion or to the Augsburg Confession, should intend leaving their homes, with their wives and children, in order to settle in another place, they shall neither be hindered in the sale of their estates after due payment of the local taxes nor injured in their honour.

France

In France Calvin won many influential converts (Huguenots). They prospered until the royal government launched a savage persecution in 1572.

St. Bartholomew's Day Massacre

If I were inclined to increase the general horror inspired by an action so barbarous as that perpetrated on the 24th of August, 1572, and too well known by the name of the *massacre of St. Bartholomew*, I should in this place enlarge upon the number, the rank, the virtues, and great

[1] A statement of Lutheran doctrines.

From *Memoirs of the Duke of Sully* (London: G. Bell, 1877), Vol. 1, pp. 85–87.

talents of those who were inhumanly murdered on that horrible day, as well in Paris as in every other part of the kingdom; I should mention at least the ignominious treatment, the fiend-like cruelty, and savage insults these miserable victims suffered from their butchers, whose conduct was a thousand times more terrible than death itself. I have writings still in my hands which would confirm the report, of the court of France having made the most pressing solicitations to the courts of England and Germany, to the Swiss and the Genoese, to refuse an asylum to those Huguenots who might fly from France; but I prefer the honour of the nation to the satisfying a malignant pleasure, which many persons would take, in lengthening out a recital wherein might be found the names of those who were so lost to humanity as to dip their hands in the blood of their fellow-citizens, and even of their own relations. I would, were it in my power, for ever obliterate the memory of a day that Divine vengeance made France groan for, by a continual succession of miseries, blood, and horror, during six-and-twenty years; for it is impossible to judge otherwise, when one reflects on all that happened from that fatal moment till the peace of 1598. It is even with regret that I cannot omit what happened upon this occasion to the prince who is the subject of these Memoirs, and to myself.

Intending on that day to wait upon the king my master,[1] I went to bed early on the preceding evening; about three in the morning I was awakened by the cries of people, and the alarm-bells, which were everywhere ringing. M. de Saint Julian, my tutor, and my valet, who had also been roused by the noise, ran out of my apartments to learn the cause of it, but never returned, nor did I ever after hear what became of them. Being thus left alone in my room, my landlord, who was a Protestant, urged me to accompany him to mass in order to save his life, and his house from being pillaged; but I determined to endeavour to escape to the College de Bourgogne, and to effect this I put on my scholar's gown, and taking a book under my arm, I set out. In the streets I met three parties of the Life-guards; the first of these, after handling me very roughly, seized my book, and, most fortunately for me, seeing it was a Roman Catholic prayer-book, suffered me to proceed, and this served me as a passport with the two other parties. As I went along I saw the houses broken open and plundered, and men, women, and children butchered, while a constant cry was kept up of, "Kill! Kill! O you Huguenots! O you Huguenots!" This made me very impatient to gain the college, where, through God's assistance, I at length arrived, without suffering any other injury than a most dreadful fright. The porter twice refused me entrance, but at last, by means of a few pieces of money, I prevailed on him to inform M. La Faye, the principal of the college and my particular friend, that I was at the gate, who, moved with pity, brought me in, though he was at a loss

[1] King Henry of Navarre, who became King Henry IV of France.

where to put me, on account of two priests who were in his room, and who said it was determined to put all the Huguenots to death, even the infants at the breast, as was done in the Sicilian vespers. However, my friend conveyed me to a secret apartment, where no one entered except his valet, who brought me food during three successive days, at the end of which the king's proclamation prohibiting any further plunder or slaughter, was issued. . . .

In 1598 King Henry IV granted a measure of toleration to the Huguenots. (As in Germany, the settlement did not prove permanent and further religious persecutions occurred in the seventeenth century.)

Edict of Nantes

We ordain that the Catholic, Apostolic and Roman faith be restored and re-established in all those districts and places of this our Realm . . . in which its exercise has been interrupted, there to be freely and peaceably exercised. . . .

And to leave no occasion for trouble or difference among our subjects: We permit those of the so-called Reformed Religion to live and abide in all the towns and districts of this our Realm . . . free from inquisition, molestation or compulsion to do anything in the way of Religion, against their conscience . . . provided that they observe the provisions of this Edict. . . .

We also permit those of the aforesaid Religion to practise it in all the towns and districts of our dominion, in which it had been established and publicly observed by them on several distinct occasions during the year 1596 and the year 1597 up to the end of August, all decrees and judgements to the contrary notwithstanding.

We most expressly forbid to those of this religion the practice thereof, in respect of ministry, organization, discipline or the public instruction of children, or in any respect, in our realm and dominion, save in the places permitted and granted by this edict.

The practice of this religion is forbidden in our court and suite, in our domains beyond the mountains, in our city of Paris, or within five leagues thereof.

From Henry Bettenson, ed., *Documents of the Christian Church*, 2nd ed. (London: Oxford University Press, 1963), pp. 302–303.

XII

VOYAGES OF DISCOVERY
The New World
  From *Letter of Columbus*
The Indies
  From *Letter of King Manoel (1499)*
  From *Journal of Gaspar Correa*
Exploration and Anthropology
  From Montaigne. *Of Cannibals*

SCIENTIFIC METHOD
Bacon on Empiricism
  From *The Great Instauration*
Descartes on Deduction
  From *Discourse on Method*

SCIENTIFIC ACHIEVEMENT
Astronomy
  From Copernicus. *Commentariolus*
  From Galileo. *The Starry Messenger*
  From Galileo. *Letters on Sunspots*
  From Galileo. *Letter to the Grand
    Duchess Christina*
Synthesis
  From *Newton's Principia*
  From *Bodin's Methodus*

WITCHCRAFT—SUPERSTITION
AND PERSECUTION
The Prevalence of Witches
  From *Bodin's Demonology*
The Frailty of Women
  From *The Hammer of Witches*
  *Confession of Françoise Secretain
    (1598)*
  Trial of Geillis Duncane (1591)

NEW WORLDS FOR OLD—EXPLORATION, SCIENCE, AND SUPERSTITION

THE SIXTEENTH AND seventeenth centuries were an age of vastly broadening horizons for the peoples of Western Europe.

Explorers discovered a New World across the Atlantic and a new sea route to the fabulously wealthy East Indies. After the first voyages of discovery, later adventurers—part merchants, part pirates, part conquerors—quickly established the foundations of the great European overseas empires. (The Spanish and Portuguese were first; then English Dutch, and French soon followed.)

During the same period, major advances occurred in many fields of natural science. The most striking of all were those in astronomy, discoveries that changed the whole picture of the universe and humanity's place in it. Copernicus proposed a heliocentric theory—that the sun, not the earth, was at the center of the universe. Galileo turned his newly invented telescope on the heavens and found evidence to support Copernicus. Bacon and Descartes wrote on scientific method. All the new knowledge flowed together in the great synthesis presented by Isaac Newton in his Principia *(1687).*

But the new ideas penetrated only slowly among the masses of the people. Most of them clung to a prescientific, magical view of the world that found expression in the prevalent "witchcraft delusion" of the early modern period. The persecution of witches was not a mere eccentricity of the age. It expressed the fears and tensions of a time when old, taken-for-granted certainties about religious truth and the natural order of things were everywhere being called into question. Sometimes we can see the tension in a particular individual, as in the readings from Jean Bodin given below. Bodin, nowadays remembered mainly as a great political theorist, was conscious that he lived in a "golden age" of scientific achievement; but he was also obsessed by the study of demonology and wrote extensively on the evils of witchcraft.

VOYAGES OF DISCOVERY

The New World

From *Letter of Columbus*

All these islands are very beautiful, and distinguished by a diversity of scenery; they are filled with a great variety of trees of immense height, and which I believe to retain their foliage in all seasons; for when I saw them they were as verdant and luxuriant as they usually are in Spain in the month of May,—some of them were blossoming, some bearing fruit, and all flourishing in the greatest perfection, according to their respective stages of growth, and the nature and quality of each: yet the islands are not so thickly wooded as to be impassable. The nightingale and various birds were singing in countless numbers, and that in November, the month in which I arrived there. There are besides in the same island of Juana [Cuba] seven or eight kinds of palm trees, which, like all the other trees, herbs, and fruits, considerably surpass ours in height and beauty. The pines also are very handsome, and there are very extensive fields and meadows, a variety of birds, different kinds of honey, and many sorts of metals, but no iron. In that island also which I have before said we named Española [Hispaniola], there are mountains of very great size and beauty, vast plains, groves, and very fruitful fields, admirably adapted for tillage, pasture, and habitation. The convenience and excellence of the harbours in this island, and the abundance of the rivers, so indispensable to the health of man, surpass anything that would be believed by one who had not seen it. The trees, herbage, and fruits of Española are very different from those of Juana, and moreover it abounds in various kinds of spices, gold, and other metals. The inhabitants of both sexes in this island, and in all the others which I have seen, or of which I have received information, go always naked as they were born, with the exception of some of the women, who use the covering of a leaf, or small bough, or an apron of cotton which they prepare for that purpose. None of them, as I have already said, are possessed of any iron, neither have they weapons, being unacquainted with, and indeed incompetent to use them, not from any deformity of body (for they are well-formed), but because they are timid and full of fear. They carry however in lieu of arms,

From *Select Letters of Christopher Columbus,* R. H. Major, ed. (London: The Hakluyt Society, 1847), pp. 5–9.

420

canes dried in the sun, on the ends of which they fix heads of dried wood sharpened to a point, and even these they dare not use habitually; for it has often occurred when I have sent two or three of my men to any of the villages to speak with the natives, that they have come out in a disorderly troop, and have fled in such haste at the approach of our men, that the fathers forsook their children and the children their fathers. This timidity did not arise from any loss or injury that they had received from us; for, on the contrary, I gave to all I approached whatever articles I had about me, such as cloth and many other things, taking nothing of theirs in return: but they are naturally timid and fearful. As soon however as they see that they are safe, and have laid aside all fear, they are very simple and honest, and exceedingly liberal with all they have; none of them refusing any thing he may possess when he is asked for it, but on the contrary inviting us to ask them. They exhibit great love towards all others in preference to themselves: they also give objects of great value for trifles, and content themselves with very little or nothing in return. I however forbad that these trifles and articles of no value (such as pieces of dishes, plates, and glass, keys, and leather straps) should be given to them, although if they could obtain them, they imagined themselves to be possessed of the most beautiful trinkets in the world. It even happened that a sailor received for a leather strap as much gold as was worth three golden nobles, and for things of more trifling value offered by our men, especially-newly coined blancas, or any gold coins, the Indians would give whatever the seller required; as, for instance, an ounce and a half or two ounces of gold, or thirty or forty pounds of cotton, with which commodity they were already acquainted. Thus they bartered, like idiots, cotton and gold for fragments of bows, glasses, bottles, and jars; which I forbad as being unjust, and myself gave them many beautiful and acceptable articles which I had brought with me, taking nothing from them in return; I did this in order that I might the more easily conciliate them, that they might be led to become Christians, and be inclined to entertain a regard for the King and Queen, our Princes and all Spaniards, and that I might induce them to take an interest in seeking out, and collecting, and delivering to us such things as they possessed in abundance, but which we greatly needed. They practise no kind of idolatry, but have a firm belief that all strength and power, and indeed all good things, are in heaven, and that I had descended from thence with these ships and sailors, and under this impression was I received after they had thrown aside their fears. Nor are they slow or stupid, but of very clear understanding; and those men who have crossed to the neighbouring islands give an admirable description of everything they observed; but they never saw any people clothed, nor any ships like ours. On my arrival at that sea, I had taken some Indians by force from the first island that I came to, in order that they might learn our language, and communicate to us what they knew respecting the country; which plan succeeded excellently, and was a great advantage to us, for in a short time, either by gestures and signs, or by words, we were enabled to understand each other. These men are still travelling with me, and although they have been with us now a long time, they continue to entertain the idea that I have descended from heaven; and on our arrival at any new place they published this, crying out immediately with a loud voice to the other Indians, "Come, come and look upon beings of a celestial race": upon which both women and men, children and adults, young men and old, when they got rid of the fear they at first entertained, would come out in throngs, crowding the roads to see us.

The Indies

Columbus always believed that he had discovered a new westward route to the East Indies. It was the Portuguese Vasco da Gama, however, who really found a new way to the East by sailing round the Cape of Good Hope. King Manoel of Portugal wrote this letter to King Ferdinand and Queen Isabella of Spain.

From *Letter of King Manoel (1499)*

Most high and excellent Prince and Princess, most potent Lord and Lady!

Your Highnesses already know that we had ordered Vasco da Gama, a nobleman of our household, and his brother Paulo da Gama, with four vessels to make discoveries by sea, and that two years have now elapsed since their departure. And as the principal motive of this enterprise has been with our predecessors, the service of God our Lord, and our own advantage, it pleased Him in His mercy to speed them on their route. From a message which has now been brought to this city by one of the captains, we learn that they did reach and discover India and other kingdoms and lordships bordering upon it; that they entered and navigated its sea, finding large cities, large edifices and rivers, and great populations among whom is carried on all the trade in spices and precious stones, which are forwarded in ships (which these same explorers saw and met with in good numbers and of great size) to Mecca, and thence to Cairo, whence they are dispersed throughout the world. Of these [spices, etc.] they have brought a quantity including cinnamon, cloves, ginger, nutmeg, and pepper, as well as other kinds, together with the boughs and leaves of the same; also many fine

From *A Journal of the First Voyage of Vasco de Gama,* E. G. Ravenstein, ed. (London: The Hakluyt Society, 1898), pp. 77–79.

stones of all sorts, such as rubies and others. And they also came to a country in which there are mines of gold, of which [gold], as of the spices and precious stones, they did not bring as much as they could have done, for they took no merchandise with them.

As we are aware that your Highnesses will hear of these things with much pleasure and satisfaction, we thought well to give this information. And your Highnesses may believe, in accordance with what we have learnt concerning the Christian people whom these explorers reached, that it will be possible notwithstanding that they are not as yet strong in the faith or possessed of a thorough knowledge of it, to do much in the service of God and the exaltation of the Holy Faith, once they shall have been converted and fully fortified in it. And when they shall have thus been fortified in the faith, there will be an opportunity for destroying the Moors of those parts. Moreover, we hope, with the help of God, that the great trade which now enriches the Moors of those parts, through whose hands it passes without the intervention of other persons or peoples, shall, in consequence of our regulations, be diverted to the natives and ships of our own kingdom, so that henceforth all Christendom, in this part of Europe, shall be able in a large measure to provide itself with these spices and precious stones.

From the beginning, contacts between Europeans and non-European peoples involved bloody clashes as well as peaceful trading. The following incident occurred in 1502 after a party of Portuguese had been killed at Calcutta.

From *Journal of Gaspar Correa*

The captain-major [Vasco da Gama], on arriving at Calecut, was in a passion because he found the port cleared, and in it there was nothing to which he could do harm, because the Moors, knowing of his coming, had all fled, and hid their vessels and sambuks in the rivers. . . . The King of Calecut thought that he might gain time, so that the captain-major should not do him harm; and when his fleet arrived he sent him a Brahman of his in a boat with a white cloth fastened to a pole, as a sign of peace. This Brahman came dressed in the habit of a friar, one of those who had been killed in the country; and on reaching the ship, he asked for a safe conduct to enter. When it was known that he was not a friar,—for the captain-major and everyone had been joyful, thinking that he was one of our friars,—seeing that he was not, the captain-major gave him a safe conduct, and bade him enter the ship. . . . He then ordered all the fleet to draw in close to the shore, and all day, till night, he bombarded the city, by which he made a great destruction. . . .

From *The Three Voyages of Vasco de Gama*, H. E. J. Stanley, ed. (London: The Hakluyt Society, 1869), pp. 328–332.

Whilst they were doing this business, there came in from the offing two large ships, and twenty-two sambuks and Malabar vessels, which came from Coromandel laden with rice, which the Moors of Calecut had ordered to be laden there, as its price there was very cheap, and they gained much by it; and they came to fetch the port, thinking that our ships, if they had come, would already be at Cochym, and not at Calecut; but our fleet having sighted them, the caravels went to them, and the Moors could not fly, as they were laden, and the caravels brought them to the captain-major, and all struck their sails. Six nakhodas of the sambuks then came to the captain-major, saying they were from Cananor, and mentioned the names of the factor and of Ruy de Mendanha, and other Portuguese, at which the captain-major was pleased. He then ordered the boats to go and plunder the small vessels, which were sixteen, and the two ships, in which they found rice, and many jars of butter, and many bales of stuffs. They then gathered all this together into the ships, with the crews of the two large ships, and he ordered the boats to get as much rice as they wanted, and they took that of four of the small vessels, which they emptied, for they did not want more. Then the captain-major commanded them to cut off the hands and ears and noses of all the crews, and put all that into one of the small vessels, into which he ordered them to put the friar, also without ears, or nose, or hands, which he ordered to be strung round his neck, with a palm-leaf for the King, on which he told him to have a curry made to eat of what his friar brought him. When all the Indians had been thus executed, he ordered their feet to be tied together, as they had no hands with which to untie them: and in order that they should not untie them with their teeth, he ordered them to strike upon their teeth with staves, and they knocked them down their throats; and they were thus put on board, heaped up upon the top of each other, mixed up with the blood which streamed from them; and he ordered mats and dry leaves to be spread over them, and the sails to be set for the shore, and the vessel set on fire: and there were more than eight hundred Moors; and the small vessel with the friar, with all the hands and ears, was also sent on shore under sail, without being fired. These vessels went at once on shore, where many people flocked together to put out the fire, and draw out those whom they found alive, upon which they made great lamentations.

Exploration and Anthropology

Europeans were fascinated by the discovery of new peoples whose life-styles were so sharply different from their own. Montaigne wrote about the Indians of South America.

From Montaigne. *Of Cannibals*

These nations, then, seem to me barbarous in this sense, that they have been fashioned very little by the human mind, and are still very close to their original naturalness. The laws of nature still rule them, very little corrupted by ours; and they are in such a state of purity that I am sometimes vexed that they were unknown earlier, in the days when there were men able to judge them better than we. I am sorry that Lycurgus and Plato did not know of them; for it seems to me that what we actually see in these nations surpasses not only all the pictures in which poets have idealized the golden age and all their inventions in imagining a happy state of man, but also the conceptions and the very desire of philosophy. . .

For the rest, they live in a country with a very pleasant and temperate climate, so that according to my witnesses it is rare to see a sick man there; and they have assured me that they never saw one palsied, bleary-eyed, toothless, or bent with age. They are settled along the sea and shut in on the land side by great high mountains, with a stretch about a hundred leagues wide in between. They have a great abundance of fish and flesh which bear no resemblance to ours, and they eat them with no other artifice than cooking.

They have their wars with the nations beyond the mountains, further inland, to which they go quite naked, with no other arms than bows or wooden swords ending in a sharp point, in the manner of the tongues of our boar spears. It is astonishing what firmness they show in their combats, which never end but in slaughter and bloodshed; for as to routs and terror, they know nothing of either.

Each man brings back as his trophy the head of the enemy he has killed, and sets it up at the entrance to his dwelling. After they have treated their prisoners well for a long time with all the hospitality they can think of, each man who has a prisoner calls a great assembly of his acquaintances. He ties a rope to one of the prisoner's arms by the end of which he holds him, a few steps away, for fear of being hurt, and gives his dearest friend the other arm to hold in the same way; and these two, in the presence of the whole assembly, kill him with their swords. This done, they roast him and eat him in common and send some pieces to their absent friends. This is not, as people think, for nourishment, as of old the Scythians used to do; it is to betoken an extreme revenge. And the proof of this came when they saw the Portuguese, who had joined forces with their adversaries, inflict a different kind of death on them when they took them prisoner, which was to bury them up to the waist, shoot the rest of their body full of arrows, and afterward hang them. They thought that these people from the other world, being men who had sown the knowledge of many vices among their neighbors and were much greater masters than themselves in every sort of wickedness, did not adopt this sort of vengeance without some reason, and that it must be more painful than their own; so they began to give up their old method and to follow this one.

I am not sorry that we notice the barbarous horror of such acts, but I am heartily sorry that, judging their faults rightly, we should be so blind to our own. I think there is more barbarity in eating a man alive than in eating him dead; and in tearing by tortures and the rack a body still full of feeling, in roasting a man bit by bit, in having him bitten and mangled by dogs and swine (as we have not only read but seen within fresh memory, not among ancient enemies, but among neighbors and fellow citizens, and what is worse, on the pretext of piety and religion), than in roasting and eating him after he is dead. . . .

So we may well call these people barbarians, in respect to the rules of reason, but not in respect to ourselves, who surpass them in every kind of barbarity.

Their warfare is wholly noble and generous, and as excusable and beautiful as this human disease can be; its only basis among them is their rivalry in valor. They are not fighting for the conquest of new lands, for they still enjoy that natural abundance that provides them without toil and trouble with all necessary things in such profusion that they have no wish to enlarge their boundaries. They are still in that happy state of desiring only as much as their natural needs demand; anything beyond that is superfluous to them. . . . Truly here are real savages by our standards; for either they must be thoroughly so, or we must be; there is an amazing distance between their character and ours.

The men there have several wives, and the higher their reputation for valor the more wives they have. It is a remarkably beautiful thing about their marriages that the same jealousy our wives have to keep us from the affection and kindness of other women, theirs have to win this for them. Being more concerned for their husbands' honor than for anything else, they strive and scheme to have as many companions as they can, since that is a sign of their husbands' valor.

Our wives will cry "Miracle!" but it is no miracle. It is a properly matrimonial virtue, but one of the highest order. In the Bible, Leah, Rachel, Sarah, and Jacob's wives gave their beautiful handmaids to their husbands; and Livia seconded the appetites of Augustus, to her own disadvantage; and Stratonice, the wife of King Deiotarus, not only lent her husband for his use a very beautiful young chambermaid in her service, but carefully brought up her children, and backed them up to succeed to their father's estates. . . .

Three of these men, ignorant of the price they will pay some day, in loss of repose and happiness, for gaining knowledge of the corruptions of this side of the ocean; ignorant also of the fact that of this intercourse will come their ruin (which I suppose is already well advanced: poor wretches, to let themselves be tricked by the desire for new things, and to have left the serenity of their own sky to come and see ours!)—three of these men were at Rouen, at the time the late King Charles IX was there. The king talked to them for a long time; they were shown our ways, our splendor, the aspect of a fine city. After that, someone asked their opinion, and wanted to know what they had found most amazing. They mentioned three things, of which I have forgotten the third, and I am very sorry for it; but I still remember two of them. They said that in the first place they thought it very strange that so many grown men, bearded, strong, and armed, who were around the king (it is likely that they were talking about the Swiss of his guard) should submit to obey a child, and that one of them was not chosen to command instead. Second (they have a way in their language of speaking of men as halves of one another), they had noticed that there were among us men full and gorged with all sorts of good things, and that their other halves were beggars at their doors, emaciated with hunger and poverty; and they thought it strange that these needy halves could endure such an injustice, and did not take the others by the throat, or set fire to their houses. . . .

All this is not too bad—but what's the use? They don't wear breeches.

SCIENTIFIC METHOD

Bacon on Empiricism

Francis Bacon (1561–1626) called for a new science based on empirical observation and experimentation.

From *The Great Instauration*

Since . . . satisfaction with the present induces neglect of provision for the future, it becomes a thing not only useful, but absolutely necessary, that the excess of honour and admiration with which our existing stock of inventions is regarded be in the very entrance and threshold of the work, and that frankly and without circumlocution, stripped off, and men be duly warned not to exaggerate or make too much of them. For let a man look carefully into all that variety of books with which the arts and sciences abound, he will find everywhere endless repetitions of the same thing, varying in the method of treatment, but not new in substance, insomuch that the whole stock, numerous as it appears at first view, proves on examination to be but scanty. And for its value and utility it must be plainly avowed that that wisdom which we have derived principally from the Greeks is but like the boyhood of knowledge, and has the characteristic property of boys: it can talk, but it cannot generate. . . . Observe also, that if sciences of this kind had any life in them, that could never have come to pass which has been the case now for many ages—that they stand almost at a stay, without receiving any augmentations worthy of the human race; insomuch that many times not only what was asserted once is asserted still, but what was a question once is a question still, and instead of being resolved by discussion is only fixed and fed; and all the tradition and succession of schools is still a succession of masters and scholars, not of inventors and those who bring to further perfection the things invented. In the mechanical arts we do not find it so; they, on the contrary, as having in them some breath of life, are continually growing and becoming more perfect. . . .

From *The Great Instauration* in *The Works of Francis Bacon*, J. Spedding, R. L. Ellis, and D. D. Heath, eds. (Boston, Mass.: Taggard and Thompson, 1863), Vol. 8, pp. 25–27, 31–34, 44–47, 53.

There is none who has dwelt upon experience and the facts of nature as long as is necessary. Some there are indeed who have committed themselves to the waves of experience, and almost turned mechanics; yet these again have in their very experiments pursued a kind of wandering inquiry, without any regular system of operations. And besides they have mostly proposed to themselves certain petty tasks, taking it for a great matter to work out some single discovery;—a course of proceeding at once poor in aim and unskillful in design. As for those who have given the first place to Logic, supposing that the surest helps to the sciences were to be found in that, they have indeed most truly and excellently perceived that the human intellect left to its own course is not to be trusted; but then the remedy is altogether too weak for the disease; nor is it without evil in itself. For the Logic which is received, though it be very properly applied to civil business and to those arts which rest in discourse and opinion, is not nearly subtle enough to deal with nature; and in offering at what it cannot master, has done more to establish and perpetuate error than to open the way to truth. . . .

For my own part at least, in obedience to the everlasting love of truth, I have committed myself to the uncertainties and difficulties and solitudes of the ways, and relying on the divine assistance have upheld my mind both against the shocks and embattled ranks of opinion, and against my own private and inward hesitations and scruples, and against the fogs and clouds of nature, and the phantoms flitting about on every side; in the hope of providing at last for the present and future generations guidance more faithful and secure. Wherein if I have made any progress, the way has been opened to me by no other means than the true and legitimate humiliation of the human spirit. For all those who before me have applied themselves to the invention of arts have but cast a glance or two upon facts and examples and experience, and straightway proceeded, as if invention were nothing more than an exercise of thought, to invoke their own spirits to give them oracles. I, on the contrary, dwelling purely and constantly among the facts of nature, withdraw my intellect from them no further than may suffice to let the images and rays of natural objects meet in a point, as they do in the sense of vision. . . . And by these means I suppose that I have established for ever a true and lawful marriage between the empirical and the rational faculty, the unkind and ill-starred divorce and separation of which has thrown into confusion all the affairs of the human family. . . . I have sought on all sides diligently and faithfully to provide helps for the sense—substitutes to supply its failures, rectifications to correct its errors; and this I endeavour to accomplish not so much by instruments as by experiments. For the subtlety of experiments is far greater than that of the sense itself, even when assisted by exquisite instruments; such experiments, I mean, as are skilfully and artificially devised for the express purpose of determining the point in question.

To the immediate and proper perception of the sense therefore I do not give much weight; but I contrive that the office of the sense shall be only to judge of the experiment, and that the experiment itself shall judge of the thing.

But I design not only to indicate and mark out the ways, but also to enter them. And therefore the third part of the work embraces the Phenomena of the Universe; that is to say, experience of every kind, and such a natural history as may serve for a foundation to build philosophy upon. For a good method of demonstration or form of interpreting nature may keep the mind from going astray or stumbling, but it is not any excellence of method that can supply it with the material of knowledge. Those however who aspire not to guess and divine, but to discover and know; who propose not to devise mimic and fabulous worlds of their own, but to examine and dissect the nature of this very world itself; must go to facts themselves for everything. Nor can the place of this labour and search and worldwide perambulation be supplied by any genius or meditation or argumentation; no, not if all men's wits could meet in one. This therefore we must have, or the business must be for ever abandoned. But up to this day such has been the condition of men in this matter, that it is no wonder if nature will not give herself into their hands. . . .

I have made a beginning of the work—a beginning, as I hope, not unimportant:—the fortune of the human race will give the issue;—such an issue, it may be, as in the present condition of things and men's minds cannot easily be conceived or imagined. For the matter in hand is no mere felicity of speculation, but the real business and fortunes of the human race, and all power of operation. For man is but the servant and interpreter of nature: what he does and what he knows is only what he has observed of nature's order in fact or in thought; beyond this he knows nothing and can do nothing. For the chain of causes cannot by any force be loosed or broken, nor can nature be commanded except by being obeyed. And so those twin objects, human Knowledge and human Power, do really meet in one; and it is from ignorance of causes that operation fails.

Descartes on Deduction

René Descartes (1596–1650) emphasized rigorous deductive logic. His method led him to a belief in a perfect God who ordained immutable laws of nature and to a view of the human person as an intricate mechanism animated by a rational soul (a "ghost in a machine," as later critics put it).

From *Discourse on Method*

As a multitude of laws often only hampers justice, so that a state is best governed when, with few laws, these are rigidly administered; in like manner, instead of the great number of precepts of which Logic is composed, I believed that the four following would prove perfectly sufficient for me, provided I took the firm and unwavering resolution never in a single instance to fail in observing them.

The *first* was never to accept anything for true which I did not clearly know to be such; that is to say, carefully to avoid precipitancy and prejudice, and to comprise nothing more in my judgment than what was presented to my mind so clearly and distinctly as to exclude all ground of doubt.

The *second*, to divide each of the difficulties under examination into as many parts as possible, and as might be necessary for its adequate solution.

The *third*, to conduct my thoughts in such order that, by commencing with objects the simplest and easiest to know, I might ascend by little and little, and, as it were, step by step, to the knowledge of the more complex; assigning in thought a certain order even to those objects which in their own nature do not stand in a relation of antecedence and sequence.

And the *last*, in every case to make enumerations so complete, and reviews so general, that I might be assured that nothing was omitted.

The long chains of simple and easy reasonings by means of which geometers are accustomed to reach the conclusions of their most difficult demonstrations, had led me to imagine that all things, to the knowledge of which man is competent, are mutually connected in the same way, and that there is nothing so far removed from us as to be beyond our reach, or so hidden that we cannot discover it, provided only we abstain from accepting the false for the true, and always preserve in our thoughts the order necessary for the deduction of one truth from another.

I had long before remarked that, in (relation to) practice, it is sometimes necessary to adopt, as if above doubt, opinions which we discern to be highly uncertain, as has been already said; but as I then desired to give my attention solely to the search after truth, I thought that a procedure exactly the opposite was called for, and that I ought to reject as absolutely false all opinions in regard to which I could suppose the least ground for doubt, in order to ascertain whether after that there remained aught in my belief that was wholly indubitable. Accordingly, seeing that our senses sometimes deceive us, I was willing to suppose that there existed nothing really such as they presented to us; and

From René Descartes, *Discourse on Method*, John Veich, trans. (Edinburgh: William Blackwod and Sons, 1873), pp. 61–62, 74–77, 83–87, 96–100.

because some men err in reasoning, and fall into paralogisms, even on the simplest matters of Geometry, I, convinced that I was as open to error as any other, rejected as false all the reasonings I had hitherto taken for demonstrations; and finally, when I considered that the very same thoughts (presentations) which we experience when awake may also be experienced when we are asleep, while there is at that time not one of them true, I supposed that all the objects (presentations) that had ever entered into my mind when awake, had in them no more truth than the illusions of my dreams. But immediately upon this I observed that, whilst I thus wished to think that all was false, it was absolutely necessary that I, who thus thought, should be somewhat; and as I observed that this truth, *I think, hence I am,* was so certain and of such evidence, that no ground of doubt, however extravagant, could be alleged by the Sceptics capable of shaking it, I concluded that I might, without scruple, accept it as the first principle of the Philosophy of which I was in search.

In the next place, I attentively examined what I was, and as I observed that I could suppose that I had no body, and that there was no world nor any place in which I might be; but that I could not therefore suppose that I was not; and that, on the contrary, from the very circumstance that I thought to doubt of the truth of other things, it most clearly and certainly followed that I was; while, on the other hand, if I had only ceased to think, although all the other objects which I had ever imagined had been in reality existent, I would have had no reason to believe that I existed; I thence concluded that I was a substance whose whole essence or nature consists only in thinking, and which, that it may exist, has need of no place, nor is dependent on any material thing; so that "I," that is to say, the mind by which I am what I am, is wholly distinct from the body, and is even more easily known than the latter, and is such, that although the latter were not, it would still continue to be all that it is.

After this I inquired in general into what is essential to the truth and certainty of a proposition; for since I had discovered one which I knew to be true, I thought that I must likewise be able to discover the ground of this certitude. And as I observed that in the words *I think, hence I am,* there is nothing at all which gives me assurance of their truth beyond this, that I see very clearly that in order to think it is necessary to exist, I concluded that I might take, as a general rule, the principle, that all the things which we very clearly and distinctly conceive are true, only observing, however, that there is some difficulty in rightly determining the objects which we distinctly conceive.

In the next place, from reflecting on the circumstance that I doubted, and that consequently my being was not wholly perfect (for I clearly saw that it was a greater perfection to know than to doubt,) I was led to inquire whence I had learned to think of something more perfect than myself; and I clearly recognised that I must hold this notion from some Nature which in reality was more perfect.... for to receive it from nothing was a thing manifestly impossible; and, because it is not less repugnant that the more perfect should be an effect of, and dependence on the less perfect, than that something should proceed from nothing, it was equally impossible that I could hold it from myself: accordingly, it but remained that it had been placed in me by a Nature which was in reality more perfect than mine, and which even possessed within itself all the perfections of which I could form any idea; that is to say, in a single word, which was God.

I would here willingly have proceeded to exhibit the whole chain of truths which I deduced from these primary.... But because I have essayed to expound the chief of these discoveries in a Treatise which certain considerations prevent me from publishing, I cannot make the results known more conveniently than by here giving a summary of the contents of this Treatise.[1] ...

I pointed out what are the laws of nature; and, with no other principle upon which to found my reasonings except the infinite perfection of God, I endeavoured to demonstrate all those about which there could be any room for doubt, and to prove that they are such, that even if God had created more worlds, there could have been none in which these laws were not observed. Thereafter, I showed how the greatest part of the matter of this chaos must, in accordance with these laws, dispose and arrange itself in such a way as to present the appearance of heavens; how in the meantime some of its parts must compose an earth and some planets and comets, and others a sun and fixed stars.... So that even although he had from the beginning given it no other form than that of chaos, provided only he had established certain laws of nature, and had lent it his concurrence to enable it to act as it is wont to do, it may be believed, without discredit to the miracle of creation, that, in this way alone, things purely material might, in course of time, have become such as we observe them at present; and their nature is much more easily conceived when they are beheld coming in this manner gradually into existence, than when they are only considered as produced at once in a finished and perfect state.

From the description of inanimate bodies and plants, I passed to animals, and particularly to man.... I had shewn what must be the fabric of the nerves and muscles of the human body to give the animal spirits contained in it the power to move the members, as when we see heads shortly after they have been struck off still move and bite the earth, although no longer animated; what changes must take place in the brain to produce waking, sleep, and dreams; how light, sounds,

[1] In his treatise *Du Monde,* Descartes put forward a heliocentric theory of the universe. He suppressed the treatise because a similar theory put forward by Galileo was censured by the church (see p. 439).

odours, tastes, heat, and all the other qualities of external objects impress it with different ideas by means of the senses; how hunger, thirst, and the other internal affections can likewise impress upon it divers ideas; what must be understood by the common sense *(sensus communis)* in which these ideas are received, by the memory which retains them, by the fantasy which can change them in various ways, and out of them compose new ideas, and which, by the same means, distributing the animal spirits through the muscles, can cause the members of such a body to move in as many different ways, and in a manner as suited, whether to the objects that are presented to its senses or to its internal affections, as can take place in our own case apart from the guidance of the will. Nor will this appear at all strange to those who are acquainted with the variety of movements performed by the different automata, or moving machines fabricated by human industry, and that with help of but few pieces compared with the great multitude of bones, muscles, nerves, arteries, veins, and other parts that are found in the body of each animal. Such persons will look upon this body as a machine made by the hands of God, which is incomparably better arranged, and adequate to movements more admirable than is any machine of human invention. . . .

I had after this described the Reasonable Soul, and shewn that it could by no means be educed from the power of matter, as the other things of which I had spoken, but that it must be expressly created; and that it is not sufficient that it be lodged in the human body exactly like a pilot in a ship, unless perhaps to move its members, but that it is necessary for it to be joined and united more closely to the body, in order to have sensations and appetites similar to ours, and thus constitute a real man. I here entered, in conclusion, upon the subject of the soul at considerable length, because it is of the greatest moment: for after the error of those who deny the existence of God, an error which I think I have already sufficiently refuted, there is none that is more powerful in leading feeble minds astray from the straight path of virtue than the supposition that the soul of the brutes is of the same nature with our own; and consequently that after this life we have nothing to hope for or fear, more than flies and ants; in place of which, when we know how far they differ we much better comprehend the reasons which establish that the soul is of a nature wholly independent of the body, and that consequently it is not liable to die with the latter; and, finally, because no other causes are observed capable of destroying it, we are naturally led thence to judge that it is immortal.

SCIENTIFIC ACHIEVEMENT

Astronomy

Nicolaus Copernicus (1473–1533) noted a "defect" in the cosmologies handed down from the ancient world. The assumption that the earth was the center of the universe made it impossible to provide a wholly adequate mathematical explanation of the observed movements of the planets. This led Copernicus to formulate a radically different hypothesis.

From Copernicus. *Commentariolus*

Having become aware of these defects, I often considered whether there could perhaps be found a more reasonable arrangement of circles, from which every apparent inequality would be derived and in which everything would move uniformly about its proper center, as the rule of absolute motion requires. After I had addressed myself to this very difficult and almost insoluble problem, the suggestion at length came to me how it could be solved with fewer and much simpler constructions than were formly used, if some assumptions (which are called axioms) were granted me. They follow in this order.

Assumptions

1. There is no one center of all the celestial circles or spheres.
2. The center of the earth is not the center of the universe, but only of gravity and of the lunar sphere.
3. All the spheres revolve about the sun as their mid-point, and therefore the sun is the center of the universe.
4. The ratio of the earth's distance from the sun to the height of the firmament is so much smaller than the ratio of the earth's radius to its distance from the sun that the distance from the earth to the sun is imperceptible in comparison with the height of the firmament.
5. Whatever motion appears in the firmament arises not from any motion of the firmament but from the earth's motion. The earth to-

From "Commentariolus" in *Three Copernican Treatises*, Edward Rosen, trans. (New York: Columbia University Press, 1939), pp. 57–60.

gether with its circumjacent elements performs a complete rotation on its fixed poles in a daily motion, while the firmament and highest heaven abide unchanged.

6. What appears to us as motions of the sun arise not from its motion but from the motion of the earth and our sphere, with which we revolve about the sun like any other planet. The earth has, then, more than one motion.

7. The apparent retrograde and direct motion of the planets arises not from their motion but from the earth's. The motion of the earth alone, therefore, suffices to explain so many apparent inequalities in the heavens.

Having set forth these assumptions, I shall endeavor briefly to show how uniformity of the motions can be saved in a systematic way. However, I have thought it well, for the sake of brevity, to omit from this sketch mathematical demonstrations, reserving these for my larger work. But in the explanation of the circles I shall set down here the lengths of the radii; and from these the reader who is not unacquainted with mathematics will readily perceive how closely this arrangement of circles agrees with the numerical data and observations.

Accordingly, let no one suppose that I have gratuitously asserted, with the Pythagoreans, the motion of the earth; strong proof will be found in my exposition of the circles. For the principal arguments by which the natural philosophers attempt to establish the immobility of the earth rest for the most part on the appearances; it is particularly such arguments that collapse here, since I treat the earth's immobility as due to an appearance.

The Order of the Spheres

The celestial spheres are arranged in the following order. The highest is the immovable sphere of the fixed stars, which contains and gives position to all things. Beneath it is Saturn, which Jupiter follows, then Mars. Below Mars is the sphere on which we revolve; then Venus; last is Mercury. The lunar sphere revolves about the center of the earth and moves with the earth like an epicycle. In the same order also one planet surpasses another in speed of revolution, according as they trace greater or smaller circles. Thus Saturn completes its revolution in thirty years, Jupiter in twelve, Mars in two and one half, and the earth in one year, Venus in nine months, Mercury in three.

In ancient and medieval cosmologies the heavenly bodies were regarded as perfect spheres, made of a finer substance than the earth—more pure, more perfect, not subject to change or decay. Galileo (1564–1642) turned a telescope on the heavens and saw a different picture.

From Galileo. *The Starry Messenger*

Great indeed are the things which in this brief treatise I propose for observation and consideration by all students of nature. I say great, because of the excellence of the subject itself, the entirely unexpected and novel character of these things, and finally because of the instrument by means of which they have been revealed to our senses.

Surely it is a great thing to increase the numerous host of fixed stars previously visible to the unaided vision, adding countless more which have never before been seen, exposing these plainly to the eye in numbers ten times exceeding the old and familiar stars.

It is a very beautiful thing, and most gratifying to the sight, to behold the body of the moon, distant from us almost sixty earthly radii, as if it were no farther away than two such measures—so that its diameter appears almost thirty times larger, its surface nearly nine hundred times, and its volume twenty-seven thousand times as large as when viewed with the naked eye. In this way one may learn with all the certainty of sense evidence that the moon is not robed in a smooth and polished surface but is in fact rough and uneven, covered everywhere, just like the earth's surface, with huge prominences, deep valleys, and chasms.

Again, it seems to me a matter of no small importance to have ended the dispute about the Milky Way by making its nature manifest to the very senses as well as to the intellect. Similarly it will be a pleasant and elegant thing to demonstrate that the nature of those stars which astronomers have previously called "nebulous" is far different from what has been believed hitherto.

I have observed the nature and the material of the Milky Way. With the aid of the telescope this has been scrutinized so directly and with such ocular certainty that all the disputes which have vexed philosophers through so many ages have been resolved, and we are at last freed from wordy debates about it. The galaxy is, in fact, nothing but a congeries of innumerable stars grouped together in clusters. Upon whatever part of it the telescope is directed, a vast crowd of stars is immediately presented to view. Many of them are rather large and quite bright, while the number of smaller ones is quite beyond calculation.

But it is not only in the Milky Way that whitish clouds are seen; several patches of similar aspect shine with faint light here and there throughout the aether, and if the telescope is turned upon any of these it confronts us with a tight mass of stars. And what is even more remarkable, the stars which have been called "nebulous" by every astron-

From Stillman Drake, trans., *Discoveries and Opinions of Galileo* (New York: Doubleday, 1957), pp. 27–28, 49–50. Copyright © 1957 by Stillman Drake. Reprinted by permission of Doubleday & Company, Inc.

omer up to this time turn out to be groups of very small stars arranged in a wonderful manner. Although each star separately escapes our sight on account of its smallness or the immense distance from us, the mingling of their rays gives rise to that gleam which was formerly believed to be some denser part of the aether that was capable of reflecting rays from stars or from the sun.

But what surpasses all wonders by far, and what particularly moves us to seek the attention of all astronomers and philosophers, is the discovery of four wandering stars not known or observed by any man before us. Like Venus and Mercury, which have their own periods about the sun, these have theirs about a certain star that is conspicuous among those already known, which they sometimes precede and sometimes follow, without ever departing from it beyond certain limits.[1] All these facts were discovered and observed by me not many days ago with the aid of a spyglass which I devised, after first being illuminated by divine grace. Perhaps other things, still more remarkable, will in time be discovered by me or by other observers with the aid of such an instrument. . . .

Galileo's discovery of varying spots on the surface of the sun contradicted the view that heavenly bodies were immutable. Some Aristotelian philosophers simply refused to believe the evidence of the telescope.

From Galileo. *Letters on Sunspots*

Well, if alteration were annihilation, the Peripatetics would have some reason for concern; but since it is nothing but mutation, there is no reason for such bitter hostility to it. It seems to me unreasonable to call "corruption" in an egg that which produces a chicken. Besides, if "corruption" and "generation" are discovered in the moon, why deny them to the sky? If the earth's small mutations do not threaten its existence (if, indeed, they are ornaments rather than imperfections in it), why deprive the other planets of them? Why fear so much for the dissolution of the sky as a result of alterations no more inimical than these? . . .

But I shall not go on; I reserve to another time the examination of the Peripatetic arguments, merely remarking that it appears to me not entirely philosophical to cling to conclusions once they have been discovered to be manifestly false. These men are persuaded that if Aristotle were back on earth in our age, he would do the same—as if it were a sign of more perfect judgment and a more noble consequence of deep learning to defend what is false than to learn the truth! People like this, it seems to me, give us reason to suspect that they have not so

[1]Galileo refers here to his discovery of the four moons of Jupiter.

From Stillman Drake, trans., *Discoveries and Opinions of Galileo* (New York: Doubleday, 1957), 142–143. Copyright © 1957 by Stillman Drake. Reprinted by permission of Doubleday & Company, Inc.

much plumbed the profundity of the Peripatetic arguments as they have conserved the imperious authority of Aristotle. It would be enough for them, and would save them a great deal of trouble, if they were to avoid these really dangerous arguments; for it is easier to consult indexes and look up texts than to investigate conclusions and form new and conclusive proofs. Besides, it seems to me that we abase our own status too much and do this not without some offense to Nature (and I might add to divine Providence), when we attempt to learn from Aristotle that which he neither knew nor could find out, rather than consult our own senses and reason. For she, in order to aid our understanding of her great works, has given us two thousand more years of observations, and sight twenty times as acute as that which she gave Aristotle.

I have demonstrated that the sunspots are neither stars nor permanent materials, and that they are not located at a distance from the sun but are produced and dissolved upon it in a manner not unlike that of clouds and vapors on the earth. That is all I have to say to Your Excellency on this subject for the present; let it seal all the new discoveries I have made in the heavens, and let me now return freely and without interruption to the studies which I shall shortly publish together with the consideration of other celestial novelties.

Galileo's observations convinced him that Copernicus's heliocentric theory was true, not just as a mathematical hypothesis but as a description of actual physical reality. His assertion of this position led to a conflict with the church. Galileo defended his views in the following letter, but in the end he was forced by the Inquisition to renounce them.

From Galileo. *Letter to the Grand Duchess Christina*

Some years ago, as Your Serene Highness well knows, I discovered in the heavens many things that had not been seen before our own age. The novelty of these things, as well as some consequences which followed from them in contradiction to the physical notions commonly held among academic philosophers, stirred up against me no small number of professors—as if I had placed these things in the sky with my own hands in order to upset nature and overturn the sciences. They seemed to forget that the increase of known truths stimulates the investigation, establishment, and growth of the arts; not their diminution or destruction.

Showing a greater fondness for their own opinions than for truth, they sought to deny and disprove the new things which, if they had cared to look for themselves, their own senses would have demon-

From Stillman Drake, trans., *Discoveries and Opinions of Galileo* (New York: Doubleday, 1957), pp. 175, 177, 181–183, 191–193. Copyright © 1957 by Stillman Drake. Reprinted by permission of Doubleday & Company, Inc.

strated to them. To this end they hurled various charges and published numerous writings filled with vain arguments, and they made the grave mistake of sprinkling these with passages taken from places in the Bible which they had failed to understand properly, and which were ill suited to their purposes. . . .

Persisting in their original resolve to destory me and everything mine by any means they can think of, these men are aware of my views in astronomy and philosophy. They know that as to the arrangement of the parts of the universe, I hold the sun to be situated motionless in the center of the revolution of the celestial orbs while the earth rotates on its axis and revolves about the sun. They know also that I support this position not only by refuting the arguments of Ptolemy and Aristotle, but by producing many counter-arguments; in particular, some which relate to physical effects whose causes can perhaps be assigned in no other way. In addition there are astronomical arguments derived from many things in my new celestial discoveries that plainly confute the Ptolemaic system while admirably agreeing with and confirming the contrary hypothesis. Possibly because they are disturbed by the known truth of other propositions of mine which differ from those commonly held, and therefore mistrusting their defense so long as they confine themselves to the field of philosophy, these men have resolved to fabricate a shield for their fallacies out of the mantle of pretended religion and the authority of the Bible. These they apply, with little judgment, to the refutation of arguments that they do not understand and have not even listened to. . . .

The reason produced for condemning the opinion that the earth moves and the sun stands still is that in many places in the Bible one may read that the sun moves and the earth stands still. Since the Bible cannot err, it follows as a necessary consequence that anyone takes an erroneous and heretical position who maintains that the sun is inherently motionless and the earth movable.

With regard to this argument, I think in the first place that it is very pious to say and prudent to affirm that the holy Bible can never speak untruth—whenever its true meaning is understood. But I believe nobody will deny that it is often very abstruse, and may say things which are quite different from what its bare words signify. Hence in expounding the Bible if one were always to confine oneself to the unadorned grammatical meaning, one might fall into error. Not only contradictions and propositions far from true might thus be made to appear in the Bible, but even grave heresies and follies. Thus it would be necessary to assign to God feet, hands, and eyes, as well as corporeal and human affections, such as anger, repentance, hatred, and sometimes even the forgetting of things past and ignorance of those to come. These propositions uttered by the Holy Ghost were set down in that manner by the sacred scribes in order to accommodate them to the capacities of the common people, who are rude and unlearned. . . .

Hence I think that I may reasonably conclude that whenever the Bible has occasion to speak of any physical conclusion (especially those which are very abstruse and hard to understand), the rule has been observed of avoiding confusion in the minds of the common people. . . . Who, then, would positively declare that this principle has been set aside, and the Bible has confined itself rigorously to the bare and restricted sense of its words, when speaking but casually of the earth, of water, of the sun, or of any other created thing? Especially in view of the fact that these things in no way concern the primary purpose of the sacred writings, which is the service of God and the salvation of souls—matters infinitely beyond the comprehension of the common people.

This being granted, I think that in discussions of physical problems we ought to begin not from the authority of scriptural passages, but from sense-experiences and necessary demonstrations; for the holy Bible and the phenomena of nature proceed alike from the divine Word. . . . For that reason it appears that nothing physical which sense-experience sets before our eyes, or which necessary demonstrations prove to us, ought to be called in question (much less condemned) upon the testimony of biblical passages which may have some different meaning beneath their words.

I do not wish to place in the number of such lay writers some theologians whom I consider men of profound learning and devout behavior, and who are therefore held by me in great esteem and veneration. Yet I cannot deny that I feel some discomfort which I should like to have removed, when I hear them pretend to the power of constraining others by scriptural authority to follow in a physical dispute that opinion which they think best agrees with the Bible, and then believe themselves not bound to answer the opposing reasons and experiences. In explanation and support of this opinion they say that since theology is queen of all the sciences, she need not bend in any way to accommodate herself to the teachings of less worthy sciences which are subordinate to her; these others must rather be referred to her as to their supreme empress, changing and altering their conclusions according to her statutes and decrees. . . .

Let us grant then that theology is conversant with the loftiest divine contemplation, and occupies the regal throne among sciences by dignity. But acquiring the highest authority in this way, if she does not descend to the lower and humbler speculations of the subordinate sciences and has no regard for them because they are not concerned with blessedness, then her professors should not arrogate to themselves the authority to decide on controversies in professions which they have neither studied not practiced. Why, this would be as if an absolute despot, being neither a physician nor an architect but knowing himself free to command, should undertake to administer medicines and erect buildings according to his whim—at grave peril of his poor patients' lives, and the speedy collapse of his edifices.

Synthesis

Isaac Newton (1642–1727) succeeded in explaining a great mass of observed phenomena by postulating a few simple laws.

From *Newton's Principia*

We offer this work as the mathematical principles of philosophy; for all the difficulty of philosophy seems to consist in this—from the phænomena of motions to investigate the forces of nature, and then from these forces to demonstrate the other phænomena; and to this end the general propositions in the first and second book are directed. In the third book we give an example of this in the explication of the System of the World; for by the propositions mathematically demonstrated in the former books, we in the third derive from the celestial phænomena the forces of gravity with which bodies tend to the sun and the several planets. Then from these forces, by other propositions which are also mathematical, we deduce the motions of the planets, the comets, the moon, and the sea. I wish we could derive the rest of the phænomena of nature by the same kind of reasoning from mechanical principles; for I am induced by many reasons to suspect that they may all depend upon certain forces by which the particles of bodies, by some causes hitherto unknown, are either mutually impelled towards each other, and cohere in regular figures, or are repelled and recede from each other; which forces being unknown, philosophers have hitherto attempted the search of nature in vain; but I hope the principles here laid down will afford some light either to this or some truer method of philosophy. . . .

Rules of Reasoning in Philosophy

Rule I. *We are to admit no more causes of natural things than such as are both true and sufficient to explain their appearances.*

To this purpose the philosophers say that Nature does nothing in vain, and more is in vain when less will serve; for Nature is pleased with simplicity, and affects not the pomp of superfluous causes.

Rule II. *Therefore to the same natural effects we must, as far as possible, assign the same causes.*

As to respiration in a man and in a beast; the descent of stones in Europe and in America; the light of our culinary fire and of the sun; the reflection of light in the earth, and in the planets.

Rule III. *The qualities of bodies, which admit neither intension nor remission of degrees, and which are found to belong to all bodies within the reach of*

From *Sir Isaac Newton's Mathematical Principles of Natural Science*, Andrew Motte, trans., revised by Florence Cajori (Berkeley, Calif.: University of California Press, 1934), pp. 398–400, 13–14. Reprinted by permission of the publisher.

our experiments, are to be esteemed the universal qualities of all bodies what-soever.

For since the qualities of bodies are only known to us by experiments, we are to hold for universal all such as universally agree with experiments and such as are not liable to diminution can never be quite taken away. We are certainly not to relinquish the evidence of experiments for the sake of dreams and vain fictions of our own devising; nor are we to recede from the analogy of Nature, which uses to be simple, and always consonant to itself. We no other way know the extension of bodies than by our senses, nor do these reach it in all bodies; but because we perceive extension in all that are sensible, therefore we ascribe it universally to all others also. That abundance of bodies are hard, we learn by experience; and because the hardness of the whole arises from the hardness of the parts, we therefore justly infer the hardness of the undivided particles not only of the bodies we feel but of all others. That all bodies are impenetrable, we gather not from reason, but from sensation. The bodies which we handle we find impenetrable, and thence conclude impenetrability to be an universal property of all bodies whatsoever.

Lastly, if it universally appears, by experiments and astronomical observations, that all bodies about the earth gravitate towards the earth, and that in proportion to the quantity of matter which they severally contain; that the moon likewise, according to the quantity of its matter, gravitates towards the earth; that, on the other hand, our sea gravitates towards the moon; and all the planets mutually one towards another; and the comets in like manner towards the sun; we must, in consequence of this rule, universally allow that all bodies whatsoever are endowed with a principle of mutual gravitation. For the argument from the appearances concludes with more force for the universal gravitation of all bodies than for their impenetrability; of which, among those in the celestial regions, we have no experiments, nor any manner of observation. Not that I affirm gravity to be essential to bodies: by their *vis insita* [inherent force] I mean nothing but their *vis inertiæ* [force of inertia]. This is immutable. Their gravity is diminished as they recede from the earth.

Rule IV. *In experimental philosophy we are to look upon propositions collected by general induction from phænomena as accurately or very nearly true, notwithstanding any contrary hypotheses that may be imagined, till such time as other phænomena occur, by which they may either be made more accurate, or liable to exceptions.*

This rule must follow, that the argument of induction may not be evaded by hypotheses.

The Laws of Motion

Law I: *Every body continues in its state of rest, or of uniform motion, in a right line, unless it is compelled to change that state by forces impressed upon it.*

Projectiles continue in their motions, so far as they are not retarded by the resistance of the air, or impelled downwards by the force of gravity. A top, whose parts by their cohesion are continually drawn aside from rectilinear motions, does not cease its rotation, otherwise than as it is retarded by the air. The greater bodies of the planets and comets, meeting with less resistance in freer spaces, preserve their motions both progressive and circular for a much longer time.

Law II: *The change of motion is proportional to the motive force impressed; and is made in the direction of the right line in which that force is impressed.*

If any force generates a motion, a double force will generate double the motion, a triple force triple the motion, whether that force be impressed altogether and at once or gradually and successively. And this motion (being always directed the same way with the generating force), if the body moved before, is added to or subtracted from the former motion, according as they directly conspire with or are directly contrary to each other; or obliquely joined, when they are oblique, so as to produce a new motion compounded from the determination of both.

Law III: *To every action there is always opposed an equal reaction: or, the mutual actions of two bodies upon each other are always equal, and directed to contrary parts.*

Whatever draws or presses another is as much drawn or pressed by that other. If you press a stone with your finger, the finger is also pressed by the stone. If a horse draws a stone tied to a rope, the horse (if I may say so) will be equally drawn back towards the stone; for the distended rope, by the same endeavor to relax or unbend itself, will draw the horse as much towards the stone as it does the stone towards the horse, and will obstruct the progress of the one as much as it advances that of the other. If a body impinge upon another, and by its force change the motion of the other, that body also (because of the equality of the mutual pressure) will undergo an equal change, in its own motion, towards the contrary part. The changes made by these actions are equal, not in the velocities but in the motions of the bodies; that is to say, if the bodies are not hindered by any other impediments. For, because the motions are equally changed, the changes of the velocities made toward contrary parts are inversely proportional to the bodies.

Like many of his contemporaries, Jean Bodin (1530–1596) reflected on the relationship between ancient and modern science.

From *Bodin's Methodus*

Once there was a golden age, afterwards a silver, then a bronze, and then an iron. At length clay followed. But this opinion must be adjusted, for if anyone examines the meaning of historians, not of poets, certainly he will decide that there is a change in human affairs similar

From John Bodin, *Method for the Easy Comprehension of History*, Beatrice Reynolds, trans. (New York: Columbia University Press, 1945), pp. 296, 301–302.

to that in the nature of all things; nor is there anything new under the sun, as that sage master of wisdom says. The age which they call "golden," if it be compared with ours, would seem but iron. . . .

Some one will say, however, that the ancients were inventors of the arts and to them the glory ought to go. They certainly did discover many things—especially the power of the celestial bodies, the calculated courses of many stars—but yet not all—the wonderful trajections of fixed stars and of those called "planets." Then they noted carefully the obscurities of nature and explained many things accurately, and yet they left incomplete many of these things which have been completed and handed down to posterity by men of our time. No one, looking closely into this matter, can doubt that the discoveries of our men ought to be compared with the discoveries of our elders; many ought to be placed first. Although nothing is more remarkable in the whole nature of things than the magnet, yet the ancients were not aware of its use, clearly divine, and whereas they lived entirely within the Mediterranean basin, our men, on the other hand, traverse the whole earth every year in frequent voyages and lead colonies into another world, as I might say, in order to open up the farthest recesses of India. Not only has this discovery developed an abundant and profitable commerce (which formerly was insignificant or not well known) but also all men surprisingly work together in a world state, as if in one and the same city-state. Indeed, in geography, one of the most excellent arts, one may understand how much advance has been made from the fact that information about India which used to seem fabulous to many (for Lactantius and Augustine said that men who believed in the antipodes were crazy) have been verified by us, as well as the motion of the fixed stars and the trepidation of the great sphere. Moreover, what is more remarkable than that abstraction and separation of forms from matter (if I may speak thus)? From this the hidden secrets of nature are revealed; hence healthful medicines are daily brought forward. I pass over the method of investigating celestial-longitude from equal hours, which could not be calculated by the ancients from the normal to the ecliptic without great error. I will not dwell upon the catapults of our ancestors and the ancient engines of war, which, of course, seem like some boyish toy if compared with our [instruments]. I omit finally countless arts, both handicraft and weaving, with which the life of man has been aided in a remarkable way. Printing alone can easily vie with all the discoveries of all the ancients.

So they who say that all things were understood by the ancients err not less than do those who deny them the early conquest of many arts. Nature has countless treasures of knowledge which cannot be exhausted in any age. Since these things are so and since by some eternal law of nature the path of change seems to go in a circle, so that vices press upon virtues, ignorance upon knowledge, base upon honorable, and darkness upon light, they are mistaken who think that the race of men always deteriorates.

WITCHCRAFT—SUPERSTITION AND PERSECUTION

The Prevalence of Witches

Bodin thought that a major threat to society came from the machinations of witches.

From *Bodin's Demonology*

But those greatly err who think that penalties are established only to punish crime. I hold that this is the least of the fruits which accrue therefrom to the state. For the greatest and the chief is the appeasing of the wrath of God, especially if the crime is directly against the majesty of God, as is this one. . . . Now, if there is any means to appease the wrath of God, to gain his blessing, to strike awe into some by the punishment of others, to preserve some from being infected by others, to diminish the number of evil-doers, to make secure the life of the well-disposed, and to punish the most detestable crimes of which the human mind can conceive, it is to punish with the utmost rigor the witches. . . . Now, it is not within the power of princes to pardon a crime which the law of God punishes with the penalty of death—such as are the crimes of witches. Moreover, princes do gravely insult God in pardoning such horrible crimes committed directly against his majesty, seeing that the pettiest prince avenges with death insults against himself. Those too who let the witches escape, or who do not punish them with the utmost rigor, may rest assured that they will be abandoned by God to the mercy of the witches. And the country which shall tolerate this will be scourged with pestilences, famines, and wars; and those which shall take vengeance on the witches will be blessed by him and will make his anger to cease. Therefore it is that one accused of being a witch ought never to be fully acquitted and set free unless the calumny of the accuser is clearer than the sun, inasmuch as the proof of such crimes is so obscure and so difficult that not one witch in a million would be accused or punished if the procedure were governed by the ordinary rules.

From *De la Démonomanie des Sorciers*, G. L. Burr, trans. in *University of Pennsylvania Translations and Reprints* (Philadelphia: University of Pennsylvania Press, 1897), Vol. 3, No. 4, pp. 5–6.

The Frailty of Women

In 1486 two Dominican Inquisitors explained why most witches were women.

From *The Hammer of Witches*

Why Superstition is Chiefly Found in Women.

As for the first question, why a greater number of witches is found in the fragile feminine sex than among men; it is indeed a fact that it were idle to contradict, since it is accredited by actual experience, apart from the verbal testimony of credible witnesses. And without in any way detracting from a sex in which God has always taken great glory that His might should be spread abroad, let us say that various men have assigned various reasons for this fact, which nevertheless agree in principle. Wherefore it is good for the admonition of women, to speak of this matter; and it has often been proved by experience that they are eager to hear of it, so long as it is set forth with discretion.

For some learned men propound this reason; that there are three things in nature, the Tongue, an Ecclesiastic, and a Woman, which know no moderation in goodness or vice; and when they exceed the bounds of their condition they reach the greatest heights and the lowest depths of goodness and vice. . . .

Others again have propounded other reasons why there are more superstitious women found than men. And the first is, that they are more credulous; and since the chief aim of the devil is to corrupt faith, therefore he rather attacks them. See *Ecclesiasticus* xix: He that is quick to believe is light-minded, and shall be diminished. The second reason is, that women are naturally more impressionable, and more ready to receive the influence of a disembodied spirit; and that when they use this quality well they are very good, but when they use it ill they are very evil.

The third reason is that they have slippery tongues, and are unable to conceal from their fellow-women those things which by evil arts they know, and, since they are weak, they find an easy and secret manner of vindicating themselves by witchcraft. See *Ecclesiasticus* as quoted above: I had rather dwell with a lion and a dragon than to keep house with a wicked woman. All wickedness is but little to the wickedness of a woman. And to this may be added that, as they are very impressionable, they act accordingly.

There are also others who bring forward yet other reasons, of which preachers should be very careful how they make use. For it is true that in the Old Testament the Scriptures have much that is evil to say about

From *Malleus Maleficiarum*, M. Summers, trans. (London: John Rodker, 1928), pp. 41–44.

women, and this because of the first temptress, Eve, and her imitators; yet afterwards in the New Testament we find a change of name, as from Eva to Ave (as S. Jerome says), and the whole sin of Eve taken away by the benediction of Mary. Therefore preachers should always say as much praise of them as possible.

But because in these times this perfidy is more often found in women than in men, as we learn by actual experience, if anyone is curious as to the reason, we may add to what has already been said the following: that since they are feebler both in mind and body, it is not surprising that they should come more under the spell of witchcraft.

During the centuries of persecution many thousands of persons in many parts of Europe—most of them women—confessed to offenses like the following ones. Often the confessions were made under torture; sometimes they were given voluntarily.

Françoise Secretain confessed in 1598 under threat of torture after having been accused by an eight-year-old child, Loyse Maillat. (Françoise was condemned to death by burning but died in prison before the sentence was carried out.)

Confession of Françoise Secretian (1598)

First, that she had wished five devils on Loyse Maillat.

Second, that she had long since given herself to the Devil, who at that time had the likeness of a big black man.

Third, that the Devil had four or five times known her carnally, in the form sometimes of a dog, sometimes of a cat, and sometimes of a fowl; and that his semen was very cold.

Fourth, that she had countless times been to the Sabbat and assembly of witches near the village of Coyrieres in a place called Combes by the water; and that she went there on a white staff which she placed between her legs.

Fifth, that at the Sabbat she had danced, and had beaten water to cause hail.

Sixth, that she and Groz-Jacques Bocquet had caused Loys Monneret to die by making her eat a piece of bread which they had dusted with a powder given to them by the Devil.

Seventh, that she had caused several cows to die, and that she did so by touching them with her hand or with a wand while saying certain words.

Another example comes from sixteenth-century Scotland.

From Henry Boguet, *An Examen of Witches,* M. Summers, ed. (London: John Rodker, 1929), p. 5.

Trial of Geillis Duncane (1591)

Within the towne of Trenent, in the kingdome of Scotland, there dwelleth one David Seaton, who, being deputie bailiffe in the said towne, had a maid called Geillis Duncane, who used secretlie to absent and lie forth of hir maister's house every other night: This Geillis Duncane tooke in hand all such as were troubled or grieved with anie kinde of sicknes or infirmitie, and in short space did perfourme many matters most miraculous; which things, for asmuche as she began to do them upon a sodaine, having never done the like before, made her maister and others to be in great admiration, and wondered thereat: by meanes whereof, the saide David Seaton had his maide in great suspition that shee did not those things by naturall and lawfull waies, but rather supposed it to bee done by some extraordinarie and unlawfull meanes. Whereupon, her maister began to grow verie inquisitive, and examined hir which way and by what meanes shee was able to performe matters of so great importance; whereat shee gave him to aunswere: nevertheless, her maister, to the intent that hee might the better trie and finde out the truth of the same, did with the help of others torment her with the torture of the pilliwinkles[1] upon her fingers, which is a grievous torture; and binding or wrinching her head with a cord or roape, which is a most cruell torment also; yet would she not confess anie thing; whereuppon, they suspecting that she had beene marked by the Devill (as commonly witches are), made diligent search about her, and found the enemies mark to be in her fore crag, or fore part of her throate; which being found, she confessed that al her doings was done by the wicked allurements and entisements of the Devil, and that she did them by witchcraft. After this her confession, she was committed to prison, where shee continued a season, where immediately shee accused these persons following to bee notorious witches, and caused them forthwith to be apprehended, one after another, viz. Agnes Sampson the eldest witche of them all, dwelling in Haddington; Agnes Tompson of Edenbrough; Doctor Fian alias John Cuningham, master of the schoole at Saltpans in Lowthian, of whose life and strange acts you shal heare more largely in the end of this discourse. These were by the saide Geillis Duncane accused, as also George Motts wife, dwelling in Lowthian; Robert Grierson, skipper; and Jannet Blandilands; with the potter's wife of Seaton: the smith at the Brigge Hallis, with innumerable others in those parts, and dwelling in those bounds aforesaid; of whom some are alreadie executed, the rest remaine in prison to receive the doome of judgement at the Kinges Majesties will and pleasure.

[1]An instrument of torture similar to the thumbscrews later in use.

From *Pitcairn's Criminal Trials in Scotland* in G. L. Burr, *University of Pennsylvania Translations and Reprints* (Philadelphia: University of Pennsylvania Press, 1897), Vol. 3, No. 4, pp. 19–20.

XIII

SOCIAL CONDITIONS
Germany
From *Simplicissimus*
Spain
From *Letter to the Queen of Spain*
France
From *Report of the Estates of Normandy (1651)*
From *Letters of the Abbess of Port-Royal*

FOUNDATIONS OF ABSOLUTISM
Rationalism
From Thomas Hobbes. *Leviathan*
Divine Right
From Bossuet. *Politics Drawn from the Very Words of Holy Scripture*
Patriarchy
From Robert Filmer. *Patriarcha*
From David Hunt. *Parents and Children in History*
From *Journal of Jean Héroard*

THE COURT OF LOUIS XIV
Portrait of a Monarch
From *Memoirs of the Duke of Saint-Simon*
Life at Versailles
From *Memoirs of the Duke of Saint-Simon*
From *Letter of the Duchess of Orleans*
From W. H. Lewis. *The Splendid Century*

ABSOLUTISM IN PRACTICE
Religion
From *Revocation of the Edict of Nantes 1685*
From *Memoirs of the Duke of Saint-Simon*

From *Declaration of the Gallican Church*
From Louis XIV. *Letter to His Heir*
Military Organization
From Voltaire. *The Age of Louis XIV*
Economy and Local Administration
From *Colbert's Memoranda*
From *Colbert's Correspondence*

EASTERN EUROPE
The Turkish Menace
From *The Present State of the German and Turkish Empires*
Peter the Great
From *Gilbert Burnett's History*
From *Von Korb's Diary*
From *De Missy's Life of Peter*

THE SEARCH FOR ORDER—ABSOLUTISM AND ARISTOCRACY

THE SEVENTEENTH CENTURY was a time of great intellectual vitality but also of much political instability. Historians often refer to the age as one of "general crisis." Frequent wars caused widespread devastation. A perceptible worsening of climatic conditions, marked by colder and wetter summers, led to a series of bad harvests and recurring famines. The economic expansion of the sixteenth century came to a halt. In many countries peasant uprisings or aristocratic rebellions occurred.

In these circumstances there was a widely felt need for stability and order. One consequence was that theories of royal absolutism became popular among political thinkers. They ranged from the severely rationalist arguments of Thomas Hobbes to various religious doctrines of divine right and patriarchal authority. (Modern political philosophers are usually most impressed by the rationalist arguments, but seventeenth-century people usually found the religious ones more simple and satisfying.)

During the reign of Louis XIV (1643–1715), France became the model of a centralized, absolute monarchy. Royal authority was supported by a large army, a loyal church, and a network of local government officials who were closely supervised by the central government. Louis coped with the problem of an unruly aristocracy by inducing many French nobles to take up residence in the great palace he built at Versailles and to pass their days in the intricate ritual of court life that grew up there. The king's great finance minister, Jean Colbert—following the common "mercantilist" doctrine of the seventeenth century—aimed to enhance France's wealth and power by increasing the country's manufactures and reducing dependence on imports from abroad. For a time it seemed that France might dominate all western Europe.

Meanwhile, in eastern Europe, two other absolutist states experienced changing fortunes. The Turks, who throughout the seventeenth century had threatened to invade the Christian lands of the west, were finally defeated at Vienna in 1683. And Russia took the first major steps toward westernization under Peter the Great. These events helped to shape the course of European history in the modern world.

SOCIAL CONDITIONS

Germany

Jacob von Grimmelshausen, who served as a soldier in the Thirty Years' War, wrote a picaresque novel about the adventures of a "Simpleton" in those grim times.

From *Simplicissimus*

The Fate of a Farm

When these horsemen took over my father's smoky house, the first thing they did was to bring in their horses; then each one started to destroy everything and tear everything to pieces. Some were killing the cattle, and broiling or roasting the carcasses; others were going through the house, determined not to miss any thing good there might be for them to find; even the privy was not safe from their investigations, as if we had hidden there Jason's Golden Fleece. Others were making great bundles of linen and clothes and all sorts of stuff, as if they were going to open a flea market someplace, and what they weren't going to carry away with them they pulled to pieces. Some shoved their swords through the piles of straw or hay as if they hadn't had enough pigs to kill; others shook the feathers out of the mattresses and filled them with bacon and salt meat and other things as if they expected to sleep on them better that way. Others were breaking down the stoves and the window panes, as if they thought that summer was going to last forever. They were smashing the tableware and carrying away with them these useless pieces of copper or pottery or pewter. They burnt beds, and the tables, and the chairs, and the benches, when they could have found plenty of dry fire-wood in the yard. Of pots and of pans they shattered the lot; either because they didn't want to eat anything but roast meat any more, or because they only planned to stay with us for one single meal. Our maid underwent such treatment in the stables that she could hardly walk coming out. Is it not shameful to have such things happening? As for the groom, they laid him on the ground, they put a funnel into his mouth, and they poured in a whole tubful of foul matter. They called this "a little drink in the Swedish manner"; but he didn't find it at all to his taste. They also forced him to guide them on another raid, where they captured both people and cattle whom they brought into our yard. Among them they got my father, and my mother, and my sister Ursula.

Then they started to take the flints out of the cocks of the pistols in order to use them as thumbscrews, and to torture the poor beggars as if they were sorcerers who needed to be punished before being burnt. As a matter of fact, the soldiers had already shoved one of the captured peasants into the oven and they were trying to keep him warm in there (so he would tell them the hiding place of his little hoard). They had tied a cord around the head of another, and they were tightening the cord with a garrot, so that with every turn they gave it, the blood gushed out of his mouth, his nose and his ears. In short, each man was busy working out some new kind of torture for the peasants and so each victim had his own particular kind of torment.

However it seemed to me at the time that my father was the luckiest of them all, because he admitted with roars of laughter what the others were forced to reveal in the midst of sufferings and fearful plaints.

This kind of honor was his, no doubt, because he was the head of the family. The soldiers put him before a great fire, they tied him so that he couldn't move his arms or his legs, and they rubbed the soles of his feet with damp salt; then they had our old goat lick it off. He was so tickled by this that he nearly died of laughter. It all seemed to me so pleasant and so silly—I had never seen nor heard my father laugh so long—that, either because his laughter was contagious, or else because I couldn't understand what was going on, I had to laugh too. That is how my father told the raiders what they wanted to know, and revealed the hiding place of his treasure which consisted of gold and pearls and jewels; a much richer hoard than one would have expected a peasant to own.

I cannot say anything about the treatment of the women, the maids, and the young girls who had been captured, because the soldiers didn't let me see what they were doing to them. I know only that one heard sighs and groans in various corners, and I thought that my mother and my sister Ursula were probably no better off than the others.

Spain

This letter written by an anonymous official in mid-seventeenth century survives in the Spanish Archivo Histórico Nacional.

From *Letter to the Queen of Spain*

Señora, every day the occupation of my office brings me to many places in which I see and recognize necessities and miseries that until these times were never seen or heard of; towns that only a few years ago had one thousand *vecinos* [heads of families] do not have five hundred today, and in those that had five hundred there are scarcely signs of one hundred. In all these places there are innumerable persons and families that pass one or two days without eating, and others who merely eat herbs that they have gathered in the countryside as well as other types of sustenance never heard of or used before; and this, Señora, is not rumor or wild fancy, but something that Your Majesty can easily recognize and see.... And therefore, it is certain, Señora, that there have been many deaths and illnesses everywhere this year, and everyone has assured me that these have been caused by mere want. La Mancha, Señora, has been depopulated and many families have emigrated to Madrid, where there have now gathered more poor people than have ever been seen. La Alcarria is deserted, prostrate, and poor; parents cannot help their children, nor brothers their brothers, even though they are watching them die. And in places where poor people were never seen, today they roam about in great gangs. The rest of the province of Toledo is in the same condition, and if it was not for that pastor and prelate (the Cardinal Pascual de Aragon) who gives so many lavish and repeated alms and helps with so many necessities, it is certain that one would see misfortunes never imagined, but since it is not possible to help everyone, many are experiencing these misfortunes already.

And consequently, Señora, today most of the kingdom is in the same state of affairs, and I only wish that it were possible for Your Majesty to visit your kingdom so that you could see these conditions first hand and feel sympathy for them. . . .

From O. and P. Ranum, eds., *The Century of Louis XIV* (New York: Walker and Company, 1972), pp. 200–201, trans. R. Kagan. Reprinted by pemission of the publisher.

France

From *Report of the Estates of Normandy (1651)*

Saint-Quentin. Of the 450 sick persons whom the inhabitants were unable to relieve, 200 were turned out, and these we saw die one by one

From the translations in Cecile Augon, *Social France in the XVII Century* (London: Methuen and Co. Ltd., 1911), pp. 171–172, 189.

as they lay on the roadside. A large number still remain, and to each of them it is only possible to dole out the least scrap of bread. We only give bread to those who would otherwise die. The staple dish here consists of mice, which the inhabitants hunt, so desperate are they from hunger. They devour roots which the animals cannot eat; one can, in fact, not put into words the things one sees. . . . This narrative, far from exaggerating, rather understates the horror of the case, for it does not record the hundredth part of the misery in this district. Those who have not witnessed it with their own eyes cannot imagine how great it is. Not a day passes but at least 200 people die of famine in the two provinces. We certify to having ourselves seen herds, not of cattle, but of men and women, wandering about the fields between Rheims and Rhétel, turning up the earth like pigs to find a few roots; and as they can only find rotten ones, and not half enough of them, they become so weak that they have not strength left to seek food. The parish priest at Boult, whose letter we enclose, tells us he has buried three of his parishioners who died of hunger. The rest subsisted on chopped straw mixed with earth, of which they composed a food which cannot be called bread. Other persons in the same place lived on the bodies of animals which had died of disease, and which the curé, otherwise unable to help his people, allowed them to roast at the presbytery fire.

From *Letters of the Abbess of Port-Royal*

(1649) This poor country is a horrible sight; it is stripped of everything. The soldiers take possession of the farms and have the corn threshed, but will not give a single grain to the owners who beg it as an alms. It is impossible to plough. There are no more horses—all have been carried off. The peasants are reduced to sleeping in the woods and are thankful to have them as a refuge from murderers. And if they only had enough bread to half satisfy their hunger, they would indeed count themselves happy.

(1652) People massacre each other daily with every sort of cruelty. . . . The soldiers steal from one another when they have denuded every one else, and as they spoil more property than they carry off, they are themselves often reduced to starvation, and can find no more to annex. All the armies are equally undisciplined and vie with one another in lawlessness. The authorities in Paris are trying to send back the peasants to gather in the corn; but as soon as it is reaped the marauders come to slay and steal, and disperse all in a general rout.

FOUNDATIONS OF ABSOLUTISM

Rationalism

From Thomas Hobbes. *Leviathan*

In the first place, I put for a general inclination of all mankind, a perpetual and restless desire of power after power, that ceaseth only in death. And the cause of this, is not always that a man hopes for a more intensive delight, than he has already attained to; or that he cannot be content with a moderate power: but because he cannot assure the power and means to live well, which he hath present, without the acquisition of more.

Hereby it is manifest, that during the time men live without a common power to keep them all in awe, they are in that condition which is called war; and such a war, as is of every man, against every man.

Whatsoever therefore is consequent to a time of war, where every man is enemy to every man; the same is consequent to the time, wherein men live without other security, than what their own strength, and their own invention shall furnish them withal. In such condition, there is no place for industry; because the fruit thereof is uncertain: and consequently no culture of the earth; no navigation, nor use of the commodities that may be imported by sea; no commodious building; no instruments of moving, and removing, such things as require much force; no knowledge of the face of the earth; no account of time; no arts; no letters; no society; and which is worst of all, continual fear, and danger of violent death; and the life of man, solitary, poor, nasty, brutish, and short.

The final cause, end, or design of men, who naturally love liberty, and dominion over others, in the introduction of that restraint upon themselves, in which we see them live in commonwealths, is the foresight of their own preservation, and of a more contented life thereby;

From Thomas Hobbes, *Leviathan* (London: Andrew Crook, 1651), Chs. 11, 13, 17, 18.

that is to say, of getting themselves out from that miserable condition of war, which is necessarily consequent, as hath been shown, to the natural passions of men, when there is no visible power to keep them in awe, and tie them by fear of punishment to the performance of their covenants.

The only way to erect such a common power, as may be able to defend them from the invasion of foreigners, and the injuries of one another, and thereby to secure them in such sort, as that by their own industry, and by the fruits of the earth, they may nourish themselves and live contentedly; is, to confer all their power and strength upon one man, or upon one assembly of men, that may reduce all their wills, by plurality of voices, unto one will: which is as much as to say, to appoint one man, or assembly of men, to bear their person; and every one to own, and acknowledge himself to be author of whatsoever he that so beareth their person, shall act, or cause to be acted, in those things which concern the common peace and safety; and therein to submit their wills, every one to his will, and their judgments, to his judgment. This is more than consent, or concord; it is a real unity of them all, in one and the same person, made by covenant of every man with every man, in such manner, as if every man should say to every man, *I authorize and give up my right of governing myself, to this man, or to this assembly of men, on this condition, that thou give up thy right to him, and authorize all his actions in like manner*. This done, the multitude so united in one person, is called a COMMONWEALTH, in Latin CIVITAS. This is the generation of that great LEVIATHAN, or rather, to speak more reverently, of that *mortal god*, to which we owe under the *immortal God*, our peace and defence. For by this authority, given him by every particular man in the commonwealth, he hath the use of so much power and strength conferred on him, that by terror thereof, he is enabled to form the wills of them all, to peace at home, and mutual aid against their enemies abroad. And in him consisteth the essence of the commonwealth; which, to define it, is *one person, of whose acts a great multitude, by mutual covenants one with another, have made themselves every one the author, to the end he may use the strength and means of them all, as he shall think expedient, for their peace and common defence*.

And he that carrieth this person, is called SOVEREIGN, and said to have *sovereign power*; and every one besides, his SUBJECT.

A *commonwealth* is said to be *instituted*, when a *multitude* of men do agree, and *convenant, every one, with every one*, that to whatsoever *man*, or *assembly of men*, shall be given by the major part, the *right* to *present* the person of them all, that is to say, to be their *representative*; every one, as well he that *voted for it*, as he that *voted against it*, shall *authorize* all the actions and judgments, of that man, or assembly of men, in the same manner, as if they were his own, to the end, to live peaceably amongst themselves, and be protected against other men.

From this institution of a commonwealth are derived all the *rights*, and *faculties* of him, or them, on whom the sovereign power is conferred by the consent of the people assembled.

First, because they covenant . . . they that have already instituted a commonwealth, being thereby bound by covenant, to own the actions, and judgments of one, cannot lawfully make a new covenant, amongst themselves, to be obedient to any other, in any thing whatsoever, without his permission. And therefore, they that are subjects to a monarch, cannot without his leave cast off monarchy, and return to the confusion of a disunited multitude; nor transfer their person from him that beareth it, to another man, or other assembly of men: for they are bound, every man to every man, to own, and be reputed author of all, that he that already is their sovereign, shall do, and judge fit to be done.

Secondly, because the right of bearing the person of them all, is given to him they make sovereign, by covenant only of one to another, and not of him to any of them; there can happen no breach of covenant on the part of the sovereign; and consequently none of his subjects, by any pretence of forfeiture, can be freed from his subjection.

Thirdly, because the major part hath by consenting voices declared a sovereign; he that dissented must now consent with the rest; that is, be contented to avow all the actions he shall do, or else justly be destroyed by the rest. For if he voluntarily entered into the congregation of them that were assembled, he sufficiently declared thereby his will, and therefore tacitly covenanted, to stand to what the major part should ordain.

Fourthly, because every subject is by this institution author of all the actions, and judgments of the sovereign instituted; it follows, that whatsoever he doth, it can be no injury to any of his subjects; nor ought he to be by any of them accused of injustice. For he that doth anything by authority from another, doth therein no injury to him by whose authority he acteth: but by this institution of a commonwealth, every particular man is author of all the sovereign doth: and consequently he that complaineth of injury from his sovereign, complaineth of that whereof he himself is author; and therefore ought not to accuse any man but himself; no nor himself of injury; because to do injury to one's self, is impossible. It is true that they that have sovereign power may commit iniquity; but not injustice, or injury in the proper signification.

Fifthly, and consequently to that which was said last, no man that hath sovereign power can justly be put to death, or otherwise in any manner by his subjects punished. For seeing every subject is author of the actions of his sovereign; he punisheth another for the actions committed by himself.

Divine Right

From Bossuet. *Politics Drawn from the Very Words of Holy Scripture*

There are four characters or qualities essential to royal authority: First, royal authority is sacred; second, it is paternal; third, it is absolute; fourth, it is ruled by reason. . . .

Royal Authority Is Sacred.

God established kings as his ministers and rules peoples by them.

We have already seen that all power comes from God. "The prince," St. Paul adds, "is the minister of God to thee for good. But if thou do that which is evil, be afraid; for he beareth not the sword in vain; for he is the minister of God, a revenger to execute wrath upon him that doeth evil." [Rom. 13:4]

Thus princes act as ministers of God, and as his lieutenants on earth. It is by them that he exercises his rule. . . .

Thus we have seen that the royal throne is not the throne of a man, but the throne of God himself. . . .

The person of kings is sacred.

It thus appears that the person of kings is sacred and that to make an attempt on their lives is a sacrilege.

God has had them anointed by his prophets with a sacred unction as he has his pontiffs and his altars anointed.

But without the external application of this unction, they are sacred by their office, as being the representatives of the divine majesty, deputized by his providence to the execution of his designs. . . .

The title of Christ is given to kings; and they are everywhere called christs, or the anointed of the lord.

Royal Authority Is Paternal and Its Proper Character Is Goodness.

After what has been said, this truth has no need of proof.

We have seen that kings take the place of God, who is the true father of the human species. We have also seen that the first idea of power which exists among men is that of the paternal power; and that kings are modeled on fathers.

From J. B. Bossuet, *Politics Drawn from the Very Words of Holy Scripture* (1709), in Brian Tierney, Donald Kagan, and L. Pearce Williams, eds., *Great Issues in Western Civilization*, 3rd. ed., Vol II, pp. 613–615 (adapted), trans. L. Pearce Williams. Copyright © 1967, 1972, 1976 by Random House, Inc. Reprinted by permission of the publisher.

Everybody is also in accord, that the obedience which is owed to the public power can be found in the ten commandments only in the precept which obliges him to honor his parents.

Thus it follows from this that the name of king is a name for father and that goodness is the most natural character of kings. . . .

It is a royal right to provide for the needs of the people. He who undertakes it at the expense of the prince undertakes royalty: this is why it has been established. The obligation to care for the people is the foundation of all the rights that sovereigns have over their subjects.

Royal Authority Is Absolute.

Without this absolute authority, he cannot do good nor can he repress evil: it is necessary that his power be such that no one can hope to escape him; and finally the only defense of individuals against the public power ought to be their innocence. . . .

Princes, then, must be obeyed in the same way as justice itself; otherwise there can be no order and no finality in men's affairs.

They are gods, and participate in some sense in the divine independence. "I have said, You are gods, and you are all children of the Most High." [Ps. 81:6.]

There is no one save God alone who may judge their decisions and their lives. . . . The prince may himself redress his own errors when he sees that he has committed a wrong; but against his authority there can exist no remedy save in his authority itself.

There Can Be No Coactive Power Opposing the Prince.

A "coactive power" is a power to compel and execute that which is legitimately commanded. Legitimate command belongs to the prince alone; to him alone, therefore, belongs the "coactive power."

It is for this reason that St. Paul gives the sword to him only. "If you do not act rightly, be afraid; for it is not for nothing that he has the sword." [Rom. 13:4.] . . .

Thus it is that for the good of the state, all its force has been united in a single person. Let force exist elsewhere, and you divide the state and destroy the public peace; you set up two masters, contrary to this maxim of the Gospel: "No man can serve two masters." [Matt. 6:24.]

The prince is by his office the father of his people; he is placed by his grandeur above all petty interests; even more: all his grandeur and his natural interests are that the people shall be conserved, for once the people fail him he is no longer prince. There is thus nothing better than to give all the power of the state to him who has the greatest interest in the conservation and greatness of the state itself.

Kings Are Not by This Above the Laws.

". . . And it shall be, when he sitteth upon the throne of his kingdom, that he shall write him a copy of this law in a book out of that which is before the priest the Levite: and it shall be with him and he shall read therein all the days of his life: that he may learn to fear the Lord his god, to keep all the words of this law and these statutes to do them: that his heart be not lifted up above his brethren and that he turn not aside from the commandment to the right hand, or to the left: to the end that he may prolong his days in his kingdom, he, and his children." [Deut. 17. 18–20]

It should be noticed that this law does not include only religion, but the law of the realm as well to which the prince was subject as much as any other, or even more than others by the justness of his will.

This is something princes find difficult to understand. "What prince can you find me," asks St. Ambrose, "who believes that what is not good is not permitted, who considers himself bound by his own laws. . . ."

Kings therefore are subject like any others to the equity of the laws both because they must be just and because they owe to the people the example of protecting justice; but they are not subject to the penalties of the laws: or, as theology puts it, they are subject to the laws, not in terms of its coactive power but in terms of its directive power.

Patriarchy

Bossuet observed that royal power was "paternal." Sir Robert Filmer built a whole political theory around this idea.

From Robert Filmer. *Patriarcha*

As Adam was lord of his children, so his children under him had a command and power over their own children, but still with subordination to the first parent, who is lord-paramount over his children's children to all generations, as being the grandfather of his people.

I see not then how the children of Adam, or of any man else, can be free from subjection to their parents. And this subjection of children being the fountain of all regal authority, by the ordination of God himself; it follows that civil power not only in general is by divine institution, but even the assignment of it specifically to the eldest parents, which quite takes away that new and common distinction which refers

From Robert Filmer, *Patriarcha* (London: Richard Chiswell, 1680), Ch. 1.

only power universal and absolute to God, but power respective in regard of the special form of government to the choice of the people.

This lordship which Adam by command had over the whole world, and by right descending from him the patriarchs did enjoy, was as large and ample as the absolutest dominion of any monarch which hath been since the creation.

It may seem absurd to maintain that kings now are the fathers of their people, since experience shows the contrary. It is true, all kings be not the natural parents of their subjects, yet they all either are, or are to be reputed, the next heirs to those first progenitors who were at first the natural parents of the whole people, and in their right succeed to the exercise of supreme jurisdiction; and such heirs are not only lords of their own children, but also of their brethren, and all others that were subject to their fathers. And therefore we find that God told Cain of his brother Abel, "His desires shall be subject unto thee, and thou shalt rule over him."

If we compare the natural rights of a father with those of a king, we find them all one, without any difference at all but only in the latitude or extent of them: as the father over one family, so the king, as father over many families, extends his care to preserve, feed, clothe, instruct, and defend the whole commonwealth. His war, his peace, his courts of justice, and all his acts of sovereignty, tend only to preserve and distribute to every subordinate and inferior father, and to their children, their rights and privileges, so that all the duties of a king are summed up in an universal fatherly care of his people.

Because many seventeenth-century authors insisted that a king was like the father of a family, some modern historians have suggested that a study of actual family relationships might help us to a better understanding of seventeenth-century society and government.

From David Hunt. *Parents and Children in History*

Why did adults find it necessary to insist so emphatically on the obedience of children? Eriksonian theory suggests the beginnings of an answer. In his most thorough attempt to relate the second phase of childhood to the quality of social life, Erikson writes:

> We have related basic trust to the institution of religion. The basic need of the individual for a delineation of his *autonomy* in the adult order of things seems, in turn, to be taken care of by the *principle of "law and order,"* which in daily life as well as in the high courts of law apportions to each his privileges and his limitations, his obligations and his rights. The sense of autonomy which

arises, or should arise, in the second stage of childhood, is fostered by a handling of the small individual which expresses a sense of rightful dignity and lawful independence on the part of the parents. . . .

In short, parents need certain specific cultural and political supports if they are to accept with equanimity the first manifestations of infantile will. If we look for a moment at the kinds of reinforcements available to parents of the old regime, I think we can understand why they reacted as they did to the second stage of childhood.

In the seventeenth century, childrearing took place in a hierarchical society characterized by a very uneven distribution of wealth and dominated by forces of political and religious authoritarianism. It was not a social order in which most individuals found it possible to maintain "a sense of rightful dignity and lawful independence." For the vast majority of French subjects in this period, the concept of "law and order" could hardly have had much relation to their own very precarious existence. Such a social order naturally influences styles of childrearing. The adult who in his own life had little experience of genuine self-determination and only limited opportunity to observe it in the conduct of others, was not able to tolerate his child's efforts to be self-determining. The difficulty parents experienced in dealing with infantile will grew out of the inequitable character of their experience "in marriage, in work, and in citizenship."

Admittedly, these are sweeping statements. One might well object that I am arguing almost tautologically: if the society is authoritarian, methods of childrearing (and probably every social relationship) will also be authoritarian. All known societies contain some element of hierarchy. For generations, historians have been debating about the nature of the social system whose character I seem to be taking for granted. Many have argued that individuals of the old regime were used to the graded ranks into which they were born and did not feel differences in status and power as hindrances to close personal ties or to living a satisfying and happy life. These historians claim that modern criticisms of the old regime are anachronistic. With our legalistic and bureaucratic notion of the way a society works, we lack the means to understand a world held together by mutual loyalties, a shared tradition, the "existential bond" between master and servant.

Paternalism is implicit in these defenses of the old regime. To its champions, this system worked like a large family. Rulers were similar to benevolent parents, often autocratic, but at the same time attentive to the welfare of their "children." A study of childrearing, and particularly of the stage of autonomy, can give us an especially informative slant on the problem. If the concept of paternalism has been called into question, then presumably the best setting in which it might be evaluated would be within the family itself. Here the human consequences of old regime hierarchy should be most characteristically demonstrated.

It happens that we have a detailed account of the infancy of Louis XIII of France, recorded in the diary of the court doctor, Jean Héroard. (Louis was born in 1601.)

From *Journal of Jean Héroard*

9 Oct. 1603   Awake at 8.00. He is obstinate, is whipped for the first time.

5 Sept. 1604   At 8.15 the king arrives and wants to make him give a kiss. He flies into such a bad temper that he is whipped for it by His Majesty. Mme de Montglat also whipped him five or six times. The king asked him, "What was that for?" He answered angrily, "For you . . ." The king left. "I want papa," he said. The king came back and kissed him. At 10.00 the king and queen took him to Mass.

13 Oct. 1604   At 3.30 he is taken through the great gallery to the garden of pines. . . . The king wants to take his hand, he does not want to. The king takes his hat off his head and throws it on the ground, really angry. The king goes away and leaves him. He calms down, goes to find the king, and without a word takes his hand.

23 Oct. 1604   (Louis wanted to play with his drum, "one of his great pleasures.") So he goes to the king unwillingly, by compulsion. The king says to him, "Take off your hat." . . . He is reluctant to remove it. The king takes it off and he is irritated. Then the king takes from him his drum and drumsticks, which is still worse. "My hat, my drum, my drumsticks." The king to spite him puts the hat on his own head. "I want my hat." The king hits him with it on the head; he is really angry with the king and the king with him. The king takes him by the wrists and lifts him in the air stretching out his little arms. "Hey, you're hurting me, Hey, my drum, Hey, my hat." The Queen gives him back his hat and drumsticks; it was quite a little tragedy. He is taken away by Mme de Montglat bursting with rage . . . will not kiss or hug Mme de Montglat . . . finally is whipped. . . . His nurse takes him aside alone and says, "Monsieur, you have been obstinate, it won't do, you must obey papa." He answers, gasping, "Kill Mamanga (his governess) she is bad. I will kill everybody. I will kill God."

7 Dec. 1604   He goes to the king and is very well behaved. The king and queen go hunting. Mlle de Ventelet says to him, "Monsieur who is the master of papa?" He answers, "God is." "And who is your

From *Journal de Jean Héroard sur l'enfance et la jeunesse de Louis XIII* (Paris: Firmin, Didot Frères, 1868), Vol. I, pp. 55, 74, 85, 93, 95, 106, 194, 251, trans. B. Tierney.

master?" "I don't want to say." It was never possible to make him acknowledge a master. The day before, the King made him very angry when he said, "I am the master and you are my servant." He was extremely irritated by that word.

26 July 1606   The king, pointing to Monsieur the first president and other deputies of Normandy, says to him, "See those people, you will command them after me." He answers coldly, "Good, papa." He is very subdued with the king, whom he fears.

12 Feb. 1607   At 8.45 undressed and put to bed, says his prayers, "God give a good life to father, my good friend, and mother, my good friend." Mme de Montglat asks him, "Do you love your father?" "I love him more than Pataut" (his nurse's dog). "Monsieur, you shouldn't speak so. You should say you love him more than yourself." "More than myself! Hey. One ought not to love himself. One should love other people but not himself."

THE COURT OF LOUIS XIV

Portrait of a Monarch

The Duke of Saint-Simon lived for many years at the court of Louis XIV and left a detailed account of day-to-day life there.

From *Memoirs of the Duke of Saint-Simon*

His natural talents were below mediocrity; but he had a mind capable of improvement, of receiving polish, of assimilating what was best in the minds of others without slavish imitation; and he profited greatly throughout his life from having associated with the ablest and wittiest persons, of both sexes, and of various stations. He entered the world (if I may use such an expression in speaking of a King who had already completed his twenty-third year), at a fortunate moment, for men of distinction abounded. His Ministers and Generals at this time, with their successors trained in their schools, are universally acknowledged to have been the ablest in Europe; for the domestic troubles and foreign wars under which France had suffered ever since the death of Louis XIII had brought to the front a number of brilliant names, and the Court was made up of capable and illustrious personages. . . . Glory was his passion, but he also liked order and regularity in all things; he was naturally prudent, moderate, and reserved; always master of his tongue and his emotions. Will it be believed? he was also naturally kind-hearted and just. God had given him all that was necessary for him to be a good King, perhaps also to be a fairly great one. All his faults were produced by his surroundings. In his childhood he was so much neglected that no one dared go near his rooms. He was often heard to speak of those times with great bitterness; he used to relate how, through the carelessness of his attendants, he was found one evening in the basin of a fountain in the Palais-Royal gardens. . . .

His Ministers, generals, mistresses, and courtiers soon found out his weak point, namely, his love of hearing his own praises. There was nothing he liked so much as flattery, or, to put it more plainly, adulation; the coarser and clumsier it was, the more he relished it. That was

From *The Memoirs of the Duke de Saint-Simon*, ed. F. Arkwright (New York: Brentano's, n.d.), Vol. V, pp. 254, 259–263.

the only way to approach him; if he ever took a liking to a man it was invariably due to some lucky stroke of flattery in the first instance, and to indefatigable preserverance in the same line afterwards. His Ministers owed much of their influence to their frequent opportunities for burning incense before him. . . .

It was this love of praise which made it easy for Louvois to engage him in serious wars, for he persuaded him that he had greater talents for war than any of his Generals, greater both in design and in execution, and the Generals themselves encouraged him in this notion, to keep in favour with him. I mean such Generals as Condé and Turenne; much more, of course, those who came after them. He took to himself the credit of their successes with admirable complacency, and honestly believed that he was all his flatterers told him. Hence arose his fondness for reviews, which he carried so far that his enemies called him, in derision, "the King of reviews"; hence also his liking for sieges, where he could make a cheap parade of bravery, and exhibit his vigilance, forethought, and endurance of fatigue; for his robust constitution enabled him to bear fatigue marvellously; he cared nothing for hunger, heat, cold, or bad weather. He liked also, as he rode through the lines, to hear people praising his dignified bearing and fine appearance on horseback. His campaigns were his favourite topic when talking to his mistresses. He talked well, expressed himself clearly in well-chosen language; and no man could tell a story better. His conversation, even on the most ordinary subjects, was always marked by a certain natural dignity.

His mind was occupied with small things rather than with great, and he delighted in all sorts of petty details, such as the dress and drill of his soldiers; and it was just the same with regard to his building operations, his household, and even his cookery. He always thought he could teach something of their own craft even to the most skilful professional men; and they, for their part, used to listen gratefully to lessons which they had long ago learnt by heart. He imagined that all this showed his indefatigable industry; in reality, it was a great waste of time, and his Ministers turned it to good account for their own purposes, as soon as they had learnt the art of managing him; they kept his attention engaged with a mass of details, while they contrived to get their own way in more important matters.

His vanity, which was perpetually nourished—for even preachers used to praise him to his face from the pulpit—was the cause of the aggrandisement of his Ministers. He imagined that they were great only through him, mere mouthpieces through which he expressed his will; consequently he made no objection when they gradually encroached on the privileges of the greatest noblemen. He felt that he could at any moment reduce them to their original obscurity; whereas, in the case of a nobleman, though he could make him feel the weight of his displeasure, he could not deprive him or his family of the advantages due to his birth. For this reason he made it a rule never to admit a *seigneur* to his Councils, to which the Duke de Beauvilliers was the only exception. . . .

But for the fear of the devil, which, by God's grace, never forsook him even in his wildest excesses, he would have caused himself to be worshipped as a deity. He would not have lacked worshippers. . . .

Life at Versailles

From *Memoirs of the Duke of Saint-Simon*

Very early in the reign of Louis XIV the Court was removed from Paris, never to return. The troubles of the minority had given him a dislike to that city; his enforced and surreptitious flight from it still rankled in his memory; he did not consider himself safe there, and thought cabals would be more easily detected if the Court was in the country, where the movements and temporary absences of any of its members would be more easily noticed. . . . No doubt that he was also influenced by the feeling that he would be regarded with greater awe and veneration when no longer exposed every day to the gaze of the multitude.

His love-affair with Mademoiselle de la Vallière, which at first was covered as far as possible with a veil of mystery, was the cause of frequent excursions to Versailles. This was at that time a small country house, built by Louis XIII to avoid the unpleasant necessity, which had sometimes befallen him, of sleeping at a wretched wayside tavern or in a windmill, when benighted out hunting in the forest of St. Leger. . . . The visits of Louis XIV becoming more frequent, he enlarged the *château* by degrees till its immense buildings afforded better accommodation for the Court than was to be found at St. Germain, where most of the courtiers had to put up with uncomfortable lodgings in the town. The Court was therefore removed to Versailles in 1682, not long before the Queen's death. The new building contained an infinite number of rooms for courtiers, and the King liked the grant of these rooms to be regarded as a coveted privilege.

He availed himself of the frequent festivities at Versailles, and his excursions to other places, as a means of making the courtiers assiduous in their attendance and anxious to please him; for he nominated beforehand those who were to take part in them, and could thus gratify some and inflict a snub on others. He was conscious that the substantial favours he had to bestow were not nearly sufficient to produce

From *The Memoirs of the Duke de Saint-Simon*, ed. F. Arkwright (New York: Brentano's, n.d.), Vol. V, pp. 271–274, 276–278.

a continual effect; he had therefore to invent imaginary ones, and no one was so clever in devising petty distinctions and preferences which aroused jealousy and emulation. The visits to Marly later on were very useful to him in this way; also those to Trianon, where certain ladies, chosen beforehand, were admitted to his table. It was another distinction to hold his candlestick at his *coucher;* as soon as he had finished his prayers he used to name the courtier to whom it was to be handed, always choosing one of the highest rank among those present. . . .

Not only did he expect all persons of distinction to be in continual attendance at Court, but he was quick to notice the absence of those of inferior degree; at his *lever,* his *coucher,* his meals, in the gardens of Versailles (the only place where the courtiers in general were allowed to follow him), he used to cast his eyes to right and left; nothing escaped him, he saw everybody. If any one habitually living at Court absented himself he insisted on knowing the reason; those who came there only for flying visits had also to give a satisfactory explanation; any one who seldom or never appeared there was certain to incur his displeasure. If asked to bestow a favour on such persons he would reply haughtily: "I do not know him"; of such as rarely presented themselves he would say, "He is a man I never see"; and from these judgements there was no appeal.

He always took great pains to find out what was going on in public places, in society, in private houses, even family secrets, and maintained an immense number of spies and tale-bearers. These were of all sorts; some did not know that their reports were carried to him; others did know it; there were others, again, who used to write to him directly, through channels which he prescribed; others who were admitted by the backstairs and saw him in his private room. Many a man in all ranks of life was ruined by these methods, often very unjustly, without ever being able to discover the reason; and when the King had once taken a prejudice against a man, he hardly ever got over it. . . .

No one understood better than Louis XIV the art of enhancing the value of a favour by his manner of bestowing it; he knew how to make the most of a word, a smile, even of a glance. If he addressed any one, were it but to ask a trifling question or make some commonplace remark, all eyes were turned on the person so honored; it was a mark of favour which always gave rise to comment. . . .

He loved splendour, magnificence, and profusion in all things, and encouraged similar tastes in his Court; to spend money freely on equipages and buildings, on feasting and at cards, was a sure way to gain his favour, perhaps to obtain the honour of a word from him. Motives of policy had something to do with this; by making expensive habits the fashion, and, for people in a certain position, a necessity, he compelled his courtiers to live beyond their income, and gradually reduced them to depend on his bounty for the means of subsistence. This was a plague which, once introduced, became a scourge to the whole country, for it did not take long to spread to Paris, and thence to the armies and the provinces; so that a man of any position is now estimated entirely according to his expenditure on his table and other luxuries. This folly, sustained by pride and ostentation, has already produced widespread confusion; it threatens to end in nothing short of ruin and a general overthrow.

The obsession with status and precedence at Louis XIV's court appears in the following letter. (The Duchess of Orleans was married to the king's brother, the much younger Duchess of Burgundy to the king's grandson.)

From *Letter of the Duchess of Orleans*

4th January, 1704, Versailles.

To the DUCHESS OF HANOVER.

I must really tell you how just the King is. The Duchesse de Bourgogne's ladies, who are called Ladies of the Palace, tried to arrogate the rank and take the place of my ladies everywhere. Such a thing was never done either in the time of the Queen or of the Dauphiness. They got the King's Guards to keep their places and push back the chairs belonging to my ladies. I complained first of all to the Duc de Noailles, who replied that it was the King's order. Then I went immediately to the King and said to him, "May I ask your Majesty if it is by your orders that my ladies have now no place or rank as they used to have? If it is your desire, I have nothing more to say, because I only wish to obey you, but your Majesty knows that formerly when the Queen and the Dauphiness were alive the Ladies of the Palace had no rank, and my Maids of Honour, Gentlemen of Honour, and Ladies of the Robe had their places like those of the Queen and the Dauphiness. I do not know why the Ladies of the Palace should pretend to anything else." The King became quite red, and replied, "I have given no such order, who said that I had?" "The Maréchal de Noailles," I replied. The King asked him why he had said such a thing, and he denied it entirely. "I am willing to believe, since you say so," I replied, "that my lackey misunderstood you, but as the King has given no such orders, see that your Guards don't keep places for those ladies and hinder my servants from carrying chairs for my service," as we say here. Although these ladies are high in favour, the King, nevertheless, sent the majordomo to find out how things should be done. I told him, and it will not happen again. These women are becoming far too insolent now that they are in favour, and they imagined that I would not have the courage to report the matter to the King. But I shall not lose my rank nor prerogatives on account of the favour they enjoy. The King is too just for that.

From G. S. Stevenson, ed., *The Letters of Madame*, (New York: D. Appleton and Co., 1924), pp. 232–233.

In the next reading a modern author comments on the ritual of court etiquette.

From W. H. Lewis. *The Splendid Century*

Court etiquette was a life study. Who for instance could guess that at Versailles it was the height of bad manners to knock at a door? You must scratch it with the little finger of the left hand, growing the finger nail long for that purpose. Or could we know that you must not *tutoyer* an intimate friend in any place where the King was present? That if the lackey of a social superior brought you a message, you had to receive him standing, and bareheaded? You have mastered the fact that you must not knock on a door, so when you go to make your first round of calls in the great houses in the town, you scratch: wrong again, you should have knocked. Next time you rattle the knocker, and a passing exquisite asks you contemptuously if you are so ignorant as not to know that you give one blow of the knocker on the door of a lady of quality? Who could guess that if you encounter the royal dinner on its way from the kitchens to the table, you must bow as to the King himself, sweep the ground with the plume of your hat, and say in a low, reverent, but distinct voice, *La viande du Roi?* Many times must the apprentice courtier have echoed the psalmist's lament, "Who can tell how oft he offendeth?" And it behoved you not to offend, for the King had an eye like a hawk or shall we say, like a school prefect, for any breach of etiquette, and not even the most exalted were safe from his reproof. One night at supper his chatterbox of a brother put his hand in a dish before Louis had helped himself: "I perceive," said the King icily, "that you are no better able to control you hands than your tongue." Once at Marly, Mme. de Torcy, wife of a minister, took a seat above a duchess at supper. Louis, to her extreme discomfort, regarded her steadfastly throughout the meal, and when he reached Mme. de Maintenon's room, the storm broke; he had, he said, witnessed a piece of insolence so intolerable that the sight of it had prevented him from eating: a piece of presumption which would have been unendurable in a woman of quality. It took the combined efforts of Mme. de Maintenon and the Duchess of Burgundy the rest of the evening to pacify him. Decidedly not a king with whom to take liberties, or even make mistakes. . . .

From W. H. Lewis, *The Splendid Century* (New York: Morrow, 1954), pp. 39–40. Copyright © 1954 by W. H. Lewis. Reprinted by permission of William Morrow & Company and Methuen London.

ABSOLUTISM IN PRACTICE

Religion

The Edict of Nantes (1598) had granted a measure of toleration to French Protestants. Its revocation was followed by renewed persecutions.

From *Revocation of the Edict of Nantes (1685)*

1. Be it known that of our certain knowledge, full power, and royal authority, we have, by this present perpetual and irrevocable edict, suppressed and revoked, and do suppress and revoke, the edict of our said grandfather, given at Nantes in April 1598, in its whole extent. . . .

2. We forbid our subjects of the R.P.R.[1] to meet any more for the exercise of the said religion in any place or private house, under any pretext whatever. . . .

3. We likewise forbid all noblemen, of what condition soever, to hold such religious exercises in their houses or fiefs, under penalty to be inflicted upon all our said subjects who shall engage in the said exercises, of imprisonment and confiscation.

4. We enjoin all ministers of the said R.P.R., who do not choose to become converts and to embrace the Catholic, apostolic, and Roman religion, to leave our kingdom and the territories subject to us within a fortnight of the publication of our present edict, without leave to reside therein beyond that period, or, during the said fortnight, to engage in any preaching, exhortation, or any other function, on pain of being sent to the galleys. . . .

7. We forbid private schools for the instruction of children of the said R.P.R., and in general all things whatever which can be regarded as a concession of any kind in favor of the said religion.

---

[1]"Religion prétendue réformée," i.e., "the so-called reformed religion."

From F. A. Isambert, *Recueil général des anciennes lois françaises* (Paris, 1821–23), trans. in J. H. Robinson, *Readings in European History* (Boston: Ginn and Co., 1906), Vol. II, pp. 289–291.

From *Memoirs of the Duke of Saint-Simon*

The first-fruits of this dreadful plot were the wanton revocation of the Edict of Nantes, without a shadow of a pretext, and the proscriptions which followed it; its ultimate results were the depopulation of a fourth part of the kingdom and the ruin of our commerce. For a long time the country was given over to the authorised ravages of dragoons, which caused the deaths of, literally, thousands of innocent people of all ages and both sexes. Families were torn asunder; men of all classes, often old and infirm, highly respected for their piety and learning, were sent to toil in the galleys under the lash of the overseer; multitudes were driven penniless from their homes to seek refuge in foreign countries, to which they carried our arts and manufactures, enriching them and causing their cities to flourish at the expense of France.

After Louis XIV's death it was proposed that the Huguenot exiles be recalled. Saint-Simon then took a very different line.

I reminded [the Regent] of the disturbances and civil wars caused by the Huguenots from the reign of Henry II to that of Louis XIII; pointing out that even when they were comparatively quiet they had formed a body apart within the State, having their own chiefs, courts of justice specially appointed to deal with their affairs, even when they concerned Catholics, with strong places and garrisons at their disposal; corresponding with foreign Powers; always complaining and ready to take up arms: subjects, in short, merely in name, and yielding just as much or as little allegiance to their Sovereign as they thought fit. I recapitulated the heroic struggles by which his grandfather, Louis XIII, had at last beaten down this Hydra; thereby enabling his successor to get rid of it once for all by the mere expression of his will, without the slightest opposition.

I begged the Regent to reflect that he was now reaping the benefit of these struggles in a profound domestic tranquility; and to consider whether it was worth while, in time of peace when no foreign Power was thinking about the question, to make a concession which the late King had rejected with indignation when reduced to the utmost extremities by a long and disastrous war. I said, in conclusion, that if Louis XIV had made a mistake in revoking the Edict of Nantes it was not so much in the act itself as in the mode of carrying it out.

From *The Memoirs of the Duke de Saint-Simon*, ed. F. Arkwright (New York: Brentano's, n.d.), Vol. V, pp. 296, 437.

*Throughout his reign Louis XIV commanded the support of the established
Catholic church (which, in the past, had often been hostile to the claims of absolute monarchy).*

From *Declaration of the Gallican Church*

We, the archbishops and bishops assembled at Paris by order of the
King, with other ecclesiastical deputies who represent the Gallican
Church, have judged it necessary to make the regulations and the dec-
laration which follows:

That St. Peter and his successors, Vicars of Jesus Christ, and the
whole Church herself, have received power of God only in things spiritual, and pertaining to eternal salvation, not in things civil or temporal, the Lord Himself having said, "My kingdom is not of this
world," and also "Render unto Caesar the things that be Caesar's, and
unto God the things that are God's"; as also firmly declareth the Apostle, "Let every soul be subject unto the higher powers; for there is no
power but of God; the powers that be are ordained of God; whosoever
therefore resisteth the power, resisteth the ordinance of God."

Therefore kings and princes are in no wise subjected by God's appointment to any ecclesiastical power in temporal things; neither can
the authority of the Keys of the Church directly or indirectly depose
them, or their subjects be dispensed from the obedience and fidelity of
their oaths to the same; and this doctrine we affirm to be necessary for
the maintenance of public peace, no less profitable to the Church than
to the State, and to be everywhere and every way observed as agreeable
to the Word of God, to the tradition of the Fathers and the example of
the Saints. . . .

From F. A. Isambert, *Recueil général des anciennes lois françaises* (Paris, 1821–23),
trans. in T. C. Mendenhall, B. D. Henning and A. S. Foord, *Ideas and Institutions in European History* (New York: Holt, Rinehart and Winston, 1948), Vol.
I, p. 318.

Under Louis XIV the church became virtually a department of government.

From Louis XIV. *Letter to His Heir*

I have never failed, when an occasion has presented itself, to impress
upon you the great respect we should have for religion, and the deference we should show to its ministers in matters specially connected
with their mission, that is to say, with the celebration of the Sacred
Mysteries and the preaching of the doctrine of the Gospels. But because people connected with the Church are liable to presume a little
too much on the advantages attaching to their profession, and are willing sometimes to make use of them in order to whittle down their most

From J. Longnon, ed., *A King's Lessons in Statecraft,* H. Wilson, trans. (New
York: Albert and Charles Boni, 1925), p. 149.

rightful duties, I feel obliged to explain to you certain points on this question which may be of importance.

The first is that Kings are absolute *seigneurs,* and from their nature have full and free disposal of all property both secular and ecclesiastical, to use it as wise dispensers, that is to say, in accordance with the requirements of their State.

The second is that those mysterious names, the Franchises and Liberties of the Church, with which perhaps people will endeavour to dazzle you, have equal reference to all the faithful whether they be laymen or tonsured, who are all equally sons of this common Mother; but that they exempt neither the one nor the other from subjection to Sovereigns, to whom the Gospel itself precisely enjoins that they should submit themselves.

Military Organization

Voltaire, writing in the mid-eighteenth century, looked back on the reign of Louis XIV as a time of order and grandeur.

From Voltaire. *The Age of Louis XIV*

He was the legislator of his armies as well as of his people as a whole. It is surprising that, before his time, there was no uniform dress among the troops. It was he who, in the first year of his administration, ordered that each regiment should be distinguished by the color of its dress or by different badges; this regulation was soon adopted by all other nations. It was he who instituted brigadiers and who put the household troops on their present footing. He turned Cardinal Mazarin's guards into a company of musketeers and fixed the number of men in the companies at five hundred; moreover, he gave them the uniform which they still wear today.

Under him there were no longer constables, and after the death of the Duke of Epernon, no more colonel generals of infantry; they had become too powerful, and he quite rightly wanted to be sole master. Marshal Grammont, who was only colonel of horse of the French Guards under the Duke of Epernon and who took his orders from this colonel general, now took them only from the King, and was the first to be given the title of Colonel of the Guards. The King himself installed his colonels at the head of the regiments, giving them with his own hand a gilt gorget with a pike, and afterward, when the use of pikes was abolished, a spontoon, or kind of half-pike. In the King's Regiment, which he created himself, he instituted grenadiers, on the scale of four to a company in the first place; then he formed a company of grenadiers in each regiment of infantry. He gave two to the French Guards. Nowadays there is one for each battalion throughout the whole infantry. He greatly enlarged the Corps of Dragoons, and gave them a colonel general. The establishment of studs for breeding horses, in 1667, must not be forgotten, for they had been completely abandoned beforehand and they were of great value in providing mounts for the cavalry, an important resource which has since been too much neglected.

It was he who instituted the use of the bayonet affixed to the end of the musket. Before his time, it was used occasionally, but only a few companies fought with this weapon. There was no uniform practice and no drill; everything was left to the general's discretion. Pikes were then thought of as the most redoubtable weapon. The first regiment to have bayonets and to be trained to use them was that of the Fusiliers, established in 1671.

The manner in which artillery is used today is due entirely to him. He founded artillery schools, first at Douai, then at Metz and Strasbourg; and the Regiment of Artillery was finally staffed with officers who were almost all capable of successfully conducting a siege. All the magazines in the kingdom were well stocked, and they were supplied annually with eight hundred thousand pounds of powder. He created a regiment of bombardiers and one of hussars; before this only his enemies had had hussars.

In 1688 he established thirty regiments of militia, which were provided and equipped by the communes. These militia trained for war but without abandoning the cultivation of their fields.

Companies of cadets were maintained in the majority of frontier towns; there they learned mathematics, drawing and all the drills, and carried out the duties of soldiers. This institution lasted for ten years, but the government finally tired of trying to discipline these difficult young people. The Corp of Engineers, on the other hand, which the King created and to which he gave its present regulations, is an institution which will last forever. During his reign the art of fortifying strongholds was brought to perfection by Marshal Vauban and his pupils, who surpassed Count Pagan. He built or repaired a hundred and fifty fortresses.

To maintain military discipline, the King created inspectors general and later directors, who reported on the state of the troops; from their reports it could be seen whether the war commissioners had carried out their duties.

He instituted the Order of Saint-Louis, an honorable distinction which was often more sought after than wealth. The Hôtel des Invalides put the seal on his efforts to merit loyal service.

It was owing to measures such as these that he had, by 1672, a hundred and eighty thousand regular troops, and that, increasing his forces as the number and strength of his enemies increased, he finished with four hundred and fifty thousand men under arms, including the troops of the navy.

Before his time such powerful armies were unknown. His enemies could scarcely muster comparable forces, and to do so they had to be united. He showed what France, on her own, was capable of, and he always had either great successes or great resources to fall back on.

Economy and Local Administration

Louis XIV's finance minister, Colbert, strove to build up French commerce and manufactures.

From Colbert's Memoranda

A Memorandum, 1669

The commerce of all Europe is carried on by ships of every size to the number of 20,000, and it is perfectly clear that this number cannot be increased, since the number of people in all the states remains the same and consumption likewise remains the same. . . .

Commerce is a perpetual and peaceable war of wit and energy among all nations. Each nation works incessantly to have its legitimate share of commerce or to gain an advantage over another nation. The Dutch fight at present, in this war, with 15,000 to 16,000 ships, a government of merchants, all of whose maxims and power are directed solely toward the preservation and increase of their commerce, and much more care, energy, and thrift than any other nation.

The English with 3,000 to 4,000 ships, less energy and care, and more expenditures than the Dutch.

The French with 500 to 600.

Those two last cannot improve their commerce save by increasing the number of their vessels, and cannot increase this number save from the 20,000 which carry all the commerce and consequently by making inroads on the 15,000 to 16,000 of the Dutch.

A Memorandum, 1670

[Formerly] the Dutch, English, Hamburgers, and other nations bringing into the realm a much greater quantity of merchandise than that which they carried away, withdrew the surplus in circulating money, which produced both their abundance and the poverty of the realm, and indisputably resulted in their power and our weakness.

We must next examine the means which were employed to change this destiny.

Firstly, in 1662 Your Majesty maintained his right to 50 sols per ton of freight from foreign vessels, which produced such great results that we have seen the number of French vessels increase yearly; and in seven or eight years the Dutch have been practically excluded from port-to-port commerce, which is carried on by the French. The advantages received by the state through the increase in the number of sailors and seamen, through the money which has remained in the realm by this means and an infinity of others, would be too long to enumerate.

At the same time, Your Majesty ordered work done to abolish all the tolls which had long been established on all the rivers of the kingdom, and he began from then on to have an examination made of the rivers which could be rendered navigable in order to facilitate the descent of commodities and merchandise from inside the realm toward the sea to be transported into foreign lands. Although everything that invites the universal admiration of men was still in disorder in these first years and although the recovery work was a sort of abyss, Your Majesty did not delay in beginning the examination of the tariffs of the *cinq grosses fermes* and scrutinized the fact that the regulation and levying of these sorts of duties concerning commerce had always been done with a great deal of ignorance on the basis of memoranda by tax farmers, who, being solely concerned with their own interests and the increase in the profits from their tax farms while they possessed them, had always overvalued the commodities, merchandise, and manufactured items of the realm which they saw leaving in abundance, and favored the entrance of foreign merchandise and manufactured items, in order to have a greater quantity of them enter, without being concerned about whether money was as a result leaving the realm, for they were indifferent to this as long as their tax farms produced gain for them during the period of their possession.

Finally, after having thoroughly studied this matter, Your Majesty ordered the tariff of 1664, in which the duties are regulated on a completely different principle, that is to say, that all merchandise and man-

"A Memorandum, 1670": From P. Clement, *Lettres, instructions et mémoires de Colbert* (Paris: Imprimerie Nationale, 1870). Translated excerpts in O. and P. Ranum, *The Century of Louis XIV* (New York: Walker, 1972), pp. 120–123. Reprinted by permission of Walker and Company, Inc.

ufactured items of the realm were markedly favored and the foreign ones priced out of the market, though not completely; [for] having as yet no established manufacturers in the realm, this increase in duties, had it been excessive, would have been a great burden for the *peuple,* because of their need for the aforesaid foreign merchandise and manufactured items; but this change began to provide some means of establishing the same manufactures in the realm; and to this end:

The fabric manufacture of Sedan has been reestablished, and enlarged to 62 from the 12 looms there were then.

The new establishments of Abbeville, Dieppe, Fécamp, and Rouen have been built, in which there are presently more than 200 looms.

The factory for barracan was next established at La Ferré-sous-Jouarre, which is made up of 120 looms;

That of little damasks from Flanders, at Meaux, consisting of 80 looms;

That for carpeting, in the same city, made up of 20 looms . . .

That for tin, in Nivernois;

That for French lace, in 52 cities and towns, in which more than 20,000 workers toil;

The manufacture of brass, or yellow copper, set up in Champagne;

That for camlet of Brussels, in Paris, which will become large and extensive;

Brass wire, in Burgundy;

Gold thread of Milan, at Lyons . . .

[*Many other new enterprises were listed.*]

And since Your Majesty has wanted to work diligently at reestablishing his naval forces, and since for that it has been necessary to make very great expenditures, since all merchandise, munitions and manufactured items formerly came from Holland and the countries of the North, it has been absolutely necessary to be especially concerned with finding within the realm, or with establishing in it, everything which might be necessary for this great plan.

To this end, the manufacture of tar was established in Médoc, Auvergne, Dauphiné, and Provence;

Iron cannons, in Burgundy, Nivernois, Saintonge, and Périgord;

Large anchors, in Dauphiné, Nivernois, Brittany, and Rochefort;

Sailcloth for the Levant, in Dauphiné;

Coarse muslin, in Auvergne;

All the implements for pilots and others, at Dieppe and La Rochelle;

The cutting of wood suitable for vessels, in Burgundy, Dauphiné, Brittany, Normandy, Poitou, Saintonge, Provence, Guyenne, and the Pyrenees;

Masts, of a sort once unknown in this realm, have been found in Provence, Languedoc, Auvergne, Dauphiné, and in the Pyrenees.

Iron, which was obtained from Sweden and Biscay, is currently manufactured in the realm.

Fine hemp for ropes, which came from Prussia and from Piedmont, is currently obtained in Burgundy, Mâconnais, Bresse, Dauphiné; and markets for it have since been established in Berry and in Auvergne, which always provides money in these provinces and keeps it within the realm.

In a word, everything serving for the construction of vessels is currently established in the realm, so that Your Majesty can get along without foreigners for the navy and will even, in a short time, be able to supply them and gain their money in this fashion. And it is with this same objective of having everything necessary to provide abundantly for his navy and that of his subjects that he is working at the general reform of all the forests in his realm, which, being as carefully preserved as they are at present, will abundantly produce all the wood necessary for this.

A Memorandum, 1672

If the King conquers all the provinces subject to and forming part of the States of the United Provinces of the Netherlands, their commerce becoming commerce of the subjects of the King, there would be nothing more to desire; and if afterwards His Majesty, examining what would be most advantageous to do for the commerce of his old and new subjects, thought it for the good of his service to divide the advantages of this commerce by cutting down a part of that of the Dutch so as to transfer it into the hands of the French, it would be easy to find the necessary expedients to which the new subjects would be obliged to submit.

"A Memorandum, 1672": From Charles W. Cole, *Colbert and a Century of French Mercantilism* (New York: Columbia University Press, 1939), p. 320. Copyright 1939 by Oxford University Press. Reprinted by permission.

Much of Colbert's voluminous correspondence was concerned with the supervision of local government officials.

From *Colbert's Correspondence*

To the Count de Grignan, Lieutenant-General of Provence, Paris, 25 December, 1671

I have informed the King of the disorderly conduct in which the Assembly of the Towns of Provence has persisted; and, as His Majesty

Colbert's Correspondence: From P. Clement, *Lettres, instructions et mémoires de Colbert* (Paris: Imprimerie Nationale, 1870), translated in T. C. Mendenhall, B. D. Henning and A. S. Foord, *Ideas and Institutions in European History* (New York: Holt, Rinehart and Winston, 1948), pp. 315–316, 321.

is not disposed to countenance it longer, he has given the orders necessary to prorogue it and, at the same time, has dispatched ten *lettres-de-cachet*, to commit the ten most discontented deputies to Granville, Cherbourg, Saint-Malo, Morlaix and Concarneau.

To the Same, Versailles, 31 December, 1671

I have made a complete report to the King of all which has transpired in the Assembly of the Towns of Provence since the 20th of the month. You will see, through the orders which His Majesty sends, how little pleased he is with the conduct of those who have served as deputies this year. And, as soon as His Majesty has accepted their offer of 450,000 livres, his desire is that, following the orders which you will receive, you send to the provinces of Normandy and Brittany ten of those deputies who have displayed the most ill-will toward the good of his service. All of Provence will see the troublous extremities in which the obstinacy of these deputies has placed them. I very much doubt whether His Majesty will see fit to call them together for a long time, and in any case, he will give them sufficient leisure to repent the bad conduct to which they held. However, with your own conduct, His Majesty is very satisfied.

To M. de Creil, Intendant of Rouen, Saint-Germain, 3 February 1673

Of all the abuses which come before us from the *généralités*[1], there is none at present which seems more important to the Council than that [practised] by the assistants to the Receivers of the *Tailles*[2], who, under the name of the Receivers, make assessments, in conjunction with the magistrates, to defray the court costs and fees and which they apply to their own profit. As was provided by the order of the Council of 4 July 1664, concerning the regulation of this disorder, pray inform me if it is known or practised in the *généralité* of Rouen, and particularly apply yourself to finding out if any of the Receivers of *Tailles* or Commissioners of Revenue are guilty of this, in order that you may either apply the necessary remedy through your authority or advise me about it.

To M. de Bezons, Intendant of Limoges, 16 November 1680

The King having been advised by M. de Marillac, intendant in the *généralité* de Poitiers, that a man named Baudoin has been guilty of a

---

[1]Administrative districts.
[2]Land taxes.

great many frauds in several parishes of the province of Saintonge, under the pretext of collecting for the *corvées* to repair roads, and on the strength of a commission of the tribunal of the King's lands at Paris giving him permission, His Majesty gave *Sieur* de Marillac verbal powers to institute proceedings against Baudoin; and, this having been done, he has been condemned to the galleys for life and forced to make restitution to those whom he had swindled.

As *Sieur* de Marillac has informed me that in the process of trying Baudoin, he learned that, in the *généralité* of Limoges, there are several other people who have similar commissions and who, under the same pretext, are plaguing the people, I feel free to request that you hunt them down, throughout the entirety of the *généralité* of Limoges, in order to halt their depredations. If you have the facilities there to try them and to make examples of them, the King will, upon your request, send you the authority to try them and to impress the maximum penalties. . . .

To M. d'Herbigny, Intendant of Grenoble, Versailles, 16 November, 1680

I was surprised to learn, by your letter of the 28th last, that you had levied on the *élection* of Vienne an assessment of 4,700 livres, for the construction, subject to my approval, of a bridge to facilitate the transportation of the harvest to Grenoble.

You know as well as I that it is not permissible to make such an assessment on the people without a writ of the King affixed with the Great Seal, and you must take care to do nothing contrary to that general usage of the realm, and never to give so bad an example to the authorities of that province, who are only too much inclined to go beyond the bounds, and to those who will succeed to your position.

To M. Morant, Intendant of Aix, Sceaux, 1 July, 1682

I shall report at the next meeting of the Council on the suggestion which you have sent concerning the public works and the tolls; I am certain that His Majesty will agree with them. You ought afterwards to apply yourself to repairing the roads and to forcing the *seigneurs* to repair and maintain those roads on which they levy the tolls.

As you fully appreciate the importance of these public works to the good of the province, I am sure that you will give them your complete attention. . . .

EASTERN EUROPE

The Turkish Menace

An anonymous seventeenth-century observer reflected rather cynically on the probable reaction of Louis XIV to a Turkish invasion of Germany.

From *The Present State of the German and Turkish Empires*

Some perhaps will ... retort that though Vienna had been taken by the Turk, there was no great fear of his further progress into Germany: Because Louis the King of France surnamed the Great for the things he has done already, would oppose him in such a case with a puissant army, and force him back again to the great loss of the Turks, and his own immortal glory.

This indeed would be great in Louis the Great; and in truth in such a conjuncture of affairs he would be the only prince of Europe in a capacity to stop the progress of such a potent enemy. But first, we may justly question whether he would in such a case be willing, or not, till such time as he were forced to it, for his own defence. For every one knows that knows anything, that clipping the wings of the Austrian eagle (or House of Austria) will extremely add to the splendour of the French monarchy. Whilst then the Turks were invading Germany on the one side, would not both self-preservation, honour and interest invite the French King to be busy on the other? And divide perhaps Germany with the Turks, since in all likelihood he could do no better.

All Europe knows into what extreme distress the States of Holland were brought by the French King's first and second campaign against the Hollanders: And had Germany been invaded by the Turks, the lillies [emblem of the French monarchy] perhaps had ere now taken such deep roots in Holland, that it had not been easy (to say no more) to pull them out again. But as Germany was then in peace with the Turks, the Emperor united all the German princes together, for their common interest, and set on foot in the beginning of winter, an army of near 40,000 horse and foot.... The good success whereof occa-

From *The Present State of the German and Turkish Empires* (London, 1684), pp. 38–44.

sioned a great change in the affairs of Holland. For then the French thought it no longer secure for them to remain there, and deserted on a sudden the cities they had taken in it partly by force; partly by a free surrender, so that after having caused the citizens to redeem their liberties with great sums of money the French retreated from their new conquests, which they had never done, if the forces of Germany had been diverted by a Turkish invasion.

Out of all this discourse, we may gather that although the French King were able alone to beat the Turks out of Germany, in case they had succeeded in their designs; it's not certain whether he would have been willing to do it, at least till he had been himself possest of the best part of Germany, of Flanders, and Holland likewise. . . .

Peter the Great

Peter the Great combined westernizing reforms with savage repression in his rule of Russia (1682–1725). Bishop Burnett met the emperor on his visit to England in 1698.

From *Gilbert Burnett's History*

He is a man of a very hot temper, soon inflamed and very brutal in his passion. He raises his natural heat by drinking much brandy, which he rectifies [i.e., distills] himself with great application. He is subject to convulsive motions all over his body, and his head seems to be affected with these. He wants not capacity, and has a larger measure of knowledge than might be expected from his education, which was very indifferent. A want of judgment, with an instability of temper, appear in him too often and too evidently.

He is mechanically turned, and seems designed by nature rather to be a ship carpenter than a great prince. This was his chief study and exercise while he stayed here. He wrought much with his own hands and made all about him work at the models of ships. He told me he designed a great fleet at Azuph [i.e. Azov] and with it to attack the Turkish empire. But he did not seem capable of conducting so great a design, though his conduct in his wars since this has discovered a greater genius in him than appeared at this time.

. . . He was, indeed, resolved to encourage learning and to polish his people by sending some of them to travel in other countries and to draw strangers to come and live among them. He seemed apprehensive still [i.e. ever] of his sister's [i.e. the Princess Sophia's] intrigues.

From J. H. Robinson, *Readings in European History* (Boston: Ginn and Co., 1906), Vol. II, pp. 303–306, 310–312.

There was a mixture both of passion and severity in his temper. He is resolute, but understands little of war, and seemed not at all inquisitive that way.

After I had seen him often, and had conversed much with nim, I could not but adore the depth of the providence of God that had raised up such a furious man to so absolute an authority over so great a part of the world. David, considering the great things God had made for the use of man, broke out into the meditation, "What is man, that thou art so mindful of him?" But here there is an occasion for reversing these words, since man seems a very contemptible thing in the sight of God, while such a person as the tsar has such multitudes put, as it were, under his feet, exposed to his restless jealousy and savage temper.

While Peter was traveling abroad, his sister, Sophia, was involved in a rebellion of the Moscow guard, the Streltsi. *(Von Korb was an Austrian diplomat stationed in Moscow.)*

From *Von Korb's Diary*

How sharp was the pain, how great the indignation, to which the tsar's Majesty was mightily moved, when he knew of the rebellion of the Streltsi, betraying openly a mind panting for vengeance! He was still tarrying at Vienna, quite full of the desire of setting out for Italy; but, fervid as was his curiosity of rambling abroad, it was, nevertheless, speedily extinguished on the announcement of the troubles that had broken out in the bowels of his realm. . . . Nor did he long delay the plan for his justly excited wrath; he took the quick post, as his ambassador suggested, and in four weeks' time he had got over about three hundred miles[1] without accident, and arrived the 4th of September, 1698,—a monarch for the well disposed, but an avenger for the wicked.

His first anxiety after his arrival was about the rebellion,—in what it consisted, what the insurgents meant, who dared to instigate such a crime. And as nobody could answer accurately upon all points, and some pleaded their own ignorance, others the obstinacy of the Streltsi, he began to have suspicions of everybody's loyalty. . . . No day, holy or profane, were the inquisitors idle; every day was deemed fit and lawful for torturing. There were as many scourges as there were accused, and every inquisitor was a butcher. . . . The whole month of October was spent in lacerating the backs of culprits with the knout and with flames; no day were those that were left alive exempt from scourging or scorching; or else they were broken upon the wheel, or driven to the gibbet, or slain with the ax. . . .

To prove to all people how holy and inviolable are those walls of the

[1]German miles, each equivalent to about five English.

city which the Streltsi rashly meditated scaling in a sudden assault, beams were run out from all the embrasures in the walls near the gates, in each of which two rebels were hanged. This day beheld about two hundred and fifty die that death. There are few cities fortified with as many palisades as Moscow has given gibbets to her guardian Streltsi.

[In front of the nunnery where Sophia was confined] there were thirty gibbets erected in a quadrangle shape, from which there hung two hundred and thirty Streltsi; the three principal ringleaders, who tendered a petition to Sophia touching the administration of the realm, were hanged close to the windows of that princess, presenting, as it were, the petitions that were placed in their hands, so near that Sophia might with ease touch them.

From *De Missy's Life of Peter*

The tsar labored at the reform of fashions, or, more properly speaking, of dress. Until that time the Russians had always worn long beards, which they cherished and preserved with much care, allowing them to hang down on their bosoms, without even cutting the moustache. With these long beards they wore the hair very short, except the ecclesiastics, who, to distinguish themselves, wore it very long. The tsar, in order to reform that custom, ordered that gentlemen, merchants, and other subjects, except priests and peasants, should each pay a tax of one hundred rubles a year if they wished to keep their beard; the commoners had to pay one kopeck each. Officials were stationed at the gates of the towns to collect that tax, which the Russians regarded as an enormous sin on the part of the tsar and as a thing which tended to the abolition of their religion.

These insinuations, which came from the priests, occasioned the publication of many pamphlets in Moscow, where for that reason alone the tsar was regarded as a tyrant and a pagan; and there were many old Russians who, after having their beards shaved off, saved them preciously, in order to have them placed in their coffins, fearing that they would not be allowed to enter heaven without their beards. As for the young men, they followed the new customs with the more readiness as it made them appear more agreeable to the fair sex.

From the reform in beards we may pass to that of clothes. Their garments, like those of the Orientals, were very long, reaching to the heel. The tsar issued an ordinance abolishing that costume, commanding all the boyars (nobles) and all those who had positions at the court to dress after the French fashion, and likewise to adorn their clothes with gold or silver according to their means.

The dress of the women was changed, too. English hairdressing was substituted for the caps and bonnets hitherto worn; bodices, stays, and skirts, for the former undergarment. . . .

The same ordinance also provided that in the future women, as well as men, should be invited to entertainments, such as weddings, banquets, and the like, where both sexes should mingle in the same hall, as in Holland and England. It was likewise added that these entertainments should conclude with concerts and dances, but that only those should be admitted who were dressed in English costumes. His Majesty set the example in all these changes.

XIV

CROWN AND PARLIAMENT
Earlier Views
From Fortescue. *The Governance of England (1471)*
From *Elizabeth's "Golden Speech" (1601)*
From James I. *Speech to Parliament (1610)*
From *Petition of Grievances (1610)*

CIVIL WAR
Two Modern Views
From C. H. George. *Revolution*
From J. H. Hexter. *Storm Over the Gentry*
Charles I. The Break with Parliament
From *Petition of Right (1628)*
Commons Protestation (1629)
Acts of Parliament (1641)
Abolition of Ship Money
Case of the Five Members
Militia Ordinance
A "Royal Martyr"?
Declaration of Sovereignty
Act Establishing a Court to Try the King
Charles's Defense
The Sentence
Last Words

OLIVER CROMWELL
War and Religion
From *Letters and Speeches*
Authority and Consent
Dismissal of the Rump Parliament
From *Clarendon's History*
From *Ludlow's Memoirs*
Cromwell's Deathbed Prayer
A Royalist View
From *Clarendon's History*

SOCIETY AND RELIGION
Social Legislation
From *Acts and Ordinances*
Radical Dissent
From *The Free-Man's Freedom Vindicated*
From *A Fiery Flying Roll*
From Winstanley. *Letter to Lord Fairfax*
A Digger Song (1649)
Women's Roles
From *Domesticall Duties*
From *Hudibras*
Women's Petition (1649)
From Mary Cary. *The New Jerusalem's Glory*
From George Fox. *A Collection of . . . Epistles*
From *The Sufferings of the People Called Quakers*
From *Dorothy Osborne's Letters*

FROM RESTORATION TO REVOLUTION: ENGLAND AND HOLLAND
Restoration
From *John Evelyn's Diary*
The "Glorious Revolution"
From *John Evelyn's Diary*
Patterns of Government
From *Observations Upon the United Provinces of the Netherlands*
From *The Bill of Rights (1689)*

THE SEARCH FOR ORDER— CONSTITUTIONALISM AND OLIGARCHY

WHILE MANY COUNTRIES of Europe turned to absolutist governments in the seventeenth century, the English reshaped their medieval institutions into a new kind of constitutional regime.

England inherited from the late Middle Ages a system of government based on cooperation between king and parliament. The king conducted affairs of state; parliament levied taxes and enacted laws. The relative powers of crown and parliament were not clearly defined, but the system worked well enough so long as no serious policy differences arose between the king's government and the wealthy, powerful classes represented in the House of Lords and the House of Commons.

Signs of strain began to appear under James I (1603–1625). Under Charles I (1625–1649) the religious and financial policies of the crown came under attack in the House of Commons from the first years of the reign. When parliament refused grants of taxes to support policies of which it disapproved, Charles turned to extra-parliamentary expedients. But this only embittered the situation still more. By 1642 the two sides had become so estranged that England drifted into a civil war.

Charles's adversaries entered the conflict with the declared purpose of defending the ancient rights and institutions of England. But, during the war, ideas much more radical than those of the parliamentary leaders emerged and found support. The leaders of parliament soon quarreled with the generals of the army that they had created. The war ended with the execution of the king, the dissolution of parliament, and the establishment of a military dictatorship under Oliver Cromwell.

When Cromwell died, Charles II (1660–1685) was welcomed back to England with almost universal support. However, the "Restoration" of 1660 was a restoration of parliament as well as of monarchy, and tensions between crown and parliament persisted under Charles II.

The final resolution of the situation came in the next reign. James II (1685–1688) converted to Catholicism and married a Catholic wife. The unwelcome prospect that a permanent Catholic line of succession to the throne would be established united royalist and parliamentary supporters in a common cause. They offered the throne to Prince William of Holland and his wife Mary (a daughter of James II). When William took power he promised to rule in cooperation with parliament and a Bill of Rights was enacted to define the future pattern of English government.

CROWN AND PARLIAMENT

Earlier Views

Sir John Fortescue used the phrase "political and regal dominion" to describe the English system of limited monarchy as it had developed by the fifteenth century.

From Fortescue. *The Governance of England (1471)*

There are two kinds of kingdom, of which one is a lordship, called in Latin *dominium regale,* and the other is called *dominium politicum et regale.* And they differ in that the first king may rule his people by such laws as he makes himself. And therefore he may set upon them tallages and other impositions such as he wills himself without their assent. The second king may not rule his people by other laws than those that they assent to. And therefore he may set upon them no impositions without their own assent. . . .

But, blessed be God, this land is ruled under [the] better law; and therefore the people thereof are not in such penury nor thereby hurt in their persons but are wealthy and have all things necessary to the sustenance of nature. Wherefore they are mighty and able to resist the adversaries of this realm and to beat other realms that do or would do them wrong. Lo, this is the fruit of the *ius politicum et regale* under which we live.

From Sir John Fortescue, *The Governance of England,* ed. C. Plummer (Oxford: Clarendon Press, 1885), pp. 109–114.

Queen Elizabeth I's last parliament was much aggrieved by royal grants of commercial monopolies. The queen won over the members with a gracious speech.

From *Elizabeth's "Golden Speech" (1601)*

Mr. Speaker,

You give me thanks; but I doubt me, that I have more cause to thank you all, than you me. And I charge you, to thank them of the

From H. Townshend, *Historical Collections* (London, 1680), pp. 264–266.

lower house from me: for had I not received a knowledge from you, I might have fallen into the lapse of an error, only for lack of true information.

Since I was queen, yet did I never put my pen unto any grant, but that, upon pretext and semblance made unto me, it was both good and beneficial to the subject in general; though a private profit to some of my ancient servants, who had deserved well at my hands. But the contrary being found by experience, I am exceedingly beholding to such subjects as would move the same at the first. . . . And I take it exceedingly gratefully from them; because it gives us to know that no respects or interests had moved them other than the minds they bear to suffer no diminution of our honour and our subjects' loves unto us. The zeal of which affection, tending to ease my people, and knit their hearts unto me, I embrace with a princely care; for (above all earthly treasure) I esteem my people's love, more than which I desire not to merit.

That my grants should be grievous to my people and oppressions privileged under colour of our patents, our kingly dignity shall not suffer it: yea, when I heard it, I could give no rest unto my thoughts until I had reformed it. . . .

To be a king and wear a crown is a thing more glorious to them that see it than it is pleasing to them that bear it: for myself, I was never so much enticed with the glorious name of a king, or royal authority of a queen, as delighted that God had made me his instrument to maintain his truth and glory and to defend this kingdom (as I said) from peril, dishonour, tyranny, and oppression.

There will never queen sit in my seat with more zeal to my country, care for my subjects, and that sooner with willingness will venture her life for your good and safety, than myself. For it is not my desire to live nor reign longer than my life and reign shall be for your good. And though you have had, and may have many princes, more mighty and wise, sitting in this state; yet you never had, or shall have any that will be more careful and loving.

James I (1603–1625) liked to lecture his parliaments about the immensity of royal power. In 1610 he emphasized his role as "father" of the country.

From James I. *Speech to Parliament (1610)*

The state of Monarchy is the supremest thing upon earth; for kings are not only God's lieutenants upon earth and sit upon God's throne, but even by God himself they are called gods. There be three principal similitudes that illustrate the state of Monarchy: one taken out of the Word of God and the two other out of the grounds of policy and phi-

From *The Works of the Most High and Mighty Prince James* (London: James Montague, 1616), pp. 529–531.

losophy. In the Scriptures kings are called gods, and so their power after a certain relation compared to the Divine power. Kings are also compared to the fathers of families, for a king is truly *parens patriae* [father of his country], the politic father of his people. And lastly, kings are compared to the head of this microcosm of the body of man.

Kings are justly called gods for that they exercise a manner or resemblance of Divine power upon earth. . . .

As for the father of a family, they had of old under the Law of Nature *patriam potestatem* [paternal power], which was *potestatem vitae et necis* [power of life and death], over their children or family. . . . Now a father may dispose of his inheritance to his children at his pleasure, yea, even disinherit the eldest upon just occasions and prefer the youngest, according to his liking; make them beggars or rich at his pleasure; restrain or banish out of his presence, as he finds them give cause of offence, or restore them in favour again with the penitent sinner. So may the King deal with his subjects.

And lastly, as for the head of the natural body, the head hath the power of directing all the members of the body to that use which the judgment in the head thinks most convenient. . . . It is sedition in subjects to dispute what a king may do in the height of his power; but just kings will ever be willing to declare what they will do, if they will not incur the curse of God. I will not be content that my power be disputed upon, but I shall ever be willing to make the reason appear of all my doings, and rule my actions according to my laws.

The House of Commons responded with complaints about extra-parliamentary taxation and legislation.

From *Petition of Grievances* (1610)

The policy and constitution of this your kingdom appropriates unto the Kings of this realm, with the assent of the Parliament, as well the sovereign power of making laws as that of taxing or imposing upon the subjects' goods or merchandises, wherein they have justly such a propriety as may not without their consent be altered or changed. . . .

We therefore, your Majesty's most humble Commons assembled in Parliament, following the example of this worthy care of our ancestors and out of a duty to those for whom we serve, finding that your Majesty, without advice or consent of Parliament, hath lately in time of peace set both greater impositions and far more in number than any your noble ancestors did ever in time of war, have with all humility presumed to present this most just and necessary petition unto your Majesty, That all impositions set without the assent of Parliament may be quite abolished and taken away. . . .

[Also] it is apparent both that proclamations have been of late years much more frequent than heretofore, and that they are extended not only to the liberty but also to the goods, inheritances, and livelihood of men: some of them tending to alter some points of the law and make them new. . . .

By reason whereof there is a general fear conceived and spread amongst your Majesty's people that proclamations will by degrees grow up and increase to the strength and nature of laws; whereby not only that ancient happiness, freedom, will be as much blemished (if not quite taken away) which their ancestors have so long enjoyed, but the same may also (in process of time) bring a new form of arbitrary government upon the realm.

We therefore, your Majesty's humble subjects the Commons in this Parliament assembled . . . have thought it to appertain to our duties, as well towards your Majesty as to those that have trusted and sent us to their service, to present unto your Majesty's view these fears and griefs of your people, and to become humble suitors unto your Majesty that thenceforth no fine or forfeiture of goods or other pecuniary or corporal punishment may be inflicted upon your subjects . . . unless they shall offend against some law or statute of this realm in force at the time of their offence committed.

CIVIL WAR

Two Modern Views

Some historians think the English civil war was caused mainly by social and economic problems; others emphasize religious and constitutional issues.

From C. H. George. *Revolution*

At this point of analysis the Marxian hypothesis proves useful in explaining the division in the nature of English rulership, as it does later for the same split in French power. For if one looks very closely into the economic self-interest of the leading oligarchies of power, their conflicts help explain the loss of the medieval sense of alliance between the wellborn, the priests, and the rich. The increasing opportunities for wealth and power in business, farming, and the State, induced an increasing competition which placed great strain on the social structure and political mechanisms of old England. The traditional ruling barons used their status to grab trading and industrial "monopolies" from the Court; they were hated by excluded entrepreneurs from the towns, and in turn were themselves divided into peers who made out at Court and those "Country" aristocrats who did not. The lesser country aristocracy were also increasingly divided in their relations to one another and the government by the new economics of estate management and its relation to the cloth industry. Finally, the masses of the economically undistinguished in town and village found almost nothing they liked in the emerging order of things—the "drones" at Court, monopolists, enclosing landlords, rack-renters, price-riggers, usurers, and the like, meant unemployment, depopulation, dislocation, pauperism, and a generally terrifying rise in insecurities about the most basic needs of life. Bread and shelter and dignity of person were harder to come by in Stuart England than they had been in the England of the Plantagenets.

There were also religious issues which divided the ruling classes, though they were not of great importance. This was not a "Puritan" revolution. . . .

From Charles H. George, *Revolution: European Radicals from Hus to Lenin* (New York: Scott, Foresman, 1971), pp. 71–72.

From J. H. Hexter. *Storm Over the Gentry*

And now one final word before we emerge at last from the storm over the gentry. The two scholars whose combined but clashing efforts raised that storm have at least one thing in common. It is the main purpose of both Professor Tawney and Professor Trevor-Roper to show that the seventeenth-century revolution in Britain was closely related to prior shifts in the personnel of the landowning classes and shifts in the dimensions of their estates, their incomes, and their economic prospects. That a revolution prepared by conflicts over Parliamentary privilege, royal prerogative, judicial independence, arbitrary arrest, power of taxation, and the rule of law in England, triggered by a religious upheaval in Scotland, and traversed by the complex lines of fission that separated Anglican from Puritan, courtier from country man, was indeed closely related to the matters that have especially engaged their attention, neither Tawney nor Trevor-Roper has proved. And what such masters of the materials of seventeenth-century history and of historical forensics cannot prove when they set their minds to it, is not likely ever to be proved. Yet the destruction left in the wake of the storm over the gentry need not enduringly depress us. At least one amateur of seventeenth-century history observes the havoc with a sense of relief, even of emancipation. He takes faith and freedom rather seriously himself; and he has not felt that in so doing he is necessarily eccentric. He is inclined to think that a good many men in the mid-seventeenth century took them seriously too. For such a one it is something of a relief to feel that the outcome of the storm over the gentry licenses him to turn part of his attention from rent rolls, estates accounts, and recognizances of debt to what a very great scholar [William Haller] calls *Liberty and Reformation in the Puritan Revolution*.

From J. H. Hexter, "Storm Over the Gentry," *Encounter* 56 (1958), p. 32. Copyright © 1958 by J. H. Hexter, reprinted by his permission.

Charles I. The Break with Parliament

The House of Commons attacked the policies of Charles I (1625–1649) from the beginning of the reign.

From *Petition of Right* (1628)

To the King's Most Excellent Majesty

Humbly show unto our Sovereign Lord the King the Lords Spiritual and Temporal and Commons in Parliament assembled, that whereas it

From S. R. Gardiner, ed., *The Constitutional Documents of the Puritan Revolution*, 2nd ed. (Oxford: Oxford University Press, 1899), pp. 66–69.

is declared and enacted by a statute made in the time of the reign of King Edward the First commonly called Statutum de Tallagio non Concedendo that no tallage or aid should be laid or levied by the King or his heirs in this realm without the good will and assent of the archbishops, bishops, earls, barons, knights, burgesses and other the freemen of the commonalty of this realm; and by authority of Parliament holden in the five and twentieth year of the reign of King Edward the Third it is declared and enacted, that from henceforth no person should be compelled to make any loans to the King against his will because such loans were against reason and the franchise of the land. . . .

Yet, nevertheless of late divers commissions directed to sundry commissioners in several counties with instructions have issued, by means whereof your people have been in divers places assembled and required to lend certain sums of money unto your Majesty. . . .

And where also by the statute called the Great Charter of the Liberties of England it is declared and enacted, that no freeman may be taken or imprisoned or be disseised of his freehold or liberties or his free customs or be outlawed or exiled or in any manner destroyed, but by the lawful judgement of his peers or by the law of the land.

And in the eight and twentieth year of the reign of King Edward the Third it was declared and enacted by authority of Parliament, that no man, of what estate or condition that he be, should be put out of his land or tenement, nor taken, nor imprisoned, nor disherited, nor put to death without being brought to answer by due process of law.

Nevertheless against the tenor of the said statutes and other the good laws and statutes of your realm to that end provided, divers of your subjects have of late been imprisoned without any cause shown. . . .

They do therefore humbly pray your most excellent Majesty that no man hereafter be compelled to make or yield any gift, loan, benevolence, tax or such like charge without common consent by Act of Parliament, and that none be called to make answer or take such oath or to give attendance or be confined or otherwise molested or disquieted concerning the same or for refusal thereof. And that no freeman in any such manner as is before mentioned be imprisoned or detained.

Members of the House of Commons accused Charles's ministers of "popery" during a turbulent session in 1629.

Commons Protestation (1629)

This day, being the last day of the Assembly, as soon as prayers were ended the Speaker went into the Chair, and delivered the Kings com-

From W. Notestein and F. H. Relf, eds., *Commons Debates for 1629* (Minneapolis: University of Minnesota Press, 1921), pp. 101–106.

mand for the adjournment of the House until Tuesday sevennight following.

The House returned him answer, that it was not the office of the Speaker to deliver any such command unto them, but for the adjournment of the House it did properly belong unto themselves; and after they had settled some things they thought fit and convenient to be spoken of they would satisfy the King.

The Speaker told them that he had an express command from the King as soon as he had delivered his message to rise; and upon that he left the Chair, but was by force drawn to it again by Mr. Denzil Holles, son of the Earl of Clare, Mr. Valentine, and others. And Mr. Holles, notwithstanding the endeavour of Sir Thomas Edmondes, Sir Humphrey May, and other Privy Councellors to free the Speaker from the Chair, swore, Gods wounds, he should sit still until they pleased to rise. . . .

Sir John Eliot. God knows I now speak with all duty to the King. It is true the misfortunes we suffer are many, we know what discoveries have been made; how Arminianism creeps in and undermines us, and how Popery comes in upon us; they mask not in strange disguises, but expose themselves to the view of the world. In search whereof we have fixed our eyes not simply on the actors (the Jesuits and priests), but on their masters, they that are in authority, hence it comes we suffer. The fear of them makes these interruptions. You have seen prelates that are their abettors. That great Bishop of Winchester, we know what he hath done to favour them; this fear extends to some others that contract a fear of being discovered, and they draw from hence this jealousy. This is the Lord Treasurer, in whose person all evil is contracted. I find him acting and building on those grounds laid by his Master, the late great Duke of Buckingham, and his spirit is moving for these interruptions. And from this fear they break Parliaments lest Parliaments should break them. I find him the head of all that great party the Papists, and all Jesuits and priests derive from him their shelter and protection.

In this great question of Tonnage and Poundage, the instruments moved at his command and pleasure; he dismays our merchants, and invites strangers to come in to drive our trade, and to serve their own ends.

The Remonstrance was put to the question, but the Speaker refused to do it; and said he was otherwise commanded from the King.

Whereupon Mr. Selden spake as followeth:

"You, Mr. Speaker, say you dare not put the question which we command you; if you will not put it we must sit still, and thus we shall never be able to do any thing; they that come after you may say they have the Kings command not to do it. We sit here by commandment of the King, under the great Seal of England; and for you, you are by his Majesty (sitting in his royal chair before both Houses) appointed our Speaker, and yet now you refuse to do us the office and service of a Speaker."

Then they required Mr. Holles to read certain Articles as the Protestations of the House, which were jointly, as they were read, allowed with a loud *Yea* by the House. The effect of which Articles are as followeth:

First, Whosoever shall bring in innovation in Religion, or by favour or countenance, seek to extend or introduce Popery or Arminianism or other opinions disagreeing from the true and orthodox Church shall be reputed a capital enemy to this Kingdom and Commonwealth.

Secondly, Whosoever shall counsel or advise the taking and levying of the Subsidies of Tonnage and Poundage, not being granted by Parliament, or shall be an actor or instrument therein, shall be likewise reputed an innovator in the government, and a capital enemy to this Kingdom and Commonwealth.

Thirdly, If any merchant or person whatsoever shall voluntarily yield or pay the said subsidies of Tonnage and Poundage, not being granted by Parliament, he shall likewise be reputed a betrayer of the liberties of England and an enemy to the same.

These being read and allowed of, the House rose up after they had sitten down two hours.

The King hearing that the House continued to sit (notwithstanding his command for the adjourning thereof) sent a messenger for the serjeant with the mace, which being taken from the table there can be no further proceeding; but the serjeant was by the House stayed, and the key of the door taken from him, and given to a gentleman of the House to keep.

After this the King sent Maxwell with the black rod for the dissolution of Parliament, but being informed that neither he nor his message would be received by the House, the King grew into much rage and passion, and sent for the Captain of the Pensioners and Guard to force the door, but the rising of the House prevented the bloodshed that might have been spilt.

After this episode Charles ruled without parliament for eleven years. Then a rebellion in Scotland forced him to summon a new parliament and to accept statutes guaranteeing a substantial role for parliament in future English government.

Acts of Parliament (1641)

Act Against Dissolving the Long Parliament

Whereas great sums of money must of necessity be speedily advanced and provided for the relief of His Majesty's army and people

From S. R. Gardiner, ed., *The Constitutional Documents of the Puritan Revolution*, 2nd ed. (Oxford: Oxford University Press, 1899), pp. 144–145, 158–159.

in the northern parts of this realm . . . which credit cannot be obtained until such obstacles be first removed as are occasioned by fears, jealousies and apprehensions of divers His Majesty's loyal subjects, that this present Parliament may be adjourned, prorogued, or dissolved, before justice shall be duly executed upon delinquents, public grievances redressed, a firm peace between the two nations of England and Scotland concluded, and before sufficient provision be made for the re-payment of the said monies so to be raised . be it declared and enacted by the King, our Sovereign Lord, with the assent of the Lords and Commons in this present Parliament assembled, and by the authority of the same, that this present Parliament now assembled shall not be dissolved unless it be by Act of Parliament to be passed for that purpose. . . .

Triennial Act

Whereas by the laws and statutes of this realm the Parliament ought to be holden at least once every year for the redress of grievances, but the appointment of the time and place for the holding thereof hath always belonged, as it ought, to His Majesty and his royal progenitors: and whereas it is by experience found that the not holding of Parliaments accordingly hath produced sundry and great mischiefs and inconveniences to the King's Majesty, the Church and Commonwealth; for the prevention of the like mischiefs and inconveniences in time to come:

Be it enacted by the King's Most Excellent Majesty, with the consent of the Lord's spiritual and temporal, and the Commons in this present Parliament assembled . . . that in case there be not a Parliament summoned by writ under the Great Seal of England, and assembled and held before the 10th of September, which shall be in the third year next after the last day of the last meeting and sitting in this present Parliament . . . and so from time to time, and in all times hereafter, if there shall not be a Parliament assembled and held before the 10th day of September, which shall be in the third year next after the last day of the last meeting and sitting in Parliament before the time assembled and held . . . that then in every such case as aforesaid, the Parliament shall assemble and be held in the usual place at Westminster. . . .

Extra-parliamentary taxes that the king had levied were declared illegal. One of the most unpopular was "Ship Money."

Abolition of Ship Money

Be it therefore declared and enacted by the King's Most Excellent Majesty and the Lords and the Commons in this present Parliament assembled, and by the authority of the same, that the said charge imposed upon the subject for the providing and furnishing of ships commonly called Ship-money ... and the said judgment given against the said John Hampden, were and are contrary to and against the laws and statutes of this realm, the right of property, the liberty of the subjects, former resolutions in Parliament, and the Petition of Right made in the third year of the reign of His Majesty that now is.

From S. R. Gardiner, ed., *The Constitutional Documents of the Puritan Revolution*, 2nd ed. (Oxford: Oxford University Press, 1899), p. 191.

The Acts of 1641 did not settle the issue of ultimate sovereignty. Rather, the crisis worsened. A Scottish Presbyterian army was encamped in the northern counties of England. A Catholic rebellion broke out in Ireland. When parliament continued to attack royal policies and claimed a right to appoint the king's ministers, Charles tried to arrest five leading members of the House of Commons on charges of treason.

Case of the Five Members

And as his Majesty came through Westminster Hall, the Commanders, etc., that attended him made a lane on both sides the Hall (through which his Majesty passed and came up the stairs to the House of Commons) and stood before the guard of Pensioners and Halbedeers (who also attended the king's person) and, the door of the House of Commons being thrown open, his Majesty entered the House, and as he passed up towards the Chair he cast his eye on the right hand near the Bar of the House, where Mr. Pym used to sit; but his Majesty not seeing him there (knowing him well) went up to the Chair, and said, "By your leave, Mr. Speaker, I must borrow your chair a little." Whereupon the Speaker came out of the Chair and his Majesty stepped up into it; after he had stood in the Chair a while, casting his eye upon the members as they stood up uncovered, but could not discern any of the five members to be there, nor indeed were they easy to be discerned (had they been there) among so many bare faces all standing up together. Then his Majesty made this speech.

"Gentlemen, I am sorry for this occasion of coming unto you. Yesterday I sent a Serjeant at Arms upon a very important occasion, to apprehend some that by my command were accused of high treason; whereunto I did expect obedience and not a message. And I must declare unto you here that, albeit no king that ever was in England shall be more careful of your privileges, to maintain them to the uttermost of his power, than I shall be; yet you must know that in cases of trea-

From John Rushworth, *Historical Collections* (London, 1721), Vol. 4, pp. 477–478.

son no person hath a privilege. And therefore I am come to know if any of these persons that were accused are here. For I must tell you, Gentlemen, that so long as these persons that I have accused (for no light crime, but for treason) are here, I cannot expect that this House will be in the right way that I do heartily wish it. Therefore I am come to tell you that I must have them wheresoever I find them. Well, since I see all the birds are flown, I do expect from you that you shall send them unto me as soon as they return hither. But I assure you, on the word of a king, I never did intend any force, but shall proceed against them in a legal and fair way, for I never did intend any other.

"And now, since I cannot do what I came for, I think this no unfit occasion to repeat what I have said formerly, that whatsoever I have done in favor and to the good of my subjects, I do mean to maintain it.

"I will trouble you no more, but tell you I do expect as soon as they come to the House you will send them to me; otherwise I must take my own course to find them."

After this abortive attempt the houses of parliament raised an army on their own authority, without royal consent, and civil war broke out.

Militia Ordinance

Whereas there hath been of late a most dangerous and desperate design upon the House of Commons, which we have just cause to believe to be an effect of the bloody counsels of Papists and other ill-affected persons, who have already raised a rebellion in the kingdom of Ireland; and by reason of many discoveries we cannot but fear they will proceed not only to stir up the like rebellion and insurrections in this kingdom of England, but also to back them with forces from abroad.

For the safety therefore of His Majesty's person, the Parliament and kingdom in this time of imminent danger.

It is ordained by the Lords and Commons now in Parliament assembled, that Henry Earl of Holland shall be Lieutenant of the County of Berks, Oliver Earl of Bolingbroke shall be Lieutenant of the County of Bedford, &c.

And shall severally and respectively have power to assemble and call together all and singular His Majesty's subjects, within the said several and respective counties and places, as well within liberties as without, that are meet and fit for the wars, and them to train and exercise and put in readiness, and them after their abilities and faculties well and sufficiently from time to time to cause to be arrayed and weaponed, and to take the muster of them in places most fit for that purpose.

From S. R. Gardiner, ed., *The Constitutional Documents of the Puritan Revolution,* 2nd ed. (Oxford: Oxford University Press, 1899), pp. 245–246.

A "Royal Martyr"?

By 1648 Charles was defeated A majority of parliament intended to retain him as king, though with limited powers. But the army generals were deter-mined to put Charles on trial and execute him. In December 1648, the gener-als "purged" parliament of all its more moderate members. The surviving remnant o "rump tnen enacted these decrees.

Declaration of Sovereignty

(Resolved) That the commons of England, in parliament assembled, do declare that the people are, under God, the original of all just power. And do also declare, that the commons of England, in parliament as-sembled, being chosen by and representing the people have the su-preme power in this nation. And do also declare, that whatsoever is enacted, or declared for law, by the commons in parliament assembled, hath the force of a law; and all the people of this nation are concluded thereby, although the consent of king, or house of peers, be not had thereunto.

From W. Cobbett, *Parliamentary History of England* (London, 1868), Vol. 3, col. 1257.

Act Establishing a Court to Try the King

Whereas it is notorious that Charles Stuart, the now King of England, not content with the many encroachments which his predecessors had made upon the people in their rights and freedom, hath had a wicked design totally to subvert the ancient and fundamental laws and liberties of this nation, and in their place to introduce an arbitrary and tyran-nical government, and that besides all other evil ways and means to bring his design to pass, he hath prosecuted it with fire and sword, . . . be it enacted and ordained by the [Lords] and Commons in Parlia-ment assembled, and it is hereby enacted and ordained by the author-ity thereof, that the Earls of Kent, Nottingham, Pembroke, Denbigh and Mulgrave, the Lord Grey of Wark, Lord Chief Justice Rolle of the King's Bench, Lord Chief Justice St. John of the Common Pleas, and Lord Chief Baron Wylde, the Lord Fairfax, Lieutenant-General Crom-well. &c. [in all about 150], shall be and are hereby appointed and re-quired to be Commissioners and Judges for the hearing, trying and judging of the said Charles Stuart.

From S. R. Gardiner, ed., *The Constitutional Documents of the Puritan Revolution*, 2nd ed. (Oxford: Oxford University Press, 1899), pp. 357–358.

Charles prepared a speech in his own defense but was not allowed to deliver it at the trial.

Charles's Defense

Having already made my protestations, not only against the illegality of this pretended Court, but also, that no earthly power can justly call me (who am your King) in question as a delinquent, I would not any more open my mouth upon this occasion, more than to refer myself to what I have spoken, were I in this case alone concerned: but the duty I owe to God in the preservation of the true liberty of my people will not suffer me at this time to be silent: for, how can any free-born subject of England call life or anything he possesseth his own, if power without right daily make new, and abrogate the old fundamental laws of the land which I now take to be the present case? . . .

And admitting, but not granting, that the people of England's commission could grant your pretended power, I see nothing you can show for that; for certainly you never asked the question of the tenth man in the kingdom, and in this way you manifestly wrong even the poorest ploughman, if you demand not his free consent; nor can you pretend any colour for this your pretended commission, without the consent at least of the major part of every man in England of whatsoever quality or condition, which I am sure you never went about to seek, so far are you from having it. Thus you see that I speak not for my own right alone, as I am your King, but also for the true liberty of all my subjects, which consists, not in the power of government, but in living under such laws, such a government, as may give themselves the best assurance of their lives, and property of their goods; nor in this must or do I forget the privileges of both Houses of Parliament, which this day's proceedings do not only violate, but likewise occasion the greatest breach of their public faith that (I believe) ever was heard of. . . .

This I intended to speak in Westminster Hall on Monday, January 22, but against reason was hindered to show my reasons.

From John Rushworth, *Historical Collections* (London, 1721), Vol. 7, pp. 1403-1404.

The Sentence

[He is author of the] unnatural, cruel, and bloody wars, and therein guilty of high treason, and of the murders, rapines, burnings, spoils, desolations, damage, and mischief to this nation acted and committed in the said war, and occasioned thereby. For all which treasons and crimes this Court doth adjudge that he, the said Charles Stuart, as a

From John Rushworth, *Historical Collections* (London, 1721), Vol. 7, p. 1425.

tyrant, traitor, murderer, and public enemy to the good people of this nation, shall be put to death by the severing of his head from his body.

[After the sentence was read], His Majesty then said, Will you hear me a word, Sir?

PRESIDENT OF THE COURT. Sir, you are not to be heard after the sentence.

HIS MAJESTY. No, Sir?

PRESIDENT. No, Sir, by your favour, Sir. Guards, withdraw your prisoner.

HIS MAJESTY. I may speak after sentence, by your favour, Sir, I may speak after sentence, ever. By your favour, hold—I am not suffered to speak, expect what justice other people may have. . . .

On the scaffold Charles was finally allowed to speak.

Last Words

[As] for the people—truly I desire their liberty and freedom as much as anybody whosoever. But I must tell you that their liberty and freedom consists in having of government those laws by which their lives and goods may be most their own. It is not for having share in government. That is nothing pertaining to them. A subject and a sovereign are clean different things, and therefore, until they do that—I mean that you do put the people in that liberty as I say—certainly they will never enjoy themselves.

Sirs, it was for this that now I am come here. If I would have given way to an arbitrary way, for to have all laws changed according to the power of the sword, I needed not to have come here. And therefore I tell you (and I pray God it be not laid to your charge) that I am the martyr of the people.

From *England's Black Tribunal* (London, 1720).

OLIVER CROMWELL

War and Religion

From *Letters and Speeches*

[*On army officers, 1645*]

I had rather have a plain russet-coated captain that knows what he fights for, and loves what he knows, than that which you call a gentleman and is nothing else. I honour a gentleman that is so indeed.

[*On the battle of Naseby, 1645*]

Sir, this is none other but the hand of God; and to Him alone belongs the glory, wherein none are to share with Him. The General [Fairfax] served you with all faithfulness and honour: and the best commendations I can give him is, that I dare say he attributes all to God, and would rather perish than assume to himself. Which is an honest and a thriving way, and yet as much for bravery may be given to him, in this action, as to a man.

[*On tolerance, 1645*]

Presbyterians, Independents, all had here the same spirit of faith and prayer; the same pretence and answer; they agree here, know no names of difference: pity it is it should be otherwise anywhere. All that believe, have the real unity, which is most glorious, because inward and spiritual, in the Body, and to the Head. As for being united in forms, commonly called Uniformity, every Christian will for peace-sake study and do, as far as conscience will permit; and from brethren, in things of the mind we look for no compulsion, but that of light and reason.

[*On Catholics, 1650*]

For that which you mention concerning liberty of conscience, I meddle not with any man's conscience. But if by liberty of conscience, you mean a liberty to exercise the Mass, I judge it best to use plain dealing and to let you know, Where the Parliament of England have power, that will not be allowed of.

From Thomas Carlyle, ed., *The Letters and Speeches of Oliver Cromwell*, 3 vols. (New York: G. P. Putnam's Sons, 1904), Vol. 1, pp. 154, 204, 218, 468–469 Vol. 2, p. 15.

[On the massacre at Drogheda (Ireland), 1649]

... The enemy retreated, divers of them, into the Mill-Mount: a place very strong and of difficult access, being exceedingly high, having a good graft, and strongly palisadoed. The Governor, Sir Arthur Ashton, and divers considerable Officers being there, our men getting up to them, were ordered by me to put them all to the sword. And indeed, being in the heat of action, I forbade them to spare any that were in arms in the town, and, I think, that night they put to the sword about 2,000 men, divers of the officers and soldiers being fled over the Bridge into the other part of the Town, where about one hundred of them possessed St. Peter's church-steeple, some the west gate, and others a strong round tower next the gate called St. Sunday's. These being summoned to yield to mercy, refused, whereupon I ordered the steeple of St. Peter's Church to be fired, where one of them was heard to say in the midst of the flames: "God damn me, God confound me; I burn, I burn."

The next day, the other two towers were summoned, in one of which was about six or seven score; but they refused to yield themselves, and we knowing that hunger must compel them, set only good guards to secure them from running away until their stomachs were come down. From one of the said towers, notwithstanding their condition, they killled and wounded some of our men. When they submitted, their officers were knocked on the head, and every tenth man of the soldiers killed, and the rest shipped for the Barbadoes. The soldiers in the other tower were all spared, as to their lives only, and shipped likewise for the Barbadoes.

I am persuaded that this is a righteous judgment of God upon these barbarous wretches, who have imbrued their hands in so much innocent blood; and that it will tend to prevent the effusion of blood for the future, which are the satisfactory grounds to such actions, which otherwise cannot but work remorse and regret.

Authority and Consent

In 1653 Cromwell dismissed the remnant or "rump" of parliament and became, in effect, a military dictator. Although he experimented with several types of assemblies, he never created a representative body that could legitimize his power.

Dismissal of the Rump Parliament

Calling to Major-General Harrison, who was on the other side of the House, to come to him, he told him, that he judged the Parliament

From C. H. Firth, *The Memoirs of Edmund Ludlow* (Oxford: Oxford University Press, 1894), Vol. 1, pp. 352–354.

ripe for a dissolution, and this to be the time of doing it. The Major-General answered, as he since told me, "Sir, the work is very great and dangerous, therefore I desire you seriously to consider of it before you engage in it." "You say well," replied the General, and thereupon sat still for about a quarter of an hour; and then the question for passing the Bill being to be put, he said again to Major-General Harrison, "this is the time I must do it"; and suddenly standing up, made a speech, wherein he loaded the Parliament with the vilest reproaches, charging them not to have a heart to do any thing for the publick good, to have espoused the corrupt interest of Presbytery and the lawyers, who were the supporters of tyranny and oppression, accusing them of an intention to perpetuate themselves in power, had they not been forced to the passing of this Act, which he affirmed they designed never to observe, and thereupon told them, that the Lord had done with them, and had chosen other instruments for the carrying on his work that were more worthy. This he spoke with so much passion and discomposure of mind, as if he had been distracted. Sir Peter Wentworth stood up to answer him, and said, that this was the first time that ever he had heard such unbecoming language given to the Parliament, and that it was the more horrid in that it came from their servant, and their servant whom they had so highly trusted and obliged: but as he was going on, the General stept into the midst of the House, where continuing his distracted language, he said, "Come, come, I will put an end to your prating"; then walking up and down the House like a madman, and kicking the ground with his feet, he cried out, "You are no Parliament, I say you are no Parliament; I will put an end to your sitting; call them in, call them in": whereupon the serjeant attending the Parliament opened the doors, and Lieutenant-Colonel Worsley with two files of musqueteers entered the House; which Sir Henry Vane observing from his place, said aloud, "This is not honest yea it is against morality and common honesty." Then Cromwell fell a railing at him, crying out with a loud voice, "O Sir Henry Vane, Sir Henry Vane, the lord deliver me from Sir Henry Vane." Then looking upon one of the members, he said, "There sits a drunkard", and giving much reviling language to others, he commanded the mace to be taken away, saying, "What shall we do with this bauble? here, take it away." Having brought all into this disorder, Major-General Harrison went to the Speaker as he sat in the chair, and told him, that seeing things were reduced to this pass, it would not be convenient for him to remain there. The Speaker answered, that he would not come down unless he were forced. "Sir," said Harrison, "I will lend you my hand"; and thereupon putting his hand within his, the Speaker came down. Then Cromwell applied himself to the members of the House, who were in number between 80 and 100, and said to them, "It's you that have forced me to this, for I have sought the Lord night and day, that he would rather slay me than put me upon the doing of this work."

The following account concerns a man who refused to pay a tax levied by Cromwell without parliament's consent

From *Clarendon's History*

Maynard, who was of counsel with the prisoner, demanded his liberty with great confidence, both upon the illegality of the commitment, and the illegality of the imposition, as being laid without any lawful authority. The judges could not maintain or defend either, but enough declared what their sentence would be; and therefore the Protector's Attorney required a farther day to answer what had been urged. Before that day, Maynard was committed to the Tower, for presuming to question or make doubt of his authority; and the judges were sent for, and severely reprehended for suffering that license; and when they with all humility mentioned the law and *Magna Charta*, Cromwell told them, their *magna farta* should not control his actions, which he knew were for the safety of the commonwealth. He asked them who made them judges; [whether] they had any authority to sit there but what he gave them; and that if his authority were at an end, they knew well enough what would become of themselves; and therefore advised them to be more tender of that which could only preserve them; and so dismissed them with caution, that they should not suffer the lawyers to prate what it would not become them to hear.

From Lord Clarendon, *The History of the Rebellion and Civil Wars in England* (Oxford: Oxford University Press, 1839), Vol. 6, pp. 351–352.

Ludlow was a parliamentary general who regarded Cromwell as a usurper.

From *Ludlow's Memoirs*

Then I drew near to the council-table, where Cromwell charged me with dispersing treasonable books in Ireland, and with endeavouring to render the officers of the army disaffected, by discoursing to them concerning new models of Government. I acknowledged that I had caused some papers to be dispersed in Ireland, but denied that they justly could be called treasonable. . . .

'You do well,' said he, 'to reflect on our fears . . . I now require you to give assurance not to act against the Government.' I desired to be excused in that particular, reminding him of the reasons I had formerly given him for my refusal, adding, that I was in his power, and that he might use me as he thought fit. 'Pray then,' said he, 'what is it

From C. H. Firth, *The Memoirs of Edmund Ludlow* (Oxford: Oxford University Press, 1894), Vol. 2, pp. 10–11.

that you would have? May not every man be as good as he will? What can you desire more than you have?' 'It were easy,' said I, 'to tell what we would have.' 'What is that, I pray?' said he. 'That which we fought for,' said I, 'that the nation might be governed by its own consent.' 'I am,' said he, 'as much for a government by consent as any man; but where shall we find that consent? Amongst the Prelatical, Presbyterian, Independent, Anabaptist, or Leveling Parties?' I answered, 'Amongst those of all sorts who had acted with fidelity and affection to the publick.'

Cromwell's Deathbed Prayer

Lord, though I am a miserable and wretched creature, I am in Covenant with Thee through grace. And I may, I will, come to Thee for Thy People. Thou hast made me, though very unworthy, a mean instrument to do them some good, and Thee service; and many of them have set too high a value upon me, though others wish and would be glad of my death. Lord, however Thou do dispose of me, continue and go on to do good for them. Give them consistency of judgment, one heart, and mutual love. And go on to deliver them, and with the work of reformation; and make the Name of Christ glorious in the world. Teach those who look too much on Thy instruments to depend more upon Thyself. Pardon such as desire to trample upon the dust of a poor worm, for they are Thy people too. And pardon the folly of this short Prayer: Even for Jesus Christ's sake. And give us a good night, if it be Thy pleasure. Amen.

From Thomas Carlyle, ed., *The Letters and Speeches of Oliver Cromwell*, 3 vols. (New York: G. P. Putnam's Sons, 1904), Vol. 3, p. 217.

A Royalist View

From *Clardendon's History*

He was one of those men, *quos vituperare ne inimici quidem possunt, nisi ut simul laudent;* [whom his very enemies could not condemn without commending him at the same time:] for he could never have done half that mischief without great parts of courage, industry, and judgment. He must have had a wonderful understanding in the natures and humours of men, and as great a dexterity in applying them; who, from a private and obscure birth, (though of a good family,) without interest or estate, alliance or friendship, could raise himself to such a height, and compound and knead such opposite and contradictory tempers,

From Lord Clarendon, *The History of the Rebellion and Civil Wars in England* (Oxford: Oxford University Press, 1839), Vol. 6, pp. 349–350.

humours, and interests into a consistence, that contributed to his designs, and to their own destruction; whilst himself grew insensibly powerful enough to cut off those by whom he had climbed, in the instant that they projected to demolish their own building. What Velleius Paterculus said of Cinna may very justly be said of him, *ausum eum, quæ nemo auderet bonus; perfecisse, quæ a nullo, nisi fortissimo, perfici possent:* [he attempted those things which no good man durst have ventured on; and achieved those in which none but a valiant and great man could have succeeded.] Without doubt, no man with more wickedness ever attempted any thing, or brought to pass what he desired more wickedly, more in the face and contempt of religion, and moral honesty; yet wickedness as great as his could never have accomplished those trophies, without the assistance of a great spirit, an admirable circumspection and sagacity, and a most magnanimous resolution.

SOCIETY AND RELIGION

Social Legislation

Many people came to resent the harsh enforcement of Puritan legislation by Cromwell's military government.

From *Acts and Ordinances*

Whereas the Acts of Stage-Playes, Interludes, and common Playes, condemned by ancient Heathens, and much less to be tolerated amongst Professors of the Christian Religion is the occasion of many and sundry great vices and disorders, tending to the high provocation of Gods wrath and displeasure ... It is ordered and ordained ... That all Stage-players and Players of Interludes and common Playes, are hereby declared to be, and are, and shall be taken to be Rogues, and punishable, within the Statutes of the thirty ninth year of the Reign of Queen Elizabeth, and the seventh year of the Reign of King James.

And because the prophanation of the Lords-day hath been heretofore greatly occasioned by May-Poles, (a Heathenish vanity, generally abused to superstition and wickedness.) The Lords and Commons do further Order and Ordain, That all and singular May-Poles, that are, or shall be erected, shall be taken down and removed. . . .

And be it further Enacted by the authority aforesaid, That if any man shall from and after the Four and twentieth day of June aforesaid, have the carnal knowledge of the body of any Virgin, unmaried Woman or Widow, every such man so offending ... as also every such woman so offending ... shall for every such offence be committed to the common Gaol, without Bail or Mainprize, there to continue for the space of three Months. . . .

And it is further Enacted and Declared, That every person and persons which upon the said Lords Day, days of Humiliation or Thanksgiving, shall be in any Tavern, Inn, Alehouse, Tobacco-house or Shop,

From C. H. Firth and R. S. Rait, eds., *Acts and Ordinances of the Interregnum* (London: His Majesty's Stationery Office, 1911), Vol. 1, p. 421, Vol. 2, pp. 385, 388, 861.

or Victualling-house (unless he lodge there, or be there upon some lawful or necessary occasion) ... and every person or persons which upon the said days shall be dancing, prophanely singing, drinking, or tipling in any Tavern, Inn, Alehouse, Victualling-house, or Tobacco-house or Shop, or shall harbor or entertain any person or persons so offending; or which shall grinde or cause to be ground in any Mill, any Corn or Grain upon any the said days, except in case of necessity, to be allowed by a Justice of the Peace, every such Offender shall forfeit and pay the sum of ten shillings for every such offence, to be levied as aforesaid.

Whereas the Publique Meetings and Assemblies of People together in divers parts of this Nation, under pretence of Matches for Cock-Fighting, are by experience found to tend many times to the disturbance of the Publique Peace, and are commonly accompanied with Gaming, Drinking, Swearing, Quarreling, and other dissolute Practices, to the Dishonor of God, and do often produce the ruine of Persons and their Families; For prevention thereof, Be it ordained by His Highness the Lord Protector, by and with the Advice and Consent of His Council, That from henceforth there shall be no Publique or Set-meetings or Assemblies of any persons within England or Wales, upon Matches made for Cock-Fighting. ...

Radical Dissent

During the civil war period many new religious sects appeared. Sometimes they combined religious dissent with political radicalism. The "levellers" argued for egalitarian democracy.

From *The Free-Man's Freedom Vindicated*

Adam ... and ... Eve ... are the earthly original fountain of all and every particular and individual man and woman in the world since, who are, and were, by nature all equal and alike in power, dignity, authority, and majesty, none of them having by nature, dominion or magisterial power one over or above another; neither have they, or can they exercise any, but merely by institution or donation, or assumed by mutual consent and agreement. ... And unnatural, irrational, sinful, wicked, unjust, devilish, and tyrannical, it is for any man whatsoever, spiritual or temporal, clergyman or layman, to appropriate and assume unto himself a power, authority, and jurisiction to rule, govern or reign over any sort of man in the world without their free consent, and

From John Lilbourne, *The Free-Mans Freedom Vindicated* (London, 1646).

whosover doth it . . . do thereby, as much as in them lies, endeavour to appropriate and assume unto themselves the office and sovereignty of God (who alone doth, and is to, rule by his will and pleasure) and to be like the Creator, which was the sin of the devils, not being content with their first station, would be like God, for which sin they were thrown down into Hell. . . .

From *A Fiery Flying Roll*

Thus saith the Lord: Be wise now therefore, O ye Rulers, &c. Be instructed, &c. . . . Yea, kisse Beggers, Prisoners, warme them, feed them, cloathe them, money them, relieve them, release them, take them into your houses, don't serve them as dogs without doore, &c.

Owne them, they are flesh of your flesh, your owne brethren, your owne Sisters, every whit as good (and if I should stand in competition with you) in some degrees better than your selves.

Once more, I say, owne them; they are your self, make them one with you, or else go howling into hell; howle for the miseries that are coming upon you, howle.

The very shadow of levelling, sword-levelling, man-levelling, frighted you, (and who, like your selves, can blame you, because it shook your Kingdome?) but now the substantiality of levelling is coming.

The Eternall God, the mightly Leveller is comming, yea come, even at the door; and what will you do in that day. . . .

From Abiezer Coppe, *A Fiery Flying Roll* (London, 1649).

The "Diggers" advocated a communistic utopia and began to dig up common lands to put their ideas into practice.

From Winstanley. *Letter to Lord Fairfax*

Our digging and ploughing upon George-hill in Surrey is not unknown to you, since you have seen some of our persons, and heard us speak in defence thereof: and we did receive mildness and moderation from you and your council of war both when some of us were at Whitehall before you and when you came in person to George-hill to view our works: we endeavour to lay open the bottom and intent of our business as much as can be, that none may be troubled with doubtful imaginations about us, but may be satisfied in the sincerity and universal righteousness of the work.

We understand that our digging upon that common is the talk of the whole land; some approving, some disowning, some are friends filled with love, and sees the work intends good to the nation, the

From *A Letter to the Lord Fairfax* (London: Giles Calvert, 1649).

peace whereof is that which we seek after; others are enemies filled with fury, and falsely report of us that we have intent to fortify ourselves, and afterwards to fight against others and take away their goods from them, which is a thing we abhor: and many other slanders we rejoice over, because we know ourselves clear, our endeavour being no otherwise but to improve the commons, and to cast off that oppression and outward bondage which the creation groans under, as much as in us lies, and to lift up and preserve the purity thereof.

And the truth is, experience shows us that in this work of community in the earth, and in the fruits of the earth, is seen plainly a pitched battle between the lamb and the dragon, between the spirit of love, humility, and righteousness, which is the lamb appearing in flesh; and the power of envy, pride, and unrighteousness, which is the dragon appearing in flesh, the latter power striving to hold the creation under slavery, and to lock and hide the glory thereof from man: the former power labouring to deliver the creation from slavery, to unfold the secrets of it to the sons of men, and so to manifest himself to be the great restorer of all things.

And these two powers strive in the heart of every single man, and make single men to strive in opposition one against the other, and these strivings will be till the dragon be cast out, and his judgment and downfall hastens apace, therefore let the righteous hearts wait with patience upon the Lord, to see what end he makes of all the confused hurley-burleys of the world. . . .

A Digger Song (1649)

> You noble Diggers all, stand up now, stand up now,
> You noble Diggers all, stand up now,
>   The waste land to maintain, seeing Cavaliers by name
>   Your digging do disdain and persons all defame.
> Stand up now, stand up now.
>
> Your houses they pull down, stand up now, stand up now,
> Your houses they pull down, stand up now;
>   Your houses they pull down to fright poor men in town
>   But the gentry must come down, and the poor shall
>   wear the crown.
> Stand up now, Diggers all! . . .
>
> To conquer them by love, come in now, come in now,
> To conquer them by love, come in now;
>   To conquer them by love, as it does you behove,
>   For He is King above, no power is like to love.
> Glory *here*, Diggers all.

From C. H. Firth, *Clarke Papers* (London: Camden Society, 1891–1901), Vol. 2, p. 221.

Parliamentary leaders and army generals had no sympathy with such extreme views. The Leveller and Digger movements were both suppressed.

Women's Roles

This view of family structure comes from 1634.

From *Domesticall Duties*

But what if a man of lewd and beastly conditions, as a drunkard, a glutton, a profane swaggerer, an impious swearer and blasphemer, be married to a wise, sober, religious matron, must she account him her superior and worthy of an husband's honor?

Surely she must. For the evil quality and disposition of his heart and life doth not deprive a man of that civil honor which God hath given unto him. Though an husband in regard of evil qualities may carry the image of the devil, yet in regard of his place and office, he beareth the Image of God: so do Magistrates in the Commonwealth, Ministers in the Church, Parents and Masters in the Family. Note for our present purpose, the exhortation of St Peter to Christian wives which have infidel husbands, 'Be in subjection to them: let your conversation be in fear'. If Infidels carry not the devil's image and are not, so long as they are Infidels, vassals of Satan, who are? Yet wives must be subject to them.

From William Goudge, *Of Domesticall Duties* (London, 1634), p. 274.

During the civil war some women were drawn into political activities. The following lines were written in a satirical vein by a Royalist.

From *Hudibras*

> Women, that were our first apostles,
> Without whose aid we'd all been lost else;
> Women, that left no stone unturned
> In which the Cause might be concerned;
> Brought in their children's spoons and whistles,
> To purchase swords, carbines and pistols. . . .
> What have they done, or what left undone,
> That might advance the Cause at London?
> Marched rank and file, with drum and ensign,
> T' entrench the City for defence in;
> Raised ramparts with their own soft hands,

From Samuel Butler, *Hudibras,* ed. T. R. Nash (New York: D. Appleton and Company, 1847), pp. 245–247.

To put the enemy to stands;
From ladies down to oyster-wenches
Laboured like pioneers in trenches,
Fell to their pickaxes and tools
And helped the men to dig like moles.
Have not the handmaids of the City
Chosen of their members a committee
For raising of a common purse
Out of their wages, to raise horse? . . .

In 1649 John Lilbourne, the Leveller, and three companions were arrested. A large group of London women petitioned for their release.

Women's Petition (1649)

The Humble Petition of divers well-affected women of the Cities of London and Westminster, etc. Sheweth, that since we are assured of our creation in the image of God, and of an interest in Christ equal unto men, as also of a proportional share in the freedoms of this Commonwealth, we cannot but wonder and grieve that we should appear so despicable in your eyes, as to be thought unworthy to petition or represent our grievances to this honorable House.

Have we not an equal interest with the men of this Nation, in those liberties and securities contained in the Petition of Right, and the other good laws of the land? Are any of our lives, limbs, liberties or goods to be taken from us more than from men, but by due process of law and conviction of twelve sworn men of the neighborhood?

And can you imagine us to be so sottish or stupid, as not to perceive, or not to be sensible when daily those strong defenses of our peace and welfare are broken down, and trod under foot by force and arbitrary power?

Would you have us keep at home in our houses, when men of such faithfulness and integrity as the FOUR PRISONERS our friends in the Tower are fetched out of their beds, and forced from their houses by soldiers, to the affrighting and undoing of themselves, their wives, children and families? Are not our husbands, ourselves, our children and families by the same rule as liable to the like unjust cruelties as they? . . . Doth not the Petition of Right declare that no person ought to be judged by Law Martial (except in time of war) . . . ? And are we Christians and shall we sit still and keep at home, while such men as have borne continual testimony against the unjustice of all times, and unrighteousness of men, be picked out and delivered up to the slaughter . . . ?

No. . . . Let it be accounted folly, presumption . . . or whatsoever in

From J. O'Faolain and L. Martines, *Not in God's Image* (New York: Harper and Row, 1973), pp. 266–267.

us . . . we will never forsake them, nor ever cease to importune you . . . for justice . . . that we, our husbands, children, friends and servants may not be liable to be thus abused, violated and butchered at men's wills and pleasures. . . .

Some radical religious groups held that women could be preachers and minis ters. Mary Cary was associated with the "Fifth Monarchy" sect. George Fox was the founder of the Quakers.

From Mary Cary. *The New Jerusalem's Glory*

And if there be very few men that are thus furnished with the gift of the Spirit; how few are the women! Not but that there are many god, women, many who have indeed received the Spirit: but in how small measure is it? how weak are they? and how unable to prophesie? for i' is that that I am speaking of, which this text says they shall do; which yet we see not fulfilled. . . . But the time is coming when this promise shall be fulfilled, and the Saints shall be abundantly filled with the spirit; and not only men, but women shall prophesie; not only aged men, but young men; not only superiours, but inferiours; not only those that have University learning, but those that have it not; even servants and handmaids.

From M. Cary, *The New Jerusalem's Glory* (London, 1656), p. 238.

From George Fox. *A Collection of . . . Epistles*

And there are Elder Women in the Truth, as well as Elder Men in the Truth; and these Women are to be teachers of good things; so they have an Office as well as the Men, for they have a Stewardship, and must give account of their Stewardship to the Lord, as well as the Men. Deborah was a judge; Miriam and Huldah were prophetesses; old Anna was a prophetess. . . . Mary Magdalene and the other Mary were the first preachers of Christ's Resurrection to the Disciples . . . they received the Command, and being sent, preached it: So is every Woman and Man to do, that sees him risen, and have the Command and Message. . . . And if the Unbelieving Husband is sanctified by the Believing Wife, then who is the Speaker, and who is the Hearer? Surely such a Woman is permitted to speak and to work the Works of God, and to make a Member in the Church; and then as an Elder, to oversee that they walk according to the Order of the Gospel.

What, are Women Priests? Yes, Women Priests. And can Men and Women offer Sacrifice without they wear the holy Garments? No:

From J. O'Faolain and L. Martines, *Not in God's Image* (New York: Harper and Row, 1973), pp. 265–266.

What are the holy Garments Men and Women must wear? . . . the Priest's Surplice? Nay. . . . It is the Righteousness of Christ . . . this is the Royal Garment of the Royal Priesthood, which everyone must put on, Men and Women.

The claim of women to play traditionally male roles in church affairs seemed to many people subversive of all established order and to deserve harsh punishment.

From *The Sufferings of the People Called Quakers*

The earliest account of the Sufferings of this People in Cambridge-shire bears Date in the same Month wherein Oliver Cromwell had assumed the Title of Protector, viz. in December, 1653, when Elizabeth Williams and Mary Fisher, the one about fifty and the other about thirty Years of Age, came from the North of England to Cambridge .. Complaint was forthwith made to William Pickering, then Mayor, that two Women were preaching: He sent a Constable for them and examined them . . . He asked their Names: They replied, their Names were written in the Book of Life. He demanded their Husbands Names: They told him, they had no husband but Jesus Christ, and he sent them. Upon this the Mayor grew angry, called them Whores, and issued his Warrant to the Constable to whip them at the Market-Cross until the Blood ran down their Bodies . . . The Executioner commanded them to put off their Clothes, which they refused. Then he stript them naked to the Waste, put their Arms into the Whipping-post, and executed the Mayor's Warrant far more cruelly than is usually done to the worst of malefactors, so that their Flesh was miserably cut and torn . . . and in the midst of their Punishment they sang and rejoiced, saying, "The Lord be blessed, the Lord be praised, who hath thus honoured us, and strengthened us thus to suffer for his Name's sake."

From J. Besse, *A Collection of Sufferings of the People Called Quakers* (London, 1753), Vol. 1, pp. 84–85.

Even in such troubled times many people lived tranquil lives; most females continued to carry out traditional roles; some young women made happy marriages. The letters of Dorothy Osborne, written from her father's country house, to William Temple, the young man she would eventually marry, remind us of this side of life.

From *Dorothy Osborne's Letters*

You ask me how I pass my time here. . . . I rise in the morning reasonably early, and before I am ready I go round the house till I am weary

From E. A. Parry, ed., *Letters from Dorothy Osborne to Sir William Temple 1652–1654*, 3rd ed. (London: Griffith, Farren, Okeden and Welsh, 1888), pp. 37, 61, 80, 91, 100, 170, 290.

of that, and then into the garden till it grows too hot for me. About ten o'clock I think of making me ready, and when that's done I go into my father's chamber, from whence to dinner, where my cousin Molle and I sit in great state in a room, and at a table that would hold a great many more. . . . The heat of the day is spent in reading or working, and about six or seven o'clock I walk out into a common that lies hard by the house, where a great many young wenches keep sheep and cows, and sit in the shade singing of ballads. I go to them and compare their voices and beauties to some ancient shepherdesses that I have read of, and find a vast difference there; but, trust me, I think these are as innocent as those could be. I talk to them, and find they want nothing to make them the happiest people in the world but the knowledge that they are so. Most commonly when we are in the midst of our discourse, one looks about her, and spies her cows going into the corn, and then away they all run as if they had wings at their heels. . . . When I have supped, I go into the garden, and so to the side of a small river that runs by it, when I sit down and wish you were with me. . . .

I can assure you we are seldom without news, such as it is; and at this present we do abound with stories of my Lady Sunderland[1] and Mr. Smith; with what reverence he approaches her, and how like a gracious princess she receives him, that they say 'tis worth one's going twenty miles to see it. All our ladies are mightily pleased with the example, but I do not find that the men intend to follow it. . . .

Nothing can alter the resolution I have taken of settling my whole stock of happiness upon the affection of a person that is dear to me, whose kindness I shall infinitely prefer before any other consideration whatsoever, and I shall not blush to tell you that you have made the whole world besides so indifferent to me that, if I cannot be yours, they may dispose of me how they please. Henry Cromwell[2] will be as acceptable to me as any one else. . . .

[*The next letter refers to Oliver Cromwell's seizure of power in 1653.*]

But, bless me, what will become of us all now? Is not this a strange turn? . . . Tell me what I must think on't; whether it be better or worse, or whether you are at all concern'd in't? For if you are not I am not, only if I had been so wise as to have taken hold of the offer was made me by Henry Cromwell, I might have been in a fair way of preferment, for, sure, they will be greater now than ever. Is it true that Algernon

[1]Lady Sunderland was the sister of Algernon Sidney, a radical parliamentary leader.

[2]Dorothy's father had been a royalist commander, but this did not discourage Henry Cromwell, the second son of Oliver Cromwell, from becoming one of her suitors.

Sydney was so unwilling to leave the House, that the General was fain to take the pains to turn him out himself? Well, 'tis a pleasant world this. If Mr. Pim were alive again, I wonder what he would think of these proceedings, and whether this would appear so great a breach of the Privilege of Parliament as the demanding the 5 members? But I shall talk treason by and by if I do not look to myself. 'Tis safer talking of the orange-flower water you sent me. . . .

The less one knows of State affairs I find it is the better. My poor Lady Vavasour is carried to the Tower, and her great belly could not excuse her, because she was acquainted by somebody that there was a plot against the Protector, and did not discover it. She has told now all that was told her, but vows she will never say from whence she had it. . . .

I have sent you my picture because you wished for it; but, pray, let it not presume to disturb my Lady Sunderland's. Put it in some corner where no eyes may find it out but yours, to whom it is only intended. 'Tis not a very good one, but the best I shall ever have drawn of me; for, as my Lady says, my time for pictures is past, and therefore I have always refused to part with this, because I was sure the next would be a worse. There is a beauty in youth that every one has once in their lives; and I remember my mother used to say there was never anybody (that was not deformed) but were handsome, to some reasonable degree, once between fourteen and twenty. It must hang with the light on the left hand of it; and you may keep it if you please till I bring you the original.

[*Dorothy lived contentedly with her husband for forty years. But she experienced two misfortunes typical of the hazards of seventeenth-century life. Just before her marriage she suffered a severe attack of smallpox which left her face permanently disfigured. Later she had six children, but only one of them lived to maturity.*]

FROM RESTORATION TO REVOLUTION: ENGLAND AND HOLLAND

Restoration

From *John Evelyn's Diary*

May 29, 1666 This day, his Majesty, Charles the Second came to London, after a sad and long exile and calamitous suffering both of the King and Church, being seventeen years. This was also his birthday, and with a triumph of above 20,000 horse and foot, brandishing their swords, and shouting with inexpressible joy; the ways strewed with flowers, the bells ringing, the streets hung with tapestry, fountains running with wine; the Mayor, Aldermen, and all the Companies, in their liveries, chains of gold, and banners; Lords and Nobles, clad in cloth of silver, gold, and velvet; the windows and balconies, all set with ladies; trumpets, music, and myriads of people flocking, even so far as from Rochester, so as they were seven hours in passing the city, even from two in the afternoon till nine at night.

The "Glorious Revolution"

From *John Evelyn's Diary*

June 25, 1686 Now his Majesty, beginning with Dr. Sharp and Tully, proceeded to silence and suspend divers excellent divines for preaching against Popery.

November 29, 1686 I went to hear the music of the Italians in the new chapel, now first opened publicly at Whitehall for the Popish Service. . . . The throne where the King and Queen sit is very glorious, in a closet above, just opposite to the altar. Here we saw the Bishop in his

From *Diary of John Evelyn*, ed. W. Bray, 4 vols. (London: Henry G. Bohn, 1862), Vol. 1, p. 365, Vol. 2, pp. 265, 273, 286, 291, 295–297.

mitre and rich copes, with six or seven Jesuits and others in rich copes, sumptuously habited, often taking off and putting on the Bishop's mitre, who sat in a chair with arms pontifically, was adored and censed by three Jesuits in their copes. . . . I could not have believed I should ever have seen such things in the King of England's palace, after it had pleased God to enlighten this nation; but our great sin has, for the present, eclipsed the blessing, which I hope He will in mercy and His good time restore to its purity.

February 3, 1687   Most of the great officers, both in the court and country, Lords and others, were dismissed, as they would not promise his Majesty their consent to the repeal of the test and penal statutes against Popish Recusants.

June 10, 1688   A young Prince born, which will cause disputes.
About two o'clock, we heard the Tower-ordnance discharged, and the bells ring for the birth of a Prince of Wales. This was very surprising, it having been universally given out that her Majesty did not look till the next month.

September 30, 1688   The Court in so extraordinary a consternation, on assurance of the Prince of Orange's intention to land, that the writs sent forth for a Parliament were recalled.

October 7, 1688   In the mean time, [the king] called over 5,000 Irish, and 4,000 Scots, and continued to remove Protestants and put in Papists at Portsmouth and other places of trust, and retained the Jesuits about him, increasing the universal discontent. It brought people to so desperate a pass, that they seemed passionately to long for and desire the landing of that Prince, whom they looked on to be their deliverer from Popish tyranny, praying incessantly for an east wind, which was said to be the only hindrance of his expedition with a numerous army ready to make a descent. To such a strange temper, and unheard-of in former times, was this poor nation reduced, and of which I was an eye-witness.

November 5, 1688   I went to London; heard the news of the Prince having landed at Torbay, coming with a fleet of near 700 sail, passing through the Channel with so favourable a wind, that our navy could not intercept, or molest them. . . .
These are the beginnings of sorrow, unless God in His mercy prevent it by some happy reconciliation of all dissensions among us. This, in all likelihood, nothing can effect except a free Parliament; but this we cannot hope to see, whilst there are any forces on either side. I pray God to protect and direct the King for the best and truest interest of his people!

December 18, 1688   I saw the King take barge to Gravesend at twelve o'clock—a sad sight! The Prince comes to St. James's and fills Whitehall with Dutch guards. A Council of Peers meet about an expedient to call a Parliament; adjourn to the House of Lords. The Chancellor, Earl of Peterborough, and divers others taken. . . .

All the world go to see the Prince at St. James's, where there is a great Court. There I saw him, and several of my acquaintance who came over with him. He is very stately, serious, and reserved.

Patterns of Government

Sir William Temple (Dorothy Osborne's husband) became ambassador to Holland and wrote this account of Dutch government.

From *Observations upon the United Provinces of the Netherlands*

In the first constitution of this government, after the revolt from Spain, all the power and rights of Prince William of Orange, as Governor of the Provinces, seem to have been carefully reserved. But those which remained inherent in the Sovereign, were devolved upon the assembly of the States-General, so as in them remained the power of making peace and war, and all foreign alliances, and of raising and coining of monies: in the Prince, the command of all land and sea forces, as Captain-general and Admiral, and thereby the disposition of all military commands, the power of pardoning the penalty of crimes, the chusing of magistrates upon the nomination of the towns; for they presented three to the Prince, who elected one out of that number. Originally the States-General were convoked by the council of State, where the Prince had the greatest influence: nor, since that change, have the States used to resolve any important matter without his advice. Besides all this, as the States-General represented the sovereignty, so did the Prince of Orange the dignity, of this State, by public guards, and the attendance of all military officers; by the application of all foreign ministers, and all pretenders at home; by the splendor of his court and magnificence of his expence; supported not only by the pensions and rights of his several charges and commands, but by a mighty patrimonial revenue in lands and sovereign principalities and lordships, as well in France, Germany, and Burgundy, as in thy several parts of the Seventeen Provinces; so as Prince Henry was used to answer some that would have flattered him into the designs of a more arbitrary power, that he had as much as any wise Prince would desire in that

From *The Works of Sir William Temple*, 4 vols. (London, 1814), Vol. 1, pp. 118–119.

State; since he wanted none indeed, besides that of punishing men, and raising money; whereas he had rather the envy of the first should lie upon the forms of the government, and he knew the other could never be supported, without the consent of the people, to that degree which was necessary for the defence of so small a State against so mighty Princes as their neighbours.

From *The Bill of Rights (1689)*

Whereas the said late King James II having abdicated the government, and the throne being thereby vacant, his Highness the prince of Orange (whom it hath pleased Almighty God to make the glorious instrument of delivering this kingdom from popery and arbitrary power) did (by the advice of the lords spiritual and temporal, and diverse principal persons of the Commons) cause letters to be written to the lords spiritual and temporal, being Protestants, and other letters to the several counties, cities, universities, boroughs, and Cinque Ports, for the choosing of such persons to represent them, as were of right to be sent to parliament, to meet and sit at Westminster upon the two and twentieth day of January, in this year 1689, in order to such an establishment as that their religion, laws, and liberties might not again be in danger of being subverted; upon which letters elections have been accordingly made.

And thereupon the said lords spiritual and temporal and Commons, pursuant to their respective letters and elections, being now assembled in a full and free representation of this nation, taking into their most serious consideration the best means for attaining the ends aforesaid, do in the first place (as their ancestors in like case have usually done), for the vindication and assertion of their ancient rights and liberties, declare:

1. That the pretended power of suspending laws, or the execution of laws, by regal authority, without consent of parliament is illegal.

2. That the pretended power of dispensing with the laws, or the execution of law by regal authority, as it hath been assumed and exercised of late, is illegal.

3. That the commission for erecting the late court of commissioners for ecclesiastical causes, and all other commissions and courts of like nature, are illegal and pernicious.

4. That levying money for or to the use of the crown by pretense of prerogative, without grant of parliament, for longer time or in other manner than the same is or shall be granted, is illegal.

5. That it is the right of the subjects to petition the king, and all commitments and prosecutions for such petitioning are illegal.

From *The Statutes: Revised Edition* (London: Eyre and Spottiswoode, 1871), Vol. 2, pp. 10–12.

6. That the raising or keeping a standing army within the kingdom in time of peace, unless it be with consent of parliament, is against law.

7. That the subjects which are Protestants may have arms for their defense suitable to their conditions, and as allowed by law.

8. That election of members of parliament ought to be free.

9. That the freedom of speech, and debates or proceedings in parliament, ought not to be impeached or questioned in any court or place out of parliament.

10. That excessive bail ought not to be required, nor excessive fines imposed, nor cruel and unusual punishments inflicted.

11. That jurors ought to be duly impaneled and returned, and jurors which pass upon men in trials for high treason ought to be freeholders.

12. That all grants and promises of fines and forfeitures of particular persons before conviction are illegal and void.

13. And that for redress of all grievances, and for the amending, strengthening, and preserving of the laws, parliament ought to be held frequently.

And they do claim, demand, and insist upon all and singular the premises, as their undoubted rights and liberties. . . .

Having therefore an entire confidence that his said Highness the prince of Orange will perfect the deliverance so far advanced by him, and will still preserve them from the violation of their rights, which they have here asserted, and from all other attempt upon their religion, rights, and liberties:

The said lords spiritual and temporal, and commons, assembled at Westminster, do resolve that William and Mary, prince and princess of Orange, be, and be declared, king and queen of England France, and Ireland. . . .

Upon which their said Majesties did accept the crown and royal dignity of the kingdoms of England, France, and Ireland, and the dominions thereunto belonging, according to the resolution and desire of the said lords and commons contained in the said declaration.

About the Editors

After serving in the Royal Air Force, Brian Tierney received his B.A. and Ph.D. from Cambridge University. He has taught at Catholic University, Washington, D.C., and at Cornell, where he is now Bryce and Edith M. Bowmar Professor in Humanistic Studies. He has been the recipient of Guggenheim Fellowships and of fellowships from the American Council of Learned Societies and the National Endowment for the Humanities. Professor Tierney has been awarded the honorary degrees of Doctor of Theology by Uppsala University, Sweden, and Doctor of Humane Letters by Catholic University. A specialist in medieval church history, he has published many articles and several books, among them *Foundations of the Conciliar Theory; Medieval Poor Law;* and *Origins of Papal Infallibility, 1150–1350.* He is coeditor with Donald Kagan and L. Pearce Williams of *Great Issues in Western Civilization.* His most recent work is *Religion, Law, and the Growth of Constitutional Thought, 1150–1650.*

Joan W. Scott received her Ph.D. in history from the University of Wisconsin. She has taught at the University of Illinois at Chicago Circle, Northwestern University, the University of North Carolina at Chapel Hill, and Brown University, where she is currently Nancy Duke Lewis University Professor and professor of history. She also is director of Brown's Pembroke Center for Teaching and Research on Women. Professor Scott has held fellowships from the Social Science Research Council, the National Endowment for the Humanities, and the American Council of Learned Societies. She has directed seminars for college teachers sponsored by the National Endowment for the Humanities and has served as a consultant for projects in labor history and women's history. Her fields of research are nineteenth-century French social history and European women's history. She has written numerous articles on both topics and was awarded a prize by the Berkshire Conference of Women Historians for "Women's Work and the Family in Nineteenth Century Europe," coauthored with Louise Tilly. She is author of *The Glassworkers of Carmaux: French Craftsmen and Political Action in a Nineteenth Century City,* which won the American Historical Association's Herbert Baxter Adams prize in 1974. She is coauthor, with Louise Tilly, of *Women, Work and Family.*

A NOTE ON THE TYPE

The text of this book has been set on the Linotron 202 in a typeface called "Baskerville." The face is a facsimile reproduction of types cast from molds made for John Baskerville (1706-75) from his designs. John Baskerville's original face was one of the forerunners of the type-style known as "modern face" to printers—a "modern" of the period A.D. 1800.

Composed by P & M Typesetting, Waterbury, Connecticut. Printed and bound on Cameron press by Banta Company, Harrisonburg, Virginia.

Text design by Barbara Sturman. Cover design by Mary Chris Welch.